Computing

Wiley Series in Computing and Information Processing

Hugh J. Watson, University of Georgia-Athens, Series Editor

Computing

With End-User Applications and BASIC

NANCY STERN

Hofstra University

ROBERT A. STERN

Nassau Community College

WILEY

JOHN WILEY AND SONS

New York Chichester Brisbane Toronto Singapore

To Melanie and Lori

Trademark Acknowledgments:

1-2-3 is a registered trademark of Lotus Development Corporation
dBASE IV is a registered trademark of Ashton-Tate Corporation
BASICA, IBM, and PC-DOS are registered trademarks of International Business Machines Corp.
MS-DOS, GW-BASIC, and QuickBASIC are registered trademarks of Microsoft Corporation
WordPerfect is a registered trademark of WordPerfect Corporation

Library of Congress Cataloging in-Publication Data:

Stern, Robert A.
    Computing with end-user applications and BASIC / Robert A. Stern and Nancy Stern.
       p.   cm.
    Includes bibliographical references
    1.End-user computing.   2. BASIC (Computer program languuage)
    I. Stern, Nancy B.   II. Title.
    QA76.9.E53S75   1990   004'.01'9--dc20   89-28441
    ISBN 0-471-51849-2

Printed in the United States of America

10 9 8 7 6

Sponsoring Editor: Joe Dougherty, Wiley
Managing Editors: Susan Nelle, BMR and Raleigh Wilson, BMR
Development Coordination: Elaine Brett
Production Coordination: Jane E. Granoff
Cover and Text Design: Paul Quin
Illustration: Paul Quin and Winston Sin
Copy Edit: Kay Nelson and Susan Defosset
Photo Research: Monica Suder
Page Makeup: Curtis Philips
Index: Susan Coerr

Brief Contents

Contents

END-USER COMPUTING

Computing Today

Computing in Business

Chapter 3   Page 49

**Productivity Tools:
Word Processing,
Spreadsheets, and
Database Management**

Storage and Files

Using Data
Communications
and Networks

Part III   Page 183

SOFTWARE

Chapter 8   Page 185

System Software and Specialized Application Packages

Chapter 9   Page 215

Software Development Languages and Tools

SYSTEMS

Chapter 10   Page 251

Systems Analysis and Design

Chapter 11   Page 285

Database Management Systems

Management Information Systems

Social Issues and Technological Trends

Page GR-1

Developing Graphs with Lotus 1-2-3

Page MAC-1

Creating and Using Macros In Lotus 1-2-3

Tutorial   Page DB-1

Using dBASE IV

APPENDICES

How This Book Differs from the Titles Currently on the Market

Dramatic changes in information processing strategies and technologies have resulted in many different approaches to teaching introductory courses. Where there once was general consensus, there is now fragmentation.

Although no book can be all things to all people, we believe we have developed an approach that is not only unique, but may also help to bring back some of the consensus to the introductory computing market. The major features of this book are:

- An end-user orientation
- Tutorials on the major productivity tools
- Micro-minicomputer-mainframe balance
- A focus on computing and applications, not hardware
- An emphasis on database management systems
- A proven pedagogic approach
- Functional use of color

An End-User Orientation

The main objective is to teach computing concepts to people who will be end-users, those that need some background in *why* computers are such an integral part of organizations today as well as *how* they can use them. Our approach is to strike a proper balance between the *why* and the *how* of computer use.

We emphasize that there are three levels of end-user involvement in most organizations, depending on the individual's role and level of expertise. On the lowest level, some end-users simply input or edit data; we provide tutorials explaining how this is done using the major productivity tools. At the next level are the computer users and professionals who design applications, providing the formatting that enables data to be entered and accessed efficiently and effectively. At the third level are those managers who use information made available by the applications and their designers for decision-making purposes, and who may not have any expertise in the application software itself.

In order to introduce students to hands-on computer use as early in the course as possible, an overview of the three major productivity tools is provided in Chapter 3. This is an ideal introduction to the tutorials designed to be used in the laboratory.

Tutorials for the Major Productivity Tools

Most end users need to be proficient in the three basic productivity tools—word processing, spreadsheets, and database management systems. Because few introductory texts provide hands-on tutorials, many schools now require two books for their first computer course—one on concepts and one on how to use the three basic packages.

Our book not only combines tutorials with basic concepts, it provides a significant amount of information on how and why these tools are effectively used in organizations. A data disk that is referenced in the tutorials and that can be used for hands-on work and for homework assignments is available from Wiley.

Micro-Minicomputer-Mainframe Balance

Most books are heavily oriented toward either mainframes or microcomputers. We provide a proper balance among the levels of computing. We use the more familiar, easy-to-grasp micro concepts to introduce students to the other levels of computing power. We make it clear that microcomputers, minicomputers, mainframes, and supercomputers are conceptually similar, differing primarily in speed, cost, and capacity.

Moreover, we focus on the ways in which micros, minis, and mainframes can be linked or networked to provide capabilities that far surpass those of any single level of computing and make the type of computing power almost transparent to the user.

A Focus on Computing and Applications, Not Hardware

Application-oriented processing is the focus here; hardware, or devices, is highlighted mainly to illustrate how it can accomplish the tasks at hand. We emphasize throughout that software drives the hardware. That is, the approach to applications design is to first decide what needs to be done, then choose the software most appropriate to accomplish those tasks, and only then focus on the hardware that can be used with the selected software. Several chapters cover some aspect of applications design: Chapter 9 on Software Development Languages and Tools introduces students to the steps used to create a program; Chapter 10 considers similar procedures used at the Systems Analysis level; Chapter 11 on Database Management Systems illustrates systems design at the level of designing databases; and Chapter 12 on Management Information Systems deals with systems design at the highest managerial level.

An Emphasis on Database Management Systems

Database management systems are likely to be the most important decision-making tool for managers. Accordingly, we provide consistent and focused coverage of DBMSs throughout the text as well as in selected chapters. Students are introduced to database concepts early in the book—Chapter 3 is an overview of the basic productivity tools: word processing, spreadsheets, and database management systems. Basic database terms and data hierarchy concepts are introduced in Chapter 6 on Storage, and Chapter 11 on Database Management Systems reinforces this earlier information and provides in-depth coverage of DBMSs, using illustrations from dBASE IV. There is full tutorial coverage of dBASE IV as well.

Proven Pedagogic Approach

We have retained our well-known pedagogic approach, which has gained a reputation for reinforcing computing concepts and increasing student comprehension. The easy-to-read pedagogical style is augmented by:

- Chapter opening outlines
- Chapter objectives
- Self-quizzes with solutions within each chapter
- "In a Nutshell" boxes that provide brief summaries of terminology or concepts
- "Looking Ahead" boxes that provide a glimpse of future applications
- Chapter summaries
- Chapter quizzes with solutions
- Review questions
- Key terms
- Problem-solving applications

Functional Use of Color

Color is used in this book as both a design tool and as a study aid. Each module has its own unique color scheme, and color is used on headings to emphasize each chapter's structure.

Within each module's illustration program, a particular color is used to identify each of the following elements in information systems: input, processing, output, hardware, operating systems, and users; and three different colors are used to identify the three levels of users.

Color tabs along the top of the book identify the modules, and colored tabs along the side of the book identifies the tutorials.

How This Book Is Organized

Computing with End-User Applications and BASIC is actually three books in one. The first book contains four modules: Computing, Hardware, Software, and Systems. These four modules cover the principles of computing and information processing. The second book contains six step-by-step tutorials on DOS 3.3, WordPerfect 5.0, Lotus 1-2-3, Lotus 1-2-3 graphics, Lotus 1-2-3 macros, and dBASE IV. The third book is a full appendix on "Structured BASIC Programming for the PC."

Each chapter was carefully crafted to provide an easy-to-read narrative reinforced with numerous photographs and illustrations. Technological concepts and terms are consistently illustrated with familiar, everyday examples to make it easy for students to learn and retain the information.

Each chapter has the following organization: a chapter outline to highlight the order of concepts, a list of behaviorally stated chapter objectives, text that has a clear structure emphasized with headings in color, self-quizzes at appropriate intervals, and a chapter summary. This is followed by end-of-chapter pedagogy: a list of key terms, a chapter test, a series of review questions keyed to the chapter objectives, and problem-solving applications that require students to use the three productivity tools.

Each tutorial begins with the hardware and software requirements for that software package, an outline of the keystrokes and concepts that will be covered, and a brief introduction to the package. The emphasis is not only on *how* to use these tools, but *why* they are so effective for decision making. The tutorial is divided into several lessons, each designed to fit one laboratory session. Each lesson ends with exercises that the student can use to reinforce what was learned in that lab session.

The main body of the tutorial consists of hands-on, step-by-step instructions designed to help the student master specific procedures. Color is used for specifying the procedures covered, as well as for keystrokes that the student will type. There are numerous screens illustrating what happens at each step, so that students know what their screens should look like.

For each productivity tool, templates and command summaries are provided, as well as brief highlights of how versions of each package differ.

Supplements

Student Activities Workbook (0-471-51930-8)

This student supplement features industry and software case studies and the all new visual course guide. The former provide students with engaging hands-on software exercises and real-world problems, while the latter presents scaled down, annotated transparencies which students can further annotate for use as a study and learning aid. The Student Activities Workbook also includes such traditional student review material as detailed study tips and chapter-by-chapter learning guides which feature chapter overviews, outlines, key terms (with definitions and text page references), and self-tests (20 short answer, 10 matching, and 40 multiple choice questions) complete with solutions.

Getting Started with VP-Planner Plus (0-471-51920-0)
Getting Started with dBASE III Plus (0-471-51921-9)

These brief, hands-on tutorials emulate the text tutorials in their step-by-step coverage of VP-Planner and dBASE III Plus commands and functions. Each of the two manuals comes complete with an educational version of the appropriate software and can be bundled with either of the Stern & Stern texts for little or no extra cost to students.

Instructor's Manual (0-471-51157-9)

This carefully crafted instruction ancillary includes the following chapter-by-chapter elements:

- chapter overview
- chapter objectives

- chapter outline
- chapter highlights/lecture notes (annotated with transparency master references)
- key chapter terms defined (with text page references)
- solutions to all end-of-chapter exercises (enlarged so that these can be used as transparency masters)
- classroom discussion topics
- individual and group assignments
- recommended long-term projects
- Additional hands-on exercises to accompany text tutorials

Other key Instructor's Manual elements include sections containing sample course syllabi, teaching tips, and suggestions for the use of the Supplementary Video Program and Student Activities Workbook. The Instructor's Manual is also available on disk.

Test Bank (0-471-51156-0)

This instructor ancillary features approximately 2,000 true/false and multiple choice questions. References to text pages on which question topics are discussed (i.e. answered) are included, and all questions are graded for level of difficulty. The Text Bank is also available on disk.

Transparency Master (0-471-51158-7)

Over 200 transparency masters featuring both art and text are included in this instructor ancillary. Key figures/topics from the text and Instructor's Manual are included, as well as all new material designed to supplement the lecture process.

Selected Transparency Acetates (0-471-51931-6)

Approximately 40 of the most critical transparency masters are available in acetate form and may be used with the Student Activities Workbook to facilitate more active student involvement in class lectures.

Supplementary Video Program

A variety of stimulating videos—such as thorough introductions to the personal computer and individual application—will be made available to adopters of either of the Stern & Stern texts.

Data Disk

Available for use with tutorials included in the Stern & Stern texts, this data disk contains WordPerfect, Lotus, dBASE, and ASCII files and may be duplicated for use by students. Note: This data disk must be used when working with the tutorials.

How to Obtain Supplements

To obtain any of the supplements described above, contact your local Wiley representative or write to the following address:

Stern End User
John Wiley & Sons, Inc.
605 Third Ave
New York, NY 10158

Author Access

We update our books every 2-3 years and welcome your comments, suggestions and even criticisms. We are also available to answer any queries you might have. Our Bitnet address is ACSNNS@HOFSTRA. Our CompuServe e-mail address is 76505,1222. Our University address is: BCIS Dept./Hofstra University/Hempstead, NY 11550/516-560-5716.

Acknowledgments

To a team committed to excellence and quality.

We are pleased to work with Joseph Dougherty at John Wiley and Sons and Susan Nelle at BMR, who put together the developmental and production team of researchers, writers, reviewers, and developmental editors so that we were able to complete this book in one year. Their efforts are truly appreciated, and have without doubt contributed to the overall *raison d'etre* of this book.

The team included editors, managers, and marketing personnel, who participated in an initial brainstorming session; the Wiley sales representatives, who contributed their insight and marketing knowledge about the changing introductory course; the more than 200 instructors who responded to our survey, and who were hand-picked for their expertise and experience with information processing and with teaching tutorials in the lab environment; more than 30 reviewers, who painstakingly read, annotated, and reviewed each chapter and tutorial. We wish to acknowledge and thank writers Ric Williams, Ken Knecht, Jim Schuman, Greg Harvey, and Richard Pitter, who helped to develop and write this book.

Special thanks go to Elaine Fritz Brett, who not only did an excellent job as the major developmental editor, but who truly understood and helped to realize our vision for this book.

Finally, we wish to thank Jane Granoff, production supervisor, who made sure that a quality product was produced and did so with grace and good humor.

Reviewers

Doug Bock
  Southern Illinois University at Edwardsville
Joyce Capen
  Central Michigan University
Marilyn Meyer
  Fresno City College
Judith Ernst
  South Florida Community College
Prof. Bob Young
  Los Angeles City College
Sandra Stalker
  North Shore Community College
Jeanne Ross
  University of Lowell
Ruth Robbins
  University of Houston, Downtown
Floyd Johnson
  Kearney State College
Vivek Shah
  Southwest Texas State University
Paul Chase
  Becker Junior College

Judy Read Smith
  Portland Community College
Charles Biondi
  Cumberland Community College
Ron Thorn
  Northeast Louisiana University
Dr. Virgil Brewer
  Eastern Kentucky University
Peggy Griffey
  Clatsop Community College
Katherine Sundahl
  University of Missouri, Columbia
Lindsay Graves
  Pima Community College
Liang Wee
  University of Arizona
Bangren Tsay
  California State University, Chico
Dr. Ruth Malmstrom
  Raritan Valley Community College

Marketing Survey Respondents

James Wenger
  Emporia State University
Susan Brender
  Boise State University
Jim Nichols
  Lincoln University
Sharon Lichti
  South Oregon State College
Linda Gammiel
  Weber State College
Donald Dawley
  Miami University
George Clark
  Florida A&M University
Peter Guiliani
  Franklin University
G. Larry Brown
  Piedmont Virginia Community College
William W. Johnson
  Wayne Community College
Beverly Simon
  Middlesex County College
Jim Lawaich
  Brookdale Community College
Barbara Herring
  Wayne Community College
Jack Bregglio
  Rancho Santiago Community College
Jeanne Cipar
  Minneapolis Community College
Karen E. Hilles
  Santa Monica College

Samual Gale
  Kingsburgh Community College
Jim Payne
  University of Tulsa
Charles Biondi
  Cumberland Community College
Pat Boyd
  Umpqua Community College
Peggy Griffey
  Clatsop Community College
David Hawkins
  Georgia College
Dr. Barbara Mason
  Wichita State University
Floyd Johnson
  Kearney State College
Virgil Brewer
  Eastern Kentucky University
Jeanne Ross
  University of Lowell
Ron Thorn
  Northeast Louisiana University
Donald Labudde
  Northeastern Illinois University
Robert Otto
  Western Kentucky University
Vic Broquard
  Illinois Central College
Vivek Shah
  Southwest Texas State University
Ruth Robbins
  University of Houston, Downtown

James Kelley
  University of the Virgin Islands
Bonnie Bailey
  Maryland State University
Paul Chase
  Becker Junior College
Judith Ernst
  South Florida Community College
Linda Lujan
  Arapahoe Community College
Marilyn Meyer
  Fresno City College
Judy Read Smith
  Portland Community College
Raymond Marves
  Florida Community College at Jacksonville

Richard Manthei
  Joliet Junior College
Lindsay Graves
  Pima Community College
Karen Watterson
  Shoreline Community College
Raymond Vogel
  Schenectady County Community College
Sandra Stalker
  North Shore Community College
Marilyn Popyk
  Henry Ford Community College
Dr. Ruth Malmstrom
  Raritan Valley Community College

About the Authors

Dr. Nancy Stern is currently Professor and Chairperson of the Business Computer Information Systems Department at Hofstra University in Hempstead, New York. She holds an A.B. degree from Barnard College, an M.S. from New York University, and a Ph.D. from the State University of New York at Stony Brook. She is the coauthor of several other information processing texts including *Structured COBOL Programming*, 4th ed., *370/360 Assembler Language Programming*, and *RPG II and RPG III Programming*. She is also the author of *Flowcharting: A Self-Teaching Guide*. Dr. Stern is advisory editor of the Wiley Series on Information Processing Systems, as well. One of her major interests is the history of computing; she has written several articles and books on computing history and is currently Assistant Editor-in-Chief of the *Annals of the History of Computing*.

Robert A. Stern is an attorney and a Professor of Mathematics and Computer Processing at Nassau Community College in Garden City, New York. He holds a B.S. in Industrial Engineering and a B.S. in Business Administration, both from Lehigh University, an M.S. in Operations Research from New York University, and a J.D. from St. John's University School of Law. He is the coauthor of the texts mentioned above. Mr. Stern has had diverse business experience as a systems analyst, an industrial engineer, and an attorney.

COMPUTING

Computing Today

When you have completed this chapter, you will be able to:

✔ List and describe the functions of the four hardware components of a computer system.

✔ Describe the two basic categories of software and give examples of each.

✔ Describe the tradeoffs between purchasing packaged programs and having programs custom-designed.

✔ List the four main categories of computer systems and the criteria that differentiate them.

✔ List the components of a microcomputer system.

✔ List five benefits of using computers.

✔ List five practices that protect a computer system from errors and breakdowns.

Chapter Outline

Throughout seven thousand years of recorded history—from the ancient banking societies of China to the high court of France—all organizations have used information systems to help people maintain records and make decisions. Early information systems consisted of scribes using brush, ink, and paper, with fast runners to deliver the results. As technologies changed, so did information systems. Today, businesses use computerized systems to record their activities, and they communicate the results using such technologies as telephones and satellite signals.

The computer has created a revolution in the production, processing, and transfer of information, primarily because of its ability to handle enormous amounts of data quickly. And the changes continue. In a single decade, computers have changed from being primarily large systems dedicated to churning out payrolls and financial reports for major companies staffed by technically trained specialists, to being available to individual workers in the form of small, powerful desktop computers that everyone can use to increase their own personal productivity.

In Chapter 1, we will look at the various elements that make up these computerized information systems—whether they are large, company-wide systems, or small, personal systems. This chapter is an overview of computing; each of the topics discussed will be covered in depth in later chapters.

The Computer System and How It Processes Data

The word *system* has several commonly used meanings. There are, for example, telephone systems, nervous systems, grading systems, and betting systems. For our purposes, a **computer system** is a group of devices, commonly called **hardware**, that together with sets of instructions, called programs or **software**, perform information-processing functions. The main purpose of all computer systems is to process data quickly and efficiently so that the information obtained is timely, meaningful, and accurate. As shown in Figure 1–1, a computer system consists of four components: input devices, the processor, output devices, and storage devices.

1. **Input devices**: the part of the system that accepts data from the user

2. The **processor**: the part that transforms input data into useful information

3. **Output devices**: the part that produces the processed data, called information

4. **Storage devices**: the part that stores the program, input, or output so that it can be used again later.

The actual reading of incoming data (the processing) and the creating of output are performed by several devices that together constitute a computer system. When people use the term *computer,* they are really referring to hardware, or a group of machines, called a computer system. Computer systems come in various sizes from micro to mini to large mainframes to supercomputers.

Figure 1–2 shows these four components in a standard microcomputer system and a typical large mainframe computer system. Even though these systems appear to be dramatically different, they process data in the same way—their differences are primarily those of speed and the quantity of data handled.

Every business—and each computer user—has individual needs, so each computer system is specially designed, or configured, to include the component devices that meet those specific needs. In the overview of system components that follows, we will describe some of the common devices that are used in computer system configurations.

1–1 A computer system consists of four components: input devices, the central processing unit, output devices, and storage devices.

Input Devices for Reading Incoming Data

There are many different types of input devices: keyboards, disk drives, tape drives, optical readers, and so on. Each input device reads a specific form of data—for example, keyboards read typed letters, numbers, and symbols; optical readers read typed or handwritten characters. The input device converts the data into electronic pulses that are transmitted to the CPU for processing.

Different businesses are apt to have various types of input devices. An insurance company, for example, may use terminals and tape drives as input devices, while a supermarket may use electronic cash registers and optical scanners that read bar codes on food products.

Output
Printers
CRT

Processing
CPU

Storage
Main Memory
Storage Devices

Input
Stored data
Keyboard

1–2 Large mainframe systems and personal microcomputer systems have the same functional components—only the scale and speed are different.

The Central Processing Unit (CPU)

The **central processing unit**, or **CPU**, is the part of the computer system that controls all computer operations. It reads data from an input device into **primary storage**, or main memory; processes the data according to program specifications; and produces information by activating an output device.

The CPU must be linked by cables or other communication channels to all input and output devices in the computer system. The **program**, or set of instructions for processing data, is read into the CPU before input can be entered and processed.

The processor reads each character of an instruction or data item into a storage position. A single storage position is called a **byte** of storage. The letter **K** is often used as an abbreviation for a **kilobyte**, which is approximately 1,000 bytes (actually 1,024 bytes). We say that the main memory or primary storage capacity of the CPU in a microcomputer is, for example, about 640K. Some larger systems measure their storage capacities in **gigabytes** or billions of bytes.

The amount of primary storage is important to computer users because it determines how much data the computer can process at one time. For example, one of the earliest popular home computers, the Apple IIe, had only 64K of main memory. If you loaded a word processing program into an Apple IIe, it might use several thousand bytes of memory; then every letter you typed and each formatting instruction you entered would use more bytes. Within just a couple of pages, you could use up all the available memory. Then you would find that your work would stop for a couple of

In a Nutshell

Units of Storage

Byte	one storage position
Kilobyte	approximately 1000 storage positions
Megabyte	approximately 1 million storage positions
Gigabyte	approximately 1 billion storage positions

minutes while the processor stored everything you typed onto a floppy disk, and freed some memory so that you could continue typing.

If you use a more current microcomputer, you will find that such delays are very infrequent. You can type almost indefinitely without interruption, because you probably have at least 256K of primary storage, if not 640K, and most of it is available for data.

An important characteristic of primary storage is that once a computer is turned off, or if the power fails, *data and programs in primary storage are lost.* This is processing memory, not storage memory. Thus, before turning off a computer, information should be stored using a storage device.

Output Devices for Producing Outgoing Information

Each output device of a computer system accepts information from the CPU and converts it to an appropriate output form. A printer, for example, is an output device that prints reports or graphs based on information that the CPU has processed and produced.

Auxiliary Storage for Storing Programs and Data

Once the central processing unit has processed data, **auxiliary storage** (or **secondary storage**) devices keep the data in electronic form so that it can conveniently be used again. Examples of auxiliary storage are a floppy disk or the packs of large, hard disks used on minicomputers and mainframes. In contrast to primary storage, auxiliary storage retains programs and data for future use.

The Stored-Program Concept

Before computer hardware can actually read data, process it, and produce information, it must read into memory a set of instructions called a program, which actually controls the processing to be performed. Programs, like data, are stored in the computer's primary storage. We say, then, that computers are **stored-program devices**, since they require a set of instructions to be stored before data can be processed.

Computer professionals called **programmers** prepare these instructions, or programs, for each application. The total set of programs that enable the computer system to process data is referred to as software.

In order for the computer to perform particular operations, an appropriate program must be entered in the CPU. Typically, these programs are stored on disks. A computer system for a medium-sized company, for example, may have hundreds of programs for use in a variety of application areas such as payroll, accounting, inventory control, and sales forecasting. A home computer system may have dozens of programs for typing reports, playing games, balancing the checkbook, and so on.

Most large computer systems and even some microcomputers can store more than one program in the CPU at the same time, thereby permitting several different jobs to be run at the same time. This concept is known as **multiprogramming** on large computer systems, and **multitasking** on micro-computers. Some large computers are also shared by numerous users who access the computer using terminals at remote locations—a concept known as **time-sharing**. These concepts will be considered in detail later.

Computers use two types of software, or programs: **operating system software** to monitor, or supervise, the overall operations of the computer system; and **application software** to manipulate input data in order to provide users with meaningful information, or output.

Operating System Software

Computers need a series of control programs, called an **operating system**, to move files in and out of storage and to run programs. Some computers have built-in operating systems, but these cannot easily be updated. Most computer vendors either provide their own operating system or enable users to purchase one of the more popular operating systems. The IBM PC and PS/2, for example, have their own operating systems (PC–DOS or OS/2), but they can also use other operating systems such as UNIX or XENIX. Some Apple computers use Apple DOS, while the Apple Macintosh family uses an operating system called Finder. Similarly, mainframes have numerous operating systems that control their overall operations.

Each of these operating systems has unique ways to process and store data. A disk that is formatted for one operating system cannot even be read by another system, even if the disk physically fits into the disk drive. Programs are written for a particular operating system as well. We say that programs or data that are designed for different operating systems are not compatible; that is, they cannot be used together. This is often a problem for users. For example, a Macintosh user cannot loan computer games to an IBM XT user; and at the mainframe level, programs written for a UNISYS mainframe cannot run unmodified on an IBM mainframe.

In a Nutshell

Types of Software		
	Operating System	supervises or controls the overall operations of a computer
	Applications	designed to satisfy a user need
	– packaged	inexpensive, designed for a wide range of users, good documentation
	– customized	more apt to satisfy specific user needs, expensive and time-consuming to develop

1–3 A typical office computer will be loaded with several application programs. Each packaged program comes with disks and user manuals. *Courtesy:* Hewlett-Packard Company.

In recent years, compatibility problems have been at least partially solved with the development of special devices or software that allow users to send data from one operating system to another.

Application Programs for End-Users

Application software manipulates input data to perform a given job, such as prepare a report, update a master payroll file, or print customer bills. Typically, programs are acquired in one of two ways: packaged (or off-the-shelf) programs purchased from a vendor, or custom programs designed especially for an individual organization's unique needs.

Packaged programs are sold or leased by computer vendors, self-employed programmers, or software houses, and are designed for general use in many companies. Some programs allow limited customization. Because they are designed for a broad range of users, they may not exactly meet any one user's needs. They are, however, relatively inexpensive and are supplied with extensive reference manuals called documentation (Figure 1–3).

Custom programs are written by programmers within an organization, by outside consultants, or by self-employed programmers. These programs are designed to exactly meet the needs of users, but they are very expensive and time-consuming to develop.

Programs are designed to meet the needs of people known as **users**—people who are not computer professionals but who need information to do their jobs successfully, such as the personnel who handle customer orders or managers making budget decisions. Although users are more likely to be satisfied with custom programs than packaged programs, the expense and time required to develop custom programs is often not justified. As a result, users frequently buy packaged programs and then either have computer professionals modify the package or sacrifice some of their specific needs to the general design of the package.

Designing Information Systems

Whether an organization uses packaged or custom-designed programs, the most important part of creating a useful computer system is to design the overall **information system**—which includes choosing all the programs to be used, defining how they will be used for each specific application, and providing detailed documentation of the procedures to be used by all levels of users. Well-designed information systems help employees do their jobs more effectively by supplying them with timely, accurate information.

For example, McDonald's, the fast-food chain, effectively uses information systems to provide faster service to customers and to deliver accurate, timely information to managers. Employees at electronic cash registers enter customers' orders, which appear immediately on a video display terminal over the cook's head and are then stored in auxiliary memory for later inventory analysis (see Figure 1–4). The system provides McDonald's with two immediate benefits: first, customers receive faster service, and second, store managers have accurate, detailed information to help them plan food deliveries, create employee schedules, forecast future sales, and so on.

Effective information systems are not created overnight, however. Computer professionals must work closely with those who will actually be using the system to ensure that computer hardware and software meet the organization's actual information needs. Typically, organizations have complex information needs as data moves between the accounting, marketing, and production areas, which makes creating information systems challenging to

1–4 A complex information system. Orders from the cash registers automatically appear overhead at the cook's workstation—and are also sent to managers at headquarters.

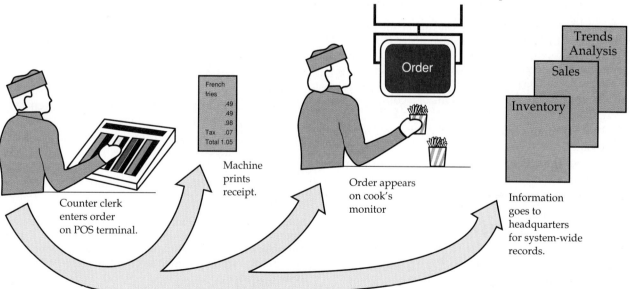

French fries
.49
.49
.98
Tax .07
Total 1.05

Machine prints receipt.

Counter clerk enters order on POS terminal.

Order

Order appears on cook's monitor

Trends Analysis

Sales

Inventory

Information goes to headquarters for system-wide records.

everyone involved. One reason the McDonald's system is so effective is that it serves the *combined* information needs of three groups in the organization:

1. The **cooks** (production) receive orders accurately and quickly.

2. **Store managers** receive accurate sales information (accounting) and are able to schedule timely deliveries (inventory).

3. Information from all stores is sent to corporate headquarters; then **senior managers** can see quickly which products are doing well and which are doing poorly, and create strategic plans and advertising campaigns.

The Systems Analyst's Role

Specially trained computer professionals called **systems analysts** study the information needs of various groups in an organization and work with user groups to design a system plan. They then supervise the work of programmers who actually write the software needed to meet the specifications in the system design. Systems analysts are trained to serve as a communications bridge, or facilitator, between programmers, who may not understand the business needs of users, and the users themselves, who rarely have sophisticated technical experience.

Managers are always seeking good, business-savvy systems analysts who can match computer technologies to business needs in creative and effective ways, because effective information systems enable employees to be more productive and organizations to be more profitable.

The User's Role

Systems analysts cannot design information systems by themselves, however. If users do not become *actively* involved with the systems analyst from system design through programming, testing, and final implementation, an information system may turn out to be unreliable, expensive, and ineffective in the organization. The user's role is to ensure that the system is easy to use and that it meets specific business needs.

SELF-TEST At the end of each chapter in this text, and sometimes at the end of a subsection, there is a series of self-test questions, followed by solutions. The purpose of these quizzes is to provide you with a method of evaluating your understanding of the chapter.

1. The four hardware components of a computer system are: _____, _____, _____, and _____.
2. (T *or* F) Primary storage is memory used for processing.
3. (T *or* F) The CPU cannot process data until a program has been entered.
4. The most common form of auxiliary storage is _____.
5. The computer professionals who write programs are called _____.
6. The capability to execute more than one program at a time is called _____ on mainframe computers, and _____ on microcomputers.
7. The two basic categories of software are _____ and _____.
8. (T *or* F) Custom programs are always written by a company's own programmers.
9. (T *or* F) Packaged programs are generally less expensive than custom programs.
10. The computer professional who works with users to design the overall information system for an organization is called a _____ _____.

SOLUTIONS 1) input devices, the processor, output devices, storage devices. 2) True. 3) True. 4) magnetic disk. 5) programmers. 6) multiprogramming; multitasking. 7) operating system software; application software. 8) False. 9) True. 10) systems analyst.

From Micros to Mainframes

Computer professionals can design information systems to run on any type of computer system. Computer systems available today are classified (in order of increasing size) as microcomputers, minicomputers, mainframes, and supercomputers. However, computers are quickly becoming more powerful, so terms such as *microcomputer* and *supercomputer* are relative— that is, supercomputers are simply the fastest, most powerful computers available at the moment and microcomputers are the smallest. Many microcomputers today can do the work that it took a whole room full of hardware to do two decades ago, and today's supercomputer may be tomorrow's microcomputer!

For many years, the one real difference between microcomputers and other computers such as minicomputers, mainframes, or supercomputers was that the larger systems could do multiprogramming; that is, they could execute more than one program at a time. However, this distinction is eroding as new operating systems become available that enable microcomputers to perform multiprogramming or multitasking as well. Now, micros and supercomputers differ basically only in degree with regard to five factors: the size of the system, its cost, speed, storage capacity, and the number of input/output devices they can handle.

Microcomputer Hardware

A **microcomputer**, or micro, is the smallest and least expensive of all computers; most often it can sit comfortably on a desk. Some are now even made as briefcase-sized portables, called laptops (Figure 1–5). But do not let the prefix "micro" fool you—the amount of memory available in microcomputers is increasing rapidly, with the result that the sophistication and speed of new applications is astonishing. "Micro" refers mainly to the computer's

1–5 A portable microcomputer, the Toshiba T1000 laptop. *Courtesy:* Toshiba.

1–6 On Macintosh micro-computers, the **mouse** can be used to select items on the screen. *Courtesy:* Apple Computer, Inc.

desktop or laptop size. We define a microcomputer as a device with primary storage capacity from 256K (approximately 256,000 bytes) to several mega-bytes, and with a basic cost of under $100 to several thousand dollars.

Many computers that fit our category of "micro" can have additional storage capacities if they include add-on memory boards, and many micros cost more than several thousand dollars if they are purchased with numer-ous peripheral devices and sophisticated software. These ranges are not definitive, but they provide a handy guide for determining which machines are typically classified as micros.

The minimum configuration consists of the following items: input dev-ices, microprocessor and CPU, output devices, and disk drives.

Input Devices.   Most input is done with either a keyboard or a mouse. A **keyboard**, which resembles a typewriter keyboard, is the basic unit for entering data and for coding or using program instructions.

A **mouse** is a hand-held device that you slide around the desktop to electronically move an arrow on the computer screen. In some cases, the user points the arrow at a picture, or **icon**, on the screen, and then pushes a button on the mouse to execute the command that the icon represents. In other cases, the mouse is used to select an item from an on-screen menu. This eliminates the need to type commands, which makes microcomputers very *user-friendly*, a term that means easy to learn and use. Apple's Macintosh computers were the first to make extensive use of the mouse (Figure 1–6).

Microprocessor and CPU.   The central processing unit, or CPU, includes a microprocessor chip and primary memory. A microprocessor is a tiny silicon chip, about the size of a child's fingernail, on which electronic cir-cuitry has been etched (Figure 1–7). The microprocessor in the CPU manages the computer processing and the transfer of data to and from primary

1–7 The microprocessor from a desktop computer is a small chip of silicon etched with circuits. Here it sits on a flower to show its small size. *Courtesy:* NCR.

storage, commonly called **random access memory (RAM)**. The amount of RAM and the quality and sophistication of the microprocessor vary with each microcomputer.

In addition to RAM, the CPU contains **read-only memory (ROM)**, which consists of prewired instructions that *cannot* be altered by programmed instructions. Examples of ROM instructions are built-in procedures for starting the system or for calculating a square root.

Output Devices.   Common output devices for micros are **cathode ray tubes (CRTs)**, also called **video display terminals (VDTs)** or **monitors**, and **printers**. A cathode ray tube is a TV-like screen that displays your instructions and the computer's responses.

Output on paper is called **hard copy**, and various printers are available that produce text and graphics on paper. The print quality available from hard-copy output can vary considerably. Terms like "letter-quality," "near-letter quality," and "draft quality" refer to how the printer works and the resulting quality of output.

A **letter-quality printer** produces the best output. Each letter is composed of solid lines, just like typewriter output. There are several ways to achieve letter quality: **impact printers** work just like typewriters, with a key striking the paper through an inked ribbon; **thermal printers** use a heat process on specially treated paper; and **laser printers** use laser technology to produce very high-quality characters.

Near-letter-quality printers and **dot-matrix printers** produce output by creating letters and figures out of individual dots. Dot-matrix printers are the least expensive, although their output is fairly crude. They are most commonly used with home computers.

Near-letter-quality printers use the same method, but they improve the quality by moving the print head over letters more than once so that the spaces between dots get filled in with other dots.

Some printers can produce either simple dot-matrix output, called **draft-quality output**, or near-letter-quality output. Draft-quality is useful for checking interim output—it runs faster because the print head goes over the characters only once.

Although letter-quality or near-letter-quality output is used by many businesses for formal correspondence, laser printers are quickly becoming standard business equipment (Figure 1–8). They are almost silent, much faster than other printers, and produce high-quality print. A typical laser printer for a microcomputer costs about $2,000—as compared to a typical dot-matrix printer, which costs several hundred dollars and is considerably slower and noisier.

Disk Drives for Storage.   A secondary storage medium is needed to store programs and data so that they will be retained even after the computer is shut off. The two most popular types of media for storing files and programs for micros are floppy disks and hard disks.

A **floppy disk**, interchangeably called a *diskette,* a *disk,* or a *floppy,* is a small flexible Mylar disk coated with iron oxide on which data is stored. Floppies have been in existence since the early 1970s and were originally

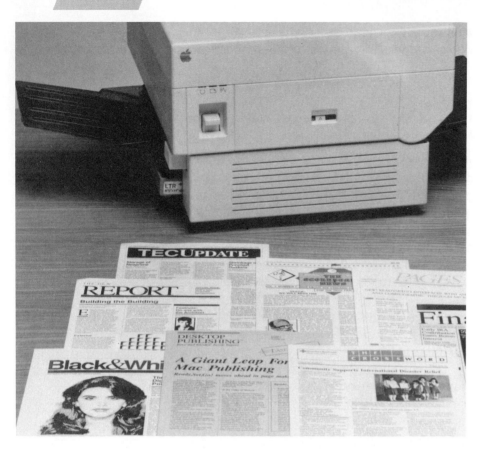

1–8 Laser printers can print not only letters, but graphic images as well. *Courtesy:* Apple Computer, Inc.

eight inches in diameter. Today, as shown in Figure 1–9, floppies are widely available in two sizes—the 3½-inch version, which is encased in rigid plastic; and the floppy 5¼-inch size, which has a flexible plastic covering. The original 8-inch diskette is not commonly used any more. Contrary to what you might expect, the smaller-sized diskettes store more data than the larger ones. For example, 3½-inch diskettes usually store 720,000 bytes of data (720K) but can store up to 1.4 megabytes (or more), while 5¼-inch diskettes store from the usual 360,000 bytes (360K) up to 1.2 megabytes.

A basic rule of thumb about storage is that you can never have enough. A page of text, for example, uses about 2,000 characters, which means that a 5¼-inch disk can store about 300 pages of text, which may not be sufficient for some tasks. Moreover, large programs may need to be stored on numerous disks.

1–9 Hard plastic 3½-inch storage disks (left) and the flexible 5¼-inch disk (right). These disks can store both programs and data. *Courtesy:* IBM.

Basic Components of a Micro

Input devices	keyboard, mouse
Microprocessor	8088, 8086, 80286, 80386, 80486 chips
Output	monitors, printers
Disk drives for storage	hard disks, 5¼-inch and 3½-inch floppy disks

Users who prefer not to have to move disks in and out of their computers frequently choose micros with built-in hard disks. **Hard disk drives** that can store between 10 and 100 million characters are available for microcomputers, and some hard disks have even greater capacities.

The hard disk has several advantages over a floppy disk. Hard disks access information faster than floppies, and because of their hard construction, they store data more densely and provide greater protection from environmental conditions such as dust. There is no need for the user to deal extensively with dozens or hundreds of floppy disks; everything can be stored on the hard disk unit. However, there is a price to pay for these benefits: hard disk drives cost two to ten times as much as floppy disk drives.

Micros Come in Different Forms

In the late 1970s and early 1980s, when micros were first marketed, smaller firms such as Radio Shack, Commodore, and Apple dominated the market. When the huge marketing success of these machines became evident, major manufacturers such as IBM and AT&T began to design and manufacture micros that have also become highly competitive.

IBM.   IBM is currently the front runner in the micro field and has set a *de facto* standard for microcomputer hardware and software. The IBM market is segmented into the older Personal Computer and the newer Personal System/2 series (Figure 1–10). The basic differences between the two series are that the PS/2 is designed with greater expansion capabilities, has module components, and has more advanced internal circuitry than the original PC, which makes it capable of running operating systems that can handle more than one program at a time. PS/2s have also standardized the use of the smaller, higher-density 3½-inch floppy disks for better storage. There are numerous versions of both the PC (e.g., XT, AT) and the PS/2 (models 30, 50, 70, 80). The model names or numbers refer to their capabilities; some of the PS/2 models are considerably faster than PCs.

Several companies such as Compaq, Leading Edge, and Wyse have capitalized on the success of IBM-PCs by manufacturing comparable machines called PC-compatibles or **clones**. PC-compatibles are built on the IBM standard, but they often provide additional features not available on IBM systems, such as faster processors, sometimes at a lower price. Some of these computers are portable as well.

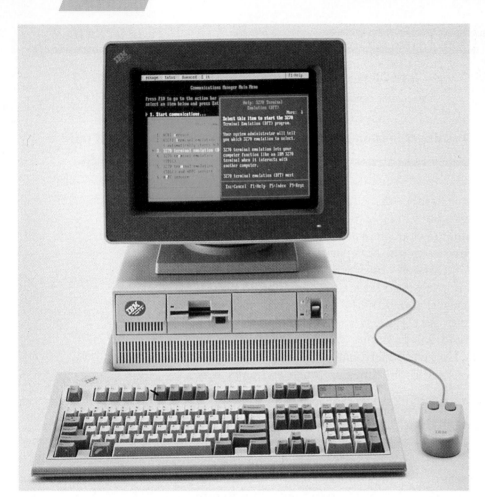

1–10 A desktop micro, the PS/2 from IBM, with color monitor, keyboard, and mouse. *Courtesy:* IBM.

Apple and Macintosh.   Apple has surprised some industry observers with the success of its competitive and easy-to-use Macintosh. The Macintosh offers excellent graphics capability with powerful word processing, database, and spreadsheet software. Combined with Apple's laser printers, the Macintosh has become the favored system at many colleges as well as for users needing desktop publishing capability.

The Intermediate Range: Minicomputers

Minicomputers are larger than micros and provide more computing power than micros without incurring the prohibitive expense associated with some mainframe systems. The minicomputer's size prevents it from being portable, but it can be moved more easily than a mainframe. Although some are kept in special computer rooms with dust and humidity controls, most minicomputers do not need elaborate environmental protection.

Minicomputers have storage capacities ranging from 100 MBs to 1 or more gigabytes. Also, minicomputers can generally support hundreds of terminals in a multiprogramming environment.

Some minis, like Digital Equipment Corporation's VAX (Figure 1–11), are called *superminis* because their capability is so close to that of mainframes.

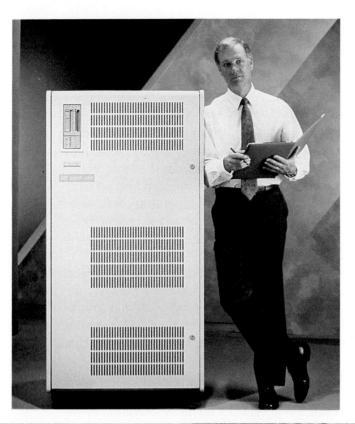

1–11 This VAX 6000 minicomputer is referred to as a supermini because its power is close to that of a mainframe. *Courtesy:* Digital Equipment Corp.

1–12 A mainframe computer, such as the NCR V-8800 shown here, is usually housed in a secure and climate-controlled room. *Courtesy:* IBM.

Pricing begins at several thousand dollars and can range into the hundreds of thousands of dollars. The minicomputer's reasonable price as compared to larger systems makes it available to small organizations such as scientific laboratories, research groups, colleges, and engineering firms.

Mainframes and Mainframe Families

A **mainframe computer** is faster, more powerful, and more expensive than a minicomputer. Mainframes are so named because they were first built by placing computer components on a chassis, or "main frame." A mainframe computer like the one in Figure 1–12 is generally found in a special computer room where environmental factors such as temperature, humidity, and dust are closely monitored. Because of the computer's cost and the value of the information stored there, these rooms usually have a security system that allows only authorized personnel to enter.

A mainframe's primary storage is measured in megabytes or **gigabytes** (one billion bytes); this capacity can often be substantially increased, depending on the system's configuration. Mainframes process data at several million instructions per second (called **MIPS**). More than 1,000 remote workstations or terminals can be connected to a typical mainframe computer.

IBM introduced the concept of building entire families of compatible mainframe computers—small, medium, and large—all with interchangeable software and computing abilities suggested by their sizes. Organizations could start with a small, relatively inexpensive system and add to it, building a larger computer system as computing needs grew. For example, many colleges purchased relatively small VAX minicomputer systems and then expanded their storage capacity or upgraded to a larger, compatible system as their computing requirements and funds increased. A major advantage to such families of computers is that all data and software on the smaller systems can be used on each successively larger system—a concept known as **upward compatibility**.

Supercomputers for Number Crunching

Supercomputers are the fastest, largest, and costliest computers available. Their speed is in the 1.2 to 2 billion instructions-per-second range and is expected to keep increasing in the future.

The supercomputer can process data from more than 10,000 individual workstations. To do this, however, a supercomputer needs a smaller computer to coordinate its input and output. The smaller computer, either a mainframe or a minicomputer, acts as a **front-end processor** and frees the supercomputer for the high-speed processing of large numbers, which it does best.

Supercomputers are usually too expensive and too large for typical business applications—prices start at about $4 million, with the Cray-2 selling for approximately $17 million. They tend to be used primarily for scientific, "number-crunching" applications in weather forecasting, aircraft design, nuclear research, seismic analysis, and so on, where rapid analysis of huge amounts of data is needed.

1–13 A Cray-2 Super-computer, showing the distinctive horseshoe-shaped computing unit. *Courtesy:* Cray Research, Inc.

Only large computer manufacturers such as Fujitsu, Hitachi, and Control Data Corporation build supercomputers. One company, Cray Research, specializes in supercomputers and offers extremely sophisticated hardware and processors. Figure 1–13 shows a supercomputer. Figure 1–14 provides an analysis of how supercomputers are used in the United States.

Using Computers in Organizations

Organizations spend a great deal of money and resources designing, developing, implementing, and maintaining information systems so that they will be effective in providing essential management support. In addition to the costs of hardware and software are hidden organizational costs such as training users, upgrading systems, purchasing new furniture, telecommunications costs, support costs, overhead, and so on—hidden costs that can sometimes constitute 80 percent of the total computer system cost! Despite these costs, organizations use computers because of the significant benefits they provide.

The Benefits of Using Computer Systems

Organizations purchase and maintain computer systems for five basic reasons:

1. Computers Are Fast. Most modern computers perform operations such as addition, subtraction, and so on, in speeds measured in fractions of a second. Microcomputer speeds are typically measured in **microseconds**, or millionths of a second. Mini and mainframe computer speeds are measured in **nanoseconds**, or billionths of a second. And supercomputer speeds are measured in **picoseconds**, or trillionths of a second.

1–14 This chart shows the most common uses for supercomputers in the United States.

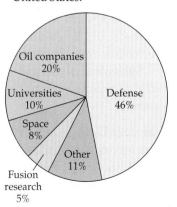

Defense 46%
Oil companies 20%
Universities 10%
Space 8%
Other 11%
Fusion research 5%

2. Computers Are Accurate.   Electronic technology is so precise that when a computer is programmed correctly and when input is entered properly, the accuracy of the output is virtually guaranteed. Some computers have checking mechanisms for ensuring the accuracy of data, but even these mechanisms are often seen as unnecessary. This is not to say that output from a computer is always correct; rather, when inaccuracies occur, it is most often the result of bad input or a programming error—almost never the result of a computer error.

3. Computers Have Large Storage Capacities.   Data and information previously stored in a room full of file cabinets can be compactly stored on just a few computer devices, such as disks, in a fraction of the space. Moreover, the data can be accessed or read quickly and in a variety of useful forms.

4. Low Cost for Large-Volume Jobs.   The overall cost of computers for large applications is often far less than if clerks were to do the job manually. In fact, many tasks performed today, such as oil exploration, genetic research, and molecular studies, either could not be accomplished or would be too expensive to do manually.

5. Intangible Benefits.   Many benefits are not directly related to tangible factors such as greater speed or lower cost. Intangible benefits are hard to measure, but they can easily be demonstrated. For example, the quality of computer-produced information may improve the decision-making process; similarly, they may speed up the flow of information through organizations. Such benefits can enhance a company's reputation or service by helping it respond more quickly to customer requests and questions.

Practical Steps for Ensuring a System's Usefulness

Computer systems should be designed to minimize errors and breakdowns, which damage a company's relations with customers or make employees' work more difficult. Mistakes occur as a result of programming errors, input errors, and poor system management.

Security is also an issue in designing information systems. Computer software and the company's critical data need protection from natural disasters such as fire, flood, and earthquakes, as well as from people working against the organization's interests. Users sometimes use computers as tools for white-collar crime or even for revenge, and computer hackers make news when they penetrate huge networked systems with tricks that overwork the system or contaminate data. The resulting errors and computer failures could be avoided if the computer system and its software and data were made more secure.

Systems analysts and users can ensure that computing systems successfully accomplish organizational goals by following these recommended practices:

Validate Data.   The overwhelming majority of "computer errors" result from errors in input. Users need to check the data entered into the computer to make sure that it is relatively error free. Moreover, programmers should include tests in their programs to check input for reasonableness. Examples of unreasonable input data might be dollar amounts in the billions or nineteenth-century dates.

Involve Users in Planning.   Users are apt to resist a computerized system if they were not involved in working with the systems analysts and programmers in the design of the system. Without the cooperation of users, information systems will almost always fail to meet expectations.

The two main reasons that computers fail to satisfy user needs are that either users do not understand a system's limitations and potential, or systems analysts do not fully understand user needs.

A major goal of this book is to help future business people understand what they can reasonably expect from an *information* system. Indeed, many business programs in colleges and universities are designed to bridge this communication gap between users and computer professionals such as systems analysts. Such understanding helps to minimize fear and resistance.

Set Realistic Development Goals.   In their enthusiasm, computer professionals may underestimate the time and resources needed to build an information system and fail to provide for unanticipated delays and obstacles. Such optimism, in the end, can create difficulties for users working within a fixed budget and a projected schedule for computer use.

Guarantee Security.   As the number of users working with computers continues to grow, the need for proper control and security measures increases dramatically. Many organizations now link terminals and microcomputers at remote locations to central computers, which gives the system even greater exposure to potential security problems. To maintain the integrity of programs and data, users and computer professionals must work together to prevent unauthorized people from accessing their systems.

Develop Written Standards and Guidelines.   Because the computer field is constantly changing, there are few established practices and techniques for formalizing and standardizing the system development process or its hardware and software components. Systems analysts need to be systematic and scientific when they develop systems. They also need to develop written documentation that records the rationale for the system's design, detailed specifications for all facets of the design, and comprehensive guidelines for using the system. Developing information systems and documentation that follow acknowledged standards makes those systems easier to use, evaluate, maintain, and modify.

SUMMARY

A *computer system* is a group of machines that, together with programs, perform information processing functions by operating on data so that results are timely, meaningful, and accurate. A computer system consists of four parts: *input devices,* the *processor, output devices,* and *auxiliary storage devices.* Before computer systems can actually read data, process it, and produce information, they must read in a set of instructions called a *program.* Computer professionals, called *programmers,*

write these programs for each application. There are two types of programs: *operating system programs* and *application programs.* The term *software* is used to describe all programs.

The most important step in creating a useful computer system is to design an *information system,* which is a set of organized procedures for accomplishing business functions. Systems analysts design information systems that meet business needs. They cannot create information systems by themselves, however. People who actually use information systems, called *users*, need to work with systems analysts to build a useful information system. Users are not only clerical workers and data entry operators but also managers who use information to improve their decision-making process.

Common computer systems available today are, in order of increasing size, *microcomputers, minicomputers, mainframes,* and *supercomputers.* The major differences between these machines are in their size, capacity, cost, speed, and the number of input/output devices they can handle. A microcomputer is the smallest and least expensive of all computers. Minicomputers are larger than micros and provide more computing power than micros without incurring the prohibitive expense often associated with mainframe systems. A mainframe is faster, more powerful, and more expensive than a minicomputer and can handle more than 1,000 remote workstations or terminals. Supercomputers are the fastest, largest, and costliest computers available and can handle over 10,000 individual workstations or terminals.

Organizations purchase computers for five basic reasons: computers are fast, accurate, and have large storage capacities, they can often do large jobs at a low cost, and they provide intangible benefits such as improving the quality of information and moving it more quickly through organizations.

Users and computer professionals can ensure that computer-produced information is beneficial to organizations by following these practices:

◆ Users should validate the data that is entered, and programmers should include tests for reasonableness in their programs.

◆ Computer professionals and users should work together in planning an information system.

◆ Computer professionals and users should have realistic development goals.

◆ Computer professionals and users should work together to guarantee security.

◆ Computer professionals should develop written standards and guidelines for using an information system.

KEY TERMS

Application software	Front-end processor
Auxiliary storage	Gigabyte
Byte	Hard copy
Cathode ray tube	Hard disk drive
Central processing unit (CPU)	Hardware
	Icon
Clone	Impact printer
Computer system	Information system
Custom program	Input devices
Dot-matrix printer	Keyboard
Draft-quality output	Kilobyte (K)
Floppy diskette	Laser printer

Letter-quality printer	Output devices
Mainframe computer	Packaged program
Megabyte (MB)	PC-compatible
Microcomputer	Picosecond
Microprocessor	Primary storage
Microsecond	Printer
Millions of instructions per second (MIPS)	Processor
	Program
Minicomputer	Programmers
Monitor	Random-access memory (RAM)
Mouse	Read-only memory (ROM)
Multiprogramming	
Multitasking	Secondary storage
Nanosecond	Software
Near-letter-quality printer	Storage devices
	Stored-program device
Operating system	Systems analyst
Operating system software	Thermal printer
	Time-sharing
Output devices	Upward compatibility
Packaged program	Users
PC-compatible	Video display terminal (VDT)
Operating system	
Operating system software	

CHAPTER SELF-TEST

1. Computers take incoming data called _____, process it, and produce outgoing information called _____.

2. The main unit of a computer system is called the _____.

3. The set of instructions that specifies what operations a computer is to perform is called a _____.

4. Most modern mainframes and minicomputers can perform operations at speeds that are measured in _____. Supercomputers perform operations at speeds measured in _____.

5. The overwhelming majority of so-called "computer errors" result from _____.

6. The communications gap that frequently results in poorly designed computer applications relates to poor communication between _____ and _____.

7. (T *or* F) The reading of input data by an input unit of a computer system is performed under the control of a CPU.

8. Another term for a CPU's primary storage is _____.

9. A single storage position is called a _____ of storage.

10. The letter K is used to represent approximately __(no.)__ bytes of storage; the designation MB is used to represent __(no.)__ bytes of storage.

11. A common auxiliary storage medium for computers is _____.

12. (T *or* F) Most large companies use supercomputers.

13. (T *or* F) IBM was the first manufacturer of microcomputers.

SELF-TEST SOLUTIONS: 1) input; output. 2) central processing unit (CPU). 3) program. 4) nanoseconds; picoseconds. 5) errors in input. 6) users; computer professionals. 7) True. 8) main memory or random access memory (RAM). 9) byte. 10) 1,000 (actually 1,024); 1,000,000 or one million (one megabyte). 11) disks. 12) False. Most large companies use mainframes; supercomputers are used for specific scientific functions and by a relatively small number of organizations. 13) False. IBM manufactures micros, but numerous smaller companies like Apple, Commodore, and Radio Shack manufactured them first.

REVIEW QUESTIONS

1. List the four hardware components of a computer system and briefly describe each.

2. Why are computers called "stored-program devices"?

3. What are the two categories of computer programs, and what is meant by "compatibility"?

4. What are the five factors that differentiate micros, minis, mainframes, and supercomputers?

5. Describe at least four different categories of printers used with microcomputers.

6. What are the two most common sizes of microcomputer diskettes?

7. What is meant by a "family" of computers?

8. What tasks are supercomputers designed to perform?

9. List five benefits of using computer systems.

10. Do you think microcomputers will continue to have a large home market? Explain your answer.

PROBLEM-SOLVING APPLICATIONS

1. Find an article from a local newspaper that describes a computerized system that failed to meet its objectives. Describe the circumstances and see if you can provide some reasons why the failures occurred. What recommendations would you make for avoiding similar problems in the future?

2. Find an article from a local newspaper that describes direct and substantive benefits derived from a specific computerized system.

3. Indicate the major reasons why some people have negative reactions to the use of computers.

4. Indicate some of the ways in which small businesses might use micros. Indicate some of the ways in which larger business might use micros.

Computing in Business

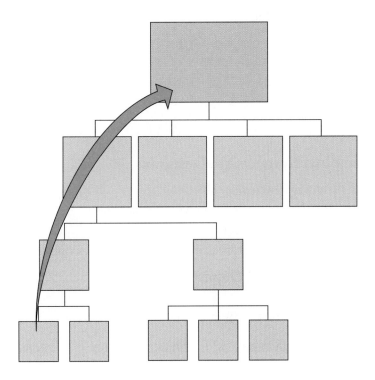

When you have completed this chapter, you will be able to:

- ✔ List and describe four common business productivity tools.
- ✔ List four functional areas of a business.
- ✔ Describe three differences between a traditional information processing organization and a top-down MIS organization.
- ✔ List advantages and disadvantages for centralized, decentralized, and distributed computing facilities.

Chapter 2

Chapter Outline

The growing number of microcomputers and minicomputers in business have given employees at all levels—from clerical workers with specialized tasks to executives with broad informational needs—direct access to computing power and information. Employees are now more effective and productive in their jobs because they have computing power to assist them in creating, storing, retrieving, organizing, summarizing, communicating, and making decisions about information.

For example, using desktop microcomputers, a product manager can analyze marketing statistics to determine which products have the most potential, prepare a report by typing it on the computer, and turn the final statistical relationships into a graph that is electronically incorporated into the report. The report can then be circulated to co-workers for comment and subsequently revised by retyping only those sections that need to be changed. The marketing executive to whom the product manager reports can use the statistics in the report to construct an electronic model that projects the financial results of following one course of action as opposed to another.

Desktop computers also give business people access to large databases that can assist them in being more effective. For example, paralegal clerks in law offices can find computerized information in a fraction of the time it formerly took them to search by hand through whole libraries of legal volumes. Financial analysts can quickly scan a series of graphs depicting the performance of various stocks to determine which are doing well.

Productivity Tools

How do computers enable clerks, professionals, and managers to work more effectively? A number of computer applications are commonly called **productivity tools** because they can be used by almost any kind of worker to do his/her job more effectively. The most common productivity tools are used for word processing, creating spreadsheets and graphics, accessing databases, and communicating via electronic mail. This chapter is an overview of these tools; they will be discussed in detail in Chapter 3.

Word Processing

Employees whose jobs used to require many hours a day typing now spend fewer hours at the keyboard because they use electronic **word processing** (Figure 2–1). If you use a standard office typewriter, the document must be completely retyped whenever you need to make a change or correction. Word processing software saves impressive amounts of time and energy, because words are recorded electronically, making them easy to change. This also minimizes the need for rekeyboarding every time you need a new version.

Using word processing software, writing becomes more like working with soft clay than like working with hammer, chisel, and stone. With word processing, there is no more erasing, inserting, or cutting and pasting by hand. You can rearrange words and sentences, and make deletions and

```
L[········1·········2·········3·········4·········5·········]·········7····
¶
¶
PROPOSAL TO NATIONAL INSURANCE CORPORATION¶
Corporate Training¶
The Corporate Training department has identified an
objective to redesign and reformat over 5000 pages of
textual and graphic information which constitutes the
company's training documentation.  In addition to
redesigning this substantial amount of information, the
department will also add new sections to the current
training curriculum.  The training documentation is
currently available in a variety of media, mostly on much
copied papers.  The documentation is somewhat out of date
since the collection of materials dates back twelve years.
According to the Director of Training, there is no orderly
fashion or design for this information.  The corporation has
hired a consultant, Ms. Judy Mason who has designed a
specific format and process for the training documentation.
Ms. Mason will become a member of the National Insurance
                                                   ═CT0Z01.DOC═
COMMAND: Copy Delete Format Gallery Help Insert Jump Library
         Options Print Quit Replace Search Transfer Undo Window
Edit document or press Esc to use menu
Pg1 Co1              {}              ?              NL        Microsoft Word
```

2–1 Word processing software makes writing and assembling a training manual easier. When modifications are needed, the time required to add, subtract, and/or revise material will also be greatly reduced.

insertions with simple keystrokes. As one novelist put it about her word processing program, "Once I learned it could do the two most time-consuming tasks—insert and delete text—I was free to spend my time creating and thinking."

Spreadsheet and Graphic Analysis Programs

The electronic **spreadsheet** is one of the most important and widely used business tools to come along in the era of microcomputers. In the paper form of ledger sheets, spreadsheets have always been a tool available to accountants; as an electronic tool, they have made a powerful form of analysis available to everyone with access to a computer.

Spreadsheets use a row-and-column format for calculation, exactly like ledger sheets used by accountants. The user creates the format of the spreadsheet by entering column and row labels, then filling in data in the boxes, or cells, formed where rows and columns cross. Formulas can also be entered in cells, to tell the program to add rows or columns, or to carry out any mathematical function the user desires.

A common use for spreadsheets is for budgeting or for cash flow statements, for example. It is not as useful to know how much you will spend in an entire year as it is to have the total amount for each budget category "spread" across twelve months, so that you know how much money you need in each month.

One reason spreadsheets are so popular is that they allow the user to instantly recalculate the effect of a change. If you reviewed your budget for the next twelve months and decided you would reduce your expenses by moving to a cheaper apartment and by not taking a trip you had planned, you could simply make those changes and then get new totals in seconds.

Spreadsheets allow you to manipulate projected costs much more easily than you can with ledger sheets. For instance, if you were an architect designing a house for a client on a fixed budget, you could do all the planning you wanted by using your microcomputer. (How many square feet can the client afford? Solid brass or plated fixtures? Three bedrooms or two?) Each time you make a change in the design, the spreadsheet automatically recalculates all the related figures and computes to see whether you

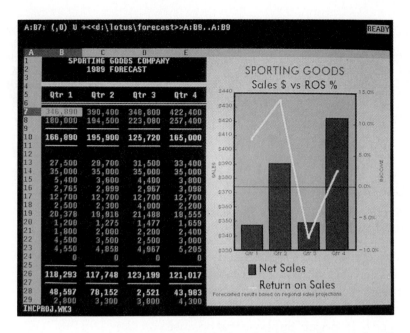

| A:B7: (,0) U +<<d:\lotus\forecast>>A:B9..A:B9 | | | | READY |

```
         A        B        C        D        E
                SPORTING GOODS COMPANY
1
2                  1989 FORECAST
3
4
5              Qtr 1    Qtr 2    Qtr 3    Qtr 4
6
7            346,890  390,400  348,800  422,400
8            180,000  194,500  223,080  257,400
9
10           166,890  195,900  125,720  165,000
11
12
13            27,500   29,700   31,500   33,400
14            35,000   35,000   35,000   35,000
15             5,400    3,600    4,400    3,800
16             2,765    2,899    2,967    3,098
17            12,700   12,700   12,700   12,700
18             2,500    2,300    4,000    2,200
19            20,378   19,916   21,488   18,555
20             1,200    1,275    1,477    1,659
21             1,800    2,000    2,200    2,400
22             4,500    3,500    2,500    3,000
23             4,550    4,858    4,967    5,205
24                 0        0        0        0
25
26           118,293  117,748  123,199  121,017
27
28            48,597   78,152    2,521   43,983
29             2,800    3,300    3,800    4,300
INCPROJ.WK3
```

SPORTING GOODS
Sales $ vs ROS %

■ Net Sales
Return on Sales
Forecasted results based on regional sales projections

2–2 Spreadsheets hold lots of information, but often a graph makes it easier to understand the relationships between the data elements. *Courtesy:* Lotus Development Corp.

are still on budget. This kind of analysis is called "what-if" analysis. *What if* I made the closet bigger? *What if* I added two hundred square feet? *What if* I added a fireplace?

Spreadsheets are also linked to **graphics** so that results can be displayed pictorially. For instance, while a sales manager can compare monthly sales of the top three salespeople during a year by analyzing three columns of numbers, many people find that looking at a graph that displays the same information is easier and has more impact. Figure 2–2 illustrates the difference between looking at the same data on a spreadsheet and in graphic chart form.

Accessing Databases

Walk into almost any office and you will find large numbers of filing cabinets with drawers full of file folders. The cost in paper, file folders, files, and—most of all—clerical time to prepare file folders, copy documents, and file them can add up to over $3,000 per drawer. At these prices it makes sense to look for other means for storing data. For legal documents, insurance forms, patient records, shipping invoices, and other high-volume records and documents, the solution is electronic filing.

Electronic filing may be defined as computer-assisted storage and retrieval of data or information. A concept central to electronic filing—and to a great deal of this book—is that of a database. A **database** consists of several electronically stored files (such as the student and course files in Figure 2–3), that can be cross-referenced. In other words, a database is a collection of files, and a file is a collection of records. When files are cross-referenced, users can retrieve data in many ways. For example, using the student and course files in a college database, you could ask for a listing of the students in each course in the French department. The database software first checks the course file to find the names of all courses in the French department, and

Sort course list
for French courses.

Use course numbers
to find enrollment logs.

Use student ID numbers
to find name and address.

2–3 This database of three related tables allows cross-referencing by key identification number to assemble a list of French students.

then checks the student file to find all students registered in those courses; it would then list the students in each course in the French department.

Electronic filing may not seem particularly useful at first until you need information that is important to you. For example, assume that you have just graduated from college and need to find a job. Suppose that because you like to travel and also like to work with computers, you decide that you want to be a systems analyst for an airline. Fortunately, your college job placement office maintains a database of potential employers. This database contains, among other things, information on company names, products, locations, managers' names, and so on. You can sort the companies in the database to find airlines, search those airlines to find those located in the state where you want to work (e.g., California), and print the results, including the name, address, and phone number of the managers you should contact in that state. Then, by combining the information from the database with a letter typed in a word processing package, you can send your resume and cover letter to any number of prospective employers in an afternoon of work!

Communicating via Electronic Mail

Electronic mail consists of using electronic means to send, store, and deliver messages that you would otherwise deliver verbally by phone or send by mail. Figure 2–4 shows an electronic mail program running on an Apple

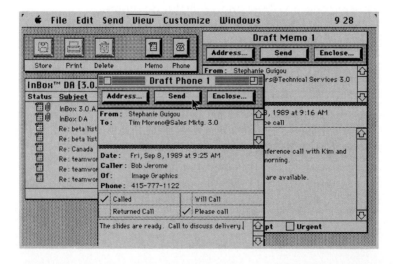

2–4 Using In-Box on the Apple Macintosh, a person can write, send, re-route, or annotate mail electronically.

Macintosh. Electronic mail is useful when you consider that the principle activity of middle- and upper-level managers is transferring information either by person-to-person contact or by written documents. Consider also that half the conversations executives have are composed of one-way information transfers; that is, no discussions are needed. Obviously, managers could send written memos or letters, or use the telephone to communicate with others; however, electronic mail is not slowed by the one- or two-day delays that regular mail generally takes. Also, it almost always reaches its destination, unlike telephone calls, which require someone to answer the phone. Electronic mail also enables managers to distribute information or delegate tasks to entire groups at once with a single message, and thus be more productive.

As you can see, computers do not do anything that was not done before by hand—typing correspondence, making calculations, filing documents, or phoning a colleague. Instead, computers enable you to do business tasks more efficiently, search for information more quickly, and analyze your decision alternatives more effectively.

How Business Computer Systems Are Organized

Today, because many computer professionals, clerks, and managers operate their own computers, their information systems must be organized toward a common purpose if the computers are to benefit the organization. People in different functional areas of a company interact with one another to get their work done, and they often need access to the same data, although it may be used in very different ways. A close look at the tasks and structure of organizations shows that they consist of four major functional areas, often called *departments* or *divisions*, which, when working together, enable the organization to produce goods and services and, hopefully, produce a profit. These four functional areas are:

◆ **Marketing**—the area concerned with sales, advertising, pricing, and moving goods to market.

◆ **Accounting and Finance**—the area concerned with generating and investing money and with accounting operations and payroll.

◆ **Production**—the area concerned with purchasing raw materials, manufacturing products, inventory control, and production scheduling.

◆ **Human Resources**—the area concerned with recruiting personnel, managing personnel policies and benefits, and meeting legal requirements for employment.

An organization's four functional areas (which could be expanded to include other groups such as Research and Development, or Building Maintenance) are reflected in its **organization chart**, a schematic drawing showing the hierarchy of formal relationships between groups of employees. The organization chart in Figure 2–5 illustrates the major functional areas of a typical business. The role of managers, of course, is to coordinate those

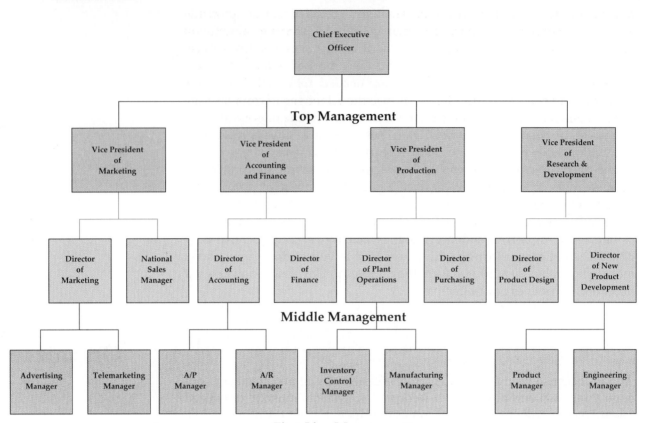

Top Management

Middle Management

First-Line Management

functional areas for the common goal of producing company products and profits.

The company employees working at each level tend to use computers for different purposes, reflecting the kind of decision making performed at each level. At the first-line management level, both workers and managers use computers for *operational* purposes—to do specific tasks such as enter orders, pay invoices to vendors, and so on. Middle managers and the people who work for them use computers to do *tactical analysis*—the data input at the operational level is now used to make decisions such as when to order new inventory, when to raise a product's price, and so on. At the top management level, computers assist executives in *strategic planning*—the analysis done at the middle management level is used to set long-term strategy for the company.

How do managers accomplish their specific business objectives? Basically, they assign specific tasks to employees. We call this integration of tasks and procedures a **business system**—for example, when clerks produce a monthly payroll they use an accounting business system to pay employees.

Two different approaches may be used to computerize a business system so that it becomes an effective information system: the traditional approach, which designs systems to meet the needs of each functional area, independent of other departments' systems; and the top-down management

2–5 Operational needs of first-line management tend to be very specific, whereas the tactical analysis needs of middle management and the strategic planning needs of top management require more general, integrated information

information system approach, in which the needs of the overall organization are considered first, while the needs of functional areas are met secondarily in a way that integrates the information needs of all areas.

Traditional Business Computer Systems

Systems analysts design traditional business systems or information systems on the assumption that *an organization is the sum of its functional areas, or parts.* In other words, the belief is that if each functional area does its work efficiently, the entire organization will run smoothly. Many organizations have used this approach successfully. However, any computer system that a functional area uses must serve the area's current interest—indeed, many organizations have suffered because they used computer systems that did not provide for changing business goals.

While the traditional systems approach is extremely useful in satisfying the needs and requirements of operating staff and managers in functional areas, what do you do if you are a top-level executive and need broad-based sales information across all your company's divisions? How do you get a company-wide sales forecast? How do you analyze your product mix to develop corporate strategies?

These questions point to a fundamental weakness in traditional business systems: even if a business system is helping all the company's functional areas to meet their objectives, the information needs of top-level executives may not be satisfied—which endangers the future of the company. Department managers need the day-to-day information provided by traditional business systems so they can run their departments or divisions effectively, but top executives must look at trends in information across a number of functional areas so they can develop business perspectives and create competitive strategies. Traditional business systems are not designed to provide the cumulative, integrated, historically based business information that executives need.

Looking Ahead

Working at Home in the Electronic Age

Workers in the 1990s have options that were unavailable in 1980—many sophisticated jobs can be done from home offices with nothing more than a microcomputer hooked up to a company's central computer. Such connections are done by modem—a small box that translates magnetic computer code into audio signals that can be transmitted across telephone wires.

With this connection, stockbrokers can follow investments and send buy and sell orders, journalists can send word processed copy to their newspapers, and executives can access company databases and analyze the financial performance of their companies. Workers can spend a quiet day at home catching up on important analysis; they can avoid time-consuming conversations with colleagues, while still being able to send messages to them by their company's electronic mail system.

This innovative approach to employment allows some workers to work part time at the office and part time at home, or to have a whole new career entirely run from an electronic home office.

Top-Down Management Information Systems (MIS)

Business information systems designed to integrate the information needs of the entire organization, beginning with the company-wide goals set by high-level managers, are called **Management Information Systems (MIS)**. Systems analysts develop them using a *top-down design*. Rather than focus on the business needs of each functional area, MIS analysts view an organization as though it were one complete unit with one set of specific corporate objectives—for example, the objective of gaining a market share increase of 5 percent while making a profit of 14 percent of sales.

MIS developers begin by designing a system around the information needed to meet top managers' company-wide goals and then design the information systems needed in each functional area to accomplish those goals. In other words, MIS developers view the company as an integrated entity with goals that are separate from but part of the collective goals of all the independent functional areas (Figure 2–6).

Decision Support Systems.   A common type of management information system is the **decision support system (DSS)**, which helps managers make quantitative "what-if" analyses to evaluate business alternatives. Decision support systems provide special analytic computing tools that allow managers to communicate with company databases by using normal English rather than special commands, to create financial models that test planning assumptions, to produce preformatted reports, and to use project management software. With these tools, managers can more easily monitor, track, and analyze activities within and between functional areas.

Executive Information Systems.   Many analysts formerly believed that it was only a matter of time before almost all company executives began using decision support systems to help them make top-level decisions. However, early DSSs met with little top management approval. They were

2–6 Each level of management has different information needs and uses the MIS system differently as a result.

relatively complicated to use, requiring a significant amount of computer expertise. In addition, their designers failed to take into account that even if executives had the time, they were not interested in doing highly technical analyses. Rather, they needed extremely flexible and easy-to-use systems that provided summary financial, reporting, and planning information from both inside and outside the organization—information specifically tailored to their information needs, organizational responsibilities, and management style.

Many executives now have such useful **executive information systems (EIS)** at their fingertips—systems that create and deliver critical information such as reports, charts, and text drawn from a wide variety of internal and external sources. For example, when executives in one typical corporation turn on their desktop computers in the morning, a menu appears on the screen that allows them to:

♦ Read memos, reports, and messages

♦ Review selected financial data

♦ Review external data, such as economic indicators, competitive information, or financial markets

♦ Analyze sales and financial results with a wide range of "pushbutton" statistical tools for exploring ratios, trends, and relationships in their data, and for evaluating the level of risk and uncertainty associated with their decision alternatives

♦ Access personnel data to keep tabs on who's who in the organization and how each function is performing against benchmarks

♦ Track the progress of key projects and development schedules.

When executives at Avon, the $3 billion cosmetic firm, used their EISs, they discovered that by eliminating some low-priced items from their Christmas line they had inadvertently cut their profitability. Without the EIS, which flagged the problem, the senior managers felt they would not have been able to correct the problem in time for the next Christmas season!

Traditional business systems, top-down management information systems, decision support systems, and executive information systems are all examples of how organizations use increasingly powerful and easy-to-use computer technology to find innovative ways of increasing productivity, controlling costs and, ultimately, creating a competitive advantage in the marketplace. However, businesses are also using a very advanced concept called **artificial intelligence** to manage information better. Artificial intelligence is an advanced form of programming that simulates human thought—the ability not only to weigh alternatives and make decisions, but also to go back and correct past procedures when new information proves them invalid. By far the most practical and exciting use for artificial intelligence in businesses is that of expert systems.

In a Nutshell

How Systems Are Organized

Traditional approach	Each functional area is designed independently. Successful in satisfying user needs at the department level; less successful in satisfying overall management needs.
MIS approach	Top-down, in that management needs are given priority. Functional area needs are then satisfied.
Advances using the MIS approach	Decision Support Systems Executive Information Systems Expert Systems

Expert Systems

Expert systems are integrated computer programs that compile all the decision-making rules and knowledge required for a specific decision to imitate the thinking process of experts. For example, one system called the Nervous Shock Advisor gives attorneys advice on the outcome of legal cases in the areas of nervous shock, emotional distress, and emotional suffering. When plaintiffs contend that they have suffered emotional distress, the system advises attorneys whether the claim is potentially valid, based on judgments reached in previous court cases.

Expert systems are best used in business situations where tasks require expensive, or scarce, experts to make decisions quickly and consistently over a long period of time. For example, when the Campbell Soup Company's lead cook decided to retire, the company faced a potential crisis. The lead cook had been responsible for operating the complicated machines used to cook soup and was the only employee who fully understood the system. Rather than lose his experience, the company built an expert system based on his knowledge and did not suffer when the cook finally retired.

How Business Computer Systems Are Designed

No matter how effective or state-of-the-art business information systems may be, they inevitably become obsolete or ineffectual as business needs change. Experience shows that as a company grows or changes, its information system must be redesigned to keep pace. If a system is unable to help managers make appropriate decisions because the information it provides is insufficient, inaccurate, or late, it is time for management to think about redesigning the system.

In one instance, top managers in a health maintenance organization discovered that because of rapid growth, the volume of health claims would soon quadruple from 250,000 claims a year to well over a million claims, making the paperwork literally unmanageable. They hired a team of systems analysts to determine precisely why the current set of operations were

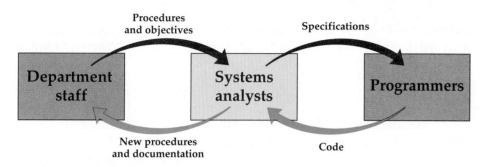

Procedures
and objectives

Specifications

Department
staff

Systems
analysts

Programmers

New procedures
and documentation

Code

2–7 System design involves users in defining objectives. Computer professionals then design and write the software.

not satisfactory and how they could be redesigned so that the department's growth objectives could be met.

Systems analysts, who may be either company employees or outside consultants, redesign business information systems by analyzing existing procedures and identifying basic problem areas. The new, more efficient business system normally uses computers for processing data. Once a new system is designed, analysts provide programmers with specifications for writing the computer programs that will be integrated into the new system. Systems analysts are then responsible for implementing the new system and writing procedural documentation for it so that it functions smoothly and effectively. This procedure is illustrated in Figure 2–7.

If the new system does not function smoothly or fails to meet functional objectives, the most likely reason is that the analysts did not communicate well with users. As you saw in Chapter 1, the single most common reason for computer systems not meeting the needs of users is that analysts and business people did not understand each other's respective needs. In practice, this means that business people are responsible for learning the potential applications as well as the limitations of computer systems, and systems analysts are responsible for being aware of the information needs and business functions of both users and the company as a whole.

Types of Computer Configurations

Computer professionals organize their computer or MIS facilities in many ways to match a company's overall structure. Three common configurations are centralized, decentralized, and distributed systems. Figure 2–8 illustrates how each type of computer implementation might be integrated into the overall organization.

How did such different configurations evolve? Originally, a single mainframe located in the information processing (or MIS) department served all the functional needs of the company. As minicomputers and microcomputers became increasingly powerful and inexpensive, however, managers in functional areas began purchasing their own computers so that they could have more control over them. In this way, computer facilities often became decentralized. Many companies then linked their decentralized systems together to create an integrated design that is referred to as a distributed system. We will discuss each type of facility, because each has its own advantages and disadvantages, and fosters different degrees of communication between users and analysts.

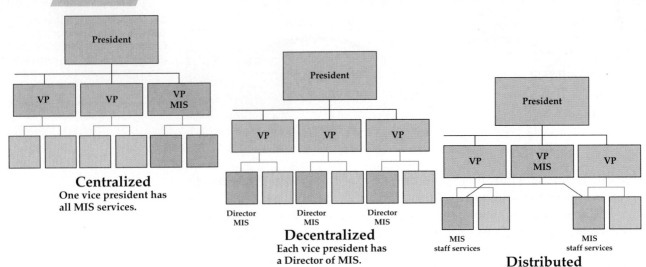

Centralized
One vice president has
all MIS services.

Decentralized
Each vice president has
a Director of MIS.

Distributed
Each department has its own MIS
service, reporting both to functional
VP and the VP of MIS.

Centralized Systems: The Traditional Use for Mainframes

Single computer facilities that serve the entire information needs of an organization are referred to as **centralized information processing**. This approach is still widely used in many companies. A centralized facility exists within the organization in one of three ways:

◆ **As a Subdivision of the Accounting or Finance Department.** When computers were first used in business organizations, they were primarily employed to satisfy accounting and financial needs. It was quite natural for information processing to become a subdivision of one of these departments. Even today, the primary function of a computer facility in many organizations is to serve these departments.

The main disadvantage of placing a computer facility within a department such as accounting or finance is that a specific department tends to get greater attention and priority, even when numerous other functional areas require computerization. For example, if the computer facility is in the accounting department, an accounting application is apt to be given higher priority, even though the marketing application may require more immediate attention.

◆ **As a Separate Department.** When computer services exist in a separate department, the director is typically a corporate-level manager reporting either to an executive vice-president or to the president. As a result, the director is better able to manage the information needs of the organization as a whole. Figure 2–9 shows some of the ways in which a director of computing services may fit into different organizational structures.

◆ **As a Time-Sharing Facility.** When computer services are needed, but the acquisition of major computing hardware is simply too expensive, companies outside the organization may supply computer time and computer support on an as-needed or regularly scheduled basis. In this way, an organization

2–8 The organization of centralized, decentralized, and distributed computer facilities. Equipment configurations usually mirror staff organization.

2–9 In major corporations, the director of computing services may report to various senior officers. This chart shows the distribution of reporting arrangements.

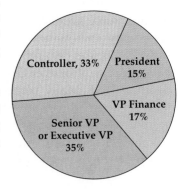

can minimize its need for hardware and computer professionals and rely either solely or predominantly on some outside source.

However, centralized systems have two built-in problems. First, a single, often overworked, computer staff must serve all departments. As a result, the computer staff has only limited knowledge of specific user needs in each of the functional areas, and communication between computer professionals and individual users is difficult. Second, it is also difficult to determine the actual computer costs to attribute to each department. As a result, a company with a centralized system cannot effectively assess the benefits or value of computerization for each of its functional areas.

Centralized systems are almost always found in medium to large companies, since they rely primarily on mainframes. Smaller companies using microcomputers typically have some form of decentralized computer system.

Decentralized Systems: Using Micros and Minis

To meet the computing needs of departments better and allocate resources more effectively, many companies have established separate computer facilities for each department; this is called a **decentralized system**. The advantages of this approach are that each department can purchase the precise equipment it needs, hire a staff of computer professionals that know of its specific requirements, and be responsible for its own computer costs.

A major disadvantage of decentralized computing, however, is that it tends to isolate each department so that there is no integration or coordination of a company's data, hardware, software, and systems support. Each department may use the same data or software for different purposes, or may need an expensive piece of hardware but be able to use it for only a small amount of the time. Moreover, there is inevitably a duplication of effort and equipment in the decentralized approach.

Decentralization also reduces the ability of the company's top-level managers to obtain information on the company as a whole. Because the various hardware systems do not communicate with one another, it is impossible to design a top-down management information system in this environment.

Recent advances in hardware and software have made it possible for large and small companies to derive the benefits of both centralized and decentralized processing. A facility that combines the advantages of both is called a distributed system.

Integrating Micros, Minis, and Mainframes in a Distributed Environment

Top management wants a cost-effective computing system that integrates the work of all functional areas and provides decision-making information about the company as a whole, and other computer users commonly want to send data, files, and messages to their co-workers. As a consequence, the most rapidly growing computer configuration is that of the **distributed system**. Distributed systems consist of terminals, micros, or minis linked in a system called a **network** to a centralized computer, usually a mainframe.

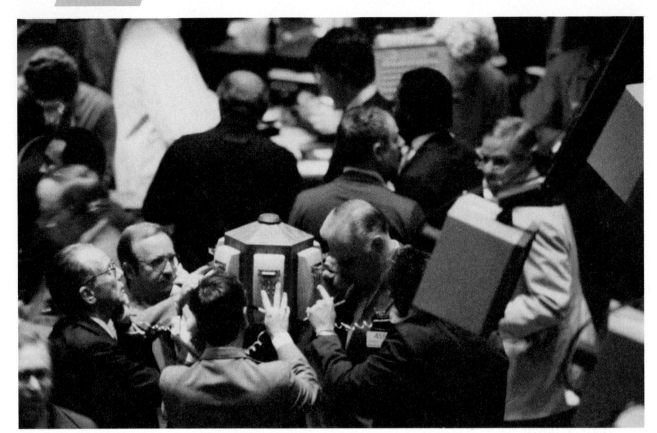

Figure 2–10 shows a well-known application of a distributed information processing network.

The distributed approach is applicable to all levels of computing—from a small company that has only microcomputers linked in a network, to a medium-sized company that has a mini networked to micros, to a Fortune 500 company that has huge mainframe systems linked to minis and micros.

Distributed systems have the advantages of both centralized and decentralized systems while minimizing their disadvantages. Each department's local data is processed by equipment and software designed to meet its special requirements; at the same time, a central computer can assess the cost of each functional area's information needs and ensure that computing efforts are not duplicated. In addition, top-level managers can obtain the integrated information that supports their decision making.

Note, too, that it is relatively easy and inexpensive to expand a distributed system—you simply add micros as workstations to do tasks such as word processing, budgeting, sales forecasting, and so on. Systems analysts then link these micros to a central computer, creating a distributed network. Micros are now so prevalent in distributed systems that the combined total of their processing, measured in MIPS (millions of instructions per second), sometimes doubles or triples the MIPS of the organization's mainframe!

Distributed systems are not without pitfalls, however. They demand a high level of technical and organizational skills from system managers, since the system must serve all functional areas and all levels of computer exper-

2–10 A distributed computer system serves traders on the floor of the New York Stock Exchange. *Courtesy:* New York Stock Exchange.

Centralized Systems	Decentralized Systems	Distributed Systems
1. Results in standardized equipment and procedures for the company as a whole. 2. Computer specialists work as a group—procedures become more professional; supervision of activities is improved. 3. Reduces duplication of effort.	1. Direct control by users minimizes the traditional communication gap; computer professionals better understand department's needs. 2. Response to user needs is more direct; pressure from other departments is minimized. 3. Easier to assess the effectiveness of each facility.	1. Combines the advantages of centralized and decentralized data processing. 2. Employs an intregrated approach to systems. 3. The best method for accommodating growth.
1. Difficult to assess needs, costs, and effectiveness of the system. 2. Difficult to determine priorities for computer use. 3. Management-level resistance exists because control of activities is in the hands of the system manager.	1. There is duplication of data files, processing, and reporting. 2. Lack of standardization. 3. Costs are usually higher. 4. Management control is more difficult.	1. Requires sophisticated hardware and software control. 2. Requires strict adherence to standards. 3. Many users make system vulnerable to accidents and vandalism.

tise. In addition, as the system inevitably expands, strict procedural and design standards must be followed as each piece of hardware or software is added. Also, because such systems typically have so many users—many of them off-site—with access to input and output, system designers and managers have to provide a high level of security.

2–11 Advantages and disadvantages of different types of computer facilities.

Figure 2–11 provides an overview of the advantages and disadvantages of each type of facility.

The Organization of Computing Departments

Computing departments are structured and staffed in various ways to meet the needs of the organizations they support. For example, the computer facility's manager may have one of any number of titles—director, manager, or vice president; and the department he or she manages may be called Management Information Services, Information Services, Computer Information Systems, or Information Processing. Regardless of the title, these managers are responsible for the entire computer facility and its staff of computer professionals.

Types of Computer Specialists

There are five principal categories of computer specialists commonly found in computing departments. Figure 2–12 shows some typical salary ranges.

♦ **Systems Manager and Systems Analysts**. The systems manager supervises the activities of an organization's systems analysts. As we discussed earlier, systems analysts are responsible for analyzing existing business procedures, determining basic problem areas or inefficiencies, and designing a more efficient information system, or computerized set of procedures. The

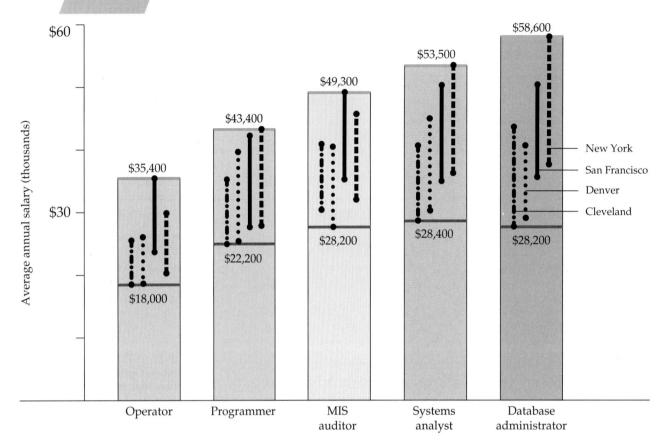

2–12 The salaries of computer professionals vary by job and location as well as experience. Ranges are for workers with less than 4 and more than 6 years experience. *Source:* EDP.

systems manager assigns specific tasks to individual analysts and evaluates their progress.

◆ **Programming Manager and Programmers**. The programming manager directs the activities of an organization's programmers. The programmer receives the job requirements from a systems analyst and is responsible for writing, testing, and documenting programs that will integrate into the business system as a whole.

Smaller companies that cannot afford a full staff of computer analysts and programmers may hire a different type of computer professional called a **programmer analyst**, who designs business systems *and* writes all the necessary programs as well. The programmer analyst is responsible for the entire design, including all the programming and implementation.

◆ **Operations Manager and Operators**. Operations managers are responsible for the overall operations of the computer center. They supervise computer operators, who in turn perform data entry and control procedures. Operations managers are accountable for the efficient and effective use of computer equipment. An operations manager must ensure that input errors are kept to a minimum and that the computer system is relatively secure from breakdown, fire, power outages, unauthorized use, and inadvertent misuse.

◆ **Auditors**. Auditors are the accounting and computer specialists responsible for assessing the effectiveness and efficiency of the computer system and for maintaining the overall integrity of a system's programs and data.

◆ **Database Administrator**. The database administrator oversees the structure, design, and control of all information processing files and is responsible for organizing and designing the database and associated computer files. The database administrator is accountable for efficient design of the database and for implementing proper controls and techniques necessary for accessing it.

Common Organizational Structures

In small companies the entire staff of computer professionals may consist of one or two microcomputer specialists who are responsible for every computer-related function—from customizing software packages and designing the information systems to purchasing hardware. Large companies, however, usually have a department of people with various specialties. In these companies, computer facilities are usually organized in one of two basic ways: 1) systems analysts reporting to a systems manager, and programmers reporting to a programming manager, or 2) programmers reporting to systems analysts.

The left-hand structure in Figure 2–13 illustrates an organization in which programmers and analysts report to different supervisors and work together as peers designing programs for a new system. Under this structure, analysts have less actual control over the programmers working on a specific application, but the advantage is that there is usually a free exchange of ideas between the two groups.

The right-hand structure in Figure 2–13 illustrates an organization in which programmers report directly to systems analysts. As supervisors, systems analysts act as project managers, assigning programmers to write programs for new systems and then monitoring their progress and evaluating their results. In this instance there is one overall manager for both systems and programming.

2–13 Two common organization structures for programmers and systems analysts. Independent reporting increases staff flexibility, but working in teams makes for greater coordination and closer control.

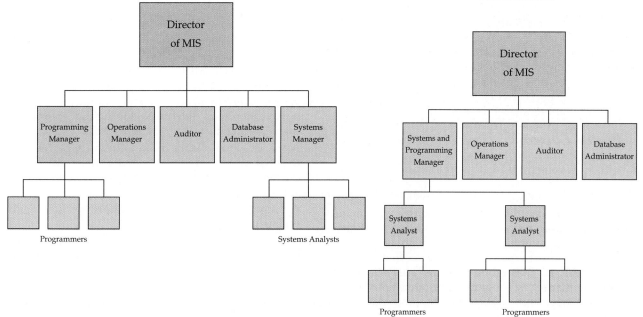

Clearly a wide variety of models are available to company executives for designing a management information system that meets their unique needs. The key to the success of these important business systems is the creativity and know-how of the systems analysts who put it all together and the ability of these analysts to work closely with users to accurately determine their information processing needs.

SUMMARY

Information systems in a business must be organized toward a common purpose if they are to benefit the organization. One way to organize information systems is to design them to satisfy functional area needs of the organization. A close look at the tasks and structure of organizations shows that organizations consist of several functional areas, including *marketing, accounting and finance, production,* and *human resources.* Information systems that are designed primarily to support the needs of functional areas are called *traditional business systems.* Information systems designed for high-level managers using a *top-down design approach* are called *Management Information Systems (MIS).*

Two kinds of MIS systems exist: *Decision Support Systems (DSS)* and *Executive Information Systems (EIS).* DSSs commonly provide middle managers quantitative analysis tools, while EISs provide executives with broad-based and historical information. Organizations are also increasingly using artificial intelligence tools for designing *expert systems* that take advantage of scarce or expensive expertise in organizations.

Systems analysts design information systems when current business systems become either too expensive or too inefficient to operate, or when systems are unable to help managers make appropriate decisions because information provided is insufficient, inaccurate, or late. Systems analysts begin developing a new business information system by analyzing the existing business procedures, providing programmers with specifications for new computer programs, implementing and then documenting the new system so that it functions smoothly and effectively.

Computer professionals organize computer facilities in three common configurations: *centralized, decentralized,* and *distributed systems.* A centralized facility may appear within the organization in one of three ways: as a *subdivision* of the accounting or finance department, as a *separate department,* or as a *time-sharing facility.* Distributed facilities maximize the advantages of both centralized and decentralized facilities while minimizing their disadvantages.

Common information processing staff members include systems managers, systems analysts, programming managers, programmers, operations managers and operators, EDP auditors, and database administrators. Information processing directors can organize computer facilities with programmers and systems analysts reporting to different supervisors or programmers reporting directly to systems analysts.

KEY TERMS

Artificial intelligence	Information systems
Auditor	Management information system (MIS)
Business functions	
Centralized data processing	Network
Database	Operations manager
Database administrator	Organization chart
Decentralized system	Productivity tools
Decision support system	Programmer
Distributed system	Programmer analyst
Electronic filing	Systems manager
Electronic mail	Top-down design
Electronic spreadsheet	Traditional business system
Expert systems	Word processing
Graphics	

CHAPTER SELF-TEST

1. The productivity tool that allows managers to manipulate data in a format similar to a ledger sheet is called a _____.

2. A database is a collection of many _____ that are cross-referenced.

3. The productivity tool that allows people in a company to communicate via their computers is called _____ _____.

4. The four functional areas common to most companies are: _____, _____, _____, and _____.

5. With a *(centralized, decentralized)* computer facility, it is difficult to determine the actual computer costs to attribute to each department.

6. A management information system that attempts to satisfy the needs of each department as well as the needs of the company as a whole is likely to use a _____ computer facility.

7. A programmer analyst is a computer professional who usually _____.

8. A person responsible for the structure, design, and control of information processing files is called a _____.

9. In some computer organizations, programmers report to _____. In other organizations, programmers report directly to _____.

10. (T *or* F) The title "database administrator" can be another name for the position of "director of information processing."

11. (T *or* F) It is possible for a centralized information processing facility to use a time-sharing arrangement with an outside firm.

12. (T *or* F) With a decentralized information processing facility, there is apt to be duplication of files, processing, and reporting.

13. (T *or* F) The programming staff always reports directly to the information processing manager.

14. The most difficult information system to manage is one that is (centralized, decentralized, distributed).

SOLUTIONS 1) spreadsheets. 2) files. 3) electronic mail. 4) marketing, accounting and finance, production, and human resources. 5) centralized. 6) distributed. 7) both designs the system and writes the programs. 8) database administrator. 9) a programming manager; systems analysts. 19) False. 11) True. 12)True. 13)False. 14) distributed.

REVIEW QUESTIONS

1. List four common productivity tools and briefly describe how each is used in business.

2. Name the four common functional areas of a business.

3. List three ways a top-down Management Information System differs from a traditionally organized business information system.

4. What is a decision support system? An expert system?

5. List and briefly describe the three alternatives for structuring a company's computing facilities. List at least two advantages and disadvantages of each.

6. List five professional roles for computer professionals and briefly describe the responsibilities of each.

7. What are the advantages and disadvantages of having programmers report to systems analysts as opposed to having each group report to their own managers?

PROBLEM-SOLVING APPLICATIONS

1. College campuses have computer facilities to meet various functional needs—the financial and accounting systems, computer science instructional facilities, student registration information, statistical analysis for research projects, and so on. Review your college's bulletin and catalog and see if you can discover whether your campus has a centralized, decentralized, or distributed computer system. You may find that some functions are centralized, while others, such as specialized research facilities, have decentralized facilities.

2. Assume you have just been appointed Chief Operations Officer for a medium-sized manufacturing company. It has a centralized computing facility that the functional areas are rapidly outgrowing, and one of your immediate goals is to update the computing organization to meet your needs and those of your functional area vice presidents. Draw an organization chart that you think would work for you.

Productivity Tools: Word Processing, Spreadsheets, and Database Management

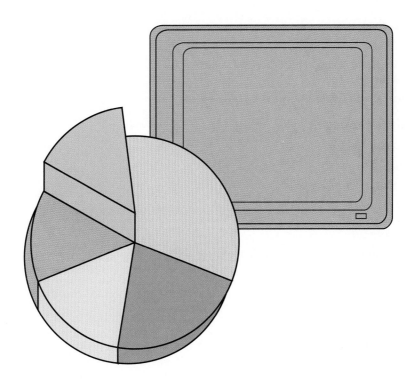

When you have completed this chapter, you will be able to:

- ✔ List and describe the three most common end-user productivity tools.

- ✔ Describe how the three productivity tools are used for each of the four levels of use: keyboarding, editing, formatting, and managerial decision-making.

- ✔ Describe the advantages of word processing over typing, spreadsheets over ledger sheets, and electronic databases over paper filing systems.

- ✔ Describe the difference between flat-file databases and relational databases.

Chapter 3

Chapter Outline

If you have used a microcomputer, you are probably already acquainted with at least one application software package—you have probably used a word processing package to write reports and term papers. This chapter discusses those application software packages called **productivity tools**.

As the name implies, these software packages increase your productivity by providing the tools necessary to do a specific type of task efficiently. For example, earlier generations of students had to type their papers on a typewriter, then read and edit them, then retype them, then proofread them, then retype them, and so on. With word processing, you type a paper only once, edit and proof it on the screen, and then print it in any format you choose. You save many hours, allowing you to spend more time on writing style and content, and less on tedious keyboarding. Moreover, most word processing packages include spelling checkers and thesauruses, as well as other tools that make document preparation easier.

The categories of end-user productivity tools discussed in this chapter are word processing, spreadsheets, and database management. All of the packages discussed here are typically used on microcomputers for both business and personal applications.

Using Productivity Tools

End-user productivity tools can be used at four general levels:

1.   The lowest level is that of entering data, often in the form of typing, which is usually called **keyboarding**.

2.   The second level is **editing**. Special editing features allow the data already entered in a document, spreadsheet, or database to be altered, deleted, replaced, moved, or copied.

3.   The third level is that of **formatting** or design. Formatting refers to the way output is arranged to make it pleasing to look at and easy to read and understand. Printing a report with appropriate headings, page numbers, well-labeled columns, and so on, is an example of formatting.

4.   The fourth level is the **manager's use of output** to support decision making. Generally, managers do not have time to obtain a working knowledge of the software used in their departments; however, they can manipulate and analyze data that others have entered, edited, and formatted.

As we introduce each of the productivity tools, we will describe how they are used at each of these four levels.

Microcomputer Basics

To understand how productivity tools are used, you will first need a brief introduction on how to use a microcomputer.

The Keyboard

Keyboard entry is by far the most common way to enter data into a computer, and so you should be familiar with the keyboard your microcomputer

Function keys   Alphanumeric keyboard   Numeric keypad
                                                                          and cursor keys

Function keys

Alphanumeric keyboard   Cursor keys   Numeric keypad

uses. Computer keyboards resemble the keyboards on electric typewriters. The standard personal computer keyboard usually consists of three or four main areas: the **alphanumeric keys** (those with letters, numbers, and symbols on them), the **function keys** (numbered F1 through F10 or F12), the **cursor control keys** (arrows pointing in four directions), and a **numeric keypad** (rather like an adding machine keyboard) (Figure 3–1). These last two areas are sometimes combined and the [Num Lock] key used to switch between the cursor control keys and the numeric keypad. In addition, there are a number of special keys with labels like [Shift] (sometimes labeled with an up arrow), [Esc], [Ctrl], and [Alt].

The function keys are assigned specific tasks by each software package. For example, in WordPerfect on an IBM-compatible computer, the F10 key is used to save a file (record it on disk); in another popular word processing package, WordStar, the F1 key is used for saving. Most application packages include a keyboard template—a plastic or cardboard plate that fits over the function keys—to tell users how function keys and other additional key combinations work (Figure 3–2). This text has a template for WordPerfect included at the back to use with the WordPerfect tutorial.

The Screen and the Cursor

The most important element on the screen when you are using an application is the **cursor**. It is usually a small blinking underline or rectangle (Figure 3–3). The cursor indicates where your input will actually appear on the

3–1 These typical micro-computer keyboards have four main groups of keys: the alphanumeric keys, the numeric keypad, 10 or 12 computer-related function keys, and the cursor control keys.

WordPerfect	Shell	Spell	Screen	Move	Ctrl	Text In/Out	Tab Align	Footnote	Font	Ctrl	Merge/Sort	Macro Define		
	Thesaurus	Replace	Reveal Codes	Block	Alt	Mark Text	Flush Right	Math/Columns	Style	Alt	Graphics	Macro		
	Setup	♦Search	Switch	♦Indent♦	Shift	Date/Outline	Center	Print	Format	Shift	Merge Codes	Retrieve		
	Cancel	♦Search	Help	♦Indent		List Files	Bold	Exit	Underline		Merge R	Save	Reveal Codes	Block
	F1	F2	F3	F4		F5	F6	F7	F8		F9	F10	F11	F12

[Esc] [F1] [F2] [F3] [F4] [F5] [F6] [F7] [F8] [F9] [F10] [F11] [F12]

screen. You can move the cursor around by using the cursor control keys (the arrow keys) or a mouse. The mouse is moved on your desktop and has buttons to activate the cursor and select menu items. The four arrow keys move the cursor one character or line at a time in the direction indicated by the arrow.

3–2 Many software packages provide a template that fits over the function keys and identifies the commands that have been assigned to them.

Accessing Software

Programs are stored as files on disks. We are going to describe the way software is accessed on the two most popular kinds of microcomputers: IBMs and their compatibles, and the Apple Macintosh family. We will describe both how programs are started and how to display the contents of a disk; that is, how to display the files electronically recorded on it.

First of all, note that a microcomputer file can be one of two kinds: *program files* are the files which contain sets of instructions that operate on data; *data files* are the output or input files you create with the application. For example, WP.EXE is the name of the WordPerfect word processing program; it must be loaded and run in order to generate a document. A report that you have typed and named REPORT1.TXT is a data file because it consists of data that has been outputted by the program. Notice that *data* in this sense is not limited to numbers—anything to be processed by the computer is data.

On IBM Microcomputers and Compatibles.   Programs on IBM and IBM-compatible computers are normally started from the disk operating system (DOS) prompt, which appears on the screen when you start the system. If you are using a dual-floppy-disk system, this is normally the A> prompt; if the system you use has a hard disk, the prompt is normally C>. To start a program, you must type a command that usually consists of some

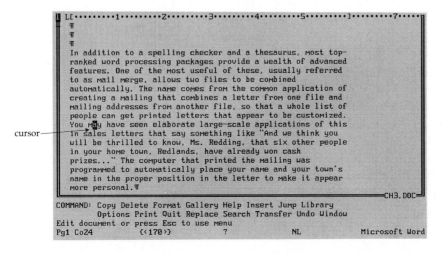

cursor

```
L[••••••••1•••••••••2•••••••••3•••••••••4•••••••••5•••••••••]••••••••••7••••
  ¶
  ¶
  ¶
  In addition to a spelling checker and a thesaurus, most top-
  ranked word processing packages provide a wealth of advanced
  features. One of the most useful of these, usually referred
  to as mail merge, allows two files to be combined
  automatically. The name comes from the common application of
  creating a mailing that combines a letter from one file and
  mailing addresses from another file, so that a whole list of
  people can get printed letters that appear to be customized.
  You may have seen elaborate large-scale applications of this
  in sales letters that say something like "And we think you
  will be thrilled to know, Ms. Redding, that six other people
  in your home town, Redlands, have already won cash
  prizes..." The computer that printed the mailing was
  programmed to automatically place your name and your town's
  name in the proper position in the letter to make it appear
  more personal.¶
                                                          CH3.DOC
COMMAND: Copy Delete Format Gallery Help Insert Jump Library
         Options Print Quit Replace Search Transfer Undo Window
Edit document or press Esc to use menu
Pg1 Co24         {<170>}              ?              NL        Microsoft Word
```

3–3 In most productivity packages, the cursor appears as a blinking underline or blinking upright bar.

form of the program's name. For example, to load and start the word processing package WordPerfect, you type *WP,* while to start the spreadsheet software Lotus 1-2-3, you can type either *LOTUS* or *123.*

To display a list of the files on a DOS disk, you type the command DIR and press [Enter]; this displays a **directory**, or list of all files on the current disk drive (Figure 3–4). Each file name may consist of a name of up to eight characters, a period, and an extension of up to three characters. Here are some file names you might see displayed:

◆ CHAPTER1.DOC   Good name for Chapter 1 of a report

◆ BUDGET91.WK1   Good name for a 1991 budget spreadsheet (the .WK1 extension is assigned by the Lotus 1-2-3 package)

◆ USERDATA.DBF   Good name for a user database (the .DBF extension is assigned by the dBASE package)

◆ COMMAND.COM   Standard DOS operating system file which is used for starting up the computer

You can usually determine a file's type by looking at its extension. For example, .COM and .EXE files are files that run an application, .DOC and .TXT usually indicate text files, .WKS and .WK1 are spreadsheet files, and .DBF indicates a database file. Some programs—such as Microsoft Word, Lotus 1-2-3, and dBASE IV—automatically assign an extension of their own whenever you save a file. For example, if you create a spreadsheet in Lotus 1-2-3 and name it BUDGET91, Lotus 1-2-3 will automatically save it as BUDGET91.WK1. The .WK1 extension is added so that you can more easily tell your spreadsheet files from your other data files, such as text files.

On an Apple Macintosh.   To start a program on an Apple Macintosh, you position the cursor on a little picture, or icon, that represents a software package; then you click the mouse button.

To see a directory listing, you position the cursor on the icon that represents the disk and then click the mouse button; a directory listing then appears on the screen (Figure 3–4).

Common Features of Application Packages

Certain features are common to all the application programs we will be examining. Among these features are the ability to create a data file, to save that file in a specific format on disk, to retrieve it and display it on the screen, to edit or modify it, and to print results in a variety of formats.

All application packages have **default settings**. To make it easy for you to begin using the package, its manufacturers set each feature at a commonly used value. For example, in a word processing package, the left margin might "default" to column 10. This means that unless you alter the position of the left margin, it will automatically start at the tenth column. In most cases, you can change defaults to suit the type of work you do. As you become more sophisticated in using a package, you will learn how to change the default settings to meet your particular needs.

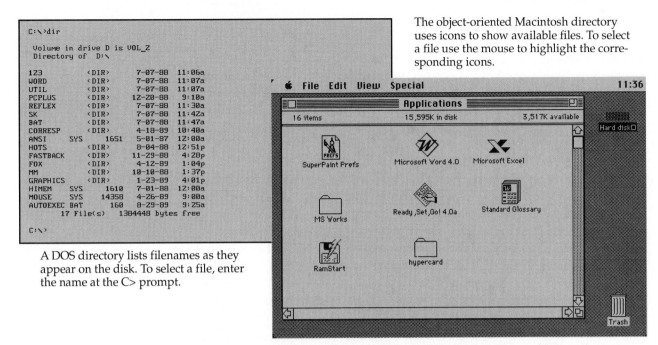

The object-oriented Macintosh directory uses icons to show available files. To select a file use the mouse to highlight the corresponding icons.

A DOS directory lists filenames as they appear on the disk. To select a file, enter the name at the C> prompt.

3–4 It is often useful to see a directory listing of the files on a disk before you start to use an application program.

Most application packages have on-line **help screens**. When you press a key specified by that package, the screen displays information about the functions that are currently being used. These help screens are particularly useful when you are first learning to use a package. For example, if you are changing the margins for printing and you get confused, you can ask for help; the package will display a screen that explains how to change margins.

Another feature common to most application packages is that they are **case-insensitive** for commands and file names. This means that you can type commands and file names in either upper- or lowercase and get the same result. Some aspects of applications *are,* however, case sensitive. For example, if you want to search for a word in a word processing document, the package can distinguish between MacGregor and Macgregor.

As you learn more about application packages, you will see that there are many similarities between different types of software; recognizing these similarities will help you to learn new packages more quickly.

SELF-TEST

1. Three major categories of end-user productivity tools are _____, _____, and _____.
2. The level of using productivity tools that consists of typing in data is also called _____.
3. (T *or* F) The keys with little arrows on them are called function keys.
4. (T *or* F) Some keys on the keyboard are assigned special tasks by each software package.
5. Three examples of file name extensions are: _____, _____, and _____.
6. (T *or* F) All software packages have default settings that assume certain initial values; the user can typically override them.

SOLUTIONS   1) word processing, spreadsheet packages, database management systems. 2) keyboarding. 3) False. They are cursor control keys. 4) True. 5) Any of these: .COM, .EXE., .DOC, .TXT, .WKS, .WK1, .DBF. 6) True.

Word Processing Packages

Word processing is probably the most commonly used microcomputer application. Nearly everyone needs to create written documents. **Word processing** vastly simplifies the task of writing and revising these documents because they have to be keyboarded only once; editing can then be done quickly and as many times as necessary. In most offices, word processing packages on microcomputers have virtually replaced typewriters for creating memos, letters, business reports, and other documents.

Word processing is particularly well suited for repetitive documents such as personalized form letters or contracts, because once a standard document is entered, it can be called up on the screen and edited for a special use in seconds. For that reason, word processing has been embraced by journalists and other professional writers and editors who find that it frees them to concentrate on what they are trying to communicate. Figure 3–5

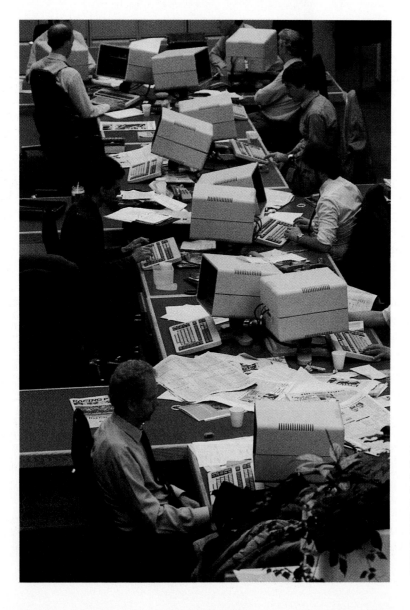

3–5 Word processing software lets reporters write and rewrite stories easily— and then it feeds right into electronic page makeup software. *Courtesy:* Atex Publishing Systems, a division of Eastman Kodak Company's Electronic Pre-Press Systems, Inc.

shows news reporters preparing copy on an Atex production system in the newsroom of the **The Times** in London, England.

Level 1: Keyboarding

In word processing, keyboarding is roughly equivalent to using a typewriter, although a number of extra keys or key combinations are used to produce the desired result. Being familiar with the standard layout of a typewriter keyboard is helpful, and the ability to type without looking at the keyboard ("touch type") is a distinct advantage.

Most word processing packages allow even beginners to start typing immediately, using the built-in default settings for margins, tabs, line spacing, and character size. For the most part, you can type text just as you would with a typewriter, using the [Tab], [Shift], and [Backspace] keys as usual. There is one major difference, however: on a typewriter you press the Carriage Return key at the end of each line, but in a word processing package, the [Enter] key (similar to Carriage Return) is used only at the end of paragraphs or after short lines that are not part of a longer paragraph. When you type using a word processing package, text you are keying in a paragraph wraps around to the next line when it reaches the end of the current line. This feature, called **word wrap**, automatically moves the cursor from the right margin to the left margin of the next line when the line is full, so there is no need to press the [Enter] key. When you insert or delete text, the word wrap feature automatically reformats the paragraph to fill the lines again.

Usually an on-screen **status line**, at either the top or the bottom of the screen, helps you keep track of your place within a document. The status line typically tells you the page number, line number within that page, and position number within that line. It may also show where margins and tabs have been set, as well as other information that varies, depending on the word processing package. The most popular word processing packages are WordPerfect, Microsoft Word, and WordStar.

Level 2: Editing

When you enter text, you can make corrections as you go along by pressing the [Backspace] or [Delete] key to erase newly entered characters. But sometimes text must be corrected later, after the document is partially or completely typed. Editing—changing text after it has been entered—can be done both during keyboarding or at any time after keyboarding. Although keyboarding is usually simple and straightforward, editing with a word processing package can be somewhat more complex. Even beginners will quickly master basic editing techniques to use during keyboarding, such as backspacing to delete what was just typed. However, there may be several ways to accomplish a particular editing task, and each method has its advantages. It is well worth the initial investment of time and energy to learn to use a word processing package's more advanced editing features.

Among the features that make editing easier is the ability to quickly move the cursor to precisely where you want it in the text. Most word processing packages have special keystroke sequences that allow you to scroll through a document. **Scrolling** means that the text flows rapidly past on the screen. You can scroll a line at a time, or you can skip from the top of one page to the top of the next one. You can quickly move to the beginning or end of a line or to the beginning or end of a document. In addition, there are usually some intermediate shortcuts such as moving the cursor a single word or paragraph at a time.

In long documents, the fastest way to find a particular word or place in the text is to use the **search feature** and let the computer do the looking for you. Linked to that feature is another, **search and replace**, which searches for every instance of a specified word or phrase and replaces it with another, either automatically or after pausing for you to verify the change. For example, suppose you have been using the term *personal computer* in a term paper, and you have decided that you want to use *microcomputer* instead. You know that the term appears as many as 25 times in your paper, and if you go through looking for each one of them, you may miss some instances. Instead, you use the command for search and replace. When a screen query asks what you want to search for, you type *personal computer*. When it then asks what to replace it with, you type *microcomputer*. It then asks whether you want it to replace automatically or whether you want to review each instance to make sure the change should be made. If you tell it to replace automatically, the operation is over in seconds, and you can be sure every misspelling has been caught. In addition to doing the replacement, the package will reformat each paragraph to fill the lines properly with the shorter term.

Most word processing packages give you the option of working in either **Insert mode** or **Typeover mode** (the exact names of these modes vary depending on the package). During the actual typing process, these two modes are virtually indistinguishable. However, when you are making changes or corrections to a document, the difference quickly becomes obvious. In Insert mode, text is moved to the right as new characters are typed. In Typeover mode, text that is currently on the screen will be overwritten by the new text you enter.

Just as there are shortcuts for moving the cursor, there are shortcuts for moving, copying, or deleting text. You can usually mark a **block** of text of any size to delete it or move it to a different location. Figure 3–6 shows a

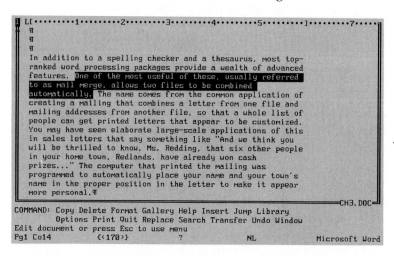

3–6 Microsoft Word has versions for both IBM-compatibles and for the Macintosh. It is a powerful word processing package that allows for sophisticated document formatting.

block highlighted using Microsoft Word. Most programs also allow you to delete or move an entire sentence, paragraph, or page, or bring a block of text in from another document. The ease with which text can be reorganized is one of the most convenient features of word processing.

Occasionally everyone makes a mistake, and most of today's word processing packages allow you to cancel a command or "undelete" text. Not all word processing programs have these options, and even when they are included, their effectiveness may be limited. For that reason and many others, it is always wise to save your work frequently. This is a lesson most new users learn the hard way: after pages of keyboarding, the electricity may go or someone may accidentally kick the electric plug out of the socket—and you will find that hours of work are lost. Some word processing packages limit your risk of losing work by automatically saving your document at regular intervals. Even so, it is best to develop the habit of saving text often as you are entering it. Once a document is saved on a disk, it can be retrieved whenever you want to use it.

A number of other features can help improve accuracy when you are writing or editing with word processing. Most packages include a **spelling checker**; many include an electronic thesaurus, and some even include a grammar checker. Spelling checkers compare the words in your document with an electronic dictionary. The spelling checker indicates any words in the document that are not in the dictionary so that you can check them for accuracy. WordPerfect, a popular word processing package, has an easy-to-use spelling checker (Figure 3–7).

Of course, spelling checkers cannot catch every error—for example, they cannot tell the difference between two correctly spelled words, such as *there* and *their*, and they cannot verify technical or specialized words not commonly found in dictionaries. Many spelling checkers permit you to add words to the dictionary.

Another word processing tool, the thesaurus, is a dictionary of words with similar meanings. If you find that you are overusing a term—"technique," for example—the thesaurus will offer you alternatives: strategy, methodology, approach, and so on. These alternatives can be automatically substituted for the original word with one or two keystrokes.

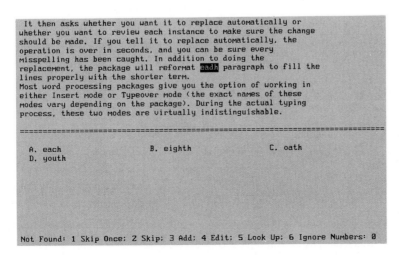

3–7 WordPerfect, like many word processing packages, includes an integrated spelling checker. When it encounters a word not in its dictionary, the word is highlighted and a list of similar words in the dictionary is displayed. You can then choose to correct your word, add it to the dictionary, or skip it (for example, if it is a proper name).

Level 3: Formatting

The third level of word processing use involves formatting the document. The default values of a word processing package (such as margins, page length, and so on) can be changed to meet the needs of a particular document or the standards of a particular company.

A few years ago, word processing software put formatting codes on the screen rather than showing what the printed output would actually look like. If you wanted a word to be in boldface, for example, the screen would show the boldface code before and after the word, but the word would look just like all the other words. Current versions of most word processing packages are now **WYSIWYG**—an acronym for "what you see is what you get," pronounced *wizzy-wig*. This new term has actually entered common usage in computer journalism. A WYSIWYG word processing package displays the text on the screen in exactly the same format as how the printed output will look.

Page Formatting.   Many of the formatting features available in word processing packages are similar to those that people first used on typewriters. For example, margins, tabs, and line spacing can all be set and changed at will.

Of course, word processing offers many other formatting features that usually are not available on typewriters. One of these is **justification**. Documents usually have left justification; all the lines at the left margin start in the same column. When only right justification is turned on, the right-hand margin lines up, but the left margin is uneven.

You can also automatically center text on a line (or on a page) or have it both right- and left-justified, so that both right and left margins line up. The text you are reading right now is both right- and left-justified; the text in the figure captions is not. Figure 3–8 demonstrates various types of justification.

In a Nutshell

Common Features of Word Processing Packages		
	Word wrap	Automatic wrapping of text to a new line when a line is full—no need to press the [Enter] key at the end of each line
	Status line	On-screen information about the document and current control settings such as Caps Lock mode
	Editing	Ability to change, add, or delete text both during keyboarding and afterward
	Block moves	Ability to mark a block of text and move, copy, or delete it, even between documents
	Justification	Ability to make both left and right margins align
	Spelling checker	Ability to compare each word with an electronic dictionary to catch errors
	Thesaurus	Ability to look up words of similar meaning to substitute for the current word

```
     Of course, word processing offers many other
     formatting features that usually are not available
     on typewriters. One of these is justification.
     Documents usually have left justification: all the
     lines at the left margin start in the same column.

     Of  course,  word   processing   offers   many   other
     formatting  features  that usually are not available on
     typewriters.  One  of  these  is  left  and  right
     justification.  When  a  document  is  left-  and
     right-justified, both margins line up.

              Of course, word processing offers many other
         formatting features that usually are not available
         on typewriters. One of these is justification. When
          right justification is turned on, the right margin
                                                 lines up.
```

3–8 The ability to arrange and format text in a wide variety of ways allows word processing packages to generate sophisticated output.

Page numbers and running heads—those lines above the text that give the chapter and book title—can also be programmed to print on every page, or to alternate between even- and odd-numbered pages.

Character Formatting.   Word processing packages normally offer a great deal of versatility in type style. These styles are usually limited only by the sophistication of the printer being used. Several type sizes and typefaces, or fonts, are normally available. These fonts may use proportional spacing (which allows more space for wide characters such as m and w and less for narrow ones like i and l). This enables right and left margins to be perfectly aligned. This textbook is formatted with proportionally spaced fonts.

With most of these packages, underlining and double underlining can be accomplished automatically, text can be boldfaced or italicized, and superscripts and subscripts are usually available (Figure 3–8).

Advanced Features.   In addition to a spelling checker and a thesaurus, most top-ranked word processing packages provide a wealth of advanced features. One of the most useful of these, usually referred to as **mail merge**, allows two files to be combined automatically. The name comes from the common application of creating a mailing that combines a letter from one file and mailing addresses from another file, so that a whole list of people can get printed letters that appear to be customized. You may have seen elaborate large-scale applications of this in sales letters that say something like "And we think you will be thrilled to know, Ms. Redding, that six other people in your home town, Redlands, have already won cash prizes...." The computer that printed the mailing was programmed to automatically place your name and your town's name in the proper position in the letter to make it appear more personal.

Most sophisticated word processing packages can also keep track of footnotes, automatically moving them to the bottom of the page on which their reference number occurs and renumbering them as other footnotes are added or deleted. Anyone who has ever typewritten a report with footnotes would appreciate this feature.

Tables of contents can be automatically created from headings in the document, and indexes can be generated automatically. Some programs even include the ability to update cross-references within a document automatically. For example, if we wrote in this chapter that Chapter 8 will describe other software applications, and then later added a chapter, so that the software chapter became Chapter 9, the reference to Chapter 8 would automatically be changed to read Chapter 9.

Other common advanced features include automatic column formatting and split screens. Split screens divide the screen into two or more parts so that you can examine two sections of a document (or two separate documents) at the same time. In addition, many sophisticated word processing packages allow you to preview the document before you print it.

The most elaborate formatting features are those referred to as **desktop publishing** tools. Many newer word processing packages offer advanced capabilities that allow users to do page design at a level used in publications such as newsletters, magazines, and books. Not only can pages be beautifully formatted, but drawings and logos can also be loaded in electronically from graphics packages and incorporated in the design of the document. Specialized desktop publishing software packages will be described in detail in Chapter 8.

Level 4: The Manager's Use of Word Processing

In many offices, managers now use personal computers in place of dictating or handwriting their notes. For people with good typing skills, it is generally faster to keyboard a letter than to write it in longhand or dictate it, and the ability to *see* what is being communicated can cut down on revision time. In many instances, managers themselves enter the data for a letter, report, or other document and then transmit it to the clerical staff to proofread, format, and print.

Even in offices where managers still dictate letters, the ability to revise without rekeyboarding can save time, and spelling checkers can correct errors that might otherwise be missed.

SELF-TEST

1. (T *or* F) The main reason word processing saves work as compared to typing documents is that the keyboarding needs to be done only once.
2. The feature in word processing that fills lines and automatically starts new lines without the user pressing the [Return] or [Enter] key is called _____ _____.
3. (T *or* F) There are usually several different ways to do any editing task.
4. The feature that looks through the document for the occurrences of a word or phrase is called the _____ feature.
5. When this feature also substitutes a new word or phrase, it is called the _____ and _____ feature.
6. The term WYSIWYG is an acronym for _____.
7. The feature that aligns all the lines on both the left and the right margins is called _____.
8. (T *or* F) Mail merge combines data in one file with data in another file for customized mailings.

SOLUTIONS 1) True. 2) word wrap. 3) True. 4) search. 5) search; replace. 6) What you see is what you get. 7) justification. 8) True.

Spreadsheet Packages

Businesses have traditionally used large ledger pages filled with figures to keep track of financial transactions. These pages, called spreadsheets, are divided into grids of columns and rows. The columns and rows usually are labeled to identify their contents. Totals often appear across the bottom and right-hand columns of the sheet. **Spreadsheet packages** computerize such record keeping. They are used not only for financial planning and analysis but also for any type of numerical analysis—predicting inventory levels or tracking the progress of your college grade point average, for example. In fact, any data that can be represented in column-and-row format can be used in a spreadsheet.

As with the traditional ledger spreadsheet, a computer spreadsheet (often called a **worksheet**) is divided into columns and rows. Each column is identified by a letter and each row by a number. The intersection of a specific column and row creates a **cell**. Cells are identified by addresses. For example, the cell in column B, row 10, is referred to as cell B10. A spreadsheet created in the popular spreadsheet package Quattro is shown in Figure 3–9.

When you set up a spreadsheet like the one in Figure 3–9, you can enter a value in any cell (in cell E6, total salary income; in cell D7, total interest income; and so on), and you can also enter a mathematical formula (in cell D9, the sum of cells D7 and D8). If you change any value—such as showing income in the dividends cell, D8—the cell containing the formula, D9, will instantly recalculate. The use of formulas makes it possible to reuse a spreadsheet. For example, if you prepare a monthly budget for a period of several months, you can use the same spreadsheet for each month by simply changing the numeric values. The computer will automatically recompute the totals.

Because spreadsheets make it possible to determine almost instantaneously the results of a change in a single value or group of values, they have become favorite tools of financial planners. They are ideally suited to asking "What-if?" questions: "What if we raised the price of product A by 10% and sales dropped by 2% as a consequence?" "What if I took a five-year car loan at 9.9%, or a three-year loan at 6.9%—what would the difference in interest be, and what would my monthly payments be?"

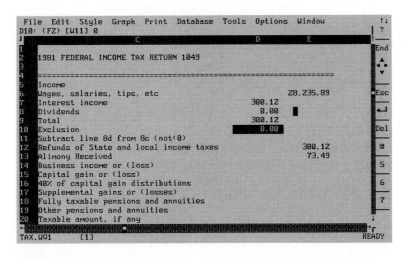

3–9 Traditional ledger worksheets are largely being replaced by computer spreadsheets like this one, created in Quattro.

Setting up a spreadsheet is somewhat more time-consuming than manually preparing a ledger sheet, but the payoff is the quick, accurate results you get when you enter formulas and experiment with alternative plans. You can also use the same format over and over, updating and revising as you need to.

Popular spreadsheets include Lotus 1-2-3 from Lotus Development Corporation, Quattro from Borland, and Supercalc from Computer Associates—all available for IBM and IBM-compatible microcomputers, and Excel for both the Macintosh and IBMs.

The typical maximum size of a spreadsheet is about 256 columns wide by 8,192 rows long. Columns have single letter identification, then begin with double letters; in other words, columns X, Y, and Z are followed by columns AA...AZ, BA...BZ, CA...CZ, and so on.

Level 1: Keyboarding

You can store three types of data in a cell: labels, values, and formulas. Labels identify the information contained in a particular column or row. For example, if you have a column containing the gross pay of employees, you might label it GROSS PAY. The values are the numbers that you enter into a cell. Formulas are mathematical calculations that the spreadsheet will execute and then display the result of that cell. For example, assume that column C of a spreadsheet has one number in each of the three cells C1, C2, and C3. If you want to have the total of the three numbers stored in cell C4, you can place the formula +C1+C2+C3 in C4. The spreadsheet automatically calculates the sum and inserts it into C4. If you later change the values of C1, C2, or C3, the revised sum is automatically placed in C4. This automatic recalculation is an enormous improvement over handwritten ledgers.

At the top or bottom of the screen are usually a number of indicators, one of which tells you which cell currently contains the cursor. Whether it contains a formula, a label, or a value, the actual contents of that cell are also displayed. In spreadsheets, the cursor is a highlighted box that fills the entire cell.

Most spreadsheets have a number of indicators indicating the specific mode you are in, such as READY, EDIT, and CALC. On many spreadsheets, READY indicates that you can enter data, EDIT tells you that the cell already has data in it and that you can change it, and WAIT lets you know that the program is performing processing operations and you cannot enter data until it is finished.

Many spreadsheet commands are available—for example, commands that allow you to change the width of a column, insert a row or column, format data to display as percentages or with decimal values, print all or part of a spreadsheet, and so on. These commands are available on menus, which in most spreadsheets appear only when you summon them, usually by pressing the slash key [/]. A list of commands then appears at the top of the screen, and you may select the appropriate command either by moving the cursor to it and pressing [Enter] or by typing the first letter of the command. These menus are hierarchical; in other words, each menu normally leads to a second submenu showing more detailed choices. Function

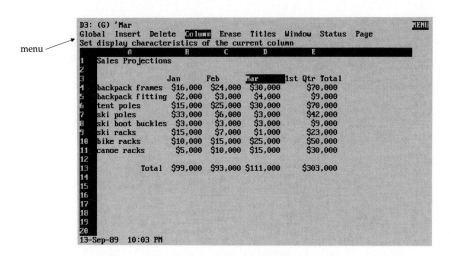

menu

```
D3: (G) 'Mar                                                        MENU
Global  Insert  Delete  Column  Erase  Titles  Window  Status  Page
Set display characteristics of the current column
          A            B         C         D         E
1   Sales Projections
2
3                     Jan       Feb      Mar      1st Qtr Total
4   backpack frames  $16,000  $24,000  $30,000      $70,000
5   backpack fitting  $2,000   $3,000   $4,000       $9,000
6   tent poles       $15,000  $25,000  $30,000      $70,000
7   ski poles        $33,000   $6,000   $3,000      $42,000
8   ski boot buckles  $3,000   $3,000   $3,000       $9,000
9   ski racks        $15,000   $7,000   $1,000      $23,000
10  bike racks       $10,000  $15,000  $25,000      $50,000
11  canoe racks       $5,000  $10,000  $15,000      $30,000
12
13          Total    $99,000  $93,000 $111,000     $303,000
14
15
16
17
18
19
20
13-Sep-89  10:03 PM
```

3–10 Spreadsheet packages have a number of simple menus, like this one in Lotus 1-2-3, that allow you to choose from a number of commands.

keys provide access to still other commands, such as performing calculations and accessing help screens. Figure 3–10 shows a Lotus 1-2-3 screen where a menu of commands has been accessed.

As previously mentioned, you can enter three types of information into a worksheet: labels, values, and formulas. Most programs automatically assume the type of data you are entering by its first character. For example, a spreadsheet package will assume you are entering a value if your entry begins with a number. It will assume you are entering a formula if you enter one of the following characters: + . (@ # $

If you begin an entry with any character other than these or a number, the spreadsheet treats the data as a label. However, you can override these assumptions if you need to use a number or character in a label—for instance, 1991 BUDGET can be entered as a label by keying "1991 BUDGET."

Once you have entered the data, you will usually want to complete the calculations and print the spreadsheet. Calculations may be done in either of two ways: automatically as you enter data, or manually by pressing a CALC function key that performs recalculation—F9 in Lotus 1-2-3, for example.

By using the Print command, you can either print an entire spreadsheet or specify a range of rows and columns to be printed. You can also print with or without the borders containing the row and column addresses. In addition, you can get a printout of any formulas so that you can check the validity of your spreadsheet's underlying assumptions.

Level 2: Editing

There are several ways to navigate through a spreadsheet. One method is to use the cursor control keys. If you know the address of the cell you want to edit, you can use the GOTO function key to go directly to that cell. Another alternative is to use the program's search feature to find specific data.

Once you are at the cell you want to edit, you must first enter EDIT mode, usually by pressing a function key. Editing does not normally occur in the cell itself, but rather in an area reserved at the top or bottom of the screen for displaying the contents of the active (or currently selected) cell. If you make a mistake or change your mind, most packages allow you to press [Esc] or another key to "escape" and leave your data unchanged.

In a Nutshell

Common Features of Spreadsheets

Formulas	Do mathematical calculations; then display the result in the specified cell
Functions	Specialized mathematical calculations. Common functions are:

@SUM (range)	Totals the values in a list
@AVERAGE (range)	Finds the average
@MAX (range)	Finds the largest value in a list
@MIN (range	Finds the smallest value in a list
@COUNT(range)	Counts the number of items in a list
@SQRT (number)	Finds the square root

Search	Looks for specified label, value, or formula

Your editing does not need to be limited to a single cell. You can specify a range of cells to copy, move, delete, or otherwise manipulate. Generally, a range consists of a block of several rows and columns of data.

Once a spreadsheet has been designed, it is frequently necessary to add one or more rows or columns. The Insert feature performs this task. You will be asked whether you want to insert a row or a column, and for the position for the insertion; after the new column or row is inserted, the column letters and row numbers of the spreadsheet are automatically adjusted, even in formulas that reference specific cells.

Level 3: Formatting

Some spreadsheets are designed by individuals for their own work; in this case, the same person formats the spreadsheet, enters the data, and makes decisions based on the calculations done by the spreadsheet. Other spreadsheets are designed for many people to use, and a trained specialist may design these. Similarly, the data in the spreadsheet's cells might be entered by someone other than the final user; if a spreadsheet is designed for the executive level, for example, an executive's assistant might key in current data, leaving the executive to change certain values to ask "What-if?" questions.

Whoever designs and uses the spreadsheet, the formatting is done before data is entered. However, when the first pass of a spreadsheet is completed and printed, formatting changes may be needed to make it more readable. You can change the format of an entire spreadsheet (often referred to as *global formatting*), or change the format of a single column or a range of cells. Column widths and data formatting are the elements most commonly changed. For example, you might want column A to be 20 characters wide because it will contain long text labels, while column B might be a currency column 9 characters wide, and so on. Or you might decide to show the results of calculations with two decimal places rather than rounded to whole numbers.

Labels are a critical part of a spreadsheet's design. They can be formatted to print flush left, flush right, or centered. Unlike values, they can extend beyond the right margin of the cell they occupy, as long as there is nothing in the neighboring cells.

If each cell had to be formatted individually, spreadsheet design would be very tedious. Spreadsheets have a Copy command that allows you to easily copy a format or data from one group of cells into other rows or columns. Once the first cell in a row has been formatted, you can copy its format across the rest of the spreadsheet.

The spreadsheet designer is often responsible for entering formulas where calculations are desired. Formulas in spreadsheets use two types of addressing: **relative addressing** and **absolute addressing**. In most spreadsheet packages, relative addressing is the default value. To illustrate these two concepts, we will return to the earlier example of the formula +C1+C2+C3, which was used to place the sum of these three cells in C4. If you copied the formula in C4 to D4, the program would automatically adapt the formula to be +D1+D2+D3, to total the D column; this is an example of relative addressing. There are times, however, when you actually want to copy a formula *exactly* as it is—you actually want the +C1+C2+C3 total to appear in cell D4 without making an accommodation for the column letter. In this case, you override the default and tell the program to use absolute addressing—to pick the formula up literally.

Spreadsheets include a special category of formulas called **functions**. These allow spreadsheet designers to include complex formulas. Functions typically begin with the @ symbol; for example, the adding function for adding cells C1, C2, and C3 could be typed as @SUM(C1..C3) instead of C1+C2+C3. This is a big timesaver when you want to add many cells in a column or row—it is easier to type @SUM(C1..C55) than to code +C1+C2+C3 ... through +C55. Some functions are very specialized; for example, you can use the @MAX or @MIN functions to have the spreadsheet package find the largest or smallest numbers in a row or column, which can be useful if you want your spreadsheet to indicate the outside limits in your analysis.

Most spreadsheets can also graph data automatically, for more visual impact. The types of graphs available, as well as the quality of their appearance on the screen and their printed output, vary greatly from one program to another. Usually, you must first specify a range of cells to graph; then enter a special Graph mode and select the type of graph you want. Figure 3–11 shows a pie chart created using Excel from Microsoft.

Some of the newer packages are capable of creating three-dimensional spreadsheets. In these packages, spreadsheets can be electronically linked to one another. If a cell is updated in one of these linked spreadsheets, the corresponding cells on the linked sheets also are updated. This linking of spreadsheets allows not only the graph but also the data itself to be three-dimensional.

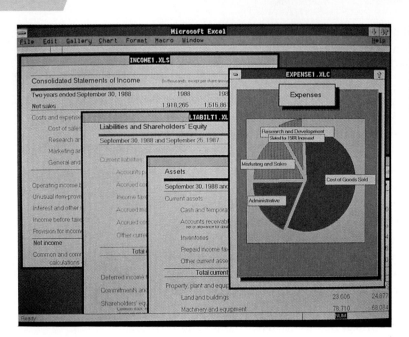

3–11 A pie chart generated from an Excel spreadsheet. Note that the pull-down menus used to define chart parameters are still visible in other windows on the screen. *Courtesy:* Microsoft Corp.

Level 4: The Manager's Use of Spreadsheets

The most common managerial use of spreadsheets is probably for "What-if?" analysis. Spreadsheets are so helpful in decision making that many managers are accomplished spreadsheet designers themselves. In some cases, however, useful spreadsheets are designed for executives by specialists, and the executives then use them independently.

Spreadsheets have taken much of the guesswork out of planning because they can immediately recalculate, reflecting changes made at any point in the spreadsheet. For example, a manager can easily calculate the effect of various supplier price increases on company profits.

The visual impact of spreadsheet-generated charts and graphs can also help managers get their point across more dramatically. Most spreadsheet packages can use data in spreadsheets to create bar graphs, pie charts, and so on, all of which can be understood at a glance. With a spreadsheet, a manager can create professional-looking financial reports quickly and with a minimum of training. Figure 2–2 in Chapter 2 illustrated the impact of translating data into graphic representation.

SELF-TEST

1. Another word for an electronic spreadsheet is a _____.

2. The location formed where a row and column cross is called a _____.

3. The three forms of spreadsheet data are: _____, _____, and _____.

4. (T *or* F) When we say that spreadsheet menus are hierarchical, we mean that menus can have sub-menus.

5. (T *or* F) Once a spreadsheet is set up, you cannot insert new rows or columns, so it is important to get it right the first time.

6. (T *or* F) Absolute addressing in a copy function means that the cell addresses will be copied exactly.

7. @SUM is an example of a special kind of formula called a _____.

SOLUTIONS   1) worksheet. 2) cell. 3) labels, values, formulas. 4) True. 5) False. 6) True. 7) function.

Database Management Systems

Before they began using computers, businesses kept large amounts of data in paper form in folders in filing cabinets. For example, a manufacturer might have one filing cabinet containing information on parts in stock and another cabinet containing information on parts suppliers. Each part would be assigned a part number, and the folders in the parts cabinet would be arranged according to this number. Each folder would contain information about a single part, including the names of suppliers for that part. Each folder in the supplier cabinet contained all the needed information, including the address, for a supplier. If the name of a specific supplier changed, that supplier's file had to be altered. In addition, each reference to that supplier in the parts file had to be altered also. Maintaining such paper filing systems, which were really large databases, was a time-consuming, error-prone operation.

With the advent of computers, **database management systems** (or DBMSs) have been developed to allow data to be stored electronically, and to manage the editing, updating, accessing, and modification of both the data and the file structure itself. Database management systems are one of the most important applications of computer systems, and they are now used extensively on mainframes, minicomputers, and microcomputers. Chapter 11 will describe DBMSs in detail. At this point, we will provide a brief overview of them so that you will understand the function of this important productivity tool.

A **database** consists of a collection of related **files** that are stored on disk. Each file is composed of **records** that contain individual data items, called **fields**. Figure 3–12 illustrates this relationship among fields, records, files, and databases.

The DBMS manages the database and allows you to access it in a wide variety of ways. On microcomputers, databases are managed with one of two kinds of software packages: **file management systems** or **relational database management systems**. Other structures exist but are less common.

File management systems work much like traditional paper filing systems. They can only access a single file at a time. If you want to determine the names of all the suppliers of a particular part who are in California, you need to get the list of the parts suppliers from the parts file and then look up each of those records in the supplier file. Examples of file management systems are Filemaker II from Claris for the Macintosh, Reflex from Borland, and Q & A from Symantec for IBMs and IBM-compatibles. File management systems are mostly used for small home or personal databases that do not require elaborate output.

Name	Soc. Sec. No.	Department	Salary
Arthur Jones	379-52-5366	Purchasing	34000
Janacek Mitslav	212-36-1200	Sales	32950
Mario Ferrano	642-12-1130	Accounting	21600

Record shows information on one employee

Field shows one type of information

3–12 A file is made up of records containing individual fields of information. A database is a collection of files cross-referenced for access. In this case, employee (Social Security) numbers may also be used to access an address file, sales files, and retirement benefits files.

Viewing Customer table with form F: Record 1 of 315   Main

```
                    Borland Order Information Form

          Customer Identification                  Customer Demographics
    Customer ID #:  5
    Customer's Name: George Bartelshay          Age: 38
         Address: 518 Pine St                    Sex: M
    City, State, Zip: Manchester,  4JT           Credit Balance:
         Country: England                             900.00

                    Product Order Information

    Product Code  Description      Language   Quan    Price

    PB1-E         Paradox 3.0      English    1       725.00
    PB12-E        Paradox OS/2     English    1       725.00
    TLC-E         Turbo C          English    2       149.95
    TLP-E         Turbo Pascal     English    1       149.95
```

3–13 A report screen in Borland's Paradox database shows records from several files assembled to give complete information about sales to one customer. *Courtesy:* Borland International.

Relational database management systems are organized so that separate data files are linked. Tables containing information on orders placed can be linked to a table of customer addresses and another containing demographic data. Figure 3–13 shows information from these tables assembled using the relational database program Paradox from Borland. The relationships are highly flexible and can be defined as needed—even after the files have been created. In the parts inventory example, if you need to know all the California suppliers of a particular part, you simply instruct the DBMS to search the database for those suppliers.

Relational databases are easier to maintain because each item of information occurs only one time, and it is not necessary to update it in several different places. This decreases the number of mistakes that are made.

Figure 3–14 shows the Control Center of the relational database package dBASE IV. Other well-known relational databases are Paradox from Borland, R:BASE from Microrim, and Oracle from Oracle Corporation—all for IBMs and compatibles; as well as 4th Dimension from ACIUS, Inc., and FoxBase+ from Fox Software for the Macintosh.

Designing the Database

Databases require much more advance planning and design than most other software packages. The first task of the designer is to design the file structure that will contain the data. Database designers give each field in a record a unique name and specify the maximum number of characters the field can contain. The size corresponds as closely as possible to what is normally needed, and information can usually be abbreviated to save data entry time and memory storage space. For example, the state name in an address can be stored as the two-letter postal code with no periods so that it can be a field two characters long.

Normally, data is stored in the database in the order in which it is entered, and the next record is assigned the next available record number. However, to make working with a database easier, it is often desirable to **index** files on several key fields. When a field is indexed, the DBMS can then directly access records by that field. For example, employee information is conveniently accessed in an employee's record by Social Security Number

3–14 In dBASE IV, the Control Center allows you to efficiently access the various functions, such as File Creation and Report Writer. *Courtesy:* Ashton-Tate Corp.

for some purposes, by last name for others, and perhaps by job classification or pay grade for another. The database designer would index the records by all these fields. The index serves the same purpose as an index in the back of a book. To locate an entry, it is easier to go to the index than to search sequentially through the text or file of records.

One of the most useful features of databases is the ability to query them. For example, if you have a database containing customer information and want to mail a brochure only to those customers in a specific zip code range (for example, 52240-52245), you can instruct the DBMS to locate and print only those records. In the relational database Paradox, for instance, data from several different tables can be accessed and displayed at the same time.

Level 1: Keyboarding

Once the database is designed, data entry may be done by a specially trained clerical employee or by personnel performing some other job such as telephone order-taking. Data is entered on the input screen for each field in sequence. When the data for all of the fields has been entered, the new record is stored in the database.

Level 2: Editing

Data can be edited during input or by calling the record up later in Edit mode. Editing done after keyboarding is usually done to update a record. For example, a customer has moved and has a new address and telephone number; or an employee has received a raise and has a new hourly payroll rate.

Level 3: Formatting

In business applications, databases are usually customized by information managers or programmers, who create special input and output screens to make data entry and access easier. The original database designer often does screen formatting, but advanced users sometimes design their own special-

In a Nutshell

Common Features of Database Management Systems		
Establish indexes for direct access of records	Arranges records in order by data in a key field
Customize screens for input and access	Allows for design of internal data structure as well as special input and output screen displays
Display data in any form	Displays data in any format or order on screen
Edit previously entered data	Calls back records already entered so they can be updated or altered
Design a report according to user specifications	Allows for design of customized print reports that are formatted for user convenience

purpose screens. The order in which fields are displayed can be arranged for the convenience of the user and need not reflect the way information is stored.

Newcomers to databases often have trouble understanding that there is no relationship between the internal structure of the information and the way it is displayed on the screen. A record may be inputted and stored in a certain order: last name, first name, street address, city name, state name, zip code, phone number, birth date, and so on. However, an output screen designed for someone using the file for some special purpose—such as telemarketing, for example—would be arranged for the convenience of the user: the phone number might be at the top, and information not relevant to the calls might not even be displayed. The screen might even display information from another file altogether, perhaps a record of products already purchased by that customer. This is a primary advantage of relational databases—once data is captured, information can be displayed, indexed, cross-referenced, and generally made much more useful than a simple record in paper or flat-file form.

Information stored in a database often needs to be made available, usually in printed form, to individuals who do not have access to the database itself, or as a record that can be used for some specialized purpose. Payroll records are an example of this type of report. DBMSs can generate customized, attractively formatted reports.

Many database management systems consist of very complex programs—so complex, in fact, that they include their own programming languages. In the past, database programs have often been quite daunting, but as they have become more powerful, they have also become more user-friendly. Most now include menus and allow even newcomers to generate programs automatically.

Level 4: The Manager's Use of Databases

Managers most commonly make use of databases in either of two ways to get information: on screen or on paper. Database designers, particularly in medium to large companies, may create special management-level screen displays that allow managers to access data for special decision-making purposes. On the other hand, some managers like to manipulate the data themselves. They may want to sort an indexed database on screen to view information.

Managers may query databases to obtain a variety of valuable information. For example, assume a manager is interested in knowing the names of all employees in the purchasing department who have been with the company more than 10 years. The manager can query the database for this information, sort it on the screen by one field (possibly by the length of time with the company or last name of employee), and print the list. The ability to query a database efficiently can supply useful management information.

The sophistication of today's DBMS packages makes it possible for systems analysts to design true top-down management information systems—systems that are designed around the goals and informational needs of top managers.

Integrated Packages

Newer versions of productivity packages add features to make them more competitive in the software marketplace. As a consequence, the distinction between types of productivity tools is sometimes blurred. For example, word processing packages often have graphing and calculating capabilities; small databases can usually be created within spreadsheets; and so on.

A number of software companies have taken this concept all the way and produced what are called **integrated packages**, which combine all three

Looking Ahead

Transferring Files Between Programs

Software manufacturers are beginning to recognize the need for file compatibility—the ability to transfer data painlessly from one application to another. In some instances, the file formats of leading programs have become the de facto standards. The .WK1 format of Lotus 1-2-3 is one such standard among spreadsheets, while the .DBF of dBASE is the database standard. In word processing, most packages can create unformatted ASCII files—files that are stripped of that program's unique codes, leaving only the computer's internal codes for letters, numbers, and symbols. These ASCII files can be moved between applications.

Another de facto standard is that of PostScript coding for text files that are intended for desktop publishing applications. Many word processing packages allow files to be output in PostScript. Virtually all desktop publishing packages and laser printers have adopted PostScript, and the Linotronic phototypesetting system is PostScript based. Such compatibility means that text can be written in a word processing package from one software company, formatted in a desktop publishing package from another company, and output on a variety of printers from different manufacturers.

As users master more applications, the demand for file compatibility will grow.

of the productivity tools—word processing, spreadsheets, and database management—in one package so that users can easily move data from one application to another. For example, in such packages you can move data in a database file to a spreadsheet so that you can analyze it conveniently. Or you can create a spreadsheet, represent it in a graphic form such as a bar chart, and place the bar chart in the word processing part of the package, where you can use it in a report.

Symphony by Lotus, Framework by Ashton-Tate, Microsoft Works, and Enable from Enable Software, Inc. are examples of integrated packages.

Other Productivity Tools

Microcomputer users also have a number of other tools available to them that we will not describe in detail here. For example, a number of desktop utilities can perform useful functions such as keeping your appointment calendar, providing a list of telephone numbers that you can have your computer dial for you, simulating a calculator by using the numeric keypad on the keyboard, and organizing the files on your disks in various ways not available with most operating systems. Productivity tools for such special purposes will be described in Chapter 8.

Once you have been introduced to each of the three major productivity tools, you may want to experiment with some of these other specialized software packages that can increase your personal productivity, depending on your specific needs.

SUMMARY

End-user productivity tools can be divided into three main categories: *word processing*, *spreadsheet packages*, and *database management systems*. These tools allow the user to perform a variety of tasks efficiently. Users interact with productivity tools at four levels: *keyboarding* or data entry, *editing*, *formatting*, and for *managerial decision making*.

Word processing is extremely useful in creating documents. The user easily can enter, edit, and print documents in a wide variety of formats. Blocks of text can be deleted, copied, and moved to other locations. Different type styles or fonts can be used (depending on the capabilities of the software package and the printer), headings can be centered, and headers, footers, and footnotes can be inserted automatically.

Spreadsheets replace the traditional handwritten ledger. They are divided into rows and columns; the intersection of a row and column is a *cell*. Cells can contain *labels*, *values*, or *formulas*. Formulas can be inserted so that the spreadsheet calculates results automatically. When a value is modified, related values are automatically recalculated.

Database management systems allow users to access, update, modify, and print information in databases efficiently. *Databases* are collections of related *files*. The files are composed of *records* that are subdivided into individual data items, called *fields*.

There are two basic types of databases: *file management systems* and *relational DBMSs*. In a file management system, data is not shared among files. In relational databases, data is stored in tables in a form that makes it more accessible for cross-referencing between files. The user defines the relationships between the data, which allows for a great deal of flexibility in the ways information can be accessed.

Databases can be queried to locate data that meets specified criteria. For example, a database could be queried to determine all employees who will be retiring in the next five years.

Integrated packages combine all three productivity tools so that users can easily move data between applications. There are also a number of desktop utilities that help users organize their work, as well as other productivity tools designed for special purposes.

KEY TERMS

Absolute addressing	Insert mode
Alphanumeric keys	Integrated package
Block	Justification
Case-insensitive	Keyboarding
Cell	Mail merge
Control keys	Manager's use of output
Cursor	Numeric keypad
Database	Query
Default setting	Record
Database management system	Relational database management system
Desktop publishing	Relative addressing
Editing	Scrolling
End-user productivity tool	Search feature
Field	Search and replace
File	Spelling checker
File management system	Spreadsheet packages
Formatting	Status line
Function keys	Typeover mode
Functions	Word processing
Help screen	Word wrap
Index	Worksheet
	WYSIWYG

CHAPTER SELF-TEST

1. The three major categories of end-user productivity tools are _____, _____, and _____.

2. The _____ of a word processing screen provides information such as the position of the cursor, which page you are on, and so forth.

3. When a document is _____, the characters line up at the right margin.

4. _____ software allows the user to manipulate columns and rows of numeric data efficiently.

5. In spreadsheets, columns are identified by _____, and rows are identified by _____.

6. The intersection of a row and column in a spreadsheet is called a(n) _____.

7. Cells in spreadsheets can contain three kinds of data: _____, _____, and _____.

8. In a database management system, a file is composed of a group of related _____ that contain related data items called _____.

9. In a(n) _____ DBMS, data is stored in tables that provide a great deal of flexibility.

SOLUTIONS   1) word processing; spreadsheet packages; database management systems. 2) status line. 3) right-justified. 4) Spreadsheet. 5) letters; numbers. 6) cell. 7) labels, values, formulas. 8) records; fields. 9) relational.

REVIEW QUESTIONS

1. What is the purpose of help screens in application packages?

2. What are the benefits of using word processing over simply typing a document on a typewriter?

3. What types of page formatting tasks can be performed by most word processing packages?

4. Assume you have created a document in which you repeatedly referred to the date of an upcoming meeting as being March 24. However, the meeting has been changed to March 28. What would be an efficient way of changing each occurrence of March 24 to March 28?

5. If you were a high-school teacher, what type of end-user productivity tool might you find most useful in helping to keep track of and calculate student grades? Why?

6. Name at least two advantages that spreadsheet packages have over traditional handwritten ledgers.

7. What is the purpose of placing formulas in spreadsheet cells?

8. Explain the difference between absolute and relative addressing in spreadsheets.

9. List three tasks that can be performed by a database management system.

10. Briefly explain the difference between a file management system and a relational DBMS.

11. What is meant by querying a database?

PROBLEM-SOLVING APPLICATIONS

1. Based on magazine reviews, brochures from computer stores, manuals, or other information, compare the graphics features of the latest versions of two leading spreadsheet programs. One of these should be Lotus 1-2-3; the other should be either Microsoft Excel or Borland's Quattro. How many kinds of graphs does each offer? What kinds are available in each? (Good sources for reviews include *InfoWorld, PC, PC World,* and *PC Computing,* most of which should be available in campus and public libraries.)

2. Go to a local small business that uses one or more personal computers and find out how those computers are being used. What type of computer does the business use? What software is used on the computer, and for what types of work?

3. Go to a local bank or other institution that uses several personal computers. What types of computers are used? Are they all the same or is there a mixture of types? What software is used? Is there standardization of programs throughout the institution, or are different users allowed to select their own programs? Find out how word processing, database management packages, and spreadsheets are used, and by which personnel. Do the managers use the software in a different way than the clerical staff?

HARDWARE

CHAPTER 4

Processing Data

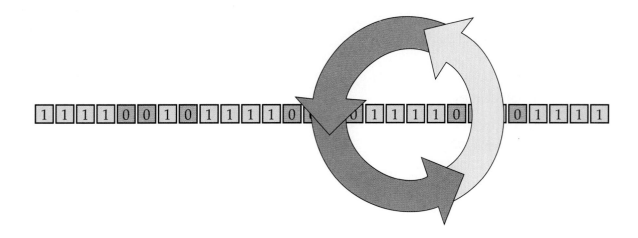

When you have completed this chapter, you will be able to:

✔ List and describe the functions of the three components of the CPU.

✔ Distinguish between primary storage and secondary storage, and between volatile and nonvolatile memory.

✔ Define these terms: binary numbers, bit, byte, word.

✔ Describe batch processing and interactive processing and give examples of each.

✔ List five criteria used to evaluate the processing capability of computer systems.

Chapter Outline

4-1 The four basic parts of any computer system are input, processing, storage, and output. Here, those parts are shown on a desktop PC and a large mainframe system. *Courtesy*: IBM.

This chapter introduces the operations of the **central processing unit (CPU)**, which we could call the brain of a computer. Every part of the human body has a specialized function, but all those functions are organized and directed by the brain. The CPU has a very similar function in computer systems.

As you learned in Chapter 1, a computer system has four components: input devices, the central processing unit, output devices, and auxiliary or secondary storage devices. Figure 4–1 shows these components on an IBM PS/2 microcomputer system and an IBM 3081 mainframe system. Remember that the only real difference between microcomputers, minicomputers, and mainframes is that of degree—particularly with respect to speed and capacity. The traditional definitions of these three categories of computers are continually blurring as the power of micros approaches that of minis, and the power of minis approaches that of mainframes.

The role of the CPU, also called the **processor** (or microprocessor in a micro), is to read input from an input device into storage, to process input data according to program specifications, and to produce information by activating an output unit and transmitting information to it.

The Components of the CPU

A CPU has three components: the **control unit**, the **arithmetic-logic unit**, and **main memory** or **primary storage**.

The Control Unit

The control unit of the CPU monitors the operations performed by the entire computer system. It controls the transmission of data between main memory and input and output devices. It also fetches (copies) each instruction from primary storage, places it in an **instruction register**, or temporary

Control unit

Main memory

Arithmetic logic unit

Buses move data among the parts of the CPU.

Central processing unit

storage location within the CPU, and executes it. The control unit then returns all results to primary storage.

The movement of data between the control unit and main memory occurs on electronic paths called **buses**. Figure 4–2 illustrates how buses move data between the parts of the CPU.

The Arithmetic-Logic Unit (ALU)

If an arithmetic or logic operation is to be performed, the control unit transmits the required data to registers in the arithmetic-logic unit, or ALU, which then operates on the data. The ALU performs arithmetic functions such as addition or subtraction, and logic functions such as the comparison of two numbers (Is number A equal to number B?). The ALU also uses specialized storage areas called **registers** in which data is held while operations are performed on it. For example, if a logic function such as "Is number A equal to number B?" is called for, the two numbers are placed in registers by the control unit and compared by the ALU; the answer is then returned to the control unit.

Primary Storage

Primary storage, or main memory, holds instructions and data needed for processing. Computer main memory is typically on computer chips that are **volatile**, which means that data held there disappears when the computer is turned off or loses power. A small number of micros use magnetic bubbles for main memory rather than microprocessor chips; this type of memory is **nonvolatile**, meaning that data stored in it can be retained for some time even after the power is shut off.

Here is how primary storage works when you use a computer application, regardless of whether it is on a micro, mini, or mainframe: when you start the application, the control unit copies the software program from a disk or another secondary storage medium into primary storage, where it remains available for as long as you keep it loaded or keep the computer on. As you work, the data you input is also held in primary storage. When you save your data, the control unit copies the finished work to a disk from primary storage. When you exit or complete the application, the data you have input as well as the finished work is removed from main memory, and you then have room for loading a new application and new data.

4–2 The **bus** moves data within the central processor to and from current memory (RAM). The efficiency of the bus is a factor in determining the efficiency of the CPU itself.

How Data Flows Through the CPU

Let us illustrate how the CPU manages an application program such as dBASE IV (Figure 4–3).

1. You insert the dBASE IV diskette into your disk drive (an input device), or change to the hard disk directory that holds dBASE IV. You give the dBASE command to load the program. This triggers the control unit to transmit or copy the program to primary storage, or main memory. The program must be loaded into main memory to be executed.

2. You want a report that relates the weekly salary rates of all employees, which is already stored on a data disk in a file called EMPLOYEE.DBF. You put this data disk in a disk drive and then instruct dBASE to use the EMPLOYEE.DBF file. The control unit copies the file from the data disk into main memory.

3. Now you use the dBASE application package and tell it you want a listing of every employee, grouped by department, with each weekly salary rate and an average salary rate for each department.

4. The control unit fetches the appropriate instructions from the dBASE program, which has been loaded into main memory. Since finding an average is an arithmetic function, the control unit gives the data, and the instruction which averages it, to the arithmetic-logic unit (ALU). The ALU operates on the data to find the average salary rate for each department and then returns the completed figure to the control unit, which transmits it into memory.

5. The control unit monitors the program instructions that then display the average salary figure on your computer screen (an output device).

If there were an unexpected power failure during this procedure, you would have to start over from the beginning, because the dBASE program, the employee data, and your instructions would have disappeared from primary storage. Your dBASE program and data would still be on the disks, however.

4–3 The control unit manages the movement of data in and out of memory, and to and from the ALU.

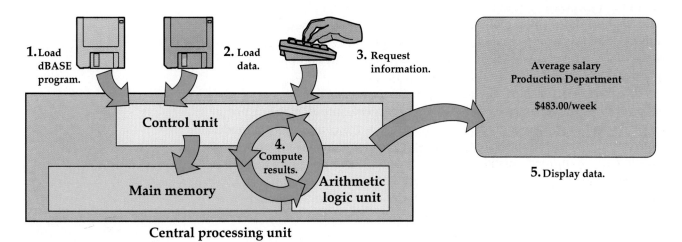

How Data Is Stored

As we have seen, primary storage is used for temporarily storing programs and data while processing is occurring. Remember, however, that primary storage is volatile—whatever was in it will disappear when the power goes off. Long-term, semi-permanent data storage is referred to as secondary storage.

Secondary Storage

Secondary storage is recorded magnetically and does not disappear when the power goes off. Disks and magnetic tapes are examples of secondary storage media that can hold programs and data permanently (or at least until they are erased), ready to be called into the CPU's memory when needed.

All microcomputers have one or two floppy disk drives as secondary storage devices; they are used either for loading programs and data into primary storage or for saving data from primary storage. Many micros also contain a hard disk, which is a secondary storage device that may be built into the computer case with the CPU or easily installed after purchase. Hard disks contain many times as much storage space as floppy disks; for example, the data from about 60 standard 360K double-density, double-sided diskettes can be stored on a single 20-MB microcomputer hard disk. This allows you to store many applications and data files on a hard disk, where the CPU can access them more quickly.

Like microcomputers, large-capacity computers also require secondary storage for the large amounts of data and numerous program applications that organizations use. For example, a large gas company employing thousands of people world-wide might use several different secondary storage devices storing millions or even trillions of bytes of data on large-volume hard disks or on magnetic tape. These and other mass storage devices will be discussed in detail in Chapter 6.

Integrated Circuits and Silicon Chips

The current revolution in microcomputer technology began with the development of tiny integrated circuit chips, called **microprocessors**, that contain the CPU. A single silicon chip no bigger than a child's fingernail is imprinted with thousands of integrated circuits. Each integrated circuit consists of hundreds of electronic components. Figure 4–4 shows an enlarged schematic of a microprocessor chip to give you a sense of the complexity of the circuitry etched on it.

Integrated circuit chips, also called processors, are used in large computers as well as microcomputers; the CPUs of larger computers consist of a large number of processor chips. Chips for all types of computers are made from a semiconductor material called silicon, a nonmetallic element occurring in glass-like quartz rocks. The material itself is a poor conductor of electricity, but a thin sliver, or chip, is coated with an emulsion that is etched in a way that leaves electrical conducting material behind in paths that form circuitry.

4–4 Circuits etched on a silicon chip make it a microprocessor, the heart of a computer system. Here, an engineer works on an enlarged schematic of the Intel 80386. *Courtesy*: Calypso Color.

Each particular CPU is designed to manage a certain amount of primary storage capacity—you may be able to expand the main memory in your microcomputer, for example, but only to a certain level. Storage capacity is measured in **kilobytes** (K), or thousands of bytes; **megabytes** (MB), or millions of bytes; or, for larger systems, **gigabytes** (GB), or billions of bytes. For example, IBM PCs, PS/2s, and their compatibles typically come with 640K to 2MB of main memory, with the capability of expanding further. Figure 4–5 shows the main circuitry board, or motherboard, of the PS/2 Model 30; notice its array of memory chips.

The capacity for main memory in high-end microcomputers is now in a range formerly considered to be available only on minicomputers. As microprocessors become even more powerful and inexpensive, the distinctions between classes of computers will continue to disappear.

In a Nutshell

Measurements for Memory Capacity

Term	Abbreviation	Number of Bytes
kilobytes	K	thousands
megabytes	MB	millions
gigabytes	GB	billions

4–5 Main memory in a microcomputer is handled by RAM chips on the main circuit board. *Courtesy*: IBM.

RAM

RAM, or **random-access memory**, is the volatile memory described earlier as primary storage, or main memory, which is used to store programs and data during processing. It can store as many programs and data files as can fit within the computer's memory capacity. When the user quits the application, the memory it took up immediately becomes available for new work.

The term *random-access memory* comes from the fact that the control unit accesses data or main memory randomly without the need to search through each storage location in sequence.

ROM

Not all memory in a computer is volatile. When you turn your computer on or load a software program into it, your computer must have some preset instructions available to tell it what to do. These permanent, nonvolatile instructions are programmed onto **ROM** chips—ROM is an abbreviation for **read-only memory**. Other names for ROM chips are **firmware**, or **prewired functions**. ROM chips have many functions; for example, they tell the computer what to do when the power is turned on; they will check to see that the cable to the printer is connected; and they will tell the control unit what each key on the keyboard means. Unlike RAM, users cannot normally store their own instructions in ROM.

When you start up an IBM PC or PS/2 microcomputer with no operating system, you will find that the computer is ready to run BASIC programs. This is because the BASIC interpreter program is built in as part of ROM.

Types of ROM

PROM	programmable read-only memory
EPROM	erasable programmable read-only memory
EEPROM	electronically erasable programmable read-only memory

Any program *could* be put into a computer in ROM form, which would save you time because you would not need to move disks in and out. However, ROM has, in the past, been much more expensive than the volatile memory chips used for primary storage. In addition, software vendors would have to create new chip circuitry and new ROM chips every time they updated their program, and users would have to open the computer case and replace chips when they wanted to update their applications.

There are, however, three new types of ROM chips that *do* allow programming by vendors or users: PROM, EPROM, and EEPROM. PROM and EPROM chips must be removed from the computer for programming, and erasing old programs on EPROM chips requires the use of a special process. The newest ROM chip, EEPROM, allows program information to be changed by software without removing the chips from the computer.

Other Types of Memory

As computers become used for more and more applications, every computer owner will eventually want a more powerful and faster system. The whole computer industry is in a headlong rush to satisfy the rapidly increasing demand for computer components to do every job from running home appliances to managing bionic body parts. New forms of main memory are continually under development, and some will eventually either replace or supplement integrated circuits.

Magnetic bubble memory consists of magnetized spots on a thin film of semiconductor memory (see Figure 4–6). Data stored in bubble memory cannot be accessed as quickly as in integrated circuits, but bubble memory

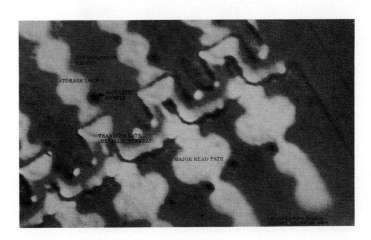

4–6 Programs and data can be stored in magnetic "bubbles" on a thin film. Bubble memory is slower than chips, but the contents are not lost when the current is cut off. Here the bubbles are magnified 300 times. *Courtesy*: Bell Labs.

4–7 This is the surface of a cache memory chip, the IBM 9370. Data stored on these chips can be retrieved very quickly, speeding computer operations. *Courtesy*: IBM.

has one major benefit: it is nonvolatile, so data is retained in memory for a period of time after the power is shut off. This is particularly important for computer applications in environments that are susceptible to frequent blackouts or power surges.

Cache memory is a type of memory that can double the speed of a computer. It is based on a scheme of storing and retrieving data that is different from traditional microprocessor memory. The tradeoff is that cache memory is very expensive. Cache memory is used extensively in minicomputers as well as for some micros, particularly for storing the most frequently referenced data and instructions. It also has great potential for supercomputers and larger mainframes as well. Figure 4–7 shows a cache memory chip.

4–8 The optical disk stores large amounts of data for quick retrieval. Here one is shown against a background of all the magnetic tapes needed to store the same information. *Courtesy*: 3M.

Laser and optical memories are nonmagnetic alternatives that use light energy rather than magnetic fields to store characters. Lasers burn holes in a disk's surface to represent bits of information. CD-ROM (compact disk read-only memory) disks use the same technology as CD audio disks, and as their name implies, cannot at this point be written to—only read. They are suitable for storing large amounts of data that need frequent reference. Figure 4–8 shows an example of an optical disk, another form of nonmagnetic memory that may someday replace traditional disk devices for auxiliary storage.

Looking Ahead

Optical Computing

An entirely new computer technology based on transmitting data by light rather than electricity is on the drawing board and may produce a revolutionary new generation of computers by the end of this century. This approach, called **optical computing**, has a number of advantages, the primary one being speed: light in an optical fiber travels 500 times faster than does electricity in a chip, and light in an optical integrated circuit travels 150 times faster than in an electronic integrated circuit.

Another advantage is that of storage, which is expected to use the principles of holographics. Have you seen a holographic image? Light creates an image that appears to be three-dimensional—you can walk around it because you can see it from different directions. It is predicted that optical chips will be coated with a holographic emulsion; a complete set of data can be read by a beam of light from one direction, but with a slight shift in the direction of the beam, another complete set can be read, and so on—so that 125 gigabytes of data may be stored on a single chip! Storage of data on the chip is done in the same way—by beaming data down from a number of different directions.

Experts say that we will see hybrids of electronic and optical computing introduced by 1995, and that applications are likely to be in the communications industry, aerospace, and advanced robotics.

SELF-TEST

1. The three components of the central processing unit are the _____, _____, and _____.
2. The _____ is the CPU component that manages the processing of data.
3. Logic processes, such as the comparison of two numbers, are carried out by the _____.
4. (T *or* F) During processing, data or instructions are held in temporary storage places called *registers.*
5. The electronic paths on which data moves between the CPU and memory are called _____.
6. (T *or* F) Secondary storage is volatile, while primary storage is nonvolatile.
7. The small silicon chips that contain the CPU of a microcomputer are called _____.
8. (T *or* F) The CPU can process an unlimited amount of data in its transactions—the user simply adds more memory chips to upgrade the RAM as desired.
9. Three alternatives to the microprocessor form of memory are: _____, _____, and _____.
10. Of these three, which ones are nonmagnetic?

SOLUTIONS 1) control unit; arithmetic-logic unit (ALU); main memory or primary storage. 2) control unit. 3) arithmetic-logic unit (ALU). 4) True. 5) buses. 6) False. It is the other way around. 7) microprocessors. 8) False. There is an upper limit on how much memory each CPU is designed to handle. 9) magnetic bubble memory; cache memory; laser and optical memory. 10) laser and optical memory, CD-ROM disks, optical disks.

How Data Is Represented

People communicate with one another in written language by using characters consisting of letters of the alphabet (A to Z), digits (0 to 9), and special symbols such as the dollar sign ($), percent sign (%), and so on. Computers are capable of reading all these characters into primary storage, but the characters must be converted into a form that permits high-speed internal processing.

Numbering Systems

All computers use some variation of the **binary numbering system** for representing each character. In the binary numbering system, there are only two possible digits: 0 and 1. The 1 represents the presence of an electrical impulse or signal; we call this the "on state." The 0 represents the absence of such a signal, and we call this the "off state." Figure 4–9 shows three ways in which the computer uses this on/off principle.

The numbering system we use everyday is called the **decimal system**, and it is based on units of ten. To call it by its mathematical name, it is a base-10 numbering system. Computers use a binary-coded system for representing data and instructions; since the binary numbering system is based on only two states, on and off, it is called a base-2 numbering system.

Most numbering systems, including the decimal system, are called "positional" because the physical location or position of a digit within the number affects its value. For example, in a positional numbering system, the number 23 has a different value than the number 32 even though the digits are the same. In positional numbering systems, the *place value* is critical.

The decimal or base-10 system has the following positional values:

...	10^3	10^2	10^1	10^0	Exponential value of position
	1000	100	10	1	Decimal value of position

A 1 in the second or tens position and a 0 in the units position (10) is the number following 9. After we reach 9, there are no more single digits; therefore we proceed to the next position, the tens position, initializing the units position with 0. Ten, then, is the decimal number following 9.

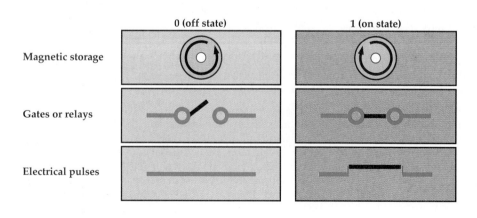

4–9 Computers use the on/off principle and the binary numbering system for all processing.

In the base-10 or decimal system, each position has a value that is a factor of 10. The first position has a value of 10^0 or 1, the second has a value of 10^1 or 10, . . .; the seventh position would have a value of 10^6 or 1,000,000, and so on.

The binary numbering system has a base of 2, so each position has a place value that is a factor of 2. We have, then:

...	2^4	2^3	2^2	2^1	2^0	Exponential value of position
	16	8	4	2	1	Decimal value of position

Any number raised to the zero power is 1; therefore, the units position has a place value of 2^0 or 1. The second position has a value of 2^1 or 2 (any number raised to the first power is the number itself). The third position has a value of 2^2 or 2 x 2 = 4; and so on.

As noted, in the binary numbering system, we have only two digits, 0 and 1. To represent the number 2 in binary we have already, in effect, run out of digits; therefore we must initialize the units position and proceed with the position adjacent to the units position—the 2's position. That is, 10 in binary is 2 in decimal.

We say, then, that 10_2 (10 in base 2) = 2_{10} (2 in base 10). In our illustration the subscript represents the base. The number 3 in base 2 would be 11; to represent a 4 we must initialize the two rightmost positions and place a 1 in the next or 4's position. Therefore 100 in binary is a 4 in decimal. A 5 would be 101. Notice that the sequence is 0, 1; then you proceed to the next position and initialize the previous one (10, 11, 100, and so on).

Using the binary numbering system, the computer can represent any decimal number with a series of on-off circuits, where "on" is represented by a binary 1, and "off" is represented by a binary 0.

Bits and Bytes

The smallest unit in binary code is the **bit**, short for binary digit—a single on- or off-state signal. A group of eight bits is called a **byte**. Typically, one character is represented in one byte. Clusters of consecutive bytes are a **word**, the term for a unit of data.

Figure 4–10 illustrates the relationship of these three binary units. The term *word* in this context should not be confused with the English-language meaning—it is simply a unit of data that corresponds to the number of bits that can be transferred to a register in the CPU's control unit in a single operation. The number of bytes in a word varies from system to system. The larger the word size, the faster the computer. Word sizes include 8 bits, 16, 32, 64, and even 128 bits.

Coding Systems

No matter what size word is being used, every number and character and symbol needed to do a computer's work must be represented in some coded binary form. There are two commonly used coding schemes: **ASCII** and **EBCDIC**.

4–10 Eight bits make up one byte, or character. The number of bytes in a word depends on the size of the CPU bus used.

Bits can be on or off.

Eight bits form a byte.

1	1	1	1	0	0	1	0

Two bytes (16 bits) form a word on the IBM PC.

1	1	1	1	0	0	1	0
1	1	1	0	1	1	1	0

Four bytes (32 bits) form a word on the IBM PS/2

1	1	1	1	0	0	1	0
1	1	1	0	1	1	1	0
0	1	1	0	0	1	1	1
1	0	1	1	0	1	1	1

ASCII.   ASCII, an acronym for American Standard Code for Information Interchange, is used in virtually all microcomputers and some larger computers as well. (It is pronounced **ass-key**.) ASCII is always the form in which data is transmitted over communications lines. Some computers use 7-bit ASCII, while others use 8-bit ASCII. Both are shown and contrasted to EBCDIC in Table 4–1. This abbreviated table does not include lowercase letters or symbols.

EBCDIC.   EBCDIC, pronounced *eb-c-dick,* is an acronym for Extended Binary Coded Decimal Interchange Code. It is the standard for most IBM and IBM-compatible mainframe computers, and it uses an 8-bit code. See Table 4–1 for the EBCDIC code for numbers and letters. Note that the rightmost four binary digits in all computer codes correspond to the binary values 0 to 9.

Character	EBCDIC	8-bit ASCII	7-bit ASCII	Character
0	1111 0000	0101 0000	011 0000	0
1	1111 0001	0101 0001	011 0001	1
2	1111 0010	01010010	011 0010	2
3	1111 0011	0101 0011	011 0011	3
4	1111 0100	0101 0100	011 0100	4
5	1111 0101	0101 0101	011 0101	5
6	1111 0110	0101 0110	011 0110	6
7	1111 0111	0101 0111	011 0111	7
8	1111 1000	0101 1000	011 1000	8
9	1111 1001	0101 1001	011 1001	9
A	1100 0001	1010 0001	100 0001	A
B	1100 0010	1010 0010	100 0010	B
C	1100 0011	1010 0011	100 0011	C
D	1100 0100	1010 0100	100 0100	D
E	1100 0101	1010 0101	100 0101	E
F	1100 0110	1010 0110	100 0110	F
G	1100 0111	1010 0111	100 0111	G
H	1100 1000	1010 1000	100 1000	H
I	1100 1001	1010 1001	100 1001	I
J	1101 0001	1010 1010	100 1010	J
K	1101 0010	1010 1011	100 1011	K
L	1101 0011	1010 1100	100 1100	L
M	1101 0100	1010 1101	100 1101	M
N	1101 0101	1010 1110	100 1110	N
O	1101 0110	1010 1111	100 1111	O
P	1101 0111	1011 0000	101 0000	P
Q	1101 1000	1011 0001	101 0001	Q
R	1101 1001	1011 0010	101 0010	R
S	1110 0010	1011 0011	101 0011	S
T	1110 0011	1011 0100	101 0100	T
U	1110 0100	1011 0101	101 0101	U
V	1110 0101	1011 0110	101 0110	V
W	1110 0110	1011 0111	101 0111	W
X	1110 0111	1011 1000	101 1000	X
Y	1110 1000	1011 1001	101 1001	Y
Z	1110 1001	1011 1010	101 1010	Z

Table 4–1 EBCDIC, the code used in IBM mainframes, uses eight bits. ASCII, which is used in microcomputers and for data transmission, comes in either a 7-bit or 8-bit code. These are the codes for numbers and upper case letters.

Error-Checking with the Parity Bit

Data is constantly moving from one part of the computer to another, and often from one computer to another. Data is transmitted as electronic impulses in the on state and off state, so slight irregularities in the electrical power supply occasionally cause errors to enter the stream of data. One way to verify that data was accurately transmitted would be to transmit it twice and compare the two transmissions, but that would double processing time and costs. The **parity bit** is an alternative solution to this problem.

The parity bit is a single bit attached to each byte; the code itself determines whether the parity bit is a 0 or a 1. There are even-parity and odd-parity computers. In even-parity computers, an even number of bits must always be "on" at any given time; in odd-parity computers, an odd number of bits must always be on.

With even-parity computers, if the number of 1 bits in any byte is odd, the parity bit is automatically turned on or set to 1. Also, in an even-parity computer, if the number of 1 bits is even, the parity bit is set to 0. This means that when all the 1 bits are added up, there is always an even number of them. This concept is called **even parity**. Figure 4–11 shows the EBCDIC code for the number 2, including the parity bit for even-parity computers.

When a transmission is sent to a computer that uses even parity to do error checking, the receiving computer checks to see that there are always an even number of 1 bits. If a byte contains an odd number of on bits, it asks for retransmission.

Computers using **odd parity** work in exactly the same way except that the parity bit is used to ensure an odd number of 1 bits.

Parity checking is guaranteed to detect an error only if exactly one bit is transmitted incorrectly. If, however, two bits were transmitted incorrectly, the error would not be detected, because the number of 1 bits would still be even for even-parity computers and odd for odd-parity computers. Although the chance for double transmission errors is very remote, some systems do protect against it. To guard against the possibility of multiple errors, a scheme called **longitudinal parity** can be used. In this scheme, a **check byte** is added to the end of each record that is transmitted, where each bit of the check byte is used to preserve the appropriate parity of each bit position in each byte of the record.

Parity checking can detect errors, but it cannot correct them. A number of encoding schemes are now available that both detect and correct single or multiple errors when large volumes of data are transmitted over communications lines. Because they are much more elaborate than parity checks, these encoding schemes require a great deal of additional processing at the receiving end. Their major use is for the long-distance transmission of data to a site where retransmission would be difficult—the transmission of data to a space probe, for example.

Thus far we have described the technical detail of data transmission. Now, we will take a look at how data is processed at the operating level.

4–11 Parity bits are added to each byte to keep the number of on bits even (as shown here) or odd depending on whether you use an even or odd parity computer.

Methods of Processing Data

There are basically three stages for processing data with a computer: input the data, process the data, and output the information. There are two basic models for processing data: batch processing and interactive processing.

Batch Processing

Businesses typically produce all payroll checks for each pay period at the same time. This is an example of **batch processing**—holding all data until output is needed and then processing it all at once. There are a number of ways data is entered before processing can be done. In a very large-scale operation, data is often entered on computers or terminals that are not even connected to the main CPU. This type of data entry is called an **off-line operation**. For example, payroll information might be keyboarded at several different corporate sites and then transmitted to the computer at corporate headquarters every Thursday so that paychecks can be printed on Friday in a batch-processing operation.

In a small company that uses microcomputers, the payroll data disk could be updated on any microcomputer, then processed elsewhere with the help of the payroll program disk. The payroll example in Figure 4–12 illustrates batch processing on a microcomputer.

Batch processing is an effective way to make efficient use of expensive computer time. Not only is it more efficient to do a single processing task on a large data file all at once, but there are also physical advantages to batch processing when special forms such as checks are used for output and have to be specially loaded in the printer. However, there are disadvantages as well: the data available in the main computer is less timely—it is only up to date at the time the entire batch is processed. Batch processing is not appropriate for an application that needs to process or report on current data quickly.

4–12 In batch processing, the computer stores all data until output is needed, then performs all operations at one time.

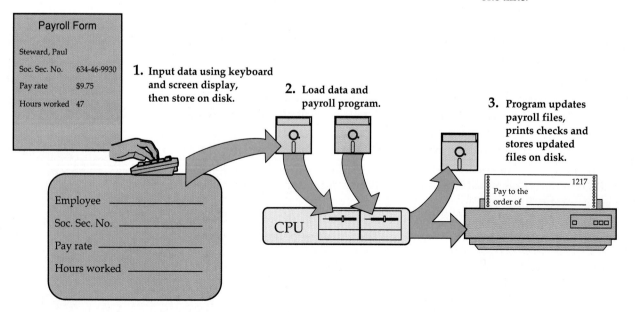

Payroll Form

Steward, Paul

Soc. Sec. No.   634-46-9930

Pay rate $9.75

Hours worked   47

1. Input data using keyboard and screen display, then store on disk.

2. Load data and payroll program.

3. Program updates payroll files, prints checks and stores updated files on disk.

Employee

Soc. Sec. No.

Pay rate

Hours worked

CPU

1217

Pay to the order of

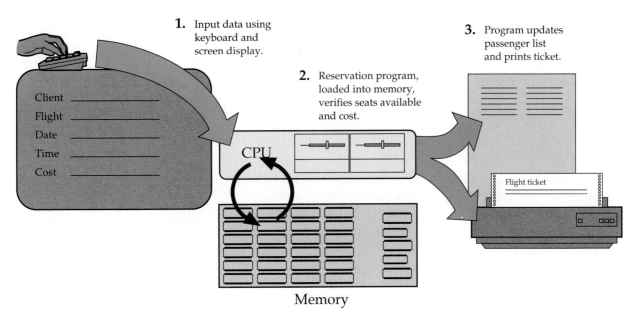

1. Input data using keyboard and screen display.

2. Reservation program, loaded into memory, verifies seats available and cost.

3. Program updates passenger list and prints ticket.

Client _____
Flight _____
Date _____
Time _____
Cost _____

CPU

Flight ticket

Memory

4–13 An airline reservation system is an example of interactive or real-time processing; the computer completes each task immediately, keeping all records current and available.

Other examples of appropriate tasks for batch processing are producing transcripts of grades at the end of the semester, or producing stock inventory reports at the end of the day. If an inventory manager uses yesterday's inventory report, he or she must keep in mind that changes in stock made during the day will not be in the report. If there is no great need for up-to-the-minute accuracy on reports, then batch processing is the most efficient method for producing those reports.

Interactive Processing

Batch processing is a good idea only if there is no urgency about processing records as soon as the data is transacted or entered. It may be that payroll files need to be current only at the end of a payroll period when it is time to produce checks; in such a case, batch processing is feasible. On the other hand, airline reservations systems, for example, must be updated instantly so that the airline knows at all times how many seats have been sold; ticket agents can then stop selling tickets when a flight has been fully booked. An airline reservations system is an example of a system that uses interactive processing (Figure 4–13).

In interactive processing, data must be processed immediately, as soon as it is transacted, so that updated information can be quickly provided to all system users. In airline reservations systems, there are terminals at many sites, for example, at travel agencies and airport airline desks. Although the terminals are off-site at remote locations, they communicate directly and instantly with the central computer via communications lines such as telephones and satellites. These systems immediately update ticket information on all flights. Updating information is called an **on-line operation**, and the person at the remote terminal is said to be "on-line" with the main computer. Because updated information that is produced interactively is available almost instantly, as with our airline reservation example, this type of processing is often also referred to as *real-time processing*. For interactive

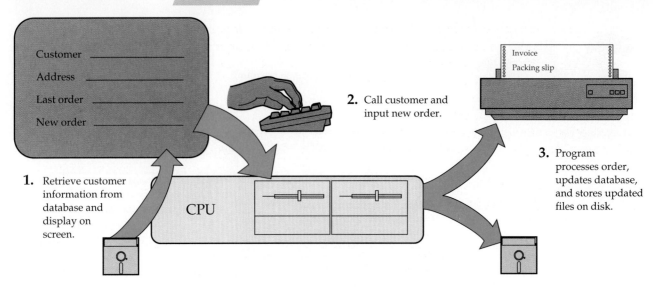

Customer _____

Address _____

Last order _____

New order _____

1. Retrieve customer information from database and display on screen.

CPU

2. Call customer and input new order.

Invoice

Packing slip

3. Program processes order, updates database, and stores updated files on disk.

4–14 In transaction processing, all facets of a transaction, including output, are completed at one time.

processing, the central computer must be linked to all terminals at all times, and a program must be resident in the main CPU to process the data that is being input at the various terminals.

A form of interactive processing is **transaction processing**. Transaction processing allows a user to input data and complete a transaction on the spot. Figure 4–14 shows how transaction processing is used for telephone sales. The marketer retrieves names of customers from the customer database and then makes sales calls asking for reorders of company products. When a customer places a new order over the phone, the marketer inputs the order information; the computer retrieves the customer information from the customer database and processes all data to produce a customer invoice and a packing slip to be used by the warehouse for packing and shipping the order.

Transaction processing such as in the example above may be part of a larger company-wide information system, or the processing could be done as an independent subsystem off-line—that is, not under the control of the company's main computer. If this were the case, data could then be periodically batched and sent to the main computer to update the database. In other words, in many applications one kind of processing may be combined with others so that the most efficient information system is created.

Evaluating the Processing Capacity of Computer Systems

Choosing an appropriate computer system can be extremely difficult for novices; in this world of rapidly changing technology, it is a challenge even for technical experts. One of the most important ways to compare systems is to look at processing speeds—how fast can this system do the work you plan to do?

There are other considerations besides speed, however. For example, the rule of thumb for choosing simple personal microcomputer systems is to begin by identifying the software applications that you need to use and then to look for microcomputers that can run that software. It is more important to have a broad range of useful software applications available than it is to have the latest, fastest technology, which may not yet be supported by software. In other words, while speed is desirable, it is useless if you cannot do the work you need to do.

Larger computer systems have more complicated selection criteria, however, because an apparently small difference in processing time or capability may save or cost a company hundreds of thousands of dollars in direct and indirect costs.

If current trends continue, the cost of computer system memory will continue to decline (Figure 4–15). In other words, as time goes on, the cost of chips declines while their capacity goes up, resulting in more power for your money.

Following are some of the criteria used for evaluating the processing capacity of microcomputer systems. On a larger scale, the same criteria also apply to evaluating minicomputer and mainframe systems.

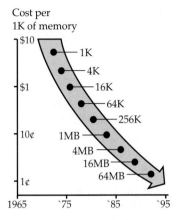

4–15 This graph shows how the cost of memory is declining and chip capacity is increasing.

Chip Technologies

Microprocessor chips have come a long way in just a few years. The design of the whole system depends on several features that the microprocessor provides. Figure 4–16 contrasts some of the most commonly used microprocessors.

Clock Speed

The CPU's clock generates clock pulses that synchronize the computer's operations. Processing actions occur at each "tick" of the electronic clock. The speed of the clock determines the speed at which the CPU can process data. Speed is measured in megahertz (MHz); one megahertz is a million pulses per second. Notice in Figure 4–16 that the range in IBM systems

4–16 Microprocessors are evaluated on a number of design features that affect speed and capacity. Some of the most critical factors are shown here, along with popular microcomputers that use each chip.

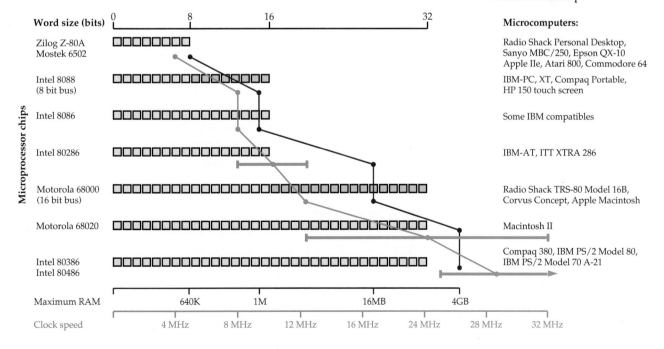

varies from 8 MHz for the IBM PC and IBM XT, to 32 MHz or more for the PS/2 Model 80 system.

Processing Speed

Processing speed, or the time required to access data in memory, is measured in microcomputers in microseconds, or millionths of a second. For example, the IBM PC family can perform about 4.75 million operations per second. At the opposite end of the scale, processing speeds for supercomputers are measured in picoseconds, or trillionths of a second. The supercomputer Cray-2 can theoretically process data at the rate of 200 million operations per second.

Coprocessors are special chips that can be added to micros to speed up certain kinds of operations; one common type is the math coprocessor, which is used to speed up the processing of mathematical operations for applications such as statistical analysis.

Word Size

Earlier we defined the unit "word" as a group of consecutive bytes. A word is a cluster that can be simultaneously processed, so the larger the word, the faster the speed at which the system can process data. Notice the variation in word size in Figure 4–16. Larger systems have word sizes of 64 or even 128 bits.

Bus Technology

Buses, as you will recall, are the electronic tracks on which data moves between memory and the CPU. The more bytes the bus can handle, the more data passes through, and the faster the processing speed. Notice in Figure 4–16 that IBM used the Intel 8088 chip in its PCs and XTs; it has a clock speed of 8 MHz, and the word size is 16 bits. However, because the data bus can move only 8 bits at a time, processing slows at that stage.

Parallel Processing

One of the areas in which microcomputers are breaking new ground is that of **parallel processing**, or the use of many microprocessor chips to do processing tasks simultaneously. At the same time the industry has been producing chips that can process more data at a high speed, it has also been developing computers that can handle multiple chips. In effect, these computers have multiple CPUs. Mainframe computers have been doing this for some time, but in recent years many more computers can perform parallel processing as the price of chips has come down.

In a Nutshell

Measurements of Processing Speeds

Microsecond	millionth of a second, in microcomputers	
Nanosecond	billionth of a second, in minicomputers, mainframes	
Picosecond	trillionth of a second, in supercomputers	

Computers with parallel processors are most useful for managing huge databases—the ones used by airlines and banks, for example. Parallel processing divides a task up into parts in a way that requires special instructions within the software application packages. With such packages now widely available, more systems can take advantage of the speed and power of parallel processing.

Computers that use 12 or 30 microprocessors are produced by a number of companies; the biggest parallel system thus far, the Connection Machine by Thinking Machines Corporation, has more than 65,000 processors!

What the Future Holds

Ten years ago, if we had thought about the technological developments that are available today, we would have assumed that they would not be available for use until the next century. For example, more and more complex applications are available for everyday use, mostly because of the rapid increase in memory capacity available in personal systems. Well-known word processing packages that seemed marvelous five years ago have now been upgraded through several versions and are capable of producing book- and magazine-quality publications because the increased memory in ordinary systems makes sophisticated graphics displays available.

A recent development in CPU design is known as **RISC technology**, an acronym for reduced instruction set computers. With the RISC approach, CPUs have fewer and simpler instructions programmed into ROM but are still capable of complex tasks by combining simple instructions. This is another development that greatly reduces processing time. Both Sun and NeXT workstations use RISC technology for advanced design and scientific

4-17 This Sun SPARC computer uses RISC technology to manage complex graphics—and even synthetic sound. *Courtesy*: Sun Microsystems, Inc..

analysis applications (Figure 4–17). Standard micros use CISC technology, which is an abbreviation for Complex Instruction Set Computers.

The availability of new types of memory will undoubtedly lead to a new generation of computers. Nonvolatile memory in forms such as bubble memory, laser-generated memory, and optical memory will make new applications available for the first time, and if history repeats itself, these new memory forms will become available at prices which continue to decrease over time.

SUMMARY

The brain of the computer is the central processing unit, or *CPU*. The CPU has three major components, the *control unit*, which manages the operations of the CPU, including movement of data; the *arithmetic-logic unit*, or *ALU*, which does all mathematical and comparison functions; and *primary storage*, or memory.

The control unit moves data in and out of primary storage, or *main memory*, via *buses* (electronic tracks), and data is temporarily stored in transit in *registers*.

Primary storage is also called *RAM* (for random-access memory), and in most computers is *volatile*—that is, data copied into RAM disappears when the power goes off. The CPU also has *ROM* (for read-only memory), which contains the basic operating instructions for the CPU and usually cannot be altered by users. Some newer ROM chips are programmable *(PROM)*; erasable and programmable *(EPROM)*; or even electronically erasable and programmable *(EE-PROM)*, which do not need to be removed to be erased and programmed.

Secondary or *auxiliary storage* is on disks, magnetic tape, and other magnetic media, and is nonvolatile.

The most important technological advance in this generation of computers is the *microprocessor*, the tiny silicon chip imprinted with thousands of *integrated circuits* that make up the CPU of a microcomputer. Central processing units of minis, mainframes, and supercomputers consist of a large number of such chips.

There are other forms of memory available: *magnetic bubble memory*, which is magnetic but nonvolatile; *cache memory*, which speeds up the computer impressively but is very expensive; and *laser and optical memory*, which are nonmagnetic and nonvolatile forms based on tiny laser-generated holes on the surface of a disk.

Data is represented in a computer as a series of electrical impulses, or *bits*, that represent either the on state (1), or the off state (0). Computer codes, therefore, are all based on some version of the *base-2* or *binary numbering system*.

A *bit*, short for binary digit, is a single on or off signal. A group of eight bits is called a *byte*, and this is the most basic processing unit of information. Typi-

cally, one character is represented in one byte of 8 bits. Several groups of bytes make up a *word*—the size depends on the computer's design.

The two most commonly used coding systems for representing data are *ASCII* and *EBCDIC*. ASCII is mostly used on microcomputers, and EBCDIC is primarily used on mainframes, particularly those from IBM. ASCII is the code typically used for transmitting data from one computer to another.

Computers are designed to check data transmission by the use of a *parity bit*, which is added to ASCII or EBCDIC computer codes. In even-parity computer systems, all the on bits (1's), including the parity bit, must add up to an even number; in odd-parity computers, all the on bits (1's), including the parity bit, must add up to an odd number. When the 1-bits do not add up properly, the CPU knows that an error has occurred and asks for retransmission of that byte.

There are two basic kinds of information processing: *batch processing* and *interactive processing*. In batch processing, a large amount of input is processed at the same time, and in interactive processing, data is processed immediately when it is entered to provide immediate output of some kind and to maintain files that are always up to date.

Input for batch processing is *off-line*—the user doing the input is not in direct communication with the central CPU; in interactive processing, the person doing the input is *on-line*, or in direct communication with the central CPU at all times.

When transactions are processed on-line and interactively, it is called *transaction processing*.

Computers are evaluated according to the capabilities of their chip technology: their *clock speed*; the *word size* used in processing; the *speed of processing*; their *bus technology*, or the number of bits the buses can transport at one time; and their ability to perform more than one task simultaneously *(parallel processing)*.

The next generation of CPUs will provide computer capability far beyond what we have available today—and this will happen faster than we can imagine.

KEY TERMS

Arithmetic-logic unit (ALU)	Longitudinal parity
ASCII	Magnetic bubble memory
Batch processing	Main memory
Binary numbering system	Megabyte
Bit	Microprocessor
Bus	Nonvolatile memory
Byte	Odd parity
Cache memory	Off-line operation
Central processing unit (CPU)	On-line operation
Check byte	Optical memory
CD-ROM	Parallel processing
Control unit	Parity bit
Coprocessor	Positional numbering system
Decimal system	Prewired function
EBCDIC	Primary storage
EEPROM	Processor
EPROM	PROM
Even parity	RAM (random-access memory)
Firmware	Register
Gigabyte	RISC technology
Instruction register	ROM (read-only memory)
Integrated circuits	Transaction processing
Interactive processing	Volatile memory
Kilobyte	Word
Laser memory	

CHAPTER SELF-TEST

1. The term *CPU* is an abbreviation for _____.
2. Both large mainframe systems and personal computer systems have the same four components: _____, _____, _____, and _____.
3. The CPU's three components are the _____, _____, and _____.
4. The CPU copies data from an input device into _____, where it is stored during processing.
5. The part of the CPU that does math and logic functions is the _____.
6. Data moves between the CPU and main memory on electronic paths called _____.
7. (T *or* F) If data is stored in volatile memory, it will be lost if the power goes off.
8. Some microcomputers have an internal hard disk that can hold large amounts of data. Is this primary storage or secondary storage?
9. Is the data on an internal hard disk volatile or nonvolatile?
10. A kilobyte is _____ (no.) bytes.
11. (T *or* F) Many microcomputers have expandable memory capacities, but there is a limit to how much memory each CPU is designed to handle.
12. RAM stands for _____.

13. Is RAM volatile or nonvolatile?
14. Magnetic bubble memory's advantage over standard microprocessor memory is that it is _____.
15. ROM stands for _____.
16. There are now three kinds of more flexible ROM memory: _____, which stands for ____; _____, which stands for _____; and _____, which stands for _____.
17. What is the advantage of EEPROM chips over EPROM chips?
18. Numbering systems in which the place held by a digit within a number affects the number's value are called _____.
19. The numbering system that uses base-2 is called _____, and the numbering system that uses base-10 is called _____.
20. Two commonly used coding systems are ASCII and EBCDIC. The one used by IBM mainframes is _____; the one used by most microcomputers is _____.
21. The two basic types of processing are _____ and _____. When an entire transaction is completed on the spot, including output, it is called _____ processing.

SOLUTIONS 1) central processing unit. 2) input devices, the central processing unit, output devices, and secondary or auxiliary storage. 3) control unit; arithmetic-logic unit; primary storage or memory. 4) primary storage or main memory. 5) arithmetic-logic unit (ALU). 6) buses. 7) True. 8) secondary or auxiliary storage. 9) nonvolatile. 10) approximately 1000 (actually 1024). 11) True. 12) random-access memory. 13) volatile. 14) nonvolatile. 15) read-only memory. 16) PROM or programmable read-only memory; EPROM or erasable programmable read-only memory; EEPROM or electronically erasable ready-only memory. 17) EEPROM chips can be erased and reprogrammed without removing them from the computer. 18) positional numbering systems. 19) binary code; decimal code. 20) EBCDIC; ASCII. 21) batch processing; interactive processing; transaction processing.

REVIEW QUESTIONS

1. List and briefly describe the three components of the CPU.
2. What is the function of primary storage, and how does secondary storage differ from it?
3. What does RAM stand for? ROM?
4. Name two alternative magnetic forms of memory, and one nonmagnetic alternative.
5. What kinds of computers use ASCII coding? What kinds use EBCDIC?
6. How does the parity bit work in error checking? Describe this for even-parity machines and for odd-parity machines.
7. Define batch processing and interactive processing. Define an off-line operation and contrast it to

an on-line operation. Which is used for batch processing and which for interactive processing?

8. List five processing criteria used for evaluating computer systems.

PROBLEM-SOLVING APPLICATIONS

1. Find out how much memory the computer you use has. Has it been upgraded beyond the amount that it came with originally?

2. Check Figure 4–16 to see what kind of microprocessor chip your computer uses. If your brand is not there, check your computer's documentation. Is it slower or faster than a standard IBM PC—in clock speed? in word size?

3. Again, using Figure 4–16, predict which computer will produce output faster—the Radio Shack TRS-80 or the IBM AT?

4. Consult newspapers or journals written 5 to 10 years ago to see if you can find projections regarding computer capability in the 1990's. Compare and contrast the predictions with the reality.

Input And Output

When you have completed this chapter, you will be able to:

✔ Describe how input data is transmitted and stored in the CPU.

✔ Distinguish between input that is already machine readable and data that must be reentered before it can be input to the CPU.

✔ Name at least two business applications of data entry methodologies and five examples of machine readable input forms.

✔ Describe the main technologies used for screen displays and printers and the reasons they are winning out over older technologies.

Chapter 5

Chapter Outline

We use computers because we expect them to produce some form of useful information, or output. In Chapter 1 we discussed the distinction between data and information, and this is a good time to review it.

Individual bits of **data**—such as today's date or the record of the sale of a box of nails—are typically entered into the computer, which uses application programs to process it in some way. Each application is designed to produce some particular kind of output—a summary of all sales for a given day, for example. This output, or processed data, is **information**, and it differs from raw data in that it can be used for decision making.

If you manage inventory, for example, it is not enough to know how many boxes of nails were sold today; you may also need to know how many boxes are now in inventory at the end of the day, what the average number of boxes sold per day is, the projected date on which all the boxes of nails will be sold, and how long it takes to restock nails by ordering from your nail vendor. This is *information*, because it allows you to decide when to reorder nails.

This chapter will summarize how **input** data is entered and how **output** information is produced. We will discuss all the various ways that data can be input for processing and the variety of hardware devices used for input and output, both for microcomputers and for large mainframes. As with the technology used in CPUs and microprocessor chips, the technology for inputting and outputting is changing rapidly, so we will review the whole spectrum from traditional keypunch technology to the latest cutting-edge laser technology.

Like all devices that access the CPU, input and output devices are called **peripheral devices**. As we will see in the next chapter, secondary storage devices—which serve as input/output devices—are also peripheral devices.

Inputting Data

Input to a computer frequently comes from documents such as purchase orders, vendor invoices, or payroll change reports. These documents are prepared where the original action occurs—at the "source" of a transaction—so they are called **source documents** (Figure 5–1). The source of a purchase order, for example, is the purchasing department, while payroll change requests may originate in the human resources or payroll department.

In order for data recorded on a source document to be processed by a computer, it must be in a form that can be read by an input device. In Chapter 4 you learned that computers understand only binary coded data— a bit of data that signals either an on state or an off state, represented by 0's for off and 1's for on. Many input devices are designed to read input and transmit it to a CPU in binary coded form; these input devices can read or scan magnetic spots, printed characters, black-and-white stripes, holes in paper cards, electronic pulses, flashes of light, magnetic fields that move clockwise or counterclockwise, positive or negative voltage, current flowing or stopped, pitted surfaces or smooth—even the human voice can be read by some devices and transmitted in binary coded form to the CPU.

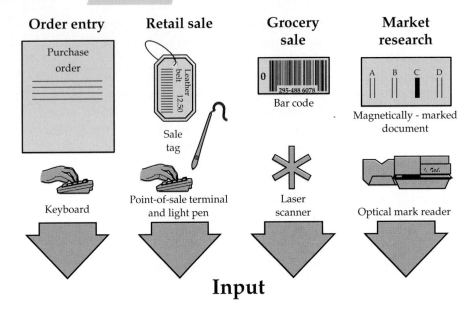

Input

5–1 The wide range of source documents has given rise to a variety of input devices and methods.

The trend in input procedures is to increase productivity and reduce data errors by reducing the number of times data is recorded, or input. For example, in a company that does not have efficient input procedures, an employee salary raise might involve as many as three inputs: first, the department manager fills out a handwritten form requesting the raise; then the handwritten request goes to the human resources department for verification, and that department then types up a list of raises, including this one; then the list goes to the accounting department, which finally inputs the same information into the computer.

In a more efficient computer environment, the originating department would enter the salary raise on its own computer, which is connected electronically to the central computer. The human resources department could verify the request electronically, and the accounting department would implement the raise without ever reentering the data. As you read the summary of input devices, notice the improvement in productivity it represents over older methods of collecting, re-entering, and storing data.

Some input devices are designed to accept keyboarding or some other form of human input; they then convert input data into computer-readable form. For example, when you use a word processing package to type a term paper, the keyboard on your personal computer is an input device that accepts letters, numbers, and symbols; the signals from the keyboard are processed by the computer's CPU, and by the time this data reaches the floppy disk in your disk drive, your keyed input has been translated into binary coded data.

Many input systems, however, have been designed to reduce the amount of human involvement in the process of inputting data; they use data that is already in machine-readable form. The bar codes on grocery items that are scanned in checkout lines (Figure 5–2) are an example of a form of input that eliminates the need for a checkout clerk to key in product

5–2 A laser scanning device at the supermarket checkout stand reads the bar codes on packages. The computer then looks up the price and computes the total cost of purchases. It also adjusts inventory records. *Courtesy*: IBM.

codes and prices; not only is the scanning done more quickly, but the rate of error is also greatly reduced.

Let us take a look at the wide range of input devices used in business. The most common ones are shown in Figure 5–3. Some of them are used for processing large amounts of data such as in payroll, order processing, and inventory, while others are special-purpose devices such as the grocery store scanners that are used in systems that can dramatically improve productivity.

Keyboards and Other Manual Input Devices

Input devices can be categorized into two basic types: those that require human interaction with the computer and those that can accept data directly in machine-readable form. First, we will look at the types of input devices that require manual input.

Keypunch Cards and Readers   The first input media used by mainframes was paper-based, and some systems that use **keypunch cards** and **paper tape** can still be found, although they are rapidly being replaced by more efficient magnetic systems. Keypunch cards have either 80 or 96 columns. Data is keyed in by using a keypunch machine that punches small holes in the card's columns, where the combination of holes punched represents a letter, number, or special character. Processing keypunch cards with a card reader is an older example of batch processing, described in Chapter 4. Keypunch operators input data from source documents, and periodically all cards for an action such as payroll are processed together using a card reader linked to a CPU.

Keyboard Input   For preparing large quantities of input data, most companies use **key-to-disk** or **key-to-tape** methods very similar to those used on a microcomputer. Operators enter data from source documents by typing on

Device

Use

Keyboard

Light pen

Touch screen

Mouse

Enters data into mainframe from remote locations.

Disk pack

5 1/4" disk

3 1/2" disk

Tape

Stores data as magnetic spots, or bits, to be used later for accessing and updating records. Magnetic storage devices are available for all types of computers.

Optical disk

Stores data as laser marks, or bits, for access later on. Now mostly used for permanent storage.

Bar code and scanner

0

295-488 6078

Enters data stored as printed bars of different widths.

Optical reader

AaBbCcDd

Number 137

Price 24.95

Rfeia fleaclk enlilije chpsdvej nasxfeclk nonzda oidi nlvmljv cnjim lnxi slnxi mb kfihf

Enters data stored on typed pages or even handwritten forms.

Magnetic ink character recognition reader

Hard Rock Bank & Trust
ANYWHERE, U.S.A. 54321

⑈123456789⑆   123456780⑈   ⑈000000 1500⑈

Enters data imprinted with magnetic ink. This system is mostly used on bank checks.

5–3 Examples of input devices. Each input device reads in a different form of data for processing by the CPU.

In a Nutshell

Why Magnetic Storage Has Replaced Keypunch Cards

- ◆ Cards can be bent, stapled, folded, or mutilated, which makes data unreadable.
- ◆ Cards may not process properly when heat and humidity are high.
- ◆ Card readers are very slow mechanical input devices.
- ◆ Unlike disks, cards cannot be reused.
- ◆ Even the smallest disks can hold the equivalent of thousands of cards of data.

a keyboard; the keystrokes are captured on magnetic disks or tapes as tiny magnetized spots.

Many companies use terminals rather than microcomputers to do data entry, however. A **terminal** is most often a remote keyboard and monitor that is connected to a separate CPU by cable or telephone. Data from terminals can be processed either in batches or interactively.

A specialized form of interactive terminal is the **automatic teller machine (ATM)** (Figure 5–4), which is now almost universally offered to bank customers. ATMs are on-line banking devices in which data entered at the point of transaction automatically and immediately updates banking records. Customers can withdraw money, deposit cash or checks, or electronically transfer money from one account to another, often on a 24-hour basis. To protect the customer's funds, the bank provides plastic cards that have magnetic strips encoded with account information; the customer inserts the card and then keys in a secret password. If the card and password match, the customer is allowed to proceed with a transaction.

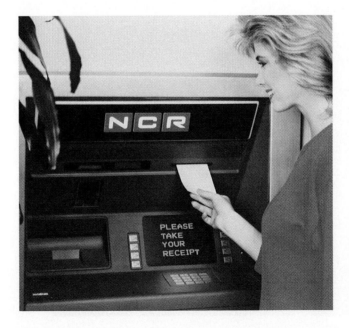

5–4 An automatic teller machine allows bank customers to deposit and withdraw funds. Customers access their accounts using a magnetic card and an individual password. *Courtesy*: NCR.

5–5 The mouse can be used to move a cursor on the screen and select items from a menu using touch buttons. *Courtesy*: Apple Computer, Inc.

The Mouse　　A **mouse** is a small hand-held device that contains a ball-type roller on the bottom and one or more buttons on the top (Figure 5–5). It first entered the marketplace on a large scale with Apple's Macintosh microcomputers, but has since been added as a useful tool for most computer systems. Because a mouse is easy to use and reduces the need for typing, it is considered to be a very **user-friendly** input device.

The mouse is normally used to select choices from a **menu** on a screen; it is ideally suited for quickly giving a series of instructions to the computer. Using a mouse, however, does not eliminate the need to use a keyboard for entering text. In word processing applications, for example, the text is entered via the keyboard but may then be formatted in various ways by using the mouse to make selections from menus that offer choices in type font and page layout. The mouse may then be used again to give the computer printing instructions from a menu that offers choices about which pages and how many copies to print.

Graphics application packages—software for creating diagrams and illustrations—make particularly good use of the mouse, because it can be used to trace or draw patterns.

5–6 Light pens are used to select menu items by touching the desired item on the screen with the pen. *Courtesy*: Light-Pen Company.

Light Pen   Light pens are similar to the mouse in that they are used to respond to screen prompts, reducing the need for keying data (Figure 5–6). Light pens use a laser beam to transmit signals to the CPU. They can be used to "write" directly on the screen, to select menu choices by touching the screen, or to modify illustrations displayed on the screen.

Touch-Sensitive Screen   Another user-friendly input device is the **touch-sensitive screen** (Figure 5–7). The screen displays choices and instructions, and you simply touch the desired choice—much as you would press elevator buttons to choose your floor.

Voice-Recognition Device   The most user-friendly form of input device is the one that can "hear" the human voice and correctly interpret a small vocabulary of words. This new **voice-recognition** technology is finding early application in on-site order entry and inventory control. The human voice differs widely from person to person, so this technology still has problems with high error rates. It is expected that this problem will be resolved within a few years.

Note that light pens, touch-sensitive screens, and voice recognition devices minimize the need for keying data. This makes them ideally suited for people who do not like to type, or for people with eye-hand coordination problems such as children and the handicapped.

Point-of-Sale Terminals   One major consumer-oriented application of input devices is the **point-of-sale terminal (POS)**. Broadly defined, a point-

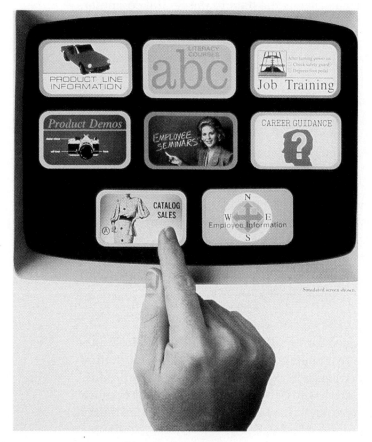

5–7 Touch screens respond to selections made by pointing with your finger. *Courtesy*: IBM.

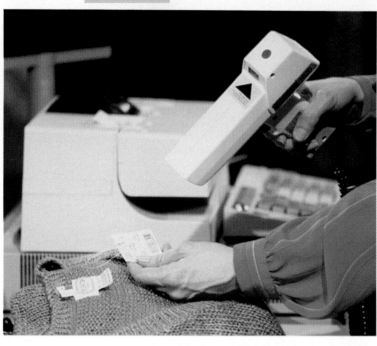

5–8 Point-of-sale terminals are used in retail stores along with hand-held scanners to enter sales information, update inventories, and print customer receipts. *Courtesy:* IBM.

of-sale system uses terminals in retail establishments to enter data at the actual location where a sale is transacted. For example, department stores have POS terminals scattered through many departments (Figure 5–8); at the point of sale, the purchase is recorded and the terminal produces a sales slip for the customer. The terminal sends the data to the central computer, which verifies the account number and updates the account for a credit card purchase; it also updates inventory records as well as sales data. Other retail businesses that commonly use POS terminals are fast-food restaurants, supermarkets, and hotels.

Touch-Tone Telephones and Portable Keying Devices Some computer systems are equipped to accept input data directly from any Touch-Tone telephone. For example, many banks allow their checking account customers to pay bills by telephone; a customer simply responds to a series of instructions that request the account number to be entered, then the company to be paid (usually identified with a code number), the amount to be paid, and the date on which to pay it.

Portable keying devices also use the telephone to send input data to the CPU. A salesperson working at a distance from the main office, for example, can enter orders from a pay phone using either the Touch-Tone telephone or a special order entry keyboard (Figure 5–9). The CPU receiving the order then generates a shipping order and customer invoice.

Devices for Reading Machine Code

Many input devices are designed for inputting data that is already in machine-readable form. Systems that operate on machine-readable input have two main advantages: first, because nobody has to keyboard data, productivity is increased and there are fewer errors; and second, input is much faster because the computer does not have to translate it into internal binary

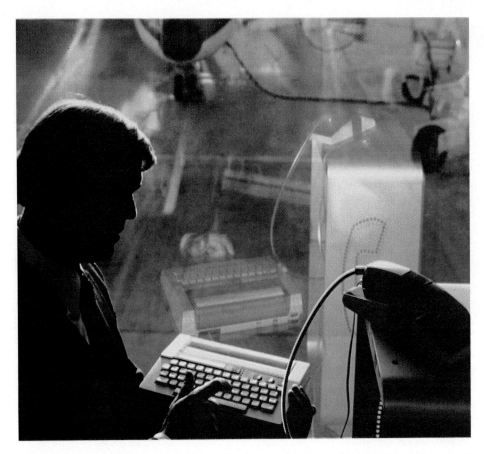

5–9 With portable keying devices, salespeople can dial in customer orders to the home office. *Courtesy*: Texas Instruments.

code. Following is an overview of the main categories of devices that read machine code in some form.

Optical Character Recognition Devices   **OCRs**, or **optical character recognition devices**, read typed or even handwritten data on a source document. This has a number of useful applications. Whole books or manuscripts can be read into magnetic storage on floppy disks, for example, so that revisions can be made without completely retyping the document. A very inexpensive OCR device is one that reads the monospaced type produced by typewriters; it can be purchased for approximately $300. OCRs that read typeset material like the text in this book, which has proportional letter spacing and several different typefaces, are much more sophisticated and expensive—from $20,000 to $300,000, depending on the speed at which the equipment can read the source documents.

Some business applications use special OCR type that many devices can easily read. The ISBN (International Standard Book Number) is printed on the back cover of this book using an OCR type. Bookstores often use OCR scanning devices to read the ISBN and record the sale.

OCR scanning has a relatively high error rate because source documents may have smudges, erasures, overprinting, or misaligned type. As the reliability of these devices improves and the cost decreases, they will be used even more widely to avoid reentering existing source documents. Some inexpensive scanners are already widely available for microcomputers.

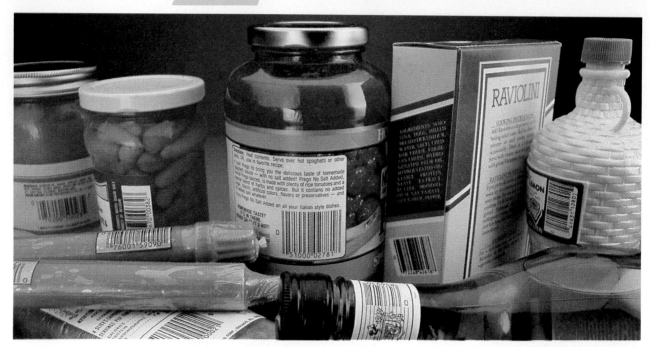

Bar Code Readers Most grocery stores have begun to use optical **bar code readers** for their checkout procedures. These devices read the black-and-white bars that you see on most food packaging. These bars form a code called the **Universal Product Code (UPC)** (Figure 5–10). The UPC includes coding for the manufacturer as well as for the product.

5–10 Groceries and other retail products now have bar codes included in their packaging so that stores can automatically record sales as customers check out. *Courtesy*: NCR.

The bar code reader has a scanning device that translates black-and-white (or light-and-dark) bars of different widths into electrical impulses. The electronic cash register uses the UPC information to look the price up from an auxiliary storage device. Checkout clerks no longer have to memorize the changing prices of hundreds of products and key them in—the bar code data is already in machine-readable form.

A novel application of bar codes is one used by the New York City Marathon; for a number of years runners have been assigned individual bar codes to wear on their shirts. As a runner finishes the marathon, a scanning device uses the bar code to record the runner's name and order of finish.

Optical Mark Readers An **optical mark reader**, sometimes called a mark-sense reader, detects the presence of pencil marks on predetermined grids. Students are familiar with one type of mark-sense source document: the computer-scored test answer sheet (Figure 5–11). The test-taker marks the answer by filling in a bar or circle under the letter of choice.

Other applications of mark-sense readers include payment forms and market research forms that request the customer or respondent to fill in answers to brief queries. Because grids must be filled in accurately with no stray pencil marks, this input device has limited versatility and therefore limited use.

Magnetic Ink Character Reader Banks use **magnetic ink character readers (MICRs)** to read the magnetic ink numbers printed at the bottom of checks. When checks are printed for the bank's customers, they contain

| Last | | | | | | | | STUDENT'S NAME | First | | | | M.I. |

END-OF-COURSE TEST

A Ⓐ Ⓑ Ⓒ Ⓓ

1 Ⓐ Ⓑ Ⓒ Ⓓ   11 Ⓐ Ⓑ Ⓒ Ⓓ   21 Ⓐ Ⓑ Ⓒ Ⓓ   31 Ⓐ Ⓑ Ⓒ Ⓓ   41 Ⓐ Ⓑ Ⓒ Ⓓ

2 Ⓕ Ⓖ Ⓗ Ⓙ   12 Ⓕ Ⓖ Ⓗ Ⓙ   22 Ⓕ Ⓖ Ⓗ Ⓙ   32 Ⓕ Ⓖ Ⓗ Ⓙ   42 Ⓕ Ⓖ Ⓗ Ⓙ

3 Ⓐ Ⓑ Ⓒ Ⓓ   13 Ⓐ Ⓑ Ⓒ Ⓓ   23 Ⓐ Ⓑ Ⓒ Ⓓ   33 Ⓐ Ⓑ Ⓒ Ⓓ   43 Ⓐ Ⓑ Ⓒ Ⓓ

4 Ⓕ Ⓖ Ⓗ Ⓙ   14 Ⓕ Ⓖ Ⓗ Ⓙ   24 Ⓕ Ⓖ Ⓗ Ⓙ   34 Ⓕ Ⓖ Ⓗ Ⓙ   44 Ⓕ Ⓖ Ⓗ Ⓙ

5 Ⓐ Ⓑ Ⓒ Ⓓ   15 Ⓐ Ⓑ Ⓒ Ⓓ   25 Ⓐ Ⓑ Ⓒ Ⓓ   35 Ⓐ Ⓑ Ⓒ Ⓓ   45 Ⓐ Ⓑ Ⓒ Ⓓ

6 Ⓕ Ⓖ Ⓗ Ⓙ   16 Ⓕ Ⓖ Ⓗ Ⓙ   26 Ⓕ Ⓖ Ⓗ Ⓙ   36 Ⓕ Ⓖ Ⓗ Ⓙ   46 Ⓕ Ⓖ Ⓗ Ⓙ

7 Ⓐ Ⓑ Ⓒ Ⓓ   17 Ⓐ Ⓑ Ⓒ Ⓓ   27 Ⓐ Ⓑ Ⓒ Ⓓ   37 Ⓐ Ⓑ Ⓒ Ⓓ   47 Ⓐ Ⓑ Ⓒ Ⓓ

5–11 A computer-scored test answer sheet allows the student to fill in answers using a pencil. An optical mark reader is then used to compute the score.

these inked numbers, which identify the account and check number. After the check has been used in a transaction and returned to the bank, it is encoded with the amount of the check. Figure 5–12 shows the kinds of numbers used on bank checks.

Large batches of checks are accumulated by the bank and read by a high-speed MICR, which reads, sorts, and transmits the characters to a medium such as disk or tape. In the United States, hundreds of millions of checks are processed with MICR devices each day. Note that these units can read only digits and some special characters, but not alphabetic characters.

Detecting Data Entry Errors

All computer operations are subject to a certain number of errors. Errors come from many sources: incorrect input by an operator, flaws in pro-

5–12 Cancelled checks have magnetic numbers imprinted along the bottom, identifying the bank, account number, and check amount.

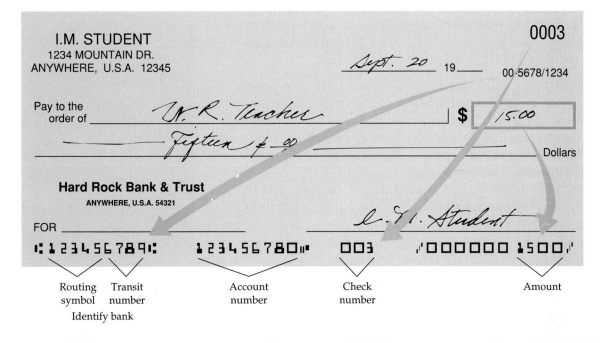

I.M. STUDENT
1234 MOUNTAIN DR.
ANYWHERE, U.S.A. 12345

Sept. 20   19___   00-5678/1234

0003

Pay to the order of ___ W. R. Teacher ___ $ 15.00

___ Fifteen & 00 ___ Dollars

Hard Rock Bank & Trust
ANYWHERE, U.S.A. 54321

FOR ___   I. M. Student

⑆1234567891⑆   123456780⑈   003   ⑆000000 1500⑆

Routing symbol   Transit number

Identify bank

Account number

Check number

Amount

grams—even the hardware itself can introduce errors if the technology is not yet perfected. The most common source, however, is human error in inputting data. Human beings, like hardware, have not yet been perfected, so computer systems need some built-in procedures to protect users from the serious consequences of errors.

For example, if you deposit $250 in your checking account, and the person who keys in the amount of the check either misses or adds a zero, you either have an extra $2250 ($2500 – $250) that must be painfully removed at a later date, or your checks bounce because the bank thinks you have $225 ($250 – $25) less than you really do. The cost to the bank is not only in your lost goodwill but also in the expense of correcting the multiple errors that result from the single misplaced zero.

Data Verification   Checking the validity of data is called **data verification**. A common approach is to keyboard the data from source documents, store the input on a disk or tape, and then have a second person keyboard the same input. The two data sets are then compared; if they do not match, the operator determines which data was incorrectly entered and what corrections are necessary. This is a costly procedure because it essentially duplicates the data entry procedure. However, it is often a justifiable expense because it can detect up to 90% of the errors in input, and the cost of correcting errors is higher than the cost of data verification.

A modification of this procedure is to have an operator key in input for each transaction and then have the computer echo the transaction back to the user for immediate verification. Many automatic teller machines do this for you: the amount of money you have just keyed in is displayed on the screen, and you are asked to press an "OK" key to verify that you keyed in the correct amount.

Control Listings   A second method used to minimize data entry errors is to produce an unprocessed listing of all input, which is called a control listing or audit trail. A clerk familiar with the input is assigned the task of checking the listing to verify that the correct number of records were entered, that certain data passes a visual check of correctness, and so on. This is less expensive than entering the data twice (double-entering it), but it is highly dependent on the skill and alertness of the clerk.

Software Controls   Many applications contain their own programming controls that are designed to validate data. For example, a payroll program could ensure that (1) each hourly rate entered falls within preestablished limits, (2) the name and Social Security number are included for each employee and are present on the company employee list, (3) the hours worked fall within reasonable limits, and so on.

Programmed controls reduce the number of mistakes and the risk of dishonest employees intentionally entering a high hourly rate or high number of hours worked to collect extra pay. They do not, however, prevent errors that fall within the predetermined parameters. No procedure, however sophisticated, will eliminate errors entirely; the only hope is to minimize their occurrence.

SELF-TEST

1. (T *or* F) Data is more useful for decision making than is information.
2. Input and output devices—as well as storage devices—are categorized as _____ devices.
3. A _____ _____ is an originating form containing data; examples of such forms include a purchase order or payroll change request.
4. (T *or* F) A source document is always in printed form.
5. (T *or* F) An important way to improve productivity is to reduce the number of times data is entered.
6. Data from terminals can be processed in two ways: _____ and _____.
7. Two hand-held input devices that reduce the need for keying are the _____ and the _____.
8. The device that can read printed material into storage is called an _____ _____ _____ _____.
9. UPC symbols on packaged goods are read by devices called _____ _____ _____.
10. (T *or* F) Most programs perform some type of verification of input data before processing it.

SOLUTIONS 1) False. 2) peripheral. 3) source document. 4) False. Bar-coded or even handwritten documents for example, can be source documents. 5) True. 6) in batches; interactively. 7) mouse; light pen. 8) optical character recognition device (OCR). 9) bar code readers. 10) True.

Outputting Information

The purpose of computing is to add value to the input data; input data is processed, organized, and presented in some way to provide meaningful information that enables users to make decisions or take action of some sort. For information to have this added value, it must meet five criteria: it must be *accurate, timely, complete, concise,* and *relevant*.

There is a long-standing expression in the computer industry: "Garbage in, garbage out"—meaning that inaccurate data will produce useless output information. It is important to maintain **accuracy** through the entire computing process because it is remarkably easy to corrupt perfectly good data. For example, if you construct a spreadsheet to help you make sales decisions, you might inadvertently put in a formula that adds the wrong two figures, and your decision will be affected by an incorrect total.

The second criterion for information is **timeliness**. The computer, with its high-speed processing capabilities, can produce error-free output within seconds or minutes of data input. However, timeliness is second in importance to accuracy. It is better to produce accurate output tomorrow than incorrect output today.

The third measure of information quality is **completeness**. Unlike human beings, computers do not tire before the job is done, and they can therefore provide a complete analysis of the data, no matter how cumbersome or tedious the task.

Because information is so easy to produce on a computer, users and programmers sometimes produce too much of it. **Conciseness** pays off because you can go straight to the information you need without wading through pages of irrelevant material. The last criterion is therefore **relevance**. The information provided must have a bearing on the decision-making application for which it was intended.

Types of Output Information

We use output devices daily, usually without even noticing that a sophisticated computer program is managing the application. Many local libraries, for example, have converted their card catalogs from stacks of drawers full of file cards to a few computer screens. To find out whether your library has a certain book, you simply follow a few on-screen instructions and type in the author's last name or some other identifier, and the closest titles in the library's collection appear on the screen. In this case the computer is producing **soft copy**, or screen display output.

This is in contrast to **hard copy**, or printed output. Some libraries have the capability of printing a bibliography of titles on a subject you are interested in. You can key in a few parameters, and the computer gives you a printed list of all the books that fall within your criteria.

There are endless varieties of special-purpose output, such as airline tickets, electronic bank teller transaction slips, library overdue notices, book manuscript from a word processor—the applications areas are boundless.

Most routine business output, however, can be classified into five categories: *responses to individual queries, special reports, exception reports, periodic summary reports,* and *transaction reports.*

Inquiries are usually on-demand searches in a database for a particular piece of information. For example, a human resources department might need to know the date of employment for Justine Oxley, whose Social Security number is 342-00-0228. Or a customer service representative might check to see whether the part a customer needs is currently in inventory.

Special reports are generated on a one-time or unscheduled basis in response to a management request. For example, a marketing manager might notice an unaccountable jump in sales in a geographic area and request a listing of individual orders for that area to determine whether the jump is a trend or a one-time exception.

Exception reports are listings of all events or data items that fall outside some management-assigned tolerance for variability. For example, the manager of a sales force might regularly receive a listing of all salespeople whose expense accounts were either over or under the expected range. Both situations may require some management intervention.

Periodic summary reports can be daily, weekly, monthly, quarterly, or even yearly. These include sales summaries, end-of-month inventory reports, the company's financial reports, cost of sales analyses—all the standard working reports needed by all of the company's functional departments. They are used by either the operating staff or by managers for decision-making purposes.

Transaction reports are detailed reports of transactions at the operations level; examples of transaction reports are complete listings of payroll checks, orders received, and invoices scheduled for payment.

In the following sections, we will discuss several types of output devices. Figure 5–13 shows some of the most common output devices. Most output devices are designed to produce either hard copy or visual displays of information. We will discuss these two types of output devices in detail,

Device	Use

Printer — Prints reports, fills in forms.

Cathode ray tube — Displays keyed, computer-stored, or computer-produced information.

Disk pack

5 1/4" disk

3 1/2" disk

Tape

Stores keyed or computer-produced information for later use.

Optical disk — Stores data as laser marks, or bits, for later use. Now mostly used for permanent storage.

Plotter — Draws computer-produced color graphs and charts.

Microfilm — Stores miniaturized printed reports, forms, and other data on film.

5–13 Examples of common output forms and devices. Output devices convert data stored in the CPU to meaningful information.

and then briefly describe two other forms of output devices: those for audio output and for microfilm output.

Screen Displays

Screen display output is usually associated with some form of interactive processing—a combination of input and output. The screen typically provides an array of options called a menu: you choose one; then the screen provides more detailed options and eventually gives you the exact information you need.

Until recently, most programs on IBM computers used the keyboard to call up menus and make menu choices; the Macintosh and more recent IBM applications use the mouse to "pull down" menus from key words at the top of the screen and to move the cursor to the chosen options you select with the mouse's button. Figure 5–14 shows examples of the contrasting menu approaches from these two types of software.

Two graphic user interface programs make extensive use of a mouse for making selections from menus: IBM's new Presentation Manager, used with the OS/2 operating system; and Microsoft's Windows, designed for both IBM's DOS operating system and the Apple Macintosh.

Application programs usually require several levels of menus. For example, in the library book catalog program discussed above, the user chooses one of the major modules of the program; a submenu for that

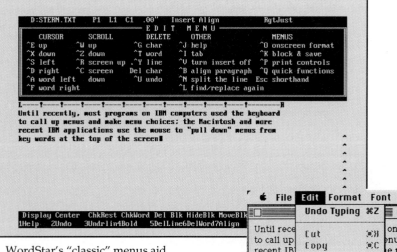

5–14 Two contrasting menu approaches.

WordStar's "classic" menus aid users in making menu selections with their keyboards.

Microsoft Word on the Macintosh uses the newer "pull-down" menu technology.

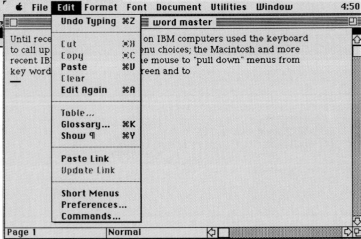

program then appears, and it may have further submenus. After entering the author's name on a submenu, the books closest to your specifications appear on the screen.

A variety of screen display devices are available, and the technologies used to produce them are becoming quite sophisticated. For example, early personal computer screens were always "black and white," but today's Macintosh II can produce 16.7 *million* colors on the screen.

CRTs   The most common form of display monitor is the CRT, or **cathode ray tube**. This is the type of monitor used with microcomputers. CRTs contain an electron "gun" that fires a beam of electrons, lighting up tiny points of phosphor that then glow for a short period of time. Each tiny point of light is called a **pixel**, or picture element; each character you see on the screen is made up of many pixels. The gun constantly scans the screen, relighting the pixels so rapidly that you see the screen characters as continuously glowing.

The quality of what you see on the screen is affected by how many pixels your monitor is designed to display. The more pixels, the better the **resolution**, or crispness, of the characters on the screen.

CRTs that have only one color are called **monochrome monitors**, and they are typically either green or amber against a black background.

Color monitors are also very popular. The cost of color monitors is decreasing and the availability of higher levels of memory is going up, so more users are incorporating them in their systems. They are called **RGB monitors** (for red, green, blue), because they have three electron guns—one each for red, green, and blue—and the pixels each have a dot of red, green, and blue that can be activitated individually or in combination by the electron guns to create many hues and colors.

In summary, most microcomputers as well as minis and mainframes can be equipped with either a monochrome or RGB monitor. Figure 5–15 shows a pie chart displayed on an RGB monitor. Color monitors cost as much as several hundred dollars more than monochrome monitors, require more

5–15 Whereas monochrome monitors can only display colors as shades of gray, color monitors allow the user to display any number of color combinations as shown in this pie graph. *Courtesy*: IBM.

5–16 The most common flat screen display is the liquid crystal display (LCD). Here it is shown on a Radio Shack portable computer. *Courtesy*: Radio Shack.

internal memory than monochrome monitors, and need special adapter cards to allow the CPU to process color.

A variety of adapter cards can be plugged into a microcomputer's motherboard to create color graphics on the screen and to allow them to be sent to laser or other printers. These include color graphics adapters (CGAs), multicolor graphics adapters (MCGAs), enhanced graphic adapters (EGAs), and video graphics arrays (VGAs). Each of these categories of graphics card represent different standards of resolution—that is, different numbers of pixels and colors that affect the crispness of images and the number of hues available.

Flat-Screen Technologies   You may have noticed that the monitor on your personal computer is actually deeper than it is wide or tall; this is the shape required for the electron gun inside. However, it is not a very practical shape or weight for portable computers. Thanks to new **flat-screen technologies**, small laptop computers can go everywhere and do almost as much work as desktop computers. Most current flat screens are monochrome.

One technology, **electroluminescent (EL) display**, is not used much because it requires too much power for battery-operated laptops. The most common flat screen is the **liquid crystal display (LCD)**, which is based on running a current through liquid crystals sandwiched between two sheets of polarized material. Characters on the screen are created when crystals arrange themselves so that light does not shine through; the image is dark against a lighted background. An LCD screen is shown in Figure 5–16.

Some of the newest laptops use **gas plasma displays**, even though they require more power than LCDs. They have excellent resolution and display graphics superbly, although the only color is an orange-red (Figure 5–17). Gas plasma displays sandwich a neon/argon gas mixture with grids of vertical and horizontal wires. Pixels are located at the points where horizontal and vertical wires cross.

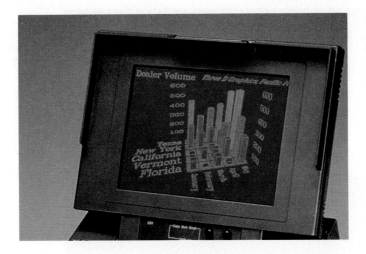

5–17 This Toshiba laptop display uses gas plasma technology, which can be clearly identified by its distinctive orange color. *Courtesy*: Toshiba America, Inc.

Printers

In Chapter 1 you were introduced to the basic forms of printers for hard copy output: letter-quality and near-letter quality, impact and nonimpact, and some of the nonimpact forms of printing such as thermal and laser printers. In this section we will discuss printers in more detail so that you have an understanding of which kinds are used for microcomputers or larger systems, and what the issues are in choosing printers.

Printers can be classified as impact (strike-on) or nonimpact printers. Both kinds of printers are used for the whole range of computers—there are inexpensive impact printers that are commonly used for microcomputers, and high-speed impact printers that are used with large mainframes. Until recently, the nonimpact technologies that we will cover were exclusively designed for high-speed output for mainframes, but some nonimpact technologies—laser printing, thermal transfer printing, and ink-jet printing—are rapidly entering the microcomputer market because of their typographic and illustration capabilities, and because their cost has decreased dramatically. Figure 5–18 compares impact and non-impact printers.

Purchasers of printers must consider the form of paper output needed for their applications. For example, printers are usually designed for feeding paper by either **friction feed** or **tractor feed**, although some may include attachments that allow for both methods. Friction-feed printers feed a sheet

Impact printers	Non impact printers
1. Inexpensive 2. Can produce carbon copies	1. Can be used for high-speed output 2. Can produce high-quality output 3. Almost noiseless 4. Fewer mechanical parts, less breakdown
1. Slow 2. Noisy 3. Subject to mechanical breakdown	1. The printers are expensive 2. Paper and toner supplies are expensive 3. Cannot produce carbon copies

5–18 Advantages and disadvantages of impact and non-impact printers.

5–19 Continuous-form paper moves through the tractor feed on a dot-matrix printer. *Courtesy*: Radio Shack.

at a time through; they are used for high-quality output such as correspondence and reports, often on company letterhead paper.

Tractor-feed printers use **continuous-form paper** (Figure 5–19) that feeds through without interruption. Continuous-form paper has small holes on either side that fit onto sprockets on the printer; the sprockets feed the paper through at the right speed. Continuous-form paper can be designed to do special business tasks. For example, most companies use continuous-form checks to pay their bills and payroll by computer, and the checks may be designed with one or more carbon copies for filing. Pressure-sensitive mailing labels are also available on continuous forms so that they can be used on computer printers. Most business forms that go through a computer's printer are some type of continuous form—invoices, purchase orders, shipping labels, and so on. These forms are perforated so that they can be separated, and many include backup sheets on chemically treated paper that creates carbon copies.

Impact Printers   **Impact printers** use some form of strike-on method to press a carbon or fabric ribbon against the paper, much as typewriters do. At the inexpensive end, designed for microcomputers or terminals for larger systems, are impact printers that print one character at a time; these are called **serial printers**. At the high-speed end, designed to be used with large computer systems, are **line printers**, which print a line at a time and include band printers, chain printers, and drum printers.

For mainframes, **band printers** use a flexible stainless-steel print band that is photoengraved with print characters and prints one line at a time. The band rotates horizontally until the characters to be printed are properly aligned. They are popular because they are inexpensive, produce high-quality output, run at high speed, and have removable bands that allow type fonts to be changed easily.

Chain printers are mainframe printers that have one print hammer for each print position in a line. The chain revolves horizontally past all print

Inked ribbon

Paper

Raised characters
on flexible chain are
in constant motion

Hammer strikes as
character moves
behind paper.

Paper

Hammer strikes as
character moves
behind paper.

Inked ribbon

Raised characters
on print drum are
in constant motion

positions. As a character on the chain passes the position where it is to print, the hammer presses the paper against the ribbon to produce a character image. Chain printers have two disadvantages: they are relatively expensive, and some have chains that are difficult to change.

Finally, **drum printers** use a cylindrical steel drum embossed with print characters. Each column on the drum contains all the characters, and the columns and drum rotate at high speed to print a line at a time. Many organizations have been replacing their drum printers with newer band printers, which are more versatile and tend to last longer. Figure 5–20 shows how chain and drum printer mechanisms work.

Dot-matrix printers are impact printers that create characters from a rectangular grid of pins. The pins press against a carbon ribbon to print on paper. The characters are rather crude, but readable. Many offices use a form of dot-matrix printer that is called a **near-letter-quality printer** because it overprints in a slightly offset pattern that fills in the lines to create much better quality type. Figure 5–21 illustrates the difference between the standard dot-matrix type (sometimes called draft-quality type) and near-letter-quality type.

Daisywheel printers print fully formed characters from a flat disk that has petal-like projections containing individual characters (Figure 5–22). They are the slowest type of printer, but they produce letter-quality output. Many offices use daisywheel printers for their public correspondence because the quality of the output is similar to that of standard typewriter output. The daisywheels themselves are also interchangeable so that a variety of typefaces can be used on the same printer.

In summary, the high-speed line printers used with mainframes are most likely to be band printers. The disadvantages of impact printers in contrast to nonimpact printers is that they are usually slower, noisier, and

5–20 Impact printers all use some form of strike-on method to print. The chain printer hammer (left) strikes as the chain rotates past the paper, while drum printers create lines of type by rotating column sections of the drum (right).

5–21 Dot-matrix printers can usually be adjusted to print draft-quality characters as at left, or near-letter-quality characters, as at right.

Computers   Computers

more subject to mechanical breakdowns. However, because they are also relatively inexpensive, they continue to be widely used.

Nonimpact Printers   There are three commonly used types of nonimpact printers: thermal printers, ink-jet printers, and laser printers.

Thermal printers create whole characters on specially treated paper that responds to patterns of heat produced by the printer. They can produce print in only one color. Thermal printers are less popular than ink-jet and laser printers because they are slow; in addition, their paper is expensive and deteriorates over time. **Thermal transfer printers**, however, use a heat-and-wax method that produces high-quality output, in color, and on regular paper. It is less expensive than the older thermal technology.

Ink-jet printers are used with both microcomputers and large computer systems. Their technology is based on shooting tiny dots of ink onto the paper. Since any color of ink can be used, they are well suited for graphics applications. Figure 5–23 shows a Hewlett-Packard ink-jet printer with color output.

Laser printers began as high-speed printers for large mainframe systems, but their versatility and high-quality output have made them popular for all models of computers. Laser printers beam whole pages at a time onto a drum; then the paper is passed over the drum and the image is picked up with toner, like that used in xerographic copiers. Many laser manufacturers are introducing lower-priced models for microcomputers. At the high-priced end, color laser printers that produce near-photographic-quality images are being used in the graphics industry for color proofing of books and magazines.

One application that has developed largely because of the availability of laser printers is **desktop publishing**, which uses hardware systems costing

5–22 A daisy-wheel printer uses a revolving, petal-like print head to produce clear, precise letters. *Courtesy*: Qume Corp.

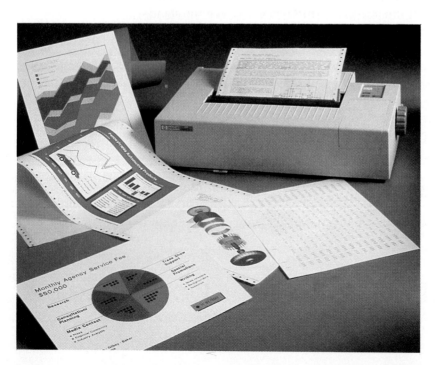

5–23 An ink-jet printer with color output. Ink-jet printing is particularly well-adapted to color printing. *Courtesy*: Hewlett-Packard Company.

as little as $10,000 to produce professional-quality publications (Figure 5–24). Desktop publishing is discussed in more detail in Chapter 8.

Note that nonimpact printers cannot be used to print on continuous forms if they include backup or carbon sheets; the printing will only make a visible impression on backup sheets if a strike-on method is used.

5–24 Desktop publishing systems allow the user to combine sophisticated graphics and word-processed text, with high-resolution laser printers to produce professional-looking output. *Courtesy*: Aldus Corporation.

Plotters   **Plotters** are printers that are specially designed to produce high-quality line drawings in colors. They use two methodologies to produce graphics. Pen plotters move pens containing different colors of ink over the paper, and electrostatic plotters use electrostatic charges to produce images on the paper. Plotters have many applications, particularly for presentation graphics (charts and graphs for business meetings) and engineering drawings.

Other Forms of Output

Not all output from computers is on a screen or from a printer. Two other forms of output deserve mention.

Audio Response Units   An **audio response unit** provides users with a verbal response using a voice simulator or a series of prerecorded messages. Some makes of automobiles give you voice messages if you leave your key in the ignition or your parking lights on. Many banks use audio response units to assist tellers who need to find out whether an account has funds to cover a check. The teller keys in the customer's account number and the amount of the check using a Touch-Tone phone. The computer then determines whether there are enough funds in the account and selects the appropriate verbal response to "speak" to the teller.

Voice simulators are also useful as an aid to blind people. Figure 5–25 shows a word processing application designed to give audio feedback to blind typists who cannot visually verify the correctness of their keyboarding.

5–25 A blind person "reads" using the Kurzweil Reading Machine to scan characters and give audio output. *Source*: Pat Goudvis.

Computer Output Microfilm Units   Microfilm and microfiche (generically called **microforms**) have a long and useful history as noncomputerized storage media for information. These are miniaturized photographic copies of documents that take up little storage space (Figure 5–26). Reading microforms requires special equipment that enlarges the images to readable size.

Libraries use microforms to store images of newspapers and magazines that they would otherwise be unable to keep because of space limitations, and medical facilities use miniaturized X-rays for the same reasons.

5–26 A stack of documents can be reduced to a small roll of microfilm for easier storage. *Courtesy*: Kodak.

Looking Ahead

Talking to Your Computer

Voice simulators as output devices will increasingly be used together with voice recognition input devices for interactive processing, as the technology improves. Imagine managing your bank account with the use of voice simulation and recognition. You are sitting comfortably in your favorite chair. You ask your computer/telephone to call your bank and find out what your current balance is. After your computer/phone tells you what it is, you then ask the computer to pay your phone bill for you. Prepare yourself—such applications are just around the corner!

In recent years, as computers produce huge amounts of printed reports that need to be stored as archival material, companies have recognized the value of microfilm to store important computer output. **Computer output microfilm (COM) units** can be linked to a CPU and can create output on microfilm or microfiche at very high speeds. COM output requires special microfilm readers for users to look at the output.

SUMMARY

Individual bits of raw *data* are input into computers, then processed and used to produce output in the form of *information*. Information is processed data that is analyzed and formatted in a way that helps users make decisions and take action.

Data is input from original documents called *source documents*. The data that comes from source documents must be entered in some way into a storage medium for processing. Sometimes source documents must be rekeyed so that they can be read by a CPU, while other source documents have a form of machine-readable code that does not require keyboarding.

The trend in input procedures is to reduce the number of times data is entered; in efficient information systems, data is often passed from department to department electronically so that each department can take appropriate action without reentering the facts.

Older keypunch technology involved using special input equipment that punched holes in paper cards to record data; it was then fed to the CPU via a card reader for batch-mode processing.

Keypunch methodologies have largely been replaced by *key-to-disk* or *key-to-tape technologies*. Operators use keyboards to type documents into magnetic storage on disks or tapes. Many companies use terminals or microcomputers for data entry.

Automatic teller machines (ATMs) are examples of interactive terminals, because they process data while the customer waits, and then immediately update banking records.

Special input devices allow input to be entered in a very user-friendly way that is easy to learn. The *mouse*, for example, can be moved around the desktop to manipulate the screen cursor, and *light pens* can be used to make selections from menus displayed on the screen.

Even friendlier input methodologies are *touch screens*, which users touch to make menu selections and *voice-recognition devices*, which can recognize spoken words as input. All these devices minimize the need for keyboarding.

Portable keying devices and *Touch-Tone telephones* are useful for sending data over telephone lines.

A number of scanning devices can read various forms of input directly and then convert them to machine-readable form: *optical character recognition devices (OCRs)*, which read typed or typeset words; *bar code readers*, which read the Universal Product Code (UPC) or bar code on merchandise; *optical mark readers*, which read pencil marks made on special computer-entry forms; and *magnetic ink character readers (MICRs)*, which are used by banks to read the magnetic ink numbers on checks.

There are four commonly used ways to detect input errors: *double-keyboarding* for electronically comparing output; *echo-printing* each transaction and then visually checking the data to detect errors; *visually checking control listings* of unprocessed data; and using *programmed error controls* that verify which data falls within predetermined parameters.

Output information, to be useful, must meet the criteria of *accuracy, timeliness, completeness, conciseness,* and *relevance*. Standard business output falls into five categories: *inquiries, special reports, exception reports, periodic reports,* and *transaction records* that provide detailed output.

Output hardware includes *printers* for *hard copy output,* and *screens* for *soft copy output.* Screens are usually associated with *interactive output,* and usually present *menus* of choices for the user to respond to.

The most common kind of screen or monitor is the *CRT,* or *cathode ray tube,* which can be either *monochrome* or *color.* Small laptop computers use *flat-screen technologies* such as *electroluminescent (EL) displays, liquid crystal displays (LCDs),* or *gas plasma displays.*

Printers can be classified as *impact* or *nonimpact.* Impact printers include slower printers such as *dot-matrix* and *daisywheel printers* for micros, as well as high-speed *line printers* such as *band printers, chain printers,* and *drum printers* for mainframes.

Nonimpact printers currently in use are primarily *thermal printers, ink-jet printers,* and *laser printers.* The availability of laser printers has made possible a whole new industry called *desktop publishing.*

Plotters are printers that are designed for color graphics for presentations and engineering drawings.

Two other forms of output are *audio response units* that simulate the human voice or play prerecorded messages in response to input; and *computer output microfilm (COM)* units, which output *microform* information for compact storage.

KEY TERMS

Audio response unit
Automatic teller machine (ATM)
Band printer
Bar code reader
Cathode ray tube (CRT)
Chain printer
Computer output microfilm (COM) unit
Continuous-form paper
Daisywheel printer
Data
Data verification
Desktop publishing
Dot-matrix printer
Drum printer
Electroluminescent (EL) display
Flat-screen technology
Friction feed
Gas plasma display
Hard copy
Impact printer
Information
Ink-jet printer
Input
Key-to-disk

Key-to-tape
Keypunch card
Laser printer
Light pen
Line printer
Liquid crystal display (LCD)
Magnetic ink character reader (MICR)
Menu
Microform
Monochrome monitor
Mouse
Near-letter-quality printer
Nonimpact printer
Optical character recognition (OCR)
Optical mark reader
Output
Paper tape
Peripheral device
Pixel
Plotter
Point-of-sale terminal (POS)
Portable keying device

Resolution
RGB monitor
Serial printer
Soft copy
Source document
Terminal
Thermal printer

Thermal transfer printer
Touch-sensitive screen
Tractor feed
Universal Product Code (UPC)
User-friendly
Voice-recognition device

CHAPTER SELF-TEST

1. Information differs from data in that it can be used for _____.
2. Input and output devices are called _____ devices.
3. A purchase order used as input to a computer system would be called a _____ _____.
4. (T *or* F) Some input units can read source documents directly; others require source documents to be converted to some machine-readable form.
5. Input devices that can read printed characters directly from a source document are called _____ _____ _____ devices.
6. (T *or* F) Output that is displayed on a CRT screen is referred to as soft copy.
7. (T *or* F) Flat-screen gas plasma displays are always capable of producing on-screen color graphics.
8. (T *or* F) Daisywheel printers are faster than line printers like band printers.
9. Impact printers that form characters using pins in a rectangular patterns are called _____ printers.
10. (T *or* F) Daisywheel printers produce letter-quality output.
11. The most versatile of the three types of line printers is the _____ printer.
12. (T *or* F) Laser printers use a technology similar to that of copiers.
13. Two advantages of impact printers are _____ and _____.
14. (T *or* F) Plotters are used to reproduce photographic images.
15. The computer device that creates microfilm output is the _____ _____ _____ unit.

SOLUTIONS 1) decision making. 2) peripheral. 3) source document. 4) True. 5) optical character recognition (OCR) or optical scanning. 6) True. 7) False. 8) False. 9) dot-matrix. 10) True. 11) band. 12) True. 13) They are inexpensive and they can produce carbon copies. 14) False. 15) computer output microfilm (COM).

REVIEW QUESTIONS

1. Name three categories of peripheral devices.
2. Name two examples of source documents that must be keyboarded and two examples of source documents that already have machine-readable code ready for input.

3. List and describe two hand-held input devices.
4. List and describe three ways of detecting input errors.
5. What are the five qualities that make information useful for decision making?
6. List and describe five types of reports.
7. Define the following terms related to screen display: CRT, pixel, resolution, monochrome, and RGB.
8. List and describe three types of flat-screen technologies.
9. For impact printers and nonimpact printers, list at least two advantages and three disadvantages.
10. List and describe two nonmagnetic forms of output.

PROBLEM-SOLVING APPLICATIONS

1. In Lotus 1-2-3, design a small form that will do multiplication. Design the form so that two cells will accept input of numbers that you will multiply, and a third cell that will produce the multiplication output. Which cells have data in them and which have information?
2. See how many different input technologies you can identify around you in one day: key-to-disk or key-to-tape, mouse, light pen, touch-sensitive screen, voice-recognition device, portable keying device, OCR, bar code reader, optical mark reader, or magnetic ink character reader. See whether you can identify additional types of input devices.
3. Based on the information in this chapter, which kind of printer would you choose if you needed high-speed, high-quality output? What would you choose if all you needed was an inexpensive printer for your company or school's mainframe? What kinds of questions would you ask to arrive at a purchasing choice?

Storage and Files

When you have completed this chapter, you will be able to:

- ✔ Define the following terms and their relationships: field, key field, record, master file, database.

- ✔ List and describe the two types of secondary storage for mainframe systems, and the advantages and disadvantages of each.

- ✔ Describe the three main types of disk drives available for microcomputers.

- ✔ Describe how disk and tape devices read and write data.

Chapter 6

Chapter Outline

Computers have become faster, more powerful, and more accessible to individuals and organizations. As a consequence, the amount of data and information available in our society is multiplying at an overwhelming rate.

Television often shows a fantasy version of what is available to users of large computers systems. On *Matt Houston* reruns, for example, we see Houston and his sidekick lawyer ask their computer for personal histories on any person that happens to relate to their investigations. The computer instantly provides detailed records of suspicious people—from parking tickets to the charities the suspects contribute to—as well as photographs of the subjects and all their associates.

The databank that would be needed to support such far-ranging inquiries does not yet exist, at least in the hands of private investigators, and the huge amount of storage capacity that would be needed to store millions of scanned photographs is not practical at this time. However, even small users—such as the student who gathers scientific data on which to base a report—need to store a lot of data before they can produce information that can be analyzed or used to print a report.

We have covered how data is processed in the CPU and the variety of ways in which it is input and output. In this chapter we will describe how data is stored. This is an increasingly important aspect of computerization, because as software capabilities increase, business projects become more ambitious. Only the most efficient storage methods will enable us to retrieve information from our increasingly vast data libraries.

How Data Is Organized and Retrieved

Business operations involving computers all use some form of database management, which will be presented in detail in Chapter 11. In this chapter we will discuss how data is stored, and we will introduce you to one basic database concept: **data hierarchy**. Data hierarchy refers to the organization of data at different levels so that it can be stored and retrieved efficiently. Employee records are a good example. Stored in computer files are records of all employees, including their home addresses, Social Security numbers, hiring dates, number of dependents claimed for payroll tax deductions, whether they are U.S. citizens, their current salary, and so on.

The Hierarchy of Data

The whole file of employee records is called the **master file** (Figure 6–1). Master files are permanent files that are updated as changes occur; in this case, updates would include salary changes to existing records, the addition of new employees, the deletion of employees that leave, and so on.

All the data about each employee is a **record**. So a master file is made up of many records—in this case, one for each employee of the company.

6–1 A master file holds any number of individual records made up of fields of information.

Soc. Sec. No.	Last Name	First Name	Address	City	State	Zip	Dep.	Salary	US Citizen
001-02-0123	Munoz	Frank	17 Florence Ave.	Centerville	IA	34567	2	2430	y
524-60-1771	Lambeth	Charles	633 Page St.	Centerville	IA	34567	1	2033	y
020-03-1234	Willis	Marlene	4412 West 12th	Centerville	IA	34567	0	3212	y

Key Field �⎯⎯⎯⎯⎯⎯⎯⎯⎯⎯ Fields ⎯⎯⎯⎯⎯⎯⎯⎯⎯⎯ Records

The data in each record is different but always of the same type: Social Security number, home address, and so on. Each such unit of data is stored in a **field**. An employee record would have a separate field for last name, first name, street address, city, state, zip code, date of hire, dependents claimed, and so on. So a record is made up of a number of fields.

Records can be either fixed-length, with all records the same size, or variable-length, with the record lengths differing. **Fixed-length records** have fields that are always the same size—for example, 20 characters for each last name, 40 characters for each address, and so on. This method for representing data is the easiest because you always know where to find a field; however, it can be an inefficient use of storage space because many fields will have data that requires fewer than the allotted number of characters. **Variable-length records** use only as much storage per field as is needed, so they are more efficient for storage than fixed-length records. Their disadvantage is that because the length of each record is different, they require extra processing.

Each record in a file has one or more **key fields** that uniquely define the record so that it can be accessed quickly and easily. In our example, the key field is the Social Security number field. The database program retrieves and orders records by this field.

To review: records are made up of a number of fields, and a master file is made up of a number of records. The **database** itself is made up of a collection of master files that are related in some way; a company's database might include master files for employees, sales data, product information, inventory, and so on.

There are a number of ways these master files can relate. For example, salespeople generate orders for which they will receive commissions. For each order the company receives, data is input to the sales master file; it includes the salesperson's Social Security number and the product ID number, which is used to retrieve employee data and product information. Two kinds of output can be produced: the salesperson gets a commission report by product, and the payroll department gets the data needed to produce a commission check.

Types of Data Fields

To make it easier for database software to manipulate the data in fields, database designers designate the data as one of three types (Figure 6–2).

Alphanumeric data fields can contain any kind of data—numbers, letters, or special symbols. Most of the fields in Figure 6–2 are alphanumeric. Numbers often appear in these fields, but they are not used for mathematical operations; for example, the number in a street address would not be added, subtracted, or multiplied for any purpose.

Numeric data fields can have only numbers in them. If an alphabetic letter is entered in a numeric field, the database program knows it is an error

6–2 Alphanumeric fields may contain any kind of data, numeric fields hold only numbers, and logic fields allow only Yes/No or True/False responses.

Soc. Sec. No.	Last Name	First Name	Address	City	State	Zip	Dep.	Salary	US Citizen
001-02-0123	Munoz	Frank	17 Florence Ave.	Centerville	IA	34567	2	2430	y

———————— Alphanumeric fields ————————   Numeric fields   Logic field and rejects the input. The data in numeric fields can have mathematical operations performed on it; for example, the number of dependents field can be multiplied by the standard deduction to determine how much tax to withhold in each paycheck.

Logic data fields allow only Yes/No or True/False responses. This allows database users to get reports on only the records that meet some condition. The field USCITIZEN is an example of a logic field.

How Files Are Organized

Many master files contain thousands or hundreds of thousands of records. How the records are organized on the storage disks can make a big difference in the efficiency of any particular application. There are three common ways to organize records in a file: sequentially, by index, or by direct access. Each method is appropriate for certain kinds of applications.

Sequential Files

In a **sequential file**, records are physically stored in some sequence or order. For example, the employee records, if stored sequentially, could be in numeric order by Social Security number. If a file is used over and over in the same order, and if it is not subject to a large number of additions and deletions that disturb the order of records, sequential order can be an efficient way to organize the data. Processing time is reduced because the disk drive does not need to search for records that are out of order. However, if records are added and deleted frequently, significant processing time is involved in having the computer put them back in order again.

Sequential files can only be accessed sequentially. This means that if you need to query the database to determine the salary for an employee with Social Security number 080-36-2822 and it is the 765th record on the disk, you must read past the first 764 records to access the desired record. We will see later that tapes must be processed sequentially, while disks can be processed either sequentially or by using one of the other two methods of file organization: indexed or direct access.

Indexed Files

The **indexed-file method** of organization is the one most commonly used for storing records on disks; it uses an index based on the key field of the records. As each record is created, the computer also creates an index that keeps track of the record's key field and the disk location of that record (Figure 6–3). The records may be randomly placed in the file, but they can be quickly located by referencing the index. To understand this technique, think about how difficult it would be to find this section on indexed files by sequentially paging through the book, but how easy it is if you simply look in the index to see what page describes indexed files.

The index itself consists of two matched lists: the key field for each record and the disk address of that record. The indexed file method for accessing records has two advantages: it allows for frequent updating of large amounts of data without the need to re-sort the records into a new

6–3 An indexed file contains a "directory" of key fields and the disk addresses of the corresponding records.

Key field	Disk address
001-02-0123	Surface 1 Track 6 Sector 3
020-03-1234	Surface 1 Track 14 Sector 5
066-04-2345	Surface 2 Track 11 Sector 2

sequence; and it also allows records to be located quickly without the need for sequentially reading through the disk. It is not, however, feasible to use this method for data stored on magnetic tape.

Direct-Access Files

In a **direct-access file**, the key field is used in some way as the address itself, eliminating the need to look for it in the index. As a simplified example, in a three-digit key field, the first digit may provide the disk surface number, with the last two digits providing the track number where the record is located (there will be more on disk addresses later in this chapter). Alternatively, some mathematical operation can be performed on the key field that will result in a unique location number for each record.

Direct access is most appropriate for on-line operations that require the highest-possible speed for retrieval and updating of data. Examples are bank automatic teller machines and airline ticket reservation systems. Direct access is not appropriate for data stored on magnetic tape or for applications that require retrieving records in sequential order.

Primary and Secondary Storage

Chapter 4 discussed **primary storage**, the CPU's temporary memory that holds data and programs during processing. Most often, primary storage, also called random-access memory (RAM), is **volatile**; that is, data in primary storage is not written on any magnetic medium while it is being processed, and so it disappears when the computer is turned off. Chapter 4 also described some forms of primary memory—such as bubble memory and optical memory—that are nonvolatile, but at this time none of them are in common use.

Secondary storage, however, is **nonvolatile** because data is written magnetically on some medium such as a disk or tape. Both application software programs and data input files need to be stored and then read into primary storage when they are needed.

When a program or data file is put into primary storage, or RAM, we say it is **read into memory**; what actually happens is that the file is copied from the disk to RAM. It does not disappear from the disk—the file remains there unchanged unless you write over it later.

When output of some kind is to be stored after processing, we say that we will **write** it **to disk**. Once again, the output is simply copied from RAM to the disk. Most applications hold the file—or at least the portion you are working on—in RAM until you close the file or exit the application.

Because RAM—primary storage—is volatile, beginning computer users sooner or later lose the work they did because they forgot to **save** it by writing it to disk before they left the application. Once you exit an application, RAM clears that data away to leave room to process more work, and your previous work is lost forever unless you have saved it.

A Brief History of Secondary Storage

The first medium used for large-scale computer storage was the keypunch card described in Chapter 5. It had some advantages that keep it in limited use even today, but cards are bulky and easily damaged.

Keypunch cards were replaced by magnetic tapes, which resemble reel-to-reel audio tapes. Magnetic tapes store data more efficiently than cards. The data on one card can be stored in less than $\frac{1}{10}$–inch of tape. Figure 6–4 shows the relative capacities of commonly used storage media.

Magnetic tapes are ideally suited to batch processing—holding input data and then processing a large batch all at once—which was once the major form of computer use. Operations such as payroll processing and end-of-month sales statements are best processed all at one time and therefore still use batch processing techniques. Batch processing is most often performed on sequential files, which is the only method of file organization used with tapes.

But we now expect computers to do interactive processing as well—to produce some result on the spot. Imagine calling your travel agent for airline tickets to Europe and then having to wait for a day or two to find out whether you can get on the flight. This is what would happen if the input from all the travel agents in the country had to be batch processed at the same time. As noted, tape is not a good medium for interactive processing because it can only be processed sequentially; if needed data is at the end of the tape, the computer has to read the entire tape before that data becomes available for processing.

Disk storage is now the primary medium used with all types of computers, from microcomputers with floppy disks to mainframes with disk mechanisms that make more than a billion characters of data available at one time. Because all disk mechanisms are designed to go directly to the requested disk address, they are referred to as **direct access storage devices**. Tape

6–4 Common storage media and the amount of data they hold. Except for the optical disk, all these store data magnetically.

Medium	Storage capacity	Medium	Storage capacity
5 1/4" disk	360 K-1.2 MB	Magnetic tape	1-10 MB
3 1/2" disk	720 K-1.4 MB	Disk pack	20 MB-1GB
Hard disk	10-100 MB	Optical disk	800 MB

continues to have an important role as the primary medium for backup storage, however.

In this chapter we are going to describe how data is stored on disks and tape, and discuss the hardware associated with each.

Storage on Disks

You are already familiar with disk storage from using your microcomputer—you are probably using either the 5¼-inch **floppy disk** most commonly used on IBM PCs and compatibles, or the 3½-inch diskette in a hard plastic cover that was made popular by Apple when it introduced the Macintosh line. Because they hold so much more data than 5¼-inch disks, 3½-inch disks are now used on most newer micros, including the IBM PS/2 family and their compatibles, as well as for most laptops. Figure 6–5 shows these two familiar disks and the features that distinguish each. Other sizes of diskettes exist but are less common. (Note that we use the terms *floppy disk*, *diskette*, and *disk* interchangeably when referring to disk storage media for micros.)

How Microcomputer Disks Store Data

Inside a disk jacket is a thin, flexible plastic disk that has a metal oxide coating capable of retaining magnetic bits of data. The larger 5¼-inch disks are enclosed in a flexible jacket, while 3½-inch disks are enclosed in rigid plastic, which makes them the more durable form.

Figure 6–6 illustrates how data is stored on the disk. Each disk contains two surfaces, or sides; on each surface there are a number of invisible concentric circles called **tracks**, and the tracks are segmented into wedge-shaped **sectors**. Even though tracks get successively smaller toward the hub of the disk, each contains the same amount of data; data is just recorded more densely. This is similar to the tracks on a long-playing record album.

Microcomputer disks are **soft-sectored** when you buy them—that is, the sectors are not already defined on the disks. Sector definition differs among operating systems, so sectors are defined for the first time when you format,

6–5 The 5¼-inch and 3½-inch floppy disks have similar features. However, sliding panels and a hard case give the 3½-inch disk more protection.

or initialize, your new disks using your operating system. Other types of computer systems may require sectors to be already defined; these are called **hard-sectored** disks. Soft-sectored disks have a small hole near the center hub that tells the disk drive where the tracks begin. Hard-sectored disks have evenly spaced holes around the hub, one for each predetermined sector (Figure 6–7).

Notice in Figure 6–5 that diskettes have a notch or tab for write protection. This feature allows you to protect the data on 5¼-inch disks by covering the notch, which prevents the disk from being written to, accidentally or otherwise. In other words, when the notch is covered, you can read the data, but you cannot make any changes to it. On 3½-inch disks, the write-protect tab is movable so that you simply slide it for write protection.

Most microcomputers now use double-sided, double-density disks, which can hold up to 360 K, or approximately 368,640 bytes, for a low-density 5¼-inch disk; or 720 K for the high-density disk used by IBM AT micros and compatibles. (To do this math yourself, 1 K = 1024 bytes; 1024 x 360 K = 368,460 bytes.) The smaller 3½-inch disks commonly hold two to four times as much data, which accounts for their popularity; the 3½-inch disks for IBM PS/2 microcomputers, for example, hold from 720 K to 1.44 MB.

To contrast the capacities of these two disk sizes, consider the number of book or manuscript pages that could be stored on each type of disk. If the manuscript page held about 2,000 characters per page, the book on the 5¼-inch disk would be about 180 pages long, leaving space for invisible formatting codes. A 720K 3½-inch disk could hold a book manuscript of about 360 pages.

The smaller 3½-inch disks are gaining in popularity not only because of their larger storage capacities, but also because their rigid plastic casing protects them better. Their movable write-protect tab is also an advantage.

Taking Care of Diskettes   Disks are fairly durable, but they can be damaged or electronically altered, making your data meaningless. Figure 6–8 illustrates five rules for protecting the data on your diskettes.

1.   Do not expose disks to magnetic fields. Three common sources of magnetic damage are telephones, television sets, and copiers. Disks usually go through X-ray equipment at the airport undamaged, but many people pass them around the scanners by hand just in case.

2.   Keep 5¼-inch diskettes in their paper sleeves. This protects the window where the magnetic disk itself is exposed. The disk's magnetic material can be damaged if it gets scratched or if foreign material such as food or dust gets on it. Store disks in boxes to keep objects from being piled on top of them, which may warp the disk.

3.   On soft 5¼-inch diskettes, write on the label with felt-tip pens, not pencils or ballpoint pens; hard points can press through the jacket and damage the disk. Avoid touching the disk surface itself, because fingerprints can damage it.

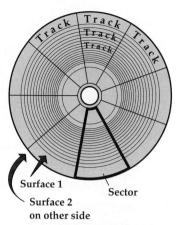

6–6 A floppy disk has concentric tracks like an LP record. The disk's tracks contain bytes of data. The FORMAT command divides the disk into wedges called sectors.

6–7 The sectors on a hard-sectored disk are pre-defined to meet the specifications of a particular disk drive. Evenly spaced holes around the hub of the disk indicate the beginning of each sector.

1. Keep disks away from magnetic fields.

2. Store flexible 5 1/4" disks inside paper sleeves.

3. Use a felt-tip pen to write on labels. Ballpoint pens will scratch the disk inside.

Felt-tip is soft.

4. Keep food and liquid away from disks.

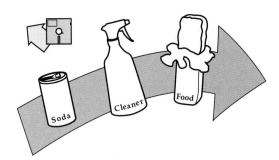

Soda   Cleaner   Food

5. Don't leave disks in heat or sun.

4.   Do not spill anything on the disk; do not use any cleaning liquids on it.

5.   Do not leave disks in heat or sunlight; for example, do not leave them in the back window of your car—the disk can become distorted by the heat and your data will be destroyed.

6–8 These five simple rules will protect your disks and their data from the most common sources of damage.

Backing Up Your Disks   Remember, disks are replaceable—it is the data on them that is valuable. The best way to protect your data is to back up your disk files onto another disk or other medium (such as a tape cartridge) on a regular basis. Most computer users develop systematic backup procedures. To the beginner, these procedures may seem paranoid—as if you were protecting yourself against the possibility of computer failure occurring the same day that the building you work in burns down. Trust the voice of experience: most people learn to back up the hard way, after losing invaluable data and spending many hours and a lot of money restoring it.

One good rule of thumb is never to use your original application disks; make a copy for everyday use and store the original.

If you have data files that are constantly changing, you may want to have two sets of backup files, alternating between them each time you back up; this allows you to go back one "generation" just in case something goes wrong with the backup itself.

Store your backup copies and original application disks someplace safe —separate from where you store your disks that are in everyday use.

How Disk Drives Access Data

Disk drives that use double-sided disks have two **read/write heads**, one for each side of the diskette (Figure 6–9). Older, single-sided disk drives have a read/write head that can access only one side of the diskette. For reading or writing data, the read/write head makes contact with the disk through the window cut in the disk's sleeve (Figure 6–5).

When a particular item of data is to be accessed or read, the disk address of the data is looked up on a file allocation table. The disk drive then whirls the disk inside its sleeve to locate the correct sector, while the arm moves the read/write head to the track containing the data. The same thing happens when you write something to a disk—the disk drive locates an available sector/track address on which to write the data.

Types of Disk Drives for Microcomputers

Microcomputers have one or two disk drives visible on the outside of the computer's case. You insert disks into these drives as shown in Figure 6–10, and then close the gate or lever, which puts the read/write head in contact with the disk, ready for data transfer. Disk drives may be either full-height as in Figure 6–10, or half-height. When there are two disk drives, the left-hand or top one is usually labeled as drive A, while the right-hand or bottom one is called drive B.

Many microcomputers also have a large-capacity internal hard disk, usually called drive C. Hard disks have a capacity several times that of a floppy disk—the smallest hard disks hold 10 MB, and the largest ones currently available can hold more than 100 MB, with even larger capacities probably available by the time you read this book.

Hard disks are made of a rigid metal substance coated with a metal oxide, just like floppy diskettes. Data is stored on a hard disk in sectors and tracks, just like on diskettes. Hard disks are sealed into sterile containers, because the distance from the read/write head to the disk is so small that

Window for recording data

Read/write heads

6–9 The floppy disk is inserted between two read/write heads so data can be read and written on both sides of the disk.

6–10 Insert disks carefully and completely into their slot, then close the lever or gate to secure them in place.

6–11 Fixed disks, or internal hard disks, are made of a rigid material, and hold many times more data than a floppy disk. *Courtesy*: Seagate Technology.

even a cigarette smoke particle is bigger. When foreign substances get between the read/write head and the disk, a **head crash** may occur—a dreaded catastrophe among computer users because everything on the disk may be lost.

There are two types of microcomputer hard disks. The older kind is called simply a **hard disk** or internal hard disk; IBM also calls it a **fixed disk**. This type of disk is built into the computer's box (Figure 6–11). In the early 1980s, **hard cards** became available. Hard cards are circuit boards with hard disks built into them. Because they are boards, they can be added by plugging them into the computer's internal expansion slots (see Figure 6–12).

Some microcomputer users opt to buy an **external hard disk**, which is a fixed disk in a separate box (Figure 6–13). It operates just like an internal hard disk but has the advantage of being portable; you unplug it from one computer and move it to another one.

There are many advantages to hard disks. To begin with, the operating system can be copied onto the hard disk. If you have an IBM-compatible microcomputer, for example, you can start your computer directly from the hard disk without inserting your disk operating system (DOS) diskette in drive A. In other words, when you turn your computer on, the computer boots itself up.

6–12 Hard cards are an alternative to fixed hard disks. They can easily be added after purchase to upgrade a microcomputer system. Here, the protective cover for the disk has been removed. *Courtesy*: Plus Development Corp.

Another benefit is that you can copy your applications directly to the hard disk, eliminating the need to load and unload diskettes. It is important to create a directory or subdirectory for each application (a separate, labeled disk area), so that you can find your way around this large data storehouse and keep your related files together.

At one time you needed a mainframe to process large databases, because they simply would not fit on diskettes. Now that hard disks have such large capacities, many such databases can be managed quite satisfactorily on microcomputers.

Disk Drives for Minicomputers and Mainframes

Medium and large systems may need access to enormous amounts of data. Consider, for example, the storage needs of the Social Security system, with records on every man, woman, and child in the United States. New technologies have been developed to accommodate the demanding needs of larger systems.

Minicomputers and mainframes, like personal computers, use magnetic disks as their major storage medium, although disks for these systems have far greater storage capacities and are larger in size. These disks are addressed just as floppy disks are, with data located by surface number, sector number, and track number. Of course, many more tracks are available on these larger disks; 200 tracks is a common number, and at the high end, IBM 3380 mainframe disks have 1,770 tracks on each surface. A single computer can instantly access any of the disk devices attached to it, and it may have as many as 100 disks available.

Most hard disks currently in use are fixed disks that cannot be removed from the disk drive, similar to the internal hard disks on microcomputers. They are most often separate stand-alone units.

A somewhat older technology that is still in use is that of removable **disk packs**, which are removable sets of hard disks mounted together on a center spindle (Figure 6–14). Data is recorded on both sides of each disk, but the top and bottom surfaces of a pack are not used because they are more exposed and tend to get damaged. An 11-disk pack, then, has 20 usable surfaces. Disk packs are being replaced by fixed disks because of the potential for deterioration in data when disk packs are moved on and off the system.

Read/Write Head Design   Some disk mechanisms for large systems use moving heads. In this design, all the read/write heads in a stack of disks are attached to a single access mechanism that moves directly to a specific disk address. This method is relatively slow, because all the access arms must move together.

A faster technology is that of fixed-head disks (Figure 6–15). These devices have fixed access arms with separate read/write mechanisms for each track on the disks. The disk, rather than the head, whirls to bring the correct sector to the arm; the read/write mechanism for the correct track then retrieves or outputs the data, depending on the application.

Other disk devices combine the technologies of both moving- and fixed-head access to produce a high-capacity, rapid-access device.

6–13 Another way to upgrade a microcomputer system is to add an external hard disk. It is as accessible as an internal hard disk, and can be moved from machine to machine. *Courtesy*: Jasmine Technologies, Inc.

6–14 Disk packs are sets of 14-inch disks mounted together on a spindle. The packs are enclosed in a sterile case that can be easily mounted or removed from the computer system. *Courtesy*: New York Stock Exchange.

6–15 The fixed-head read/ write device for mainframe disks is one of the fastest technologies for data retrieval.

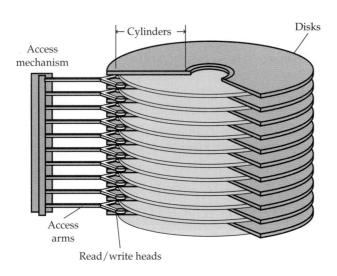

Criteria for Evaluating Disk Storage Systems There are three major criteria for evaluating disk-based storage systems: the storage capacity of the disk, the transfer rate for data, and the access time needed to locate data. Figure 6–16 summarizes these and other characteristics of four commonly used IBM systems.

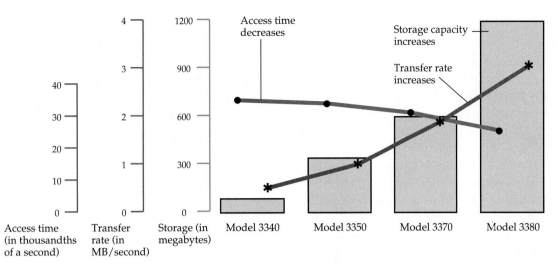

Storage capacity, measured in megabytes or gigabytes, indicates the amount of data each disk can hold. Storage capacity varies from 100 MB to 1+ GB. **Access time** is the time needed to locate a disk record; it is measured in thousandths of a second. Access time varies from 50 thousandths of a second to 25 thousandths of a second.

Data on a disk is not available for processing until it is copied from the disk to main memory (primary storage), where the CPU has access to it. The **transfer rate** refers to the speed at which data is transferred from the disk to main memory, and it is measured in megabytes per second. Transfer rate varies from .5 MB/sec. to 3 MB/sec.

When a system processes large amounts of data, saving even ten thousandths of a second per record can add up to significant amounts of time and may have benefits that more than outweigh a higher price.

6–16 Disk storage systems are evaluated by storage capacity, data transfer rate, and access time. Here is a comparison of four IBM systems.

SELF-TEST

1. A master file is a collection of _____, which in turn is a collection of _____.
2. (**T** *or* **F**) Mathematical operations cannot be done on numbers in alphanumeric data fields.
3. (**T** *or* **F**) In direct-access systems, the key field acts as the record's index.
4. (**T** *or* **F**) Sequential data files are not appropriate for batch processing operations.
5. (**T** *or* **F**) Data recorded on magnetic media is non-volatile.
6. (**T** *or* **F**) When a file is read from secondary storage into primary storage, it is erased from secondary storage in the process.
7. (**T** *or* **F**) Magnetic tapes are not appropriate for interactive processing because the computer would have to sequentially search through the tape to find a record.
8. Magnetic tapes have been replaced for the most part by _____.
9. Microcomputers usually use soft-sectored disks; the sectors are put on the disk when it is _____.

10. Double-sided, double-density 5¼-inch disks hold about _____ K of data.
11. Three common sources of magnetic fields that can destroy data on disks are: _____, _____, and _____.
12. The mechanism that enables data on a disk to be read or data to be written to a disk is called the _____ _____.
13. Which size of disk are newer microcomputer systems using—5¼-inch or 3½-inch?
14. (**T** *or* **F**) Hard disks are enclosed in sterile containers to keep out foreign material.
15. (**T** *or* **F**) Hard disks are always installed in the original microcomputer and cannot be added later.

SOLUTIONS 1) records; fields. 2) True. 3) True. 4) False. 5) True. 6) False. 7) True. 8) magnetic disks. 9) initialized or formatted. 10) 360 K (High-density 5¼-inch disks can hold approximately twice as much). 11) television sets, telephones, copiers. 12) read/write head. 13) 3½-inch disks. 14) True. 15) False.

Storing Data on Tape

At one time, almost all computer systems of any size stored their data on reels of magnetic tape. Tape has some limitations, however, mainly because it can only be processed sequentially. It is still a good medium for sequential batch processing, where the computer may need to read an entire tape for updating all or most of the records. But it is usually not practical to update master files on tape, where records need to be processed randomly or where numerous additions and deletions are required. If a new record must be inserted at a certain location—in key field order, for example—there is no space available for the insertion, so a new master file must be created to put all the added records in sequence.

Figure 6–17 demonstrates a typical process for updating a master file on tape. Changes are made off-line using key-to-disk or key-to-tape input devices; these are put in a **transaction file**. Then the transaction file and the master file are input to the CPU, where the two data files are processed. Because tape storage is sequential, the CPU must output the revised master file to a new tape. Note, however, that although this is a time-consuming process, it has an automatic backup feature—at the end of the update procedure, there is a new master file *and* an old master. If something should happen to the new master, it can easily be recreated from the transaction file and the old master file. This is one main advantage of tapes over disks. With disk processing, records are rewritten when they are updated; unless back-up procedures are implemented on a regular basis, the "old" information is lost when a rewrite is performed.

Disks, on the other hand, can store data randomly, and data can be located anywhere on the disk by searching for the record's key field. This makes it easy to update the master file right on the disk by simply adding records. The design of the disk drive's access arms and read/write heads allows fast access to any spot on the disk, whereas the tape drive has to wind through a tape to get to a particular record.

Because disks can be used for both batch and on-line processing, many organizations use disks for *all* their processing. Tapes are still in wide use, however, for backing up disk files on all sizes of systems, from microcom-

6–17 Tape files cannot be directly updated. Changes must be entered in a transaction file, which is then merged with the old master file to create an updated tape.

Transaction file of changes entered on disk.

Master file on original tape.

Update procedure creates a new master file.

New tape with updated master file data.

puters to mainframes, because tape is both fast and inexpensive. Many microcomputer systems have built-in or external tape cartridge drives, which are ideal for backing up large-capacity hard disks (Figure 6–18). Backing up hard disks onto floppy disks is very time-consuming and may involve several boxes of diskettes, while a single tape cartridge can contain all of the hard disk's files.

A typical mainframe magnetic tape is 2,400 to 3,600 feet long, but larger and smaller sizes exist. Most tapes are ½-inch wide. The tape is made of plastic with an iron oxide coating that can be magnetized to represent data. Large volumes of data can be condensed into a relatively small area. The average tape, which costs between $20 and $25, can store more than 100 million bytes. After the data on a tape has been processed, a tape, like a disk, can be reused repeatedly to store new files.

6–16 An external tape cartridge drive can back up the contents of a hard disk to a tape cartridge quickly and economically. *Courtesy*: Radio Shack.

How Data Is Represented on Tape

Data is represented on tape in a way similar to the CPU's internal code. There are nine longitudinal tracks or recording surfaces on a tape, each capable of storing magnetized bits. EBCDIC is the code used for storing data on IBM mainframes, and ASCII is used by most other systems.

Tape density is the measure of how many characters, or bytes, can be represented on an inch of tape. It is measured in **bits per inch (bpi)**. The term *bytes per inch* would be more accurate, since it is a measure of the number of characters per inch—this time-honored term is actually a misnomer. The most common tape densities are 800 bpi, 1,600 bpi, or 3,250 bpi, although some tapes have densities of 6,250 bpi or more. The densities that can be read by a particular system depend on the design of the tape drives.

How Tape Drives Read and Write Tape

Data on a magnetic tape is read by a single read/write head similar to those used to read disks. The drive resembles an audio reel-to-reel mechanism. Figure 6–19 shows how bytes are recorded on tape by the read/write head.

As with disk drives, the head is programmed either to read data from the tape to the CPU's memory or to write data from the CPU onto the tape. Tapes contain a file-protection ring whose function is similar to that of the

Parity bit

Each row is a byte

6–19 The read/write head is positioned above the tape to read or record data. Bytes of data are stored in 9 tracks on the tape: 8 rows store 8 data bits and the parity bit is stored in the top (or 9th) row.

Magnetic tape   **Magnetic disk**

1. Less expensive	1. Fast access to records
2. Ideal for sequential processing	2. Direct updating can be preferred
3. Old master gives automatic backup	3. Can add data to existing disk

1. Update requires new tape	1. More expensive
2. Slow access to records	2. Read/write heads can crash and destroy files
3. Not suitable for on-line interactive processing	3. Separate backup procedure required
4. Records must be retrieved in sequence	

6–20 Advantages and disadvantages of magnetic tape and disk storage.

write-protect notch on diskettes: it is used to minimize the chance of inadvertently writing over valuable tape data. If the ring is not in place, data cannot be written on the tape, although the data on the tape can be read.

Data can be read or written at speeds of 100,000 to 300,000 characters per second, or approximately 200 inches per second.

Figure 6–20 compares the advantages and disadvantages of disk and tape storage systems.

SELF-TEST

1. (T *or* F) When the master file is on tape, updates cannot be made directly to that tape.
2. Even in systems that process data on disks, tapes are often used for _____.
3. The most commonly used computer codes for representing data are _____ and _____.
4. Tape _____ is the measure of how much data can fit on an inch of tape, and it is measured in bpi, which stands for _____ _____ _____.

5. Disks can be used for both batch and on-line processing, but tapes are useful only for _____ processing.
6. Data on tape drives, like data on disk drives, is read and written by a mechanism called the _____ _____.

SOLUTIONS 1) True. 2) backing up. 3) EBCDIC, ASCII. 4) density; bits per inch. 5) batch. 6) read/write head.

Backup Procedures for Disks and Tape

All computer users must back up their data—whether they are personnel maintaining multiple databases for huge corporations or are students writing term papers. The cost of recreating data from source documents—or even of losing it altogether—can put the profitability of a corporation or the student's grade at risk.

Imagine the chaos that would result if a bank lost all its checking account records, even for a day. Many corporations not only make multiple backup copies of data but also store daily or weekly backup copies at a separate, secure site. If there were a disaster such as a fire or earthquake, the data at one of the sites would be likely to survive. There have also been instances of data destruction by disgruntled employees, which is another reason backup is essential.

The goal of backing up data is to be able to recreate the master file in its latest form if the need arises. Remember that the master file, particularly when it is in interactive disk form, is being continuously updated. A backup tape is just a copy of the master file at a particular point in time. Backup systems must also retain all update records between backup tape runs; alternatively, a backup system could simultaneously create a second or duplicate master file.

Operators often maintain two previous generations of backup tapes or disks in addition to the present one—just in case the backup itself has data problems or the program used had errors in it.

Maintaining quality data backup also requires keeping a data entry log and carefully labeling all the tapes and disks involved. Learning such procedures is an important part of the training needed by computer professionals.

Maintaining Disks and Tapes

The large numbers of disks or tapes required by a company's information system must be maintained in some order so that they can be retrieved when they are needed. They are usually kept in a special library and may even require a specialized librarian (Figure 6–21), whose job it is to make sure disks or tapes are not misused or misplaced.

6–21 Large collections of disks and tapes used for storage are frequently managed by a specialized librarian. *Courtesy*: Hewlett-Packard.

Looking Ahead

Optical Disk Storage

Two new forms of laser technology show promise for eventually outperforming the diskettes we now use in microcomputers. A single 12-inch **optical disk** can store the text of the entire *Encyclopedia Britannica,* and optical disks can also store photographic images. Optical disks were first used by the entertainment industry for storing movies to be sold to the home market, but videotape has won out in that market so far.

A more compact form of optical disk is the **CD-ROM disk** (an abbreviation for compact disk read-only memory), which is slightly less than 5 inches in diameter. It can hold more than 800 million bytes of data. Audiophiles are familiar with the high-quality sound of compact disk (CD) music recordings.

The current shortcoming of both disk sizes is that they are read-only at this time. This makes them useful for storing generic data that does not change, such as encyclopedias, sets of journals, and so on. A newer form of optical disk device permits a one-time recording. This type of device is called a WORM (for write once, read many) device. Even newer optical disk devices have been announced that can be erased and reused.

As erasable, reusable optical disks become widely available and their high cost comes down, they may well become as important a storage medium as standard disks.

Maintaining large libraries of magnetic media requires a number of control measures:

- External labels are placed on the face of each disk or tape. They identify the contents and how long the files should be retained. Other specifications, such as the data density, should also be written on the label.

- The program itself can include a procedure to create a **header label** on the disk or tape before the first data record. This allows users to verify that they are using the correct disk or tape before they start processing.

- Both disks and tapes have devices that provide for protecting the files from being overwritten; on microcomputer disks, this is the write-protect notch or tab, for example.

SUMMARY

A *database* is a collection of *master files*; a master file is a collection of records; and a *record* contains a number of data *fields.* There are three kinds of data fields: *numeric fields,* which allow for mathematical operations to be done on the data; *alphanumeric fields,* which can contain any combination of letters, numbers, or symbols but cannot have mathematical operations performed on them; and *logic fields,* which provide for yes/no or true/false conditions. Records can be either *fixed-length* or *variable-length.*

Master files contain the major information for a database application and may contain thousands or hundreds of thousands of records. There are three ways to organize records in a file: *sequentially,* in a rigid sequence arranged by some key field; by using the *indexed-file method,* where the disk contains an index of all records by key field; and by using the *direct-access method,* in which the key field is transformed in some way so that it converts to a disk address, eliminating the need to search through an index to find the address.

Primary storage differs from secondary storage in that it is *volatile* memory used for processing; data disappears from primary storage if the computer is turned off. *Secondary storage* is *nonvolatile* because it is in magnetic form—bits of data in the form of magnetic signals.

Keypunch cards were the first form of large-scale secondary storage, but they were replaced by *magnetic tape* because tape holds much more information and is not as easily damaged.

Magnetic tape is best suited to batch, sequential processing, but is not very useful for on-line, interactive processing. Because of this limitation, *disk storage* is now much more widely used than tapes. Tapes are still used to back up disks.

Data is stored on disks on one or two surfaces, each of which contains magnetic *tracks*, which are concentric circles of data. The tracks are divided into wedge-shaped sections called *sectors*. Data can be located by its *surface*, *track*, and *sector address*.

Disk drives access data with *access arms* that end in a *read/write head*. When an item of data is requested, the disk address is looked up; the disk then whirls to locate the correct sector, and the head moves in and out to reach the correct track. Disk drives are said to be *random-access devices* because data need not be accessed sequentially.

Microcomputers commonly have either or both of two kinds of disk drives: those designed to accept *floppy diskettes*, and *internal* or *external hard disks* that hold larger amounts of data. Hard disks store the operating system and numerous applications programs and files for fast access, with no need to insert diskettes.

Minicomputers and mainframes use disks for large-scale, fast-access applications. Two forms of disks are used: *fixed disks*, which are becoming the most widely used, and *removable disk packs*, which are sets of disks mounted together on a spindle.

There are two kinds of access arms for minicomputer and mainframe disk devices: those with a *single moving head*, and those with a *fixed-head mechanism* for each track, which allows for very fast data retrieval.

Disk storage systems are evaluated on three criteria: *storage capacity*, *access time* to locate a disk record, and the *transfer rate* at which data is transferred from the disk to the CPU's main memory.

Magnetic tape can store up to 100 million bytes, and is ideal for backing up disk files. Tapes are described by *tape density—bits per inch (bpi)*, which actually means characters per inch. The usual range is from 800 to 6,250 bpi, although tapes with greater densities are available.

Tapes are read by a read/write head similar to those used to read disks. Data can be read or written at speeds of 100,000 to 300,000 characters per second.

Backup procedures are designed to allow the recreation of the master file at any point in time. The master file is backed up at regular intervals, and all input files are also retained, possibly in multiple copies.

It is very important to follow *disk-* or *tape-maintenance-control procedures* such as labeling each disk or tape, both externally and in software file headers that precede the first data record.

Two new forms of laser-created disks show promise for mass storage: *optical disks* and *CD-ROM* disks. At this time, most cannot be erased and reused, and they are very expensive, but these barriers are likely to be broken in the near future.

KEY TERMS

Access time	Master file
Alphanumeric data field	Nonvolatile
Bits per inch (bpi)	Numeric data field
CD-ROM disk	Optical disk
Database	Primary storage
Data hierarchy	Read into memory
Direct-access file	Read/write head
Direct-access storage	Record
Disk pack	Save
External hard disk	Secondary storage
Field	Sector
Fixed disk	Sequential file
Fixed-length record	Soft-sectored
Floppy disk	Storage capacity
Hard card	Track
Hard disk	Transaction file
Hard-sectored	Transfer rate
Head crash	Variable-length record
Header label	Volatile
Indexed file	Write-protect notch
Key field	Write to disk
Logic data field	

CHAPTER SELF-TEST

1. The main data storage file for an application is called the _____ file.

2. The three methods of disk file organization are _____, _____, and _____.

3. The primary storage medium that is most often used in CPUs is *(volatile/nonvolatile)*.

4. When a disk drive copies a record into memory, we say it reads the disk; when a disk drive copies a record onto the disk, we say it _____ to disk.

5. To a large extent, disks have replaced tapes as the major form of high-speed storage; this is because disks are suitable for both _____ processing and _____ processing.

6. When disks are manufactured with sectors already defined on them, they are called _____.

7. (T *or* F) A write-protect notch or tab is used to prevent inadvertent writing to a disk that already has valuable data on it.

8. Disk record addresses are based on three locations: the _____, _____, and the _____.

9. Microcomputer hard disks that can be added to one of the computer's expansion slots are called _____ _____.

10. (T *or* F) Microcomputers can now manage databases that at one time required mainframe capacity.

11. Most mainframe systems now use (*disk packs/fixed disks*).

12. The time needed by a disk storage system to locate a disk record is called its _____ time.

13. (T *or* F) The term bpi, or bits per inch, should actually be called bytes per inch.

14. The device on tapes that is roughly parallel to the write-protect notch on diskettes is the _____ _____ _____.

15. (T *or* F) When a master file is on disk, you can update it directly.

SOLUTIONS 1) master. 2) sequential, indexed, and direct access. 3) volatile. 4) writes. 5) batch; interactive. 6) hard-sectored. 7) True. 8) surface number; sector number; track number. 9) hard cards. 10) True. 11) fixed disks. 12) access. 13) True. 14) file-protection ring. 15) True.

REVIEW QUESTIONS

1. List and define the relationship of these terms: database, master file, record, field, key field.
2. List and define three types of data fields.
3. Describe the three major forms of file organization in a database.
4. Distinguish between primary and secondary storage.
5. List, in historical order, the three forms of storage media used by large computer systems.
6. What are the advantages of 3½-inch diskettes over the 5¼-inch size?
7. What are five rules for diskette protection?
8. List three forms of disk drives for microcomputers.
9. Which can locate a record faster—moving read/write heads or fixed heads? Why?
10. What are the three criteria for evaluating disk storage systems?
11. List at least two advantages and disadvantages associated with both tape and disk storage systems.
12. What is the purpose of backing up the master file?

PROBLEM-SOLVING APPLICATIONS

1. Use the DOS CHKDSK command to check out the storage capabilities of the microcomputer you work on most often.
If you do not have a hard disk, insert your DOS disk in drive A, and any other disk with files on it in drive B. At the A prompt, type **chkdsk b:.** *If you have a hard disk,* get to the root or main directory by typing **cd** at the prompt. At the C prompt, type **chkdsk.**
A number of lines of information will appear on your screen. How many bytes of total disk space—secondary storage—do you have? How much is available for further use? Now look at the bottom two lines. How much total RAM, or primary storage, do you have? How much is currently available?

2. Using a database program such as dBASE IV, create two versions of a small employee file for these five people:
   Matthew Jave
   Gladys Ann James
   Lloyd James
   Michael Jones
   Justine Jones
Set up the fields in these two ways: (1) name field in natural order, as above; (2) two separate fields for last name and for first name and initial. Now do the SORT function on the two files. What problems are presented by one of the file structures? What structure would work best if you planned to produce mailings with the opening "Dear Mr. Jones:"?

3. Based on what you have learned so far in this course, decide which storage system (microcomputer with a hard disk, or large disk-based system, or large tape-based system) you would choose for these situations: a) you are designing a flight simulator to train commercial pilots in handling a wide range of emergency situations; b) you need permanent, organized records of approximately 230,000 stock-trading transactions per month (the records will rarely be consulted); c) you are asked to design a computerized accounting system for a company that invoices about 200 customers a month and that projects a growth rate of about 7 percent a year.

Using Data Communications and Networks

When you have completed this chapter, you will be able to:

- ✔ Recognize the most common data communications applications on distributed computer systems.
- ✔ Consider how data communications assists business people through subscriber services, electronic mail, banking services, time sharing, and telecommuting.
- ✔ List and describe the seven major communications links for sending data between computers.
- ✔ Discuss the role of the telephone system in data communications.
- ✔ Identify the hardware used to reduce communications costs and to integrate the use of terminals.
- ✔ Discuss the speed and manner by which data physically moves through communications links.
- ✔ Identify the various types of networks.

Chapter 7

Chapter Outline

Data communications—the group of technologies that enable computers to pass data electronically to one another—is the backbone of the information age. We live in a time when being able to get the right information quickly to the right place often means the difference between success and failure. By using data communications, people can combine and use the power and resources of computers, no matter where the hardware is physically located.

For example, when trainers for Olympic athletes in colleges and universities around the country need broad-based physiological information for their athletes, they use computers in their offices to tap into a specialized sports database located in Colorado. Similarly, salespeople with small, five-hundred-dollar microcomputers in Iowa can use a telephone link to access the power and resources of a multimillion dollar mainframe facility in New York, enabling them to get immediate pricing estimates and inventory information for closing their sales quickly. Real-estate appraisers can double their earnings simply by accessing a national electronic database of public and private real-estate records so that they are able to do, in fifteen minutes, research and analysis work that once took them three hours.

These capabilities are possible because of advances in data communications that enable computers to work together, no matter where they are located. Computers near each other—either in the same room or building—can send data directly to each other through either cables or telephones. Computers stationed at a distance use a special form of data communications called **telecommunications** that can transmit data via communications facilities such as telephone systems. Highly advanced data communications technologies can now be used to quickly send—to almost anywhere in the world—not only data but also photographs, illustrations, and voice messages.

Hardware for Data Communications

Data communications systems typically consist of many remote terminals or small computers linked in some way to a large central mainframe (Figure 7–1). A **terminal** is a device for entering and/or receiving data in a data communications system; it most often includes a display screen and keyboard, and is not located at the same site as a CPU. In many instances a

7–1 Data communications hardware includes any of several types of terminals linked via modems and telephone lines to a central mainframe computer.

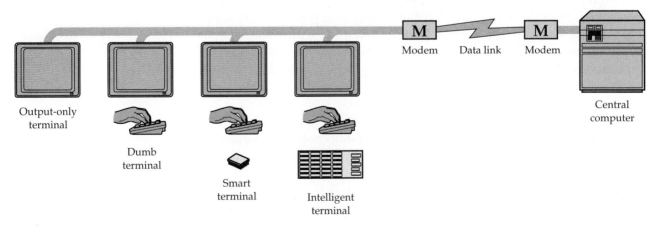

Output-only terminal

Dumb terminal

Smart terminal

Intelligent terminal

M Modem   Data link   M Modem

Central computer

In a Nutshell

Kinds of Terminals

Dumb terminals	Can only send and receive data
Smart terminals	Can send, receive, and edit data
Intelligent terminals	Can send, receive, and edit data and run applications independently

microcomputer or minicomputer functions as a terminal, so when we talk about terminals in this chapter, we are referring to any device that communicates with a central computer. While most terminals can both send and receive messages, a few are for input only or output only. The displays at airports that list arriving and departing flights, for example, are output-only terminals.

Devices designed specifically to function only as terminals look like microcomputers but may have considerably less computing power, or even none at all. Terminals are classified by their ability levels. **Dumb terminals** can only send and receive data. **Smart terminals** have some independent abilities—they can edit input, for example, before it is sent to the CPU, but they cannot run independent application programs. **Intelligent terminals** can send and receive data, and can also independently run application software without the main CPU's capability; microcomputers, when used in a data communications system, can function as intelligent terminals.

The most common links between devices in a data communications system are telephone lines. To communicate by phone, terminals or microcomputers must be attached to a **modem**—a small device that enables digital data to be transmitted over telephone lines. Later in this chapter we will discuss modems further, and also discuss the linking devices and communication facilities, such as telephone lines, that are needed for long-distance communications between terminals and the central computer.

Data Communications Applications

By combining advances in computer and data communications technologies, computer professionals can distribute computing power throughout a company, a country, or the world at large in new and exciting ways. Let us look more closely at what computer professionals can do with data communications. We will focus on distributed computer systems, time-sharing, electronic mail, subscriber services, banking services, and telecommuting.

Distributed Computer Systems

The procedure of transmitting computer power throughout an organization is called **distributed processing**. The most common distributed systems have micros, minis, or terminals linked to a central mainframe system in order to improve productivity. Many business tasks—such as receiving customer orders and sending merchandise—can take several days to complete using manual (or uncomputerized) procedures; distributed computer systems allow companies to give customers better service and reduce errors.

For example, clerks in a lumber company may manually process a written order for ten thousand feet of lumber on Tuesday and then ship the order four days later on Friday. In addition to the cost of the four-day delay, the possibility exists than an error might occur somewhere in the process—the customer might receive by mistake only a thousand feet of lumber, or a hundred thousand. By using data communications technologies, clerks can enter orders at terminals where the order is displayed for immediate verification, thus reducing both turnaround time and the possibility of error.

After the order is entered in the computer, it is processed by additional software products that integrate it with other orders to ensure the most efficient order processing procedures for the company as a whole.

The three most common distributed activities are remote data entry, remote data inquiry, and remote job entry.

Remote Data Entry.   When users enter data on a terminal where a transaction actually occurs, such as in point-of-sale systems in fast-food restaurants or supermarkets, the application is called **remote data entry**. Remote data entry applications use a central computer that may not be physically at the same site as the terminals.

Remote data entry systems can be designed to do either interactive or batch processing (Figure 7–2). As you will recall from Chapter 4, in interactive processing—also called on-line or transaction processing—the computer processes input data immediately as it is entered and quickly updates the master files. In batch processing, the computer stores the data and processes it later at a scheduled time. In batch systems, users enter data with

7–2 Remote terminals and communications equipment can be used in both interactive processing and batch processing to interface with a central computer.

a key-to-storage device that directly transmits data to a disk or tape file. The computer then processes the entire file at some later time.

Batch processing uses computers more efficiently than transaction-oriented processing for three reasons:

- A high-speed disk or tape can transmit data to a CPU much faster than a person can key it in using an on-line terminal.

- Data can be transmitted later in the day after standard working hours when the telephone or other communications rates are cheaper.

- The master file to be updated does not need to be on-line at all times, and the central computer can be used for a larger number of applications.

Designers of remote data entry systems consider factors such as cost, efficiency, and security when they decide whether to use transaction or batch processing. For example, department store systems process transactions immediately to create a charge slip that the customer can take away, and to keep data such as the customer's available credit up to date at all times. On the other hand, on-line processing of an accounts receivable file in an accounting department would be too expensive; it would also be prone to security problems because employees would always have access to it. In this instance, it would be a better choice to batch transactions; the master file will only be up to date after each batch is run, but there is no significant loss of information, and controls are easier to manage.

Remote Data Inquiry.   Various businesses rely on remote terminals for requesting information from data stored in a database linked to a central computer. Stockbrokers, for example, frequently query a central database of stock information when they want to quote a stock price to a customer. To get a price, they key in a stock code at terminals or micros on their desks. The computer receives this code immediately, accesses the price from the database, and transmits the information back to the stockbroker's terminal in seconds or even a fraction of a second.

A screen and keyboard is almost always needed—even for simple queries. Sometimes a printer is also needed for hard-copy output. Businesses generally use remote inquiry systems when customers need immediate replies to inquiries or when managers need immediate information for making decisions. Figure 7–3 shows a stockbroker and his client working with an information display system.

Typically, remote data inquiry systems require that data always be up to date. The database is updated with an on-line remote data entry system, which may use the same terminals from which queries are made. For example, from the same terminal a stockbroker not only can query the database for a stock price, but also can actually buy or sell stocks; each new transaction immediately updates the central database.

Remote Job Entry.   In a **remote job entry** application, users write or run programs from terminals. Unlike remote data entry systems in which the computer was previously programmed to process the data, for this type of system the program is supplied at the remote site *along with* the data.

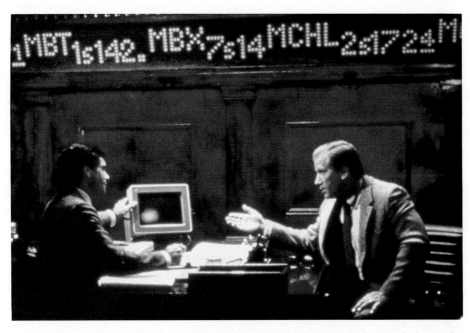

7–3 This stockbroker and his client are working with an information system to retrieve stock prices and other information. The same system can be used to buy or sell stocks and keep brokerage records. *Courtesy:* IBM.

Students who write and run programs from terminals located throughout a university or college are operating in a remote job entry environment (Figure 7–4). Engineers who have terminals linked to a CPU for solving equations and obtaining other mathematical results are also operating in a remote job entry environment.

A remote station for this type of system commonly consists of an input device, CRT display, disk drive, and printer. Students at a remote job entry station might send a program and data from the disk drive through cables to a mainframe at another location for processing. The mainframe would then transmit the output back to the CRT or printer at the station (Figure 7–5).

7–4 Students use library terminals for remote job inquiry to access the university mainframe. *Courtesy:* Apple Computer, Inc.

1. Load program from remote terminal.

2. Enter data from remote terminal.

CPU

4. Transmit information back to remote terminal, printer, or disk.

3. Process information.

7–5 Remote job applications use terminals to send programs as well as data to the central computer, and often output the information to a screen, a printer, or to local storage media, such as disks.

Similarly, users may **upload** files—send data and programs to the mainframe for storage—or **download** files—copy files already located in mainframe storage to a disk drive at their station. Using a micro, you can write programs, and create data files, and then upload them to the mainframe, where the program is executed and "bugs" are identified. When the program runs properly, you can download onto a diskette the final version of the program and its output.

A single large-scale mainframe system can handle many users entering data, querying data, and running programs from remote locations all at once through a computer processing technique called time-sharing.

Time-Sharing

Time-sharing is a concept that enables each user to independently access some partition or section of the CPU while the operating system controls the overall processing of all the programs. Because the computer is so fast, it may appear to users that all the instructions are being executed simultaneously. Actually, by interleaving instructions from various programs, a computer executes only one instruction at a time, but at very high speeds. Thus we say that programs can be executed *concurrently*, not *simultaneously*.

Because a potential danger of time-sharing is that one user will monopolize the system at the expense of other users, operating systems must allocate computer time and resources in a way that is equitable to all users. **Time-slicing** is one very common method that allocates a small amount of computer time to each user. When the allotted time is used up, the CPU transfers control to another user program and puts the first program in a "wait state" for a short time. Numerous programs may be executed at the same time in this interleaved way. Because mainframes execute instructions in speeds measured in nanoseconds (billionths of a second) or picoseconds (trillionths of a second), this method of switching from one program to another is usually not noticed by the users.

Time-sharing is also an option for small companies that need computing power but cannot afford to acquire and maintain their own systems. Smaller companies can rent or share computing resources of companies that own large systems which are not used to capacity. These smaller companies could also rent computer time from companies that specialize in providing time-sharing services. Using terminals located in their offices, employees can access the *other company's system* and enter programs or data for processing.

Time-sharing does have three disadvantages, however.

◆ When the user wants to access the system, the computer may be too busy to handle the request.

◆ Security and privacy in a time-sharing environment can be a problem and should be evaluated before such services are used.

◆ Time-sharing can become expensive if usage is high. Total costs depend on the amount of time the CPU is used, plus transmission-line costs.

Time-sharing is becoming less common as smaller organizations purchase relatively inexpensive minicomputers and microcomputers to meet their computing needs. Although minis and micros do not have the capability of larger systems, they are far less expensive and more adaptable to a smaller company's needs.

Electronic Mail

Electronic mail (E-mail) is a data communications innovation that is revolutionizing the office and the way in which business people interact with one another. With the use of terminals or computers, users can transmit copies of a document or messages to one or more locations in a matter of minutes or even seconds. To use electronic mail, you would typically have a terminal on your desk; when you are away from your desk, messages and documents "queue up" and are stored in a computer "mailbox" file on disk. When you return, you access E-mail, and the system transmits your messages, either in sequence or according to some preestablished priority code. You may then scan a summary of the messages before selecting the ones you want to read first. You can also save and delete messages, forward messages to other people, or respond to them directly, and so on. Figure 7–6 provides an example of how electronic mail transmission typically functions.

7–6   On this Macintosh desktop, the user is prepared to distribute a memo via electronic mail. In the background (left) we can also see the status of this user's "in-box"—showing the various items awaiting attention. *Courtesy:* TOPS.

In a Nutshell

Accessing Subscriber Services

The following telephone numbers for obtaining more information about popular subscriber services were current at time of publication:

CompuServe	(800) 848-8199
Prodigy	(800) 767-3664
Dow-Jones News/Retrieval	(800) 522-3567

Subscriber Services

E-mail systems are usually limited to communications within an organization, although the messages may sometimes be transmitted across the country to other company sites. But what if you want to communicate with people outside your own company, or what if you do not have access to any E-mail system? E-mail is only one of the services offered to subscribers by organizations such as CompuServe and Prodigy. **Subscriber services** typically require you to link a terminal, personal computer, or other system to a modem in order to dial up the service for sending or receiving messages and information.

A subscriber service serves as a clearinghouse for messages in much the same way as a post office serves as a clearinghouse for mail. It stores all messages until the receiving subscriber logs on and checks the mail. To successfully send and receive messages, both the person or organization transmitting a message and the person or organization receiving the message must subscribe to the same service. Bitnet, for example, is a popular subscriber service found on college campuses.

In addition to E-mail, subscribers have access to many useful databases such as the National Weather Service forecasts, stock exchange data, business information, and so on, as well as to games, shopping services, and other consumer products. Services may include electronic bulletin boards on which users can post advertisements, announcements, or inquiries about specified products.

The largest subscriber service, CompuServe Information Services, has more than 600,000 users accessing information on more than 1,000 subject areas. Specialized services include Knowledge-Index and the Dow-Jones News/Retrieval Service, and Prodigy, a service aimed specifically at home users.

To subscribe to any of these services, you must pay an initiation fee and a monthly fee, plus (except for Prodigy) a connect-time charge for use of databases. The phone time is a normal charge on your telephone bill, usually at local rates.

Subscriber services for home users have not always been successful. Since 1982, large corporations have spent—and lost—millions of dollars trying to bring computer information services (called videotex) into people's homes by linking home television sets with a central computer via telephone to give subscribers access to many of the same services. Promoters of these

Looking Ahead

Prodigy: A New Home Information System

Sears and IBM are hoping to succeed where others have failed in the home subscriber market by spending an estimated $500 million on a new subscription service called Prodigy—an all-in-one-box information system. Prodigy's most attractive feature is its flat-rate pricing: it costs an initial $49.95 plus $9.95 a month and can be used with no additional time charge from any IBM-compatible PC with a modem and graphics card. Subscribers can:

◆ Do banking and shopping
◆ Get business news and access stock quotes from Dow Jones
◆ Read *Consumer Reports* excerpts
◆ Make airline reservations
◆ Send and receive electronic messages
◆ Obtain movie, TV, video, music, and book information
◆ Play games
◆ Obtain local and national weather forecasts and ski reports

systems expected videotex to change the way people shopped, handled finances, and accessed information. Unfortunately, their attempts all failed: telephone connect charges were high, response time was slow, and the service monopolized the two most popular appliances in the household—the telephone and the television. Videotex quickly became known as a data communications flop, although new products have recently been announced.

Unlike videotex, Prodigy does not monopolize the TV because it works only with a personal computer, though it has not solved the problem of tying up the phone. Because it uses graphics freely to attract computer novices in the home market (Figure 7–7), it is slower than the older, more business-oriented services—it has an eight-second response time.

Prodigy uses advertising revenue to absorb the bulk of the service's cost, significantly reducing the tab to subscribers.

Prodigy officials promise that they will add to and improve their services. But only time will tell whether they can reach the critical mass of users

7–7 A mystery game on Prodigy, a subscriber computer service. The space at the bottom of the screen is used for "teasers" and advertising. *Courtesy:* Prodigy Services Company.

In a Nutshell

Applications for Data Communications Systems

Distributed computer systems	Micros or minis are linked to a main CPU.
Time-sharing	Separate companies share a mainframe.
E-mail	Electronic mail system.
Subscriber services	Subscribers can access databases and an E-mail service.
Banking services	Local banks provide customers with on-line access to the central database.
Telecommuting	Workers at home are linked to their company's computer.

required to enable them to provide more comprehensive services. Prodigy may be worth the wait and risk, however. Sears and IBM are hoping that Prodigy will be as successful as Minitel, the French videotex system that currently provides 8,000 services to 4.5 million subscribers and is as commonly used in France as the telephone directory system is used in this country. Prodigy may indeed have a brilliant future.

Banking Services

Many major banks use data communications to offer customers electronic banking services at their offices or homes via a terminal or personal computer equipped with a modem. For example, you dial into the service and enter an identification code. If the code is accepted, you can find out your checking and savings account balances, transfer funds, pay bills, and look up rates on products such as certificates of deposit and other investment options that the bank offers.

To provide better service in the branch office itself, banks may provide tellers with data communications systems connected to **audio response units** that give verbal rather than printed output. For example, suppose a customer wishes to cash a check at a branch office. The teller keys in the customer's account number and the amount of the check by using a Touch-Tone telephone. The computer then determines whether the account has sufficient funds to cover the check. The computer is equipped with various prerecorded phrases, words, and messages that are extracted from a file to answer a specific request; the response is then transmitted through an audio response unit. That is, the appropriate verbal response is transmitted to the teller via the telephone, and the teller either cashes the check or politely refuses, depending on the computer's audio response. Some banks allow customers to call the system themselves and query information directly. For example, customers can find out the status of their bank accounts by calling from a Touch-Tone telephone and entering their account numbers with the telephone keys.

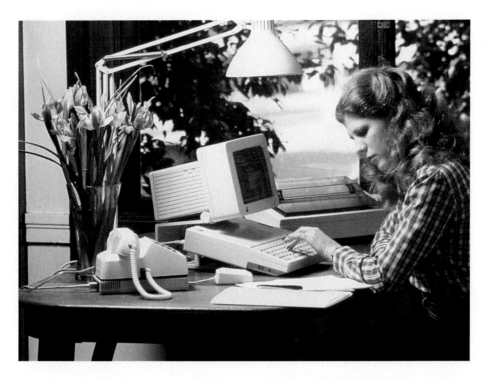

7–8 Telecommuting makes it possible to work from home entering data remotely, producing reports, or performing any tasks not requiring direct personal interaction at the office.

Telecommuting

A highly publicized use for data communications and one that may have significant social implications is **telecommuting**. Employees who have on-line terminals or microcomputers in their homes, for example, can do word processing, access corporate data, and communicate with colleagues, all without having to be physically present in the office (Figure 7–8). Often, employees can be just as effective working at home as working in an office. We know of one manager who communicated with his subordinate through E-mail and completed an important project even though he was home sick.

These are only some of the areas in which communications technologies are applied. As these technologies advance, people inevitably create new opportunities and services that, at the moment, may be only a glimmer of an idea in someone's mind!

Linking a Data Communications System

All the data communications applications we have talked about in this chapter require only three hardware elements:

◆   Central processor(s)

◆   Terminals (or microcomputers and minicomputers) at remote locations

◆   Communication channels or links

So far we have discussed CPUs and terminals extensively. The third component in a data communications system is the **communication channels** that act as the medium, or roadway, for data passing between CPUs and terminals. Communication channels fall into three basic types: hardwired, telephone lines, or alternative channels such as leased lines, micro-wave, or satellite links. We will look at each of these media in detail.

Hardwired Links

When terminals are directly and permanently linked to a central processor by cable, we say they are **hardwired**. Terminals are commonly hardwired when they are near the CPU and their locations are not expected to change. Moving a hardwired terminal requires rewiring the cable.

One main advantage of hardwired terminals is that they have immediate access to a central processor as soon as they are turned on. There is no need, as with a telephone line, to "dial up" or call the computer. Data systems are hardwired with three basic transmission media: twisted-pair cable, coaxial cable, and fiber optic cable.

Twisted-pair cable

Coaxial cable

Fiber optic cable

7–9   Three common cable types: twisted cable, coaxial cable, and fiber optic cable.

Twisted-Pair Cable.   Twisted-pair cable is the typical telephone wire used in your house and is the most common type of communication channel for small systems. It consists of bundles of pairs of copper wires that are twisted to give them physical strength (Figure 7–9). Twisted-pair cable is relatively inexpensive and has low maintenance costs. A major disadvantage of twisted-pair wiring for data communications, however, is that it is highly susceptible to electrical interference from within and outside the system. For protection from interference, shielded twisted-pair wiring is available at a slightly higher cost.

Coaxial Cable.   A **coaxial cable** is used in place of standard twisted-pair cables for high-quality data transmission. Although more expensive than twisted-pair cable, coaxial cable's major advantage is that it is sturdy enough to be laid without the wiring conduits or mechanical support elements that twisted-pair cable wiring requires. If conduits are not already in place, coaxial cable is cheaper to install and more flexible to use. Illustrated in Figure 7–9, coaxial cable consists of a central cylinder surrounded by a series of wires that carry data at very high speeds. Coaxial cable is commonly laid under the floor or in the ceiling of many computer centers. It is so sturdy that telephone companies often bury it underground or lay it across sea bottoms to provide high-quality phone transmissions.

Fiber Optic Cable.   **Fiber optic cables** are highly reliable communication channels; data can be transmitted at very high speeds with few or no errors (Figure 7–9). A fiber optic channel uses light impulses that travel through clear flexible tubing half the size of a human hair. Unlike wire cables, fiber optic cables are not subject to electrical interference. Technical innovations continue to drive down the costs of installing, using, and manufacturing fiber optics so that they are becoming competitive with traditional cabling. Some long-distance telephone companies such as Sprint have already converted to a fiber optic system, while others are in the process of converting. Figure 7–10 illustrates fiber optic technology.

But what do you do when you are not able to connect computers directly together with cable? An entire technology called telecommunications solves this problem.

Using a Telephone for Data Communications

The standard telephone system is commonly used for connecting computers over large distances; terminals can be moved virtually anywhere in the country—or even in the world—and still have access to a mainframe. Using telephone lines, salespeople can call in orders from the field and send transaction data directly to a central processor. The salesperson can use a terminal to dial the computer's phone number, and if a computer line is free, the terminal will then have direct access to the CPU.

Telephone lines have several disadvantages as the medium for data transmission, however. They are slower and have higher error rates than hardwired cables because they were designed to handle the kind of signals that are suitable for voices, not for digital computer signals. In addition, as we all know, long-distance transmission rates are expensive.

Telecommunications (or teleprocessing) is the term sometimes used to describe data communications using telephone lines. To send digital computer data over the phone, you need additional interface equipment such as modems, acoustic couplers, and, perhaps, communications controllers to supervise the signals. We will talk about each of these in depth.

7–10 Bundles of thread-like glass fibers carry encoded light beams to transmit voice and data messages virtually without interference. *Courtesy:* U. S. Sprint.

Modulation, Demodulation, and Modems.

Data in a computer is formatted as **digital signals**—or on-off electronic pulses. Because telephone lines were designed to transmit the human voice, they format data as **analog signals**—or electronic waves. For communication between computers to take place over a telephone line, the digital signal (pulse) must be converted to an analog signal (wave) before it can be transmitted. After its journey over the telephone lines, the analog signal must then be reconverted back to a digital signal so that it can be used by the receiving computer (Figure 7–11). The process of converting a digital signal to an analog signal is called **modulation; demodulation** is the process of reconverting the analog signal back to a digital signal. The device that accomplishes both of these processes is a modem, short for *mo*dulator-*dem*odulator.

There are two basic kinds of modems: direct connect and acoustic couplers. **Direct-connect** modems are attached directly to computers by cable and, as shown in Figure 7–12, can be either inside the computer on a circuit board or outside the computer, linked to it by cable. Both internal and external modems work in the same way. They connect to the phone line with a standard telephone cable.

7–11 Telephone lines currently transmit only analog, or wave, signals. **Mo**dulator-**dem**odulator units, or modems, are required to convert digital signals to analog form so that data can be transmitted over phone lines. Modems also convert the analog signals back to digital form at the receiving end.

Acoustic Couplers.

When you cannot connect your modem directly to a phone line (if you are using a pay phone, for example), you can use an **acoustic coupler**, shown in Figure 7–13. The acoustic coupler sends audio signals through the telephone handset to the modem. It has two cups into

Terminal — Digital signal — Modem modulates signal — Analog transmission — Modem demodulates signal — Digital signal — Central computer

7–12a. This internal modem slips into one of the expansion slots on a micro, and a telephone cord plugs into the back (right in photo). The accompanying communication software controls the transmission. *Courtesy:* Hayes Microcomputer Products, Inc.

which the handset of your telephone is placed. The acoustic coupler sends data through the mouthpiece and receives data through the earpiece of the handset. Although this type of modem is not used very often, it is useful for transmitting data from locations with internal phone systems where there is no phone jack, such as a hotel. Acoustic couplers are frequently built into a terminal or microcomputer.

Popular Communications Software

Both direct-connect and acoustic couplers use the same **communications software** for exchanging files with a host computer. Although communication software is becoming increasingly complex with each new version, all such programs do about the same thing: they first establish the proper communications **protocols**—or standard set of rules—that regulate the way data is transmitted between two computers. Protocols specify the methods that the software will use to detect errors, the speed of transmission, and so on. Communications software can be programmed to allow for automatic dialing, using passwords and log-on codes, and so on.

Three popular software packages are SmartCom, Kermit, and Pro-Comm. Kermit and ProComm are easily the most popular communications

7–12b. This external modem for a Macintosh plugs into its own power outlet. The telephone connection is shown coming out of the bottom. *Courtesy:* Apple Computer, Inc.

7–13 Here a telephone hand set, cradled in an acoustic coupler, provides the connection between a computer modem and the telephone lines. *Courtesy:* Tandy Corp.

programs available because they are in the public domain—that is, they are free; they can be downloaded (copied) from electronic bulletin boards or obtained at no charge from software vendors. You should be aware, however, that although these programs are free, vendors sometimes add a mailing and disk charge to each order.

Other Communications Links

Although hardwired cables and standard telephones are widely used in data communications applications, numerous other channels or links can be used. These other channels have the added advantage of satisfying complex communications requirements such as error detection, priority scheduling, and networking.

Following are the most common alternatives to hardwired cables and standard telephone lines.

Leased Telephone Lines.   A leased telephone line is a private line that is dedicated to a specific organization for its individual data communications needs. A leased line may be able to handle digital data only, or it may be able to handle both voice and data communications just like a standard telephone line.

Because leased lines have frequently been designed specifically for data transmission, they produce less static and fewer transmission errors than regular telephone lines—and they are more secure from wiretapping and other security risks. Most important, the central processor is always accessible, and it can often transmit data at faster speeds than over standard telephone lines.

Microwave Stations.   A microwave station transmits data, such as radio signals, through the air rather than through wires. Microwave stations are used primarily for transmitting data at high speeds over very long distances. You may be familiar with the dish-type antennas of microwave stations that are typically located on the roofs of buildings or on hilltop locations (Figure 7–14). More than half of the telephone transmissions make use of microwave technology.

Satellite Stations.   Communications satellites in space, orbiting 22,000 or more miles above the earth, are also used as microwave relay stations (Figure 7–14). They orbit at the speed above the equator that makes them appear stationary to microwave transmitters on the ground. These satellites are used for high-volume data transmission as well as for television broadcasting and telephone transmission. A satellite can also beam transmissions to other satellites, which relay signals back to stations on earth. Several dozen satellites are currently in orbit.

With so many options for connecting terminals to CPUs, special devices are needed to coordinate communication activities and to make sure everything is working properly.

Communications Controllers.   As more terminals are given access to a central processor, data communications costs for linking and coordinating terminal activity can be higher than the cost of the CPU itself. Devices that

7–14 The satellite dish (left) relays microwave transmissions into space and receives signals sent from other stations. Microwave transmission towers (right) send signals shorter distances. *Courtesy:* Sperry (left); AT&T Bell Laboratories (right).

reduce communication costs and integrate the use of terminals are called **communications controllers.** There are two commonly used communications controllers: multiplexers and front-end processors.

Multiplexers.   A **multiplexer** is a type of hardware that collects messages from numerous terminals at one location and transmits them collectively at high speeds over one communication channel, as illustrated in Figure 7–15. Similarly, multiplexers can be used for *message switching;* that is, a multiplexer can receive collective responses from the CPU and transmit each response back to the appropriate terminal.

Multiplexing avoids two major sources of inefficiency. First, most interactive data communication is intermittent, meaning that you enter data, then wait for a response, and so on. During those "wait states," the communication channel is not being used; a multiplexer can maximize the efficient use of the channel. Second, without multiplexing, adding another terminal would require a new channel. With multiplexing, new devices can simply be connected to the multiplexer, which is itself connected to the channel. For example, if Macy's built a new branch store, each new cash register would not need to be linked directly to the central computer at the home office. By connecting each cash register to one of its multiplexers, one multiplexed line from the new branch to the home office is all that would be needed.

Front-End Processors.   As we connect more and more remote terminals to a computer unit, the host computer must spend an inordinate amount of time doing coordinating tasks rather than processing data; for example, it

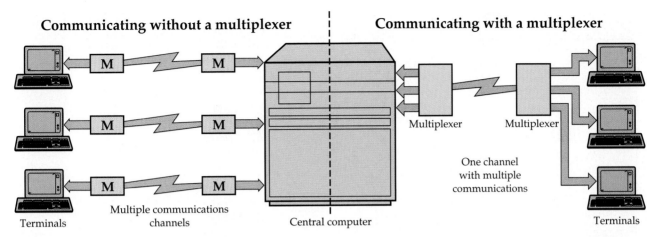

Communicating without a multiplexer   **Communicating with a multiplexer**

Terminals

Multiple communications channels

Central computer

Multiplexer   Multiplexer

One channel with multiple communications

Terminals

must keep track of which terminals are sending data; it must also check data and coordinate message switching. While it is doing these jobs, the CPU is not actually processing a user's application. **Front-end processors** are specialized data communications microcomputers or minicomputers that help host computers run more effectively by ensuring that data is routed appropriately and is error free. Moreover, front-end processors offload some of the "housekeeping" tasks from the host computer.

So far we have talked about the paths through which data moves and communications controllers such as multiplexers and front-end processors that help data move efficiently. We will now look at exactly how data moves through these channels and devices.

7–15 For some applications, each terminal has its own modem and telephone line to connect it to a central computer. Alternatively, a multiplexer can combine transmissions so that many terminals can send over a single line.

Transmitting Data

In summary, the communication channels through which data travels are comparable to highways along which cars move. This analogy is particularly apt, because, like cars, data moves in a specific direction and at a designated speed—two important characteristics of data communications transmission protocols.

Direction of Flow.   Traffic laws allow cars to move in only one of two directions on a street; similarly, data can move only in specific directions through communication channels. Although cars can only move in one of two directions on a road, electronic impulses can move in three ways, depending upon what kind of **transmission protocol** is used. The three ways are called simplex, half-duplex, and full-duplex lines or channels (Figure 7–16). Note that we are describing the way cables send and receive messages over communication links or channels which are designed to handle data. Communications software can be used to set transmission protocols.

Simplex lines permit data to flow in one direction only, like a one-way street. A simplex line is used with a device that either only sends or only receives data from a CPU but does not do both; a printer, for example, is a receive-only device. Simplex lines are used very infrequently, although some terminals or processors specifically require them. For example, an airline monitor that displays departure and arrival information might use a

Simplex transmission

Data moves one way.

Receive-only printer

Half-duplex transmission

Data moves alternatively one way, then the other.

Send-receive terminal

Full-duplex transmission

Data can move both ways at the same time.

Send-receive terminal

Central computer

7–16 Transmission protocols allow one-way, alternating, or full two-way transmission.

simplex line, because data is always transmitted in one direction only—from the CPU to the monitor.

A **half-duplex line** permits data to move in two directions, but not at the same time. When the line is being used to transmit data from a terminal to a main CPU, it cannot be used simultaneously to transmit data back from the main CPU to the terminal. With a half-duplex line, data moves first one way and then the other, rather than at the same time. This type of channel works like a CB radio, which can send or receive voice messages, but not at the same time.

Using a **full-duplex line**, data may be transmitted in both directions at the same time. A telephone is an example of a device that can make use of a full-duplex line. Using a telephone line, the main CPU can transmit messages to a terminal at the same time that the terminal is transmitting to the CPU. This type of transmission is now widely available.

Speed of Data Communications Lines.   Like speed limits set for cars on highways, transmission protocols, which are part of communications software, set the speed at which data can travel accurately across communication channels. Different kinds of channels can only handle data efficiently at certain speeds. Band width (narrow, baseband, and broadband) refers to the capacity of a channel to transmit data. Just as you would not drive eighty miles an hour over a rocky, pot-holed road, you would not send data through narrow band lines at extremely high speeds. The speed with which information is sent is commonly expressed in **baud rates** or **bits per second (bps)**—the number of bits sent through the line per second.

The final step in creating a data communications system is to put all these elements together into a coherent system called a data communications network, which consists of CPUs, terminals (which could be microcomputers or minicomputers or any input/output device), communication channels, controllers, and transmission protocols.

In a Nutshell

Speeds of Transmission Lines

Type of Line	Example	Characteristics	Range of Transmission Speed
Narrowband (low speed)	Teletype	Least costly, slow	Up to 150 bps
Baseband (voice-grade or midrange)	Telephone	Common, some noise	300 to 19,200 bps
Broadband (wideband or high speed)	Leased lines, microwave, satellite, fiber optics	More expensive, least noise	20,000 to 300,000 bps and above

SELF-TEST

1. (T *or* F) Microcomputers and minicomputers cannot be used as terminals in a data communications system.

2. (T *or* F) A multiplexer can reduce the overall cost of transmitting over communication lines.

3. (T *or* F) Remote terminals can be placed strategically at different locations but must be in the same building as the computer.

4. (T *or* F) Terminals can only be used for on-line or transaction processing.

5. (T *or* F) An accounts receivable system that uses a daily update procedure to make the master file current could use a key-to-storage device to process charge slips once a day rather than process the charges as they are transacted.

6. (T *or* F) A stock exchange would normally process changes in stock quotations once a day in a batch-processing mode.

7. (T or F) Leased private telephone lines, while generally expensive, reduce noise and interference for data communications systems.

8. Data communications systems use _____ placed strategically at key locations to enter input and/or receive output.

9. Data is transmitted to the CPU from terminals via _____ lines.

10. The process of entering data from a terminal to alter the contents of records on a file is called a(n) _____ _____ _____ operation.

11. If an accounts receivable system uses terminals to enter all sales data for charge customers, and the system has the ability to provide up-to-the-minute charge information for customer inquiries, then _____ processing is required.

12. If, in the above system, customer inquiries are answered with data that is current only through the previous day's sales, then _____ processing is being used.

13. Small companies that need data processing equipment but find the cost of acquisition and maintenance prohibitive could benefit from renting terminals with access to a central processing unit. This concept is referred to as _____.

14. If a company uses a terminal for answering inquiries, the user is said to have _____ access to the data files.

SOLUTIONS 1) False. 2) True. 3) False. 4) False. 5) True. 6) False. 7) True. 8) terminals. 9) communications. 10) remote data entry. 11) on-line, interactive, or transaction-oriented processing. 12) batch. 13) time-sharing. 14) on-line or interactive.

Data Communications Networks

A network is a data communications system that links terminals, microcomputers, minis, or mainframes so that they can operate independently but also share data and other resources. Networks that have received a lot of attention lately are *local area networks,* or LANs. They link microcomputers into computer information systems in environments in which the distance between devices is 50 miles or less. If your school links its micros to its

Star network

Terminals are linked to a central
computer. Each terminal can access
only the central computer.

Ring network

Microcomputers are linked to
each other. Any terminal can
access any other computer.

Bus network

Mainframe computers with
terminals are linked together
and to mini- or microcomputers.
Each terminal has full system access.

mainframes, it is likely to use a local area network. For distances greater than 50 miles, a wide area network, or WAN, would be used.

Networks are a combination of hardware and software components that establish the most efficient routes for messages. When there is a central processor, it is called the **host computer** or **file server**; the terminals, micros, or minis linked to it are called **nodes**. A file server is a computer dedicated exclusively to controlling the network and providing most of the data storage capacity. Computer professionals link the host and nodes into particular network configurations that are most efficient for an organization or task.

7–17 Network configurations have evolved from the star, which allows one central computer to be accessed by remote terminals, to the ring or bus, in which programs and data are shared among different computers of

Common Network Configurations

A network **configuration** refers to how the nodes and host computer are organized. The choice of which one of several different configurations to use depends on the geographic locations of nodes, the degree of communication control necessary for messages, and the speed at which data will be transmitted. Following are descriptions of three common configurations.

Star Configuration.   The **star network** is frequently used to connect one or more small computers to a large host computer that coordinates the messages between nodes (Figure 7–17). If one node becomes inoperable, it is simply bypassed. This technique of networking is often used by banks and for time-sharing in schools. In a star configuration, the reliability of the CPU is most critical, because if the central processor "goes down," the entire system is unusable—although the individual nodes may still be able to operate in a stand-alone mode if they contain independent CPUs.

Ring Configuration.   A **ring network** connects computers in a circle of point-to-point connections, with no central host computer, such as a series of desktop computers in an office (Figure 7–17). Each node handles its own applications and also shares resources over the entire network. If one node becomes inoperative, the other nodes are still able to maintain contact with one another. Such a network is best for decentralized systems in which no priorities are required.

Bus Configuration.   A **bus configuration** provides a truly interactive network, in which each node can access not only the host computer but also every other node as well (Figure 7–17). In a sense, each node can form its own star network. Bus systems are common in organizations in which some databases are decentralized and others are maintained by a central facility. For example, the Citicorp global banking network connects numerous office systems, departmental minicomputers, and large mainframes to a central bus that allows any node to access any database; an employee at a micro in Montreal can get data from a mainframe in Tokyo!

Building a Complex Network

The information needs of businesses can be so complex that they require several networks to help transmit data efficiently. For example, as mentioned above, Citicorp uses an electronic network that links microcomputers to other microcomputers so that employees in the same offices can communicate with each other, and also links employees to minicomputers and mainframes around the world so that they can send data to and receive data from any other employee and customer in the world. To build a global network, Citicorp actually combines several kinds of networks into one. Below we discuss three common types of networks.

Local Area Networks.   **Local area networks (LANs)** connect computers and terminals that are located in nearby offices or buildings—for instance, several buildings on a college campus. An example of a LAN is shown in Figure 7–18. In general, the range of a local area network is approximately 50 miles. Coaxial cables, rather than telephone lines, are used for most local area networks, but some use fiber optic cables as well. Small LANs, such as those connecting microcomputers, frequently use shielded twisted pair cabling.

The two basic types of local area networks are **baseband** (medium speed) and **broadband** (high speed). The difference between the two is the band width, which as you saw earlier is a measure of the channel's capacity. Band width determines the speed of the transmission as well as the cost, the number of simultaneous transmissions, and the ability of the channel to handle voice and data interactively.

Broadband networks are based on cable television technology. They can handle data, voice, and video transmission at very high transmission rates

7–18 A local area network (LAN) can be used to connect computers and other devices, including printers and modems, within a 50-mile radius.

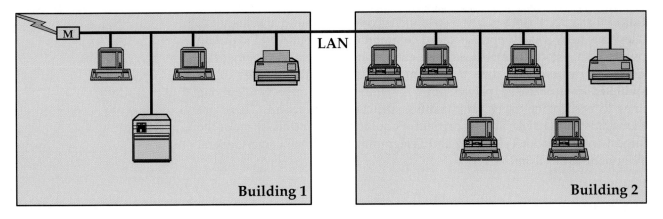

LAN

Building 1

Building 2

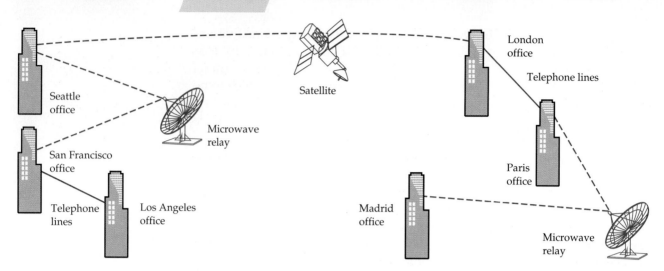

7–19 A wide area network uses many transmission modes to connect users over long distances. Public data networks make worldwide services available to small users.

along numerous channels. In this way, each channel can be dedicated to a specific kind of equipment or application.

Baseband networks are more limited but far less costly. They provide only one channel, and all the equipment attached to the cable must use this one channel.

In 1986 IBM announced a popular local area network for personal computers using a ring configuration; it is called the **token ring network** and is now the *de facto* standard for LANs. In a token ring network, a pattern of bits, or *token*, is passed from computer to computer in the network. The CPU consistently **polls**—or checks—the network several times a second to see if a token has arrived. When a computer obtains a token, it is allowed to transmit its message. Then the token is passed on. This method for transmitting messages prevents two computers from transmitting at the same time.

Wide Area Networks.   Abbreviated as **WANs, wide area networks** use microwave relays and satellites to reach users over long distances around the world, as shown in Figure 7–19. Examples of such networks in the United States are Tymnet, Telenet, and Uninet. Networks such as Telenet and Tymnet rent private telephone lines and provide cut-rate networking costs to computer users. For example, if you want to send a file to someone two thousand miles away, you can use a local phone number to sign on to Tymnet, which sends the file across country, even though you are paying only the connect rate for a local number!

Public Data Networks.   Just as telephone companies build and maintain telephone networks, companies called **common carriers** build and maintain public data networks for those who cannot afford their own networks. Common carriers specialize in offering standard telephone lines called **switched lines** or leased, private lines. A switched line connects telephone lines to each other using central office switching equipment. There are thousands of licensed common carriers of data communication. Three of the largest are American Telephone and Telegraph (AT&T), MCI, and General Telephone & Electronics (GTE).

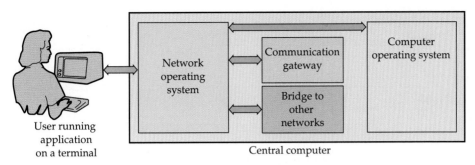

User running
application
on a terminal

Central computer

7–20 A network operating system is the interface between users and applications running on local terminals and the central computer. Networking software also connects to communication gateways and other networks.

An alternative to the major common carriers are value-added carriers who lease communications channels from the common carriers and create **value-added networks (VANs)** that add extra services over and above what the common carriers provide. Tymnet and Telenet are both value-added carriers that provide error detection, faster response time, and compatibility among different types of hardware.

Pulling all these networks together is the network software that manages each network so that it can operate separately as well as with other networks by providing the necessary communications protocols.

Three Kinds of Network Software

Networking software is really a series of programs that reside on both the host computer and nodes so that they work together. The primary function of this software is to move data between the network and storage, to control the sharing of files and records, and to control access to data. In addition, as shown in Figure 7–20, networking software can include such options as bridges to other networks and gateways to larger systems. For example, networking software from Novell, a major supplier in this area, offers most of the options specified below.

Network Operating System.   Working in conjunction with the normal computer operating system, the **network operating system** facilitates basic network management functions such as transmitting files, communicating with other systems, and performing diagnostics on the system. The most important task for the network operating system is to interact smoothly with the application software running on the network.

Bridges to Other Networks.   **Bridges** connect separate networks in a way that is transparent to the users of the networks. As shown in Figure 7–21, bridges enable a node on one side of the bridge to use the resources on the other side of the bridge as though they were located in one network. Bridges are particularly useful for connecting normally incompatible networks. For example, Novell offers a software module that acts as a bridge between many other LAN vendors' hardware. In this case, the bridged networks must all be running the same version of the Novell network operating system.

Gateways to Larger Systems.   Communication **gateways** connect small local area networks to mainframe systems. Gateways are especially useful in corporations that need to connect microcomputers, minicomputers, and

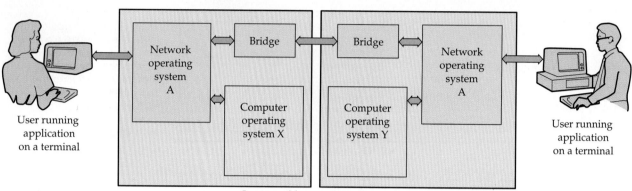

Incompatible central computers

mainframes together into complete networks. For example, many network vendors like Novell and Microsoft offer gateways between IBM microcomputers and mainframes. When connected, the microcomputer **emulates** a mainframe terminal; that is, the microcomputer acts exactly like a terminal that is totally compatible with the mainframe.

The trend is to put more and more "intelligence" into business networks, in the form of bridges, gateways, multiplexers, front-end processors, computer switching devices, public databases, and so forth. In this way, the network itself coordinates and links a wide variety of computers, terminals, and software that might otherwise be incompatible into a common system that is better able to meet business needs.

7–21 A network operating system can provide the interface between two computers with different operating environments. The network bridge allows data and programs to move between systems.

SUMMARY

Data communications is a combination of technologies that enable computers to pass data electronically to each other, no matter where they may be located. Using data communications to spread computer power throughout an organization is called *distributed processing*. The three most common distributed processing activities are *remote data entry, remote data inquiry,* and *remote job entry.* Two other distributed applications are *electronic mail* and *home banking services.* A highly publicized use for data communications and one that may have significant social implications is telecommuting.

Data communications requires *communication channels* to link CPUs and terminals (or any input and/or output device). In a data communications application, a microcomputer or minicomputer can function as a terminal. Three kinds of devices are specially designed to function as terminals: *dumb terminals,* which can only send and/or receive data; *smart terminals,* which can send and receive data and also have limited abilities such as editing; and *intelligent terminals,* which can send and receive data as well as run applications independently. In a data communications system, a microcomputer could function as an intelligent terminal.

Three basic types of communication channels exist: *hardwired, telephone lines,* and alternative channels. Hardwiring can use three basic types of cable: *twisted-pair cable, coaxial cable,* and *fiber optic cable.*

The standard telephone system is commonly used for connecting computers over large distances. *Teleprocessing* (or *telecommunications*) is the term sometimes used to describe data communications using telephone lines. To send computer data over the phone, you need additional interface equipment such as *modems, acoustic couplers,* and, perhaps, *communications controllers* to supervise the signals. Common communications controllers are *multiplexers* and *front-end processors.* Although hardwired cables and standard telephones are widely used in data communications applications, numerous other channels or links can be used, such as *leased telephone lines, microwave stations,* and *satellite stations.*

Just as traffic laws allow cars to move in only one of two directions on a street, data can move only in specific directions through communication channels, depending upon what kind of *transmission protocol* is used. Three types of communication channels include *simplex, half-duplex,* and *full-duplex. The speed with which information is sent is commonly expressed in baud rates or bits per second (bps).*

A *network* is a data communications system that links terminals, microcomputers, minis, or mainframes so that they may operate independently but also share data and other resources. A network configuration refers to how the *nodes* and *host computer* are organized. Three common configurations for networks are *star, ring,* and *bus* networks. Three common types of networks are *local area networks (LANs), wide area networks (WANs),* and *public data networks.* Pulling all these networks together is the network software, which enables each network to operate separately and with other networks by providing the necessary communications links. Networking software is really a series of programs that reside on the host computer or on a file server. These include *network operating software, bridge software,* and *gateways.*

KEY TERMS

Acoustic coupler	Hardwired
Analog signal	Host computer
Audio response unit	Intelligent terminal
Baseband	Local area network
Baud rate	(LAN)
Bits per second (bps)	Modem
Bridge	Modulation
Broadband	Multiplexer
Bus configuration	Network operating
Coaxial cable	system
Common carrier	Network
Communication channel	Node
Communications	Polling
controller	Protocol
Communications	Remote job entry
satellite	Remote data entry
Communications	Ring network
software	Simplex line
Configuration	Smart terminal
Data communications	Star network
Demodulation	Subscriber service
Digital	Switched lines
Direct-connect modem	Telecommunications
Distributed processing	Telecommuting
Download	Terminal
Dumb terminal	Time-sharing
Electronic mail (E-mail)	Time-slicing
Emulation	Token ring network
Fiber optic cable	Transmission protocol
File server	Twisted-pair cable
Front-end processor	Upload
Full-duplex line	Value-added network
Gateway	Wide area network
Half-duplex line	(WAN)

CHAPTER SELF-TEST

1. The term _____ refers to electronically transmitting data from one location or site to another using telephones or other linkages.

2. (T *or* F) Using terminals at remote locations saves manual transmittal of data, which can be very time-consuming.

3. The three types of terminals are: _____ terminals, which can only send and/or receive data; _____ terminals, which can send and receive and have some other, limited capabilities; and _____ terminals, which can send and receive data as well as run applications independently.

4. (T *or* F) Data entered at a terminal may be directly transmitted to a CPU or stored on disk or tape.

5. Processing data in _____ mode means that it is first stored and then processed at fixed intervals.

6. The immediate on-line processing of data is required only when files must be kept _____ at all times.

7. (T *or* F) Rather than immediately updating the master file, a stock exchange would be likely to store incoming stock purchases and sales on a disk or tape for future processing.

8. (T *or* F) A company that performs its updating once a day would be likely to store incoming transactions on a disk or tape for future processing.

9. Entering both a program and input from a disk at a remote location is called _____.

10. The term _____ is used to describe a technique that enables several businesses to rent computer time from a service organization; this is frequently advantageous for small companies that cannot afford their own computer.

11. (T *or* F) Minis and micros as well as mainframes may be used for data communications applications.

12. In a data communications system, a communication _____ or link is necessary for connecting a remote terminal to a CPU.

13. Most simple data communications systems use _____ or _____ as a data communications link.

14. _____ cable is the fastest but most expensive communications link available for data transmission.

15. A _____ is a private communication line offered by telephone companies for dedicated data communications use by an organization.

16. High-speed data communications use wireless _____ stations and _____ stations.

17. The speed of a communication channel is called the _____ rate.

18. When transmission is permitted both to and from a CPU over the same communication line—but *not at the same time*—the line is called _____.

19. A(n) _____ is a device that converts terminal signals in digital form to analog form for transmission over telephone lines.

20. A _____ is a device that can collect messages from numerous terminals and transmit them collectively over a single communications line.

SOLUTIONS 1) data communications. 2) True. 3) dumb; smart; intelligent. 4) True. 5) batch (or off-line). 6) current. 7) False. Stock exchanges require up-to-date information immediately. 8) True. 9) remote job entry. 10) time-sharing. 11) True. 12) channel. 13) a standard voice-grade telephone line; a cable. 14) fiber optic. 15) leased or private line. 16) microwave; satellite. 17) baud. 18) half-duplex. 19) modem or acoustic coupler. 20) multiplexer or front-end processor.

REVIEW QUESTIONS

1. List and briefly discuss the three major ways data communications technologies are used in a distributed computer system.
2. Discuss two advantages of time sharing for small companies. Discuss three disadvantages.
3. List the seven major communications links for sending data between computers. Briefly discuss two advantages and disadvantages for each.
4. List two common hardware devices used for sending data over the telephone system.
5. Briefly discuss how multiplexers and front-end processors reduce communications costs and integrate the use of terminals.
6. Describe the three ways that electronic signals can be transmitted over communication channels. Briefly identify a common use for each method.
7. List and briefly describe three common configurations for networks.
8. List and briefly describe three common networks. Which is the most popular?
9. When would you want to use a gateway? A bridge?

PROBLEM-SOLVING APPLICATIONS

1. How many computer networks are used on your campus? Using the terms from this chapter, briefly describe the type of networks and their configurations. How are they being used? Is there access to a WAN on your campus? If so, what is the WAN mostly used for?
2. Assume that you are a member of a five-person research team that will produce a report on the status of acid rain in the New England states. Each member of the team is located on a different university campus. What kind of computer network would be most useful to help the group do the research and prepare the report if each member had a terminal or networked microcomputer? If all five members were on the same campus, what kind of configuration would it have? What software would you need? How would you use the network to help prepare this report?
3. Assume that you subscribed to the Prodigy service described in this chapter. Briefly describe three services that it does not currently offer that you would like to have. How would these "wish" services be useful to you?

SOFTWARE

System Software and Specialized Application Packages

When you have completed this chapter, you will be able to:

✔ Describe these operating system features: multiprogramming, multiprocessing, virtual memory, and the virtual machine concept.

✔ Describe and compare common operating systems for microcomputers, minicomputers, and mainframes.

✔ Describe the tasks performed by specialized application packages such as integrated packages, desktop publishing, graphics, accounting, and project management software.

✔ Discuss the difference between horizontal and vertical packages.

✔ List several important considerations when purchasing software.

Chapter 8

Chapter Outline

The software developed today is much more sophisticated and diverse than packages of only a few years ago. Computer stores sell software to perform every imaginable task from creating typeset-quality publications that contain complex graphics to keeping track of daily appointments. Each of these applications has a specialized purpose. However, they all have one feature in common: they allow us to create large files of related data that we can access and manipulate as the need arises. The ability to manipulate this data on demand in highly sophisticated ways is a major reason this new generation of application software is so fascinating.

Not only must these applications perform complex tasks, but they must also be easy to use—a characteristic commonly referred to as **user-friendly**. As application packages have become easier to use, so has the operating system software that acts as an interface between us and the hardware. In recent years, the operating systems that have become available are not only user-friendly, but many are also capable of running several applications concurrently. The most important demand we make of the operating systems for our computers is that they allow us to use our time as efficiently as possible.

In this chapter, we will discuss a variety of fascinating and powerful applications, including desktop publishing, graphics packages, and accounting software. However, first we will examine some of the features of operating systems that permit us to use these applications.

Operating systems have two basic functions: to manage the computer's resources efficiently and to execute the user's instructions. The part of the operating system that manages the computer's resources—including the CPU, primary storage, and peripheral devices—is commonly called the **kernel** (or the **supervisor**). The **user interface** is the part of the operating system that permits you to communicate with the hardware—for example, to instruct it to execute a particular application package or to save a file. Figure 8–1 illustrates how the parts of the operating system are related to the end-user and to the computer hardware.

Common Operating System Features

There are a multitude of operating systems currently available. Some of them—such as DOS and the Macintosh operating system—are designed for use with microcomputers; others, such as the IBM 4381 operating system, are implemented on large computers; and still others, such as UNIX, are

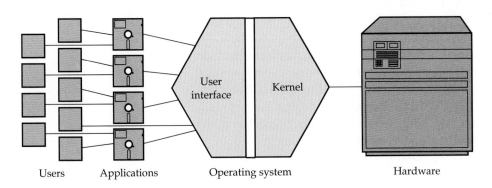

Users   Applications   Operating system   Hardware

User interface   Kernel

8–1 An operating system consists of a user interface that accepts and interprets the various activities of applications or user requests, and a kernel that controls the execution of these activities.

Single operation

Loads and runs one
program at a time.

Program   ► Loads in memory   ► Is executed   ► And is stored.

**Multiprogramming
and Multitasking**

Loads many programs
at once in microcomputer and
runs them in alternating pattern
that seems simultaneous
to the user.

Multiple   ► Share memory   ► Are executed in   ► And are stored
programs   alternating pattern   at user's command.

used at all levels—for microcomputers, minicomputers, and mainframes. In
this section, we will discuss the features of several widely used operating
systems.

Multiprogramming and Multitasking

In **multiprogramming**, several programs are placed in the computer's
primary storage at the same time. The CPU then divides its time between
these programs. It executes one program for a brief period of time, then
switches to another, and so forth, until each program is completed. New
programs are then loaded into available portions of main memory, and the
process is repeated (Figure 8–2).

On interactive systems, multiprogramming allows the CPU to juggle its
time among various users and respond to requests fairly quickly. Once
confined to mainframes, multiprogramming is becoming increasingly common on microcomputers.

When the system performs multiprogramming operations, it must divide primary storage into separate areas ("partition" it) where each application is placed so that one application cannot interfere with the others that are
processed concurrently. Generally, the operating system assigns priorities to
the various tasks that may be submitted to the CPU in order for important
tasks to be executed before those of less urgency. The requests of upper-level
management are often assigned a higher priority than those of data-entry
personnel, for example; or large, routine accounting jobs may be assigned a
lower priority than a simple query to a database that can be handled quickly.

Multitasking is a variation of multiprogramming implemented on
many high-end microcomputers. It allows the user to access several
programs at the same time, as shown in Figure 8–2. You can tell the computer to print a word processing file, sort a database, and calculate a spreadsheet simultaneously, for example. Typically, multitasking is used to allow
a single user to perform numerous tasks; multiprogamming, however, is

8–2 Multitasking, a variation
of multiprogramming, allows
a user to access several
programs at the same time.

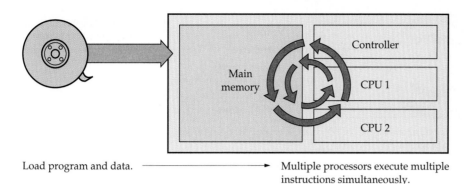

Load program and data. ⟶ Multiple processors execute multiple instructions simultaneously.

Multiprocessing

Uses two or more CPUs to process two or more instructions at the same time. Can be used to run separate programs or separate parts of one program.

usually applied to situations in which several users want to access different applications at the same time.

Multiprocessing

Multiprocessing involves linking two or more CPUs to optimize the handling of data (Figure 8–3). While one CPU is executing one set of instructions, another CPU can be executing a different set. This technique differs from multiprogramming, which executes only one program at a time but switches quickly between the different programs currently in memory. In multiprocessing, the system can actually execute several instructions and programs at the same time.

8–3 Multiprocessing enables a computer to actually run two programs simultaneously—using two processors.

Virtual Memory

Virtual memory (or **virtual storage**) allows the computer system to operate as if it has more primary storage than it actually does. When virtual memory is used, an application program is segmented into a series of modules that are stored outside main memory on a direct-access device such as a magnetic disk. When the CPU is ready to execute a specific module, the operating system moves that module from secondary storage into main memory and moves a module in main memory back to secondary storage. This process, which is referred to as **swapping**, is illustrated in Figure 8–4. Swapping allows a program to be quite large, because it is not all loaded into memory at the same time. Virtual storage is common on mainframes and minicomputers, and it is becoming available on high-end microcomputer systems well.

8–4 In virtual memory, disk storage supplements the computer's main memory, and parts of a large program are swapped back and forth.

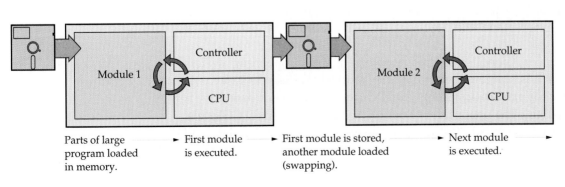

Parts of large program loaded in memory. ▶ First module is executed. ▶ First module is stored, another module loaded (swapping). ▶ Next module is executed. ▶

Virtual memory

Disk storage is use to hold a very large program, and modules are swapped to main memory for execution.

Programs loaded.   Appropriate operating system selected to run program.

Virtual machine

Different operating systems allow varied programs to be run on one machine.

8–5 A virtual machine has a second operating system, so one computer can act like two.

"Virtual Machine" Concept

In the **virtual machine** concept—primarily applied on mainframes—the real machine simulates a number of virtual machines, each capable of executing its own operating system (Figure 8–5). So, even though in reality there is only one computer system, it performs as though there were a number of separate systems. The CPU automatically chooses the appropriate operating system for you, depending on the application software. It will appear to you that an entire CPU and its peripheral devices are dedicated completely to your needs. Because of the virtual machine's ability to execute several operating systems simultaneously, it provides a great deal of flexibility. Application packages that require different operating systems can be executed on the same hardware.

Microcomputer Operating Systems

The microcomputer world is dominated by two operating system families—the DOS and OS/2 operating systems originating with IBM microcomputers, and the Apple Macintosh operating system.

PC-DOS and MS-DOS

The disk operating system IBM initially chose for its personal computer is known by the acronym PC-DOS (Personal Computer Disk Operating System). It was developed by Microsoft Corporation, which also offers a generic version called MS-DOS for users of IBM-compatible computers. We will refer to both of these operating systems as simply DOS.

DOS tells the computer how to format, read, and write information on either floppy disks or hard disks. It establishes a number of limitations, such as the number of files that can be contained in a disk directory, the number of bytes of memory that can be on a disk, and the number of bytes of memory usable by a program. In addition, it manages peripheral devices such as the printer and the keyboard. It also controls the execution of software.

You start, or "boot," a microcomputer by using operating system software, which is placed either in the A drive for dual-diskette systems or in the C drive for hard-disk systems. (On PC-compatibles, each disk drive is assigned a letter.) The operating system loads the COMMAND.COM file, which performs diagnostic tests on hardware and prompts for date and

10-16-89		File System		8:00 pm	
File	Options	Arrange	Exit	F1=Help	

```
Open (start)...
Print...
Associate...

Move...
Copy...
Delete...
Rename...
Change attribute...
View

Create directory...
Select all
Deselect all

    -BAT
    -CONFIGS
    -ADRIAN
    -QA
  ▶ -DOS4
```

	More:↑↓		*.*	More:↑↓
		ANSI .SYS	9,105	10-06-88
		APPEND .EXE	11,154	10-06-88
		ASSIGN .COM	5,753	10-06-88
		ATTRIB .EXE	18,263	10-06-88
	▶	AUTOEXEC.BAT	79	03-04-89
		CHKDSK .COM	17,787	10-06-88
		COMMAND .COM	37,556	10-06-88
		COMP .COM	9,459	10-06-88
		CONFIG .SYS	22	03-04-89
		DEBUG .COM	21,574	10-06-88
		DISKCOMP.COM	9,857	10-06-88
		DISKCOPY.COM	10,396	10-06-88
		DOSSHELL.BAT	197	03-04-89
		DRIVER .SYS	5,241	10-06-88
		EMM386 .SYS	87,776	10-06-88

```
F10=Actions Shift+F9=Command Prompt
```

8–6 DOS 4.0 provides user-friendly features such as pull-down command menus, which were unavailable in earlier versions.

time. You will then see an A> or C> prompt, depending on which drive has the operating system software in it.

Operating system commands are entered at the "command line," the line following the disk drive prompt. For example, to see the names of the files stored on the disk in drive A, type the following DIR (Directory) command at the A> prompt:

A> **DIR**

Through the years, DOS has been updated to take advantage of technological improvements. Each new version of DOS is assigned a version number. The higher the number, the more sophisticated and more recent the version. For example, when DOS 2.0 was released, it was a major improvement over DOS 1.0. DOS 2.1 contained minor improvements over 2.0. The most recent version, shown in Figure 8–6, is DOS version 4. Unlike the older versions of DOS, which required you to type specific commands, this new version allows you to select commands from a menu; in this respect, DOS version 4 is more user-friendly than its predecessors.

A number of improved user interfaces have been created in an attempt to make DOS easier to use. These improvements include software features that are more **objected-oriented** as compared to **text-oriented**. Object-oriented interfaces use graphic images, referred to as **icons**, to represent various objects, such as files. Examples of enhanced user interfaces that work in conjunction with DOS are Microsoft Windows and Desqview. Each application is opened in a **window** and several windows can be opened at once, allowing you to switch between applications. Using Windows frees you to work much as you might at your desk, spreading out several "windowed" documents to reference and work on simultaneously. This feature enables you to perform some multitasking operations not previously available using DOS. The Microsoft Windows interface is very similar to Presentation Manager, which is discussed in the next section.

OS/2

In 1987, as the computing world listened attentively, IBM announced a new line of personal computers, the PS/2 (Personal System/2) series, and a new

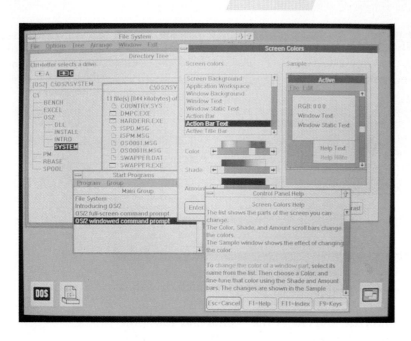

8–7 With its new operating system, OS/2, IBM introduced a new, graphically-oriented user interface called Presentation Manager. *Courtesy:* Microsoft Corporation

operating system, OS/2. Although the initial release of OS/2 still had a text-based user interface, it was soon followed by a more graphically oriented user interface known as the Presentation Manager (Figure 8–7).

OS/2 overcomes many of the limitations of DOS. For example, with OS/2, programs can use more than 640 K of RAM, which was the size limitation for programs under DOS. It also allows multitasking so that several application packages can be run at the same time. Each application runs in its own window; you can switch between windows and copy data back and forth.

Macintosh Operating System

Unlike the IBM-PC family, the original Macintosh user interface provided a graphical rather than a text-based interface between the user and the system. It is also unlike the original DOS in that there is no need to memorize a variety of commands; the Macintosh presents such commands in a menu. This approach has proved to be so popular that the IBM world, first with Microsoft Windows and more recently with the Presentation Manager, is also moving toward graphical interfaces.

As shown in Figure 8–8, when you first turn on a Macintosh, you see a "desktop" with icons representing various files. Related files can be placed in "folders." Finder, which is the Mac's graphical user interface, allows you to open and manipulate the files on the desktop. Often, the actions needed to perform a specific function are fairly self-evident. For example, if you want to delete a file, you use the mouse to place the file in the trash can. You select additional commands from pull-down menus (Figure 8–9), which are displayed when you select a main menu item.

The Macintosh's graphics capabilities have gained it widespread acceptance among publishers, designers, and journalists, who use it for applications from publishing to computer-aided design. However, its acceptance in

8–8 Two windows are currently open on this Macintosh desktop. The smaller window shows the contents of the folder called Word Processors, which is stored on the hard disk.

8–9 On a Macintosh, items are selected from "pull-down" menus. To select a command, use the mouse to position the cursor on the menu item. While holding down the mouse button, "drag" the mouse downward until the desired command is highlighted. Then release the button to execute the command.

business and industry has been slow, largely because until recently it could not run DOS applications. In addition, the original Macintoshes, unlike PC-compatible micros, did not allow for easy expansion. Most DOS-based computers have expansion slots that allow you to customize the system to meet your specific needs, while major surgery was required to add more peripheral devices to the early Macintoshes. However, the newer Macintoshes, such as the Macintosh II, have expansion slots, and special circuit boards can be added to allow them to run DOS software.

For Macintosh users who choose to use multitasking, an extension of Finder, the original graphical user interface for the Macintosh, is available; MultiFinder, as its name implies, allows you to open several applications at the same time.

UNIX—An Operating System for All Levels

UNIX was developed by AT&T's Bell Laboratories for use on minicomputers. Its development is interesting because, unlike the other operating systems discussed here, it was designed by a small group of programmers

In a Nutshell

Microcomputer Operating System Software

Macintosh	The first operating system to have a user-friendly interface, called the Finder, which allows the user to select commands from pull-down menus. Objects such as files are represented by icons. A multitasking version called MultiFinder is also available.
DOS 1.0–3.3	First operating system for IBM and IBM-compatible PCs and PS/2s. It is command-driven; that is, you must enter commands without benefit of menus or prompts. It also has strict memory limits.
DOS 4.0	Includes an optional command menu shell, mouse support, direct support of expanded memory, and support for hard disks larger than 32 MB.
	Microsoft Windows Graphical user interface for DOS. Allows several programs to be open at a time, each in its own window. Windows/386 for IBM PS/2s and compatibles introduced a true multitasking environment and eliminated the 640 K RAM limitation imposed by DOS.
OS/2	IBM's new operating system, introduced with the PS/2 family of micros. PS/2s can use DOS Windows or OS/2.
	Presentation Manager The graphical user interface for OS/2; similar in appearance and operation to Microsoft Windows under DOS.

as a simple operating system with a limited set of instructions and was originally used in research and development by experienced programmers. UNIX has two advantages: unlike most operating systems, it is available for many different types of computers—micros, minis, and mainframes; and it was specifically designed for multiprocessing, although this is now true of several other operating systems as well.

As more sophisticated microcomputers are developed to support multi-tasking and multiuser environments, UNIX is increasingly being implemented on them. Microsoft has a version of UNIX called XENIX, which is implemented on microcomputers. There are UNIX operating systems for IBM PCs and PS/2s called AIX, Macintoshes, NeXT, Apollo, and Sun minicomputer workstations. Because of the variety of implementations and its popularity among programmers (many of whom were trained to use it on university computer systems), UNIX is now widely used in business and industry and is expected to gain even more popularity in the years ahead.

8–10 Sun's Open Look user interface is one of several that make UNIX easy to use. *Courtesy:* Sun Microsystems, Inc.

The original goal of UNIX was to build an interactive programming environment that had features to help programmers develop software more efficiently. For example, it provides many **tools**, or utility programs, that perform a variety of common tasks. The user interface is contained in a **shell**, or separate software module, and is not part of the operating system itself. There are a number of commonly used UNIX shells.

A major complaint heard about UNIX is that it is not user-friendly. Its commands are often cryptic and difficult to remember. However, many computer manufacturers are now supplying user-friendly shells to make these systems easier to use (Figure 8–10).

IBM Mainframe Operating Systems

Because mainframes run large programs and are used for time-sharing, they commonly have a variety of capabilities, such as multiprocessing and virtual memory, that allow them to operate as efficiently as possible. In this section, we will discuss the operating systems originally created for IBM's S/360 and S/370 families of mainframes. Although we use IBM examples, these operating system capabilities are typical of all mainframes and mini-computers, including popular models from Digital Equipment Systems and Unisys, for example.

IBM has always designed computers with the business customer in mind. Therefore, when it developed the S/360 family of computers in the mid-1960s, the idea was to make them **upwardly compatible**. In essence, this means that if a business customer buys a small mainframe and then expands to the point where a larger system is needed, the application software and operating system that ran on the old machine will also work on a new one in the same family, saving the customer considerable money and inconvenience. If a user has a 4341 from the 4300 series, for example, and decides to trade it in for a larger model such as the 4381, all peripheral devices as well as software can still be used.

However, it is important to realize that these computers are not necessarily downwardly compatible. If you trade in a larger model in a family of computers for a smaller model, software may need to be modified.

For upward compatibility, all machines in the S/360 family have the same type of computer architecture; that is, they share CPU design features so that data is processed in the same way. In the 1970s, this architecture was carried into IBM's new line, the S/370 family. Today, there are many computers that use this architecture and can run the same operating systems, including the 9370s, 43XXs, and the powerful 30XX systems.

DOS/VS and DOS/VSE

In the mid-1960s, IBM introduced its new operating system, OS/360, for use on the S/360 family of mainframes. OS/360 replaced the existing batch-oriented operating system DOS (not to be confused with PC-DOS or MS-DOS). Many business customers objected to OS/360 because it was an entirely new system that required the customer to buy new application software and to retrain programmers.

Customers pressured IBM into creating more sophisticated versions of DOS for mainframes that incorporated some of the more desirable features of the new operating system. Several enhanced versions of DOS, such as DOS/VS (virtual storage) and DOS/VSE (virtual storage extended) were created. Originally, the operating system could process two applications simultaneously. DOS/VSE allows many applications to be run simultaneously.

In addition to upgrading DOS, IBM created two new operating systems, which currently run on many IBM mainframes. These operating systems are MVS (multiple virtual storage) and VM (virtual machine).

MVS

Multiple virtual storage (MVS) is the high-end operating system for IBM's batch-oriented mainframe systems. MVS provides for a maximum of 16 processors for multiprocessing. It carefully manages the use of virtual storage to create the illusion that primary storage is considerably larger than it actually is, and it can process many large applications efficiently and simultaneously.

VM

As previously discussed, a **virtual machine** (VM) operating system is designed to provide each user with a complete, simulated machine devoted solely to his or her needs. Each simulated machine can run a different operating system.

SELF-TEST

1. (T *or* F) When using multiprocessing, a computer system must have two or more CPUs.
2. With virtual memory, a technique called _____ is used to move program modules from secondary storage to main memory as they are needed.
3. (T *or* F) The UNIX operating system was originally designed to be used on mainframes.
4. The user interface for the Macintosh uses _____, which are symbols representing various objects or functions.
5. (T *or* F) User interfaces for DOS, such as Microsoft Windows, are actually complete operating systems in themselves.

SOLUTIONS   1) True. 2) swapping. 3) False. 4) icons. 5) False.

Specialized Application Packages

In addition to the productivity packages discussed in Chapter 3 (word processors, spreadsheets, and database management systems as well as integrated packages which combine the features of all three), there is an enormous variety of specialized software packages for computer systems. Some of the more popular ones are discussed here. All of these types of software are available on microcomputers, and many have high-end versions that run on minicomputers or mainframes.

Desktop Publishing

The phenomenon known as **desktop publishing (DTP)** was first popularized by the Apple Macintosh. The Macintosh, with its standard graphical interface, quickly found a niche in graphic design departments. It provides a perfect platform to allow designers to create complex pages consisting of both text and graphics. The ability to integrate text and graphics in a single document is essential for desktop publishing software. Figure 8–11 shows the layout of a page using the popular DTP package PageMaker on the Macintosh.

8–11 A pull-down menu is used to position a photo with text on a PageMaker screen. *Courtesy:* Aldus Corp.

The efficiency of desktop publishing is in sharp contrast to the traditional method of developing a publication. Traditionally, the customer submits a typewritten manuscript to the typesetter. A publication design is agreed upon, and the text manuscript is keyboarded using elaborate formatting codes and then output in long strips known as galleys. The galleys are checked by proofreaders and then sent to the customer to be proofread. After changes have been made, a further round of proofreading takes place. When all typographical errors have been corrected and changes made, the galleys are cut apart and pasted up in pages, leaving space for artwork. The customer must then check a copy of these page proofs. All corrections are typeset and pasted in, and, depending on the quantity of corrections, some pages may need to be completely repasted. The final pasteup is sent to the camera department, where plates for the printing press are made. The customer then checks a proof of this final stage to make certain that everything is in its proper place. Finally, the publication is sent to press to be printed. Because of the number of steps involved in traditional publishing, there are many opportunities for errors. Moreover, it is a time-consuming process both for the typesetter and the customer, who must worry about new errors that may be introduced at each stage.

Desktop publishing, however, allows the user to control all aspects of the publication process, including designing the publication, setting the type, proofreading, inserting graphics, and producing the final copy. The user takes total responsibility for the final appearance of the publication, and the time needed to produce it is greatly reduced.

DTP allows both text and sophisticated graphics to be integrated into a single file. Graphics—ranging from simple lines and geometric shapes to drawings and photographs—can be placed anywhere on the page, enlarged or reduced, and trimmed to fit the available space. Desktop publishing software allows complex pages to be formatted on the computer screen in ways not commonly available with most word processing packages. Different typefaces, styles, and sizes can be viewed on the screen just as they will appear when the document is printed. As you will recall from Chapter 3, this feature is referred to as WYSIWYG (what you see is what you get).

Many desktop publishing packages use a universal code called Post-Script, which is embedded in the document and tells the hardware how to format each page. The advantage of PostScript, which is referred to as a page description language, is that typesetting and formatting codes will always be correctly interpreted by output devices such as laser printers and phototypesetting machines. For example, if you choose the typeface Times Roman for your newsletter, it will come out looking the same whether you print it on an Apple LaserWriter or a Qume laser printer, or even a Linotronic 300 phototypesetter. This means that you can proof a publication on a laser printer, which is relatively inexpensive to use, and then send final files to the expensive phototypesetter. Because it allows files to be produced on many different printers, PostScript is currently a desktop publishing standard.

The concept of desktop publishing was first introduced by Aldus Page-Maker for the Macintosh. PageMaker was soon followed by other programs

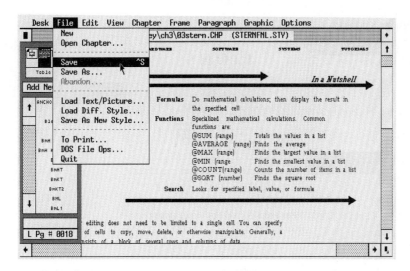

8–12 The most popular desktop publishing package used on IBM and IBM-compatible micros is Ventura Publisher, which was used to produce the layout for this textbook.

such as Ready, Set, Go! and Quark Xpress. Although desktop publishing was originally considered the exclusive domain of the Macintosh, it was not long before Xerox released Ventura Publisher (Figure 8–12), the first full-fledged desktop publishing program for IBM microcomputers; within a few months Aldus introduced an IBM version of PageMaker as well.

PageMaker has remained the single most popular package, partly because it was the first desktop publishing program and many people already know how to use it, and partly because identical versions run on both the Macintosh and PC. Not only does it include good page design tools and have the ability to integrate graphics easily, but also files created with the IBM and Macintosh versions share a common structure so that they can easily be exchanged between the two systems. Pagemaker is easy to learn and best-suited for producing short documents and graphic-intensive publications.

Xerox's Ventura Publisher, the most popular desktop publishing software for the IBM PC and PS/2 families of computers, is faster than PageMaker on the IBM, is better at handling long documents, and provides better typographic control. This textbook was written on IBM-compatible micros using the word processor WordPerfect; it was then formatted using Ventura Publisher and output to a phototypeset file ready for the printer.

Both PageMaker and Ventura Publisher (as well as many advanced word processing packages) allow users to create a unique set of design choices for each document to ensure that pages are automatically laid out with all elements treated consistently. To do this, you create what is called a **style sheet** or **template**, making choices such as what typeface to use for running heads, where to position running heads, how much space to leave above heads in text, and so on. Style sheets can usually be saved separately from the text of the publication, and reused or adapted for other documents.

The capabilities of DTP have been carried to faster and more sophisticated levels with packages such as Interleaf and FrameMaker, which are UNIX-based programs that run on minicomputer workstations from Sun or Sony. These programs are usually referred to as *electronic publishing programs* because the hardware is larger and more expensive than that needed for

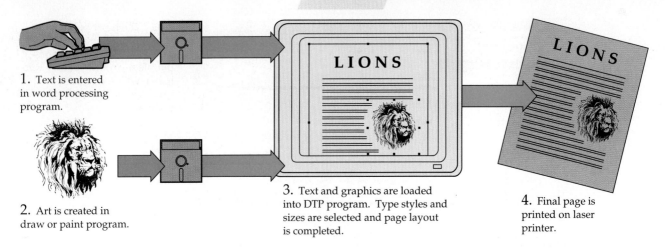

1. Text is entered in word processing program.

2. Art is created in draw or paint program.

3. Text and graphics are loaded into DTP program. Type styles and sizes are selected and page layout is completed.

4. Final page is printed on laser printer.

DTP. Typically, elaborate graphics can be created within these programs, although they also allow for importing graphics from drawing or CAD (computer-aided design) programs.

Keyboarding and Editing. Because most desktop publishing packages do not provide the sophisticated editing features included in word processing packages, it is usually preferable to enter the text using a word processing program and then "import" (move) it into the desktop publishing program for formatting. After the text is in the desktop publishing program, it can still be edited, but less efficiently.

Generally, only minimal formatting is done when text is typed by using a word processing package (Figure 8–13). The desktop publishing software formats the text as specified by the user. When the text is transferred from the word processing package to the DTP program, features such as boldface, underline, subscripts, and superscripts are usually kept, but word processing formats such as centering, right alignment, justification, and italics may have to be reentered.

DTP programs allow you to create simple graphics such as circles, rectangles, and lines. However, more sophisticated graphics must either be imported from a file created by a graphics package or pasted in after the text is printed. Graphics will be discussed later in this chapter.

Formatting and Design. Professional-quality desktop publishing software is complex, even for simple applications. It may take weeks to master all of the intricacies of such programs. Ideally, the person responsible for formatting and designing documents will have experience or training in publication design. One of the most common mistakes made by new DTP users is to assume that desktop publishing packages enable anyone to create attractive publications. In some businesses, trained designers set up formats that can be used repeatedly. The actual keyboarding and formatting is then done by the clerical staff, who follow the standard page formats provided. This textbook, for example, was designed by a professional book designer, who wrote detailed specifications for all the page elements and created a set of sample pages; these specifications were then followed by the page formatters, whose expertise is in using the Ventura Publisher program.

8–13 Desktop publishing (DTP) programs use word processing files along with graphics produced with draw or paint programs as input to produce fully formatted pages.

Managerial Decisions.   In most businesses, managers have little direct input in the desktop publishing process other than determining which documents should have the professional look of desktop publishing and which should be created by using word processing packages. However, these managers may have the final responsibility for purchasing the software. When making this decision, they should take into account the hardware available and the type of publications to be produced. One important consideration is the extent to which the publications will use graphics. An alternative managers should consider is that of using one of the more sophisticated word processing packages, which are introducing new versions that incorporate many features of DTP. Acceptable documents can often be created more quickly by using regular word processing than by providing the training time required for using most DTP programs.

Graphics

In recent years, businesses have taken to heart the old adage that "one picture is worth a thousand words" and are illustrating concepts by using programs that produce graphics (Figure 8–14). These programs fall into two major categories: graphing and charting programs, and general illustration programs. They differ not only in the types of graphics that they produce but also in the ways the graphics are generated.

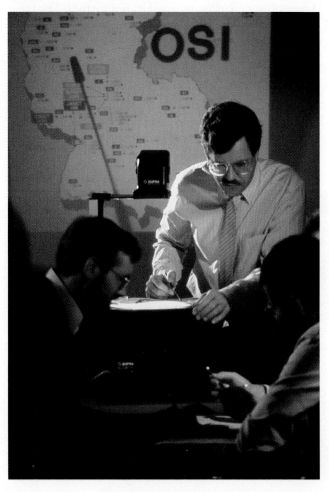

8–14 Meetings are enhanced when information is presented in graphic form, as in the facilities map shown here in the background. *Courtesy:* IBM.

Graphing and Charting Packages.

are commonly used for business graphics or **presentation graphics**; they are the types of programs most frequently associated with business uses. Presentation graphics programs are designed to produce graphic representations of data for business presentations, and their artwork can be output either as transparencies for overhead projectors, or as black-and-white or color graphs on paper. Many of these programs allow users to connect with devices that produce high-resolution color slides.

These packages are relatively limited in their scope, although many include at least some of the features commonly associated with illustration programs. The programs for IBM and compatible computers are similar to the graphics modules of Lotus 1-2-3 and other spreadsheet software, although they usually allow more choices in graph and chart styles, colors, typefaces, and output devices. The finished graphs have a more polished, professional appearance than those created using spreadsheet software. Lotus Freelance Plus and Harvard Graphics (Figure 8–15) are examples of this type of software. On the Macintosh side, Microsoft Power Point, Persuasion from Aldus, and More from Symantec are examples of sophisticated presentation graphics programs that use the Macintosh's graphics capabilities in ways not possible on IBM and compatible computers.

Generally, presentation packages operate by reading a spreadsheet or database file and automatically graphing the data in the selected format. The chart can then be enhanced with various graphic elements such as special symbols, illustrations, shading, and so on.

Illustration Packages.

When the first Macintoshes came out, they included two **illustration packages**: MacDraw and MacPaint. People were amazed at how easily they could create illustrations with this software. Since then, illustration packages have become increasingly sophisticated. However, it is only recently that such programs have begun to be taken seriously among business users, largely as a result of the importance they play in

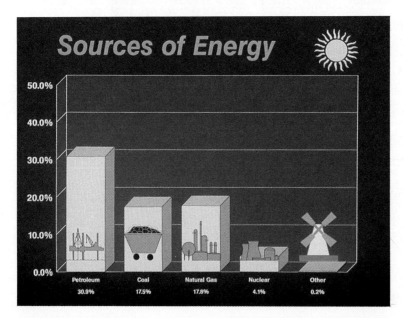

8–15 Harvard Graphics' built-in symbols and flexible options, like 3-D bar graphs, help improve the look of presentation graphics. *Courtesy:* Software Publishing

8–16 PC Paintbrush allows users to create bit-mapped graphics or combine scanned images with original artwork. *Courtesy:* ZSoft Corp.

desktop publishing. These packages can be divided into two categories: painting programs and drawing programs.

Painting programs such as MacPaint and ZSoft's PC Paintbrush (Figure 8–16) create **bit-mapped graphics**, which consist of patterns of dots. Bit-mapped graphics are similar to the output of a dot-matrix printer in which each character or drawing is actually a grouping of small dots, arranged to form the desired shape. The smaller and closer together the dots, the better the quality of the output.

You create most bit-mapped graphics manually by using a mouse to move the cursor on the screen or by using a tablet that translates, or "digitizes," drawings done on it. Optical scanners can also be used to digitize graphics that already exist on paper. Once a graphic has been scanned, it can usually be edited to change or refine it.

As the demand for higher-resolution output has grown, so has the popularity of drawing programs. Drawing programs differ from painting programs in that they use combinations of lines, arcs, circles, squares, and other shapes (objects) rather than dots to create graphics. These are referred to as **vector graphics** as opposed to bit-mapped graphics. Vector graphics can be resized—either enlarged or reduced—without altering their clarity.

The more sophisticated drawing programs, such as Adobe Illustrator (Figure 8–17), Cricket Draw, and Micrografx Designer, offer a great deal of flexibility in creating illustrations. You can exactly specify the thickness of lines; objects can be shaded to give them a three-dimensional appearance that was formerly only possible with paint programs, and they can easily be scaled, rotated, duplicated, or distorted for special effects. Micrografx Designer (Figure 8–18), in particular, is a highly sophisticated drawing program with many of the capabilities of the computer-aided design packages engineers use.

8–17 Vector graphics programs use computer-generated lines, shapes, and dot patterns. No matter how much an image is enlarged, it remains crisply drawn. *Courtesy:* Adobe Systems, Inc.

8–18 Micrografx Designer combines features typically used in CAD programs with those used in illustration packages. *Courtesy:* Micrografx, Inc.

Computer-aided design and drafting (CAD) packages are essentially drawing programs, but they offer additional features specifically required by architects and engineers, for whom they were created. Like all drawing programs, CAD programs use objects to create complex drawings, but they allow a degree of precision unavailable in the lower-level packages. They automatically calculate and display dimensions. In addition, you can precisely place objects by specifying coordinates. These programs also allow a library of symbols to be stored on disk so that you can insert, scale, and rotate them as needed. Many CAD packages are used on minicomputer or mainframe computers.

Drawing programs require more planning, patience, and skill than painting programs. However, large drawings normally take less disk space than large paintings, and take less time to print. Painting programs allow for more spontaneity, but they are far less precise. In most business and professional settings, illustration programs are usually found in graphic design or desktop publishing departments, which often need to have both types available. CAD programs are normally the domain of engineers, architects, and draftspeople.

Most managers have little, if any, direct use for illustration programs. If a scanner is available, some managers find it useful to have their company logos or signatures scanned. The logos and signatures can then be electronically integrated into letters, memos, and other documents. On the other hand, managers find that graphing and charting programs are very useful for making information accessible in attractive and instructional organizational charts and slide presentations.

Accounting Software

Many small businesses use spreadsheets for all of their financial and accounting needs, but other small businesses prefer to purchase specialized software that are specifically designed to computerize accounting procedures. A typical accounting program consists of several modules that work interactively. The three most commonly used modules are those that manage the general ledger, accounts receivable, and accounts payable (Figure 8–19). Depending upon the nature of the business, inventory or payroll modules may also be required. Other common features include a system manager program that integrates the modules, specialized report writers, and charting and graphing capabilities.

The general ledger provides for making journal entries, running a trial balance, and producing financial statements. Accounts receivable provides for invoice entry, cash receipts, and customer statements. Accounts payable includes disbursements entry and check preparation.

A good accounting program should include error-trapping procedures and good audit trails (audit trails allow users or auditors to trace transactions from the general ledger through to individual accounts). It should also provide automatic year-end closing—that is, create complete financial statements that summarize the activity for the year. And it should have the ability to maintain several open periods at a time; for example, the last transaction affecting the profits or losses of the first quarter of the year might

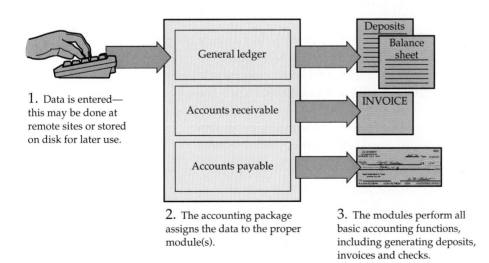

1. Data is entered— this may be done at remote sites or stored on disk for later use.

General ledger

Accounts receivable

Accounts payable

Deposits

Balance sheet

INVOICE

2. The accounting package assigns the data to the proper module(s).

3. The modules perform all basic accounting functions, including generating deposits, invoices and checks.

8–19 Accounting programs typically include general ledger, accounts receivable, and accounts payable modules.

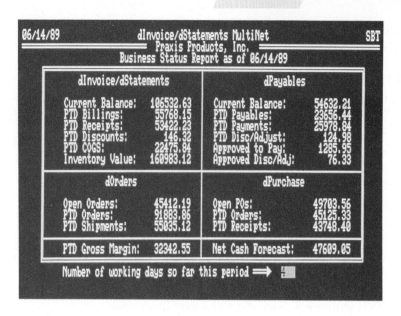

8–20 Accounting packages like this one allow small businesses to computerize their accounting procedures. *Courtesy:* SBT Corp.

not show up until one or two quarters later—errors in data entry might have occurred, for example. The package should allow these adjustments to be made after the quarter has been completed.

Accounting software comes in entry-level, midrange, and high-end configurations that are aimed at small, medium-sized, and large businesses, respectively. Accounting packages are designed for all levels of computer from micro to mainframe, and they are priced to reflect their complexity.

The capability of programs varies, and you should carefully check the capacity and reporting versatility of a package before making any purchases. Some software publishers have a line of accounting software and upgrade policies that make it possible to start out with one version and move up to a more sophisticated version as the need arises. Dac-Easy Accounting, Peachtree, and SBT (Figure 8–20) are examples of popular microcomputer accounting packages.

In most cases, an accountant or accounting clerk enters data. In larger businesses, networked versions of accounting programs make it possible for several people to enter data or to handle specific duties such as billing and writing checks.

Each module of an accounting program comes ready to run, but usually can be customized to suit the needs of a particular business. Most automatically produce statements and invoices, paychecks, and other paperwork, although a certain amount of formatting is usually necessary to match the output with specific forms.

As is the case with spreadsheets and databases, accounting programs are most widely used by managers to produce reports and business graphics. Many allow on-screen reporting, which simplifies checking the status of accounts.

Project Management Software

As the name implies, **project management software** is most likely to be used by managers who need to keep track of complex projects. Like spreadsheet

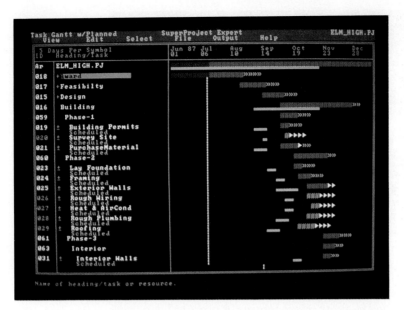

8–21 This Gantt chart produced with Super Project Expert shows how project management software can help managers schedule and track projects. *Courtesy:* Computer Associates International, Inc.

software, project management packages allow you to evaluate a number of different scenarios before you start a project. Once the project is under way, you can track its progress and reallocate tasks or personnel, or make changes to optimize resources as the need arises. Unlike spreadsheets, however, project management software provides little in the way of quantitative results except to let you know whether the final outcome is on time and within budget.

While project management packages differ in their capabilities, most include certain features. Among these are **Gantt chart** timelines (Figure 8–21) that graphically show how long projects are scheduled to take and at what points parts of the project development can overlap. Most also include the ability to create **PERT charts** (Figure 8–22), which provide an alternate approach to planning. Many packages include features such as on-screen graphics; they may also include an outliner, or software that assists writers in developing outlines for documents they are preparing.

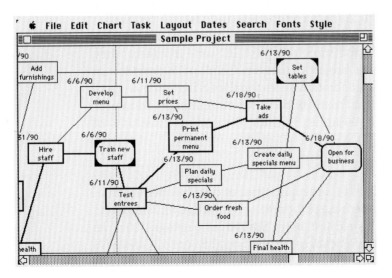

8–22 PERT charting is a project management technique used to plan large, complex projects. This PERT chart was created with MacProject.

8–23 SideKick is one of the most popular desktop organizer programs. *Courtesy:* Borland International, Inc.

Desktop Organizers and Personal Information Managers

A number of programs called **personal information managers** or **desktop organizers** have been developed to allow microcomputer users to keep track of information such as names, addresses, telephone numbers, notes, to-do lists, and appointment schedules. If a modem is attached (a device that allows computers to communicate via telephone) to your computer, most of the programs can automatically dial any number you put into the program's directory. These programs also include on-screen calculators, electronic card files and notepads, and outliners. One of the earliest—and most famous—of these useful packages was SideKick, shown in Figure 8–23. As with most desktop organizers, it remains in primary memory even when other software is in use. You access it while you are running other programs by pressing a specific combination of keys.

Such programs can be helpful to anyone who regularly uses a personal computer. They eliminate much of the clutter, such as Rolodex telephone files and note pads, from the desktop. On the other hand, because the programs use some of your computer's primary memory, you may find that you do not have enough room left for other applications. In addition, some desktop organizers may conflict with some applications and cause your computer to "crash," although this is becoming less and less of a problem.

Like so many programs for personal computers, personal information managers have grown larger and more complex. In some instances, they fulfill many of the functions of project managers. Chapter 13 provides an indepth view of what the next generation of personal information managers is apt to look like. Note, too, that many of the newer operating system user interfaces, such as Microsoft Windows, include the common features of desktop organizers.

Statistical Packages

Traditionally, statistical analysis of large quantities of data has been a time-consuming, error-prone task. Because of the computer's speed and accuracy, analyzing data was one of its earliest uses. **Statistical packages** such as IBM's Minitab, SPSS (Statistical Packages for the Social Sciences), and SAS

(Statistical Analysis System) can perform virtually any statistical operation such as determining standard deviations, variances, and so forth. Versions of statistics packages are available for micros, minis, and mainframes.

Communications Software

Chapter 7 discussed using hardware such as a modem and telephone lines to send and receive data between computer systems. Communications software allows you to set the parameters, such as the baud rate and error-checking procedures, that allow computers to communicate with one another. The baud rate determines the speed at which the data is sent. Common baud rates are 1200, 2400, and 9600 bits per second. Many communications packages include features such as auto-dialing. Some commonly used packages are SmartCom, Kermit, ProComm, Crosstalk, and Mirror.

In a Nutshell

Specialized Application Packages

Integrated Packages	Framework *(Ashton-Tate)* Symphony *(Lotus)* Enable *(Software Group)*
Desktop Publishing	PageMaker *(Aldus)* Ventura Publisher *(Xerox)* Ready, Set, Go! *(Letraset)*
Graphing and Charting	Freelance Plus *(Lotus)* Harvard Graphics *(Software Publishing)*
Illustration	MacPaint, MacDraw *(Claris)* PC Paintbrush *(ZSoft)* Illustrator *(Adobe)* Cricket Draw *(Cricket)* Corel Draw *(Corel)* Micrografx Designer *(Micrografx)*
Accounting	Dac-Easy Accounting *(Dac)* Peachtree Accounting *(Peachtree)* SBT *(SBT Corp.)* Open Systems *(Open Systems)* AccPack *(Computer Associates)*
Project Management	SuperProject Expert *(Computer Associates)* MacProject II *(Claris)*
Desktop Organizers	SideKick *(Borland)*
Statistical	Minitab *(IBM)* SAS *(SAS Institute)*
Communications	SmartCom *(Hayes)* Crosstalk *(Crosstalk Communications)* Mirror *(Softklone)* ProComm *(DataStorm)* Kermit *(public domain)*

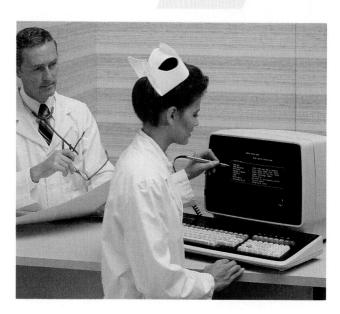

8-24 A vertical application for hospital use includes billing, inventory, maintaining patient charts, and ordering modules, all with customized entry screens. *Courtesy:* Burroughs.

Vertical Packages

The applications software discussed so far, such as desktop publishing and graphics packages, are examples of **horizontal packages**, which are useful in a broad range of business and personal situations. For example, desktop publishing software can be used to create a research paper for a graduate student or a progress report for a high-level executive. In contrast, a second group of applications, called **vertical packages**, are designed to meet the highly specialized needs of a specific industry or business (Figure 8-24).

An example of a vertical package is software used to perform the business tasks in optometrists' offices. The software might schedule appointments, maintain patient records, send bills, and keep track of employees' work schedules. However, the software attempts to take into account the needs of optometrists as compared to other groups of professionals, such as lawyers, or even closely related groups of professionals, such as dentists. Vertical packages are common in manufacturing. These programs schedule equipment and maintain inventories according to orders currently outstanding and allow for the efficient use of personnel and equipment.

Purchasing Applications Software

Choosing the correct software for a specific application can be a time-consuming process. Wrong decisions are costly, both in equipment usage and wasted staff time. Some important considerations are:

◆ **What hardware will you use?** If you must work only with existing hardware, this will narrow the field considerably. If you are in a situation where both DOS and Macintosh machines are used, you may want to get software that has versions that can be used on both—Microsoft Word and Aldus's PageMaker are examples of such packages. Although you will not be able to use the same version of software on both IBM and Macintosh micros, you will eliminate having to learn two different programs. You may also be able to move files between systems more easily.

◆ **What software meets your needs?** This seems self-evident; however, it is amazing how many people purchase software without determining whether it meets all their requirements. It is a good idea to write down your requirements and show them to the salespeople helping you select a package. Have them demonstrate how specific tasks are performed. If possible, get a demonstration package to test.

◆ **Do you already have software that can be used for the new purpose?** Sometimes people do not realize the full capabilities of the software they already own. This may be particularly true of managers in large companies. Consult with other employees who use software to perform similar tasks. Are they using any software you could adapt to your needs? For example, the word processing package WordPerfect 5.0 has a variety of desktop publishing capabilities; therefore it may not be necessary to buy separate DTP software. Using an existing package can save both time and money.

◆ **What do other people use?** Talk to people you know who use software to perform the types of tasks you want to computerize. Ask them specific questions. What do they like or dislike about the program? Would they buy the same package again? Consult some of the better-known journals such as *PC Magazine*, *PC World*, and *MacWorld*; they do comparative evaluations of software.

◆ **Is there any free software available for your application?** Free software is called *public domain software* and can be obtained from computer user groups or electronic bulletin boards. For example, there are many public domain desktop organizers and communications programs.

◆ **How difficult is it to learn?** Make certain you have realistic expectations about how long it will take you to get actual use out of the software. Also make certain that the documentation is readable and complete.

◆ **Can the new software use files from software you already own?** For example, if you are purchasing a charting and graphing program to create presentation graphics using spreadsheet output, be certain you can import files from your spreadsheet into the program.

◆ **What kind of technical support will you get?** Many software companies have "hot line" telephone numbers that provide immediate answers to your technical questions. Some manufacturers and computer stores run training sessions.

◆ **Last, where will you purchase the software?** Software for common microcomputers such as IBM-compatibles and the Macintosh is available from a variety of sources, including retail computer stores and mail-order houses. Using a retail store allows you to compare a variety of programs. The salespeople should be trained to point out the advantages and disadvantages of the various packages and help you select one to meet your needs. In addition, they may offer their own training programs, possibly even at your place of business. However, mail-order houses have several distinct advantages. They offer discounts and generally have a large inventory. Many offer next-day service. If you are a novice, getting assistance from a retail store will usually outweigh any additional cost. If you are more experienced, the money saved by ordering from a mail order house may be more important.

SELF-TEST

1. Software packages that allow users to integrate text and graphics to format professional-quality publications are called _____ _____ packages.
2. (**T** *or* **F**) Most up-to-date word processing packages have many desktop publishing features.
3. Graphics such as overhead transparencies that are used for business meetings are called _____ _____.

4. (**T** *or* **F**) CAD programs use bit-mapped graphics.
5. Software that can be used freely by anyone, without charge, is called _____ software.

SOLUTIONS 1) desktop publishing. 2) True. 3) presentation graphics, 4) False. 5) public-domain.

SUMMARY

Operating systems enable computers to run efficiently. They have two parts: the *kernel*, which manages system resources; and the *user interface*, which allows the user to communicate with the hardware. Common features of operating systems are:

♦ *Multiprogramming and multitasking*—the ability to place several programs in main memory and rapidly switch the CPU between them to execute instructions.
♦ *Multiprocessing*—using several processors concurrently to allow more than one program to be executed at a time.
♦ *Virtual memory*—swapping modules of a program between secondary storage and primary storage as needed.
♦ *Virtual machine*—creating for each user the appearance of a separate machine running its own operating system.

DOS (*MS-DOS* or *PC-DOS*) was designed as a *text-oriented operating system* to be used with IBM and IBM-compatible personal computers. Users enter specific DOS commands with DOS 3.3 or lower; beginning with DOS 4.0 users can select commands from a menu. User interface packages such as Microsoft Windows can be used to make the system more user-friendly. *OS/2*, the operating system for IBM's line of PS/2 computers, has a user-friendly graphical interface called the *Presentation Manager.*

The Macintosh was the first popular microcomputer to have a *graphical interface*, called the Finder. It uses a *mouse* to manipulate *icons*, small symbols that represent files and other objects, on a *desktop*. Multi-Finder, an extension of the Finder, provides for multi-tasking. Although a graphical interface and a mouse were first introduced on the Macintosh, both are now available on IBM microcomputer systems.

UNIX was originally developed for use by programmers in research and development. It is increasingly implemented on a wide range of systems, from microcomputers to mainframes.

Several operating systems have been developed for the IBM S 360/370 families of business mainframes and their new versions, such as 43xx, 30xx, and 9370. *MVS* provides for multiprocessing and the efficient use of virtual storage. *VM* allows several different operating systems to be used simultaneously on the same system.

Desktop publishing allows you to integrate text and graphics and create sophisticated page layouts for documents that are professional looking and of typeset quality. You create simple graphics using the DTP software; more sophisticated graphics can be created by separate graphics packages and placed into the document.

Graphics packages can be subdivided into *graphing and charting packages* and *general illustration packages*. Graphing and charting packages, often called *presentation graphics*, create many different types of charts and graphs. Often the data from a spreadsheet is used to generate the illustration. The graphs can be printed on paper, or on clear film for overhead projectors, or they can be made into slides.

Painting programs and drawing programs are types of illustration packages. *Painting programs*, such as MacPaint, create bit-mapped graphics, which consist of patterns of dots.

Drawing programs use combinations of lines, circles, squares, and so on, to create *vector graphics,* or graphics consisting of lines, arcs, and other shapes. *Computer-aided design* and drafting packages are highly sophisticated drawing packages that engineers and architects use to create complex drawings.

Accounting packages perform a wide variety of accounting functions such as *general ledger, accounts receivable,* and *accounts payable.* A wide variety of packages are available, depending on the needs and size of the company.

Project management software allows users to set up schedules and allocate personnel and resources for projects. As the project progresses, personnel and resources can be re-allocated as needed. Most packages allow you to create *Gantt* and *PERT charts.*

Desktop organizers perform many everyday tasks such as maintaining address lists, appointment schedules, and so on. On-screen notepads allow you to write reminders to yourself, and on-screen calculators perform arithmetic. These packages are held in primary memory while other applications are in use, and therefore can be called up without leaving the current program you are running.

Statistical packages perform sophisticated statistical analysis of data.

Communications packages allow you to set common communications parameters so that computers and terminals can exchange data.

Horizontal packages are developed to meet a specific need of many people in many business situations; word processing and spreadsheets are horizontal packages. *Vertical packages* are designed to meet a broad range of needs of a highly specialized market, such as for lawyers' offices or auto parts shops.

KEY TERMS

Bit-mapped graphics	Presentation graphics
Computer-aided design and drafting (CAD)	Project management software
Desktop organizer	Shell
Desktop publishing (DTP)	Statistical package
	Style sheet
Gantt chart	Supervisor
Graphing and charting package	Swapping
	Template
Horizontal package	Text-oriented
Icon	Tool
Illustration package	Upwardly compatible
Kernel	User-friendly
Multiple virtual storage	User interface
Multiprocessing	Vector graphics
Multiprogramming	Vertical package
Multitasking	Virtual machine
Object-oriented	Virtual memory
Personal information manager	Virtual storage
PERT chart	Window

CHAPTER SELF-TEST

1. The _____ is the part of an operating system that allocates computer resources.

2. _____ permits a system with more that one CPU to execute several programs simultaneously.

3. (T *or* F) Virtual machine operating systems allow you to run, on a single computer, software requiring many different operating systems.

4. When operating systems use _____, they move modules in and out of primary memory as needed to create the illusion that primary storage is larger than it really is.

5. The graphical user interface for use with OS/2 is known as the _____ _____.

6. (T *or* F) UNIX is a large, complex operating system developed to be used primarily on mainframes.

7. (T *or* F) MultiFinder is a version of the Macintosh Finder that allows users to run more than one application concurrently.

8. (T *or* F) The Apple Macintosh was unique when it first came out because it had a user-friendly graphical interface.

9. (T *or* F) Desktop publishing allows you to create documents that are similar in quality to typeset documents.

10. (T *or* F) Editing is usually easier to do in a desktop publishing package than with word processing software.

11. Freehand drawing can be done with *(bit-mapped graphics/vector graphics).*

12. (T *or* F) In desktop publishing, standard designs can be created by a professional designer, while the actual formatting of text is done by someone else who is trained to use DTP software.

13. Graphing and charting programs are commonly referred to as "business graphics" or _____ graphics.

14. _____ software is specialized drawing software that helps architects and engineers create complex designs on the screen.

15. The three types of modules most commonly used in accounting programs are _____, _____, and _____.

16. Two kinds of timelines that can be produced with project management software are _____ and _____ charts.

17. (T *or* F) Communications software is simplified word processing software that can be used to write short letters and memos.

18. *(Horizontal/vertical)* packages are developed to meet a common need in many kinds of businesses, whereas *(horizontal/vertical)* packages are designed to meet a range of needs of a particular business or industry.

19. (T *or* F) PageMaker is an example of a vertical package.

20. (T *or* F) Desktop organizers provide an interface between the user and the operating system.

SOLUTIONS 1) kernel or supervisor. 2) Multiprocessing. 3) True. 4) virtual memory. 5) Presentation Manager. 6) False. It was developed for minis and is currently used on micros and minis as well as mainframes. 7) True. 8) True. 9) True. 10) False. 11) bit-mapped graphics. 12) True. 13) presentation. 14) Computer-aided design and drafting (CAD). 15) general ledger; accounts receivable; accounts payable. 16) Gantt and PERT. 17) False. 18) Horizontal; vertical. 19) False. 20) False.

PROBLEM-SOLVING APPLICATIONS

1. If you have access to two different types of microcomputers, such as the IBM PS/2 and the Macintosh, compare how a specific operating system command is executed on each of them. For example, what command does each computer use to list the names of the files on a disk? Which method do you prefer? Why?

2. Plan either an annual report or a business proposal for a small company. Explain which of the types of application packages discussed in this chapter you might use to produce an attractive, professional-looking final document or presentation. How would these application packages tie in with the more common office packages such as word processing, spreadsheets, and database management systems?

Software Development Languages and Tools

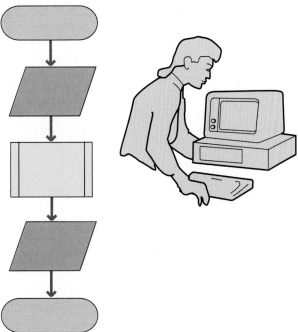

When you have completed this chapter, you will be able to:

- ✔ Evaluate the advantages and disadvantages of purchasing packaged software programs as compared with developing customized application programs.

- ✔ Explain how design tools, such as flowcharts, pseudocode, and hierarchy charts, help in developing well-structured programs.

- ✔ List the characteristics and explain the advantages of structured programming.

- ✔ Discuss the five generations of programming languages and list characteristics and examples of each.

Chapter 9

Chapter Outline

Early programmers generally wrote small, mathematically oriented programs that were designed to be used alone, not as part of an overall information system. The methods used to write these programs were similar to those used by the pioneers to build their homes. Having limited resources, those early settlers had a small number of considerations. For example, the size of the home, where it was to be located, and what materials were available for use might be their only concerns. We have come a long way in building homes since that time. Today we draw blueprints, comply with zoning laws, and have one specialist for the plumbing, another for the wiring, and so on. Such planning is necessary because homes are more complex, our resources have increased, and far more homes are being built. In addition, our expectations of what features are needed in a home have greatly expanded in the last two hundred years.

The same is true of software development. People want software that not only works but that is also user-friendly and that taps the full potential of increasingly sophisticated hardware. Moreover, the software products themselves are much more complex than in the past. As a result, a variety of software design tools, similar to blueprints, have been created to allow the programmer to develop the logic of a complex program before it is written in a programming language. In addition, hundreds of programming languages are now available, each having specific strengths. This chapter presents the tools used to design programs, along with the advantages and disadvantages of the more popular programming languages currently available (Figure 9–1).

Packaged Software vs. Customized Software

The application software packages discussed in Chapter 8 were written by commercial software developers to be sold for a profit. These packages can be purchased at computer stores or from mail-order companies. They often meet users' needs very well. However, there are times when a company may want to consider developing its own set of programs to meet specialized requirements.

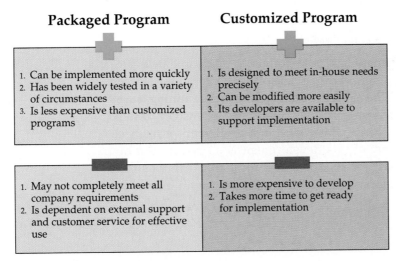

Packaged Program	Customized Program
1. Can be implemented more quickly 2. Has been widely tested in a variety of circumstances 3. Is less expensive than customized programs	1. Is designed to meet in-house needs precisely 2. Can be modified more easily 3. Its developers are available to support implementation
1. May not completely meet all company requirements 2. Is dependent on external support and customer service for effective use	1. Is more expensive to develop 2. Takes more time to get ready for implementation

Customized software has the advantage of being designed specifically to meet a company's unique needs. Companies that have information processing departments often develop these customized programs in-house, and the computer professionals that work on the software have the advantage of being familiar with the company's procedures. Also, software that is written in-house can be more readily altered as needed.

However, sometimes there may be a need to go outside the company's own information processing department for customized software. If the information processing department does not have the specialized skills or if the staff is overworked, consultants or software development companies specializing in customized programs can be hired to develop the software. Some software development companies specialize in a certain type of product, such as accounting packages, scheduling packages, and so on.

Managers must ask several questions when they are deciding whether to develop new software or to use an available commercial package:

- **Is a commercial package available that meets the user's specifications?** Some packages allow for expansion and modification according to user specifications. Any package should be rigorously tested on the company's own data before it is purchased. Computer professionals in a company often develop a series of benchmark tests to help evaluate and compare software packages. These tests are designed to ensure that the software product can perform all of the processing required. Benchmark tests allow potential users to compare the results obtained by different packages under similar circumstances.

- **Does the company already own the hardware necessary to use this software, or will new hardware need to be purchased?**

- **Does the software company provide good support?** Will the vendor be readily available to help with implementation? Many companies provide training seminars and "hot-line" telephone numbers that allow users to obtain answers to problems quickly. Programs developed in-house can also be modified in-house. This is an advantage not often available with a commercial package.

- **Does the information processing department have the skills and time to develop a customized program?** If not, are outside consultants available?

- **What is the time requirement?** It takes longer to develop a new program than to adopt an existing commercial software package. Also, the commercial software may be of higher quality because, assuming it was developed by a reputable company, it will have been extensively tested. Commercial packages are put on the market only after years of research and development. The cost of this development is shared by the numerous users who purchase the product. Most companies cannot afford such a research and development effort on their own for an individual customized program.

◆ **How does the cost of developing a new program compare with the cost of the commercial package?** There are always unforeseen problems during the development of a new program; care must be taken not to underestimate the cost of software development.

The Software Development Cycle

The creation of new software is a complex process involving a number of people. A large program cannot be efficiently written by a single programmer, so programmers often work in teams, each team writing code for a segment of the larger program. The new programs must be made to fit the existing software. In addition, the overall system must be designed in such a way that new employees can use it and modify it, even if the original team is no longer there. This complex process is described as the **software development cycle.** Figure 9–2 illustrates the following steps seven steps involved in creating a program:

1. Develop the program specifications.

2. Design a solution.

3. Code the program and translate it into machine language.

4. Debug and test the program.

5. Install the program.

6. Maintain the program.

7. Document the program.

When the users' needs change and the program's usefulness diminishes, the cycle begins all over again, and the software is redesigned to meet the new program specifications.

Developing the Program Specifications

It is impossible to develop a solution to a problem if you do not have a clear understanding of the problem itself. This fact may seem self-evident; however, a surprising amount of software has been written that does not meet the needs of the end-user because programmers did not really understand the problem to be solved. Today, **systems analysts** are assigned to projects to help avoid this potential problem and to encourage efficient software development. The systems analyst and the future users of the software join together to develop a clear understanding of the project's purpose.

The systems analyst carefully listens to the users and determines not only how their needs can be met but also how the new software can be efficiently integrated into the existing information system. The assumption is that it is the users who are most knowledgeable about the tasks that the software must perform. However, users are not generally computer professionals. On the other hand, the **programmer** has the technical skills to write the software but often does not have the business expertise or knowledge of the overall information system to determine how to create the software specifications most effectively. As a result, the systems analyst

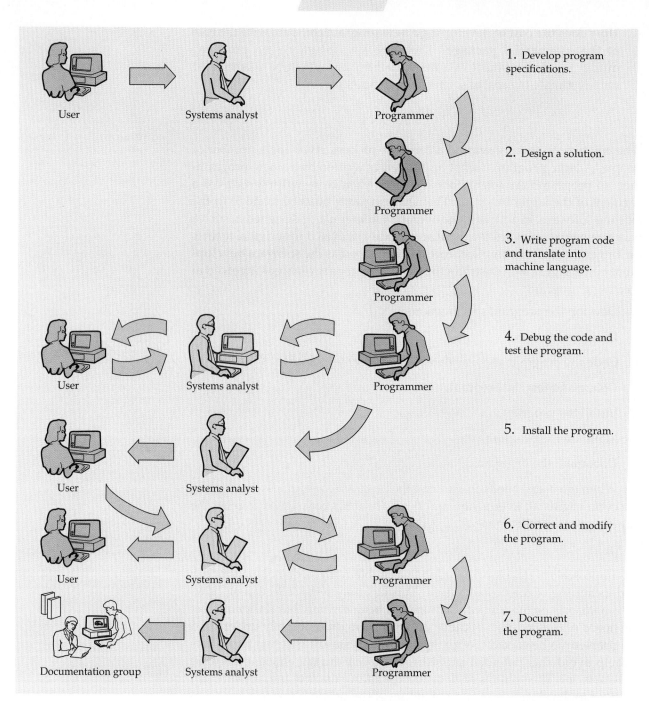

1. Develop program specifications.

2. Design a solution.

3. Write program code and translate into machine language.

4. Debug the code and test the program.

5. Install the program.

6. Correct and modify the program.

7. Document the program.

9–2 The development of well-designed programs follows these seven steps, known as the software development cycle.

must serve as the liaison between the user group and the programmer. It is the responsibility of the systems analyst—with the help of users and programmers—to develop precise specifications for the software's input, processing, and output.

In smaller companies, one computer professional, called a **programmer analyst**, may serve as both programmer and systems analyst. This person must have programming skills as well as an understanding of how to integrate new software into the information system.

Designing a Solution

After the specifications have been agreed upon, the systems analyst gives them to the programmer, who designs a solution. The programmer creates an **algorithm**, which can be thought of as similar to a recipe; it is a sequential listing of all the steps necessary to obtain the needed output from the input. These steps must be listed in the order in which they are to be performed. For example, the following simplified algorithm lists the steps necessary for preparing a customer invoice:

1. Read the account number, the unit price of the item purchased, and the quantity purchased.

2. Calculate the bill by multiplying the unit price by the quantity purchased.

3. Print the account number and the total bill.

Steps such as those described above will be accomplished by **subprograms**, or program modules, that will fit together with other subprograms to accomplish an overall procedure.

In addition to planning the logical steps in a program, the programmer should include numerous error-control routines. For example, this program is supposed to multiply the unit price by the quantity purchased. A full program should include routines that first ensure that the necessary numeric data has been entered and that it has reasonable values. For example, the unit price should not be either greater or less than the company's actual range of unit prices.

A number of problem-solving tools can be used to develop algorithms for specific tasks and to plan the logic of an overall program. Several commonly used tools are discussed here.

Flowcharts.   A **flowchart** is a pictorial representation of the logic flow to be used in a program. It illustrates the major program elements and how they are logically integrated. The flow lines in a flowchart depict the logical flow of instructions in a program. As shown in Figure 9–3, each symbol denotes either a particular operation or a series of operations to be performed by a subprogram. The programmer writes an instruction inside each symbol. Examine the flowchart in Figure 9–4, which shows the process for calculating the amount of a bill. This program will read the needed data, transfer control to a subprogram that calculates the bill, and finally print the results.

Pseudocode.   Flowcharts for large, complex programs can become extremely cumbersome to draw; it is also difficult to make modifications to a flowchart without completely redrawing it. Also, because the flowchart is so large, the logic structures can be difficult to follow. Programmers often use an alternative planning tool called **pseudocode**, that compensates for some of these shortcomings. The prefix "pseudo" means "false"; therefore, pseudocode statements are "false" code, or code-like statements, used in an actual program. Pseudocode serves a similar function as a flowchart in that it is used to plan and describe the logic to be used in a program. While

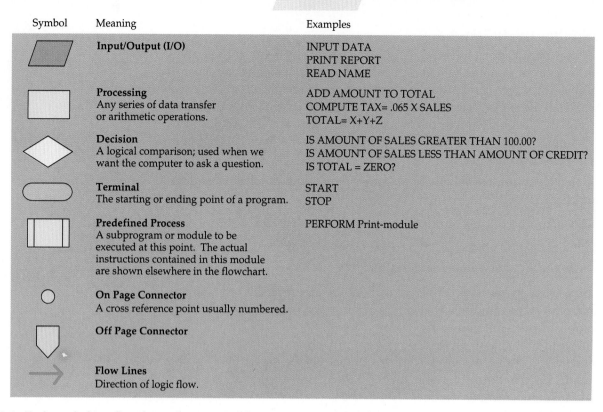

Symbol	Meaning	Examples
(parallelogram)	**Input/Output (I/O)**	INPUT DATA PRINT REPORT READ NAME
(rectangle)	**Processing** Any series of data transfer or arithmetic operations.	ADD AMOUNT TO TOTAL COMPUTE TAX= .065 X SALES TOTAL= X+Y+Z
(diamond)	**Decision** A logical comparison; used when we want the computer to ask a question.	IS AMOUNT OF SALES GREATER THAN 100.00? IS AMOUNT OF SALES LESS THAN AMOUNT OF CREDIT? IS TOTAL = ZERO?
(rounded rectangle)	**Terminal** The starting or ending point of a program.	START STOP
(predefined process symbol)	**Predefined Process** A subprogram or module to be executed at this point. The actual instructions contained in this module are shown elsewhere in the flowchart.	PERFORM Print-module
(circle)	**On Page Connector** A cross reference point usually numbered.	
(pentagon/arrow)	**Off Page Connector**	
(arrow)	**Flow Lines** Direction of logic flow.	

9–3 Each symbol in a flowchart refers to a specific computer operation.

9–4 This flowchart shows the process for calculating the amount on an invoice.

flowcharts use symbols to plan and illustrate logic, pseudocode uses words. As with flowcharts, pseudocode does not need to indicate *all* the processing details, but the overall flow of program logic should be carefully described. Figure 9–5 shows the pseudocode for calculating a customer invoice. Pseudocode is widely used in program design because it can easily represent all the programming structures that programmers need, and because its English-like language is easy to learn and understand.

Hierarchy Charts.   **Hierarchy charts** graphically demonstrate how a program can be divided into modules and how the modules relate to one another. Figure 9–6 shows a hierarchy chart for an accounting system. Each rectangle in the chart represents a program or module in the system. The main body of the program is stated at the top level. The second level subdivides the program into four accounting modules; accounts receivable, accounts payable, payroll, and financial reports. The third level represents separate modules within each program; each of these modules could be divided further. Depending on the complexity of the problem, hierarchy charts can consist of many levels.

```
Start
    Read account number, unit price, and quantity
    Perform subprogram to calculate bill
    Print account number and bill
Stop
```

9–5 In pseudocode, English words are used to express program logic.

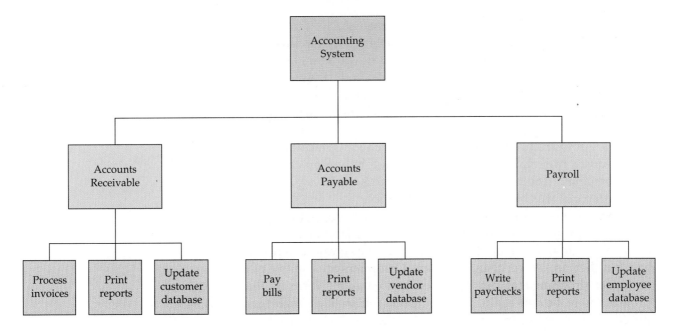

Coding the Program and Translating into Machine Language

After the logic has been designed, the programmer writes the instructions in a programming language. This process is referred to as **coding** the program. The language used depends on the system resources available, the expertise of the programmer, and the type of application. As you will learn later in this chapter, each programming language has tasks for which it is particularly well suited.

In order to be executed, a program must be in **machine language**. Each type of computer has its own such language. In each case, a machine language is a complex language that uses actual machine addresses and cumbersome operation codes (Figure 9–7). Because of the complexity of machine language and the fact that it is different for each type of computer, most programs are written in symbolic languages, such as BASIC or COBOL. **Symbolic languages** use instructions such as ADD or + instead of complex operation codes, and allow the programmer to assign names to storage locations. Thus, to add two values in a symbolic language, we might say "LET TOTAL = AMT1 + AMT2" instead of using machine language code, which might be something like 21 1047 4096. The more similar to English that a programming language is, the more **high-level** it is considered to be. Similarly, the more a language resembles machine language, the more **low-level** we say it is. BASIC and COBOL, both commonly used for programming, are relatively high-level languages.

Using symbolic languages makes software much easier to code. The program is not, however, executable in that form. That is, it cannot be executed until it has been translated or converted into machine language. The computer system itself performs this translation process, using a translator program that reads a symbolic program as input and converts it to machine language. The symbolic program is called the **source program**, and the translated program in machine language is called the **object program**.

9–6 Hierarchy charts break a large task down into increasingly smaller tasks, which then become subprograms, or modules.

9–7 Machine language code uses actual machine addresses and operation codes so that there is no need for translation.

Let total = AMT1+AMT2

Symbolic language

21 1047 4096

Machine language

The two main types of translator programs used to translate programs written in high-level languages into machine language are **interpreters** and **compilers**. Interpreters and compilers break down a single high-level instruction or language statement into several machine-language instructions.

Interpreters translate the program one statement at a time as the program is actually being run on the computer. Each statement is translated and executed before the interpreter proceeds to the next statement. This process continues until the end of the program is reached. **Compilers** translate the entire source program into machine language in one process, creating an object program. Another program, referred to as the *linking loader* or *linkage editor*, prepares the object program for execution.

Interpreters are commonly used in the simpler programming languages such as BASIC, whereas most other programming languages use compilers. Interpreters do not take up as much space in the computer's primary storage, but they are slower than compilers. Compilers are capable of creating an object program that can be stored in executable form so that if the program is to be run again, it need not be retranslated each time. Thus, programs that are to be run on a regularly scheduled basis are nearly always written in languages that can be compiled.

Debugging and Testing

It is critical for a program's logic to be correct; when the program's structure is not logical, the program will not run correctly and the output will not be accurate. The final test of a program's correctness is to run it and examine its output.

Debugging involves finding and correcting any errors—"bugs"—in a program. Debugging begins even before the program is executed. That is, all programs should first be **desk-checked**; the programmer manually traces through the program from beginning to end, visually checking for errors. Errors that can occur can be divided into two categories: **syntax errors** and **logic errors**. Syntax errors are made when the programmer violates the grammatical rules of the language; these are often caused by simple typing mistakes. Most syntax errors can be located by carefully desk-checking a program for typing mistakes. If syntax errors are not caught before the program is entered into the computer, the language's translator program will generally find them and print error messages indicating the type of error. Programs cannot be fully translated into machine language until all syntax errors are corrected.

The first step, then, is to eliminate all syntax errors. But programs without syntax errors are not necessarily correct. That is, the program may follow the grammatical rules of the language but still generate incorrect output or no output at all. This incorrect output occurs if there are logic errors; such errors may be caused by mistakes in the sequencing of instructions or by instructions that do not include all the needed steps.

Program testing becomes very important in pinpointing logic errors. Testing involves executing the program with different sets of data to determine whether it always produces correct results. A program with a logic rror sometimes outputs correct results most of the time but produces incorrect results in certain situations. For example, a payroll program may correctly calculate paychecks for employees working forty hours or less but incorrectly calculate paychecks involving overtime pay. It is critical to catch all logic errors before a program is implemented. Three techniques are useful in detecting logic errors:

1. **The programmer should recheck the logic** as outlined in the design tools (the flowchart and/or pseudocode, and the hierarchy chart). Is there a flaw in the logic? Does the logic of the actual program correspond to the logic in the design tool?

2. **The programmer should prepare test data with great care.** Test data is data that is used as input during the debugging phase. The programmer must make certain that test data incorporates all possible types of inpu the program includes a test for a specific condition, then the test data sho also include that condition.

3. **The programmer should compare computer-produced results with manually-produced test output.** If a discrepancy occurs, then the problem must be found and resolved. When a logic error is detected, the programmer must correct the source program and then retranslate it. With some types of errors, the computer prints a message flagging the error; other errors must be found by the programmer. Whenever an error occurs, the program is corrected and executed again with the test data to ensure that it now produces correct output. Usually, numerous test runs are required before a program is fully debugged.

An adage in information processing says that because of the large volume of data, anything that can possibly go wrong with input data *will* eventually go wrong. Testing a program with all types of input and including many error control routines minimizes the risks of undetected errors.

Installing the Program

After the program has been thoroughly tested and debugged, it is ready to be installed. The method used for installing or converting to a new program, particularly when it is a large one, can have a significant effect on user satisfaction. It is important for the systems analyst and the programmers to work with end-users during the conversion process to provide them with thorough training, and to ensure that the output is what is desired (Figure 9–8).

There are many ways of converting to new software. One is simply an immediate (or "cold turkey") conversion. This is often necessary, and if the program being implemented is fairly small, it can work well. For larger programs, many companies use a pilot conversion process in which the new software is implemented in only one part of the company, while the majority of the company's processing continues to be done using the old method; this allows any remaining problems to be worked out before the software has wider usage. Alternately, some companies choose the safest and most costly route, which involves continuing to use the old system along with the new one, comparing results for completeness and accuracy. This is called a

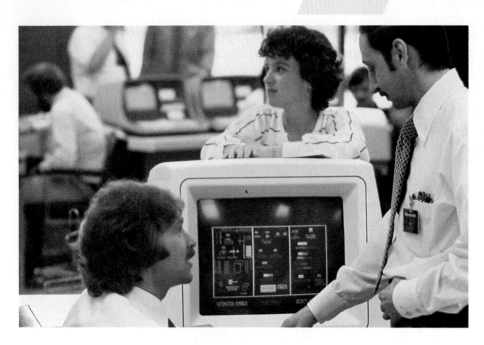

9–8 A systems analyst, programmer, and end-user gather to discuss the implementation of a pilot version of the firm's new software. *Courtesy:* Honeywell.

parallel run. The old system is discontinued only when the new system has proven itself. When the program is written in subprograms, or modules, each module may be implemented one at a time; the next module is introduced only when the procedures for the first module have been completed. In Chapter 10 you will find that the methods used to convert to an entirely new information system are very similar to those used to convert to a new program.

The approach used for conversion depends on the particular situation, the financial resources available, and the amount of testing that was performed on the software prior to installation. However, regardless of the conversion plan, it is vitally important that the systems analyst and programmer keep in close communication with the user group during this transition period.

Maintaining the Program

Studies have shown that only about 25 percent of programmers' time is spent in developing new software. The remaining 75 percent is used to maintain existing software. The types of maintenance performed falls into two broad categories: (1) modifications that involve correcting errors and making the software easier to use and more standardized, and (2) modifications that are necessary because of changing needs. If the program was designed properly, the first group of modifications will be small and can be performed when time is available. Increasing the ease of use and eliminating even minor bugs often saves significant amounts of employee time and improves user satisfaction.

All corporations have changing needs, and software is continually being modified to meet those needs. For example, an accounting department may need to have a program modified to incorporate new accounting procedures or changes in the tax laws. Often the user group may want the software to

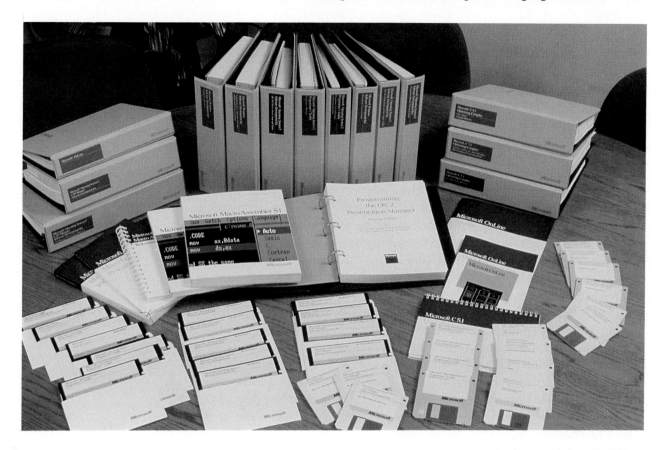

perform additional tasks that were not in the original specifications. In such a situation, new modules may need to be added to the existing program.

Documenting the Program

Documentation, which is used to explain programs to people, can take a variety of forms. Some documentation is built into the program itself as comments. Most comes in the form of manuals. Some manuals are for program users and explain how to use the program. Other documentation explains the actual methodology of the program. This documentation is vitally important to systems analysts and programmers if the program needs to be modified (Figure 9–9).

9–9 The complete package for Microsoft's Presentation Manager includes software and diagnostic disks, user manuals, and detailed documentation for programmers. *Courtesy:* Microsoft Corporation.

Structured Programming

In the early days of programming, as programmers began writing longer and more sophisticated software, they quickly ran into difficulties. Their programs consisted of long lists of instructions, one after the other. It was hard to determine where one task stopped and another started. As a result, the logic of the programs was difficult to follow and making modifications at a later time was extremely difficult. In the mid-1960s, the idea of **structured programming** was conceived to solve these problems, and it is now the standard for programming. Structured programming is a standardized approach that creates a program as a series of interrelated subprograms, or modules; it also uses a set of rules that help in creating programs that are not only standardized but are also easy to read, maintain, and modify.

Top-Down Design

Well-designed programs not only use a structured methodology, but they are also created using a **top-down design**. In top-down programming, the programmer starts with the overall problem and divides it into smaller subprograms or modules; major tasks are undertaken first, and minor tasks are left for a later, more detailed phase. As you undoubtedly know from experience, it is easier to complete a large job if you divide it into smaller tasks and complete them one at a time. This is the methodology used in top-down design. Using top-down design can be compared to developing a research paper. First, you create a general outline, going to the library to determine the main topics to be covered. From this general outline, more detailed outlines on each subtopic are created. Finally, you fill in the details and write the actual paper.

The process of using top-down design to develop a program is similar to writing a research paper. First, the required output and needed input are specified. Then the problem solution is subdivided by task. Hierarchy charts are helpful in developing the logic in a top-down program because they define the problem's subtasks and how they relate to one another. The hierarchy chart performs the same function as the outline in developing the research paper. When the final program is coded, each rectangle in the hierarchy chart can be written as a separate module.

Modules are small subprograms contained within larger ones. Each subprogram performs a specific task and is shown separately in a flowchart or in pseudocode; Figure 9–10 is an example of how a subprogram appears in flowcharts. When the subprogram symbol is encountered in the main module, control transfers to the corresponding subprogram. After the subprogram is performed, control returns to the symbol following the subprogram symbol in the main module. A given program can contain dozens of subprograms.

Coding a program in modules allows several programmers to work on the same program. Each programmer can be assigned a module or modules that best fit his or her skills. When programs are designed to be modular, the testing process is simplified because a single module or small group of modules can be tested separately; then, when all modules are separately debugged, they are combined into the entire program for more complete testing. Contrast this with the difficulty of trying to locate an error in one long program, as you must when the programming is unstructured or otherwise poorly designed.

The Four Logic Structures

In the mid-1960s two mathematicians, Corrado Bohm and Giuseppe Jacopini, proved that any programming problem, regardless of the language used, can be solved by using the appropriate combination of three basic structures: the sequence, the decision structure, and iteration (looping). Since then, a fourth structure called the case structure has been added as a

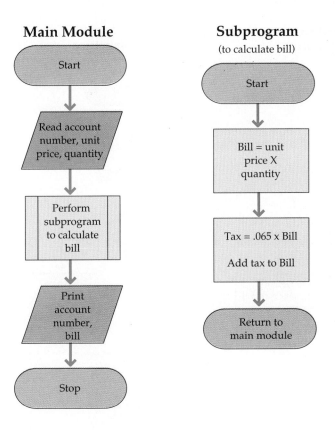

Main Module

Start

Read account number, unit price, quantity

Perform subprogram to calculate bill

Print account number, bill

Stop

Subprogram
(to calculate bill)

Start

Bill = unit price X quantity

Tax = .065 x Bill

Add tax to Bill

Return to main module

9–10 Dividing a program into modules or subprograms for specific procedural tasks simplifies program structure. These modules can then be used to build other programs.

9–11 The branch operation transfers control from one part of a program to another, making program logic very difficult to follow.

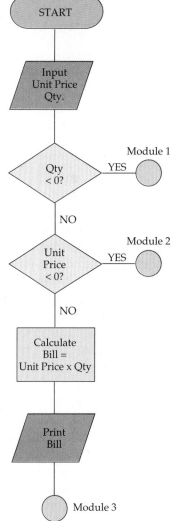

START

Input Unit Price Qty.

Qty < 0?   YES   Module 1

NO

Unit Price < 0?   YES   Module 2

NO

Calculate Bill = Unit Price x Qty

Print Bill

Module 3

logical control construct. Although the case structure is really a variant of the decision structure, it has some complex properties that make it useful in programs.

Until Bohm and Jacopini's work, the unconditional branch—also called the GOTO statement—was commonly used in programming. The unconditional branch statement, illustrated in Figure 9–11, transfers control to other statements in the program. Today computer scientists believe that unconditional branches should be avoided because they make program logic convoluted and difficult to follow. Two major principles of top-down structured programming require dividing programs into modules and avoiding the use of unconditional branches. Following is a brief description of the four logic structures currently used in structured programs.

The **sequence structure** consists of a series of statements that are executed in the order in which they occur in the program. In the absence of any other instructions to the computer, all programs are executed in sequence. The flowchart in Figure 9–4 illustrates a sequence of instructions.

The **decision structure** involves testing a condition to determine what sequence of instructions is to be executed next in a program. The action or path taken next by a program depends on the result of the test, which will always be either true or false. In Figure 9–12, the double-alternative decision structure is a modification of Figure 9–4. It tests to see if "QUANTITY > 100?" is true. If the value of QUANTITY is more than 100, control is transferred to a subprogram that calculates the discount price; otherwise, a second subprogram is called to calculate the regular price. As shown in

Sequence structure

Double-alternative decision structure

Single-alternative decision structure

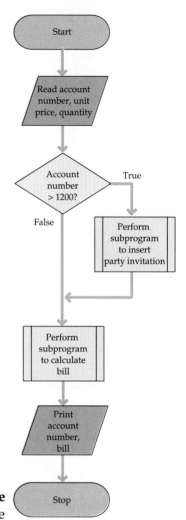

Figure 9–12, the decision structure has two variations: the **single-alternative decision structure** and the **double-alternative decision structure**. In the single-alternative decision structure, an action is taken if the condition is true; otherwise no action is taken. A double-alternative decision structure takes one action if the condition is true and another if it is false.

The **iteration** or **looping** structure permits a program to execute a series of steps repeatedly. The looping structure shown in Figure 9–12 demonstrates how iteration or looping can be depicted in a flowchart. Loops allow a specified group of instructions to be repeated as many times as required. In this example, the loop is repeated until all the bills have been processed. Iteration is extremely important in programs; often the same series of tasks must be performed hundreds and even thousands of times.

The **case structure** consists of a series of single-alternative decision structures that check for a series of conditions. When a condition is true, the specified action is taken. In the case structure in Figure 9–12, the grade code of a student (1, 2, 3, or 4), is used to determine the corresponding class (freshmen, sophomore, junior, or senior).

Case structure

Looping structure

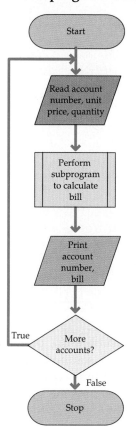

9–12 These five flowcharts illustrate logical control constructs.

We have illustrated the four structures with flowcharts. In practice, however, many programs are designed using pseudocode as a planning tool; Figure 9–13 illustrates these four logical structures using pseudocode.

All structured programs, no matter which language they are written in, use these four logical control structures to determine the sequence in which instructions are to be executed.

Advantages of Top-Down Structured Programming

Because structured programs are precisely written, they are more likely to comply with the original program specifications than are unstructured programs. They are divided into modules by tasks, making the logic easier to follow. Confining programs to the four basic structures also makes the logic of the program easier to debug. When errors do occur, it is easier to locate them because each module can be tested separately.

Structured programming also reduces the time it takes to modify and evaluate existing software. Modifying a structured program is easier because the modification is limited to the module performing the tasks being changed. If the program needs to be expanded, new modules can be more easily inserted. The remaining program is basically unchanged. Structured programming has become the standard in the computer industry because it makes programs easier to modify, expand, and debug.

Structured Walkthroughs

One method of making programs more standardized and reducing debugging time is the **structured walkthrough**. After the programmer has developed a structured solution, a group of programmers often meets to review the design; this is a structured walkthrough. During such a structured walkthrough, the programmer obtains valuable input from other informa-

---

Pseudocode Containing a Sequence Structure

```
START
    Read account number, unit price, and quantity
    Perform subprogram to calculate bill
    Print account number and bill
STOP
```

Pseudocode for a Single-Alternative Decision Structure

```
START
    Read account number, unit price, and quantity
    IF quantity is greater than 100
        THEN perform subprogram to calculate discounted bill
        ELSE perform subprogram to calculate regular bill
    END IF
    Print account number and bill
STOP
```

Pseudocode for a Case Structure

```
CASE
    WHEN 1 Class = Freshman
    WHEN 2 Class = Sophomore
    WHEN 3 Class = Junior
    WHEN 4 Class = Senior
END CASE
```

Pseudocode for a Loop

```
START
    PERFORM UNTIL no more data
        Read account number, unit price, and quantity
        Perform subprogram to calculate bill
        Print account number and bill
    END PERFORM
STOP
```

---

tion processing professionals. The group determines whether the documented solution meets the original specifications. This group may meet several times over the course of the project. Catching errors early (particularly before the program is actually coded) saves considerable time and frustration later.

9–13 In pseudocode, English words are used to express program logic. Here, the flowcharts diagrammed in Figure 9–12 are expressed with pseudocode.

SELF-TEST

1. The two graphic tools used by programmers to plan the structure of a program are _____ and _____.

2. The English-like code that programmers use to plan programs is called _____.

3. The tests that are designed to determine the capabilities of a commercial software package in real working conditions are called _____ _____.

4. (T *or* F) It is generally less expensive and quicker to develop software in-house than to purchase a commercial package.

5. In a _____ structure, statements are executed in the order in which they occur; whereas in a _____ structure, the action taken depends on whether a condition is true or false.

6. The programming methodology that begins by breaking down a complex task into smaller tasks that are executed as modules is called _____ programming.

SOLUTIONS 1) flowcharts; hierarchy charts. 2) pseudocode. 3) benchmark tests. 4) False. 5) sequence; decision. 6) top-down or structured.

The Five Generations of Programming Languages

Computer programming languages are thought of as developing in generations. Each new generation of languages has been built on the knowledge learned from its predecessors. Currently, there are five generations. However, newer generations may be added as we learn more about artificial intelligence and the thinking processes of the human brain.

The older generations of software should not be viewed as obsolete—programs are still being written and run in languages representing all the generations. In fact, some problems are more easily solved using older languages, particularly, as you will see, third-generation languages.

Machine Language: The First Generation

Machine languages are the only languages that the computer can directly execute without the need for a translation. Machine languages are referred to as **first-generation programming languages** because they were the earliest type developed. This method of programming takes a great deal of the programmer's time, and it is easy to make mistakes. Moreover, machine language is different for each type of computer. For example, the machine language instructions for an IBM 4381 are very different from those for a VAX computer or an IBM microcomputer. When programming in machine language, the programmer must be familiar with the hardware being used. Because of all of these problems, machine language is used only rarely today.

Assembly Language: The Second Generation

To overcome some of the shortcomings of machine language, **assembly languages** were developed. Assembly languages, like machine languages, are machine dependent. Each operation is given a meaningful name such as ADD or LOAD. Assembly languages also allow the programmer to assign names to storage locations, making it much easier to refer to them. The following example contains three assembly language statements, written for a specific computer, that multiply by two the value currently stored in the location named K.

```
LOAD K
MUL TWO
SAVE K
```

Assembly languages are one step removed from machine languages, so they are referred to as **second-generation programming languages**. A translator program called an **assembler** translates assembly language statements into machine language. This translator runs very efficiently because machine languages and assembly languages are so similar. Even though assembly language statements are easier to write than machine language, the language itself is still complex. Assembly language does have the advantage of allowing the programmer to interact directly with the computer hardware; therefore, today it is most commonly used in writing operating systems or other systems programs—programs that manage hardware so that applications run more efficiently.

High-Level Languages: A Focus on the Third Generation

As computers became less expensive and more powerful and the salaries of computer professionals increased proportionally, it became necessary to simplify writing programs. Starting in the 1950s, high-level languages, or **third-generation languages (3GLs)** were developed. These symbolic languages use English-like commands to instruct the computer. Some of the characteristics and application areas for commonly used high-level languages are discussed here. Third-generation languages are also called **procedural languages**, because the programmer must develop the logic necessary to carry out each procedure.

Third-generation languages require compilers (or interpreters) to translate them into machine language. Many high-level languages, such as COBOL and Pascal, are **portable**; that is, programs written in these languages can be executed on many types of computers with minimal changes.

Several organizations have developed standards for individual programming languages, such as FORTRAN and COBOL. The most well-known of these is the American National Standards Institute (ANSI).

If software developers adhere to the standards, the resulting programs are portable. For example, a program that is written for a COBOL compiler implementing the ANSI COBOL standard released in 1985 should run with only minimal changes on any COBOL compiler that meets this standard. Unfortunately, standards have not been developed for all languages. In addition, not all software developers adhere to the standards.

We will consider third-generation languages in the order in which they were developed.

FORTRAN. In the 1950s, the majority of people using computers were scientists and engineers. The types of problems they wanted to solve required a great deal of computation. Therefore, it is not surprising that the first widely used high-level language was oriented toward these types of tasks. **FORTRAN** (*FOR*mula *TRAN*slator) was developed by IBM in the 1950s and is the oldest high-level language still being used today. Although FORTRAN is very useful for scientific and engineering applications, it is not well suited for typical business applications that require large numbers of input/output operations. Originally developed for large mainframe systems, in recent years FORTRAN has been implemented on microcomputers. Figure 9–14 shows a simple FORTRAN program.

COBOL. With the increasing use of FORTRAN in the 1950s, the business community began realizing that computers could solve many of their information processing problems. FORTRAN itself was not suited for business processing, which tends to require only simple arithmetic operations, such as calculating a bill, but must often deal with enormous quantities of data; another language, therefore, needed to be developed. In 1959 a group of computer professionals formed an organization called CODASYL (*CO*nference on *DA*ta *SY*stems *L*anguage) and held a series of meetings to establish guidelines for the development of a business-oriented language. This language was to be machine independent, easy to maintain, and English-like. **COBOL**, an acronym for *CO*mmon *B*usiness *O*riented *L*anguage, was originally released in 1960. COBOL programs that were developed shortly thereafter could run on many different kinds of computers with minimal changes. This feature was very important in large businesses where a variety of hardware is often used.

In 1968 the first ANSI version of COBOL was approved. All major computer software manufacturers began developing compilers to adhere to

```
C  ***                    PAYCHECK PROGRAM                         ***
C  ***                                                             ***
C  *** This program calculates an employee's paycheck based on the ***
C  *** number of hours the employee worked and base pay per hour.  ***
C  ****************************************************************

program PayChk

character * 12 Name
real Gross, Hours, PayRat
C
C  ----------------------------------------------------------------
C  Prompt the user for the employee's name, hours worked, and rate of
C  pay per hour.
C
print*, '     PAYCHECK PROGRAM'
print*
print*
print*, 'Enter the employee''s name:  '
read*, Hours

print*, 'Enter the hourly pay rate:'
read*, PayRat
C
C  Calculate gross pay.
C
Gross = Hours * PayRat
C
C  Print the results of the paycheck calculations for this employee.
C  Then quit.
C
print*, 'Employee Name           ', Name
print*, '    Hours Worked        ', Hours
print*, '    Pay Rate            ', PayRat
print*, '    Gross Pay           ', Gross

stop
end
```

9–14 This FORTRAN program calculates each employee's paycheck amount.

this standard. A second version of ANSI COBOL was released in 1974. This version further standardized the language and made it more efficient. However, both of these early versions needed some modifications to be totally structured. In 1985, ANSI released a long-awaited new version that standardized COBOL's structured programming methodology. Most companies have implemented this new structured COBOL. Figure 9–15 shows a structured COBOL program that can process any number of input records.

PL/1. In the early 1960s, many computer professionals believed that a single language should be developed that could meet the needs of both the business and the scientific communities. **PL/1**, an abbreviation for *Programming Language/1,* was designed to meet this purpose. PL/1 combines the major advantages and features of COBOL and FORTRAN. First released in 1966, it was originally designed to be used on the IBM System 360 family of computers. Today there are several versions of PL/1, including PL/C and PL/M that can run on a variety of computers. PL/1's is most effective in organizations that require both scientific and commercial applications. For

```
00101 IDENTIFICATION DIVISION.
00102 PROGRAM-ID. SAMPLE.
00103 ENVIRONMENT DIVISION.
00104 INPUT-OUTPUT SECTION.
00105 FILE-CONTROL. SELECT EMPLOYEE-DATA    ASSIGN TO DISK.
00106               SELECT PAYROLL-LISTING ASSIGN TO SYSLST.
00107 DATA DIVISION.
00108 FILE SECTION.
00109 FD   EMPLOYEE-DATA           LABEL RECORDS ARE STANDARD.
00110 01   EMPLOYEE-RECORD.
00111      05   EMPLOYEE-NAME-IN      PICTURE X(20).
00112      05   HOURS-WORKED-IN       PICTURE 9(2).
00113      05   HOURLY-RAGE-IN        PICTURE 9V99.
00114 FD   PAYROLL-LISTING         LABEL RECORDS ARE OMITTED.
00115 01   PRINT-REC
00116      05   FILLER               PICTURE X(21).
00117      05   NAME-OUT             PICTURE X(20).
00118      05   FILLER               PICTURE X(10).
00119      05   HOURS-OUT            PICTURE 9(2).
00120      05   FILLER               PICTURE X(8).
00121      05   RATE-OUT             PICTURE 9.99.
00122      05   FILLER               PICTURE X(6).
00123      05   WEEKLY-WGAES-OUT     PICTURE 999.99.
00124 WORKING-STORAGE SECTION.
00125 01   ARE-THERE-MORE-RECORDS   PICTURE XXX VALUE 'YES'
00126 PROCEDURE DIVISION.
00127 100-MAIN-MODULE
00128      OPEN INPUT EMPLOYEE-DATA
00129           OUTPUT PAYROLL-LISTING.
00130      READ EMPLOYEE-DATA
00131           AT END MOVE 'NO ' TO ARE-THERE-MORE-RECORDS.
00132      PERFORM 200-WAGE-ROUTINE
00133           UNTIL ARE-THERE-MORE-RECORDS = 'NO '.
00134      CLOSE EMPLOYEE-DATA
00135           PAYROLL-LISTING.
00136      STOP RUN.
00137 200-WAGE-ROUTINE.
00138      MOVE SPACES TO PRINT-REC.
00139      MOVE EMPLOYEE-NAME-IN TO NAME-OUT.
00140      MOVE HOURS-WORKED-IN TO HOURS-OUT.
00141      MOVE HOURLY-RATE-IN TO RATE-OUT.
00142      MULTIPLY HOURS-WORKED-IN BY HOURLY-RATE-IN
00143           GIVING WEEKLY-WAGES-OUT.
00144      WRITE PRINT-REC.
00145      READ EMPLOYEE-DATA
00146           AT END MOVE 'NO ' TO ARE-THERE-MORE-RECORDS.
```

example, an engineering firm that has one large computer used in both engineering and business applications might use PL/1. However, in recent years PL/1's popularity has waned. A simple PL/1 program that calculates an employee's gross pay is shown in Figure 9–16.

BASIC. As the computer industry grew, the need for training more people in computer programming became increasingly apparent. Many people felt that languages such as FORTRAN and COBOL were difficult to learn. In addition, these languages were not interactive. The programmer traditionally submitted both the program and the data to the computer

9–15 This excerpt from a COBOL program shows a segment of a COBOL program listing. Note that the COBOL program is different from the others—it operates on any number of data items, whereas the others just operate on one set of data.

```
/***                        PAYCHECK PROGRAM                         ***/
/***                                                                 ***/
/***    Program Paycheck calculates an employee's paycheck based upon ***/
/***    the number of hours the employee worked and base pay per hour. ***/
/*********************************************************************/

Paycheck: procedure options (main);

declare Employee_Name character (12) varying;
declare Pay_Rate fixed decimal (6,3);
declare Gross_Pay fixed decimal (7,2);
declare Hours_Worked fixed decimal (7,3);

/* ----------------------------------------------------------------- */

    /* Prompt the user for the employee's name, hours worked, and rate of
    pay per hour. */

put page list ('                        PAYCHECK PROGRAM');
put skip (2) list ('Enter the employee''s name: ');
get data (Employee_Name);

put skip list ('Enter the number of hours worked: ');
get data (Hours_Worked);

put skip list ('Enter the hourly pay rate: ');
get data (Pay_Rate);

    /* Calculate the gross pay. */

Gross_Pay = Hours_Worked * Pay_Rate;

    /* Print the results of the paycheck calculations for this employee.
    Then quit. */

put skip list ('Employee Name          ', Employee_Name);
put skip list ('    Hours Worked       ', Hours_Worked);
put skip list ('    Pay Rate           ', Pay_Rate);
put skip list ('    Gross Pay          ', Gross_Pay);

end Paycheck;
```

9–16 This PL/1 program performs the same basic tasks as the preceding samples. Compare the syntax with the other samples.

before execution, and the program was then run in batch mode. The results were printed on paper and returned to the programmer.

Two professors at Dartmouth College, John Kemeny and Thomas Kurtz, wanted to teach students in nontechnical disciplines to write interactive programs on large time-sharing systems. In 1964, they created **BASIC** (*Beginner's All-purpose Symbolic Instruction Code*). BASIC is easy to learn and can be used by small businesses having a limited programming staff or no professional programmers at all. Because BASIC is widely implemented on microcomputers—the type of computer most commonly found in schools from junior-high to the college level—it is the language most students learn first. Newer versions, such as BASICA, Microsoft's QuickBASIC, and Borland's Turbo BASIC, continue to keep this language popular. Figure 9–17 shows a short BASIC program that calculates an employee's net pay.

```
10 REM *** THIS PROGRAM CALCULATES AN EMPLOYEE'S PAYCHECK BASED   ***
20 REM *** ON THE NUMBER OF HOURS WORKED AND THE BASE PAY PER     ***
30 REM *** HOUR.                                                  ***
40 REM
50 REM GET THE EMPLOYEE'S NAME, HOURS WORKED, AND PAY RATE.
60 INPUT "ENTER THE EMPLOYEE'S NAME "; NME$
70 INPUT "ENTER THE HOURS WORKED "; HOURS
80 INPUT "ENTER THE PAY RATE "; PAYRATE
90 REM
100 REM CALCULATE GROSS PAY.
110 LET GROSSPAY = HOURS * PAYRATE
120 REM
130 REM PRINT RESULTS
140 PRINT "EMPLOYEE'S NAME:      ";NME$
150 PRINT "HOURS WORKED:         ";HOURS
160 PRINT "PAY RATE:             ";PAYRATE
170 PRINT "GROSS PAY:            ";GROSSPAY
999 END
```

9–17 Here's the same program written in BASIC. Notice that this version of BASIC uses numbered lines. Some versions of BASIC require line numbers and others do not.

In 1978 ANSI released a standard for BASIC referred to as ANSI Minimal BASIC. However, manufacturers often did not follow this standard or included so many enhancements that the versions of BASIC on different systems varied considerably. Therefore, a program written in GW-BASIC (or BASICA, as it is called on IBM personal computers) will generally not execute on a VAX computer using VAX BASIC, without some modification. In addition, computer professionals have criticized ANSI Minimal BASIC because it is not a structured programming language. Recognizing this problem, in 1987 ANSI released a more complete standard for BASIC that incorporated structured programming features into the language. The next few years will determine whether these new standards will be widely adopted in business and industry.

Pascal.   In the mid- and late 1960s, the principles of structured programming were a major topic of discussion among computer scientists, many of whom came to believe that structured programming techniques should be taught to students from the beginning. From 1968 through 1971 Niklaus Wirth developed **Pascal** to meet the need for a relatively easy to learn, highly structured language. Figure 9–18 contains a short Pascal program. Pascal is named after the seventeenth-century mathematician Blaise Pascal, who developed the first mechanical calculator.

Computer scientists embraced Pascal as a major improvement over languages such as FORTRAN, COBOL, and BASIC, which were at that time unstructured. Because Pascal is a truly structured language and is relatively simple to learn, it is the introductory programming language for computer science students at most universities.

However, Pascal was not designed to be powerful enough for large business applications; that is, it cannot handle large quantities of business data as efficiently as COBOL. But it can perform complex mathematical operations, and some engineers and scientists have switched to it from FORTRAN.

```
program Paycheck (input, output);

{ *** This program calculates an employee's paycheck based on   ***
  *** the number of hours the employee worked and the base pay  ***
  *** per hour.                                                  ***   }

var
   Name : string;
   Hours, PayRate, GrossPay : real;

begin    { Paycheck }

   { Prompt the user to enter name, hours worked and hourly rate. }
   write ('Enter the employee''s name: ');
   readln (Name);
   write ('Enter the number of hours worked: ');
   readln (Hours);
   write ('Enter the hourly pay rate: ');
   readln (PayRate);

   { Calculate gross pay.}
   GrossPay := Hours * PayRate;

   { Print the results of the paycheck calculations for this employee.
     Then quit. }

   writeln ('Employee Name:      ', Name);
   writeln ('Hours Worked:       ', Hours:8:2);
   writeln ('Pay Rate:           ', PayRate:8:2);
   writeln ('Gross Pay:          ', GrossPay:8:2);

end.     { Paycheck }
```

Modula-2.   Niklaus Wirth originally created Pascal to be only a teaching language. As its use spread to business, its shortcomings became apparent. Wirth developed **Modula-2** as an expansion and improvement over Pascal. Introduced in 1980, it is better suited for handling the large quantities of data that are processed in business applications. Because Modula-2 retains the original emphasis on structured programming concepts that was first introduced in Pascal, some universities have begun using it in computer science courses. However, partly because there are few compilers available, its future in schools and business is still undecided.

C.   C was designed in 1972 by Dennis M. Ritchie at Bell Laboratories; the UNIX operating system, also developed at Bell Labs, was written in C. Because it provides the advantages of both assembly language and high-level languages, C is often referred to as a "middle-level" language. It is a structured language and uses high-level commands, but it also allows the programmer to interact directly with the hardware, as in assembly language. These capabilities make C well suited for systems programming that requires the programmer to write extremely efficient code that is not typically needed in normal business programming. In addition, code written in C can easily be transported from one system to another.

The C language is more difficult to learn than languages such as Pascal, but because of its power and wide implementation on microcomputers it is

9–18 This PASCAL program also calculates employee pay.

```
/***                         PAYCHECK PROGRAM                        ***/
/***                                                                 ***/
/*** Program Paycheck calculates an employee's paycheck based on the ***/
/*** number of hours worked and base pay per hour.                   ***/
/**********************************************************************/

main()
{
char    Employee_Name[40];
float   Gross_Pay;
float   Pay_Rate;
float   Hours_Worked
int     Temp;
char    c;

/* ------------------------------------------------------------- */

    /* Prompt the user for the employee's name, hours, worked, and rate
    of pay per hour. */

printf ("                          PAYCHECK PROGRAM\n");
printf ("Enter the employee's name: ");
    /* read characters into name array, one at a time */
for (Temp = 0; (Temp < 40) && ((c = getchar()) != '\r') && (c != '\n');
    Temp++) Employee_Name[Temp] = c;
Employee_Name[Temp] = '\0';        /* put in end of string character */
printf ("\n");                     /* write a newline to screen      */

printf ("Enter the number of hours worked: ");
scanf ("%f", &Hours_Worked); /* read number of hours from standard input*/
printf ("Enter the hourly pay rate: ");
scanf ("%f", &PayRate);   /* read pay rate from standard input      */

    /* Calculate gross pay. */

Gross_Pay = Hours_Worked * Pay_Rate;

    /* Print the results of the paycheck calculations for this employee.
        Then quit. */

printf ("\n\n");
printf ("Employee Name          %s\n",    Employee_Name);
printf ("   Hours Worked         %8.2f\n", Hours_Worked);
printf ("   Pay Rate             %8.2f\n", Pay_Rate);
printf ("   Gross Pay            %8.2f\n", Gross_Pay);

}
```

very popular among programmers, many of whom have switched to it from Pascal. Figure 9–19 shows the employee pay program written in C.

Ada. In 1978 the U. S. Department of Defense (DOD) held a design competition to select a programming language standard for its software. As the world's largest purchaser of computer hardware and software, the DOD realized it could save billions of dollars in development by standardizing its software language. The winning language was named for Ada, the Countess of Lovelace, who designed what we would call "programs" for Charles Babbage's computing engines in the nineteenth century.

9–19 This C program is not as readable as the others, but its translation to machine language is easier for the computer.

Ada is a general-purpose language based on the structured concepts first seen in Pascal. It is extremely powerful and sophisticated. Learning the language well enough to take advantage of its full potential can take several years. Figure 9–20 shows the program that determines an employee's net pay as it could be written in Ada.

Much of the software developed by the Department of Defense is used in **embedded systems**, or computer systems built into other systems. Computers on board aircraft, for example, are embedded systems. Embedded systems are also used in many household appliances such as microwave ovens and video cassette recorders. These systems are most commonly used in **real-time processing** where the system must respond to input quickly enough to continue an ongoing process. For example, navigational equipment on an aircraft must use real-time processing in order to continually respond to new input and feedback so that its output is not only correct but current, and therefore useful. Because Ada is well suited for real-time processing, the use of Ada in industry is growing along with the increasing automation of factory and office tasks.

Fourth-Generation Languages

As we mentioned earlier, the third-generation programming languages discussed in the previous section are all procedural languages because the programmer must list each step and must use logical control structures to indicate the order in which instructions are to be executed. **Fourth-generation languages (4GLs)**, on the other hand, are **nonprocedural languages**. These languages can be compared to the way in which you might instruct someone to cook a meal. The nonprocedural method is simply to state the needed output: fix a meal of chicken, rice, and salad. Using the procedural method, on the other hand, involves specifying each step—from preparing the shopping list to washing the dishes.

9–20 This is a sample of Ada programming, which is particularly suited for real-time processing. It can take several years to become proficient in Ada programming.

```
-- ***                    PAYCHECK PROGRAM                       ***
-- ***                                                            ***
-- ***   This program calculates an employee's paycheck based on the   ***
-- ***   number of hours worked and base pay per hour.            ***

package Paycheck_Program is
   procedure Paycheck;
end Paycheck_Program;

with Text_IO;                      -- Text_IO is a standard Ada package used
                                   -- to control text input and output.

package Paycheck_Program body is

   Employee_Name  : string (1..12);

   Gross_Pay,
   Hours_Worked,
   Pay_Rate       : real;                              continued ...
```

```
--------------------------------------------------------------------
procedure Paycheck;

begin     -- Paycheck

-- Prompt the user for the employee's name, hours worked, and rate of
-- pay per hour.

    Text_IO.Put ("                              PAYCHECK PROGRAM");
    Text_IO.New_Line;
    Text_IO.Put ("Enter the employee's name: ");
    Text_IO.Get (Employee_Name);

    Text_IO.Put ("Enter the number of hours worked: ");
    Text_IO.Get (Hours_Worked);

    Text_IO.Put ("Enter the hourly pay rate: ");
    Text_IO.Get (Pay_Rate);

-- Calculate gross pay.

    Gross_Pay              := Hours_Worked * Pay_Rate;

-- Print paycheck information for this employee. Then quit.

    Text_IO.Put ('Employee Name            ');
    Text_IO.Put (Employee_Name);
    Text_IO.New_Line;

    Text_IO.Put ('   Hours Worked          ');
    Text_IO.Put (Hours_Worked);
    Text_IO.New_Line;

    Text_IO.Put ('   Pay Rate              ');
    Text_IO.Put (Pay_Rate);
    Text_IO.New_Line;

    Text_IO.Put ('   Gross Pay             ');
    Text_IO.Put (Gross_Pay);
    Text_IO.New_Line;

end Paycheck;

end Paycheck_Program;
```

9–20 (continued)

Obviously, the nonprocedural method is easier to write, but you have less control over how each task is actually performed. For example, the dishes might be washed by hand or in a dishwasher. When using nonprocedural languages, the methods used and the order in which each task is carried out are left to the language itself; the user does not have any control over it. In addition, 4GLs sacrifice computer efficiency in order to make programs easier to write; hence they require more computer power and processing time. As the power and speed of hardware have increased and its cost has decreased, the use of 4GLs has spread.

Because fourth-generation languages have a minimum number of syntax rules, people who have not been trained as programmers can use such languages to write application programs as they need them. This saves time and frees professional programmers for more complex tasks. The 4GLs are divided into three categories: query languages, report generators, and application generators.

Query languages allow the user to retrieve information from databases by following simple syntax rules. For example, you might ask the database to locate all customer accounts that are more than 90 days overdue. Examples of query languages are IBM's Structured Query Language (SQL), Query-By-Example (QBE), and Artificial Intelligence Corporation's INTELLECT. SQL has become the de facto standard and is now part of the database management systems dBASE IV and R:BASE.

Report generators produce customized reports using data stored in a database. The user specifies the data to be in the report, how the report should be formatted, and whether any subtotals and totals are needed. For example, you might ask the system to create a list, arranged by account number, of all the company customers located in Oklahoma. Often report specifications are selected from pull-down menus, making report generators very easy to use. Examples of report generators are Easytrieve Plus by Pansophic and R&R Relational Report Writer by Concentric Data Systems.

The user can access the database when using query languages and report generators, but the database cannot be altered with these tools. With **application generators**, however, the user writes programs to allow data to be entered into the database. The program prompts the user to enter the needed data. It also checks the data for validity. Cincom System's MANTIS and ADS by Cullinet are examples of application generators.

Fourth-generation programming languages are useful for writing short, simple programs. They do not require the training of a professional programmer. Their major limitation is that, because they are nonprocedural, the programmer does not have as much control as when using high-level languages such as COBOL or Pascal. Chapter 12 discusses query languages, report generators, and application generators in more depth.

Fifth-Generation Languages

Fifth-generation languages (5GLs) are also nonprocedural languages and are also commonly used to query databases. Because these languages are still in their infancy, only a few are currently commercially available. They are closely tied to artificial intelligence and expert systems.

LISP, one of the oldest programming languages still in use, is also one of the most modern because new programming methodology has been incorporated into the language. It is used in artificial intelligence research. Currently, most expert systems are coded in LISP.

Prolog, another 5GL, was developed in 1972 in France by Alain Colmerauer and Philippe Roussel. It quickly became popular throughout Europe as it was improved and expanded. An implementation of Prolog called Microprolog brings this language to smaller microcomputers such as the IBM-PC and PS/2. In the early 1980s, the Japanese began the Fifth Generation Computer Systems Project. Its purpose is to develop a computer system that is particularly well suited for expert systems. The main language being used in this project is Prolog. The final outcome of the project is expected in the early 1990s and should have a strong effect on the practical use of Prolog in particular and 5GLs in general.

Some recent efforts to improve artificial intelligence languages have attempted to combine the best features of LISP and Prolog. Fifth-generation languages offer an area of tremendous growth in the near future.

A Comparison of Programming Languages

Machine language is the only language that computers can directly execute. If a program is written in any other language, such as assembly language or COBOL, it must be translated into machine language before being executed. Therefore machine language uses computer resources more efficiently than other languages. However, writing code in machine language takes a great deal of time, and it is easy to make mistakes. Both assembly language and machine language are different for each type of computer. Assembly language is easier to use than machine language but still requires a great deal of care and is not portable like most high-level languages.

In a Nutshell

The Five Generations of Programming Languages

Category	Characteristics
First generation: machine languages	Difficult to program in; they are dependent on the type of computer being used. However, machine language allows the programmer to interact directly with the hardware, and it can be executed by the computer without the need for a translator.
Second generation: assembly languages	Use symbolic names for operations and storage locations. Assembly language is easier to use than machine language but it is still difficult to understand. A systems program called an *assembler* translates it into machine language. Different computer architectures have their own machine and assembly languages, which means that programs written in these languages are not portable to other, incompatible systems.
Third generation: high-level languages	Use English-like instructions; many high-level languages are portable. Each has syntax rules that must be followed. Such languages are much easier to use than assembly language but they can take considerable time to learn. Two types of systems programs exist for translating them into machine language: interpreters and compilers.
Fourth-generation languages	Have simple, English-like syntax rules; commonly used to access databases.
Fifth-generation languages	Used in artificial intelligence and expert systems; also used for accessing databases.

Because assembly language allows the programmer to interact more directly with the hardware than most high-level languages, it is popular for systems programming applications such as writing operating systems. However, C also offers this advantage, and because it is a portable high-level language, it is used increasingly in systems programming.

One of the main purposes of high-level languages is to write programs that manipulate the enormous quantities of data used in business. COBOL and PL/1 are both well suited for these applications. Because these languages require large compilers, they are most commonly used on mainframes. Other languages, such as FORTRAN, Ada, and Pascal, are suited for mathematically oriented tasks. Ada has the additional advantage of being developed for use on real-time systems, which is an advantage in applications involving automation and the use of robotics in manufacturing.

Languages that are relatively easy to learn, such as BASIC and Pascal, are often used to teach programming skills to students. These languages are available on virtually all types of microcomputers as well as on minis and mainframes. Pascal has many followers among computer educators because it has always emphasized structured programming methodology. However, especially with the release of ANSI BASIC-1987, more BASIC implementations are incorporating structured features.

The increased use of fourth- and fifth-generation languages is referred to as *end-user-driven computing*. These languages allow the end-user to become both systems analyst and programmer, freeing the information processing department for more difficult tasks. These languages allow virtually anyone to write a program, but they do not yet provide the flexibility of 3GLs.

Looking Ahead

Object-Oriented Programming

As the sophistication and capabilities of new computer hardware have grown by leaps and bounds, it has become evident that new software development techniques are needed. Users anxiously await more software that harnesses the capabilities of sophisticated hardware such as the Macintosh II and the PS/2 family of computers. In addition, users' expectations of software quality have increased. They are no longer satisfied with applications that are not user-friendly or that have numerous bugs that must be worked around.

A recent approach to software development, called **object-oriented programming,** attempts to completely alter traditional software development methods, and many computer professionals believe it has the potential for satisfying some of the enormous demand for more sophisticated software. Object-oriented programming requires a new way of programming, one more closely related to how we actually think.

We typically regard the computer as a machine and data as the raw material that the computer processes. The programmer is the technician who controls the machine. The program lists all the steps the computer must take to obtain the needed output from the input. However, an object-oriented program defines the data and the set of operations that can act on that data as one unit called an *object*. The object is thought of as an actor with a specific set of skills. The programmer is the director of the show. The programmer no longer has to tell each actor exactly what steps to take but instead simply explains the ultimate task to be performed.

Critical to understanding object-oriented programming is the concept of *inheritance*. Objects can be defined and then used to build a hierarchy of descendant objects, each of which inherits access to methods used by the ancestors' objects. Objects can be reused. Even when a new object is needed, an old one can usually be modified to meet the new needs. The new object inherits the characteristics of the old object.

For example, a horse is a subclass of mammals. It "inherits" the characteristics of a mammal (body hair, live birth, nursing its young, and so on). However, it also has characteristics that distinguish it from other mammals, such as its size and shape, the way it moves, and the kinds of sounds it makes. When a programmer creates a new object, it is necessary only to add its new features; the inherited ones are already there.

To see how this makes the programmer's job easier, assume you were writing a space-war game. Both sides—the Federation and the Ferengi—have space ships, but of slightly different types. In addition, each side has non-fighting ships, such as space shuttles and cargo barges. The object *ship* has certain characteristics: X-Y coordinates, shields, warp speeds, and loyalty (Federation or Ferengi). The object *fightingShip* has everything *ship* has, plus photon torpedoes. The object *shuttlecraft* has everything *ship* has except shields and warp speeds.

Many programmers agree that object-oriented programming can greatly reduce the time needed to implement new software. In addition, because new software builds heavily on existing objects, the code is more likely to be reusable and error-free. Several object-oriented languages are currently available. The first commercially available language was Xerox's Smalltalk. Other languages include C++ (an object-oriented version of C), and Borland's Turbo Pascal, Version 5.5. The next few years will determine whether the full potential of object-oriented programming is as great as many computer professionals believe. If it is, we should see tremendous improvements in the speed of software development and the quality of the final product.

SELF-TEST

1. The second generation of programming languages are called _____ languages.
2. (T *or* F) FORTRAN was the first widely used business-oriented language.
3. (T *or* F) PL/1 was designed to incorporate the best features of COBOL and FORTRAN.
4. The programming languages _____ and _____ both developed to teach programming to students.
5. (T *or* F) In a procedural language, the programmer must specify each step needed in the programming process.

SUMMARY

The decision to purchase a *commercial software package* or develop a *customized package* depends on a number of factors, such as whether the necessary information processing personnel are available in-house, and whether there are commercial packages that meet the specified needs, are within budget, and can be installed within the required time.

If the decision is made to develop a customized package, the *software development cycle* is followed. It consists of the following steps:

1. *Develop the program specifications.* A systems analyst, with input from the program's potential users, provides the programmer with the input, output, and processing requirements.

2. *Design a solution.* The programmer creates an algorithm that lists the logic needed to obtain the output from the input. The solution is first planned using *flowcharts*, *pseudocode*, and/or *hierarchy charts*.

3. *Code the program and translate it into machine language.* Depending on the processing needs of the program and the requirements of the overall information system, a programming language is selected. The programmer uses the design solution to write the program.

   A translator program (typically a *compiler* or an *interpreter*) translates the program statements into machine language.

4. *Debug and test the program.* Program errors can be divided into two groups: *syntax* (or grammar) *errors* and *logic errors*. Syntax errors are often caused by typing mistakes, whereas logic errors are caused by a flaw in the program. Programs must be tested using data specifically designed to check for the conditions that the program will actually encounter when it is implemented.

5. *Install and convert to the program.* Conversion can occur all at once (an *immediate implementation*), or as a *pilot project* by which much of the processing is still done by the old method, or by using both the old and new systems in *parallel* until everyone is satisfied that the new program is working properly.

6. *Maintain the program.* Program maintenance involves correcting any bugs, improving the ease with which it can be used, and expanding it to meet changing needs.

7. *Document the program.* Some documentation is placed in the program to explain its logic. The majority of the documentation is contained in manuals, either for programmers to use in maintaining and modifying the program or to give the end-user instructions on using the program.

Structured programming techniques are designed to make efficient use of programmers' time and to make programs more error-free and easier to maintain. In structured programming, the programmer uses only the four basic program structures to develop a program's logic: the *sequence*, the *decision structure*, the *loop* (iteration), and the *case structure*. *Top-down design* involves developing a solution to a programming problem by dividing the program into smaller and smaller subparts. With large programs, *structured walkthroughs* are conducted so that the programmer's co-workers can study the logic of the program and offer input to improve it. It is easy to understand the logic of programs written with top-down, structured programming techniques; moreover, such programs are easier to maintain.

Programming languages can be divided into five generations: *machine language, assembly language, high-level* or *procedural languages, fourth-generation languages,* and *fifth-generation languages.* Machine language is the only language the computer can directly execute. Assembly language, halfway between machine language and high-level languages, uses symbolic words to identify instructions and storage locations. High-level languages such as *COBOL, BASIC,* and *FORTRAN* are easier to understand but still require considerable training and have strict syntax rules. Fourth-generation languages can be learned quickly, have minimal syntax rules, and are often used to access databases. They fall into three categories: *query languages, report generators,* and *application generators.* Fifth-generation languages are those used in applications of artificial intelligence and expert systems.

Object-oriented programming, which uses an entirely different logic system, may become a new generation in the next few years.

KEY TERMS

Ada
Algorithm
Application generator
Assembler
Assembly language
BASIC
Benchmark test
C
Case structure
COBOL
Coding
Compiler
Debugging
Decision structure
Desk-checking
Documentation
Double-alternative decision structure
Embedded systems
Fifth-generation programming language (5GL)
First-generation programming language
Flowchart
FORTRAN
Fourth-generation programming language (4GL)
Hierarchy chart

High-level language
Interpreter
Iteration
Logic error
Looping
Low-level language
Machine language
Modula-2
Module
Nonprocedural language
Object-oriented programming
Object program
PL/1
Pascal
Portable
Procedural language
Programmer
Programmer analyst
Program testing
Pseudocode
Query language
Real-time processing
Report generator
Second-generation programming language
Sequence structure
Single-alternative decision structure

Software development
  cycle
Source program
Structured
  programming
Structured walkthrough
Subprogram

Symbolic language
Syntax error
Systems analyst
Third-generation
  programming
  language (3GL)
Top-down design

CHAPTER SELF-TEST

1. (**T** *or* **F**) Programs must be coded before the program specifications are determined.

2. In large information processing departments, a _____ usually oversees each new project, whereas a _____ does the actual coding of the program.

3. A programming tool called a _____ uses special symbols to plan the program logic, while _____ uses English words to plan the logic.

4. Today, second-generation languages, also called _____ languages, are primarily used in systems programming.

5. (**T** *or* **F**) In structured programming, programmers attempt to avoid using iteration.

6. _____ errors are grammatical mistakes in writing a program, while _____ errors are caused by incorrect or incomplete processing steps.

7. Programming languages that are _____ can be executed on many different computers with minimal changes.

8. Because _____ has the advantages of both assembly languages and high-level languages, it is often used in systems programming.

9. The only language that computers can execute without it first being translated is _____ language.

10. (**T** *or* **F**) When using top-down design, the programmer divides a program solution into smaller and smaller subparts.

11. _____ translate and execute symbolic languages a statement at a time, whereas _____ translate the entire source program into an object program that is then executed.

12. _____ is the language most commonly used for business programs that need to access large files of data.

13. _____ was the first widely used high-level language and is used in scientific and mathematical applications.

14. Niklaus Wirth developed _____ to teach structured programming techniques to students.

15. (**T** *or* **F**) Fourth-generation languages such as SQL are often used to query databases.

16. (**T** *or* **F**) Programs are tested only after the installation and conversion process is completed.

17. _____ was developed to combine the advantages of COBOL and FORTRAN.

18. _____ languages are most commonly used in artificial intelligence and expert systems.

SOLUTIONS 1) False. 2) systems analyst; programmer. 3) flowchart; pseudocode. 4) assembly. 5) False. 6) Syntax; logic. 7) portable. 8) C. 9) machine. 10) True. 11) Interpreters; compilers. 12) COBOL. 13) FORTRAN. 14) Pascal. 15) True. 16) False. 17) PL/1. 18) Fifth-generation.

PROBLEM-SOLVING APPLICATIONS

1. Think of a job you have performed, such as writing a term paper or building a piece of furniture out of wood. Create a hierarchy chart for this task. Then create a flowchart and pseudocode to show how the job is performed. Identify any decision structures or loops.

2. Find a computer professional at your college or in business who will discuss his or her information processing department's software development cycle. What type of documentation lists the development cycle? What programming languages do they use? Why?

PART IV

SYSTEMS

CHAPTER 10

Systems Analysis and Design

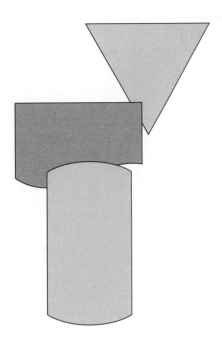

When you have completed this chapter, you will be able to:

- ✔ Identify two kinds of systems analysts and describe the skills they need to perform their jobs successfully.

- ✔ Recognize the major stages of the system life cycle.

- ✔ Discuss how business systems are analyzed and list the five steps for writing a problem definition.

- ✔ Describe the elements of a business system using four common analytical tools.

- ✔ Describe how to design a new system by modifying the elements of the old one.

- ✔ List and describe advantages and disadvantages of four types of systems conversions.

- ✔ List and describe three criteria for redesigning job descriptions in ways that motivate employees.

- ✔ Describe the major components of a Request for Proposal (RFP) and the role of the RFP in selecting new hardware.

Chapter Outline

Every business consists of a series of interconnecting functional areas that, by working together, accomplish the organization's goals. No matter how large or small a business is—whether it is a yacht-building firm or a mom-and-pop grocery store—all of them consist of functional areas that are organized to achieve business objectives. A yacht builder, for example, might need these four functional areas:

◆ Purchasing to order building materials

◆ Production to build the yacht

◆ Marketing to sell the yachts once they are built

◆ Finance and accounting to manage cash flow

Each of these functional areas consists of a series of business systems, or methods, that employees use to complete their tasks. For example, employees in purchasing might have systems for checking the quality of materials, negotiating with vendors, and ordering supplies.

Analyzing Business Systems

Managers plan, organize, and control business systems on the assumption that if each system works efficiently, the entire organization runs smoothly. To keep organizations running efficiently, managers hire **systems analysts** to examine the organization's procedures and systems and recommend how these can be made more efficient.

Note that a **business system** is a set of procedures used to achieve business goals; for example, the procedures used to check products in and out of inventory in a warehouse (Figure 10–1) and provide daily summary reports are a business system. It may or may not involve computers. Systems analysts design **information systems** to use computers to improve the effi-

10–1 Automated inventory, with bar codes and hand-held scanner, uses essentially the same procedures as the manual system it replaced. Each step just becomes more efficient. *Courtesy:* Hewlett-Packard Company.

ciency of existing business systems. An information system is a combination of the computer hardware—the computer system—and the software, output, and procedures needed to perform the functions of a business system.

Managers generally ask analysts to examine business systems for two reasons: to improve a current system or to create a new system.

◆ **To Improve a Current System.**   Frequently, managers want to make existing systems—whether computerized or manual—more effective. They may be dissatisfied with a system and want a revised one. If the payroll system, for example, is slow and has a high error rate, a manager may request an analyst to redesign it.

◆ **To Create a New System.**   When managers discover that computers can do a task that was previously impossible to do manually or was too difficult to do efficiently, they frequently ask analysts to design a new information system. For example, if marketing managers were to discover that they could use computers to perform complex statistical analyses on customer demographic data to forecast future sales, they could ask analysts to build marketing information systems for them.

The Role of the Systems Analyst

Systems analysts are basically problem solvers (Figure 10–2). The solutions they design may or may not involve computers, depending on the business needs of the organization they are evaluating. For example, analysts generally recommend that computers replace the routine and repetitive business systems that require flawless calculation, such as payroll or accounts receivable. Other times, they may determine that a procedure is best done by people—answering customers' questions, for example. Whether tasks are done by computers or people, the task of the analyst is to recommend to management the systems that will help a company run efficiently and effectively.

There are two kinds of analysts: consultants who come from outside the company, and analysts who are employees of a company. Both kinds can be equally effective, depending on the company's needs.

The Outside Consultant Analyst.   Companies hire analysts, often called computer consultants, from outside the company when they need specific expertise that is not available within the organization. For example, an airline manufacturing company that produces a significant amount of documentation might hire a systems analyst who is a desktop publishing specialist to help analyze its current documentation system and suggest more efficient ways to create maintenance manuals.

Because **outside consultants** have no ties to any internal departments or people that might bias their analysis, they are often better able to see real or potential problems than those deeply involved in the operating environment.

An Organization's Analyst.   On the other hand, an analyst employed by the organization can potentially have a greater influence on a company than an outside consultant. **Internal analysts** have a long-term commitment to the company that may help them better understand the current operating

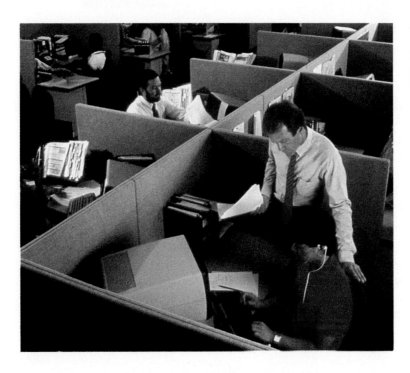

10–2 Systems analysts work closely with employees on all levels to assess system needs and potentials. *Courtesy:* Hewlett-Packard Company.

environment and thus create a more successful system. Their intimate knowledge of company procedures and their relationship with employees may help them solve business problems more effectively than can outside consultants.

Whether analysts are employed by a company or are hired as outside consultants, they go about their job in similar ways and possess similar skills. Their role is essentially advisory: they recommend to management how business systems can be improved. The decision to proceed with a new business system, however, rests with management.

Job Requirements of Systems Analysts

Systems analysts are usually experienced computer professionals. Typically, they have an MBA or an undergraduate degree and several years of project experience in writing programs for business information systems. To be effective in designing information systems, analysts must combine technical knowledge of how computer systems operate with organizational knowledge of how business systems work. They must then act much like interpreters or communications experts and translate technical issues to users as well as business needs to programmers.

Because the users of the system must live with the changes that analysts introduce, they sometimes experience stress when a new information system is put into place. Even if the new system is clearly for the better, users may fear that they might:

- Lose their jobs
- Lose their familiar routines
- Lose their status

♦   Be unsuccessful in using the new system

In addition, users sometimes wonder if they did something wrong to cause dissatisfaction with the old system. To be successful, analysts must be able to gain user confidence by convincing them that the system will, in the end, make their jobs easier, not harder, and that they will not lose their jobs. Often, simply asking users to offer suggestions for improving the system helps alleviate apprehension because their input actively involves them in the project's development. User input can also give analysts valuable insights into the needs of the organization.

Key Users Who Design Systems

Microcomputers have dramatically changed the role of the computer user in systems analysis and design. Managers often ask those users who have a strong interest and technical expertise in computers to develop systems for their work areas. Called **key users**, these people are familiar with their area's business problems and local issues, are more accessible to staff and managers than systems analysts, have some computer expertise, and can act as on-the-spot problem solvers. Consequently, these key users often need to learn systems analysis and design techniques to solve business problems quickly and independently.

For example, take the case of Margaret Cotham, an administrative assistant in the MBA office at Metropolitan Graduate School (MGS). Her boss asked her to design an information system for downloading student data files from the campus minicomputer to the department's three micros. Such a system could help the office track student progress through the MBA program, schedule future classes, and generally make it easier to compile student statistics. The chairman of the MBA program decided that he did not have enough money to hire a consultant, and because several microcomputer database and communications packages were advertised to be user-friendly, he asked Margaret to design the information system. Margaret thought computer systems were interesting and felt that the assignment was a good way to get a promotion, so she eagerly accepted the task. She quickly realized, however, that she was not sure how to design a new information system. The first thing she needed to do was analyze the current set of procedures as scientifically and objectively as possible. Before undertaking such an analysis, Margaret needed to understand the life cycle of business systems.

Understanding the Life Cycle of a Business System

Regardless of whether analysts or key users are creating entirely new information systems or improving existing ones, they must recognize that all such systems pass through five basic stages known as the **system life cycle:**

1. Planning and analysis

2. Design

3. Implementation

4. Operation and maintenance

5. Replacement

Analysts use the term *life cycle* because, like living organisms, business systems are born (planned and analyzed), grow (are designed and implemented), mature (are operated and maintained), and die (are replaced). During the life of a system, analysts must constantly modify and refine it to ensure that it works efficiently as business objectives and goals change.

Figure 10–3 provides a detailed schematic of steps involved in the system life cycle, with particular emphasis on the systems analysis and design phase. Let us start by looking at the first step of the life cycle, planning and analysis, more closely.

10–3 The life-cycle of a business system moves from planning through operation and maintenance and eventually to replacing the system with an effective one.

Planning and Analyzing Existing Business Systems

Analysts begin designing new or better systems by first analyzing the basic problem areas in existing procedures. They then present management with the results of their analysis in a **problem definition** that highlights those areas needing improvement. To write a problem definition, analysts must complete five steps:

1. Collect data about the existing system

2. Describe and analyze the elements of the system

3. Estimate current costs

4. Devise possible design alternatives

5. Obtain management approval for a new design

In the case of the MBA office, Margaret Cotham needed to write a problem definition that specifically described the current business system, including costs, and the flaws in the system that made it less effective. The report would outline in broad terms how she would redesign the system to eliminate these problems. Because the purpose of the problem definition is to present alternatives rather than a fully defined solution, she would need her boss's approval of the problem definition before she formally began designing a new system.

Collecting Data About the Existing System

Analysts begin the analysis phase by gathering as much information as they can about existing procedures and basic problem areas (Figure 10–4). Generally they use a combination of several methods for collecting data.

Reviewing Policies, Procedures, Documents, and Reports.   Analysts often begin by studying organization charts, existing written procedures, and operations manuals to find out how the business system was originally designed to function. By comparing written documents and procedures to how tasks are actually performed, they can begin to isolate problem areas. The differences between written and actual procedures often pinpoint the areas where analysts should focus attention. Analysts carefully sift through all written policies, memos, and reports to ascertain how information is currently moving through the company. For example, at MGS, Margaret began reading:

- The school's organization chart

- The school catalog that outlined degree requirements and formal registration processes

- Lists of all classes taught in her department

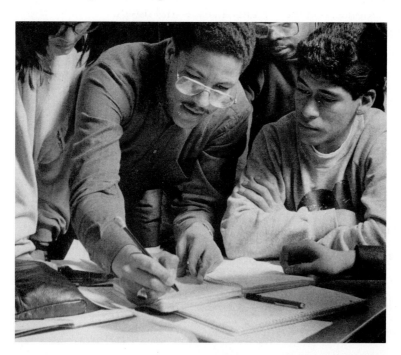

10–4 Students in this MBA program compare notes on field investigations as they analyze the current procedures and information needs of their own department— the first step in planning a business system. *Courtesy:* University of California, Berkeley.

- Office procedure manuals for tracking student progress

- All student registration reports

- All form letters the MBA staff sent to students

- All MBA department reports regarding students

Because what she read was often out of date or did not match what she knew to be common procedures in the office, Margaret quickly realized that she could not depend solely upon formal documentation to get a sense of current procedures. As a result, she began to observe employees as they worked to find out how procedures were really done.

Observing Unobtrusively.   Analysts can walk around an office and observe employee activities to objectively examine actual work procedures. They set a time for observation, select the employees they are going to observe, and inform the employees that they will be coming by. While they observe, analysts note the number, type, and importance of tasks employees are performing. For employees who do many different kinds of tasks during a normal work day, analysts may record the times for the various tasks— such as talking on the telephone, writing reports, attending committee meetings, and so on. For employees who concentrate on relatively few tasks, analysts simply note the tasks performed during the day.

Employees may be uncomfortable if they feel they are being watched; to be effective, analysts need to be unobtrusive about their observations and convey the message that the quality of people's work is not being questioned. In addition, they should do all they can to inspire confidence that a newly designed information system will be better as a result of observing employees at work.

After all observations are complete, analysts then compare what they observed to the written, formal documents studied earlier to see whether there are discrepancies between the two. At this point, they usually decide that they need more specific information. The best method for gathering additional information is to interview employees.

If a large number of people are involved in the system under study and it is not feasible to talk to all key personnel, or if the analysts suspect that employees might be reluctant to be honest in an open interview, they prepare a questionnaire.

Preparing, Distributing, and Analyzing Employee Questionnaires. Written questionnaires can supplement information obtained from documents and observations. Using questionnaires, analysts can evaluate:

- How superiors and subordinates communicate with each other

- Employee attitudes about current systems

- The degree of openness and candor about system issues

- The overall usefulness of current systems

While questionnaires are useful for gathering large amounts of statistical data that may be helpful for analyzing an existing system and proposing a new system, they can be time-consuming to create and distribute. As noted earlier, the best method for gathering information is typically to interview key employees.

Interviewing Employees. If analysts can win the confidence of employees, they can get a great deal of information. To conduct a good interview, analysts should come prepared with as much information as possible so as not to waste time; they need to ask employees specific, pertinent questions about their tasks and work flow problems. During interviews, analysts ask such questions as:

- What do you do in your job? What functions do you accomplish? How much time do you spend on each function?

- What are the most important tasks that you do?

- What do you do that could be delegated to someone at a lower level? To whom?

- What could you be doing, if you were given the proper authority, responsibility, and resources? Would you want to do any of these tasks?

- What problems do you have in doing your work?

- What solutions can you suggest to these problems?

By gathering and corroborating the results from documents, direct observation, questionnaires, and interviews, analysts can begin to determine how effectively current systems achieve business goals.

Describing and Analyzing the Elements of the System

Once Margaret had gathered data, she was prepared to describe and analyze the current MBA office system. Often the best way to analyze a system is to break it down into its seven component parts:

- Objectives
- Constraints
- Output
- Input
- Processing
- Controls
- Feedback

Figure 10–5 illustrates how these elements relate to one another. Analysts examine these components to see how they work and to isolate any problem areas. Later, when a new system is designed, each of these components will be modified as the need arises.

Reviewing Business Objectives. By the time analysts have finished collecting information, they generally have a good idea of what the current system was originally supposed to do as well as what the organization's

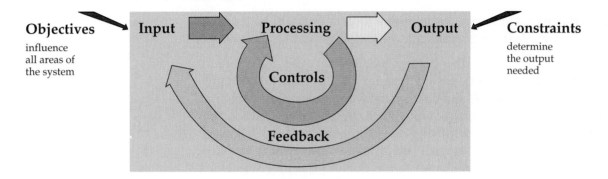

Objectives
influence
all areas of
the system

Input   Processing   Output

Controls

Feedback

Constraints
determine
the output
needed

original short- and long-term goals and business objectives are. At that point, they begin to look at how computers can support those objectives as well as what appropriate new goals might be, so that they can begin to create a new design. For example, if a department store chain has the goal of improving customer service, an analyst may begin to think about an on-line accounts receivable system that enables clerks to inquire about a customer's balance while the customer is purchasing an item.

Another common objective in companies is cost efficiency. Being able to say to managers, "I can provide you with 95 percent of what you want for 50 percent of the current system cost" is a very persuasive argument for modifying existing systems and their objectives.

In the case of MGS, the MBA program's long-term objective was to allow for a 25 percent increase in student enrollment and the hiring of four new professors over the next five years, to maintain the quality of service, and to make registration procedures as easy for students and staff as possible.

To analyze whether systems meet current objectives and to design systems that meet new objectives, analysts next look at the constraints or limitations placed upon existing systems.

Examining Constraints.   Every system has its own unique constraints which are limitations placed on it. The most common are legal, budgetary, and equipment constraints.

♦   Many systems have **legal constraints** that limit how much analysts can modify systems. For example, employers are required by law to withhold various federal, state, Social Security, and local taxes from payroll checks. Because federal and local governments dictate what the W-2 forms look like, how many copies there should be, and when they must be sent to employees, part of the payroll process cannot be modified at all.

♦   Often, managers impose **budgetary constraints** on analysts, limiting the time and money that can be spent on analyzing and designing a system. Managers may say, for example, that the computerized accounts receivable system that is about to be designed must be operational within one year and should not cost more than $100,000 to design. Cost clearly has a major effect on a system's design; sometimes analysts find in their analysis that the existing system is deficient partly because the original budgetary constraints were too restrictive. Analysts must therefore work

10–5 Breaking a business system down into its seven elements helps analysts examine the system's effectiveness and isolate problems.

with management and users to achieve a system that will be ready to function on schedule and within cost.

♦ Computer hardware and other devices that already exist in a company are **equipment constraints**. Existing systems were designed with equipment constraints in mind, and new systems are designed with similar considerations. If additional equipment is needed for a new design, system users often work with analysts to justify the purchase. If a major purchase is needed, analysts must perform a feasibility study to determine whether a substantial change to the existing computer system is justifiable. We will discuss feasibility studies at the end of this chapter.

In summary, analysts examine existing constraints when they analyze a current system. Later, when they design new systems, they determine whether the constraints are still applicable or whether different ones apply.

Examining Output.   During both the analysis and design phases of their work, analysts consider output requirements before input and processing; this is because the needs of the system users—that is, the output that will be produced by the system—is the most important element in the design. Only after output needs have been determined can input and then processing procedures be considered.

Identifying Input.   After determining output requirements, analysts examine all incoming data that serves as the basis for reports. Incoming data can be in the form of sales data, quotas, and proposed goals that are used to evaluate progress, for example. It can also be in the form of information from the field about what competitors are doing, the status of retail dealers, and so on.

Understanding the Processing.   After studying the existing output requirements and input data, analysts inspect the types of operations that are being performed on data to obtain the desired results. To fully understand an existing system, an analyst must understand all procedures and the ways in which various computations are made (Figure 10–6). For example, if a clerk needs an approval from management before making a major purchase, the analyst would examine the manager's decision-making process to see whether the clerk could make the same decision, or whether the decision could be made more efficiently or less expensively some other way.

Evaluating Controls and Feedback.   Analysts must be aware of what **controls** users implement to minimize errors. These include techniques such as double-checking computations and cross-checking data between employees.

Because errors occur even with the best of controls, **feedback** helps analysts pinpoint errors in the current system and indicates how they are handled once they are discovered. Feedback is the process of periodically evaluating a system to determine how well it meets user needs. Analysts need to know all current procedures for adjusting and correcting systems when feedback shows that errors have occurred. For example, they need to know what happens when a paycheck for an incorrect amount is issued. If

10–6 A banking system needs to provide teller receipts and ATM transaction records as well as detailed check logs, customer balance statements, and balance sheets for all levels, from the teller to the corporation. *Courtesy:* IBM.

the check is in excess of the correct amount, analysts must know the procedure for voiding the check and issuing a new one. In addition, they must know how appropriate adjustments are made, if necessary, to the employee's year-to-date figures for earnings, federal tax withheld, Social Security tax deducted, and so on.

Note that the seven components of good system analysis are also the seven considerations that will be evaluated later, when the analyst is designing a new system.

Using Structured System Charts to Describe the System

Analysts use several tools to help them depict and evaluate the components of a system. Four common tools for analyzing systems are: the structured analysis technique, system flowcharts, data flow diagrams, and automated design tools.

Using Structured Analysis.   Analysts frequently use **structured analysis**, which is a top-down method of systems analysis, to describe a system. Using this technique, they first identify the top-level function of a complex system, then analyze it and break it down into secondary-level components, and, finally, identify, analyze, and subdivide any subsequent components.

The advantage of structured analysis is that breaking the system into smaller and smaller components makes analyzing large systems easier. The disadvantage is that if the system is quite complex—such as a mainframe information system—doing structured analysis can be difficult and time-consuming.

Using Data Flow Diagrams.   Another tool analysts use to depict a system is called a **data flow diagram**. With data flow diagrams, the emphasis is on the flow of data through a system—where it originates and where it goes. Data flow diagrams clarify any phase of the system's life cycle.

Figure 10–7 shows the standard symbols used in data flow diagrams. The process symbol shows what is done to data in the current system—whether it is filed, printed out, forwarded, and so on. The source symbol indicates where data has come from. A sink symbol shows where data is going, such as to a recipient.

For example, at MGS a student course record may be sent by the MBA office (source) to the registrar (sink). The file symbol shows that data is stored—whether in a filing cabinet or on a computer disk. Vectors show the direction of the data flow. Figure 10–8 illustrates a data flow diagram depicting how a student registers for classes at MGS.

Using Systems Flowcharts.   Analysts also use a **systems flowchart** to depict system elements. The systems flowchart, like its more detailed counterpart, the program flowchart, shows the relationships between input,

10–7 These standard symbols are used in data flow diagrams.

- Process
- Source
- Destination
- Stored data
- Part of flow

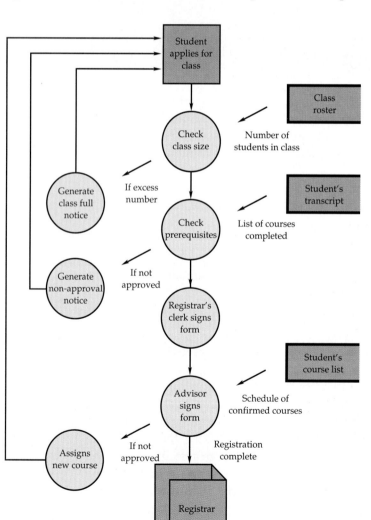

10–8 This data flow diagram shows how a student registers for a class at Metropolitan Graduate School, including what databases are needed.

processing, and output, in terms of the system as a whole. It is a general representation of the information flow within the total system.

Figure 10–9 illustrates the symbols commonly used in systems flowcharts. Analysts draw flowcharts by using either plastic templates or special automated programs. Figure 10–10 illustrates a sample systems flowchart for a payroll system. Note that it is relatively easy for managers to understand the overall processing involved by reading a systems flowchart.

Using Automated Design Tools. Sometimes analyzing a business system requires coordinating several analysts and programmers—each of whose work must be organized and cross-referenced with the other. A sophisticated approach that uses **automated design tools** is often employed for such an analysis. These tools are sometimes referred to as **computer-aided software engineering (CASE) tools**, and they focus on improving computer system development. CASE tools speed up the analysis process by enabling an analyst to integrate and organize the activities of several analysts and programmers who may be working on different components of the same system.

To appreciate how helpful CASE tools are, suppose Margaret Cotham needs to determine what long-range class enrollments are likely to be. She decides to begin be analyzing trends in all business course enrollments at MGS over the past 50 years. Even if she had ten people to help her, if they worked by hand, they would all be sitting at desks a long time, and it would be difficult to coordinate their work. CASE tools can help identify course names and enrollments and will automatically produce an organized, integrated index of courses.

One common automated design tool for microcomputers is Excelerator, which allows an analyst to diagram entire systems, from conceptual overviews down to individual data records. Excelerator uses a structured design technique—a top-down "explosion" feature—that allows analysts to start with an overview of the system, progress to finer levels of detail, and then explode the whole into different types of graphs and diagrams. Figure 10–11 shows an example of an Excelerator data flow diagram.

Analyzing a System

With an understanding of the seven basic system elements and with the ability to depict them using one of the above design tools, analysts describe the current system and begin defining system problems, preparing to recommend improvements. Specific issues they consider are the frequency, location, and relevance of processes in a business system.

Process Frequency. In thinking about a new design, analysts consider whether tasks are to be performed frequently or infrequently. Activities that occur on a by-exception basis or that occur infrequently do not usually produce cost savings when they are done on a computer rather than manually. Daily routines or procedures that rely on extensive paperwork or clerical support are well suited to computer systems.

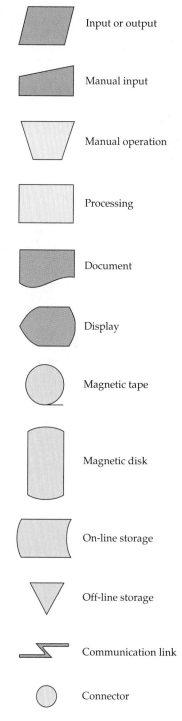

Input or output
Manual input
Manual operation
Processing
Document
Display
Magnetic tape
Magnetic disk
On-line storage
Off-line storage
Communication link
Connector

10–9 These symbols are commonly used in system flowcharts to illustrate the direction of data flow as well as its source and destination.

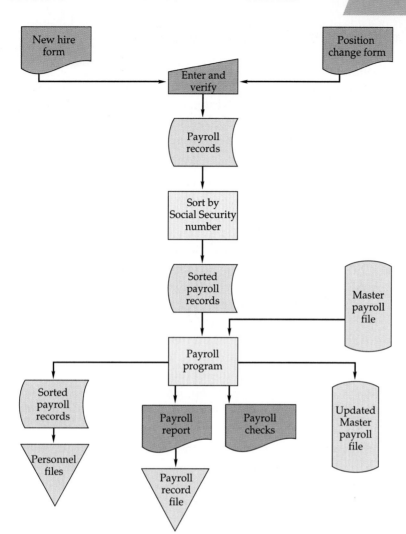

10–10 This system flowchart shows the process for updating a company's payroll records.

Process Location. Another consideration is whether process delays occur when data is transmitted from one office to another. This may indicate that a procedure is being done in the wrong location or that the transmission technique needs improvement. In manual systems, there are usually delays when information is transferred from one department to another in the form of paper documents. These delays can be significantly reduced in computerized information systems.

Process Relevance. Analysts are often surprised to find that obsolete procedures are routinely carried out in an organization's activities. For example, Margaret found that the secretaries in the MBA program were using a personal computer to develop a database of alumni names and addresses based on program records. Several years ago, MGS's development office, which solicits funds for the school, installed a sophisticated desktop publishing system, which they linked to the registrar's computers. The development office was now creating the same database in booklet form more quickly and accurately, but nobody had told the department secretaries to stop creating their own!

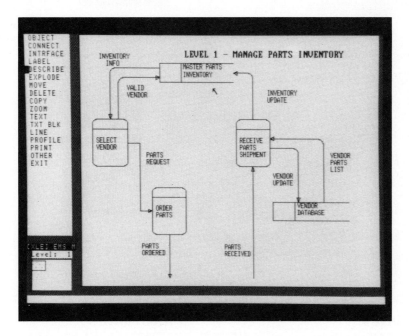

10–11 Excelerator, shown here, is an automated design tool that uses a structured design technique. Analysts start with an overview of the system and progress to finer levels of detail. *Courtesy:* Index Technology Corporation.

No set rules exist for analyzing business systems. Each activity must be assessed for its value to the total system. As a rule of thumb, well-defined, independent procedures are easiest to analyze, while procedures that interact with each other need to be broken into smaller tasks.

Developing Alternative Design Strategies

After describing and analyzing the current system, analysts generally need to outline several broad design alternatives. At this stage in the design of large systems—especially those that interact with other systems—analysts often need to outline for management the tradeoffs between a new system's cost and its potential efficiency. The most desirable system is apt to be the most expensive. Because analysts only make recommendations but do not make final decisions, they find it useful to provide management with several design alternatives to help them decide whether to build extremely effective systems at a high cost or build low-cost systems that may be less effective. For example, Margaret might suggest to her boss the five design alternatives (Figure 10–12):

◆ Purchase a new minicomputer

◆ Link three existing personal computers into a network and download data from the campus minicomputer

◆ Update and maintain student data records for the department, independent of other campus records

◆ Purchase terminals for the campus minicomputer

◆ Keep doing what they have always been doing—receiving hard-copy reports from campus computers and entering data as needed into personal computers for further analysis

Alternative 1

Alternative 2

Alternative 3

Alternative 4

Alternative 5

Note that at this stage the analyst broadly describes alternative design concepts. Once an alternative is selected by management, it will later be designed by the analyst in detail. A good way to develop design concepts is simply to ignore the costs and outline the best information system imaginable. Although the result may be economically impractical or expensive, this approach usually stimulates innovative ideas. Moreover, out of this process, affordable design alternatives often come to light.

For each alternative design, analysts prepare detailed system flowcharts or data flow diagrams documenting the output, input, and processing requirements, along with security and control procedures. They then estimate the cost of designing, implementing, and operating each alternative.

10–12 Here are five alternatives for keeping MBA records.

Providing Cost-Benefit Analysis

The most important consideration in obtaining management's approval is to demonstrate that a new design alternative will result in a cost benefit. A **cost-benefit analysis** is an integral part of an analyst's job. When presenting a new design alternative to management, the analyst outlines the costs associated with the existing system and compares these costs with those associated with a proposed system.

For proper evaluation, analysts compare the overall effects of the current and proposed systems on employee productivity and the quality of goods and services. To measure these effects, analysts use two basic methods: quantitative (numerical) and qualitative evaluation.

Quantitative Measures.   **Quantitative evaluation** assigns a **hard-dollar value** to the contribution of the current and proposed system. Hard-dollar savings are used to determine a proposed system's contribution to direct reduction of operational costs. For example, savings might include reducing the workforce, requiring less paperwork, or reducing the cost of items produced in-house such as slides, graphics, proposals, and mass mailings. A common way to ascertain hard-dollar savings is to compare the amount of work produced using the current system with the amount to be produced in the new design alternatives. For example, you may count the number of pages generated per month in a typing pool and then compare the cost per page to the cost per page for output from a word processing center with an equal number of employees. Analysts frequently use graphs for presenting managers with an overall reliable picture of the financial effects of a new system on the company as a whole.

You must remember, though, that evaluating costs is not simply a matter of comparing one set of costs with another, but also of projecting costs over a longer period. For example, while a new system may be more expensive in the first year than the current system, it may produce substantial long-term savings. Cost-benefit analyses usually project the costs of a new design for a period of three to five years (Figure 10–13).

10–13 Cost comparison charts for the five MBA department alternatives. Notice how equipment costs for alternative 1 average out over time, making labor-intensive alternatives more expensive.

Annual cost of system per year, first 3 years

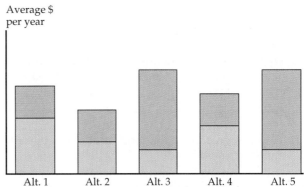
Annual cost of system per year, first 5 years

Qualitative Measures.   Qualitative evaluation assigns a soft-dollar **value** to the benefits of current and proposed systems. Soft-dollar savings reflect improvements in business processes that cannot easily be measured. Typical benefits that an organization may receive from an upgraded information system are improved customer relations, better internal communications, improved task delegation, a higher level of employee satisfaction, or a decreased need for travel. These are called soft-dollar savings because they actually do result in a better financial position; they are, however, difficult to quantify because they are indirect—for example, by how much will sales increase if customer satisfaction is improved?

Obtaining Management Approval for a Design Alternative

After analysts have completed a formal problem definition, they present their analysis and broadly stated design alternatives to management for approval. Managers may meet with an analyst several times to review and revise several design alternatives. When management actually approves a specific design alternative, analysts begin actually designing each of the new system's elements. Clear communication with management in obtaining approval of a design alternative is extremely important to analysts at this point because their credibility is often going on the line—they may be held accountable for design cost estimates. If the project runs over cost, management will want to know why!

In the case of MGS, Margaret's boss decided to approve the previously outlined option 2—to link the MBA program's three personal computers into a network and download data from the campus minicomputer.

SELF-TEST

1. The seven basic components of any system are _____, _____, _____, _____, _____, _____, and _____.

2. Like living organisms, systems are dynamic and subject to change; they are said to have a predictable _____ _____.

3. Three common types of constraints are _____, _____, and _____.

4. (T *or* F) The most effective system is usually the most expensive.

5. To determine the economic possibility of acquiring new equipment to handle business tasks, an analyst must perform a _____ study.

6. Four basic methods of collecting data are _____, _____, _____, and _____.

7. Two design tools commonly used to depict elements in a system are _____ and _____.

8. (T *or* F) An experienced systems analyst can generally computerize a system in less than a week.

9. (T *or* F) The user must work closely with the systems analyst to achieve an effectively computerized business system.

10. (T *or* F) The major reasons that the analyst studies the current system are to understand the operations required and to find the existing problem areas.

11. Errors in a system can be minimized by using _____ and _____.

12. An organized method for accomplishing a business function is referred to as a _____.

SOLUTIONS 1) objectives, constraints, outputs, inputs, processing, controls, and feedback. 2) life cycle. 3) legal, budgetary, equipment. 4) True. 5) feasibility. 6) studying procedures manuals and other documents; interviewing employees; making observations; designing and evaluating questionnaires. 7) system flowcharts; data flow diagrams (also structured analysis and automated design tools). 8) False. 9) True. 10) True. 11) controls and feedback. 12) business system.

Designing a New System

After designing the problem completely, discussing possible alternatives, and providing management with enough information to make a decision, a new design will be selected. Analysts then prepare a model of the new system by using systems flowcharts and/or other design tools.

Designing New Components

Recall that there are seven components of a system—objectives, constraints, output, input, processing, control, and feedback. When analysts design a new system, they evaluate each of these components and make modifications as necessary.

New Objectives and Constraints.   Based on the results of meetings with management, analysts list objectives and constraints for the new system. These may include some of the objectives and constraints of the existing system, but they are also likely to include new elements. For example, because the MBA program's long-range goal is to improve administrative services, Margaret and her boss agree that the new information system should meet three new objectives:

- Students should be able to register for all their classes **in one hour**.

- The administrative staff should be able to plan the next semester's courses **within the first week** of a new semester.

- Advisors should be able to determine a student's matriculation status **within 15 seconds**.

Margaret and her boss also agree that she can only spend two months building the new information system and no more than $3,000 on hardware and software. When the system is completed, she will spend 25 percent of her time maintaining the system and training users.

New Output.   Recall that output should be the first component that is designed. This helps ensure that users' needs will be satisfied. Analysts review all the reports generated by the current system and discuss with users any additional reports or changes that may be needed from a new design. For example, at this stage Margaret sat down with her boss and designed all the new forms and computer screens needed in the new system.

New Input and Processing Methods.   Analysts and users then agree on what new input will be required and what processing will be needed to create the desired output (Figure 10–14). Sometimes business systems need

10–14 New output needs may require new information in the system.

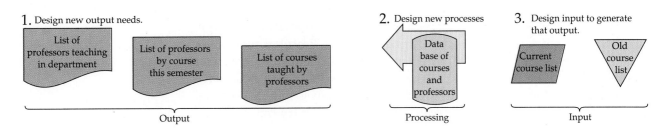

1. Design new output needs.

List of professors teaching in department

List of professors by course this semester

List of courses taught by professors

Output

2. Design new processes

Data base of courses and professors

Processing

3. Design input to generate that output.

Current course list

Old course list

Input

to be entirely redesigned or created to ensure accurate, timely input. For example, Margaret's boss wanted her new system to generate reports indicating:

- All professors teaching during any semester
- All professors who teach a particular course
- All courses a professor has taught over the years

While the campus minicomputer could easily provide the first two requests, getting a list of courses that all professors have taught over the years was more difficult. Margaret created a set of procedures that ensured proper input—in this case requiring the faculty secretary to:

- Retrieve the data from filing cabinets in storage
- Create a data file on the personal computer
- Update the data file every semester

Users and analysts must also look at all current processes and determine whether new methods might be more effective. For example, when Margaret's boss discovered that creating course schedules was much easier with the new computer system, he delegated the task to the MBA program's assistant director and then only approved or modified the schedule rather than having to create it himself.

New System Controls and Feedback.   Analysts then evaluate what controls are needed to ensure the quality of the output. They incorporate these controls into the computerized information system. They may suggest new controls as well, based on new techniques that may now be available.

When designing the new system, Margaret had to identify data she wanted from the campus minicomputer and then created periodic update schedules for downloading this data to the department's personal computers. She needed to develop procedures for ensuring data integrity as well as for updating files generated by the MBA department itself. Margaret also needed to create backup procedures to protect the department system against the possibility of a hard disk failure.

To get consistent feedback on the system, Margaret planned to meet with its users once a month to discuss problems and new ideas, and to suggest better ways to use it.

By using systems flowcharts, data flow diagrams, and automated design tools, Margaret was then prepared to begin building a model of the seven components of the new system.

Prototyping a System

A structured analysis process requires a long period of analysis and design, and the needs of users may change during that time. **Prototyping** enables analysts to provide users with all essential system elements as soon as possible, but before all of the systems interfaces and software modules have been designed (Figure 10–15). For instance, the analyst might create an on-screen menu or interactive display screen for users to try out, and then modify it to incorporate their suggestions—all before the system is actually installed.

Prototyping also allows analysts to begin an iterative process of refining the system to meet user needs before any design elements become final. If the overall design is unsatisfactory, they can change it quickly and easily. The advantages of prototyping a system are as follows:

◆ It enables users to physically sit down and begin to work with the system, so that they can find problems they might not have discovered without a working model. This helps analysts correct basic design mistakes.

◆ It makes the system easier to change if the need arises.

◆ It makes implementation easier because users have an active role in the design process; consequently, users have a better understanding of how the system will work in practice.

The disadvantages are, however, that a prototype can be difficult to manage and control, and may also be difficult to design when the information system involved is very large.

10–15 Before setting up an entire production line, a prototype of these auto assembly robots was carefully tested, first in the lab and then in a production environment. *Courtesy:* Chrysler.

The Role of Users in Designing a New System

Employees who will use the new system typically want as little to do with the design process as possible, but at the same time they want the system to meet their needs. Analysts must therefore work closely with them to learn their requirements, which are often not completely verbalized. Experienced analysts schedule frequent meetings with users to review (in small, manageable sections) the system being developed and to encourage managers to stress to employees that a satisfactory system cannot be developed without their active participation.

Refining the Process.   Unfortunately, not all relevant points can be thought of on the first design attempt. Thus, an iterative process of creating, reviewing, revising—then reviewing and revising again—is needed to produce the best system possible and to incorporate all needed data inputs, user features, and business functions. Users may feel that little progress is being made because of the repetitive nature of the design process. Analysts must assure them and their managers that iteration is a part of any design process, that the schedules and cost estimates include an allowance for the time involved, and that the need for revision does not mean a lack of planning or skill on anyone's part.

Setting Performance Standards.   Users should let analysts know early in the design process what the acceptable limits are for key system characteristics—such as response time, report run time, report costs, overall system usage cost, what processes the system will have to handle concurrently, and so on. As users become more knowledgeable about their choices, they will be better able to balance the tradeoffs offered them between system capabilities, response time, and costs. When analysts give users the option of adding or deleting a feature, they must also provide an estimate of the resulting effect on the system so that users can evaluate the inherent performance trade-offs—asking such questions as: "What am I sacrificing by taking away (or adding) this feature?"

Once an information system has been designed that satisfies business needs, analysts can then develop and implement the system so that it can be used on an ongoing basis.

Implementing a System

During the **implementation** stage of the life cycle, management approves the final design of the new system, the hardware is purchased, new software is either purchased or developed by programmers, and conversion from the old procedures to the new design is completed.

Selecting and Developing Software

When implementing new systems, most analysts use or augment hardware that already exists in the organization. Before acquiring new software, analysts first need to decide whether to purchase it or to have customized programs written, either by in-house programmers or by contracting with "software houses" that specialize in designing specific kinds of software.

Chapter 9 discussed how analysts decide whether to "make" or "buy" software. We review some considerations here.

Buying Packaged Software.   It is often better to purchase a software package than to customize your own software. The software package usually will cost less, be immediately available for use, and, if it is an established product, contain fewer errors, or bugs. In addition, businesses that buy most of their software do not need a large programming staff.

The only good reason to develop custom software is if you cannot find a package that meets your information needs—this occurs more frequently with mainframe systems in which the hardware is typically more powerful than the available software. Also, if your business system's needs are unique, a suitable off-the-shelf package may not be available.

Developing Customized Software.   When customizing software, a company can either contract for software development with a consulting firm or software house, or have its own programmers develop the software.

As noted in Chapter 9, contract programming has a number of advantages. If a consulting firm has experience in a needed specialized area, their programmers may be able to develop high-quality programs more quickly and less expensively than if they were done in-house. Contract programming, however, can be expensive.

If a business already has its own staff of programmers, it is usually less expensive to have custom software developed in-house. However, managing a large software development project is a difficult job. Not only is it hard to monitor the work of programmers, but it is also necessary to ensure that all programs eventually fit together, as defined by the software design. For large information systems, programmer teams are often formed to ease this management task. The **chief programmer** is the computer professional responsible for the overall design and coordination of all programs to be used in the information system. In smaller information systems, the analyst performs the tasks of a chief programmer. Because analysts are always responsible for the final product, they usually have project control responsibility over programmers, which means that they must ensure that the new software is appropriate and written on time.

Selecting Hardware

Analysts first attempt to design new systems by using the computer equipment that is already installed in the organization. Frequently, a new design may require additional peripherals, micros, or minis (Figure 10–16). If the analyst foresaw the need for such equipment at the problem definition stage, then it would be included in the original cost estimates and could be selected and acquired at this stage. If, however, a design alternative requires an entirely new computer system or additional hardware not originally budgeted for, analysts must suspend the design phase in order to undertake an overall **feasibility study.** We will discuss feasibility studies in more detail at the end of this chapter.

In all cases, decisions about hardware purchases should be delayed until a decision is made about how software will be acquired. As much as pos-

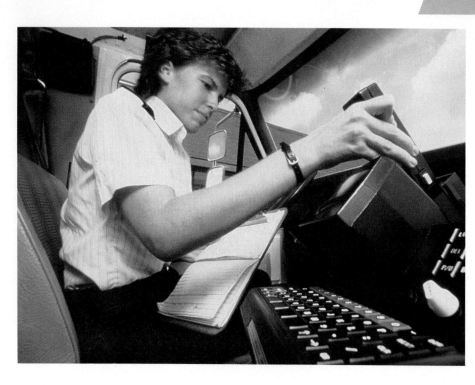

10–16 For one component of a new information system, this courier uses custom hardware—a hand-held scanner/keyboard and an on-board terminal in her truck—to feed package information to the shipper's database. *Courtesy:* Federal Express Corporation.

sible, software choices should ultimately determine which hardware is to be acquired or used. One of the main reasons that the IBM PC and PS/2 families of microcomputers have been so successful is that a wide variety of business software was developed for them.

Before any new hardware arrives, the users and systems analyst must determine the site where it will be installed and, if necessary, prepare the site. Some computer systems, for example, may require more air conditioning or a greater power supply than what is normally available in standard office space. The systems analyst's role is to determine the site requirements and oversee the schedule for preparing the site.

Obtaining Management Approval for Implementation

In very large, mainframe-oriented companies, analysts again make a presentation to management after the entire set of procedures has been designed and all programs written. This presentation includes:

◆ A detailed description of the new system

◆ An analysis of the actual design costs and the operating costs of this new system as compared to the costs estimated in the problem definition

◆ A plan for converting to the new system

If management approves the new design, then the analyst can continue with the final phase of implementation. Recall that managers typically approve a new design alternative as outlined in the problem definition because they were not satisfied with the original system; they may not, however, approve implementing a new system if the analyst's plans are unacceptable for some reason—for example, if the political situation in the company has changed or if some other major upheaval has occurred. In addition, if estimated costs differ significantly from actual costs, the analyst will need to account for the discrepancy.

Implementing the New System

After receiving management approval, analysts implement the new system. A new information system is likely to require changes to existing files in record layouts, in the media on which they are stored, or both. The process of creating computerized files is called **file conversion**. It is essential that controls be incorporated during this process to ensure the integrity of the new files. Typical controls include:

◆ Comparing record counts and batch totals of key fields before and after conversion to verify that all of the data has been correctly converted

◆ Comparing and checking randomly selected records before and after conversion

◆ Testing the information system with the new files to verify that all aspects of file conversions have been successfully completed

Redesigning Jobs

In addition to converting from one system to another, analysts need to be aware that new information systems tend to eliminate the more routine clerical tasks employees perform (Figure 10–17). They must therefore help managers redesign jobs and restructure the organization to compensate for these changes. Effective restructuring can enable organizations to undertake additional activities with the same number of employees.

For example, one financial company increased the amount of time that loan processors had available for productive work from 9 percent of their day to 50 percent by reorganizing the paperwork flow and using automated tools to handle much of the paperwork more effectively.

For employees who perform only a single routine task, the entire job must be redesigned to motivate them to use the new system.

To reap the full benefits of the new system, analysts usually advise managers about how to restructure the jobs of the employees who will be affected. Criteria for designing jobs include maintaining a job's intrinsic rewards, making use of a wide range of employees' skills, and maintaining individual autonomy insofar as possible.

Keep Intrinsic Rewards High. The job content itself should motivate the employee. That is, a job should require the employee to use a variety of skills to perform a task that is easily identifiable and relevant to both the worker and the organization. Such jobs are said to be high in intrinsic rewards, in contrast to extrinsic rewards such as higher wages or bonuses.

Continue to Use Employee Skills. Implementing an information system often leads to reclassifying jobs—and the temptation to reduce the variety of skills required for a task. This is usually false economy and reduces worker motivation. Many new systems actually warrant upgrading salaries and expanding job skills.

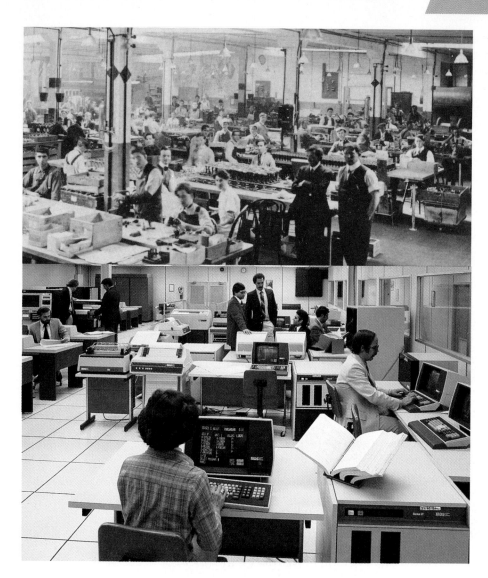

10–17 A Western Union operating room from 1914 (above) was a highly labor-intensive and mechanical operation. Today's office (below) uses computers to increase each person's productive work time and directly link operations across continents. *Courtesy:* AT&T Bell Laboratories Archive.

Increase Autonomy in New Jobs. Job freedom tends to increase employee motivation. The greatest latitude possible should be given to employees, as long as it does not interfere with the successful completion of their tasks.

Types of System Conversions

In Chapter 9 we discussed the ways programs are implemented in information systems. The same methods are used to convert to entirely new information systems. Because a new information system may affect many aspects of the company's success, it is important to implement the system with the least possible amount of disturbance. As with program implementation, the four alternative types of conversion for information systems are direct conversion, parallel conversion, phased conversion, and pilot conversion.

Direct conversion is performed when the company simply stops using the old system and begins using the new one with no overlap. If a sufficient number of prototypes have been tested, this may be an efficient way to implement the new system. However, the tradeoff is that something unexpected may occur and the company's business may slow down or even stop in some areas while the problem is being solved.

In **parallel conversion**, the old system and the new system are used simultaneously for a while; output from both are compared to make sure the new system is functioning correctly. When the new system is operating satisfactorily, the old system is discontinued. This is a slow but reliable method of conversion.

Phased conversion is a gradual implementation. It is particularly appropriate when a large, complex system has been designed in modules that can be run independently; as each module is implemented and refined, new modules can be added until the system is complete. For example, a company might implement the order processing module, then the inventory management module, and finally the accounting system module, getting each one running effectively before introducing the next module.

Pilot conversion refers to an implementation of the entire system in one part of the company—perhaps in a single department or a single division. This approach allows the analyst to work out any problems that develop while the scale of implementation is smaller and more manageable.

Documenting the System

Once the system is functioning properly, analysts provide a total record of the precise procedures and techniques it uses, as well as the technical specification for all the hardware and software used. This record is called a **documentation package**. It is typically developed throughout the analysis and design stage and finished after implementation is completed. Because documentation describes all the facets of a new design, it is similar to a procedures manual, although it may consist of several components. If there is a problem after the system is operational, analysts and users can consult the documentation, which, if it is complete, should provide the solution. See Figure 10–18 for a list of typical elements in a documentation package.

In summary, the analysis, design, and implementation of a new information system is a complex project that involves the creativity of many people, including managers and system users. The time and cost for involving these people are usually justified by the increase in profitability, productivity, and employee job satisfaction that can result from a well-designed system.

10–18 A documentation package is typically made up of five elements: logical and physical design, programming, and operations and procedures.

Logical design elements	Physical design elements	Programming elements	Operations and procedures
• Output specifications • Processing procedures • Systems and program logic • File specifications • Input specifications	• Database and file layouts • Processing procedures • Input formats • Output formats • File conversion plan	• Top-down structure charts • Pseudocode and flowcharts • File and record layouts • Code specifications	• User options • Data entry procedures • Data control procedures • Computer operations

In a Nutshell

Analyzing and Designing Business Systems

Define Problem
1. Collect data about the existing system
2. Describe and analyze the elements of the system
3. Estimate current costs
4. Devise possible design alternatives
5. Obtain management approval for one design alternative

Design new components
Create prototype system
Select and/or develop software
Select hardware
Obtain management approval for implementation
Redesign jobs if necessary
Implement system
Prepare and distribute documentation

Doing a Feasibility Study

If entirely new hardware is required for a new system, a separate feasibility study is undertaken before systems design begins. A new computer system can be expensive and can also introduce significant changes in the organization as a whole. Similarly, a large mainframe system may affect a number of otherwise independent information systems. Therefore new hardware has implications for the overall organization as well as for the information system that is being redesigned.

Because a new computer system typically affects the entire organization, analysts conduct the feasibility study with a team of systems users and managers and even other systems analysts. The feasibility study provides a top-down and more thorough technical evaluation of the proposed equipment needs for the organization than does the problem definition for an individual information system. Analysts must identify available hardware and software technologies, their capabilities and characteristics, and the cost of purchasing, renting, or leasing to create a detailed cost analysis that considers benefits to the company as a whole. If a new computer system is considered feasible, analysts then discuss the organization's needs in detail with hardware and software vendors.

Preparing a Request for Proposal

Analysts prepare a document called a **request for proposal** (RFP) to obtain specific technical information and cost bids from vendors and to ask for information about the vendor itself. A successful RFP includes two parts: (1) the description of your organization's needs, often called a **needs analysis,** and (2) a request for information regarding the vendor and the equipment proposed by the vendor in order to evaluate the proposal. To provide a thorough description of a proposed company's computer needs, an RFP contains:

- A description of your organization, including its main business, its locations, the number of its employees, and other information about departments or groups who will be using the computer system

- A description of what the computer system is supposed to accomplish

- The terms and conditions under which the procurement will be made, such as a fixed price, cost plus incentive for early delivery, warranty requests, and so on

- A budget that provides the vendor with a general idea of what the company plans to spend

- The organization's schedule for development, implementation, training, and start-up of the proposed system

- An outline of the proposed computer system's specifications

In addition to providing a description of the organization's needs and business environment, the RFP serves as a formal request for information from the vendor that analysts need to evaluate. Information requested from the vendor in an RFP includes:

- Technical specifications in the form of technical manuals or engineering specifications, sample screen formats, and so on

- Financial viability of the vendor, in the form of annual reports, track records, length of time in the business

- Available support, specifying maintenance and training programs, including frequency of training, background of instructors, and promptness and thoroughness of technical support

An RFP should also request a list of current users of the computer system the vendor proposes, with a brief description of each client's application areas. Current user information should include the client's business and the length of time the computer system has been installed. In addition, samples of documentation and manuals should be included to allow the organization to judge the quality, thoroughness, and usability of these items.

Evaluating the Proposal

Analysts also need to prepare criteria for evaluating proposals received from vendors to make fair comparisons and to facilitate the decision-making process. Evaluation criteria for proposals are often in the form of a weighted checklist based on required system features and the vendor's ability to support the customer.

The cost of operating each proposed computer system is the most important factor in rating competitive bids. However, intangible factors such as the vendor's reputation, anticipated installation date, support to be provided, and so on, must also be considered.

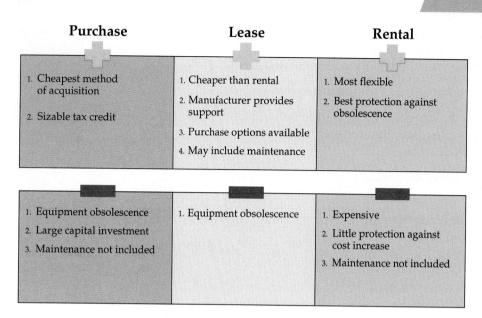

10–19 The advantages and disadvantages of the principal methods of acquiring computer equipment: purchase, lease, and rental.

Purchase

1. Cheapest method of acquisition
2. Sizable tax credit

1. Equipment obsolescence
2. Large capital investment
3. Maintenance not included

Lease

1. Cheaper than rental
2. Manufacturer provides support
3. Purchase options available
4. May include maintenance

1. Equipment obsolescence

Rental

1. Most flexible
2. Best protection against obsolescence

1. Expensive
2. Little protection against cost increase
3. Maintenance not included

Selecting a Vendor

After evaluating responses to the RFPs, analysts will then be ready to recommend a specific computer system. They must also recommend whether the system selected should be purchased, leased, or rented. Figure 10–19 indicates the main advantages and disadvantages of these three methods of acquisition.

Once analysts and users have reviewed all the bids, they make a written recommendation to management. The recommendation highlights the reasons a particular system and method of acquisition were chosen. Once a computer system is ordered, the analyst develops and supervises conversion and implementation plans.

SUMMARY

Every business consists of a series of interconnecting functional areas that together accomplish the organization's goals. To keep organizations running efficiently, managers hire *systems analysts* to examine business systems and recommend how they can be improved. Systems analysts are basically problem solvers, and the solutions they design may or may not involve computers. There are two kinds of analysts: *company employees* and *outside consultants*. As computer systems become more distributed, however, *key users* often need to quickly learn systems analysis and design techniques to help them solve business problems.

Business systems pass through five basic stages known as the system life cycle: (1) *planning and analysis*, (2) *design*, (3) *implementation*, (4) *operation and maintenance*, and (5) *replacement*. Analysts begin designing new systems by first understanding the basic problem areas in existing procedures and presenting the results in a *problem definition*.

To write a problem definition, analysts: (1) *collect data* about the existing system, (2) *describe and analyze* the elements of the system, (3) *estimate current costs*, (4) *devise possible design alternatives and their costs*, and (5) *obtain management approval* for one design alternative. Analysts use a combination of several methods for collecting data about the current system: *reviewing policies, procedures, documents, and reports; unobtrusively observing employees at work; designing and analyzing questionnaires; and interviewing employees.*

Perhaps the best way to analyze systems is to break them down into their seven component parts: *objectives, constraints, input, processing, output, controls,* and *feedback.* Analysts examine these components in order to see how they work and to isolate any problem areas. Later, when a new system is designed, each of these components will be modified as the need arises.

Analysts use several tools to help them diagnose and evaluate these seven system parts. Four common tools for analyzing systems are: *structured analysis, system flowcharts, data flow diagrams,* and *automated design tools.* Specific issues to consider when analyzing business systems are the *location, frequency,* and *relevance of tasks.*

After analyzing and describing the current system in a problem definition, analysts generally outline several broad design alternatives. For each alternative design, analysts prepare general system flowcharts or data flow diagrams outlining the *input, output,* and *processing requirements,* along with *security and control procedures* for each design alternative. They then *estimate the cost* of each alternative. To measure costs, analysts use two basic methods: *quantitative* (numerical) and *qualitative evaluation.* After analysts have completed a formal problem definition, they present their analysis and ideas to management for approval.

After management decides on a new design, analysts prepare a *model* of the new system using system charting and other design tools. A *structured analysis process* requires long planning and design periods, and during that time the needs of the user often change. *Prototyping* enables analysts to have users try out parts of a proposed system so that there will be fewer changes when the entire system is implemented.

Because users of a new information system typically want as little to do with the design process as possible, but still want the system to meet their needs, analysts must work closely with them in order to learn their often unstated requirements. Users should let analysts know early in the design process the acceptable limits for *key system characteristics*—such as *response time, report run time, report costs, overall system usage cost, usage requirements,* and so on.

As part of the design of a new system, the software packages are purchased or designed. When acquiring software, analysts first need to decide whether to purchase the software or build it in-house. Once all aspects of the new system have been completed, management approves the new system's actual design, and then conversion is undertaken.

Analysts need to be aware that because new information systems tend to eliminate the more routine, clerical tasks performed by employees, they must help managers redesign jobs and restructure the organization to compensate for these changes. Criteria for effectively designed jobs include maintaining *intrinsic rewards* in the job itself, making use of a broad range of *individual skills,* and maintaining *individual autonomy.*

There are four approaches to conversion: in *direct conversion,* the organization stops using the old system and begins using the new system with no overlap. In *parallel conversion,* the old and new systems are

used concurrently, and the output is compared at various stages to make sure the new system is running correctly. When it is, the old system is then discontinued. *Phased conversion* involves introducing one module of a large system at a time, and a *pilot conversion* is performed when the system is used in only one part of the company until all the problems are solved.

Once the system is functioning properly, analysts provide *documentation* to users that details the procedures and techniques used in the system, as well as the technical specifications of the hardware and software.

If major changes in hardware are required for a new information system, a separate *feasibility study* is undertaken before systems design begins. Analysts use the *request for proposal (RFP)* to obtain specific technical information from vendors and to ask for information about the vendor itself. Two parts to a successful RFP are: (1) the description of the organization's needs, often called a *needs analysis,* and (2) a *request for information about the vendor itself* to help evaluate the proposal.

KEY TERMS

Automated design tools	Internal analyst
Budgetary constraint	Key user
Business system	Legal constraint
Chief programmer	Outside consultant
Computer-aided software engineering (CASE) tools	Parallel conversion
	Phased conversion
	Pilot conversion
Controls	Problem definition
Cost-benefit analysis	Prototyping
Data flow diagram	Qualitative evaluation
Direct conversion	Quantitative evaluation
Documentation package	Request for proposal (RFP)
Equipment constraint	
Feasibility study	Soft-dollar value
Feedback	Structured analysis
File conversion	System flowchart
Hard-dollar value	System life cycle
Implementation	Systems analyst
Information system	

CHAPTER SELF-TEST

1. The _____ is the formal document prepared by the analyst, which defines in the utmost detail all aspects of the current system.
2. The _____ must work closely with users when creating a new system design.
3. Two types of measures of the cost of a system are _____ and _____.
4. Once analysts have fully designed a system, they must prepare a formalized, detailed record called the _____, describing that design.

5. (T *or* F) Preparing a cost-benefit analysis for a proposed system is usually the responsibility of a cost accountant.

6. Bids from _____ must be compared during a feasibility study.

7. (T *or* F) The systems analyst's role in an organization is essentially advisory.

8. (T *or* F) A new design must be based on current systems objectives, which cannot be altered in the revised system.

9. (T *or* F) Legal constraints can generally be modified in the new system.

10. (T *or* F) If an analyst suggests a new form of output in the system design, then the user should not question it because the analyst is more qualified to decide what is best for the system as a whole.

11. (T *or* F) Systems analysts should always design systems using computer equipment to replace all manual operations.

12. (T *or* F) A systems flowchart depicts the relationships between inputs, processing, and outputs for the system as a whole.

13. (T *or* F) The documentation supplied by the user describes the new system design in detail.

14. An analyst must evaluate the way a current system meets its _____.

15. Suppose, in the current system, a payroll check is incorrectly computed. The procedures used to correct the error are part of _____.

16. Four methods of collecting data on an existing system are _____, _____, _____, and _____.

17. The basic inadequacies of the present system are described in the _____.

18. _____ and _____ procedures must be integrated in a new design to ensure that the proposed system will function properly and to pinpoint any minor flaws so they may be corrected before they become major ones.

19. It is usually necessary for the systems analyst to justify a new design from a _____ basis to convince managers that it is workable.

20. A _____ is a document that analysts send to vendors to solicit technical information about computer systems.

SOLUTIONS 1) problem definition. 2) systems analyst. 3) qualitative or soft-dollar; quantitative or hard-dollar. 4) documentation package. 5) False. It is the responsibility of the systems analyst. 6) computer vendors. 7) True. 8) False. Objectives can, and frequently do, change. 9) False. Legal constraints cannot be changed. 10) False. Designing output is a joint task of both users and analysts. 11) False. New designs can include both manual and computerized components. 12) True. 13) False. Documentation is supplied by the analyst. 14) objectives. 15) controls and feedback. 16) review documents; observe employees; design and distribute questionnaires; interview employees. 17) problem definition. 18) Control; feedback. 19) cost. 20) request for proposal.

REVIEW QUESTIONS

1. What are the two common types of systems analysts? List and discuss three skills that they need to be successful in developing systems.

2. List the steps for writing a problem definition and briefly discuss their importance in analyzing existing business systems.

3. List and briefly discuss four methods of gathering data about business systems. Which method do you think is most important?

4. What are the seven component parts of a business system?

5. Briefly describe four tools analysts use to analyze systems.

6. What are three specific issues to consider when analyzing the tasks of a business system? How do these issues help analysts evaluate a system?

7. Briefly describe two common ways analysts measure the cost and benefits of business systems.

8. Briefly discuss two responsibilities that users have during the design phase of a new system.

8. What two choices do analysts have when acquiring new software? What are two advantages and disadvantages of each choice?

9. Under what conditions would an analyst need to prepare a Request for Proposal (RFP)? Is preparing an RFP part of the analysis and design process? Explain your answer.

PROBLEM-SOLVING APPLICATIONS

1. Do you think Margaret should purchase software or hire someone to write software for the MBA program's new information system? Explain your answer.

2. Which of the five possible design alternatives that Margaret provided would have required an RFP? Write a brief RFP for one of the alternatives.

3. The MBA office consists of an executive director (Margaret's boss), an administrative assistant (Margaret), a program director, a faculty chairman, a faculty secretary, and a receptionist. If Margaret and the faculty secretary will maintain the new computer system, do you think their jobs should be redesigned? If so, briefly describe how you would change their job titles and descriptions.

4. Draw a data flow diagram for the registration process in your school. Can you see areas for improvement? If so, what are they?

Database Management Systems

When you have completed this chapter, you will be able to:

- ✔ Recognize and understand database terminology.
- ✔ Describe the roles of four types of database users.
- ✔ Describe the basic components of database management systems, including data definition language, data manipulation language, general utilities, and 4GL tools such as application and report generators.
- ✔ Distinguish between the three types of database models and describe the advantages and disadvantages of each.
- ✔ List and describe common field types.
- ✔ Describe the ways in which alphanumeric, numeric, and date fields are used.
- ✔ Describe how and why files are indexed.

Chapter 11

Chapter Outline

Database management systems create, edit, update, and report from the databases on which business information systems are based. For example, all businesses normally have an accounting system, and that system has files that contain records of all sales and all customers, of purchases and vendors, of employees and their payroll data, of budgets and financial plans, and so on. A database consists of a collection of these files, which can be joined, manipulated, or otherwise accessed to provide company-wide information for top-level managers.

Each functional business area may have database needs that partially overlap with other functional areas. For example, the marketing department needs access to database records of sales and customers, as well as product records and current inventory levels. The manufacturing department needs access to database records of purchases of raw goods and vendors, as well as inventory data. Databases enable users to access and cross-reference data from different files easily and efficiently.

You were introduced to databases for microcomputers in Chapter 3, and to the way data is stored in Chapter 6. In this chapter we will deal with database management systems (DBMSs)—the software that systems analysts use to create, edit, update, and report from an organization's database.

Most large companies have their database management systems on mainframes or minicomputers; small businesses, however, often use microcomputer DBMSs. The majority of companies buy commercially available DBMS packages, because it would take hundreds or even thousands of hours to develop these powerful tools. There are numerous vendors for such packages; moreover, most DBMSs can be customized to meet each user's specifications. Later in this chapter, we will use two commercial DBMS packages to illustrate common database management concepts.

You have already been introduced to most of the terminology used to describe database management systems. The following "In a Nutshell" box provides brief definitions of these terms. We will provide more in-depth discussions of each term as we proceed through the chapter.

How Data Is Organized and Retrieved

First of all, let us review the data hierarchy concepts introduced in Chapter 6. You may want to reread the section in Chapter 6 that deals with data hierarchy. Figure 11–1 shows a graphic representation of the relationship of fields, records, files, and databases. The text that follows expands on this terminology.

Database. A **database** is a collection of related files within an organization. An organization may have more than one database consisting of related files. A database usually includes more than one file, but may contain only one. The fields within a database can be joined or otherwise interrelated for query purposes.

As an example, a school may have a database containing the names and authors of all the books in its library, a short description of each book, a list of books checked out, a list of books on order, and a list of students who are

In a Nutshell

Common Database Terms

Field: The individual units of data that are stored within a record. For example, an employee's date of hire and Social Security number are fields in each employee's record.

Record: A collection of related fields. For example, each employee has a record in an employee file, and each record contains fields of data related to that employee.

File: A collection of related records. For example, an employee file consists of employee records.

Database: A collection of related files. For example, a company's database would contain files of employees, customers, product numbers, inventory, and so on.

Key field: A field on which records can be indexed in some logical order for fast access. For example, employee records can be indexed on their employee numbers or Social Security numbers, both of which can be key fields.

Index: A file that contains two lists: the disk address of each record in the main file and the corresponding key field for that record. For example, an index for an employee file might contain all Social Security numbers and the disk address for each matching employee record. Indexing allows direct access to each record. (Also see **key field**.) That is, to access a record directly, the computer finds the key field in the index which specifies the disk address for that record.

Database management system: A software package that makes it possible to create, maintain, and access databases. Oracle, Ingres, and dBASE IV are examples of database management systems.

eligible to borrow books. Each list is to be in a separate file. This composite group of files makes up the library's database.

The same school might have another database containing information about all its employees, including salaries, dates hired, home addresses, year-to-date payments, year-to-date deductions, amounts paid to the IRS, and any other information needed to implement the school's payroll application. It is likely that the year-to-date payroll and state and federal tax-deduction information would be in one file, while the rest of the pertinent employee information would be in another file. Having the two files each containing different payroll information is more efficient because several different functional groups can access employee data—accounting and payroll, as well as the personnel department—and they each may need different data. If, instead, each record contained *all* employee data, the file would be very long, and its retrieval time extensive. Such files would also be far more difficult to access in a multi-user environment.

Database File.   A **database file** is a collection of records used in a given application, such as payroll or accounts payable. A file usually contains many records, each with the same structure. A payroll file, for example, may consist of numerous payroll records, each with a similar format.

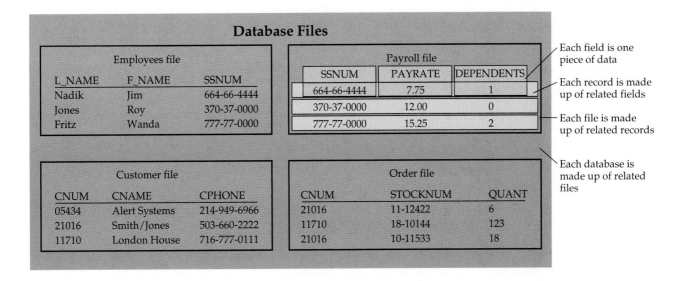

Database Files

Employees file		
L_NAME	F_NAME	SSNUM
Nadik	Jim	664-66-4444
Jones	Roy	370-37-0000
Fritz	Wanda	777-77-0000

Payroll file		
SSNUM	PAYRATE	DEPENDENTS
664-66-4444	7.75	1
370-37-0000	12.00	0
777-77-0000	15.25	2

Customer file		
CNUM	CNAME	CPHONE
05434	Alert Systems	214-949-6966
21016	Smith/Jones	503-660-2222
11710	London House	716-777-0111

Order file		
CNUM	STOCKNUM	QUANT
21016	11-12422	6
11710	18-10144	123
21016	10-11533	18

Each field is one piece of data

Each record is made up of related fields

Each file is made up of related records

Each database is made up of related files

Record.   A **record** is a collection of fields that represents one entity within a file, such as an employee record within an employee payroll file, or a record of customer information within an accounts receivable file (Figure 11–1).

All the records in the file generally have the same structure—that is, each record contains the same fields, and the fields hold the same type of information. The contents of the fields for each record, however, are different.

Field.   A **field** is a unit of data within a record (Figure 11–1). For example, the salary and number of dependents claimed would each be a field in a payroll file, and the customer name and telephone number fields would be in an accounts receivable file of customers.

Database Application.   A **database application** is a specific use for a DBMS package. For example, accounting systems and inventory systems use database packages to create, edit, update, and maintain records for reporting purposes. Figure 11–2 shows examples of applications using information from the employee file, payroll file, and accounts receivable file. Many database packages can produce customized applications. Applications are designed to accomplish a wide variety of tasks within a functional area such as marketing or accounting.

11–1 A database consists of related files; each file in turn contains records which are subdivided into fields of data.

Who Uses Databases?

Database applications are designed or used by four types of users: managers and other end-users, computer professionals such as programmers and systems analysts, data entry personnel, and the database administrator who manages the overall use of the database. Well-designed applications include special screens and reports that are adapted for the needs of each of these groups.

When applications are effectively designed, data entry personnel and managers can learn to use them without any technical training—it should

An organizations database stores data → That is processed by customized database applications ──→ To produce needed business output

11–2 DBMS software packages can be customized to produce checks, invoices, telephone directories, and other desired business output from related files in an organization's database.

not be necessary to know the specifics of the database programs to use the application. Application design itself is also becoming easy in newer DBMS packages, and experienced users can now design their own applications, even without technical training as programmers. Let us look at the ways the four types of users interact with a database application.

Managers and Other End-Users.   These are the decision makers in the company's functional areas who use database information in their work. They need menus that allow them to access information in the database, either as screen displays or as reports that give them hard-copy information in a form that best supports their decision making.

Computer Professionals.   Programmers and systems analysts customize a DBMS for a specific organization's needs; they then create new applications and maintain and update current applications. The computer professionals need screens and reports that allow them to test an application during development and revise and expand an application as needed.

Data Entry Personnel.   Employees who input data may work in the information processing department or in any of the functional departments. They

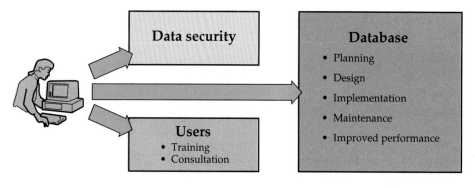

11–3 A database administrator's duties include ensuring data security, controlling the database life cycle, and supporting user needs.

need menus and screen displays for editing and updating records as well as reports in the form of listings that allow them to verify the data entered.

The Database Administrator.   You might look at the database administrator as the equivalent of the head librarian in a library, who is responsible for the books and the operation of the library. The database administrator is responsible for the databases and the information contained in them as well as for the operation and maintenance of the database management system. A list of some of the database administrator's duties is illustrated in Figure 11–3.

Parts of a Database Management System

Most database management systems have five basic components as shown in Figure 11–4: a data definition language (DDL), a data manipulation language (DML), general utilities, an application generator, and a report generator. Many DBMSs also have a data dictionary. We will consider each component in detail.

Data Definition Language

The **data definition language (DDL)** is a set of technical specifications for the database's fields and the relationships between data. Each DBMS package has its own DDL, but all have similar functions.

11–4 The five parts of a database management system allow organizations to set up and use their databases for a wide range of customized applications.

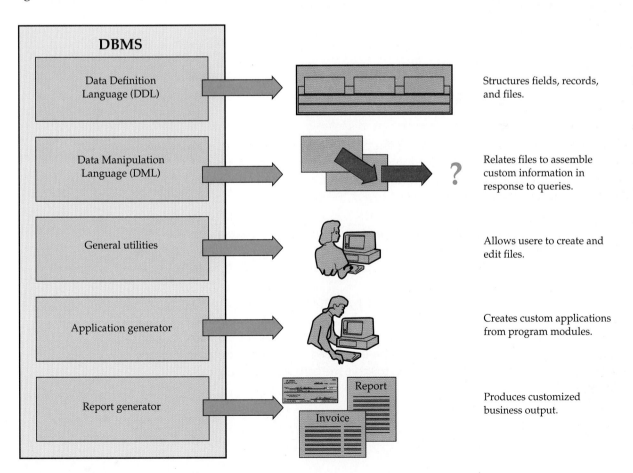

Data Definition Language (DDL)	Structures fields, records, and files.
Data Manipulation Language (DML)	Relates files to assemble custom information in response to queries.
General utilities	Allows usere to create and edit files.
Application generator	Creates custom applications from program modules.
Report generator	Produces customized business output.

Data Manipulation Language

Database management packages typically have some form of **data manipulation language (DML)** available to users that allow them to create custom-designed applications. Many of these are proprietary—that is, the DML is unique to that package. These languages—also called **query languages**—can be classified as fourth-generation languages, because they typically allow you to simply ask for a whole procedure rather than list all the steps to be followed. Query languages use simple English words such as APPEND, MODIFY, or DELETE and are therefore easier to learn than third-generation languages such as COBOL or Pascal.

One query language, **SQL** (Structured Query Language), has recently become a standard for DMLs. Because of its popularity, some databases that have their own proprietary data manipulation languages such as dBASE and R:BASE, for example, have added SQL capability in their most recent versions. Other query languages used by many DBMSs include QBE (Query by Example) and QUEL (Query Language).

Later in this chapter, we will use query language examples from Oracle and dBASE IV, so you will see the English-like nature of database query languages.

Many DBMSs also allow third-generation procedural languages such as COBOL and Pascal to be used to design applications. The DBMS's query language can be embedded within the procedural language. This allows application designers to go beyond the limitations of the package's own data manipulation language to design large and complex applications.

General Utilities

General **utilities** are the components of a DBMS that allow you to maintain the database by editing data, deleting records, creating new files, and so on.

Application and Report Generators

The **application generator** is the component of a DBMS that allows you to create applications without writing programs. It is actually a collection of program modules. You request specific tasks, and the application generator selects the appropriate program modules.

The **report generator** makes it easy to ask for and format reports. It allows you to define row and column heads, to repeat report and page headers at the top of each page, and so on. DBMS report generators allow you to create readable and attractive reports on short notice and with little computer expertise.

As you learned in Chapter 9, query languages, application generators, and report generators are all regarded as fourth-generation programming languages, because they allow people without programming experience to design computer applications. Moreover, the user need only learn English-like commands, rather than program logic, to have the computer execute full procedures.

Data Dictionary

Many DBMSs include a **data dictionary**, which is a software component that defines many aspects of the database—such as the technical specifications of the data, how data is used by end-users, who has access to specific parts of the database and their passwords, and so on. A data dictionary also maintains data integrity because as data is entered, the dictionary checks it to make sure it is within the parameters specified.

The data dictionary also controls multiple access of the data—that is, multiple users can read data in a file simultaneously, but only one user at a time can add, delete, or otherwise change a file's data. This minimizes the risk of a user attempting to change data that is being updated by someone else.

The term *locked* is used to refer to a record or file that can be read by all system users but only written to by one person at a time. For example, if you are creating an index, the whole file will be locked. On the other hand, if you are changing a field in a single record, only that record will be locked.

The data dictionary is maintained by the database administrator.

Types of DBMS Models

Three models are commonly used for database management systems: relational, hierarchical, and network. We are going to give the most attention to relational databases, because they are the most widely used on both mainframes and microcomputers.

Each of the three models has characteristics that make it appropriate for particular applications. One important difference between the three is that for hierarchical and network DBMSs, the structure often cannot be changed after data is entered, whereas relational DBMSs allow the structure to be changed at any time. On the other hand, for large, long-running applications where the same processing will take place over and over again and the structure is not expected to change, hierarchical and network DBMSs may be a better choice because they are often more quickly accessible than relational DBMSs.

In Chapter 3, you were introduced to file management systems and relational DBMSs—the most common types of database software used on microcomputers. We will explain why file management systems are not true DBMSs, and then explain how each of the three DBMS models work.

File Management Systems

File management systems are not true database management systems, because data in one file cannot be linked in any way to data in another file. A file management system is often very useful for storing simple data on a microcomputer or even a mainframe—for example, you might use a file manager to store your personal address book—but it is too limited for most large-scale database applications. Symantec's Q&A, PFS File from Software Publishing, and Reflex from Borland are three examples of microcomputer file management programs (Figure 11–5).

11–5 A file management system can be used to create and maintain individual files, such as this address listing created on the Macintosh in Reflex Plus.

File management systems are generally inexpensive and easy to use. Typically, they provide no data manipulation language and have very few utilities.

File management systems are usually limited to some maximum number of records such as 65,535; this may be too small for some applications. There may also be limitations on the size of records or the number of fields permitted.

Now we will consider the three database models.

Relational Databases

Relational database management systems are the most commonly used type of database system for all levels of computers, from micros to mainframes.

Many relational DBMS packages present files in table format to their users--with the records as rows and the fields as columns (Figure 11–6). Data is easily visualized in tabular form. Note, however, that the computer does not actually store files in table form; more often, files are stored as a sequen-

11–6 DBMS systems usually present file information in table format, as shown in this screen from dBASE IV.

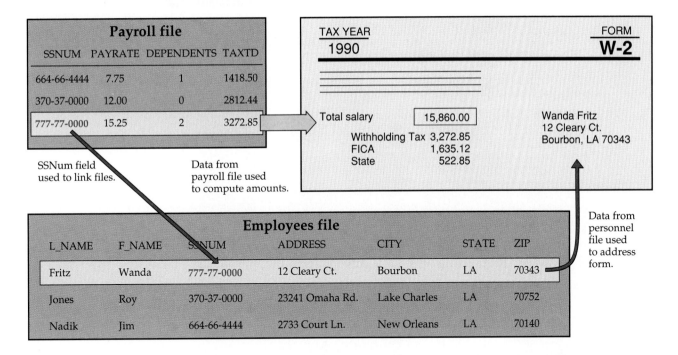

<table>
<tr><td colspan="4">Payroll file</td></tr>
<tr><td>SSNUM</td><td>PAYRATE</td><td>DEPENDENTS</td><td>TAXTD</td></tr>
<tr><td>664-66-4444</td><td>7.75</td><td>1</td><td>1418.50</td></tr>
<tr><td>370-37-0000</td><td>12.00</td><td>0</td><td>2812.44</td></tr>
<tr><td>777-77-0000</td><td>15.25</td><td>2</td><td>3272.85</td></tr>
</table>

SSNum field
used to link files.

Data from
payroll file used
to compute amounts.

TAX YEAR
1990

FORM
W-2

Total salary   15,860.00

Withholding Tax 3,272.85
FICA   1,635.12
State   522.85

Wanda Fritz
12 Cleary Ct.
Bourbon, LA 70343

Employees file

L_NAME	F_NAME	SSNUM	ADDRESS	CITY	STATE	ZIP
Fritz	Wanda	777-77-0000	12 Cleary Ct.	Bourbon	LA	70343
Jones	Roy	370-37-0000	23241 Omaha Rd.	Lake Charles	LA	70752
Nadik	Jim	664-66-4444	2733 Court Ln.	New Orleans	LA	70140

Data from
personnel
file used
to address
form.

tial stream of records. In addition, these records are not necessarily stored in the order in which they appear in a table. But relational databases can easily display data in table form in any sequence desired.

A major advantage of relational DBMSs is that they allow you to link or relate several database files. For example, the payroll department might need employees' addresses only once a year, when W-2 forms are mailed out. The payroll file includes social security numbers, but not employees' addresses. These addresses might be found in a separate personnel file that also includes social security numbers. The social security field, called SSNUM, would function as a key field to link the payroll and personnel files so that the application that generates W-2 forms can retrieve employee addresses from the personnel file (Figure 11–7).

Both files are indexed on the SSNUM field. An index, you will recall, consists of two matched lists: the key field for each record and the disk address of the corresponding record. This indexed list provides a fast way for the DBMS to access the desired data without scanning a file from beginning to end.

Suppose you wanted to produce a screen report containing employee names, departments, and tax withheld to date so that you could visually check payroll data. Figure 11–8 shows one way to display the required data using dBASE IV.

Notice that dBASE IV's programming language uses plain English words, although in very abbreviated sentences. The names this user has assigned to files and fields are also abbreviated but are easy to understand— SSNUM is social security number, PAYIND is payroll index, and so on. Let's go through the commands so that you understand how this procedural language interacts with the database.

11–7 To send W-2 forms, the DBMS uses salary information from the payroll file and then uses the SSNUM field to locate the corresponding employee address in the personnel file.

```
. SELECT 1
        Selects an initial file work area.
. USE EMPLOYEES
        Opens the EMPLOYEES personnel file as file 1.
. INDEX ON SSNUM TO EMPIND
        Indexes on SSNUM field and creates an index file called EMPIND.
. SELECT 2
        Selects a second file work area.
. USE PAYROLL
        Opens the PAYROLL file as file 2.
. INDEX ON SSNUM TO PAYIND
        Indexes on SSNUM field and creates an index file called PAYIND.
. SET RELATION TO EMPLOYEES INTO SSNUM
        Relates SSNUM for both files.
. GO TOP
        Goes to the top of the first record in the linked files.
. DISPLAY ALL FIELDS SSNUM,TAXTD,ENAME,EDEPT
        Displays fields where SSNUM in EMPLOYEES file = SSNUM in
        PAYROLL file.
```

11–8 This is a sample dBASE IV program to display merged data from employees and payroll files.

1. The SELECT command is used to assign a file work area. Each file in use must have its own work area. This command specifies work area 1.

2. The USE command opens or readies a file for access and assigns it to the previously SELECTed work area. The EMPLOYEES personnel file, is here assigned to work in area 1.

3. The INDEX command creates an index using the key field SSNUM and tells the database to place the index in a file named EMPIND.

4. A second work area is specified for the PAYROLL file, and it is indexed similarly (with SELECT/USE/INDEX).

5. SET RELATION tells the system to relate the currently SELECTed file—which is PAYROLL—with the EMPLOYEES personnel file and specifies the key field to use, which is SSNUM.

6. The GO TOP command tells the database to go to the top of the list created from the two related files—that is, to the first record in the linked files.

7. The DISPLAY command tells dBASE to create a screen display, and ALL tells it to display all records. FIELDS specifies which fields in the records to display—in this case, the SSNUM and TAXTD (tax to date) fields in the payroll file and the ENAME (employee name) and EDEPT (employee department) fields in the EMPLOYEES personnel file.

The resulting table would look like the one in Figure 11–9. It cannot be edited directly because it is not a real file.

Let us take a look at another application for a relational DBMS: how the IRS might set up files to verify that taxpayers are declaring all their income (Figure 11–10). The IRS has data from bank records as well as the data from

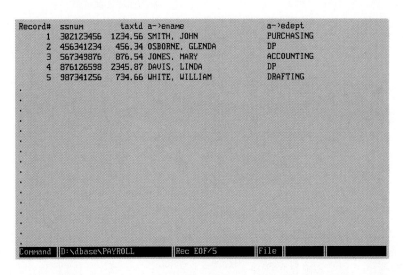

```
Record#  ssnum       taxtd a->ename         a->edept
      1  302123456  1234.56 SMITH, JOHN      PURCHASING
      2  456341234   456.34 OSBORNE, GLENDA  DP
      3  567349876   876.54 JONES, MARY      ACCOUNTING
      4  876126598  2345.87 DAVIS, LINDA     DP
      5  987341256   734.66 WHITE, WILLIAM   DRAFTING
      .
      .
      .
      .
      .
      .
      .
      .
      .
      .
      .
      .
      .
 Command  D:\dbase\PAYROLL       Rec EOF/5      File
```

11–9 This is the merged file created by the program in Figure 11–8. It can only be viewed or printed; it cannot be edited.

income tax returns submitted by each taxpayer. File 1 is a bank file, with fields for each customer name, bank account number, Social Security number, total deposits for the past year, and total interest earned. File 2 is the IRS's own data, including fields for taxpayer name, Social Security number, reported income, and reported interest earned from bank deposits. The Social Security number is the key field used to link these two files. The application compares each taxpayer's total interest earned for the year with the reported interest earned. In this way, the IRS can flag any returns in which reported interest was less than actual interest.

In summary, relational databases use key fields to link files so that users can create applications that relate appropriate data in two or more files.

Hierarchical Databases

A **hierarchical database** is organized like a tree planted upside down, with the root field at the top. For example, in Figure 11–11, the root field (the top field in the diagram) is an academic department in a college. One branch from the root field contains the Introduction to Marketing course, another contains the Managerial Accounting course, and the third contains the Business Law course.

Each data item or group of data items shown in the tree diagram is called a *segment* or, sometimes, a *record*. A segment in a hierarchical DBMS is equivalent to a file in a relational database. You could consider the segments to be arranged like a family tree in a parent-child relationship. Parent segments (Departments, for example) appear higher than the child segments

11–10 Here, the IRS uses Social Security numbers to compare individual tax records of bank income with the bank's records.

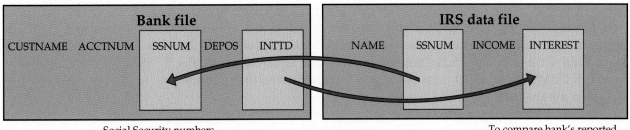

Social Security numbers are used to link files

To compare bank's reported interest with IRS records

Department segment

Course segment

Faculty segment

(Courses) in the diagram. Each parent segment can have more than one child, but a child can only have one parent. This is called a *one-to-many relationship*. Each segment lies on a hierarchical path, from the root segment following branches to the farthest child, and a given segment cannot appear on more than one path.

This means that faculty teach only one type of course. If a faculty member taught both business law and introduction to marketing, this model would not be totally effective. Similarly, if there were a Managerial Accounting Course in both the business and law departments, a hierarchical database model would require modification.

A current hierarchical database management system from IBM is called IMS/VS. The database portion of the product is called DL/1 or DB. The database can be accessed by using DL/1 commands in PL/1, COBOL, or assembler language—all procedural programming languages.

Network Databases

Network and hierarchical databases are similar in many ways. In a hierarchical database, a child can only have one parent. However, *network databases* permit more than one parent per child. A child with no parent is also permitted.

Figure 11–12 shows the department/course/faculty example for a network database. Notice that faculty who teach more than one course do not have to be listed for each course. Network DBMSs can create complex relationships among types of data and thus are suited to many different types of applications. However, users are limited to the connections that have been defined by the application's designer. Like hierarchical DBMSs, network DBMS applications must be created by experienced programmers and systems analysts.

The most popular network database architecture is called the CODASYL (Conference on Data Systems Languages) model. Its development was sim-

11–11 Segments of data in a hierarchical database are arranged in increasingly detailed levels. Each segment can have only one upward

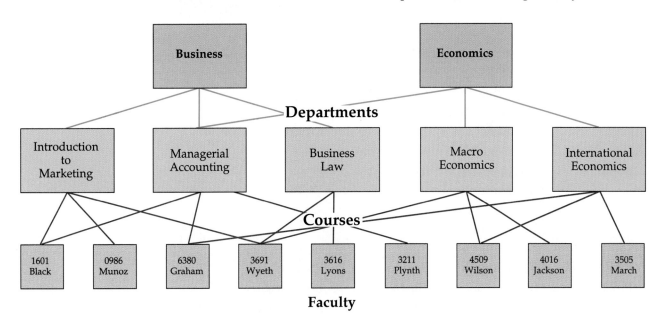

Departments

Courses

Faculty

ilar to that of the COBOL language—it was developed by a CODASYL committee. Many commercial products use the CODASYL model; one such is TOTAL from Cincom. DML (Data Manipulation Language) is used to process records in a CODASYL database. The DML commands were designed to be used in application programs written in COBOL, FORTRAN, or a similar language.

11–12 Segments of data in a network database can have multiple relationships to segments on a higher level.

---

1. The field on which relational database files are indexed is called the _____ field.
2. A collection of related files is called a _____.
3. Another term sometimes used for a file in a relational database is a _____, because it can be envisioned as having rows and columns.
4. Applications designers and users access a database by using its _____ _____ language.
5. (T *or* F) Application generators are actually a collection of program modules.
6. (T *or* F) File managers are an inexpensive form of DBMS.
7. (T *or* F) One difference between hierarchical and network databases is that in network databases, "child" records can have more than one "parent."

SOLUTIONS 1) key. 2) database. 3) table. 4) data manipulation. 5) True. 6) False. File managers are not true DBMSs because each file can only be processed independently. 7) True.

Common Database Management Systems

Table 11–1 lists some of the better-known database management systems currently available, together with the kinds of computers they run on, the type of database structure they use, and the data manipulation language (DML) they use; those that list "Proprietary" have their own unique DML.

To give you a sense of how database applications are designed with a DBMS package, we are going to outline the steps you would use to create an application in dBASE IV and then in Oracle, which are both popular relational database management systems. The dBASE IV package is used only on microcomputers, while Oracle is used on all levels of computers—often

DBMS	*Computer*	*Structure*	*DML*
DB2	Mainframe	Relational	SQL, QBE
dBASE IV	Microcomputer	Relational	Proprietary, SQL
FoxBASE+	Microcomputer	Relational	Proprietary
IDMS	Mainframe	Network	Proprietary
IMS/VS	Mainframe	Hierarchical	CICS
Ingres	Minicomputer Microcomputer	Relational	SQL QUEL
Oracle	Mainframe Minicomputer Microcomputer	Relational	SQL
PARADOX	Microcomputer	Relational	Proprietary
PFS File	Microcomputer	File Manager	Proprietary
Q&A	Microcomputer	File Manager	Proprietary
R:BASE	Microcomputer	Relational	Proprietary, SQL

Table 11–1 Common database management systems.

on networked systems that allow microcomputers to communicate with minicomputers and mainframes.

Although the language and procedures used to create applications vary between DBMSs, they are all capable of performing the operations described in these examples. We will use a common database application—a mailing list that will be used to create mailing labels.

Setting the Database File Structure

First, let us review the steps you will follow in creating the structure of the mailing list database file. You will name the fields, define the field types, determine the length of the fields, and name the file.

Naming the Fields. Your first task is to define the fields that will be in each record. The rules for naming the fields vary among database management systems. In dBASE IV, a field name can have up to 10 characters, including letters, digits, and the underline character, which is most often used as a separator (e.g., L_NAME). No spaces or punctuation are permitted. The first character must be a letter.

DBMSs sometimes have reserved words that have special meaning to the database management system and must not be used as field names. Some DBMSs, for example, have TOTAL as a reserved word. Because it is the command used to perform a summing operation on the database, it must not be used for anything else, such as a field name. DATE is a reserved word in many DBMSs, because it supplies the current date. Many other very useful words have the same restrictions.

A record in any DBMS should not contain two or more identical field names. Finally, if possible, each field name should be meaningful, giving some indication of the data it contains. Field names like NAME, ADDRESS,

CITY, STATE, ZIP, SALARY, and so on, are more useful than names like A1, B17, CC12, etc.

Defining the Field Types.   Each field must be assigned a data type. Some of the most common field types are:

- **Numeric**   Used for numeric values that are likely to be used in computations. Amount fields, for example, are typically defined as numeric because they are apt to be totalled. An account number, though likely to contain only numbers, would typically be defined as a character field because it is not used in arithmetic.

- **Alphanumeric or Character**   Used for text field. This type can consist of any alphanumeric characters; it may have a length limit. For larger amounts of text, use the memo type (explained shortly). If digits are stored in a character field, you cannot use them for arithmetic calculations without using a function to convert the value to numeric.

- **Float**   Used for very large values, such as the amount of the national debt or the distance in light years between two stars.

- **Date**   Used for dates, which are most often stored in MM/DD/YY format but can be displayed in any date format.

- **Logical**   Used to specify a yes/no or true/false condition, known as Boolean values. For example, the field could be named CITIZEN with a Y or N indicating whether each employee is a U.S. citizen. Logical fields are only one character long.

- **Memo**   Used for large amounts of character data that often contains text. A memo field is actually a 10-position pointer field that points to data stored in a separate file automatically linked to the active database file. In dBASE, the length of the text that is accessed by a memo field is limited to slightly over 64,000 characters.

Deciding on Length of the Fields.   After establishing a field name and a field type, you must decide how long each field must be; that is, how many characters or digits is it to hold? It is important to make the fields large enough to hold the anticipated data, but not any larger than necessary.

In dBASE IV, the length of three types of fields—logical, date, and memo—is already set. Logical fields are always one byte in length (to represent T or F, or Y or N), date fields are eight bytes (MM/DD/YY), and memo fields are ten bytes to point to a second file that contains the actual memo (which can be up to 64 K characters long).

Numeric fields can contain any number of digits and decimal places. They should be large enough to store the largest possible value that can be contained in the field. However, accurate calculation is limited to 20 digits for standard numeric fields and 15 digits for float fields.

Naming the File.   Different database management systems have their own rules about the number and kinds of characters permitted in a file name. In addition, if many files are used in a database application, it can be useful to provide some pattern for names, such as making the first one or two characters identical as prefixes, so that you can remember that the files belong together.

For our examples in this section we will use the name MAILLIST for the master file.

Considerations in Designing Fields

There are a number of factors to consider when you determine the type and length of each field as well as other database design features. This section will discuss several database design issues.

Data Entry Validation.   Some types of fields have built-in data entry validation: common examples are numeric, float, date, and logical fields. For example, if a data entry operator enters letters in a numeric field by mistake, the DBMS will indicate that an error has occurred, often with a beep plus a message on the screen.

Storing Dates, Times and Other Standard Types of Fields.   Usually, date values should be stored in fields designated as date type. This enables you easily to perform date comparisons and arithmetic calculations on them, such as comparing two dates to see which is more current, subtracting one date from another, or adding or subtracting a number of days from a date. You cannot easily perform such operations on dates stored in a character field.

The contents of a date field can be displayed in many formats. YY means that the year is displayed as two digits (91 for 1991); MM means that the month is displayed in two digits (02 for February), and DD means that the day of the month is two digits (01 through 31).

Format	Display
MM/DD/YY	02/16/45
MM-DD-YY	02-16-45
MM/DD/YYYY	02/16/1945
Month DD, YYYY	February 16, 1945

Storing Numbers.   If a field should always contain numbers only—a digit-only customer number field, for example—it is sometimes a good idea to make it a numeric field, even if you will not do mathematical calculations on the numbers. This reduces data entry errors, because if operators inadvertently enter a letter or symbol in the numeric field, they will get an error message.

Time values are usually stored as characters because of the colons normally used as dividers between the hours, minutes, and seconds.

Telephone numbers are typically stored as character values if parentheses or dashes are used as separators. Similarly, Social Security numbers, which may have dashes, are typically stored as character fields.

Designing the Mailing List Structure

Now you can apply what you have learned to the mailing list example. Let us say you decide to use the following fields for your mailing list:

Field Name	Type	Width
NAME	Character	30
ADDRESS	Character	25
CITY_ST_ZIP	Character	35

You intend to place the city, state, and zip code in the CITY_ST_ZIP field. We will examine the fields one at a time and discover what some of the pitfalls are.

Name.   The intention seems to be to put the complete name—first, last, and middle initial—in a single field. But if you put the first name first, how will you alphabetize the records by last name? If alphabetization is necessary, you will have to enter the last names first and then the first names.

But if the names are in last-name, first-name order, how will you print mailing labels with first name first? You could add a comma after the last name and somehow tell the database to put everything after the comma (e.g., first name) first when it prints the names on the labels. But then what about names like Smith & Co., Inc.? This would appear on the label as Inc. Smith & Co.

To eliminate all these problems, simply segment the name into two fields, first name (F_NAME) and last name (L_NAME), with the middle initial to follow the first name. With these fields you can sort into first or last name sequence as desired. Company names, as a rule, will be entered entirely in the last-name field.

You may also want to add a title field to avoid including things like Mr., Mrs., Ms., Dr., and Prof. in the first-name field. This also permits you to partially separate male names from female, in case you have a mailing you want to send just to men or to women. This would not be completely satisfactory, however, because Dr. and Prof. titles do not indicate sex.

Address.   You may not have enough room for long addresses with such additions as division names, department names, building numbers, suite numbers, mail drops, apartment numbers, and perhaps company names and job titles. It would be best to have two lines or two fields for the address.

City/State/Zip.   By including the city, state, and zip code in one field, you have made it difficult if not impossible to sort the records by state or zip code, or to use the state or zip code data in a query (for example, how many flyers will be mailed to Montana?). If mailings are done with inexpensive bulk mailing postal rates, the items must be presorted by zip code for the post office. Thus separate CITY and STATE and ZIP fields may be preferable to a single CITY_STATE_ZIP field.

Control Number.   You should consider adding a customer number or control number to the record and perhaps the mailing label as well. In some applications, this could be the only field that is always unique; thus, it may be an important key field.

A more useful mailing label record, then, would look like the left example in Figure 11–13.

Field Name	Type	Width
CONTROL	Character	15
TITLE	Character	4
L_NAME	Character	15
F_NAME	Character	15
ADDRESS1	Character	25
ADDRESS2	Character	25
CITY	Character	15
STATE	Character	2
ZIP	Character	5

Field Name	Type	Width
CONTROL	Character	15
TITLE	Character	4
L_NAME	Character	15
F_NAME	Character	15
ADDRESS1	Character	25
ADDRESS2	Character	25
ADDRESS3	Character	25
CITY	Character	15
STATE	Character	2
ZIP	Character	6
COUNTRY	Character	12

If your mailing list will include people residing in foreign countries, you need to add a country field and a third address field for province or other district names. A good structure for an international mailing list would be the right example in Figure 11–13.

11–13 Common structures for a domestic mailing list (left) and for an international mailing list (right).

Creating a Mailing List Structure

In early versions of dBASE, it was critical to get the structure exactly right before you entered data in the database, because the structure could not be modified once data was entered. dBASE IV, however, like most other current DBMSs, allows changes to the database structure to be made at any time—that is, fields can be added, and the lengths of fields can be changed. For example, you might decide at any time to expand the ZIP field of an existing database file from 5 digits to 9 digits to include the four-digit extension that the Postal Service now prefers.

Creating a Mailing List Structure in dBASE IV

The dBASE IV program provides a Control Center that presents most common application choices in menu form, from which you can make selections (Figure 11–14). Here the "Create file" command is being chosen. Alternatively, you could use the program's command mode by exiting the Control Center and typing, for example:

```
. CREATE MAILLIST
```

The period preceding the command line is the dBASE IV *dot prompt*, letting you know the program is prepared to accept a user-supplied command. When you exit the Control Center's menu, dBASE will provide this dot prompt to let you know you are in command mode.

The screen shown in Figure 11–15 would then be displayed. You then enter the specifications for the fields you have decided to use for the mailing list application. The screen then looks like the one shown in Figure 11–16.

Creating a Mailing List Structure in Oracle

Now let us design this structure using Oracle, the DBMS from the Oracle Corporation. The structure will be created using the SQL*Plus program, Oracle's enhanced version of SQL, the popular query language. The following SQL commands set the structure we just created in dBASE IV.

```
CREATE TABLE MAILLIST
(CONTROL CHAR(15),
TITLE CHAR(4),
L_NAME CHAR(15) NOT NULL,
F_NAME CHAR(15),
ADDRESS1 CHAR(25) NOT NULL,
ADDRESS2 CHAR(25),
ADDRESS3 CHAR(25),
CITY CHAR(15) NOT NULL,
STATE CHAR(2),
ZIP CHAR(9),
COUNTRY CHAR(15));
```

You can see that SQL is reasonably close to ordinary English. The statements include the field name, data type, and number of characters per field. As in English, you do have to remember punctuation rules. All the lines after the first one describe the fields in the MAILLIST record; to group them together, you enclose them in a pair of parentheses.

Notice that the word TABLE is used to describe a file. Like many DBMS packages, Oracle uses this term, as well as the terms *row* for each record and *column* for each field.

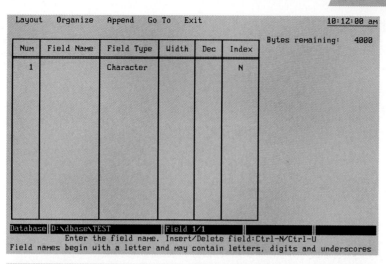

11–15 dBASE IV displays a table format for users to enter specifications for the fields within a file's records.

```
 Layout   Organize   Append   Go To   Exit                    10:12:00 am
                                              Bytes remaining:     4000
 Num  Field Name   Field Type  Width  Dec  Index
  1                 Character                     N




Database D:\dbase\TEST          Field 1/1
           Enter the field name.  Insert/Delete field:Ctrl-N/Ctrl-U
 Field names begin with a letter and may contain letters, digits and underscores
```

11–16 The fields are now fully specified for the MAILLIST file.

```
 Layout   Organize   Append   Go To   Exit                    10:15:34 am
                                              Bytes remaining:     3838
 Num  Field Name   Field Type  Width  Dec  Index
  1   CONTROL       Character    15          N
  2   TITLE         Character     4          N
  3   L_NAME        Character    15          N
  4   F_NAME        Character    15          N
  5   ADDRESS1      Character    25          N
  6   ADDRESS2      Character    25          N
  7   ADDRESS3      Character    25          N
  8   CITY          Character    15          N
  9   STATE         Character     2          N
 10   ZIP           Character     9          N
 11   COUNTRY       Character    12          N

Database D:\dbase\MAILLIST       Field 1/11
           Enter the field name.  Insert/Delete field:Ctrl-N/Ctrl-U
 Field names begin with a letter and may contain letters, digits and underscores
```

We added the SQL phrase NOT NULL to three of the fields (called columns in Oracle). NULL means that a field has no entry, so NOT NULL means that those fields must have an entry of some sort. When data is entered for each record, the L_NAME, ADDRESS1, and CITY fields must not be left blank. The data entry operator will be notified by the system if he or she attempts to bypass these fields.

Entering the Mailing List Data

Most database management systems have alternative ways to create data entry screens. Typically, there is a generic screen that can be used for any application, or you can design custom screens with the DBMS's application generator or by using whatever programming languages are provided with the DBMS.

Entering Data in dBASE IV

In dBASE IV there are three ways you can create data entry screens for entering the data in the MAILLIST file. The first alternative is to initiate data entry from the Control Center or by using command mode. The commands are:

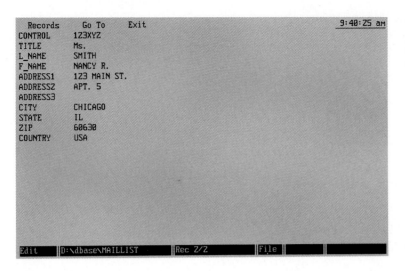

```
    Records     Go To    Exit                          9:40:25 am
CONTROL        123XYZ
TITLE          Ms.
L_NAME         SMITH
F_NAME         NANCY R.
ADDRESS1       123 MAIN ST.
ADDRESS2       APT. 5
ADDRESS3
CITY           CHICAGO
STATE          IL
ZIP            60630
COUNTRY        USA




Edit    ||D:\dbase\MAILLIST ·||Rec 2/2   ||File ||     ||
```

11–17 This is dBASE IV's generic or standard data entry screen with a record entered.

. USE MAILLIST
. APPEND

The first command activates, or opens, the file called MAILLIST, assuming you have already created a structure using the procedures we just described. The second allows you to add records to that file. The program responds to these two commands by providing the generic data entry screen shown in Figure 11–17.

However, you may want to create a custom screen (Figure 11–18) to make data entry more user-friendly. You would use dBASE IV's Forms feature, which is easier to use than Oracle's, but not as powerful. You have some control over how the data is entered. As the form is created, you can specify the number of characters to be entered, the number of decimal places, whether letters only (and whether upper- or lowercase), or digits only are required. You can also specify the range of values allowed, specific characters that must be entered, and so on.

The third alternative for creating a screen display is to use dBASE IV's proprietary programming language; with this language, an application can be created that will do anything SQL can do and sometimes more, often with about the same degree of effort.

Entering Data in Oracle

Oracle has an application generator called SQL*Forms that can be used to create a screen for data entry. SQL*Forms has many useful features common to most DBMS application generators. The data entry application can validate the data entered. For example, it might be designed to verify that the customer number that was entered appears in the existing file of customer information, or that a state abbreviation is valid. The application can also display a list of permissible data for a field and let the operator choose from that group.

SQL*Forms can also fill some fields with data determined by entries in other fields. For example, a price column can be filled automatically if other fields contain the cost and the markup percentage for that item.

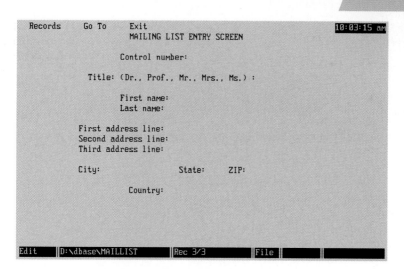

11–18 Customized data entry screens can be created with a DBMS's application generator. These screen displays can make data entry more efficient and easier to learn.

The SQL*Forms application generator allows you to design custom screens appropriate for your application. The fields to be keyed in by data entry operators can be placed anywhere on the screen, and you can add text anywhere as well, including a screen title and prompts for data entry. The data entry screen for the mailing list application shown in Figure 11–18 was designed in dBASE IV, but it could also be created using SQL*Forms or another application generator.

Modifying File Structure

Sometimes it is necessary to alter a file's structure. For example, you may find that an additional field is required, or you may want to delete a field that is never used, or you might need to change a field's size to permit more characters to be entered.

For instance, it is a simple task to make the size of a field larger. However, you should remember to make changes in the data entry screen and in any reports containing that field to accommodate its larger size. If the field is used on mailing labels, you may have to redesign the label to conform with the new size.

It is good practice to plan database structures carefully so that they are designed correctly the first time. In most DBMSs, the structure of a database can be modified, but it is considerably easier and safer to create a structure than to change it. Modifications can have unexpected effects on other parts of the application, and it can be difficult to anticipate all of those effects.

Modifying a File in dBASE IV

In dBASE IV it is a simple matter to modify the structure of a database file, using either the Control Center or command mode. To use the Control Center, you choose "Modify structure/order" and then move the cursor to the name of the database file to be modified. File names are displayed in the Control Center. To use the command mode, simply type

```
. MODIFY STRUCTURE MAILLIST
```

```
   Layout   Organize   Append   Go To   Exit               10:22:33 am
                                                    Bytes remaining:    3838
  ┌─────┬─────────────┬─────────────┬───────┬─────┬───────┐
  │ Num │ Field Name  │ Field Type  │ Width │ Dec │ Index │
  ├─────┼─────────────┼─────────────┼───────┼─────┼───────┤
  │  1  │ CONTROL     │ Character   │  15   │     │   N   │
  │  2  │ TITLE       │ Character   │   4   │     │   N   │
  │  3  │ L_NAME      │ Character   │  15   │     │   N   │
  │  4  │ F_NAME      │ Character   │  15   │     │   N   │
  │  5  │ ADDRESS1    │ Character   │  25   │     │   N   │
  │  6  │ ADDRESS2    │ Character   │  25   │     │   N   │
  │  7  │ ADDRESS3    │ Character   │  25   │     │   N   │
  │  8  │ CITY        │ Character   │  15   │     │   N   │
  │  9  │ STATE       │ Character   │   2   │     │   N   │
  │ 10  │ ZIP         │ Character   │   9   │     │   N   │
  │ 11  │ COUNTRY     │ Character   │  12   │     │   N   │
  └─────┴─────────────┴─────────────┴───────┴─────┴───────┘

 Database D:\dbase\MAILLIST          Field 1/11
          Enter the field name. Insert/Delete field:Ctrl-N/Ctrl-U
  Field names begin with a letter and may contain letters, digits and underscores
```

11–19 This is dBASE IV's standard screen display for modifying a file's structure.

Either way, you will see the screen shown in Figure 11–19. Follow the instructions at the bottom of the screen to add or delete a field. To change a field's name, width, or number of decimal positions, you move the cursor to that field and type over the old data. If you reduce a character field's width, any previous entries exceeding the new width will be truncated from the right. In other words, if the field L_NAME is shortened from 15 to 12 characters, the last name Smith-Davidson will become Smith-Davids.

Modifying a File in Oracle

In Oracle, you can use SQL to modify a table or file. To change a column, you would use the following commands:

```
ALTER TABLE MAILLIST
MODIFY (CONTROL CHAR(20));
```

The first command tells Oracle that you are going to modify the table (or file) called MAILLIST. The second command changes the width of the CONTROL column (or field) from 15 characters to 20. In Oracle, you can change a column to a smaller number of characters only if there are no entries in that column anywhere in the table. To add a new address column, you would use these commands:

```
ALTER TABLE MAILLIST
ADD (ADDRESS4 CHAR(25));
```

Editing Data in Databases

Editing data already entered in a file involves two operations: first you need to locate the record; then you change the data.

Editing Data in dBASE IV

In dBASE IV you can use the Control Center or command mode to move to the record and then use the Control Center or command mode to edit data in the ADDRESS1 field. In command mode, the commands that allow you to search for the record are:

```
. USE MAILLIST
. LOCATE FOR L_NAME = 'SMITH' .AND. F_NAME = 'FRED' .AND.
  ADDRESS1 = '127 ELM ST.'
```

These are the same criteria used in the Oracle example. To change the data, the command is:

```
. EDIT
```

If no custom screen has been designed, the generic data entry screen for that record appears, otherwise the custom screen will be displayed. You simply use the cursor keys to reach the ADDRESS1 field and type the new data over the old.

Another alternative for adding, deleting, or changing data in dBASE IV is to use the BROWSE command. BROWSE permits the entire database file to be displayed and modified. You can move through the file with the cursor keys, adding or deleting records or changing existing data. This can be useful in updating small databases.

Finally, you could write an application using dBASE IV's query language to display the data in all records or in specified records, one at a time. The operator could then be permitted to change the data in specific fields or in all fields.

Editing Data in Oracle

In Oracle you can use SQL or the SQL*Forms application to edit data in a file. The ability to edit a file is set up when you design the input screen in SQL*Forms. You can also edit in SQL. Here are the SQL commands needed to change an address:

```
UPDATE MAILLIST
SET ADDRESS1 = '1234 Main St.'
WHERE L_NAME = 'SMITH' AND F_NAME = 'FRED'
AND ADDRESS1 = '127 ELM ST.';
```

The "MAILLIST" in the first line tells the database management system which file's data is to be altered. The SET line determines the field's new data. The WHERE line determines which record(s) will be changed.

In this example, the command sequence both locates and edits the data; the database would locate all records that meet the criteria for last name, first name, and address1. It is obviously important to make sure that the criteria you set up will locate only the records you want and that other records will not be changed.

Indexing Database Files

Recall that an index consists of two matched lists: the key field for each record and, corresponding to it, the storage address for the record with that key field. Indexes are essential in relational databases. DBMS packages such as Oracle and dBASE IV use indexes to find records quickly and to link files; indexes are often useful in creating reports where the output is required in some sequence other than the one in which the file is stored. A file can have more than one index, though only one index is used at a time. That is, several key fields can be designated for a file. A payroll file, for example, could be

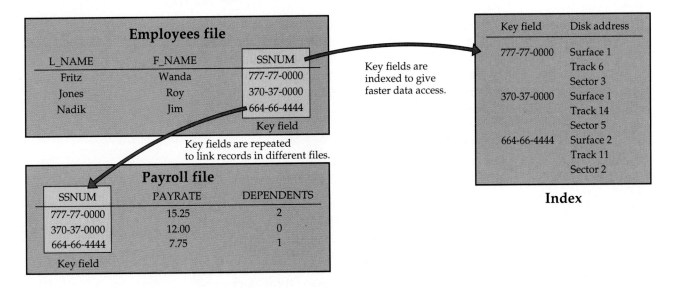

Key field	Disk address
777-77-0000	Surface 1
	Track 6
	Sector 3
370-37-0000	Surface 1
	Track 14
	Sector 5
664-66-4444	Surface 2
	Track 11
	Sector 2

Index

indexed on social security number, employee number, last name, etc. In this way, any one of the key fields could be entered in order to quickly access the corresponding record. As discussed earlier, key fields can also be used to relate records from different files. Figure 11–20 shows how key fields are used by a relational database.

11–20 Key fields have two uses: they are indexed for fast access to data, and they are used to relate records from different files.

An index uses the contents of a key field or a combination of fields to organize the records in ascending or descending order according to that key field. This makes it possible to quickly access records from the database file by the key field. The actual records in the database can be in any order; the index includes the position of each record. Once the criteria for an index are set up, most DBMS packages automatically index each new record that is added and re-sort the index into sequence by key field, so that the index is always in order and up to date.

The selection of the key field or fields on which to index a file is important, because indexes are most effective when there are no duplicate choices. For example, a name field may be a poor choice for a key field, because there are sometimes people with the same name. You can reduce (but not necessarily eliminate) duplicates by combining key fields—last name plus first name plus zip code, for example. A more reliable way is to use a field that contains unique data—such as social security number, or an assigned customer or employee number.

Creating an Index in dBASE IV

In dBASE IV, to create the same index, you would use the commands:

```
. USE MAILLIST
. INDEX ON CONTROL TO MAILIND
```

In subsequent uses of the MAILLIST file—when adding records or creating a report, for example—you must tell dBASE IV that the index exists, or it will not be used or kept up to date:

```
. USE MAILLIST INDEX MAILIND
```

When large database files are indexed in this way, accessing records by the CONTROL number field will be very fast—much faster than if the index did not exist. That is, if you enter a CONTROL number and you wish to access its corresponding record, the DBMS need not search the entire file; it simply looks up the address of the record from the index and goes directly to that location to find the corresponding record.

Creating an Index in Oracle

In Oracle, to create an index named MAILIND (for mail index) based on the contents of the CONTROL number field in the MAILLIST table, you would use the SQL command:

```
CREATE INDEX MAILIND ON MAILLIST(CONTROL);
```

Creating Reports from a Database File

Report generators are one of the most universal features of DBMS packages. All business information systems require a number of reports, and good database packages allow users easily to create attractive, clearly formatted reports, both on screen and on paper.

Creating a Report in dBASE IV

The report generator that dBASE IV has gives you more control over the appearance of your report than does Oracle's SQL*Report and is also easier to use.

For a simple report like the example above, you would use dBASE IV's command mode:

```
. USE MAILLIST INDEX MAILIND
. DISPLAY ALL FIELDS L_NAME,F_NAME,CITY FOR STATE = 'CA'
```

The FOR portion of the command restricts the DBMS to displaying only the California records, in order by control number as specified by the index.

To send this report to the printer, the commands would be:

```
. USE MAILLIST INDEX MAILIND
. LIST FIELDS L_NAME,F_NAME,CITY FOR STATE = 'CA' TO PRINT
```

Figure 11–21 shows a partial report listing as it appears on screen.

Creating a Report in Oracle

In Oracle, you can create reports in either of two ways: you can use SQL to create a simple report, or you can use the SQL*REPORT report generator to produce more complex reports—with totals and subtotals, with information grouped by some criteria, with calculated fields, with formatted headers and footers, with page titles and numbers, and so on. Report generators are discussed in more detail in Chapter 12.

To produce a simple report with SQL, you could use these commands:

```
SELECT L_NAME,F_NAME,CITY
FROM MAILLIST
ORDER ON CONTROL;
```

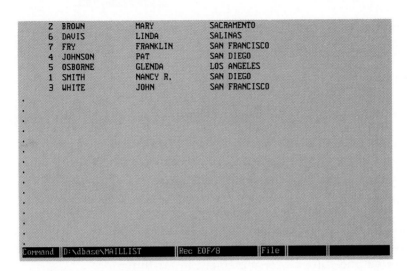

```
    2  BROWN        MARY         SACRAMENTO
    6  DAVIS        LINDA        SALINAS
    7  FRY          FRANKLIN     SAN FRANCISCO
    4  JOHNSON      PAT          SAN DIEGO
    5  OSBORNE      GLENDA       LOS ANGELES
    1  SMITH        NANCY R.     SAN DIEGO
    3  WHITE        JOHN         SAN FRANCISCO
```

```
Command  D:\dbase\MAILLIST        Rec EOF/8        File
```

11–21 The LIST ... TO PRINT command in dBASE IV sends the specified output to both the screen and the printer simultaneously.

The SELECT line determines the fields to be displayed, and the FROM line designates the file to be used. ORDER ON tells the database what index order to use. This would display or print all the names and cities in the table in the order of their control numbers. To show the names and cities only for California, you would use:

```
SELECT L_NAME,F_NAME,CITY
FROM MAILLIST
ORDER ON CONTROL
WHERE STATE = 'CA';
```

If you want to view more fields, they would be added to the SELECT line.

Selecting and Managing a Database Management System

The following factors should be considered when choosing a database management system:

◆ Compatibility with existing hardware

◆ Response time for queries, indexing, sorts, and so on, given the existing hardware

◆ Number of simultaneous users permitted by the DBMS

◆ Restrictive limitations on database, file, or record sizes

◆ The number, type, and quality of query languages and/or programming languages that can be used

◆ Capability and ease of use of the application generator

◆ Capability and ease of use of the report generator

◆ Security features

◆ Type of database models—relational, hierarchical, or network

- Suitability of the DBMS for the needed applications
- Suitability of the DBMS for the projected user's abilities
- Cost

Issues in Database Administration

Two issues in database management—database security and data integrity—are outlined briefly here. They will be discussed in more detail in Chapter 13.

Database Security

Database security refers to the measures needed to protect databases against unauthorized database manipulations on all levels. These measures would be extremely complicated and difficult to implement in far-flung, sensitive systems, such as those that support the NASA space program (Figure 11–22). These security measures are perhaps less complicated, but no less important, to small office systems.

The security offered by various database management systems ranges from nil to excellent. Of the two systems discussed in this chapter—dBASE IV and Oracle—both have log-in security, which prevents unauthorized users from accessing the database management system. Both permit the database administrator to define which files, and which fields within files, that each user can access. The dBASE IV program can make a file unreadable by anyone but the person who owns or shares it. This is called **encryption**. Various access levels can be assigned that define who can read files, update records, delete records, or add data.

11–22 The control room for this NASA flight receives data from public weather systems and secret on-board control systems. Complex information traveling to users scattered around the world, makes data security a major concern. *Courtesy:* NASA.

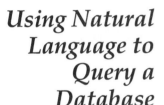

Looking Ahead

Using Natural Language to Query a Database

In the future you will be able to use natural language to query a database over the phone or on a computer terminal and get the answer the same way. Here is a fictitious example using a terminal. The computer's responses are in italics.

How much does John make?
John who?
Smith
I've got two John Smiths, one in Purchasing and one in Sales.
The one in sales.
$20,000 plus commissions.
How much was his commission in 1990?
$32,456.67

If you watch many *Star Trek* or any other science-fiction dramas, you are probably familiar with this concept. It is likely to be in full use well before the 21st century. Some current query languages have begun to approach this level of natural language communication.

Oracle has the more detailed security system, and its data dictionary keeps records of table accesses, log-ins, and other useful security information. This is because Oracle was originally designed to run on a mainframe, and large mainframe database systems need good security precautions, because so many users have access to them.

If a database management system offers no security, then network software that connects database users may offer at least log-in security, restricted access to the database management system, and restricted access to database files.

If no security is available but is required, and several users will be using the same computer or have access to other users' files, there are still solutions. For example, the databases could be stored on removable media so that they can be maintained in a secure place, or an encryption program could be written in the database's query language.

Data Integrity

Data integrity refers to the need to keep the database from being corrupted by invalid data. Corrupted data can come from many sources:

- The media itself might be corrupted by exposure to a magnetic field. This can happen if you leave a disk near a copying machine or a television, for example.

- A user might inadvertently enter a command that incorrectly changes data; for example, the intention could be to change a date in one record, but the command could be ambiguously stated so that the date is changed in all or part of the file.

♦ Simple data entry errors are inevitable. A DBMS can never eliminate all of them, but it can succeed in minimizing them. For example, the DBMS cannot find an invalid date such as 11/30/90 when it is supposed to be 11/29/90, or a price entered as $12.00 instead of $12.50. It can, however, flag invalid entries such as a date of 11/31/90 (November has only 30 days). Similarly, it can flag a negative price as an error.

The cost of recovering or restoring files from corrupted data can be very high when many records are affected. It is the responsibility of the database administrator to train users in good practices, make sure that applications are designed to protect data integrity, and manage the database authorization to limit the risks of corrupting data.

SUMMARY

Database management systems (DBMSs) are effective tools for storing and using information. They provide the capability for creating complex business information systems.

There are four types of database users: *managers* or other *end-users, computer professionals* such as systems analysts and programmers, *data entry personnel*, and *database administrators*. Database administrators have an important role in managing the database itself, defining and managing user access, and protecting the database from unauthorized access and poor database practices.

Database management systems typically include five components: a *data definition language (DDL)* used to define the technical specifications of the database, a *data manipulation language (DML)* or query language that allows users to create custom applications, *general utilities* for basic database functions, an *application generator* for creating applications such as custom input and output screens, and a *report generator* for creating custom reports. Some DBMSs also have their own proprietary DDL languages. DDLs are considered to be fourth-generation languages.

A database consists of one or more *files*. The files are made up of *records*, which in turn contain one or more *fields*. Fields are defined by type; common field types are *alphanumeric or character, numeric, date, logic*, and *menus*. Each type has characteristics that are important in designing database file structures.

There are three classifications of database management systems: *relational databases*, used on both mainframes and microcomputers, which allow files to be linked via indexed *key fields*; *hierarchical databases*, which have a branched, tree structure but allow only one "parent" record for each "child"; and *network databases*, which are similar to hierarchical databases except that multiple parents are allowed. Each type of database has strengths that make it appropriate for certain applications.

KEY TERMS

Application generator
Data definition language (DDL)
Data dictionary
Data integrity
Data manipulation language (DML)
Database
Database administrator
Database application
Database file
Database management system (DBMS)
Database security
Encryption
Field
File
File management system
File manager
Hierarchical database
Index
Key field
Network database
Query language
Record
Relational database
Report generator
SQL
Table
Utility

CHAPTER SELF-TEST

1. In relational databases, files are linked by using a(n) _____, which keeps track of key fields and their disk addresses.
2. (T *or* F) In hierarchical databases, each parent segment can have many children segments; this is called a one-to-many relationship.
3. (T *or* F) Like hierarchical databases, network databases are easy to learn, and applications can be designed by nonprogrammers.
4. (T *or* F) A file manager is generally more powerful than a relational database.
5. In a hierarchical database, a child has ___ parent(s).
6. SQL stands for _____.
7. (T *or* F) The database administrator is responsible for maintaining the data dictionary.
8. (T *or* F) It is usually better to write your own database than to buy one.
9. (T *or* F) A data dictionary contains technical information about the data stored in each record and user-access information.

10. (**T** *or* **F**) The database administrator is the only one permitted to use the database management system.

SOLUTIONS 1) index. 2) True. 3) False. 4) False. 5) one. 6) Structured Query Language. 7) True. 8. False. 9) True. 10) False.

REVIEW QUESTIONS

1. Describe the roles of four types of database users.

2. Why is a file manager not a true database management system?

3. What are the major differences between relational, hierarchical, and network DBMSs? What are the advantages and disadvantages of each?

4. List at least three considerations in choosing field types when you define a database file structure.

PROBLEM-SOLVING APPLICATIONS

1. If you were designing a dBASE IV inventory database file for a large grocery store, what fields would you include? Give the field names, types, and sizes. Explain what information would go in each field.

2. If you had a microcomputer and a personal database management system, what sort of information might you store? Would you need a file manager or a relational DBMS? Why?

3. You are a database administrator for an auto parts chain with ten stores, and you have a computer terminal in each of your stores connected to a central company microcomputer. Would you choose to use Oracle or dBASE IV? Why?

4. If you were choosing a DBMS to process bills for a public utilities company, and the procedures had not changed for thirty years and were not going to change for many years to come, would a relational DBMS necessarily be the best choice? Why or why not?

5. In what situation do you think a network database would be better than a hierarchical or relational database?

6. Make a list of all the database management systems you can find advertised in computer magazines together with their lowest price. Identify the kind of database model of each—file manager, relational, hierarchical, and network DBMS.

CHAPTER 12

Management Information Systems

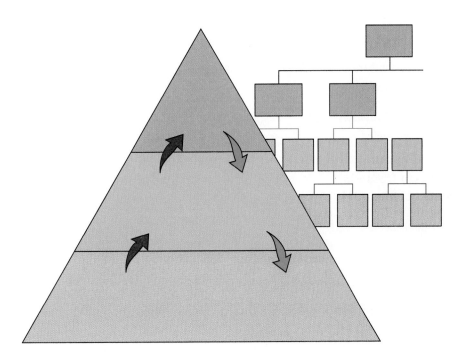

After completing this chapter, you will be able to:

✔ Define a management information system (MIS) and describe why it is needed in addition to operational-level systems.

✔ Identify the three general levels of management and the kind of information each needs.

✔ Define a decision support system (DSS) and identify its major tools.

✔ Define an executive information system (EIS) and list its characteristics.

✔ Describe the uses and components of expert systems.

✔ Describe the role of an information resources management group.

Chapter Outline

Throughout this book we have emphasized that information is data that has been organized and interpreted in such a way that it can be used as a basis for decision making. To be useful, information must be accurate, timely, complete, concise, and relevant.

A business computer system whose primary objective is to provide useful information to managers at all levels is called a **management information system (MIS)**. An MIS uses not only the data in an organization's central databases but may also incorporate data from external database services; the design of such a system may require special computer hardware and software. The goal of an MIS is to deliver to managers the timely and relevant information that they need for planning and for managing their organizations effectively.

You have already been introduced to many of the concepts in this chapter. Our discussion of management information systems is intended to help you understand how all that you have learned in the first eleven chapters fits together in the creation of an MIS that integrates all of an organization's information needs, from the highest organizational level down to the operational level.

All managers need information to help them make decisions and to assist them in achieving their personal goals, but the kind of information required differs at each level of management. For example, the day-to-day operational information that interests a line supervisor will not necessarily interest a vice president responsible for long-range planning.

One senior manager of a major food manufacturer complained to her information processing manager that, although she had all the data she could use about product sales in each department, she still did not have the information she needed—a comparison between last year's total cold cereal sales and a major competitor's total sales. As a senior manager, her job was to quickly detect trends and business patterns in the organization and industry. To get the comparative information she needed, she had to sift through 700 pages of reports and two journal articles to find and add up columns of numbers! Computer systems that detail company operations frustrated her because they did not provide her with the broadly based information that she required.

The Top-Down Approach to Information Systems

But what kinds of strategies can be used to provide managers with this information? The **traditional systems approach** does not, because it treats each business system as a separate unit. In this approach, analysts design operational-level systems with the assumption that if each business system within an organization functions efficiently, then the organization as a whole will run smoothly.

While operational-level systems are extremely useful in satisfying the needs and requirements of low-level managers and operating staff, they often do not provide the information top-level managers need. The **top-down approach**, in contrast to the traditional systems approach, views an organization as a whole with one set of specific corporate objectives originating with top management. For example, top management might set a sales goal to increase sales by 50 percent over the next five years. This goal is assumed to be that of the entire organization, and the information system is designed to provide information—appropriate for each level of management—that supports that goal.

The top-down approach assumes that by meeting the information needs of top managers, information will "trickle down" the organization to meet the needs of lower-level managers. For instance, if the main objective of an MIS is to provide top-level managers with sales forecasts, middle managers in each functional area can receive summary reports from the data generated, to compute the sales forecasts; similarly, supervisory managers can receive detailed transactional reports of the same data (Figure 12–1).

A well-designed MIS combines data from different functional areas to give managers a broad-based view of the organization. Note that while operational-level business systems are often part of an MIS, they are considered to be segments of a whole system.

Using a top-down approach alone is not sufficient for developing the information support managers need. MIS analysts must not only consider how to generate and collect the data but also how to transform it into the information managers need for decision making.

12–1 A top-down MIS approach gathers information to provide for the needs of top managers. Useful reports for other levels of management can then be generated from the same data.

Decisions at Three Levels

Organizations consist of several functional areas that work together to accomplish organizational goals. Typical departments are marketing and sales, manufacturing, accounting and finance, and research and development—all necessary components of the total enterprise. Organizations consist of a hierarchy of top managers, middle managers, and first-line managers or supervisors. A typical organization chart is shown in Figure 12–2.

Top managers oversee an entire functional area or division and coordinate the activities of middle managers; middle managers are responsible for parts of the functional areas and coordinate the activities of first-line managers; and first-line managers directly supervise the operating staff or nonmanagement employees. Within this structure, information flows vertically from top managers to lower managers and back up. Information also flows horizontally between functional areas; for example, the director of plant operations might work with the director of new product development to plan for the manufacture of a new product.

A manager's level in the organization dictates what kind of information he or she needs and where it comes from. For example, if top managers want to increase sales by 50 percent in five years, they work together to create a number of strategies such as aggressive marketing campaigns, new product designs, and faster delivery to customers. Information in the form of new goals and strategies then flows vertically (from the top down) as top managers inform middle managers of the new goals. Information then may flow back up (from the bottom up) as middle managers respond to and modify the strategies.

12–2 Within the typical organization, information flows vertically along organizational lines as well as horizontally between departments.

After developing tactics to accomplish these strategies, middle managers work with lower-level managers to implement new tasks. Information then flows back up as lower-level managers respond to or modify the tactics.

12–3 First-line managers supervise field groups, like this refinery team, as well as office workers, and need easy access to detailed production and scheduling data. *Courtesy:* NCR.

Let us look at the information needed at each level in more detail.

Operational Level

Located at the lower levels of the organization chart, first-line managers have such titles as regional sales manager, accounts receivable supervisor, and group leader. First-line managers implement and directly oversee the day-to-day operations of a business (Figure 12–3).

Because their jobs are structured, routine, and oriented toward accomplishing short-term objectives, first-line managers' major concerns may be meeting production and marketing schedules, maintaining inventory records, or monitoring the progress of clerks. To accomplish their jobs, these operating-level managers need extremely current internal information produced by transaction processing. First-line managers generally send information vertically within functional lines (Figure 12–4).

For example, in a cold cereal division of a food product company, the product managers need periodic reports that show both the number of cases of their cereal sold each month in each sales region for the last twelve months, as well as a listing of each sale made in each reporting period. This gives them the support they need to design strategies for increasing sales or correcting sales problems and to prepare reports for the director of marketing for cold cereals.

Middle-Management Level

Middle managers receive information from managers below and above them and use this information to implement the strategic plans of top management and to monitor current operations in their area (Figure 12–5). Typical titles for middle mangers are national sales manager, director of research, and director of finance.

To develop specific plans for achieving the overall strategic plans outlined by top managers, middle managers perform fairly structured activities such as formulating and managing budgets, developing training programs,

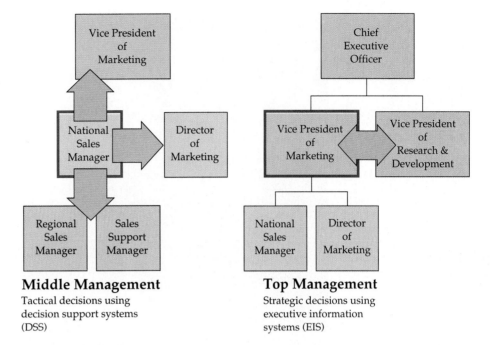

First-line Management
Operational decisions using
general business systems.

Middle Management
Tactical decisions using
decision support systems
(DSS)

Top Management
Strategic decisions using
executive information
systems (EIS)

and monitoring sales. They generally rely more on internal than external information, do a great deal of quantitative analysis, and do not need the level of detail that first-line managers require. Instead, they need summary information that provides enough detail for them to describe recent business activities in comparison with other activities, such as comparing this month's sales with last month's sales. As shown in Figure 12–4, information at the middle-management level moves both horizontally and vertically.

For example, if the director of marketing for cold cereals mentioned above needs to report how all of the division's cereals have sold across the nation, she would gather sales information from all product managers for each cereal. She might also want reports on how competitors' cold cereals sold during the same period and current market shares for each cereal and

12–4 Each level of management has its own information needs. First-line managers generally send information within organizational lines; middle managers communicate in many ways; top managers generally communicate across functional lines.

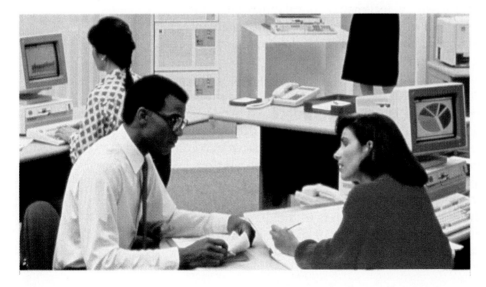

12–5 Middle managers coordinate line operators and need clear summary information. *Courtesy:* IBM.

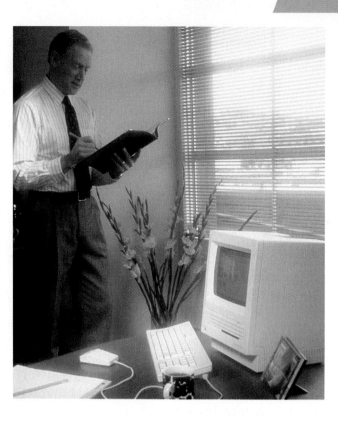

12–6 Top management needs strategic information from inside and outside the company in highly summarized form. *Courtesy:* Apple Computer, Inc.

for cold cereals collectively. This middle manager would use this information to create strategies with the product managers and to report to the division vice president.

Top-Management Level

Generally, top managers are vice presidents of functional areas or divisions who provide strategic plans to guide a firm toward its long-range goals, to establish performance objectives, and to coordinate the activities of the entire organization toward achieving these goals (Figure 12–6).

Top-management tasks vary greatly and require more initiative than middle-management tasks; for example, top managers establish financial goals for the firm, determine new markets and products, and evaluate potential mergers and acquisitions. Clearly, the decisions that top managers make have the greatest effect on the organization, although the effect may not be felt for several years. To make strategic decisions, top managers need information that is highly summarized, future-oriented, and external as well as internal. Information at the top-management level usually flows horizontally across functional lines (Figure 12–4).

The vice president of the cold cereals division, for example, must make decisions on what future products to develop, which products are not profitable and should be dropped from the product line, and what sales target will be both aggressive and achievable. To accomplish these goals, he needs not only summary reports from the middle managers in the division—the director of new product development, the director of marketing, and the director of manufacturing—but also immediate access to news of competitors' product development, long-range predictions of the cost of grains and other raw materials, marketing analyses of customers' changing preferences, and so on.

In summary, a manager's level dictates what kind of information he or she needs, and, consequently, the kind of information system to be used. Management information systems provide information reports appropriate for each level of management.

Decision Support Systems and MIS

A well-designed MIS provides whatever information managers need in the form most useful to them. Many companies are going beyond providing well-designed reports to their managers, however, and provide a **decision support system (DSS)**—a flexible information system that allows managers to access corporate and other databases and to create their own reports and applications, even their own specialized databases.

Decision support systems are often company-wide; the same tools are available to managers in all functional areas. These systems are really a collection of tools; they may include links between the corporate database and popular spreadsheet packages such as Lotus 1-2-3 so that managers can download data and ask "What-if?" questions in their own spreadsheets. Typically, a manager can do some simple DSS operations without training, but must have extensive training to become proficient in its use.

Top managers, on the other hand, are unlikely to spend the time needed to become an expert computer user, so a specialized form of DSS known as an **executive information system (EIS)** is sometimes developed for them. These systems require no expertise and are often designed around the information needs of a single executive.

Broadly speaking, then, in a company whose MIS has incorporated decision-support systems, lower-level managers generally use information derived from operational-level business systems, while middle managers use decision support systems (DSSs) that are designed to meet their quantitative and analytical needs. Top-level managers may use a specialized form of DSS called an executive information system (EIS), which provides more broadly based information to support the higher-level decisions they must make.

Advanced Tools for Decision Support Systems

Assume that you are a customer service manager for Analyze!, a major software vendor that sells more than a hundred different software products. Top management decides that Analyze! has come on hard times and therefore should concentrate only on its most profitable products. Top management wants you to reduce service on products that are not doing well—that is, those products that in your judgment require more customer service resources (such as staff time) than they are worth. To help you decide which products to cut, you need to find out:

♦   Which products bring in the most sales revenue

♦   Which products require the most telephone support with customers

Once you obtain this data, you will analyze it to find out which products do not bring in enough revenue to justify their level of customer support. If a product is expensive to support but is a best-seller, you want to continue to support it. But if a product is both expensive to support and does not sell well, you would consider no longer supporting it.

The Analyze! managers are fortunate: their company's systems analysis group designed the management information system to provide them with a number of flexible decision-support tools for obtaining and analyzing such data. These tools use **fourth-generation languages (4GLs)**, and are *relatively* easy to use. We stress the word relatively because—while 4GL tools are much simpler to use than procedural programming languages, considerable training and experience is required to use them effectively. Paradox, Oracle, and dBASE IV are examples of 4GL database management systems used on a wide variety of computers.

Four types of 4GL tools are available to the Analyze! managers that allow them to interact with the company's database: a useful query language, an application generator, a financial planning language that enables them to create statistical models for analysis, and a report generator.

Query Languages.   **Query languages** are an important element of DSS systems because they enable managers who are not familiar with computer terminology to access data. For example, as the Analyze! service manager, you can use the query language's selection commands, which are everyday terms, to find out from corporate databases which products are most profitable to your company. An example of how a query language can be implemented appears in Figure 12–7.

Application Generators.   Query languages are fine when you have a database that already contains the data that you need. But what do you do if you need to create your own database? In this case, you also need to know how much time your customer support staff spends helping customers with

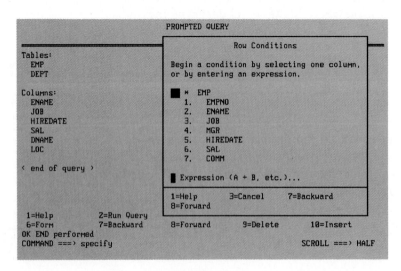

12–7 Managers can use a query language such as the one shown here, from Oracle's SQL*QMX, to access data in an MIS database.

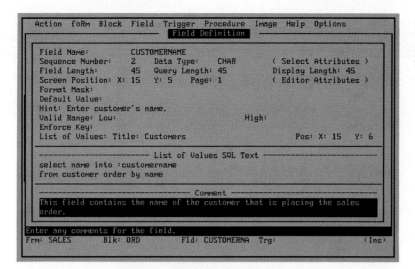

12–8 With an application generator like Oracle's SQL*Forms, you can quickly build a custom application.

each product. To get this information, it would be helpful if the employees kept track of all their service calls—and the simplest way to do that would be to have them enter data directly into a special database for the department (Figure 12–8).

Using an **application generator**, for example, you could quickly build a computerized application—an on-line transaction system with which the staff can record data about each customer service call. This particular record-keeping system might consist of five software modules that would perform various preprogrammed functions: users could choose option 1 to enter data about each call received from customers, option 2 to analyze all calls by type of product, option 3 to record which employee worked on the problem, and option 4 to record calls that are unresolved. Option 5 would call up the report generator. In other words, users simply state which function they need, and the application generator selects the appropriate modules and runs a program to meet the user's needs.

Financial Planning Languages.   You now have a month's data about Analyze! product support phone calls stored in the customer support database, and you have also used the DSS's query language to retrieve product profitability data from the corporate database. You are now prepared to analyze product data to find out which products are too expensive to support. You can use the company's MIS financial analysis tools, called **financial planning languages (FPLs)**, which provide sophisticated mathematical, statistical, and forecasting methods for analyzing data. Figure 12–9 shows a screen from the FPL program IFPS from Execucom.

Some common uses for FPLs in different functional areas are shown in Figure 12–10. FPLs enable managers to perform the "What-if?" analyses that frequently occur in business, such as: "What if the price of raw materials increased 20 percent next year?" "What if interest rates increase 2 percent next month?" "How sensitive is net income to changes in sales price?"

Using the FPL to set up a financial model of the relationship between product profitability and the cost of customer support, you can calculate

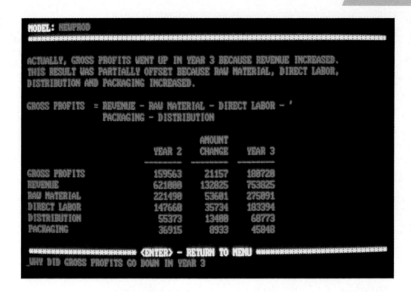

```
MODEL: NEWPROD
***************************************************************
ACTUALLY, GROSS PROFITS WENT UP IN YEAR 3 BECAUSE REVENUE INCREASED.
THIS RESULT WAS PARTIALLY OFFSET BECAUSE RAW MATERIAL, DIRECT LABOR,
DISTRIBUTION AND PACKAGING INCREASED.

GROSS PROFITS = REVENUE - RAW MATERIAL - DIRECT LABOR - '
                PACKAGING - DISTRIBUTION

                                AMOUNT
                    YEAR 2      CHANGE      YEAR 3

GROSS PROFITS       159563      21157       180720
REVENUE             621000      132825      753825
RAW MATERIAL        221490      53601       275091
DIRECT LABOR        147660      35734       183394
DISTRIBUTION        55373       13400       68773
PACKAGING           36915       8933        45848

******************* <ENTER> - RETURN TO MENU ******************
_WHY DID GROSS PROFITS GO DOWN IN YEAR 3
```

12–9 IFPS, a financial planning software package, provides managers with both the financial data they need and an on-screen analysis. *Courtesy:* Execucom Systems Corporation.

which products do not bring in enough revenue to justify their level of customer support.

Report Generators.   **Report generators** are often used as modules in a computer system built with an application generator (Figure 12–11). Report generators enable managers to concentrate on the information they want in the report and not worry about the technical structure of the database.

In Chapter 5 we identified five types of reports for computer output. Three of these types are common forms of DSS reports:

◆   **Periodic reports** are those generated at regular intervals, such as quarterly financial reports, monthly sales analyses, and weekly production reports. Two common periodic reports are the income statement and the balance sheet.

◆   **Exception reports** call attention to unusual situations. The DSS generates exception reports when certain predefined conditions occur, such as when inventory levels drop dangerously low, production output is behind schedule, or sales are low throughout an entire region.

◆   **Special reports** are the opposite of periodic reports and are prepared on an as-needed basis—that is, "on demand." Examples of special reports are revised sales forecasts, employee salary reviews, and current performance reports.

12–10 Common business uses for FPLs are shown for the four functional business areas. FPLs enable managers to do the "what-if" analyses that so frequently are needed in business.

Marketing and Sales	Accounting and Finance	Manufacturing	Research and Development
• Market planning	• Pro forma statements	• Plant location	• New product design
• Pricing analysis	• Capital budgeting	• Production scheduling	• New product testing
• Product mix	• Investment anaysis	• Labor negotiations	
• Sales forecasting	• Buy or lease decision		

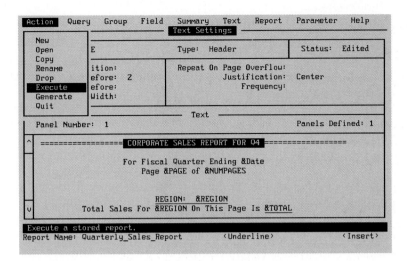

12-11 This screen from Oracle's SQL*Reportwriter shows how a report generator gives the user the ability to format professional-looking reports.

As the customer service manager, you would use the quantitative analysis you did with the DSS's financial planning language to construct bar charts illustrating the amount of support time compared with profitability for each Analyze! product. It becomes clear that five of the products require a level of support that is disproportionate to their profitability, while another three products are borderline. You then incorporate the bar charts in a two-color report of your recommendations. The report generator helps you format a professional-looking report for your manager.

As this customer support example illustrates, managers can use DSS tools to create, store, retrieve, organize, summarize, and manipulate data to create information that enables them to be effective and productive at their jobs. Note, however, that while DSS systems are reasonably user-friendly, they do require quite a bit of training.

In a Nutshell

Fourth-Generation Decision Support System Tools		
	Query languages	English-like programming languages that allow people who are not programmers to search a database.
	Application generator	Software that provides the ability to design an application using available databases.
	Financial planning languages (FPLs)	Languages that provide sophisticated mathematical, statistical, and forecasting methods for analyzing data.
	Report generators	Software that provides the ability to prepare hard-copy reports that analyze the data in the database.

SELF-TEST

1. MIS is an abbreviation for _____.
2. (T *or* F) Top-down MISs are based on completely separate databases for top management and operational-level departments.
3. (T *or* F) Top managers tend to be frustrated with operational-level computer systems.
4. (T *or* F) Operational-level systems analysis focuses on the top-down approach.
5. (T *or* F) With an MIS approach, the needs of each subsystem are met through a "trickle-down" process.
6. Many MISs provide a specialized form of DSS for executives; it is called an _____.
7. An MIS permits the user to access the database with a user-oriented _____.
8. (T *or* F) When designing an MIS, it is important to make the integrated system flexible enough to meet the changing needs of an organization.
9. (T *or* F) An MIS provides management with current information that is obtained by computerizing the interaction of the various departments within a company.
10. (T *or* F) In a company that has implemented an MIS, departmental systems usually function autonomously.
11. (T *or* F) In a company that has implemented an MIS, operational-level business systems will eventually disappear.
12. An MIS provides management with current information that is obtained from _____.
13. Three kinds of reports typical of DSSs are _____, _____, and _____.
14. (T *or* F) Advanced DSS tools for analyzing data are so easy to use that middle managers do not need training to use them.

SOLUTIONS 1) Management Information Systems. 2) False. The same databases are used, but different kinds of information are generated, appropriate for each level of decision making. 3) True. 4) False. MIS designs focus on a top-down approach. 5) True. 6) Executive Information System (EIS). 7) query language. 8) True. 9) True. 10) False. Information from various departments is combined to form the MIS database. 11) False. Operational-level business systems support MIS. 12) operational-level systems. 13) periodic reports, exception reports, special reports. 14) False. Use of advanced DSS tools requires considerable training.

Designing Management Information Systems

First of all, let us make a further distinction between decision support systems and the specialized form of DSS called executive information systems, or EISs. Here are three ways in which the two types of systems vary:

◆ A decision support system may be for company-wide use. DSSs are typically designed generically for middle-level managers and are used by a number of managers for many different purposes. Executive information systems, on the other hand, are usually designed for the unique needs of a single executive, and take his or her skills and interests into account.

◆ DSSs, while somewhat user-friendly, require quite a bit of training before a manager is effective at tasks such as building applications or creating a financial model. EISs require no computer training—the analyst designing the system creates the needed models and menus so that the executive is free to simply ask for exactly the information needed to make corporate decisions.

◆ Because DSSs are developed generically for a number of managers, they are much less expensive to develop than are EISs, which are designed for a single executive, or, on occasion, for a small group of executives.

12–12 Metaphor, a Decision Support System, can process and display information from a variety of sources. This sales graph, for instance, updates itself whenever it is called to the screen or printed in a report. *Courtesy:* Metaphor Computer Systems.

One characteristic is common to DSSs and the more sophisticated EISs. Screens are generally menu driven, and because most people can recognize no more than ten items at a time, menu screens usually contain no more than ten options.

Characteristics of DSSs

Decision support systems designed for middle managers can provide them with a wide range of tools. In addition to statistical tools for quantitative analysis, these systems may also be able to produce high-quality graphics that quickly display reports, charts, and text drawn from a wide variety of internal and external sources (Figure 12–12). This means that managers can not only gather the information they need to make decisions but also use sophisticated graphics to communicate the information on which they based their decisions.

For example, if the vice president of marketing wants to find out whether any sales regions performed poorly during the previous month, he might select a menu option called January's Performance and see a chart listing all sales regions, with problem regions highlighted in red. Then, selecting one of the highlighted regions, he might see more detailed sales information as well as a textual analysis of the problem as analyzed by the regional sales manager.

If the vice president sees a disturbing trend in several regions that deserves analysis, he can build a financial model using the financial analysis language, verify his hunch about the trend, and then create a graph that analyzes the problem. This graph can then be incorporated into a memo to district managers, and the memo can be printed on a color printer. The district managers receive a memo that gives them a vivid representation of the trend, which enhances communication between the vice president and the first-line managers in the field.

12–13 This Pilot executive information system allows the user to access custom data, update reports, and generate standard or custom charts from a simple menu. *Courtesy:* Pilot Software.

To summarize, DSSs provide managers with a broad range of data and tools for accessing data, but training is required to use them effectively. DSSs are designed to be flexible enough to permit changes and add applications as needed.

Characteristics of EISs

Executive information systems use the same tools, but computer professionals design the systems with these tools for the executives. An EIS is usually based on very sophisticated minicomputer workstations, but a systems analyst creates an individualized "turnkey system"—one that requires no computer knowledge (Figure 12–13).

Here are the design requirements for an EIS system:

1. EISs Require No Technical Knowledge to Use. EISs should present information to executives in a way that hides the technical communication links between all the hardware and software that might be accessed to compile a report. For example, if a report combines information from an external database such as Dow-Jones, and from an internal database such as payroll, the EIS graphs the information without the executive needing to think about where the information came from.

2. EISs Are Individualized. Menu options refer only to specific information or tasks that interest the executive, and the options are expressed in words and terms that he or she uses frequently. EISs often use individualized databases as well—subsets of the corporate database, databases such as industry statistics from sources outside the company, and on-line database services such as CompuServe.

3. EISs Evolve with the Executive. Each executive has an individualized style of decision making, based on his or her training and experience. One executive might be most interested in tracking production levels, while another puts a great deal of emphasis on sales goals. An effective EIS provides only the information that is meaningful to that executive.

Typically, the initial step in building an EIS is for the executive to request that the computer professional design a system that will provide information on six or seven issues of particular importance to him or her, such as changes in stock prices, information about competitors, news items on a special topic, or particular internal reports such as production forecasts. The system designer responds by designing a simple one-level system that provides those six or seven menu choices and the information in a simple form.

As executives become accustomed to accessing this information, they discover more features that they would find useful, and the designer adds them to the system. These are often second-level menu choices. For example, information about competitors might evolve into three lower-level screens, one that compares the sales of each leading product with those of each competing product, a second that compares advertising budgets of each leading product with those of their competitors, and a third that summarizes news items about competitors.

4. EIS Information Is Relevant, Complete, and Clear.   EISs should contain only information that is relevant to a specific executive, and the information should be displayed in comparative forms such as in ratios, exception reports, and historical perspectives. Any irrelevant information impedes a manager's ability to use the system quickly.

Also, the presentation style of an EIS is tailored to the individual. For example, the designer uses the type of display method with which the executive is most comfortable—it might be numerical tables, bar graphics, scatter graphs, or pie charts, for example.

To summarize, EISs are tailored to the individual executive; they use powerful systems but require no technical expertise on the part of the executive using them.

An Executive Information System in Action

To see how a high-level EIS might operate in practice, let us look at a system devised for the chief financial officer (CFO) of a large consumer products corporation (Figure 12–14). When this CFO turns on his workstation in the morning, the EIS software activates the communications link between the workstation and the mainframe and connects his workstation to the "Command Center" mainframe system. A menu then appears on his screen; the menu allows him to:

◆   Read memos, reports, and messages that have come in over the electronic mail system since he last logged on

◆   Review selected financial data that he has marked for close scrutiny

◆   Review external data, such as economic indicators, competitive information, or financial markets, that are downloaded automatically to the EIS database

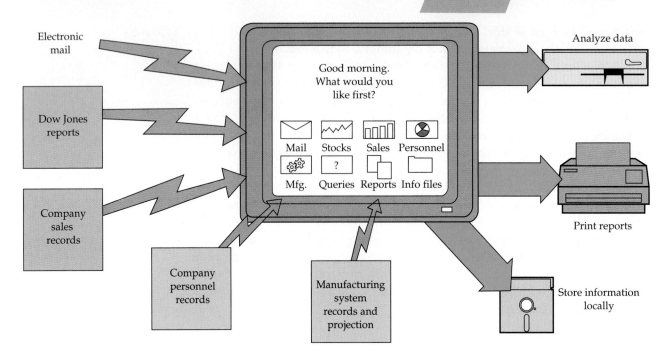

- Analyze sales and financial results, with a wide range of "push-button" statistical tools that can explore ratios, trends, and relationships in the data

- Review reports generated by existing corporate information systems that have been linked to the EIS at the mainframe level

- Select and download corporate data to microcomputer disks in forms readable by popular software products such as Lotus 1-2-3 or other spreadsheet packages

- Access personnel data to keep tabs on who's who in the organization and how each functional area is performing against benchmarks

- Track the progress of key projects and development schedules

12–14 A typical executive information system assembles data from various sources and makes it available for use at the executive's computer.

The Hardware and Software Used to Build MISs

DSSs (and the more specialized EISs) have become possible as the result of two developments in the business environment. First, managers have become more sophisticated about using computers to help them in making decisions. Second, computer technology in hardware and software has advanced sufficiently to provide them with the fourth-generation tools that allow managers to access detailed information on an individual and customized basis.

MIS Hardware

A mainframe or minicomputer is typically used as the host computer. Managers access the system through various attached terminals and worksta-

Host computer

Databases on remote computers

Data communication networks

Interactive graphics terminal

Local programs and storage

tions. Two important hardware elements in an MIS system are interactive graphics terminals and data communications networks (Figure 12–15).

An interactive graphic display provides charts and graphs to users so that they can communicate easily with the MIS software. If the graphic terminal is a microcomputer, it can process graphics itself and relieve the processing burden of the mainframe.

Data communications networks provide three advantages for management information systems:

- They allow MIS systems to use sophisticated time-sharing technologies, providing individual workstations with access to computers that have multi-programming capability.

- They allow managers to share data and reports with other managers.

- They allow managers to have access to distributed databases within the organization and to databases outside the organization, such as Dow-Jones reports and industry news.

MIS Software

To develop a top-down MIS system, systems designers typically use two types of software:

- A **database management system (DBMS)** enables managers to collect, retrieve, and analyze data from the organization's internal databases as well as from external databases. When building MIS databases, analysts need to consider all the business systems already existing in an organization, those currently under development, and those planned for future development.

When choosing software, most companies purchase DBMSs from

12–15 MIS hardware typically includes a host mainframe computer, data communications networks, and interactive graphics terminals. This equipment provides maximum access to programs and databases.

vendors. DBMSs are usually too complex or costly for organizations to create themselves, and vendor DBMSs are highly competitive with each other and very sophisticated. For example, most DBMSs already contain built-in query languages, application generators, report generators, and so on. Oracle and dBASE IV—the two examples used in the last chapter—would be appropriate DBMSs with which to build an MIS.

♦ **MIS control software** acts as an operating system for the MIS or as an interface with the hardware's operating system. This spares users such chores as coordinating and controlling all the software and data in the system.

Beyond DSSs—Expert Systems

Theoreticians have debated for years about whether machines will be able to think like people; however, no one doubts that **artificial intelligence**—simulated human decision making—in the form of expert systems is beginning to play an important role in running companies. **Expert systems** consist of a database and software that simulate the knowledge and analytical ability of an expert in a particular field.

For example, analysts at the American Express Company (AMEX) built an expert system that uses a computer to quickly determine credit limits and to approve requests for additional credit. The system helps the company provide better service to customers by allowing credit staff to approve credit more quickly. Because the American Express credit card has no set spending limit, it was difficult for the credit staff to determine appropriate levels of credit for each customer. Each time a customer made a large purchase, a merchant telephoned AMEX to authorize the charge. The AMEX employee had to search through as many as 13 databases for more information on the customer and then make a judgment call.

The expert system, called Authorizer's Assistant, now performs that search and makes recommendations to the credit employee, who makes the final authorization decision. The entire process takes only seconds while the merchant is on the phone; it had previously taken as much as half an hour.

Identifying Opportunities for Expert Systems

Expert systems are best suited to problems that require repetitive, judgmental decisions. Appropriate applications for expert systems can often be those where highly trained, expensive, or rare employees cannot always be available on site to make time-critical judgments. While expert systems are expensive to develop, their cost must be weighed against the cost to the company of keeping highly trained decision-makers available at widely scattered locations (Figure 12–16). The knowledge of that employee must be incorporated into the database on which the expert system is developed.

There are other reasons why an expert system might solve a business problem:

Time Limits.   Complex analyses that need to be done quickly in order to be useful are good candidates for expert systems. Using the AMEX example,

12–16 Oil drilling and production, often in isolated and remote locations, like this platform in the North Sea, make extensive use of expert systems. *Courtesy:* American Petroleum Institute.

if AMEX employees had half an hour to process a credit request, an expert system would not be necessary. However, because a merchant requires an answer in seconds, AMEX's expert system delivers a definite advantage.

A number of expert systems have been developed for medical diagnosis, where time can be a critical factor. When a patient exhibits an unfamiliar set of symptoms, a physician may use an expert system to diagnose an illness and to identify appropriate treatment.

Limited Number of Experts.   Repetitive but important tasks that can only be done well by a few experts are good candidates for expert systems. For example, Honeywell built an expert system to help field service technicians diagnose problems on commercial air conditioning systems. Although the technician's personal ability could range from average to excellent, the expert system ensured that service quality was uniformly high. Expert systems also help keep costs down if increased volume requires more experts. In addition, the knowledge of skilled experts is not lost if they leave the organization.

Consistent Decisions.   Tasks that require employees to make consistent decisions and remain alert over long periods of time, sometimes under difficult circumstances, are good candidates for expert systems. For example, N L Baroid, an oil drilling services company, created MUDMAN to analyze the drilling fluids, or "muds," that are pumped down shafts to facilitate drilling. On deep or difficult wells, an on-site engineer often has to sample and analyze over 20 mud parameters such as viscosity, specific gravity, and silt content at least twice a day. MUDMAN provides analytic consistency and also enables Baroid to provide better service than its competitors. When MUDMAN correctly diagnosed a mud contamination problem in the North Sea that human experts had misdiagnosed for more than a decade, one customer was so impressed that he went on to purchase additional services from Baroid.

Expert systems can apply expertise without bias and tell users what assumptions were made to make a decision and what line of reasoning was used.

The Components of an Expert System

An expert system has four basic components: a knowledge base, an inference engine, subsystems, and a user interface (Figure 12–17).

The Knowledge Base.   Created by a computer professional called a **knowledge engineer**, the **knowledge base** is the heart of the system. The knowledge base translates the knowledge from human experts into rules and strategies. Unlike a database, which consists of static relationships between fields, records, and files, a knowledge base is always changing, reflecting the advice of human experts. In fact, as more information is supplied, the basis for making decisions or the decisions themselves may actually change.

The knowledge engineer encodes knowledge by using a variety of approaches. The most common approach is to use **rules**, which express knowledge in an IF-THEN format—for example, "IF a patient's symptoms are lung infection, fever, and a cough, THEN he or she has an 80 percent probability of having pneumonia." Notice that expert systems often assign probabilities, because like human experts, they cannot be 100 percent correct. This allows the human decision maker to weigh the risk of delaying treatment against the risk of making the wrong diagnosis.

The Inference Engine.   The **inference engine** is the software that draws conclusions. It has two primary tasks—inference and control.

- The inference engine examines existing facts and rules to draw conclusions. It also adds new facts if it finds them consistent with present information and rules. For example, if it noticed that 80 percent of patients meeting the present criteria for pneumonia also shared another symptom, this symptom would be added to the knowledge base.

- The inference engine also controls the search of the knowledge base—a time-consuming process if the knowledge base is large and complex.

The Subsystems.   Two subsystems help knowledge engineers update the knowledge base and explain to users how a recommendation was made.

12–17 The principal components of an expert system are the knowledge base, the inference engine, the subsystems, and the human interface.

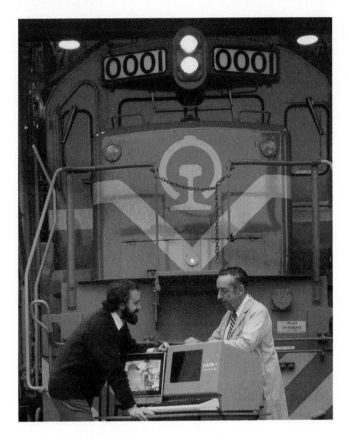

12–18 This trouble-shooting repair system for locomotives uses videotapes of diagnostic and repair sequences as part of its sophisticated user interface. *Courtesy:* General Electric.

- The **knowledge acquisition subsystem** helps the knowledge engineer define and encode the expert's problem-solving ability and also allows the engineer to easily insert and delete knowledge in the system.

- The **explanation subsystem** explains to users why the system has chosen to ask a certain question or how it has reached certain conclusions.

The User Interface.   Ideally, expert systems should communicate information with a **natural language interface** that allows users to conduct dialogues with the computer that seem as natural as talking to another human being (Figure 12–18).

Steps for Developing an Expert System

Although nontechnical managers with the proper tools can build a small-scale expert system using operational-level systems design and development methods, large systems require a team of knowledge engineers and generally a year or more to develop. Development consists of five phases (Figure 12–19).

1. Select the Problem.   To keep from wasting development time and money, knowledge engineers must correctly identify a suitable subject for an expert system. Good expert system opportunities are those that require expensive or rare experts to make fast decisions consistently over a long period of time.

1. Select the problem	2. Develop a prototype	3. Design the system	4. Test and evaluate	5. Implement and maintain
• Time limits • Available experts • Consistent results	• Establish knowledge base • Document structure and performance criteria • Schedule and prepare budget	• Inference engine • Explanation subsystem • User interface • Knowledge acquisition subsystem	• Compare with traditional system • Have other experts use system	• Train workers • Add new information

2. Develop a Prototype.   A **prototype system** is a small-scale model of an expert system. During this step, knowledge engineers learn everything about the problem they can from books and reports, and teach the human experts how to articulate their knowledge about solving certain tasks.

12–19 Here are the five phases of development for an expert system.

Knowledge engineers also select the best tool for building their expert system. The most flexible design approach is to use one of the artificial intelligence programming languages such as LISP (used extensively in the United States) or PROLOG (the standard in Europe and Japan). Alternatively, they may choose to use a commercially available **shell**, or empty expert system structure, into which they can enter the decision-making rules to create a knowledge base.

Knowledge engineers then develop a detailed design document that estimates the number of rules to be included, a more precise statement of performance criteria, and a detailed schedule and budget for the entire project.

3. Design the Complete System.   Now the knowledge engineer and the expert fine-tune the knowledge base by creating additional rules that are capable of handling the more subtle aspects of the problem.

At this point, the knowledge engineer begins to turn development over to the experts and to monitor the project rather than actively participate in it. In turn, the expert, with all the insight and experience gained during the development process, starts to implement the expert system.

4. Test and Evaluate the System.   Once the knowledge engineer and expert believe the system is complete, it can be tested against the performance criteria specified during prototyping. For example, a medical diagnostic system's recommendations can be evaluated by comparing diagnoses with later bacterial culture tests. This may result in further refinements of rules entered into the medical knowledge base. Other experts may also be invited to try the system out using other working situations.

5. Implement and Maintain the System.   Until now, the expert system has probably been isolated from users. Now is the time to integrate it into the organization's workplace and provide training for prospective users.

Maintenance of the system is an ongoing process. A major characteristic of expert systems is that knowledge engineers can continue to add *new* information or modify existing information. As a result, expert systems have much more flexibility than systems developed using traditional programming languages.

Looking Ahead

The Nervous Shock Adviser

Knowledge engineers at the University of British Columbia working with IBM have built an expert legal system that provides attorneys with expert advice on legal cases involving nervous shock, emotional distress, and emotional suffering. The system, called the Nervous Shock Advisor, advises lawyers about whether people who say they have suffered emotional distress have a viable claim. The system bases its conclusions on judgments reached in previous court cases.

After asking the attorney for specific facts about the case, the Nervous Shock Advisor:

♦ Searches a legal database and determines whether the claim is valid.
♦ Lists the factors used to arrive at its conclusion and presents a confidence-level value for each factor.
♦ Supplies references to relevant court cases that either support its conclusion or go against it.
♦ Gives references to cases that demonstrate the arguments that the defendant (that is, the opposing side) might use to present his or her side of the case.

If the system determines that the plaintiff has no case, it informs the lawyer what elements are lacking.

The system was designed to help lawyers prepare a case by presenting the basic elements that support successful litigation.

Information Resource Management

There is a significant trend occurring in business: managers are beginning to consider that information is a fundamental asset to the organization, and information, like any other asset, needs to be managed effectively. Computer professionals are restructuring and integrating piecemeal operational-level business systems by using top-down design approaches, and many corporate managers are likewise trying to integrate administrative efforts to manage information itself.

Some corporate managers suggest that although information processing departments specialize in building and maintaining systems, they do not have the expertise to manage a corporate asset like information. In some companies, a separate **information resource management (IRM)** group specializes in asset management techniques. Under the direction of a senior IRM manager, this group supervises the flow of information within an organization, applying traditional techniques such as inventory analysis, cost accounting, and budgeting (Figure 12–20). Also, as each functional area purchases its own hardware and software for local processing, an IRM manager develops a company-wide strategy for managing local computer acquisitions.

To date, IRM is only slowly being adopted in organizations. For example, although Congress has passed a Paperwork Reduction Act that advocates that all federal agencies employ IRM personnel, few people even understand what it means. The concept of IRM seems too abstract to many federal managers, who, because they see themselves inundated by an over-

12–20 An information resource manager deals with computer and information issues on all levels, in all departments, from graphics to building maintenance. *Courtesy:* Apple Computer, Inc.

supply of information, have not learned to treat it as an asset. However, large companies like FMC Corporation and Rockwell International have instituted IRM concepts with success.

Basic to the IRM concept, however, is that an IRM executive is responsible for coordinating the separate operational-level business systems and DSSs in the organization so that the integrated system works for the maximum benefit of the company.

SUMMARY

Computer systems that provide useful information to middle and top managers are called *Management Information Systems (MIS)*. MIS combines computer hardware and software into a network that delivers timely and relevant information to managers at all levels so that they can plan and control their organizations effectively.

MIS systems are designed using the *top-down approach*. Rather than focusing on the business needs of each functional area, the top-down approach views an organization as though it were one complete unit with one set of specific corporate objectives.

A manager's level in the organization dictates what kind of information he or she needs. Broadly speaking, lower-level managers generally use information derived from *operational-level business systems*, and middle and top managers both use *decision support systems (DSSs)* to meet their quantitative and analytical needs; a DSS is often designed to be used by managers across all functional areas. Top managers may use a specialized form of DSS called *executive information systems (EISs)*, which are individually tailored to deliver specific financial, reporting, and planning information needed by a particular executive.

DSSs provide middle managers with specific tools such as *fourth-generation languages (4GLs)* designed to solve specific problems or develop business applications. There are four basic DSS tools: *query languages, application generators, financial planning languages,* and *report generators.*

Four basic design requirements for EISs are: (1) they require *no technical knowledge* to use, (2) they are *individualized*, (3) they *evolve with the executive*, and (4) the *information is relevant, complete, concise, accurate, and timely*.

DSS software is typically located on a host mainframe or minicomputer, which managers access through various workstations, using interactive graphic terminals and data communications networks. To develop a top-down MIS system, analysts use two basic types of software: a *database management system* and *MIS control software*.

Expert systems consist of a database with software that processes and distills the knowledge of an expert in a particular field. Expert systems can apply expertise without bias and tell users what assumptions were made to make a decision and what line of reasoning was used. Four components comprise an expert system: the *knowledge base*, the *inference engine*, two subsystems—the *knowledge acquisition subsystem* and the *explanation subsystem*—and the *human interface*. Although nontechnical managers with the proper tools can build a small-scale expert system using traditional system design and development methods, large systems require a team of knowledge engineers and generally a year or more to develop. They require five development steps: (1) *select the problem*, (2) *develop a prototype*, (3) *design the complete system*, (4) *test and evaluate the system*, and (5) *implement and maintain* the system.

Some corporate managers suggest that information processing departments do not have the expertise to manage a corporate asset such as information. Some companies have a separate *information resource management (IRM)* group under an IRM manager that coordinates corporate information resources, including the integration of operational systems and databases as well as hardware and software acquisition and use.

KEY TERMS

Application generator	Knowledge base
Artificial intelligence	Knowledge engineer
Database management system (DBMS)	Management information system (MIS)
Decision support system (DSS)	MIS control software
Exception report	Natural-language interface
Executive information system (EIS)	Periodic report
Expert system	Prototype system
Explanation subsystem	Query language
Financial planning language (FPL)	Report generator
	Rules
Fourth-generation language (4GL)	Shell
	Special report
Inference engine	Top-down approach
Information resource management (IRM)	Traditional systems approach
Knowledge acquisition subsystem	

CHAPTER SELF-TEST

1. Four basic design requirements for EISs are _____, _____, _____, and _____.
2. (T or F) One basic difference between DSSs and EISs is that systems for higher-level managers (EISs) tend to be simpler to use.
3. (T or F) EISs are so simple to use and personalized for individual managers that they rarely require data communications technology.
4. DBMS is an abbreviation for _____.
5. (T or F) DBMSs are so complex and tailored to a particular company's computing needs that they almost always have to be designed and built in-house.

6. The computer professional who builds expert systems is called a _____.
7. The five steps of developing an expert system are _____, _____, _____, _____, and _____.
8. When determining whether a task is appropriate for development of a good expert system, knowledge engineers look for tasks done by _____, _____, or _____ employees.
9. Tasks that frequently provide good opportunities for expert systems are those that must be done _____, _____, and _____.
10. The component of an expert system that explains to users how an expert system reached certain conclusions is called the _____.

SOLUTIONS 1) it requires no technical knowledge; it is individualized; it evolves with the executive; information is relevant, complete, concise, accurate, and timely. 2) True. 3) False. Data communications technology provides managers with access to information. 4) database management system. 5) False. DBMSs are usually too complex or costly for organizations to create themselves. 6) knowledge engineer. 7) select the problem; develop a prototype; design the complete system; test and evaluate the system; implement and maintain the system. 8) highly trained; expensive; rare. 9) quickly; repetitively; over a long period of time. 10) explanation subsystem.

REVIEW QUESTIONS

1. List and describe the three levels of management. In general, what kind of information is most useful to managers at each level? Explain your answer.
2. What are the four major tools available for managers using decision support systems? Briefly discuss and provide an example of how each tool is useful to managers.
3. What are three primary design requirements for an executive information system (EIS)?
4. Briefly discuss the role of distributed computer systems in top-level decision support systems (DSS). Are they important to DSS? Explain your answer.
5. Describe the roles of the four major components of an expert system: the knowledge base, the inference engine, the two subsystems, and the human interface.

PROBLEM-SOLVING APPLICATIONS

1. Your mother bakes the best chocolate cheesecake in the world. You would like to build a cheesecake business based on your mother's baking skills. Give three reasons why her baking ability is a good candidate for an expert system. Illustrate your reasons with three specific examples of how personal judgment and expertise might be reflected in an automated recipe for chocolate cheesecake.

2. Your chocolate cheesecake expert system and your company are doing well. You have bakeries in two locations that serve six food distributors and a fleet of five trucks that serve over 50 local restaurants. You have 30 production employees, ten front-office and clerical workers (who handle all accounting on two desktop micros), and two outside sales representatives. Your business grosses close to $1 million per year and nets almost $100,000 before taxes. However, your sales reps and drivers have reported declining orders in the last few months because of growing competition. You figure you need an advantage to hold your market share, or perhaps you need to add some new dessert products.

   Briefly describe the design requirements for a DSS that you need to run and improve the business. What kind of information do you need? In what form? From what source? What tools would you use? Hardware? Software? What other systems, if any, should it communicate with?

3. Your college has hired you as an expert systems consultant and wants you to examine its administrative procedures to look for good opportunities to use an expert system. Briefly discuss two good opportunities you found at the college and explain your rationale for choosing them.

Social Issues and Technological Trends

When you have completed this chapter, you will be able to:

✔ Identify the four most common kinds of computer crime.

✔ List several hardware and software controls used for protecting computer systems.

✔ Describe two ethical issues that computer professionals sometimes face.

✔ Describe four ergonomic ways to improve the physical work environment for computer users and professionals.

✔ List and describe common career opportunities, requirements, and paths for computer professionals.

✔ Identify and describe three major technological and software trends in the computing industry.

Chapter 13

Chapter Outline

This chapter deals with the interaction of computers with society—the issues of computer crime, ethical issues in computer information systems, health and safety issues for people working with computers, and career paths for computer professionals. We will also outline several important new computer technologies that are likely to change the way we use computers.

You have probably heard a friend or neighbor complain that computers are "taking over society" and that they "know too much about us." Whether you agree with this point of view or not, serious computer professionals recognize that current information processing trends, such as the emergence of massive credit databases containing the credit history of 150 million Americans, can potentially jeopardize our personal freedoms.

Although there is no reversing the trend toward large credit databases, their existence brings up two important social and organizational issues: privacy and security. **Privacy** is an individual concern; people need assurance that their personal information, such as employment and credit history, will be used properly. **Security** is an organizational concern; businesses need safeguards that protect computer systems and data from damage or unlawful use. As a result, security protects hardware, software, and data from natural disasters such as fire, flood, and earthquake (Figure 13–1); it also guards against sabotage and espionage, as well as various kinds of theft.

Computer crime, which results from the deliberate tampering with data, has become a costly trend for organizations ranging from small businesses to multinational corporations and the federal government. We will focus on methods that companies use to protect against computer crime; such methods will also help to protect data from natural disasters.

Securing Computer Systems

One study of 283 businesses and governmental institutions found that *half* were victims of computer crime each year. Records show that while a bank robber armed with a gun steals an average of $1,600 from a bank, the white-collar criminal armed with a computer steals an average of $100,000! These statistics for white-collar crimes may in fact be low, because many organizations such as banks, fearing a loss of customer confidence, do not report all the crimes that occur.

Computer crime can be as small-scale as the unauthorized use of business computers for personal purposes, or as large as using computers to send corporate financial assets to a private Swiss bank account. Computer crime can include:

Theft of Computer Time.   This common theft may be as simple as students doing term papers on computers at work or as great as someone stealing thousands of dollars of processing time for personal profit.

Manipulation of Computer Programs or Data.   Remember the movie *War Games*, in which the protagonist changed his grades in the high school computer by using a modem at home? Unfortunately, such actions are all

13–1 Backup copies of databases and custom programs stored away from the main office allow companies to recover quickly from an otherwise crippling destruction of computers and their data. *Courtesy:* Alan Simmons.

too common. Newspapers frequently print stories about computer enthusiasts, or "hackers," breaking into public and private databases—sometimes just for the technical challenge of it! Some hackers even plant "computer viruses" that tie up CPUs by commanding them to do such time-consuming tasks as attempting to calculate the precise value of pi—thereby crippling enormous data networks.

Theft of Data and Assets.   Legally called embezzlement, computer theft often involves a trusted employee who cannot resist the temptation to steal. All too often, the theft is amazingly easy to carry out. For example, the chairman of the board and some of the executive officers of the Equity Funding Corporation—a publicly held mutual fund and insurance company—used terminals to enter insurance policies for nonexistent people. By entering bogus data over a period of years, they greatly increased the company's apparent assets. Of the 97,000 insurance policies maintained by the computer, almost two-thirds were fictitious policies with a face value of $2.1 billion! Because the company appeared to be more profitable than it actually was, the stock of Equity Funding was greatly inflated; consequently, the officers, who were large shareholders, were able to sell their shares at considerable profits. The fraud went undetected because auditors consistently accepted the computer printouts that listed policyholders as beyond question. The crime was discovered by auditors and the police only when a former employee revealed the scheme.

Users Stealing Software.   Are you stealing when you make a copy of word processing software for a friend to use? The law says you are. Yet many normally law-abiding people who would not dream of shoplifting see nothing wrong with making a copy of a $500 word processing package and giving it to a friend, despite the fact that it is in violation of the U.S. Copyright Code. **Bootlegging** software is clearly unethical, as well as illegal, yet it is so widespread that estimates suggest there may be as many as ten illegal copies for every legitimate program sold.

To prevent bootlegging, software vendors sometimes **copy protect** software so that it cannot be copied to other disks—or can only be copied a limited number of times, generally twice. Copy-protected software is becoming rarer, however, as vendors respond to complaints from users that copy protection is a nuisance. Copy protection can make it difficult to do legitimate copying, such as creating backup disks or recovering from hard-disk failure. In fact, the lack of copy protection is often a selling feature for many programs.

Limits of Legislation to Control Computer Crime

Legislators have been trying for years to enact laws to curb computer crime at the federal level, without success. The major stumbling block is the lack of a legal definition for "property" and "value" as they relate to computerized information. Prosecutors are also reluctant to take computer thieves to court because the computer security in an organization is typically so poor and computer crime laws so vague that they find it difficult to build good cases.

Because the federal government has not enacted effective laws in this area, many states are beginning to pass stronger legislation that protects companies from computer theft, deliberate destruction of data, and so on.

Hardware and Software Controls

Precautions and controls can be employed for protecting hardware and software from illegitimate use. Access to a system and its data should be controlled, and secure backup copies maintained. Most electronic network packages include measures for controlling access to sensitive files. Other ways to reduce the risk of fraud are to rotate personnel in certain jobs and to separate important tasks so that no one person could complete a fraudulent transaction.

Controlled Access to Hardware and Software.   If data or program security is important, systems analysts should ensure that unauthorized personnel cannot have physical access to the computer system. The system can be housed in a locked room to protect hardware from theft and to prevent unauthorized people from accessing data or programs. Specific physical and electronic access control techniques include keyboard locks, automatic logs, restricted access to systems, and limited after-hour use. Using passwords that change periodically can also help to keep a system secure.

Backup Copies of Data and Programs.   Creating backups consists of making extra copies of programs or data. Backups safeguard against the loss of programs or data in computer memory, on hard disks, or on diskettes. Data should be backed up each time it is updated or changed in any way.

Security for Backup Copies.   Because backups represent the safety net that will be used if original data or programs are destroyed, the backups must be protected with the same care as the originals. Protection techniques include keeping them under lock and key in a fireproof container and storing them in a location several miles from the originals. This protects files from natural disasters as well as computer crime.

Distributed Network Controls.   Distributed processing and remote databases pose specific control problems for organizations because they are vulnerable to unauthorized access to data from remote locations. For example, a company trying to discover a competitor's confidential data might tap into the competitor's network and monitor transmissions for their own benefit. Two common controls are used for protecting networks: data encryption and callback systems.

◆   **Data encryption** involves encoding data so that it cannot be understood unless it is first decoded. To encrypt data, a program uses an algorithm to scramble, or encode, data before it is sent over the network. Another program at the receiving end then decodes the data. If an unauthorized person tapped into the database, the data would not readable.

   Because data encryption is cumbersome and expensive, it is generally used only for sensitive data. Access to both the encryption and the decoding programs must be tightly controlled as well.

◆   A **callback system** ensures that a user calling in by phone is calling from an authorized telephone number. After validating a user's password, the callback system breaks the phone connection and then immediately calls a previously stored telephone number linked to the password in the system's memory. If this is not the number where the person seeking access is located, entry to the system will not be permitted.

Separation and Rotation of Functions.   Another way to ensure the security of computer systems is to segment the work done so that each task requires several different people. This separation of duties minimizes the risk of unauthorized and fraudulent use and/or modification of data as well as programs, because two or more perpetrators within the department would be required to commit a fraud. Separating tasks also reduces the risk of errors since one person can check the work of another.

   In addition to separating duties, it is advisable to have duties rotated among individuals within each group from time to time. This arrangement is likely to thwart fraudulent collusion among employees. If, for example, a particular data entry operator who enters only payroll data and a programmer who works exclusively on payroll programs intend to work together to commit a computer crime, they may find it difficult to carry it out if their jobs are periodically rotated.

Safeguards such as these help honest people stay honest. Honest computer users often confront ethical challenges as well, and these issues are often not so clearly defined.

Ethics in Computing

Ethical conduct goes beyond merely adhering to laws. All professions have a code of ethics that broadly sets standards for professionals; such ethical standards may not be covered by specific legislation. For example, what should you do if you are an analyst or programmer responsible for a program that invades privacy? Or how responsible are you if you create a software package that produces erroneous results? After all, is it reasonable to expect software packages to be totally free of errors?

There are, of course, no simple answers to questions such as these. Many people with high ethical standards have argued against holding computer professionals totally responsible for their work, because the way a system is used may not be under the programmer's or analyst's control. Some people argue that, just as Alfred Nobel cannot be held accountable for the immoral use of his invention of dynamite, computer professionals should not be held accountable for programs that are used illegally or unethically.

As the debate over these ethical issues goes on, many leaders in the computing field believe that a code of ethics is of primary importance and that it would be far better for professionals to police themselves before the government finds it necessary to pass laws. Figure 13–2 lists a section of the privacy code from the Codes of Ethics, Conduct, and Good Practice of the Institute for Certification of Computer Professionals.

Managing the Work Environment

The emergence of computers in the workplace has created a number of new organizational issues in such areas as space planning, health, and safety.

Consider what happened to a telephone company that installed an automated telephone system for its operators. Operator productivity suddenly decreased because:

◆ Light reflecting onto terminal screens from a large bank of windows bothered the operators. While the windows were a much desired change for the operators, the bright, natural light was sometimes so intense that it caused eye strain.

◆ The operators' workstations were designed for the average operator. There was little, if any, flexibility for changing the position of the screen, keyboard, or desk to satisfy individual tastes and desires.

2.2   Social Responsibility: One is expected to combat ignorance about information processing technology in those public areas where one's application can be expected to have an adverse social impact.

2.5   Integrity: One will not knowingly lay claims to competence one does not demonstrably possess.

2.8   Protection of Privacy: One shall have special regard for the potential effects of computer-based systems on the right of privacy of individuals whether this is within one's own organization, among customers or suppliers, or in relation to the general public.

Because of the privileged capability of computer professionals to gain access to computerized files, especially strong strictures will be applied to those who have used their positions of trust to obtain information from computerized files for their personal gain.

Where it is possible that decisions can be made within a computer-based system which could adversely affect the personal security, work, or career of an individual, the system design shall specifically provide for decision review by a responsible executive who will thus remain accountable and identifiable for that decision.

3.1   Education: One has a special responsibility to keep oneself fully aware of developments in information processing technology relevant to one's current professional occupation. One will contribute to the interchange of technical and professional information by encouraging and participating in education activities directed both to fellow professionals and to the public at large. One will do all in one's power to further public understanding of computer systems. One will contribute to the growth of knowledge in the field to the extent that one's expertise, time, and position allows.

3.5   Discretion: One shall exercise maximum discretion in disclosing, or permitting to be disclosed, or using to one's own advantage, any information relating to the affairs of one's present or previous employers or clients.

13–2 This selected passage is from the Code of Ethics, Conduct, and Good Practice of the Institute for Certification of Computer Professionals.

◆   Each operator was given a U-shaped desk with side panels for privacy. Because the operators were accustomed to seeing their colleagues while they worked, they felt cut off from their peers.

What can be done to help users cope with the physical, mental, and social problems caused by new office technologies? **Ergonomics** is the science of adapting machines and work environments to people. Ergonomic studies are designed to provide the best physical arrangement for people using computers and other technology for any length of time.

Reducing Office Glare.   Perhaps the most obvious problem in the work environment—and the one easiest to deal with—is office lighting. Improper lighting conditions create glare on video display terminals. There are two common ways to reduce glare: provide indirect lighting, which may almost totally eliminate the problem, and/or provide anti-reflection filters that reduce glare on the screen but also reduce the intensity of the image.

The general trend is toward eliminating all direct overhead lighting, such as fluorescent lights, and substituting softer, indirect lighting in its place.

Reducing Sound Pollution.   Well-planned offices eliminate distracting sounds yet make provisions for private conversations. Because office systems commonly result in noise created by keyboards, printers, and even the computer itself, an effective noise control program focusses on three areas: efficient sound-absorbing materials on furniture, walls, ceilings, and floors; sound-masking devices such as printer covers; and well-designed office layouts.

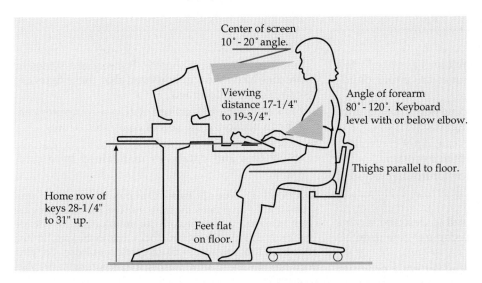

Center of screen
10° - 20° angle.

Viewing
distance 17-1/4"
to 19-3/4".

Angle of forearm
80° - 120°. Keyboard
level with or below elbow.

Thighs parallel to floor.

Home row of
keys 28-1/4"
to 31" up.

Feet flat
on floor.

13–3 Attention should be paid to workstation design and setup for the comfort and health of employees.

Designing Optimum Workstations.   Workstations should be designed to allow users the greatest economy of movement. As shown in Figure 13–3, such factors as sitting or standing heights, reach lengths, arm angles in keyboarding, and eye viewing angles all contribute to the comfort of performing necessary office tasks. Poor workstation design will ultimately result in user fatigue, a high rate of error, and slow task performance.

Reducing Hazards to Health.   Many people are concerned that computer systems in businesses can be unhealthy for employees. Consider the experience of data entry operators whose input rate is closely monitored by automated equipment. The system keeps track of the average time it takes an operator to key in an order. If management has set strict standards for acceptable performance, such close monitoring can be devastating to the health of employees. It can induce stress, other health problems, feelings of powerlessness, and even complete apathy. As a result, organizational productivity can plummet.

Another hotly debated issue is whether video display terminals (VDTs) emit harmful radiation. Numerous studies conducted in the 1970s and early 1980s failed to detect radiation above acceptable levels, but these conclusions are now being reevaluated. Questions center around the long-term biological effects of low-level radiation from VDTs on users, especially on whether prolonged exposure of pregnant women to VDTs can cause birth defects. Until conclusive evidence is available to resolve these issues, a corporate policy requiring periodic testing for malfunctioning video display terminals that emit radiation above safety limits might be appropriate.

Employees' experience with computer systems affects their attitude toward new technology. In a poorly managed computer environment, employees may believe that their computer system displaces workers, affects their health, and limits their freedoms, or they may believe that computers provide new careers, enhance employee control over tasks, and improve their decision-making ability. The perception of the effects of computers in a given business depends on the leadership and vision of the company's managers as well as the computer professionals who plan and create these systems.

SELF-TEST

1. (T *or* F) Computer crimes sometimes go unreported to the police because companies are afraid of adverse publicity.

2. (T *or* F) Computer viruses occur when data is contaminated by exposure to magnetic fields.

3. (T *or* F) The use of computers can, if not controlled, lead to invasion of an individual's privacy.

4. Examples of methods used for controlling physical access to a computer are _____, _____, _____, and _____.

5. The term _____ is used to describe scrambling techniques that make computer data unintelligible.

6. (T *or* F) Copying of commercial software program for a friend is not really an ethical or legal issue.

7. _____ is the science of adapting machines and work environments to people.

8. (T *or* F) Early in the 1970s, people worried that radiation from video display terminals might be hazardous to users' health. Subsequent scientific studies have shown, however, that these fears are completely unfounded.

9. (T *or* F) Rotating functions within a computer center can minimize the risk of computer crimes.

10. (T *or* F) Typically, programmers should have access to all files and databases maintained by a company.

SOLUTIONS 1) True. 2) False. Computer viruses are programs that tie up processing time with useless tasks; they are often introduced via network communication by outside "hackers." 3) True. 4) keyboard locks, automatic logs, limited after-hour use, passwords. 5) encryption. 6) False. Copying licensed software for others is illegal. 7) Ergonomics. 8) False. Conclusive evidence is still not available. 9) True. 10) False. Programmers should have access to files and databases on a "need-to-know" basis.

Career Opportunities in Computing

Most college graduates who have majored in the computing field begin their careers as programmers. Many organizations initially hire entry-level employees as maintenance programmers who modify existing programs to make them more current or efficient. Maintenance programming helps novices understand the types of programs typically coded in the organization and also helps them learn firsthand the need for well-documented, highly structured programs. On the other hand, maintenance work tends to be tedious unless you have an interest in "troubleshooting," and most maintenance programmers go on to become application programmers, programmer analysts, or scientific programmers.

Application programmers write, debug, and document programs for specific business tasks; they generally have a long-range goal to become systems analysts or managers—either programming, systems, or operations managers. Programmer analysts work with end-users to define and solve problems and then do the programming. Scientific programmers write, debug, and document programs for specific scientific applications; they usually have a long-range interest in increasing their knowledge of computer systems and becoming more specialized—perhaps becoming systems programmers. Systems programmers develop operating system components designed to maximize the processing efficiency of the computer system.

Requirements for Entry-Level Programming Positions

Entry-level programming jobs usually require a college degree, some knowledge of, and experience in, programming, and the right set of personal qualities.

College Degree.   Depending on the company, its requirements, and the salary offered, the degree needed might be one of the following:

- A four-year degree—Bachelor of Science (BS) in computer science or Bachelor of Business Administration (BBA) in information processing

- Associate's degree (AAS or AS) in computer science or business data processing

- Masters in Business Administration (MBA) with an emphasis on information systems, or a computer-related master's degree

In general, four-year college graduates can expect higher-paying and more responsible programming positions, but many good jobs are available for two-year graduates as well. Most organizations view a student's grade point average, particularly in computing courses, as a major factor in evaluating job applicants. An MBA or master's degree in computer science generally allows graduates to begin at a position higher than entry-level programmer.

Programming Knowledge and Experience.   This is the barrier for many graduates. Some organizations require entry-level programmers to have some business or programming experience; they can't get experience without a job, and they can't get a job without experience. If most organizations in a particular location have this requirement, it becomes nearly impossible for students to acquire the needed experience.

But the situation is rarely insurmountable. Many students can earn extra money and gain experience by working in their college's computing center, or by working part-time for local firms or for their instructors who have consulting jobs.

Personal Attributes.   The personal characteristics employers look for vary widely, but they usually include a logical mind and a demonstrated interest in problem solving. Because many organizations believe that communica-

In a Nutshell

Typical Requirements for Entry-Level Programmers

- College degree

- Programming knowledge and experience

- Personal attributes—logical mind, interest in problem solving, good communication skills

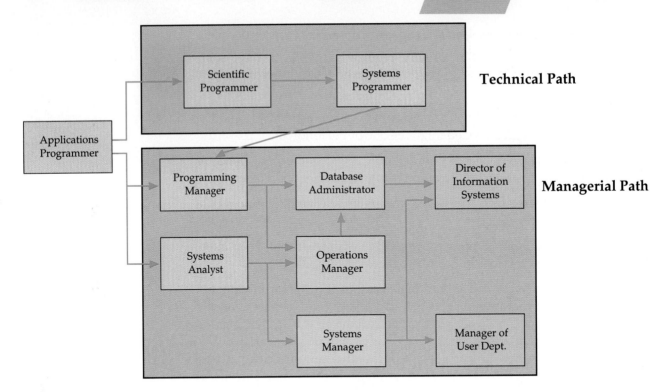

13–4 Career paths for programmers include both technical and managerial jobs.

tion barriers between users and computer professionals account for a large number of failures, they are intent on hiring individuals who are articulate, sensitive, good listeners, and able to communicate.

Companies generally use an interview to determine whether a prospective candidate has the personal attributes needed. Courses in business writing and public speaking could be useful for providing these communication skills. Sometimes a battery of tests is administered as well.

Career Paths for Experienced Programmers

After working as a programmer or in some other entry-level position for one to two years, some people are ready to advance further. The computing field is not really standardized, and various paths can be taken after you have had some programming experience (Figure 13–4). Some people bypass the entry-level stage altogether by completing a computer-related master's degree or Masters in Business Administration (MBA). The following career paths are open to an experienced programmer or a computer professional with an advanced degree:

The Lateral Move. Many programmers seek greener pastures at other organizations after they have gained experience. Most programmers with experience find that they are in demand and can obtain higher-paying jobs in prime locations with good benefits. Many choose a career path in which they change jobs every few years to earn higher salaries and to broaden their knowledge of computer systems.

The Technical Path. Programmers—particularly those with a computer science orientation—sometimes seek opportunities to expand their technical skills. After gaining some experience, they become interested in positions in the more technical areas of software engineering, compiler design, operating system design, computer graphics, sophisticated data communications design, systems programming, and so on. These jobs tend to be filled by highly skilled, experienced programming professionals.

The Management Path.   Many programmers view the computer primarily as a tool to facilitate management decision making. This tends to be particularly true of people with business-related BBA or MBA degrees, or those with extensive business experience. For these professionals, promotion to management is a primary goal. Numerous management positions are available for skilled computer professionals with good communication skills.

◆   **Programming Manager.**   The first step in management for many computer professionals is to supervise other programmers as a programming manager.

◆   **Systems Analyst and Systems Manager.**   In many organizations, a systems analyst supervises the work of programmers and also works closely with top management to determine the organization's overall needs. Even though technical responsibilities are part of the job, the position of systems analyst is considered a management-level job. In general, the more business experience systems analysts have, the more attuned they will be to the needs of specific departments and to the company as a whole. This is the most common second-level job for an experienced programmer.

After serving as a systems analyst, the computer professional could advance to systems manager. A systems manager is the individual who oversees the activities of all systems analysts in an organization. A person with systems experience and good management and communication skills is likely to be promoted to a systems manager (Figure 13–5).

◆   **Operations Manager.**   After gaining considerable experience, a computer professional may be promoted to the position of operations manager.

13–5 A systems manager needs to understand people as well as the computer programs and business systems they use. *Courtesy:* IBM.

This position has responsibility for the overall functioning of the computer and data entry operations. This is a job with general operating responsibilities in which the manager directly supervises the data entry operators, control staff, and computer operators. The operations manager has overall responsibility for the efficient and effective use of the computer equipment, and he or she makes recommendations for new acquisitions. The security and integrity of the computer system is the operations manager's responsibility as well.

◆ **Database Administrator.** A database administrator is the individual responsible for organizing, designing, and maintaining the database and all other data used by the organization. Control of the use, security, and integrity of the database is the responsibility of this professional. Some programmers and analysts typically report to a database administrator; they create, modify, and update databases.

Typically, a programmer or analyst with several years of database experience and good communication skills may be promoted into this position.

◆ **Manager of a User Department.** As user departments in an organization become more computerized, the need for computer expertise within these departments themselves increases. A primary source of failure in computer systems is poor communication between users and computer professionals, and a computer professional within the user area helps to bridge this communication gap. As a result, increasing numbers of organizations are hiring programmers and analysts to serve as technical liaisons with user departments. Often such people eventually become managers of these departments.

◆ **Information Resources Manager.** In some corporations, the information system is viewed as a valuable asset that requires its own management, separate from the information processing department. Information resource managers are responsible for coordinating the corporate computing systems and monitoring the acquisition of hardware and software by the company's functional areas. Their goal is to ensure that the computing systems of the company are integrated into an efficient and secure system.

◆ **Director of Information Systems.** The director of information systems is usually the highest-level position in a computer group. Typically, it is a vice-presidential position, but this varies considerably, depending on the organization. The director of information systems has overall responsibility for all computer operations and for the entire staff of programmers, analysts, and other computer professionals.

The director of information systems has usually had considerable experience at all levels of computing and has demonstrated management and technical skills.

Creating a Business or Consulting. Many experienced programmers are eager to form their own consulting organizations. They may begin by doing freelance programming and systems work, troubleshooting for clients, or developing packages that they then sell or lease to customers.

The advantage of establishing your own company or consulting practice is that you are working for yourself. In addition, you have the potential to earn an excellent income. The disadvantages are the obvious ones of greater risk and instability.

The most successful computer professionals, no matter what area of the profession they are in, must remain up-to-date with the latest technological and industry developments to provide the best possible solutions for business problems. Let us take a look at some of the technologies that will dramatically affect the computer systems designed in the next decade.

Where Is Computing Going?

The long-term goal of most advanced computer vendors is to create systems that are capable of handling **compound documents** that integrate data from different applications—text, data, spreadsheet, graphic, image, and voice information—into a cohesive information system. Compound document systems conceivably allow an architect, for example, to:

1. Turn on the system and orally ask it to display sketches of a new amusement park, which are stored in the database

2. Combine these sketches with photos of three proposed sites

3. Attach a written purchase order

4. Add a short oral note asking for comments

5. Send the whole package electronically across the country to the client's office

While such futuristic document systems will not appear overnight, some compound technologies, such as word processing and spreadsheets, are well established. Other technologies such as image and voice processing may not mature for many years.

Following is an overview of areas in which we can expect to see advancements in the next decade.

Image Processing Technology

Beginning computer users are often surprised by how difficult it is to combine drawings, graphics, and photographs into documents. The technical problems arise from the huge amount of storage space required to store graphics; for example, while one page of text requires about two kilobytes of storage, an 8 x 10-inch photograph can require several megabytes—enough computer space to hold two or three thousand pages of text. Image processing systems that allow users to manipulate images in databases and combine them with text are slowly maturing, however, and will become more common throughout this decade (Figure 13–6).

Current image systems often employ workstations and laser printers; in addition, they may communicate with other devices via local and wide area networks. They often contain specialized devices such as **scanners** (devices that convert pictures and text into machine-readable information), **optical disks** (platters about the size of long-playing records that can contain about

13–6 With image processing technology, products like PicturePower (shown here) allow the user to create illustrated databases that can be manipulated, searched, and viewed on screen. *Courtesy:* PictureWare, Inc.

40,000 pages of images and text), and **jukeboxes** that manipulate optical disks to process images. Scanners are now available for microcomputer users for about $200.

A good image processing system also contains software that allows users to index, compress, edit, annotate, cut, paste, and route image information. In addition, image processing systems often contain word processors that allow users to combine text and graphics (Figure 13–7).

For image systems to work effectively in organizations, three technological hurdles must be overcome: data transfer rates must increase, users must be able to write to optical disks, and software tools capable of integrating images with other office information need to be developed.

13–7 An image processing system uses advanced hardware and software components.

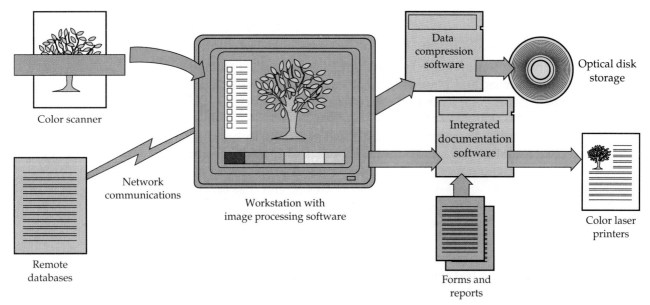

Color scanner

Remote databases

Network communications

Workstation with image processing software

Data compression software

Optical disk storage

Integrated documentation software

Forms and reports

Color laser printers

Slow Data Transfer.   The speed at which data moves between workstations through common LAN wiring such as twisted-pair and coaxial cable is sometimes too slow. These cables cannot accept information faster than 500,000 bits per second (bps), or about 31,000 bytes per second. This may sound fast, but it is too slow for image technologies that commonly use files of several million bytes. However, as LANs begin to use fiber optic cable, which is able to transfer data at much faster rates, image processing will become more practical.

Erasable Optical Disks.   For image processing technology to be effective, users must be able to write and erase data on optical disks as easily as on magnetic media. Although it costs about one dollar to store one page of image-based information on magnetic media and only about five cents to store the same information on an optical disk, optical disks are not yet fully practical because these disks can be written to only once but read any number of times (called WORM—write once, read many). Erasable disks that users can write to are becoming more common, however, and are likely to be important storage media for computers in the years ahead.

Manipulation Tools.   Traditionally, users have not had the tools to edit, manipulate, and integrate images easily with other information such as text, spreadsheets, and databases. However, public standards for using images in compound documents are being developed that allow users to pass graphic pictures, including photographs as well as drawings, back and forth between different systems.

While office imaging technologies are not yet mature, market observers such as the Gartner Group and the Yankee Group predict that vendors will overcome these hurdles gradually throughout the 1990s.

Voice Processing Technologies

Like image processing systems, voice technologies—audio response and voice recognition—are still in the early stages of development. When these technologies mature, researchers expect them to become a major method for users to communicate with each other and with computer system components.

Voice processing technology turns analog, or sound, signals into digital information that machines can understand. This process is called voice input or **voice recognition**. The technology must then be able to interpret the digital information so that it can be output in a meaningful form. It may then process the output and provide a meaningful **audio response**—that is, turn the digital information into analog signals.

Audio Response Devices

Promising audio response (also called voice output) technologies are voice store-and-forward systems and voice synthesis systems.

Voice Store-and-Forward Systems.   Voice store-and-forward systems turn analog voice signals into digital format so that voices can be stored, retrieved, and distributed like any other form of electronic information

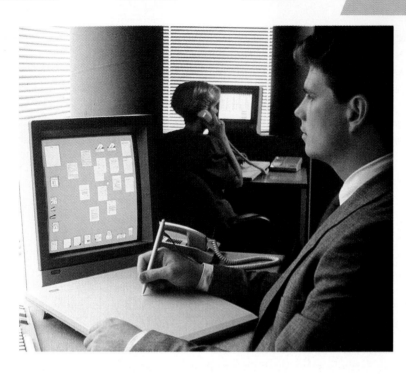

13–8 The Freestyle system allows users to add hand-written notes using a tablet, or verbal notes using a headset, to an electronic document and store or forward the information. *Courtesy:* Wang Laboratories.

(Figure 13–8). A common store-and-forward system is a **voice response system** that turns words into digital information, compresses the digitized words, stores them in libraries of words and phrases, and later uses these words to build responses. The key part of a voice response system is the algorithm used to combine the words and phrases back into meaningful responses.

You have probably used one voice response system many times: most local telephone company directory assistance programs provide digitized directory information. The directory contains a database of telephone numbers and recordings of the first ten digits, zero through nine. To hear a telephone number, the operator identifies the requested number and the system then "speaks" each digit to you. More sophisticated algorithms can combine phrases from a database of 2,000 to 3,000 words into simple sentences.

Voice Synthesis Systems.   **Voice synthesis systems** turn digital information into sound waves—an audible voice. Unlike voice response systems, which have a limited vocabulary, voice synthesis systems have a potentially unlimited vocabulary. Instead of storing words, a voice synthesis system stores the smallest units of sound used in speech (called phonemes) and uses a set of algorithms to put these basic sound units back together into words. Voice synthesis technology has two basic limitations: currently, the sound quality is poor, and it requires a heavy share of processing memory and secondary storage space.

Voice Recognition Devices

While voice output technologies are complicated, they are relatively simple when compared to voice recognition systems.

13–9 A computer trained to recognize this engineer's voice allows him to use both hands and all his attention to conduct tests. *Courtesy:* Texas Instruments.

Voice recognition turns human speech into computer-readable code (Figure 13–9). Because people talk in such hurried and varied ways, voice recognition technologies are extremely complex. Researchers may design voice recognition systems to be speaker-dependent (or independent), to recognize discrete (or continuous) speech, or both.

Speaker-Dependent Systems.   Speaker-dependent systems require users to train the system to recognize their specific speech profiles. To train the system, a user speaks into a microphone, pronouncing each word he or she wants the system to recognize. Once trained, such a system recognizes only the intonations of the user it is trained to recognize—a security benefit in some cases, since it limits access to the system. For example, a system trained by an East Indian user who speaks English with a Hindu accent will probably not understand another user who speaks English with a British accent.

Speaker-independent systems allow anyone to use the system without training the system first.

Discrete Recognition Systems.   **Discrete recognition systems** require the user to pause (possibly for only a fraction of a second) between words to help the system identify word breaks. **Continuous recognition systems** enable users to speak in a normal cadence with words running into one another.

As shown in Figure 13–10, four different combinations are possible in a voice recognition system. Currently, the most accurate systems are speaker-dependent and discrete; the most inaccurate are independent and continuous. To be effective in computer systems, voice recognition technologies must eventually become independent and continuous.

Voice Recognition Systems

	Independent	Dependent
Recognizes Discrete	**Independent/Discrete** Any user, speaking distinctly.	**Dependent/Discrete** One user, speaking distinctly. Currently most accurate.
Recognizes Continuous	**Independent/Continuous** Any user, speaking naturally. Ideal system. Currently most inaccurate.	**Dependent/Continuous** One user, speaking naturally.

13–10 Four different combinations of technologies are possible in a voice recognition system.

Technical progress is slow in developing these systems because of the numerous complexities involved. Independent and continuous systems need to be able to process large and complex vocabularies, since a literate person's vocabulary may contain 100,000 words. In addition, people talk quickly—generally up to about 145 words a minute—and they often run words and sounds together.

Researchers estimate that a fully independent/continuous system will not be developed until the end of the century at the earliest.

Personal Information Managers

Many computer experts predict that **personal information managers (PIMs)** will be an exciting breakthrough in software for the 1990s. Currently, most PIMs are used basically as desktop organizers, but more powerful PIMs allow users to enter text information randomly into computers and quickly find it again. Unlike spreadsheets (which take the place of ledgers) or databases (which take the place of filing cabinets), personal information management software has no physical counterpart. It appeals to experienced users who spend most of their time at workstations and who store most of their information in digital form.

Personal information managers are designed to handle the small bits of text information that can get lost in traditional databases. For example, data that is ideal for PIMs include comments that a client made about his or her family during a golf date, or comments that serve as informal leads to potential new clients. The biggest conceptual challenge for those managing this kind of informal text is how to store it so that it can be easily retrieved. Although various personal information managers solve this problem in slightly different ways, they all combine three types of software: text and retrieval programs, freeform databases, and hypertext applications.

Text and Retrieval Programs.   **Text and retrieval programs** store the entire contents of a document in a database. These programs retrieve text either by searching from the beginning of a document to the end or by using special search algorithms. What distinguishes full text retrieval from traditional databases is that text can be completely unstructured and unde-fined—users do not have to remember a document number or name to retrieve information. You simply enter a keyword or phrase that you know is in the document, and the retrieval system tells you which documents in the database contain the specified word or phrase. For example, you can enter a client's name in a PIM record (Ann Konn, for example) and the fact that Ann likes Bach and has a son going to the Massachusetts Institute of Technology. Then, later, in another record, you can make a note to meet Ann on Friday. When Friday comes, you can quickly locate all notes pertaining to Ann.

Freeform Databases.   Freeform database documents are structured simi-larly to the data fields and records of traditional databases: they allow you to sort, search, and manipulate documents as though they were database re-cords. These programs create an actual text database of documents—not simply a collection of text files as in search and retrieval programs. Freeform databases allow users to specify certain words or numbers in a document as data fields, sort by those fields, and use Boolean operators (such as AND, OR, and GREATER THAN) just as you would with a traditional database. For example, using a freeform database containing names and addresses of clients, a stockbroker can make notes like the following:

> Ann Konn
>
> Likes the railroad and silver industries. Wants investments with a rate of return GREATER THAN 35 percent.
>
> Gross investment to date: $1,232,500.

The stockbroker can then calculate the total investments of all his or her clients, create a list of those interested in the railroad, and sort that list by preferred rate of return!

Personal information managers that use freeform database concepts can manipulate text information extensively, but they are difficult to learn and are harder to use than search and retrieval programs. However, once mas-tered, they are also faster.

Hypertext.   Hypertext is a form of DBMS that allows users to link screens of information (text, graphics, images, and even sound) together associa-tively. Hypertext products mimic our ability to store and retrieve informa-tion referentially for quick and intuitive access. Ted Nelson, who coined the term *hypertext*, defines it as a way of creating documents that can be read in relation to other documents. A common use for hypertext is for in-depth research. While displaying one document, a hypertext application refers readers to other documents, which in turn refer them to still other docu-ments. Readers who want to check a reference might click a mouse button on the item to be referenced, and the referenced text will appear on the screen. In this way, all documents are linked to each other by association.

Many computer novices who use hypertext applications are impressed by its power. Hypercard is a popular hypertext application for the Macin-tosh. Many applications have been designed to take advantage of Hyper-

13–11 Players in the game Cosmic Osmo wander through sophisticated, inter-related hypercard stacks of graphics, text, and sound as they explore a distant planet. *Courtesy:* Activision.

card's capabilities. These range from such business-related tools as medical dictionaries to games (Figure 13–11).

Personal information managers combine search and retrieval, freeform database, and hypertext techniques to allow systems users to organize the myriad tasks, ideas, and notes—even those created haphazardly—so that they can be retrieved quickly for current projects.

Cooperative Processing Systems

Many computer experts are currently combining the strengths of mainframes, minicomputers, and personal computers into **cooperative processing** systems. A good example of a cooperative system is Prodigy, the subscriber service offered for microcomputer users by IBM and Sears. The Prodigy system consists of a central mainframe, several regional minicomputers, and software on the users' micros. Prodigy is designed so that each element of the system works in cooperation with each other element, and processing tasks are distributed to the most appropriate computer in the system.

For example, one of Prodigy's services is to allow users in any part of the country to display a map of the country with local and national weather, and even ski conditions (Figure 13–12). Rather than store the maps, weather graphics, and current weather information at the central mainframe and then send it over the network to individual users, Prodigy stores the graphics map and menu displays at the users' computers; the mainframe sends users only the current weather information via the network, and the user's software overlays it on the resident maps. This substantially reduces processing and access times as well as the amount of storage space required on the mainframe.

Cooperative systems decrease the amount of data traffic and time needed to send data over networks. Each of the system's elements is used to perform the tasks for which it is most effective.

Analysts expect that powerful, multitasking operating system software such as OS/2 will make cooperative processing more common. Multitasking

13–12 Prodigy subscribers can call up this map on their PCs at any time to access current weather information. *Courtesy:* Prodigy Services Company.

software takes advantage of increasingly powerful microcomputers and enables them to communicate and cooperate with mainframes as equals rather than simply as terminals or network nodes.

The Challenge of Computer Systems

As a result of the increasing power of image, voice, and expert systems, the day is coming when computer systems will provide many of the services now supplied by managerial support staff. Managers will rely on their computer systems to gather information, analyze it, and present it to workers and decision makers in immediately usable form.

A broad range of tools are converging on computer systems to create this level of support, which is likely to further revolutionize the work environment. These tools include compound documents, electronic messaging, interactive video teleconferencing, and intelligent networks that provide access to thousands of external public databases. They also include specialized workstation technologies such as legal, medical, and engineering expert systems that help professionals better use their creative capacities.

Such developments have significant influences on those who use computer systems, requiring them to change from being merely participants in the system to becoming system designers themselves. Successful users will be those who are able to think and plan strategically, encourage innovation, and develop computer solutions to their own business problems.

In many ways, computer systems are at the center of a technological and organizational revolution that is changing today's society. Those at the center of this revolution—those with the vision to see where computer technology is going and its power for constructive change—will be tomorrow's leaders.

SUMMARY

Organizations must be concerned about computer system security—protecting computer systems and data from natural disasters, such as earthquake and flood, and from computer crime such as embezzlement, sabotage, and espionage. *Computer crimes* can include theft of computer time, manipulation of computer programs or data, and theft of data and assets. Copying purchased software packages for other users is illegal; to prevent this practice, called *bootlegging*, software vendors sometimes *copy-protect software* so that it cannot be copied to other disks.

Many precautions and controls are available to protect hardware and software from natural disasters and illegitimate use, such as controlling physical and electronic access to business systems and ensuring that data and program backups are made. Distributed processing and remote databases pose specific control problems for organizations because they are vulnerable to unauthorized access to data. Two common controls for protecting networks are *data encryption* and *callback systems*.

Computer professionals must realize that *ethical conduct* goes beyond merely adhering to laws. It requires the professional to follow standards that may not be covered by specific legislation. Unethical activities not specifically addressed by current laws include: What should you do if you are an analyst or programmer responsible for a program that invades privacy or that replaces a labor force?

Ergonomics is the science of adapting machines and work environments to people. Ergonomic studies are designed to ensure the best physical environment for people who use computers for any length of time. Such studies provide guidelines for reducing office glare, reducing sound pollution, designing optimum workstations, and reducing hazards to health.

Most college graduates who have majored in the computing field begin their careers as programmers. Five common programming positions are: *maintenance programmers, application programmers, programmer/analysts, scientific programmers,* and *systems programmers*. Typical requirements for entry-level programmers are a college degree, programming training and experience, and appropriate personal attributes. Typical career moves after being a programmer for one to two years are: *the lateral move* to another company at the same level, *the technical path, the management path,* and *starting a business or consulting*.

The long-term goal of most advanced computer vendors is that of creating systems capable of handling *compound documents* that integrate text, data, spreadsheet, graphic, image, and voice information into a cohesive information system. For *image processing systems* to work effectively in organizations, three technological hurdles must be overcome: *data transfer rates must increase, users must be able to write to optical disks,* and *software tools capable of integrating images with other office information need to be developed.*

Like image processing systems, *voice technologies* are still in the early stages of development. Promising voice output technologies are *voice store-and-forward systems* and *voice synthesis systems*. Voice synthesis technology has two basic limitations: *poor sound quality* and *limited systems resources*. Voice recognition systems may be designed to be *speaker-dependent (or independent),* and to have *discrete (or continuous) voice recognition capabilities.*

Personal information managers (PIMs) are software packages that allow users to enter text information randomly into computers and quickly find it again. Personal information managers combine three types of software: *text and retrieval programs, freeform databases,* and *hypertext applications.*

KEY TERMS

Application programmer	Operations manager
Audio response	Optical disk
Bootlegging	Personal information manager (PIM)
Callback system	Privacy
Compound document	Programmer analyst
Copy protection	Programming manager
Continuous recognition system	Scanner
Cooperative processing	Scientific programmer
Copy protection	Security
Data encryption	Speaker-dependent (independent) system
Database administrator	Systems analyst
Director of information systems	Systems manager
Discrete recognition system	Systems programmer
Ergonomics	Text and retrieval program
Freeform database	User department manager
Hypertext	Voice recognition
Information resources manager	Voice response system
Jukebox	Voice store-and-forward system
Maintenance programmer	Voice synthesis system

CHAPTER SELF-TEST

1. A _____ programmer is responsible for modifying existing programs to make them more current or efficient.

2. A _____ programmer is responsible for writing and modifying operating systems.

3. (T *or* F) Most companies seek programmers who have a logical mind; however, since programmers are creative people, they need not possess good interpersonal and communication skills.

4. The two main promotion opportunities for programmers are _____ and _____.

5. A programmer interested in a promotion into management may seek a job as a _____, _____, or _____.

6. The title of the person who has overall responsibility for the operation of the computer center and the activities of the entire computer staff is _____.

7. (T *or* F) Computer crimes are sometimes committed by unauthorized people using a network to access a database.

8. (T *or* F) The uncontrolled use of computers could potentially lead to an invasion of privacy.

9. (T *or* F) Encryption is a major method used to preserve the privacy of data when a company operates in a data communications environment.

10. (T *or* F) Because there is no firm legal definition of "property" as related to electronic information, copying copyrighted software for others is legal.

11. Types of specialized hardware for optical computer systems are _____, _____, and _____.

12. (T *or* F) Scanners are devices that look for specific references in text.

13. (T *or* F) Voice processing systems are considered a mature technology.

14. Newer personal information managers combine three types of software: _____, _____, and _____.

SOLUTIONS 1) maintenance. 2) systems. 3) False. The best programmers possess excellent communication skills. 4) management opportunities; technical opportunities such as in compiler design, software engineering, and so on. 5) programming manager, systems analyst, operations manager. 6) director of information systems (or a similar title). 7) True. 8) True. 9) True. 10) False. Copying copyrighted software for others is illegal. 11) scanners, optical disks, jukeboxes. 12) False. Scanners translate text and graphic images into digital data that can be input into a computer system. 13) False. Researchers do not expect a mature system to be developed until the end of the century at the earliest. 14) text and retrieval programs, freeform databases, and hypertext.

REVIEW QUESTIONS

1. Do you think computer systems promote or inhibit personal freedom? Explain your answer.

2. Why are distributed computer systems particularly vulnerable to unauthorized access? What can be done about it?

3. List and discuss three health implications of replacing an organization's paper-based office system with one that relies on video display terminals.

4. Discuss three technological hurdles that vendors must overcome before image systems will become common in organizations.

5. Identify two voice output technologies. Describe two limitations of each.

6. For voice recognition systems to be effective in organizations, why must they be independent and continuous?

7. Some industry observers feel that personal information managers may represent a new breakthrough technology for office systems. Describe two features of the software that cause observers to make such a statement.

PROBLEM-SOLVING APPLICATIONS

1. You paid $498 to purchase the most powerful microcomputer word processor on the market. You show it off to your best friend, who is amazed by what it can do. He asks you if he can make a copy of the software so he can use it on his own micro. You are now faced with an ethical problem. What do you do? Explain your answer.

2. Discuss two ways that freeform databases are different from text and retrieval systems. Which type of system would be preferable for: a small legal firm specializing in environmental litigation; a yacht sales organization; a fine arts magazine publisher; an independent salesperson representing a large number of high-tech clients? Be sure to give your rationale for each.

3. Do some research and provide a brief summary and evaluation on some controversy or health issue that has been described in this chapter.

4. While researching Question 3, you probably ran across information about some current controversy regarding computer use that is not considered in this chapter. Briefly discuss this controversy.

PART V

TUTORIALS

Using DOS

Hardware needed:

✔ IBM PC, IBM PS/2, or IBM-compatible microcomputer

Software needed:

✔ DOS 2.0 or later version

✔ Student Data Disk

✔ two blank diskettes

When you have completed this tutorial, you will be able to:

✔ Turn on your computer and boot up your system

✔ Format floppy diskettes

✔ List disk directories

✔ Print the screen contents

✔ Use the ? and * wildcards

✔ Copy files and disks

✔ Create backup copies

✔ Rename files

✔ Delete files

✔ Create and manage subdirectories

Tutorial Outline

What is DOS?

DOS is the software that allows you and your applications to interact with your microcomputer's central processing unit (CPU). PC-DOS is the disk operating system designed by Microsoft for the IBM PC and IBM PS/2 families. A virtually identical operating system, MS-DOS, is used on micro-computers designed to be compatible with either of these two IBM families. We will refer to both MS-DOS and PC-DOS as DOS.

You probably have DOS release 3.0 or later on your computer. A later release is represented by a higher number. The first number represents a major revision of DOS; for example, release 4.0 is a major update of release 3.0. The second number, on the other hand, refers to a slightly changed version of a major revision. Thus, release 3.1 includes only minor changes of 3.0. Any release later than 2.0 will work for this tutorial, but the screens we show will be from release 3.3. Releases 1.0 to 3.3 are quite similar in their command structure. If you are using release 4.0, however, it may look quite different, because it is the first version to allow the user to choose commands from menus. Figure DOS–1 shows examples of releases 3.3 and 4.0 screens.

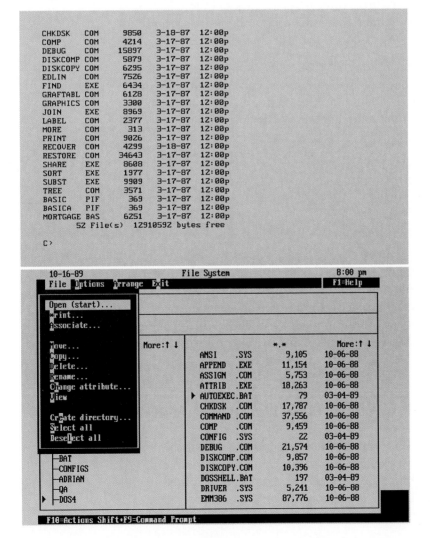

DOS–1 DOS version 4.0 has added menu choices that make it easier for new users to learn commands.

All users of IBM microcomputers and their compatibles need to learn some of the DOS commands. This is because you must have DOS up and running before you can load an application. Thus, Lesson 1 of this tutorial begins with starting up your microcomputer. You also need DOS to do all the everyday control functions necessary in microcomputing—to prepare and manage your floppy diskettes; to copy, rename, and delete files; to find out what files are on a disk and how much free space is remaining; to format and copy disks; and so on.

Before starting up your computer, however, you need to know some things about DOS files and file-naming rules.

File Naming in DOS

A file can contain a program or data. Data files are named by the user, and there are a few rules, or **file-naming conventions**, that you must follow when you name your files. All file names, including program files, usually have two parts, separated by a period. The first part can have up to eight letters, digits, or symbols; the second part, which is optional, is called the **file-name extension** and can have up to three letters, digits, or symbols. Not all symbols are permitted in file names. The following symbols are currently allowable in file names:

~ ! @ # $ ^ & ( ) - _ { } ' '

File names cannot include a space, so many people substitute an underline for a space. For example, here is what you might name a word processing file that contains the first report to your client, the ARP Corporation:

report_1.arp

Here are two examples of invalid file names:

report 1.arp

Spaces are not valid.

report_1.arpx

Extensions can have only three letters.

Notice that the file names above are typed in lowercase. You use upper- or lowercase letters for your file names. In this tutorial, we will use upper-case to highlight file names and commands, but we will show lowercase for the things you will type in—you might as well form the habit of using lowercase, because it is easier to type without having to hold down the (SHIFT) key or use the (CAPS LOCK) key.

It is wise to give files meaningful names—names that will mean something to you six months later when you are trying to remember what the file contains. If you can recognize it, you will not have to display the file in order to see what it contains.

For some applications, the file name extension for the data file is created automatically. For example, worksheets in Lotus 1–2–3 always have the extension .WK1 (or WKS in older releases). If the extension is something other than .WK1 or .WKS, Lotus will not recognize it as a spreadsheet.

Remember that a file name extension is not necessary if it is not required by your application.

The COMMAND.COM program file on the DOS disk is necessary to start, or **boot up**, the system. If you try booting up on a disk that does not include this file—as well as two "hidden" files that we will talk about when you learn to format disks—you will see an error message on your screen, and your computer will not complete the booting process. For hard disk users, COMMAND.COM and the hidden files must be on the C drive when the computer is turned on; for diskette-only users, the files must be on the disk in the A drive. Once your microcomputer is turned on with these files in the A or C drive, the DOS functions in the COMMAND.COM file are loaded into main memory and are available to you no matter what disks are moved into the disk drives. We will go through the booting-up process in Lesson 1.

Other DOS files are not required for starting up. They execute specialized functions; if you want to use one of those commands, the appropriate DOS file must be present in one of your disk drives. Table DOS–1 summarizes the commands we will cover in this tutorial, as well as the names of the files that execute those commands.

Some DOS file name extensions indicate the type of file they are:

.COM Command file

.EXE Executable program file

.BAT Batch file—a series of program files to be executed in sequence

Table DOS–1 Basic DOS commands and their file names

Command	File Used	Function
DATE	COMMAND.COM	Allows current date to be set or changed
TIME	COMMAND.COM	Allows current time to be set or changed
FORMAT	FORMAT.COM	Initializes diskettes
VER	COMMAND.COM	Displays the DOS version number
DIR	COMMAND.COM	Displays any disk's directory
TYPE	COMMAND.COM	Displays the contents of a file
COPY	COMMAND.COM	Copies files
DISKCOPY	DISKCOPY.COM	Formats a disk and copies all files from one disk to another
CHKDSK	CHKDSK.COM	Checks for disk's available space and specifies whether there are faulty files on the disk
RENAME or REN	COMMAND.COM	Renames files
DEL	COMMAND.COM	Deletes files
ERASE	COMMAND.COM	Erases files
MKDIR or MD	COMMAND.COM	Creates new directories
CHDIR or CD	COMMAND.COM	Changes the current directory
RMDIR or RD	COMMAND.COM	Removes empty directories

When you give DOS a command—FORMAT, for example—it looks for a file named FORMAT with one of the above extensions, and then it executes the instructions in that file.

Two Booting Files: AUTOEXEC.BAT and CONFIG.SYS

Two optional files, AUTOEXEC.BAT and CONFIG.SYS, are often created by users so that their computers will boot up in special ways needed by their applications. These files must be located on the same disk as the COM-MAND.COM file. When you turn on your computer, it will look for these two files and follow their instructions; but if they are not present, the computer will still boot up successfully.

The AUTOEXEC.BAT file allows users to load special functions or programs into storage as part of booting up. After executing COMMAND.-COM, the computer will look for an AUTOEXEC.BAT file and execute it if it is there. You can create this file so that it changes the default disk drive, changes to a specific subdirectory, loads application programs, and so on.

The CONFIG.SYS file, which does system configuration, allows users to customize their systems in a number of ways. For example, in release 3.1 or later, you can specify a country, and DOS will display the date, time, currency symbol, and so on, in that country's format. You can also specify how many buffers—storage areas—DOS should save. Some application packages require numerous buffer areas. Buffers are parts of RAM memory set aside by DOS to hold data that has been read, that is waiting to be written to disk, or that is on its way to the printer.

It is fairly easy for experienced users to create AUTOEXEC.BAT and CONFIG.SYS files. They can often be created with a standard word processing package. For instructions, consult a book that includes advanced DOS functions or your DOS manual.

DOS Syntax

DOS is very precise about the way commands must be entered. Though you may type them in lowercase or uppercase as you do with file names, you must follow the proper wording and spacing rules exactly. When you see a blank in the tutorial examples, you must leave a space there; if there is no blank, the command may not work if you put one there. The rules for proper wording of commands are called **syntax**. Throughout this tutorial, the commands you will use will be followed by notes about proper syntax. If you make a mistake in typing a command, DOS will let you know by displaying a message such as "Bad command or filename." If that happens, all you need to do is retype the command correctly.

You Are Ready to Begin

This tutorial will take you through the basic DOS commands in three lessons, beginning with how to start up your microcomputer. The commands we will cover are all very useful, so you might consider doing the lessons twice to make sure you can remember them without looking anything up.

Most of the procedures in this tutorial begin with instructions for how to use a particular DOS command on a microcomputer with two floppy disk drives. If you are working on a micro that has a hard disk, the commands are the same, but the disk drive orientation is somewhat different. If you have a hard disk, you will load DOS from the C drive, where it has already been installed. If you have a diskette-only system, you will load DOS from a diskette that is placed in the A drive.

Throughout the tutorial, all entries you are to type in are printed in **bold** type. And note that the Enter key is represented by the symbol, (ENTER).

Lesson 1

Starting Up and Basics

After completing this lesson, you will be able to:

✔ Turn your computer on and off, and boot up your system

✔ Set the date and time on your system

✔ Format a disk to receive data

✔ Move between disk drives

✔ List disk directories

✔ Print what is on your screen

✔ Use wildcard characters to list files

We will begin with start-up procedures for a dual diskette system that has no hard drive, then give procedures for systems that have a hard disk with one or more external floppy disk drives. (Note: To complete this lesson, you will need, in addition to the disks listed at the beginning of this tutorial, a WordPerfect disk.)

Starting Your System

If you have a dual diskette-only system, insert the DOS disk in drive A. (If you have a hard disk, skip this and the next paragraph.)

> Drive A is the upper or leftmost drive, depending on your system. Insert the DOS disk in drive A *before* you turn the switch on, because your micro will not start—or boot up—properly unless it finds the DOS disk when the power goes on. You will not hurt the micro if you forget to insert a disk, but you will have to start all over again.

Close the door on drive A.

> The "door" refers to the lever or handle on your disk drive. The disk in the drive cannot be read by DOS unless the door is closed. If you forget to close it and then try to address that drive, DOS will give you an error message such as: "Not ready error reading drive A. Abort, Retry, Fail?"

		Table DOS–2 Starting Your System
Hard-disk systems	DOS is already on drive C. Drive A should be empty.	
Dual-diskette systems	Place DOS disk in drive A before starting up the system.	

Close the door and press R for Retry, and DOS will continue with your instruction.

If you have a hard disk system, open the door on drive A.

Because DOS is typically installed on the hard disk when it is supplied, you do not need the DOS disk in the A drive. You should not have a disk in drive A when you boot up from a hard-disk system.

You now have either a DOS disk in drive A for a dual-diskette system, or no disk in drive A for a system with a hard disk (Table DOS–2). Now:

Switch on your computer.

Microcomputer switches are usually the rocker type—if it is pushed down on one side, it is ON; if it is pushed down on the other side, it is OFF. Switch locations vary, but they are always on the CPU. Look on the right or left side, or on the back. You may also have to turn on your screen, which is sometimes called the monitor. Some systems have separate switches for the monitor, printer, and other devices.

After you turn the switches on, you will hear the fan go on. A series of diagnostic tests on the hardware is then performed, and if there are no problems, a blinking cursor will appear after a few seconds in the upper left-hand corner of the screen.

What the Red Light Means

As you work your way through this tutorial, you will see that after you execute each command, a red light associated with each disk drive goes on and off, sometimes several times for one activity. This means that the disk drive is doing its work.

WARNING

Do not open a disk drive door or insert or remove disks while the red light for that drive is on.

Learn to watch the screen for the signal that the command has been completely executed. In DOS, the drive prompt that appears on the screen—A>, B>, or C>—indicates which drive is currently active.

Setting the Date and Time

Your micro may have a built-in battery-operated calendar-clock. If so, you may skip this section on setting the date and time, because the date and time on your micro are automatically kept current by the calendar-clock.

For systems without a battery-operated calendar-clock, the first words that appear on your screen ask you to supply the current date (Figure DOS–2). Respond with the current date. For example, if it is November 6, 1990, you would type 11-6-90. If you make a mistake in typing, simply back up using the (BACKSPACE) key and retype the date correctly.

```
Current date is Tue  1-01-1980
Enter new date:
```

DOS–2 When you turn your computer on, the first screen to appear is the DATE screen.

Type today's date.

The screen will then ask you to supply the current time (Figure DOS–3). Respond with the current time. For example, if it is 10:30 a.m., you would type 10:30. (You must enter the time using the 24-hour clock.)

Type current time.

The computer then responds with a copyright DOS message (Figure DOS–4). On systems with dual diskettes and no hard drive, the prompt for drive A now appears just before the cursor. It looks like this:

`A>`

If DOS was loaded from a hard disk, the C prompt will be displayed as:

`C>`

You can use the DATE and TIME commands at any time to change or verify the date and time. For example, at the DOS command:

Type **date**

DOS will display the current setting. To leave the setting as it is:

```
Current date is Tue 1-01-1980
Enter new date: 11-6-90
Current time is 0:01:13.13
Enter new time:
```

DOS–3 After you type in the date, you are queried for the time.

```
Current date is Tue  1-01-1980
Enter new date: 11-6-90
Current time is  0:01:13.13
Enter new time: 10:30

The IBM Personal Computer DOS
Version 3.3  (C) Copyright International Business Machines Corp 1981, 1987
             (C) Copyright Microsoft Corp 1981, 1986

A>
```

DOS–4 When you see the DOS copyright statement, your computer is fully booted up.

Press (ENTER)

Alternatively, if you want to change the date, type in the new date. Follow the same procedure to change or verify the time.

Resetting the System—The Warm Boot

If your computer is already on, but you need to restart, or reboot, you could turn the computer off, and then on again, but this is not a recommended procedure. Instead, you can "warm start" your system. If you have a dual-diskette system with no hard drive, make sure your DOS disk is in drive A. If you have a hard disk, open the door on drive A. To reset the system:

Press (CTRL) and, while holding it down, press (ALT). Then, while holding them down, press (DEL)

Your computer will go through the same screen sequence as if you had turned on the ON/OFF switch. Some IBM-compatible micros actually have a restart button that can be pressed instead of the (CTRL)-(ALT)-(DEL) combination.

Formatting Disks

Before disks can be used for storing data or programs, they must be prepared electronically to receive data in a form that DOS can recognize. Preparing a disk in this way is called **formatting**, or **initializing**, a disk. Your first step will be to format one of your blank disks so that you can use it to learn more about DOS commands.

WARNING

---

*If your disk is not new, it may have files on it. Formatting wipes out **all** existing files on a disk. Be sure you want them deleted before you decide to format a used disk.*

```
A>format b:
Insert new diskette for drive B:
and strike ENTER when ready
```

DOS–5 When you enter the FORMAT command, DOS reminds you to insert a diskette.

Formatting Disks if You Have a Dual-Diskette System with No Hard Drive

Your DOS disk should still be in drive A, and the door on drive A should be closed.

Insert a blank, unformatted disk in drive B and close the door.

Next, you will type the FORMAT command. If you make a mistake in typing, either use the (BACKSPACE) key to correct it or, if you have already pressed (ENTER), simply retype the command correctly. At the A> prompt:

Type **format b:**

Press (ENTER)

"Format b:" is DOS's abbreviated way of saying, "Format the disk in drive B." Be sure to include the colon after the letter B, and to press (ENTER) at the end. You must always press (ENTER) after typing a command.

As soon as you press (ENTER), a message similar to the one in Figure DOS–5 appears on your screen. Press any key when the blank disk is in the drive with the door closed. The disk drives both go to work, and you will hear whirring sounds, and the drive lights will go on and off as the formatting proceeds. DOS will indicate that formatting is occurring by displaying:

```
Formatting...
```

When formatting is finished, a message similar to the one in Figure DOS–6 appears on your screen. Since you do not want to format another disk right now:

Press **N**

The cursor will return to the A> prompt.

Your newly formatted disk is ready to use.

```
A>format b:
Insert diskette for drive B:
and strike ENTER when ready

Formatting...Format complete

     362496 bytes total disk space
     362496 bytes available on disk

Format another (Y/N)?
```

DOS–6 When formatting is complete, DOS tells you how many bytes are available on the disk, and asks whether you want to format another disk.

Formatting and Creating a Boot Disk for Dual-Diskette Systems with No Hard Disk

You format blank disks in order to copy application programs onto them or to use them to store data files. If your disk is going to contain an application and you have a dual-diskette system with no hard disk, it is useful to be able to boot up using the application disk itself. Otherwise, you have to first start with the DOS disk in drive A, turn the computer on, take the DOS disk out, and put the software application disk in.

To be able to boot up directly with your new application disk, all you have to do is add /s to the FORMAT command; this not only formats the disk, but also puts the COMMAND.COM file and two hidden system files on the disk at the same time so that it can be used as a boot disk. You will now reformat the same blank disk, this time adding the command that puts the system files on it.

Type **format b:/s**

Press (ENTER)

Make sure that your spacing is correct—the only space follows the word "format." When formatting is complete, the message in Figure DOS–7 appears on the screen. It tells you how many total bytes of space are on the disk, how many bytes are used by the system files, and how many bytes are remaining for you to use.

Your formatted system disk is now ready for you to copy a software application onto it. Ask your lab instructor for a diskette label and, with a soft, felt-tipped pen, label this disk with your name and the date. Then, when you are ready to boot up with the application disk, simply put it in drive A and turn on your computer.

Formatting Disks If You Have a Hard Drive

As noted, if the microcomputer you are working on has a hard disk, the DOS system and DOS files are probably on the hard disk. In this tutorial, we assume that your hard disk is named drive C. If yours has another letter, just

```
A>format b:/s
Insert new diskette for drive B:
and strike ENTER when ready

Formatting...Format complete
System transferred

    362496 bytes total disk space
     62464 bytes used by system
    300032 bytes available on disk

Format another (Y/N)?
```

DOS–7 When you use the /s parameter with the FORMAT command, DOS sets aside a section of disk space for the COMMAND.COM file and two hidden system files, which it copies onto the newly formatted disk.

D
O
S

substitute that letter for C in this example. Make sure that you are in drive C. If you are not:

Type **c:**

Press (ENTER)

Your cursor should now be at the C> prompt.

Insert a blank disk in drive A and close the door.

Next you will type the FORMAT command. If you make a mistake in typing, either use the (BACKSPACE) key to correct it or, if you have already pressed (ENTER), simply retype the command correctly.

WARNING

Formatting from a hard disk has one ever-present danger: If you fail to add the name of another disk drive to the FORMAT command, the hard disk will format itself. Everything on the disk, including all files and all directories, will be wiped out. If you discover your mistake before formatting begins, you have one chance to recover—when the screen says "Strike Enter when ready." With DOS 3.0 and higher, you can press the (CTRL) key and, while it is depressed, press the (BREAK) key to cancel the FORMAT command. With earlier versions of DOS, pressing any key will start the formatting, including the (ESC) key, so your only option is to turn your computer off at the ON/OFF switch and reboot after a few minutes.

At the C> prompt:

Type **format a:**

Press (ENTER)

"Format a:" is the DOS abbreviation for, "Format the disk in drive A." Be sure to include the colon after the letter A and to press (ENTER) at the end. You must always press (ENTER) after typing a command.

As soon as you press (ENTER), the message, "Insert new diskette for drive A" will be displayed on your screen. Press any key to begin formatting. Both disk drives go to work; you will hear whirring sounds, and the C and A drive lights will go on and off as the formatting proceeds. When formatting is finished, a message similar to the one in Figure DOS–6 appears on your screen. Since you do not want to format another disk right now:

Press N

The cursor will return to the C> prompt.

The disk in drive A is ready to use. Ask your lab instructor for a diskette label and, using a soft, felt-tipped pen, label this disk with your name and the date.

Note that with hard-disk systems, there is no need to put the system files on a diskette, because you will always be booting up from the hard disk in drive C.

Finding Out What Version of DOS You Are Using

Now you can find out what version, or release, of DOS you are using. If you have a dual-diskette system, put your newly formatted disk that has the COMMAND.COM file on it in drive A. At the A> prompt (or the C> prompt if you have a hard disk system)

Type ver

Press (ENTER)

Your screen will tell you what version you are using. If it is release 3.3, your screen will look like Figure DOS–8.

Note that release numbers have significance for formatting. If you are using a micro that was booted up with an earlier version, such as Version 3.1, and you then attempt to use a disk that was formatted with a later version, such as 4.0, you will get an error message. Releases are upwardly compatible; that is, you can use a release 3.1 disk in a micro booted up on release 4.0 without any difficulty. The reverse, however, does not work.

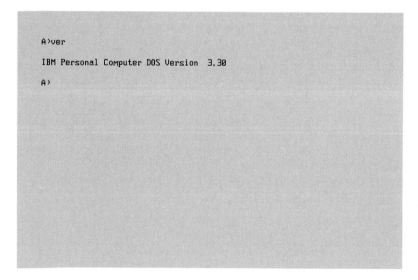

```
A>ver

IBM Personal Computer DOS Version  3.30

A>
```

DOS–8 Use the VER command to find out what version of DOS you are using.

Moving Between Disk Drives

It is very easy to go back and forth between disk drives in DOS. There are many reasons for changing disk drives, and this moving back and forth should become automatic for you. The following exercise will familiarize you with the process. If you have a dual-diskette system with no hard drive:

> ## Put your Student Data Disk in drive A and your newly formatted blank disk in drive B.

>> Make sure you close the drive doors. Since you have just formatted a disk from drive A, you should see the A> prompt on your screen. At the A> prompt:

> ## Type b:

> ## Press (ENTER)

>> Now the prompt for the B drive appears, telling you that you are in drive B. To return to drive A:

> ## Type a:

> ## Press (ENTER)

>> The A> prompt reappears.

Moving Between Disk Drives if You Have a Hard Drive

If you have a hard drive with only one floppy drive, you can still perform operations between drive A and drive B as directed in this tutorial. The computer will use the same floppy drive as both the A drive and the B drive on an alternating basis, and will prompt you to insert and remove the diskettes. To see how the computer prompts you to alternate between drive A and drive B with just one floppy drive:

> ## Place your Student Data Disk in drive A.

>> Make sure you close the drive door. Since you have just formatted a disk from drive C, you should see the C> prompt on your screen. At the C> prompt:

> ## Type a:

> ## Press (ENTER)

>> Now the prompt for the A drive appears, telling you that you are in drive A. To move to drive B:

> ## Type b:

> ## Press (ENTER)

>> Now the following prompt appears:

>> ```
>> Insert disk for drive B
>> Strike any key when ready
>> ```

> ## Remove the Student Data Disk from the floppy drive and insert your newly formatted blank diskette. Then strike any key.

The prompt for the B drive appears, telling you that you are in drive B. To return to drive A:

Type **a:**

Press (ENTER)

The following prompt appears:

```
Insert disk for drive B
Strike any key when ready
```

Remove your blank diskette from the floppy drive and insert the Student Data Disk. Then strike any key.

The prompt for the A drive appears, telling you that you are in drive A.

Listing Disk Directories

Next you will take a look at the files on the Student Data Disk. This disk should be in drive A. (Note that the instruction to press (ENTER) after typing a command will no longer be included in the rest of this tutorial. This step should be automatic for you now.) At the A> prompt:

Type **dir**

A list of files on the data disk will scroll by on the screen. This list of files is called the **disk directory**. It will look something like the directory in Figure DOS–9, although some of the file names will be different. Sometimes there are more files than your screen can hold. To ask for a single screen of files at a time:

Type **dir /p**

This time the scrolling will stop as soon as the screen is filled. You can continue listing files by pressing any key.

Press any key.

```
BUSMAIL   DBB       987    7-28-89    2:04p
BUSMAIL   DBF       987    7-28-89    3:05p
DBASE     CAT      2417    7-28-89    2:15p
36602000  FRO      5068    1-01-80   12:20a
66584010  TMP        34   10-02-89    4:10p
77744200  FRO      4780    1-01-80    3:45a
ARMAST    DBF      1006    1-01-80    7:23a
ARMAST    MDX      9216    1-01-80    7:07a
ARMAST1   DBF       620   10-02-89   10:40p
ARMAST2   DBF       620   10-02-89   10:41p
ARMAST3   DBF       620   10-02-89   10:43p
ARMASTBU  DBF       884    1-01-80    6:04a
ARTRAN    DBF       390   10-02-89   10:06p
ARTRAN    MDX      4096   10-02-89   10:06p
CATALOG   CAT       607    1-01-80   12:04a
CREDIT    FRG      4643    1-01-80    3:57a
CREDIT    FRM      2261    1-01-80    3:57a
MAIL      LBG      6073    1-01-80    4:14a
MAIL      LBL      1006    1-01-80    4:14a
UNTITLED  CAT      1874    1-01-80    4:25a
VIEW1     QBE      2980   10-02-89    9:56p
VIEW2     QBE      4062   10-02-89   10:10p
     36 File(s)    267264 bytes free

A:\>
```

DOS–9 The DIR command lists file names and their extensions, the storage space used for each file, and the date and time each was created or last modified.

```
A:\>dir /w

 Volume in drive A has no label
 Directory of  A:\

MEMO       FRM    MEMO1      TXT    MEMO2      TXT    MEMO3      TXT    MEMO4      TXT
INVOICE    FRM    README            LESSON3           LESSON7           WORDSRCH   EXM
MENU       PRG    MENU       APP    MENU       DBO    ARTRAN1    DBF    BUSMAIL    DBB
BUSMAIL    DBF    DBASE      CAT    36602000   FRO    66584010   TMP    77744200   FRO
ARMAST     DBF    ARMAST     MDX    ARMAST1    DBF    ARMAST2    DBF    ARMAST3    DBF
ARMASTBU   DBF    ARTRAN     DBF    ARTRAN     MDX    CATALOG    CAT    CREDIT     FRG
CREDIT     FRM    MAIL       LBG    MAIL       LBL    UNTITLED   CAT    VIEW1      QBE
VIEW2      QBE
        36 File(s)     267264 bytes free

A:\>
```

DOS–10   The /w parameter added to the DIR command gives you a wide-screen listing of files.

The screen will fill again. These displays will continue until the entire directory listing is complete. An alternative way to look at a file directory is to ask for a wide-screen version.

Type **dir /w**

You will see a wide-screen directory in the form shown in Figure DOS–10. This type of listing just includes file names and extensions, not storage used or date and time that each file was created.

Note that all DIR commands indicate the number of files on the disk as well as the number of bytes that are still available.

Asking for a Directory on a Different Disk Drive

You can also ask for a directory for a disk in another disk drive.

Put your DOS disk in drive A and your Student Data Disk in drive B.

At the A> prompt:

Type **dir b:**

Even though you are in the A drive, the directory listing for drive B scrolls by on the screen. Notice the command's syntax: there is a space after the command DIR, followed by the letter of the drive and then a colon.

You can use all the DOS commands to direct something to happen in a drive other than the one you are in. The **current drive** is the one designated by the prompt—if you see the A> prompt, you know that your current drive is drive A. The current drive is also called the **default drive** or **logged drive**, because it is the only drive DOS will look for when you give a command, unless you designate another drive. If you type simply dir, DOS will only list the directory for your current drive. If you type dir b:, DOS will list the directory in drive B, whether you are in drive B or not.

Looking at the Contents of a File

Sometimes you will want to look at text files that are designed to be read as is. The DOS command TYPE allows you to do this. One such file commonly found on application disks is called README. It contains pertinent information about the disk or application. Your Student Data Disk has such a file. Your Student Data Disk should be in drive B. Move to drive B by typing **b:**. At the B> prompt,

Type **type readme**

The contents of the file README will scroll by on the screen (Figure DOS–11).

The README file is actually a data file created so that it can be read by the user. Most program files, however, are not written in English, because they have been translated into special programming code for use by an application. If you ask your computer to type one of the WordPerfect program files, for example, you will get surprising results. To illustrate, put your WordPerfect disk in drive A. Move to drive A by typing **a:**. At the A> prompt:

Type **type wp.mrs**

What you will see on the screen is words mixed up with a lot of strange symbols, including Greek letters and other symbols that you will not find on the keyboard. Your computer may also beep alarmingly. Do not worry—you cannot hurt anything. To stop the TYPE command:

Press (CTRL) and then, while holding it down, press (BREAK)

The file listing and beeping will stop and your cursor will return to the A> prompt.

The TYPE command, then, is useful for displaying data files that contain text material, or a document created by a word processing program, although word processed files may contain many non-text symbols. Leave the Student Data Disk in drive B for the next exercise.

```
B>type readme

This Student Data Disk contains files that you will need

when you do the tutorials in the Stern and Stern textbook.

Back up this disk before you use any of the files.  You

will find instructions for backing up disks in the DOS

tutorial.

B>
```

DOS–11 The TYPE command displays the contents of a file. This is the README file on you Student Data Disk.

Printing from Your Screen

It is often useful to print a copy of what you see on your screen. For example, when you ask for a disk directory, you might want to print it out so that you have a record of the directory to tape to the disk's envelope. For this exercise, we will print a copy of the README file. First, make sure your printer is on and that there is paper ready to print. Move to drive B. At the B> prompt:

Type **type readme**

> The contents of the README file will appear on your screen. If you have an IBM PC or XT or compatible:

Press (SHIFT), then, while holding it down, press the key labeled "PrtSc" or "Print Screen."

> Or, if you have an IBM PS/2, simply

Press "PrtSc"

> The text that is currently on the screen will be printed. Note that it is not nicely formatted with good margins—this is simply raw, unformatted data being sent to the printer.

> You can also turn the print-screen function on and leave it on, so that it prints all your screens. Then, when you no longer want what is on the screen to print, you can turn the print-screen function off again. A key that turns a function on and off in this manner is called a **toggle** key. To make the "PrtSc" key act as a toggle, you combine it with the (CTRL) key.

Press (CTRL), then, while holding it down, press "PrtSc".

> The print-screen toggle is now on. Now take a look at how it works. At the B> prompt:

Type **dir**

> As the directory listing appears on the screen, it also goes to the printer. Everything you type from this point on will go to the printer. This is called **echo printing** because it "echoes" what appears on the screen. To turn the toggle off:

Press (CTRL), then, while holding it down, press "PrtSc"

> In other words, simply repeat the same sequence you used to turn the toggle on.

Using Wildcard Characters

Sometimes you want to look for specific files in your directory, but if there are a lot of files, it may be difficult to locate the ones you want. DOS gives you a method for narrowing your search; you can use the **wildcard characters**, the question mark (?) and the asterisk (*), to substitute for other characters in a filename. They are called wildcards because, as in poker, they can stand for any character in a file name. The question mark stands for any single character in that exact position, and the asterisk stands for any group of characters in that position.

```
A>dir memo?.txt

Volume in drive A has no label
Directory of  A:\

MEMO1    TXT     1320   9-23-89    3:01p
MEMO2    TXT     1284   9-23-89    3:05p
MEMO3    TXT     1535   9-23-89    3:16p
MEMO4    TXT     1644   9-23-89    3:24p
         4 File(s)    327680 bytes free

A>
```

DOS–12 Using the ? wildcard with the DIR command lists all files whose names match MEMO?.TXT, and have any character in the ? position.

Using the ? Wildcard

You will practice using the ? wildcard by looking for some files on your Student Data Disk: some are text files with the extension .TXT, while others are forms and have the extension FRM. You want to find the memo files with the extension .TXT. Put your Student Data Disk in drive A, and move there by typing **a:**. First, ask for a directory listing. At the A> prompt:

> ### Type dir
>
> You will see a long list of files scrolling by on the screen. There are too many to quickly find out whether a particular file is there. There may be only one or two of them on the disk, but you do not know which ones. At the A> prompt:

> ### Type dir memo?.txt
>
> This command lists all file names that begin with *memo*, have one additional character in the file name, and have an extension of .TXT. The screen shows that there are four such files (Figure DOS–12). Notice that the ? character shows you only files that begin with *memo* and have only one other character in the fifth position of the file name. Check this out. At the A> prompt:

> ### Type dir ?.wks
>
> This time, no files show up, because there are no files with only one character before the extension.

If you want to list whole groups of related files, you need the other wildcard, the * character.

Using the * Wildcard

Suppose you do not know exactly how the memo files were named, but you want to see all files on the disk related to memos. Make sure your Student Data Disk is still in drive A, and then at the A> prompt:

> ### Type dir memo*.txt

D
O
S

The same four files that you found before are displayed again. But if the disk contained a file named MEMO12.TXT, for example, it would appear here and *not* in a DIR command that used a ?, which stands for only one character. Now you will look for all the forms files, those with the extension .FRM. At the A> prompt:

Type **dir *.frm**

All the files with the extension .FRM scroll by on the screen, no matter how many characters precede the extension. As always, the directory also lists the total number of files and the amount of storage space left on the disk.

Turning Your Computer Off (Powering Down)

When it is time to turn the computer off, remove your disks, then turn the power switch for the CPU, or the CPU and the monitor, to the OFF position.

This completes Lesson 1. Do the following practice exercises before going on to Lesson 2.

Practice

1.   Turn your computer off and then boot up. Set the date and time (unless your computer has a built-in calendar-clock that does this automatically).

2.   When your computer is fully booted, reboot it with a warm boot. Reset the date and time.

3.   Move back and forth between disk drives several times. If you have two floppy-disk drives, put a disk in each drive and move between drive A and drive B; each time, ask for a directory of the disk in the current drive. If you have a hard-disk drive, put a disk in drive A and move between drive C and drive A; each time, ask for a directory of the current drive.

4.   From one drive, ask for a directory for the other drive. Move to the other drive and ask for a directory of the first drive.

5.   If you have two floppy-disk drives, put your DOS disk in drive A, and at the A> prompt use the * wildcard to ask for a directory of all files that have the .COM extension. If you have a hard drive, do the same thing from the C> prompt.

6.   Put your Student Data Disk in any drive. Use the TYPE command to look at the contents of the README data file; then use it to look at the contents of the file named MEMO1.TXT, which was created using WordPerfect 5.0.

Lesson 2

File Management

After completing this lesson, you will be able to:

✔ Copy files

✔ Copy an entire disk

✔ Create a backup copy

✔ Rename files

✔ Delete files

Copying Files

COPY is the DOS command that you will probably use the most. Think about some of the reasons you will have for copying files:

◆ to make backup copies in case the original files are lost or damaged accidentally;

◆ to give someone else a copy of data or program files;

◆ to make a different version of the same file without losing the first version;

◆ to put related files together on the same disk;

The syntax, or wording, of the COPY command is typical of other DOS commands. The syntax calls for abbreviating the English equivalent by leaving out the prepositions "from" and "to." Instead of saying "Copy from drive A to drive B," the proper wording is:

copy a:*filename* **b:***filename*

Notice that there is a space after the word *copy* and after the file name to be copied from. There is no space between the drive letters and the file names. Not all the elements of this example are needed for all uses of the COPY command. For example, if you are already in drive A, you do not need to specify the A drive. The above command sequence would then be:

copy *filename* **b:***filename*

In this COPY command, a: is assumed for the file to be copied from.

If the file name will be the same in both copies, you do not need to repeat the file name. To copy the file named MEMO1.TXT from drive A to drive B and leave the name the same, the command is:

copy memo1.txt b:

See Table DOS–3 for a summary of the minimal syntax elements needed for each copying application.

Application	Syntax	Example
To copy a file of same name in current drive to another disk	copy *(file name) (drive):*	copy memo1.txt b:
To copy a file of same name from one drive to another, where neither drive is current	copy *(drive): (file name) (drive):*	copy a:memo1.txt b:
To copy a file to another disk and rename it	copy *(drive):(file name) (drive):(new name)*	copy a:memo1.txt b:letter1.txt
To a copy a file to the same disk and rename it	copy *(file name) (new name)*	copy memo1.txt letter1.txt
To copy a file from another disk to current drive	copy *(other drive):(file name)*	copy b:memo1.txt
To copy a file from another disk and rename it	copy *(other drive):(file name) (new name)*	copy b:memo1.txt letter1.txt

Remember that DOS is very exact. If a file name has an extension, that extension must be included in the COPY command; without it, DOS will tell you "File not found."

You can use the wildcard characters * and ? with the COPY command. For example, if you want to copy all your files that have the extension .TXT, you simply use the syntax COPY *.TXT, and all .TXT files will be copied to the drive you designate.

Table DOS–3 Syntax for COPY Command Applications

Copying from One Disk to Another

If you have not already done so, boot up your computer. Then insert your Student Data Disk in drive A and your formatted blank disk, which we will refer to as your working data disk, in drive B. You have a file called MEMO2.TXT on your Student Data Disk, which you will copy to your working disk. At the A> prompt:

Type **copy memo2.txt b:**

You will see the red lights go on each disk drive as the computer does the work of copying from one drive to the other. Notice that you do not need to specify that the file is in drive A, because you are already in drive A. You also do not need to specify the name of the file after the b:, because it will have the same name. If you used the full statement, "copy a:memo2.txt b:memo2.txt," the result would be exactly the same.

Always look at the drive B directory after copying, to verify that the file was copied. At the A> prompt:

Type **dir b:**

The MEMO2.TXT file should now be listed in the directory for the new disk in drive B.

Copying to Another Disk and Renaming the File

It is often useful to change the name of a file when you copy it. For example, you might want to make a second version of a business form letter without losing the first version; or you might copy a spreadsheet so that you can use the format you designed, although you want to keep using the first one as well.

Now you will copy your MEMO2.TXT file again to your working disk in drive B, only this time you will rename it in the process. At the A> prompt:

Type **copy memo2.txt b:letter2.txt**

You could have renamed it anything, as long as you used no more than eight characters before the period, or three characters in the file name extension after the period. Check the directory of the disk in drive B to see whether you now have both files. At the A> prompt:

Type **dir b:**

Both files are listed in the directory.

Copying Files onto the Same Disk

You will sometimes want to make a second copy of a file on the same disk as the first one. DOS allows you to do this as long as you give the second file a new name. Unlike copying to another disk, where a file of the same name would be erased by the new copy, if you try to copy to a file of the same name on the same disk, DOS will give you the following message:

```
File cannot be copied onto itself.
```

You will now make a second copy of your MEMO2.TXT file on your Student Data Disk. At the A> prompt:

Type **copy memo2.txt letter2.txt**

After the copying is complete and the light on drive A is out, check the directory to see that the copying was done.

Type **dir**

Both files are listed.

Copying from Another Drive

You can also copy a file from another drive without moving drives. You can either copy it with the same name, or rename it in the process. You will now copy MEMO2.TXT from drive B to drive A and rename it REPORT2.TXT, since you already have a MEMO2.TXT file on the Student Data Disk in drive A. At the A> prompt:

Type **copy b:memo2.txt report2.txt**

Notice the syntax. Since you are already in drive A, you do not need to tell DOS to copy the file to drive A. Check the directory for drive A to make sure REPORT2.TXT was copied there. At the A> prompt:

Type **dir**

> The newly copied file REPORT2.TXT is listed.

Copying an Entire Disk to Another Disk

It is sometimes useful to copy all files from one disk to another disk. One important reason to copy an entire disk is to create a **backup** copy to use in case the original is lost or damaged. You will use your working disk to back up your Student Data Disk in the following exercise.

One way to copy all files from one disk to another is to use the * wildcard. With your Student Data Disk still in drive A, and your working disk in drive B:

Type **copy *.* b:**

> All your files on your Student Data Disk are now copied onto your working disk.

A second way to copy all files is to use the DISKCOPY command. DISK-COPY does something more than copy files—it also formats the target disk before it copies the files.

WARNING

Before you use DISKCOPY, make sure that the disk to be copied to does not have files on it that you will need, because formatting will delete them.

For this exercise, use your other blank disk, which is still unformatted. You will use DISKCOPY to format it and to create another backup copy of your Student Data Disk. The DISKCOPY command is not included in the COM-MAND.COM file, so you must put the DOS disk in drive A (or be in drive C if you have a hard disk). From drive A (or C):

Type **diskcopy a: b:**

> DOS then displays the message shown in Figure DOS–13.

```
A>diskcopy a: b:

Insert SOURCE diskette in drive A:

Press any key when ready . . .

Insert TARGET diskette in drive B:

Press any key when ready . . .
```

DOS–13 The DISKCOPY command can only be called up from the DOS disk. You are then instructed to remove the DOS disk from drive A and insert your source disk—the one you want to copy.

Insert your Student Data Disk in drive A, and your blank unformatted disk in drive B. Press any key.

The two drives go to work, formatting the disk in drive B and then copying all the files from the disk in drive A to the disk in drive B. During copying, you will see the message, "formatting while copying..." displayed on your screen. When copying is complete, you will see the message,

```
Copy complete
Copy another (Y/N)?
```

Since you do not want to copy another disk:

Press N

Label this backup "Student Data Disk Backup" and store it in a safe place so you can use it if something happens to your original Student Data Disk. You will continue to use your working disk in the following exercises.

The DISKCOPY command is particularly useful if you are planning to make more than one copy of the same disk or if you are copying entire disks onto unformatted disks. However, you should note that Microsoft, the company that created DOS, recommends that you use the * wildcard method if you are copying a disk with a great many files.

Renaming Files

The DOS RENAME command allows you to change the name of a file. The syntax of the command is very like that for the COPY command (Table DOS–4).

Renaming Files on the Same Disk

To practice renaming, you will give one of those .TXT files on your Student Data Disk a new name. Put your Student Data Disk in drive A. At the A> prompt:

Type **rename memo3.txt letter3.txt**

The light on the A drive comes on briefly, then you are returned to the A> prompt. The file has been renamed, so MEMO3.TXT will have disappeared and LETTER3.TXT now appears in the directory. Check the directory listing to see whether that happened. This is a good chance to use one of the wildcard characters to list all the files with the extension .TXT. At the A> prompt:

Type **dir *.txt**

There should be four files listed.

Table DOS–4 The Rename Command

Application	Syntax	Example
To rename a file on the same disk	rename *(file name) (file name)*	rename memo3.txt letter3.txt
To rename a file on another disk	rename *(drive):(file name) (file name)*	rename b:memo3.txt letter3.txt

Renaming Files on Another Disk

You will sometimes want to rename a file in the other drive without having to change drives. You are now in drive A. Put your working disk in drive B. You will rename the MEMO2.TXT file on your working disk. At the A> prompt:

> ### Type **rename b:memo2.txt report2.txt**
>
>> Notice that you have to designate the other drive by putting the drive letter and a colon in front of the original file name. If you did not, DOS would look in your current drive and might be unable to find a file by that name, or if it did find the file, it would rename a file in the wrong drive.

Erasing and Deleting Files

You will often find that you want to remove a file from a disk, either because it is out of date, or you do not need it any more, or because you need the space on the disk. The two DOS commands ERASE and DEL (or DELETE) are identical. Many people use the DEL command just because it is the shortest form.

WARNING

---

*You can use the wildcard characters ? and * with these two commands, but use them with extreme caution, because you may overlook an important file that falls within the category you are deleting, and you will not be able to recover once the command has been executed.*

Deleting Files on the Same Disk

You will now get rid of all the extra MEMO.TXT variations on your Student Data Disk. First, with your Student Data Disk in drive A, use the DIR and wildcard * to take a look at what is there. At the A> prompt:

> ### Type **dir *.txt**
>
>> You will see six files listed: MEMO1.TXT, MEMO2.TXT, MEMO3.TXT, MEMO4.TXT, LETTER2.TXT, and REPORT2.TXT. The two files LETTER2.TXT and REPORT2.TXT are the copies of MEMO2.TXT that you made earlier. At the A> prompt:

> ### Type **del letter2.txt**
>
>> Try the ERASE command to delete the other file. At the A> prompt:

> ### Type **erase report2.txt**
>
>> Now check the directory to see whether the two files are really gone. At the A> prompt:

> ### Type **dir *.txt**
>
>> The only files left with the .TXT extension are the original MEMO files.

Deleting Files on Another Disk

Deleting a file on another disk works just like renaming or copying—you just precede the file name with the drive name followed by a colon. To delete all the files with the extension .TXT on your working disk in drive B, use the wildcard * character.

Type **del b:*.txt**

> Check the directory for drive B to verify that all .TXT files are gone. At the A> prompt:

Type **dir b:**

> There are no .TXT files remaining on your working disk.

Deleting All Files From a Disk

You will now completely clear all the files on your working disk with a single command.

Type **del b:*.***

> DOS gives you a chance to make sure that you are really ready to part with all your files by asking for verification with the following question:

> `Are you sure (Y/N)?`

Press **Y**

> Check the directory for drive B to verify that all files are gone. At the A> prompt:

Type **dir b:**

> Your working disk is now blank again.

WARNING

Be very cautious when you are deleting files or groups of files—you will not have a chance to recover them if you make a mistake.

This completes Lesson 2. Do the following practice exercises before going on to the next lesson. When you are ready to turn the computer off, remove your disks, then turn the power switch for the CPU, or the CPU and the monitor, to the OFF position.

Practice

1. Use the COPY command to copy and rename the README file on your Student Data Disk. Make two copies on the Student Data Disk, using the names README1 and README2.

2. Use the ? wildcard to copy all README files to a blank, formatted disk.

3. Use the ? wildcard to delete all README files from the disk in #2.

4. Move to the disk drive that holds your blank, formatted disk. Then copy the README files that are on your Student Data Disk to your blank disk.

5.   On the practice disk, rename README1 with the name README.ONE. Rename README2 to README.TWO.

6.   Use the DEL command to delete README.ONE. Use the ERASE command to delete README.TWO.

Lesson 3

Managing Directories on Disks

After completing this lesson, you will be able to:

✔ Organize your files in directories and subdirectories

✔ Create new directories

✔ Move between subdirectories

✔ Copy files into a subdirectory

✔ Remove subdirectories

As you get sophisticated in your use of microcomputers, you will appreciate DOS's ability to organize files in sections and subsections, called **subdirectories**, on your disks. This is often useful on a floppy disk, but it is essential on a hard disk, which may hold the equivalent of hundreds of floppy disks and thousands of files.

Disks with numerous files work best when they are organized in tree-like directories (see Figure DOS–14). The **root directory** is the initial directory created by DOS. It is the directory that you find yourself in after turning your system on, and the one you return to if you need to use any of the DOS

DOS–14 You are going to set up two directories and two subdirectories. This can be done on a diskette or on a hard disk.

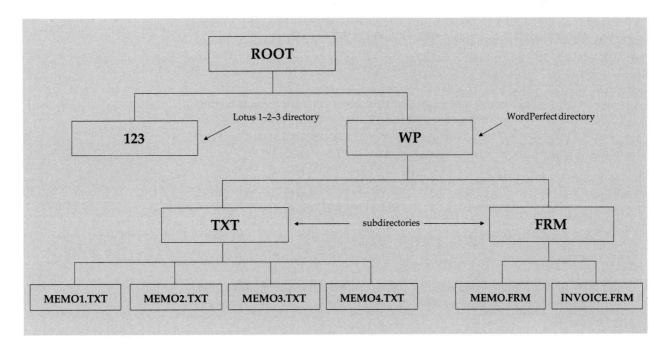

commands such as FORMAT or DISKCOPY. Any additional directories created by the user are considered to be below the root directory.

As Figure DOS–14 shows, those directories that branch off the root are called simply directories. Any directories branching from this second level or lower are referred to as subdirectories. Subdirectories make it much easier to find things on your hard disk. A good comparison is to a filing cabinet, where a drawer represents a directory, and the files within it represent subdirectories. DOS provides a similar convenience in that it enables you to group files that will be used together into a single directory.

Typically, each software package has its own directory, and you may establish directories within them for different applications of that package. For example, you might set up a directory for WordPerfect with subdirectories for text files and forms files, as shown in Figure DOS–14.

In this part of the DOS tutorial, you will practice setting up or making directories (MKDIR or simply MD), moving between or changing directories (CHDIR or CD), and removing directories (RMDIR or RD). Practice these procedures on a floppy disk, even if you are working on a computer with an internal hard disk. If you are working on a hard disk, use the root directory on the C drive to create directories on a disk in your A drive. Be sure not to tamper with the hard disk's directory structure unless you are directed to do so by your lab instructor.

Creating New Directories

You are going to set up your working floppy disk with directories for the working files for two applications: Lotus 1–2–3 and WordPerfect. You can then put the Lotus or WordPerfect program disk in drive A, and work on your files in the corresponding directory in drive B.

Put your DOS disk in drive A and your working disk in drive B. First you will set up the Lotus 1–2–3 directory. It is important to give it an easy name, because you will have to type it each time you want to move to that directory. In directory command syntax, the "branches" between directories are indicated by the **backslash** (\) character. At the A> prompt:

Type **mkdir b:\123**

Notice the backslash; it tells DOS that this new directory branches from the root directory. Notice also that there are no spaces except after the MKDIR command itself. Now take a look at the directory for drive B.

Type **dir b:**

It will look like the screen in Figure DOS–15. To set up the second directory:

Type **mkdir b:\wp**

Take another look at the root directory for drive B.

Type **dir b:**

You will now see two directories listed (Figure DOS–16). Notice that directories are identified by <DIR> in the column used for filename extensions.

```
A>dir b:

 Volume in drive B has no label
 Directory of  B:\

123          <DIR>     11-06-90  12:25p
        1 File(s)    361472 bytes free

A>
```

DOS-15 Your 1-2-3
directory is listed with a
<DIR> label.

Now you will set up two subdirectories in the directory called WP. Some of
the files on your Student Data Disk have the extension .TXT (for text), while
others have the extension .FRM (for forms). Now, within the WP directory,
make a subdirectory for each kind of file. At the A> prompt:

Type **mkdir b:\wp\txt**

> You can also use the abbreviated form of the MKDIR command, which is
> MD. Use it to create a second subdirectory.

Type **md b:\wp\frm**

> The MD form works just like the longer form.

Now you have TXT and FRM subdirectories within the WP directory.

Moving Between Subdirectories

When you decide to move to a different subdirectory, DOS requires a strict
syntax that defines the **path** it will follow along the **tree hierarchy**. The
command for changing directories is CHDIR, or its abbreviated form, CD.

```
A>dir b:

 Volume in drive B has no label
 Directory of  B:\

WP           <DIR>     11-06-90  12:32p
123          <DIR>     11-06-90  12:25p
        2 File(s)    360448 bytes free

A>
```

DOS-16 You now have two
directories on your disk.

```
B>chdir\wp\txt

B>dir

 Volume in drive B has no label
 Directory of  B:\WP\TXT
 .               <DIR>    11-06-90  12:36p
 ..              <DIR>    11-06-90  12:36p
        Z File(s)    359424 bytes free

B>
```

DOS–17 An empty sub-
directory looks like this when
you ask for a file listing.

Practice moving between subdirectories. First, move to the B drive. Then, at
the B> prompt:

Type chdir\wp\txt

This moves you to the TXT subdirectory of the WP directory. Now, to
make sure you are actually in the subdirectory of that name:

Type dir

Your screen will look like Figure DOS–17. You can see that you are in the
\wp\txt subdirectory, and that there are no files in it. Now, move to the
other WordPerfect subdirectory; this time, use the abbreviated CD command.

Type cd\wp\frm

Check the directory again to verify that you are now in the other Word-
Perfect subdirectory.

Copying Files into a Subdirectory Structure

Remove the DOS disk from drive A and insert your Student Data Disk
instead. You will copy files from the Student Data Disk into your new
subdirectories. At the B> prompt:

Type cd\wp\txt

This sets the path that DOS will follow for copying. Then move to drive
A, and at the A> prompt:

Type copy *.txt b:\wp\txt

This uses the wildcard * character to copy all files that have the extension
.TXT from drive A to the subdirectory of the WP directory. Check your
results.

Type dir b:

DOS will follow the current path that you set earlier on the B drive to give
you a list of files in that subdirectory (Figure DOS–18).

```
B>chdir \wp\txt

B>dir

    Volume in drive B has no label
    Directory of  B:\WP\TXT

    .            <DIR>      11-06-90  12:42p
    ..           <DIR>      11-06-90  12:42p
    MEMO1   TXT       1320   9-23-89   3:01p
    MEMO2   TXT       1284   9-23-89   3:05p
    MEMO3   TXT       1535   9-23-89   3:16p
    MEMO4   TXT       1644   9-23-89   3:24p
            6 File(s)    350208 bytes free

    B>
```

DOS–18 After you copy the .TXT files into the \wp\txt subdirectory, the DIR listing looks like this.

D
O
S

Now you will copy the .FRM files into the FRM subdirectory. Reset the path for DOS. First, move to drive B, and at the B> prompt:

Type cd\wp\frm

The path is now changed to the other subdirectory. Now move to drive A, and at the A> prompt:

Type copy *.frm b:\wp\frm

Now check the directory for the subdirectory.

Type dir b:

Your screen will look like the screen in Figure DOS–19.

Removing Directories

From time to time you will reorganize your disk and need to delete a subdirectory with the DOS command RMDIR (remove directory). There are two steps in deleting directories. First, the subdirectory must be empty of

```
B>dir

    Volume in drive B has no label
    Directory of  B:\WP\FRM

    .            <DIR>      11-06-90  12:36p
    ..           <DIR>      11-06-90  12:36p
    INVOICE  FRM       774   9-23-89   2:53p
    MEMO     FRM       795   9-23-89   2:47p
            4 File(s)    348160 bytes free

    B>
```

DOS–19 The DIR listing for the FRM subdirectory looks like this after files are copied into it.

files. Second, you must reposition yourself at the root directory before deleting the empty directory, because DOS can only remove directories *below* the current position. You can practice on the WordPerfect subdirectory called \WP\FRM. First, position yourself in the directory of that name. At the B> prompt:

Type cd\wp\frm

Now you are in the subdirectory you are going to delete. Check the directory, and notice that there are only two files in it, both with the extension .FRM. First, you must delete the files before you can remove the directory.

Type del *.frm

This deletes all files with a .FRM extension. There should be no files left in this directory. Check the subdirectory to make sure it is empty. You are now prepared to remove the subdirectory \WP\FRM. Reposition yourself at the root directory. At the B prompt:

Type cd\

You are now in the root directory of the disk in drive B. Now return to drive A, and put your DOS disk back in the drive, because the RMDIR command can only be called from the DOS disk. At the A> prompt:

Type rmdir b:\wp\frm

You can also use an abbreviated form of this instruction: **rd b:\wp\frm**

Check to make sure the subdirectory is really gone from the \WP directory. At the A> prompt:

Type dir b:\wp

The screen now looks like the one in Figure DOS–20. There is only one subdirectory left.

This completes Lesson 3. When you are ready to turn the computer off, remove your disks, then turn the power switch for the CPU, or the CPU and the monitor, to the OFF position.

```
A>dir b:\wp

    Volume in drive B has no label
    Directory of  B:\WP

    .              <DIR>      11-06-90  12:32p
    ..             <DIR>      11-06-90  12:32p
    TXT            <DIR>      11-06-90  12:42p
         3 File(s)    351232 bytes free

A>
```

DOS–20 One subdirectory has been deleted from the wp subdirectory.

Practice

1. On your practice disk, delete the files in the \wp\txt directory. Then delete the \wp\txt subdirectory itself.

2. Move back to the root directory on your practice disk.

3. Create a new directory for your dBASE IV data files. Call the directory \db4.

4. Copy all the files on your Student Data Disk that have the extension .db into your \db4 subdirectory. Use the * wildcard with the COPY command.

KEY WORDS

Backslash (\)
Backup
Boot up
Current drive
Default drive
Disk directory
Echo printing

File-name extension
File-naming conventions
Format
Initialize
Logged drive
Path
Root directory

Subdirectory
Syntax
Toggle
Tree hierarchy
Wildcard characters

REVIEW QUESTIONS

1. Why is it important to know whether a DOS command is included in the COMMAND.COM file or in a separate file?
2. Why is it sometimes desirable to have the COMMAND.COM file on a disk other than the DOS disk?
3. What happens if you copy a file to another disk when there is already a file with that name there?
4. What danger can you encounter in using wildcard characters to delete groups of files?
5. What is the function of the backslash (\)?
6. What is the relationship of subdirectories to directories?

Using WordPerfect

Hardware needed:

- ✔ IBM PC, IBM PS/2, or IBM-compatible microcomputer
- ✔ Hard disk drive or two floppy disk drives

Software needed:

- ✔ DOS 2.0 or later version
- ✔ Student Data Disk
- ✔ A formatted work disk
- ✔ WordPerfect 4.2 or 5.0

When you have completed this tutorial, you will be able to:

- ✔ Enter and edit a document
- ✔ Insert and delete text
- ✔ Save a document
- ✔ Print a document
- ✔ Retrieve files from disk
- ✔ Change margins, line spacing, and indents
- ✔ Boldface and underline text
- ✔ Spell check documents
- ✔ Move, copy, and delete blocks of text
- ✔ Set tab stops
- ✔ Search and replace text
- ✔ Center text
- ✔ Number pages
- ✔ Create headers and footers
- ✔ Merge form letters
- ✔ Organize and manage files
- ✔ Create a macro

WordPerfect Tutorial

Tutorial Outline

What is WordPerfect?

WordPerfect is one of the most powerful and comprehensive word processing programs available for IBM microcomputers and their compatibles. Over the years, WordPerfect has earned lavish and well-deserved praise, and is now widely acclaimed as one of the best word processing packages on the market.

This tutorial provides step-by-step instructions on how to use WordPerfect commands quickly and easily to create your reports, letters, and documents. These commands are all very basic to using WordPerfect, so you might consider doing the tutorial twice to make sure you can remember them without looking anything up.

This tutorial is designed to be used with WordPerfect 5.0. The 5.0 refers to a release number. Your school may have an earlier version of WordPerfect, release 4.2. Most of the instructions in this manual are applicable to both WordPerfect 4.2 and 5.0. Where there are differences they will be noted both where they occur and in a table at the end of this tutorial. If your school uses WordPerfect 4.2, you may wish to ask your instructor for a more detailed list of 4.2 commands.

To use this manual, you need access to a microcomputer that has an internal hard disk containing WordPerfect 5.0, or one with two floppy disk drives. If you have a hard disk (a C drive) in your computer system, it probably has been set up so that you can load DOS just by turning on the computer. If your system contains only floppy drives (A and B), you will have to turn on the computer and load DOS using a different procedure. The two procedures are summarized in the next two sections.

Starting WordPerfect on a Two-Floppy-Disk System

Place your copy of the DOS diskette into the A drive and start your system. After DOS has been loaded, the disk drive will be silent and its red lights will be off. You should then see the A> symbol, called the A prompt, on your screen. If you are unsure how to turn on your system, you should review the Using: MS-DOS tutorial before attempting this tutorial.

You are now ready to start WordPerfect. Please be aware, though, that if you learn to start the program from drive B it will greatly simplify the tasks of saving and retrieving your files. Here's how you do it.

Type **B:** then press (ENTER)

> You should see the B> prompt on the screen.

Remove the DOS disk.

Place the disk labelled WordPerfect 1 into drive A.

Type **A:WP**

Press (ENTER)

> After your computer whirrs and buzzes for a time, you will see this message prompting you to place the other WordPerfect disk in the drive:

```
Insert diskette labeled "WordPerfect 2" and press any key
```

Doc 1 Pg 1 Ln 1" Pos 1"

WP–1   The WordPerfect
screen.

Remove the WordPerfect 1 disk and replace it with WordPerfect 2 and press any key. You're now ready to skip to Lesson 1!

Starting WordPerfect on a Hard Disk

Start your system and use DOS commands to go to the directory containing WordPerfect. If you are unsure how to turn on your system and use DOS commands, you should review the Using: MS-DOS tutorial before attempting this tutorial.

Type **WP**

Press (ENTER)

If you see a message like "Invalid directory" or "Bad command or file name," WordPerfect is probably located in a different subdirectory than the one you are in—or the program is not yet on your hard disk. In either case, ask your instructor or lab assistant for help.

If you see the screen shown in Figure WP–1, you have succeeded in starting WordPerfect and are now ready to start the first lesson of the tutorial.

Lesson 1

Entering Text and Moving the Cursor

After completing this lesson, you will be able to:

✔ Identify the status line

✔ Enter text

✔ Use word wrap

✔ Move the cursor

✔ Save a document

The Status Line

Your screen should now be blank except for a line of information called the **status line**, in the lower right-hand corner. This is WordPerfect's way of telling you where the **cursor** (the small blinking dash) is on the page. The status line also sometimes provides messages, warnings, and other prompts.

The WordPerfect Keyboard

To use WordPerfect to the fullest advantage, take a few minutes to locate the following important keys on the keyboard: (ALT), (CTRL), the function keys, and the (ENTER) key. Learning where these keys are is especially important because WordPerfect is designed so that these keys can be used to make word processing quick and convenient. The following is a brief overview of how these keys are used.

The Alt, Ctrl, and Shift Keys

Pay particular attention to the (ALT), (CTRL), and (SHIFT) keys in Figure WP–2. These keys don't do anything when pressed by themselves. They are always used in combination with a second key—such as a function key—giving that key a meaning it would not have by itself. Note that there are two shift keys; each is gray and labelled (SHIFT).

WP–2 The PC XT and AT keyboards.

Function keys	Alphanumeric keyboard	Numeric keypad and cursor keys

Function keys

Alphanumeric keyboard	Cursor keys	Numeric keypad

The Function Keys

The function keys are the ten keys labelled (F1) through (F10) (or (F1) through (F12) on PC/AT and PS/2 keyboards). On the IBM PC and XT keyboards, they are located in two vertical rows on the left side. On the PC/AT and PS/2 keyboards, they are on the top row.

Each function key has four distinct uses in WordPerfect, depending on whether it is used by itself or in combination with (SHIFT), (ALT), or (CTRL). To use one of the combinations, you press the (SHIFT), (ALT), or (CTRL) key first and continue holding it down while pressing the appropriate function key once. We represent such key combinations in the tutorial with a hyphen, as in (SHIFT)-(F8) and (CTRL)-(F2).

The Enter Key

The Enter or Return key is the large gray key labeled (↵) and located just below the Backspace key (labeled (←)) on most keyboards. On some keyboards, it is labeled "Enter." In this tutorial, we refer to it as the (ENTER) key.

When typing text in WordPerfect, the (ENTER) key does *not* work like the carriage return key on a typewriter, so if you are new to word processing, you should play close attention to the section below entitled "Entering Text" in order to unlearn an old habit.

The Color-Coded Template

The WordPerfect function key template fits around the function keys and helps remind you of what each one does. Two templates are supplied with this text, one for each of the standard keyboard types. The template uses a color scheme to identify the forty functions for (F1) through (F10) and their combinations with (SHIFT), (CTRL), and (ALT). It works like this:

Red   When a name is listed in red on the template, the function key is used with the (CTRL) key. For example, notice the word "Spell" shown in red on the template, by the (F2) key. This means that to use WordPerfect's spelling checker, you would press (CTRL)-(F2).

Green   To use a function listed in green, press the (SHIFT) key with the function key.

Blue   To use a function listed in blue, press the (ALT) key with the function key.

Black   To use a function listed in black, press the function key alone.

Entering Text

WordPerfect has an automatic feature known as word wrap that eliminates the need to press the (ENTER) key at the end of a line. For example, if you are typing text and the cursor reaches the right margin, word wrap automatically moves the cursor down to a new line.

Type the paragraphs shown in Figure WP–3.

WP–3   Practice document for Lesson 1.

> WordPerfect 5 is one of the most powerful word processing programs available for IBM microcomputers and their compatibles. Over the years, WordPerfect has earned lavish and well-deserved praise, and is now widely acclaimed as one of the best word processing packages on the market.
>
> This tutorial provides step-by-step instructions on how to use WordPerfect commands quickly and easily to create your reports, letters, and documents. These commands are all very basic to using WordPerfect, so you might consider doing the tutorial twice to make sure you can remember them without looking anything up.

As you type, do not press the (ENTER) key until the end of each paragraph—let word wrap end the lines for you automatically. Press (ENTER) twice at the end of the first and second paragraphs. This will leave a blank line between paragraphs. Do not worry if you make mistakes— you will learn how to correct errors later in the tutorial.

Moving the Cursor

WordPerfect has a large variety of keys that you can use for cursor movement. With only a few keystrokes you can move word by word, to the beginning or end of a line, to the top or bottom of the screen or the page, and all the way to the beginning or end of a document. This movement needs to become automatic for you, so we are going to give you an exercise that will make it familiar. First you will use the cursor arrow keys located on the numeric keypad on the right-hand side of your keyboard.

Press the (↑) and (→) cursor arrow keys several times each.

> The cursor moved into the text you have typed.

Press the (←) and (→) cursor arrow keys.

> The cursor moved to the left or right, character by character. If you hold down the arrow keys, the cursor will move rapidly in the direction of the arrow. You can also use the (CTRL) and (HOME) keys in conjunction with the (←) and (→) keys to move the cursor more quickly.

Press the (↑) and (↓) cursor arrow keys.

> The cursor moved to the top and bottom of the text, line by line.

Hold (CTRL) while pressing the (→) or (←) key.

> The cursor moved one word to the right or left.

Press (HOME) and release it, then press the (→) or (←) key.

> Note how the cursor jumped to the left or right edge of the line. Table WP–1 shows several methods for moving the cursor through a document.

Saving a Document

Although you can see your document on screen, it actually exists only in your computer's on-line memory (RAM) and is not permanent until you

Key	Cursor Movement
↑	Up 1 line
↓	Down 1 line
←	Left 1 character
→	Right 1 character
CTRL-←	Left 1 word
CTRL-→	Right 1 word
HOME, ←	Beginning of line
HOME, →, or END	End of line
HOME, ↑ or minus key	Screen up
HOME, ↓ or plus key	Screen down
PGUP	Top of previous page
PGDN	Top of next page
HOME, HOME, ↑	Top of document
HOME, HOME, ↓	End of document
The Go-to Command:	
CTRL-HOME, any number	Go to corresponding page number
CTRL-HOME, ↑	Top of current page
CTRL-HOME, ↓	End of current page
CTRL-HOME, any letter A–Z	Next occurrence of corresponding letter

Table WP–1 Moving the Cursor.

save it to disk. Since RAM memory disappears as soon as the computer is turned off, it is essential that you save your document to a disk file if you ever want to use it again. For this exercise and others throughout the tutorial, you will need a formatted disk for saving your work. If you wish, you can use your working disk from the DOS tutorial.

Put your work disk in drive B.

If you have a hard disk computer system that does not contain a B drive, use drive A instead. When using the A drive for your Student Data Disk, however, be sure to use the proper DOS path name on your files—that is, *A:filename*—wherever *B:filename* appears in this tutorial.

Press (F10) for Save.

You should see this prompt in the lower left corner of your screen:

`Document to be saved:`

Type **B:LESSON1**

Press (ENTER)

Remember the DOS file-naming conventions—there is no space between *LESSON* and *1*, and the file name can be typed in upper- or lowercase. The B: saves it to your work disk. You will see this message on your screen:

`Saving B:\LESSON1`

It is wise when doing word processing to save your document during keyboarding every 15 minutes or so. This will protect your work against loss due to power outages or hardware problems.

Practice

Experiment moving the cursor around the LESSON1 file using each of the keystroke combinations in the left-hand column of Table WP–1.

Lesson 2

Editing Text and Basic Formatting

W
P

After completing this lesson, you will be able to:

✔ Clear the screen to type a new document

✔ Retrieve a saved file from disk in two ways

✔ Edit a document by inserting and deleting text

✔ Use the Format command to change margins and line spacing

✔ List the files stored on your disk

Clearing the Screen

The document you saved as LESSON1 should still be on the screen. To start a new lesson, you need to clear the document from the screen.

Press (F7) for Exit.

You should see this prompt in the lower left-hand corner of your screen:

`Save document? (Y/N) Yes`

(*Note:* WordPerfect 4.2 displays Y instead of Yes.) You should see this message in the lower right-hand corner of your screen:

`(Text was not modified)`

You do not need to save the document again since you already saved it in Lesson 1.

Type **N** for No.

The following prompt appears in the lower left corner of the screen:

`Exit WP? (Y/N) No`

Type **N**

The screen should now be blank except for the status line on the bottom. To verify that the screen has been cleared, press the ⬇ key on the numeric keypad. Next try pressing the ➔ key. The cursor cannot move when the screen is blank. This illustrates an important concept in Word-

Perfect: the cursor can only move through existing text or through blank space that has been created by pressing (ENTER) or the space bar.

Retrieving a Document

Because you saved the LESSON1 document in the previous Lesson, you can now retrieve it to the screen.

Press (SHIFT) and hold it down while pressing (F10) ((SHIFT)-(F10)).

This combination is called the Retrieve command. You should see this prompt in the lower left-hand corner of your screen:

`Document to be retrieved:`

Type **B:LESSON1** and press (ENTER)

The two paragraphs you typed in LESSON1 should appear on your screen (unless you misspelled the name or did not save it in the previous lesson). If you see the message "ERROR file not found," type the file name again with the correct spelling.

Editing a WordPerfect Document

You will now practice editing text in a WordPerfect document.

Inserting Text

You will begin by inserting spaces and text into your document.

Press (HOME), (HOME), (↑), or (PGUP)

This positions the cursor at the beginning of the document.

Press (ENTER) twice.

Notice that the entire document moved down two lines. Pressing (ENTER) inserts a blank line at the cursor position. WordPerfect is normally in **Insert mode**, which means that what you enter will be inserted or added to the existing document. When you press the key labeled Insert (or (INS)), this switches you into **Typeover mode**. In Typeover mode, text on the screen is replaced with the new text that you are typing. To return to Insert mode, press the Insert key again. This key is referred to as a "toggle" key. Each time you press it, the mode changes from Insert to Typeover and then back again.

Press (↑) twice.

This moves the cursor to the first line.

Type [your name] and press (ENTER)

Your name now appears at the top of the document.

Place the cursor on the "l" in "letters" in the last paragraph.

Type: **memos, tables,**

Notice that the text now extends beyond the right margin. When new text is added to a document, you can realign uneven margins by using the (↓) key.

Press ⬇

>The ⬇ realigns the margins.

You now have two versions of this document—one on disk and one on screen. The words you just typed on screen are not in the disk version yet, so you would have to save the document again if you wanted to retain this change. However, for this exercise we will not save this change.

Deleting Text

Text can be deleted two ways. The Delete ((DEL)) key on the numeric keypad will delete one letter at a time. (CTRL)-(BACKSPACE) will delete a whole word.

To practice deleting, you will delete the words you just typed ("memos, tables,").

Place the cursor on the first "m" in the word "memos"

Press (DEL) five times.

>The (DEL) key deletes the letter that the cursor is on, and the letters and spaces that follow move to the left to fill in the blank space.

Press (CTRL) and hold it down while pressing (BACKSPACE) twice.

>(CTRL)-(BACKSPACE) deletes the word the cursor is on and adjusts to the left the words that follow it. The cursor can be on any letter in the word. Press ⬇ to realign the margins.

Formatting Text

WordPerfect has many features that allow you to change the appearance, or **format**, of a document. These include changing margin widths and line spacing.

Changing Margins

WordPerfect margins are automatically set at 1 inch on the left- and right-hand sides. To change the margins, follow these steps:

Press the (PGUP) key.

>This moves the cursor to the top of the page.

Press (SHIFT)-(F8) for Format.

>The menu shown in Figure WP–4 appears. Margins are set by using the Line option. In WordPerfect, to select an option you type the number associated with the option you want. (*Note:* In Word Perfect 4.2, use option 3, Margins, to set the margins.)

Type **1** to select the Line option.

>A second menu now appears. (See Figure WP–5).

Type **7** to select the Margins option.

>The cursor now appears next to the value for the left margin. You will change the margins to 1½ inches.

Type **1.5** and press (ENTER)

>The left margin is changed from 1 inch to 1½ inches.

```
Format

  1 - Line
            Hyphenation               Line Spacing
            Justification             Margins Left/Right
            Line Height               Tab Set
            Line Numbering            Widow/Orphan Protection

  2 - Page
            Center Page (top to bottom)   New Page Number
            Force Odd/Even Page           Page Numbering
            Headers and Footers           Paper Size/Type
            Margins Top/Bottom            Suppress

  3 - Document
            Display Pitch             Redline Method
            Initial Codes/Font        Summary

  4 - Other
            Advance                   Overstrike
            Conditional End of Page   Printer Functions
            Decimal Characters        Underline Spaces/Tabs
            Language

Selection: 0
```

WP–4   The Format menu.

Type 1.5 and press (ENTER)

The right margin is changed from 1 inch to 1½ inches.

Press (F7) to Exit.

The Exit or (F7) key returns you to the document.

Press (PGDN)

The document now reformats using the new margins you have just set. You should note that only the text directly after the cursor will have new margins. Format changes such as realigning margins work only from the cursor position forward. If you want to change the margins for the entire document, you must position the cursor at the beginning of the document before formatting.

The format feature allows you to have a lot of control over margins in your document. Suppose, for example, that you now want the last paragraph to

```
Format: Line

  1 - Hyphenation                Off

  2 - Hyphenation Zone - Left    10%
                         Right   4%

  3 - Justification              Yes

  4 - Line Height                Auto

  5 - Line Numbering             No

  6 - Line Spacing               1

  7 - Margins - Left             1"
                Right            1"

  8 - Tab Set                    0", every 0.5"

  9 - Widow/Orphan Protection    No

Selection: 0
```

WP–5   The Line option menu.

have 1-inch margins. How do you change the paragraph's margins without changing the entire document?

Move the cursor to the beginning of the third paragraph.

Press (SHIFT)-(F8)

Type 1 to select the Line option.

Type 7 to select the Margins option.

Type 1 and press (ENTER)

Type 1 and press (ENTER)

Press (F7) to Exit.

Press (PGDN)

Observe that the margins have only changed in the last paragraph.

Double Spacing Paragraphs

Just as you used the Format command ((SHIFT)-(F8)) to change margins, you also use the Format command to double space text or to set any type of line spacing you want. To double space this document, follow these steps:

Move the cursor to the first character of the first paragraph.

Press (SHIFT)-(F8) for Format.

Type 1 to select Line.

(*Note:* In WordPerfect 4.2, select option 4, Spacing.)

Type 6 to select Line Spacing.

Type 2 to select double spacing, and press (ENTER)

Press (F7)

The document is now double spaced! You can set line spacing for any number you want (for example, press 3 for triple spacing).

Clear the screen without saving the margin and spacing changes you made. Refer to the procedures at the beginning of this lesson if you are not sure how to clear the screen without saving. Once the screen is blank, you are ready to learn a second way to retrieve a document.

Using the List Files Command

So far you have learned how to retrieve a document from a disk and have it displayed on the screen by pressing (SHIFT)-(F10) and typing its name. But what do you do when you do not remember its name, or are unsure how it is spelled? In such a case, WordPerfect provides the List Files command ((F5)) to list all documents currently stored on your disk. You will now retrieve the LESSON1 file using the List Files command.

Press (F5) for List Files.

Although the exact result may vary between different computer systems, you should see something similar to the following prompt in the lower left-hand corner of your screen:

```
10/06/89  10:58              Directory C:\WP50\STERN\*.*
Document size:        0   Free:   1652736   Used:   2170743        Files:   57

CHAP12  .          55027  08/03/89 10:55  ↑  CHAP13  .          64982  09/20/89 18:11
COOP    .           2688  09/08/89 12:45  |  DEF91   .89         6836  09/01/89 09:09
DEF928  .89        47569  09/28/89 13:25     DEFOSS  .            859  09/28/89 09:58
FIGURES .         377521  10/05/89 16:23     FIGURES .BK!      377452  10/05/89 16:06
FIGWP-11.PCX       42972  09/01/89 09:14     FIGWP-11.SCR        8128  09/01/89 08:20
FIGWP-9 .PCX       30805  09/01/89 09:13     FIGWP-9 .SCR        8128  09/01/89 08:03
GRAN104 .89         5809  10/05/89 16:51     GRAN104 .BK!        5809  10/05/89 16:51
LESSON11.          24465  09/22/89 17:10     LESSON3 .            959  10/02/89 18:37
LESSON3 .BK!         959  10/02/89 18:05     LESSON3-.           1044  09/28/89 10:04
LESSON3C.           1310  09/28/89 10:13     LESSON3C.BK!        1310  09/28/89 10:07
LESSON7 .           1496  10/02/89 20:08     LESSON7 .BK!        1496  10/02/89 18:59
NELLE9ZZ.89         6596  09/22/89 17:16     WP-14   .PCX       29149  09/28/89 10:13
WP-14   .SCR        8128  09/28/89 10:09     WP-15   .PCX       29993  09/28/89 10:13
WP-15   .SCR        8128  09/28/89 10:12     WP34    .PCX       12445  09/22/89 16:54
WP34    .SCR        8128  09/22/89 16:50     WP35    .PCX       14301  09/22/89 16:54
WP35    .SCR        8128  09/22/89 16:51     WPTUTOR .          91554  07/14/89 15:34
WPTUTOR .BK!      127082  10/05/89 14:19     WPTUTOR .CX2       98946  10/05/89 14:08
WPTUTOR .CX3      126845  10/03/89 11:01     WPTUTOR .CX4      111107  10/05/89 14:23
WRDSRCH .EXM         441  07/14/89 14:35

1 Retrieve; 2 Delete; 3 Move/Rename; 4 Print; 5 Text In;
6 Look; 7 Other Directory; 8 Copy; 9 Word Search; N Name Search: 6
```

WP–6 List Files.

```
Dir A:\WP50\*.*
```

Type **B:**

This indicates that you want a directory of document files on the B drive. You should type A: if you have a hard disk.

Press (ENTER)

Figure WP–6 shows a typical list of file names on a disk. The directory on your work disk will be similar but will contain different file names. Several menu options appear at the bottom of the screen to let you retrieve files, delete files, print files, copy files, and more.

To obtain a list of the files in a different directory, place the cursor on <CURRENT> <DIR>, press (ENTER), and type the name (and path if necessary). If you are in a subdirectory, you can get a list of files in the directory hierarchically above you by placing your cursor on <PARENT> <DIR> and pressing (ENTER).

Use the cursor arrow keys on the numeric keypad to move the cursor so that the file you saved earlier, LESSON1, is highlighted.

Type **1** to retrieve the highlighted file.

The List Files menu disappears and the retrieved document appears on the screen again.

This completes Lesson 2. Clear the screen to do the following practice exercise. If, after completing the exercise, you wish to exit the WordPerfect program and continue with the tutorial at a later time:

Press (F7) to Exit.

When the prompt "Save document?" appears:

Type **N**

When the prompt "Exit WP?" appears:

Type **Y**

The DOS prompt appears.

Practice

Retrieve LESSON1 and do the following:

1.   Change the left and right margins to 2 inches for the entire document.

2.   Double space the last paragraph only.

3.   Save the document as B:LESSON2.

4.   Clear the screen.

Lesson 3

Advanced Formatting and Editing

After completing this lesson, you will be able to:

✔   Use the date key

✔   Boldface and underline text

✔   Mark a block of text

✔   Use the spelling checker

✔   Examine and delete the format codes in a document

✔   Print a document

We will now be looking at some of the more advanced format and editing features of WordPerfect. To begin, insert the Student Data Disk in drive B and retrieve the document called LESSON3 using the List Files command (to use List Files, press (F5), type B: (or A: for a hard disk system), and press (ENTER)). By the time you have completed this lesson, the document will be ready for mailing to Mr. Williams.

Entering the Date

The letter shown on your screen has no date. WordPerfect can insert the current date into your document. The date that will be inserted is the date you entered when responding to the DOS date prompt (or the date stored by the computer if it has a battery-operated calendar/clock). To enter today's date on the first line, follow these steps:

Move the cursor two lines above Mr. Williams's name.

Press (SHIFT)-(F5) for the Date command.

As shown in Figure WP–7, the Date command options appear on the bottom of the screen.

Type **1** to select Date Text.

```
Lesson 3


Mr. John Williams
254 Lincoln Avenue
Sacramento, California 94843

Dear Mr. Williams,

Congradulations!  You hold the winnning ticket to this month's
Statewide Lottery ticket and will soon receive a check for
$75,000,000.

Please call us immediately at our toll-free fone number: (800)
555-0202.  And be sure to keep this form for your records!

Sincerely,



Karen Yoshino
Winner's Administrator

1 Date Text; 2 Date Code; 3 Date Format; 4 Outline; 5 Para Num; 6 Define: 0
```

WP–7 Document with the Date options.

The Date Text option inserts the current date as text, as though you had typed it yourself.

You will now begin enhancing this letter.

Boldfacing

Mr. Williams is a lucky man. He will receive $75,000,000. However, the letter forgot to mention that he will receive a Rolls Royce as well. In the letter you will add that he won a Silver Shadow Rolls Royce, and you will make this text print in bold type.

Move the cursor to the period right after the $75,000,000.

Type **and a**

Press the Bold key ((F6))

Type **Silver Shadow Rolls Royce**

Press (F6) to turn off boldface.

> Bold must be turned on before typing and off again after you finish using it. If you do not turn it off, everything you type will be boldfaced from that point on.

> The phrase "Silver Shadow Rolls Royce" is highlighted on the screen to show bold. If you cannot see boldface on your screen, adjust the contrast buttons.

Because $75,000,000 is probably the most important element in this letter, it would be nice to set it off in boldface. To boldface text that has been already entered, the text must first be marked as a **block**.

Move the cursor to the $ in $75,000,000.

Press (ALT)-(F4) for Block.

> You should see that the "Block on" signal starts flashing in the status line.

Move the cursor one space after the last zero in $75,000,000.

As you can see, $75,000,000 appears in reverse video on the screen. This is called blocking text. Now that the text has been blocked, you can boldface it.

Press �F6 for Bold.

The reverse video disappears and $75,000,000 is highlighted on the screen to show bold.

Underlining Text

Because Mr. Williams must show this letter to the courier who brings the $75,000,000 and the Rolls Royce to his door, you want to emphasize this by underlining the phrase that says that he should keep the letter. To underline text that has already been entered, the text must be blocked first.

Move the cursor to the capital P in "Please call us immediately" in the last paragraph.

Press ALT-F4 for Block.

You should see the "Block on" signal flashing on the status line.

Move the cursor one space after the "y" in "immediately".

"Please call us immediately" is now in reverse video on the screen.

Press F8 for Underline.

The block method is the only way you can underline and boldface text after it has been typed.

Similar to the way you boldface text as you type, you can also underline text as you type. Simply press the Underline key (F8) before typing, then press F8 again to turn off underline when you have finished typing text you want underlined.

When text on the screen is set as bold and underlined, it will appear high-intensity and underscored on a monochrome monitor. On color monitors, it will be in color.

Check the Spelling

You may have noticed that the letter contains three misspellings: "Congradulations," "winnnings," and "fone." You will now fix these misspellings, using WordPerfect's spelling checker.

Press CTRL-F2 for the Spell command.

This starts the WordPerfect spelling checker. The Spell Check option menu appears on the bottom of the screen (see Figure WP–8).

Type 3 to select the Document option.

As shown in Figure WP–9, when WordPerfect finds a misspelled word, it will stop and provide a list of suggested replacements. If you see the correctly spelled word in the list, press the letter next to it to have WordPerfect exchange it for the misspelled one in your document. If you do not see the correctly spelled word in the list, choose option 4 to edit the word. You can then use ← and → to move the cursor and correct the

```
Lesson 3

November 15, 1989

Mr. John Williams
254 Lincoln Avenue
Sacramento, California 94843

Dear Mr. Williams,

Congradulations!  You hold the winnning ticket to this month's
Statewide Lottery ticket and will soon receive a check for
$75,000,000.

Please call us immediately at our toll-free fone number: (800)
555-0202.  And be sure to keep this form for your records!

Sincerely,



Karen Yoshino
Winner's Administrator

Check: 1 Word; 2 Page; 3 Document; 4 New Sup. Dictionary; 5 Look Up; 6 Count: 0
```

WP–8 Document with Spell Check options.

spelling by hand. After you have corrected the spelling, you may need to reformat the paragraph.

Press Exit ((F7)) to continue the Spell Check.

Sometimes a correctly spelled word may be flagged by the spelling checker because it is a proper name or a technical word not in Word-Perfect's dictionary. For example, Royce, as a proper name, would be flagged. To indicate that the word is spelled correctly, press 2 to select the Skip option.

Spell Check is completed when the following prompt appears at the bottom of the screen:

`Word count: Press any key to continue`

Press any key and the Spell Check options appear at the bottom of the screen again.

Press Exit ((F7)) to end Spell Check.

```
254 Lincoln Avenue
Sacramento, California 94843

Dear Mr. Williams,

Congradulations!  You hold the winnning ticket to this month's
Statewide Lottery ticket and will soon receive a check for
$75,000,000.

Please call us immediately at our toll-free fone number: (800)
555-0202.  And be sure to keep this form for your records!

===============================================================================

  A. congratulations




Not Found: 1 Skip Once; 2 Skip; 3 Add; 4 Edit; 5 Look Up; 6 Ignore Numbers: 0
```

WP–9 A list of possible replacements for a misspelled word.

```
September 1, 1990

Mr. John Williams
254 Lincoln Avenue
Sacramento, California 94843

Dear Mr. Williams,

Congratulations!  You hold the winning ticket to this month's
Statewide Lottery ticket and will soon receive a check for
A:\LESSON3                                      Doc 1 Pg 1 Ln 12 Pos 10
[                                                }                      ]
[HRt]
Congratulations!  You hold the winning ticket to this month's[SRt]
[UND]Statewide Lottery[und] ticket and will soon receive a check for[SRt]
[BOLD]$75,000,000[bold] and a [BOLD]Silver Shadow Rolls Royce[bold].[HRt]
[HRt]
[UND]Please call us immediately[und] at our toll[-]free phone number: (800)[SRt]

555[-]0202.  And be sure to keep this form for your records![HRt]
[HRt]
[HRt]

Press Reveal Codes to restore screen
```

WP–10 The Reveal Codes screen.

Erasing Format Codes

Looking at the letter, you now decide that too much is underlined. You want to erase the underline under "Statewide Lottery." This underline is represented in the WordPerfect program by a **format code** that is hidden in the document. This code tells WordPerfect when to begin and end underlining. It is hidden so that it does not clutter your document display. To erase the underline, you will use the Reveal Codes command ((ALT)-(F3)) to locate the underline codes and delete them.

Place the cursor on the S in "Statewide"

Press (ALT)-(F3) for Reveal Codes.

Don't panic at Reveal Codes! As shown in Figure WP–10, the screen is divided in two with the same text on top as on the bottom. The text in the lower half shows all the codes in the letter, such as [HRt] for hard return (where you pressed the (ENTER) key), and [SRt] for soft return (where word wrap moved the cursor to the next line), and [UND] for underline.

Place the cursor on one of the underline codes and press the (DEL) key.

Notice that underline codes come in pairs, with an uppercase [UND] at the beginning of the text that is underlined and lowercase [und] following it. By deleting just one of them, you remove underlining (the second code will be automatically deleted).

Press (ALT)-(F3) again to exit Reveal Codes.

Printing the Letter

Assuming that a printer is correctly attached to your computer, you are now ready to print this letter. First you will save it to your work disk. Remove the Student Data Disk from drive B and insert your work disk.

Save this document to your work disk by using the Save command ((F10)) and press (ENTER)

```
Print

    1 - Full Document
    2 - Page
    3 - Document on Disk
    4 - Control Printer
    5 - Type Through
    6 - View Document
    7 - Initialize Printer

Options

    S - Select Printer          HP LaserJet Series II
    B - Binding                 0
    N - Number of Copies        1
    G - Graphics Quality        Medium
    T - Text Quality            High




Selection: 0
```

WP–11 The Print menu.

The document with all the changes that you made is now saved as LESSON3.

Press (SHIFT)-(F7) for Print.

The Print menu appears (see Figure WP–11).

Press **1** to print the entire document.

If the printer does not start working, it is probably not correctly hooked up.

This completes Lesson 3. Clear the screen ((F7), **N, N**) to do the following practice exercise. If, after completing the exercise, you wish to exit WordPerfect and continue with the tutorial at a later time, type (F7), **N, Y**.

Practice

Type the document in Figure WP–12 and do the following:

1. Use the Date command to enter the current date.

2. Underline the dates in the first paragraph.

3. Boldface the second paragraph.

4. Check your spelling using the spell checker.

5. Print the document.

6. Save the document as PRAC3 on your work disk.

WP–12 Practice document for Lesson 3.

Aromax Corporation
1721 North Pierce Street
Grand Junction, CO 81501

Dear Aromax Employees:

Your current Employee Health Care Card will expire on December 31, 1990. With the enclosed card, we are extending your current Employee Heath Care Card through June 30, 1991.

Due to our upcoming move to Colorado Springs early next year, we will not be issuing new Employee Health Care cards at this time. The new cards will be issued prior to June 30, 1991.

Should you have any questions regarding the Health Care Cards or your extension, please call (303) 248-6171 between 8:00 a.m. and 5:30 p.m.

Thank you for your cooperation.

Sincerely,

Health Care Claims
Administration

Lesson 4

Moving, Copying, and Deleting Text

After completing this lesson, you will be able to:

✔ Restore deleted text

✔ Move text around the document

✔ Erase or copy text

Restoring Deleted Text

If it is not already on your screen, retrieve from your work disk the letter LESSON3, which you created in the last lesson.

Press (F5) to List Files.

Retrieve your letter (LESSON3).

Be sure your edit screen is clear before you retrieve it!

You will erase the name "John" in the first line of the address.

Place the cursor on the "J"

Press the (DEL) key five times.

This erases "John" and the blank space that follows it.

Erase the word "Statewide" in the second line of the first paragraph.

Remember, you can use (CTRL)-(BACKSPACE) to delete a whole word at once.

You can also erase a whole line at once. To erase the first line in the second paragraph:

Place the cursor on the P in "Please"

Press (CTRL)-(END)

(CTRL)-(END) erases from the cursor position to the end of the line.

On second thought, you decide that you deleted too much.

Press (F1) for Cancel.

As shown in Figure WP–13, the text you just erased appears highlighted on the screen, and the Undelete menu appears on the bottom of the screen.

Type **1** to restore the text you deleted.

The last three items that you erased can be retrieved with the Cancel/Undelete command ((F1)). In order to use the Undelete command, you need to put the cursor where you want the text to be placed when you restore it.

Place the cursor on the L in the word "Lottery" in the first paragraph.

Press (F1)

Type **2** to see the previous deletion ("Statewide").

Type **1** to restore it.

Place the cursor where the word John should be restored (beginning on the W in "Williams").

Press (F1) and type **2 2 1**

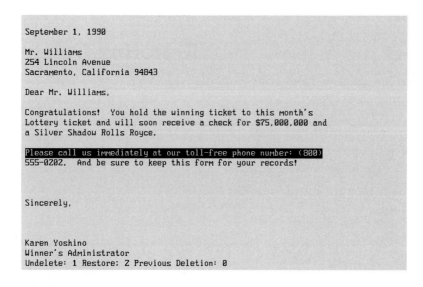

WP–13   Document with the Undelete menu.

```
  September 1, 1990

  Mr. John Williams
  254 Lincoln Avenue
  Sacramento, California 94843

  Dear Mr. Williams,

  Congratulations!  You hold the winning ticket to this month's
  Statewide Lottery ticket and will soon receive a check for $75,000,000 and
  a Silver Shadow Rolls Royce.

  Please call us immediately at our toll-free phone number: (800)
  555-0202.  And be sure to keep this form for your records!



  Sincerely,



  Karen Yoshino
  Winner's Administrator
  Move: 1 Block: 2 Tabular Column: 3 Rectangle: 0
```

WP–14 Document with the Move menu.

Moving Text

The Move command ((CTRL)-(F4)) is a powerful command in WordPerfect that allows you to do more than just move text. With it you can also delete, copy, and append text. To move text you first need to block it ((ALT)-(F4)) before using the Move command ((CTRL)-(F4)).

You will now move the name and address in LESSON3.

Put the cursor on the M of "Mr."

Press (ALT)-(F4) for Block.

Move the cursor to the space after the 3 at the end of the zip code.

Press (CTRL)-(F4) for the Move command.

As shown in Figure WP–14, the Move options appear in the lower left-hand corner of the screen.

Type **1** to move a Block.

(*Note:* In WordPerfect 4.2, select option 1, Cut Block.) Four options appear at the bottom of the screen.

Type **2** to select Copy.

Notice the message at the bottom of the screen:

Move cursor; press Enter to retrieve

WordPerfect is waiting for you to move the cursor to the new position for this text.

Use (↓) to move the cursor to the bottom of the letter.

Press (ENTER)

(*Note:* In WordPerfect 4.2, type (CTRL)-(F4), **5**.) The name and address have moved to the bottom of the letter.

W
P

Key	What the Key Does
(DEL)	Erases character above the cursor
(BACKSPACE)	Erases character to the left of the cursor
(CTRL)-(BACKSPACE)	Erases word the cursor is on
(CTRL)-(END)	Erases from the cursor to the end of the line
(CTRL)-(PGDN)	Erases from the cursor to the end of the page

Table WP–2 Keys that delete text.

Deleting Sentences, Paragraphs, and Pages

If the text you want to delete is a sentence, paragraph, or page, you can also use the Move command to delete it.

Start by deleting the first sentence in the second paragraph.

Move the cursor to the P in "Please"

Press (CTRL)-(F4) for the Move command.

The Move menu options appear in the lower left corner of the screen.

Type **1** to select Sentence.

The sentence is automatically highlighted and four new options appear at the bottom of the screen.

Type **3** to select Delete.

The sentence is deleted.

Move the cursor down one line to realign the paragraph.

You can delete an entire sentence, paragraph, or page by choosing 1, 2, or 3 from the Move menu. You can retrieve the text or "undo" the deletion by using the Cancel command ((F1)).

If you want to delete a section of text that does not fall into the category of sentence, paragraph, or page, you must block it first. Table WP–2 summarizes various ways to delete text in WordPerfect.

By this time, the document may look rather strange. Clear the screen ((F7), **N**, **N**). You are now ready to learn how to copy text.

Copying Text

Retrieve LESSON3 again. In addition to moving and deleting text, the Move command also allows you to copy text.

Place the cursor anywhere in the first sentence of the second paragraph.

Press (CTRL)-(F4) for the Move command.

The Move menu options appear in the lower left corner of the screen.

Type **1** to select Sentence.

The sentence is automatically highlighted and four options appear at the bottom of the screen.

Move	
Sentence	(CTRL)-(F4) Sentence Move (ENTER)
Paragraph	(CTRL)-(F4) Paragraph Copy (ENTER)
Page	(CTRL)-(F4) Page Move (ENTER)
Block	(ALT)-(F4), (CTRL)-(F4) Block Move (ENTER)
Delete	
Sentence	(CTRL)-(F4) Sentence Delete
Paragraph	(CTRL)-(F4) Paragraph Delete
Page	(CTRL)-(F4) Page Delete
Block	(ALT)-(F4), (CTRL)-(F4) Block Delete
Copy	
Sentence	(CTRL)-(F4) Sentence Copy (ENTER)
Paragraph	(CTRL)-(F4) Paragraph Copy (ENTER)
Page	(CTRL)-(F4) Page Copy (ENTER)
Block	(ALT)-(F4), (CTRL)-(F4) Block Copy (ENTER)

Table WP–3 Moving, Deleting, and Copying Text with the Move Command

Type **2** to select Copy.

> You should see this prompt in the lower left corner of your screen:

`Move cursor; press Enter to retrieve`

Move the cursor to the space after the exclamation point that ends the paragraph.

Press (ENTER)

> You have made a copy of the first sentence and placed it after the second one.

Table WP–3 summarizes the ways to move, delete, and copy text using the Move command.

This completes Lesson 4. Clear the screen without saving the document ((F7), **N**, **N**) and do the following practice exercises. If you wish to exit WordPerfect after completing the exercise, type (F7), **N**, **Y**.

Practice

Retrieve the document called PRAC3 from your work disk using the List Files ((F5)) command, and do the following:

1. Move the second paragraph, starting with the word "Due," to the beginning so that it is the first paragraph in the letter.

2. Delete the new second paragraph.

3. Undelete the second paragraph and restore it.

4. Make a copy of the address and place it beneath the word "Administration" in the closing.

5. Save the edited file as PRAC4.

Lesson 5

Tabbing and Indenting Text

After completing this lesson, you will be able to:

✔ Set paragraph indents

✔ Set indents on left and right margins at once

✔ Set tab stops

✔ Create hanging paragraphs

WordPerfect has three different kinds of indent commands: 1) Tab, 2) Indent, and 3) Left/Right indent. To learn about each kind of indent, you will type the three paragraphs in Figure WP–15.

Indenting Text

Begin by clearing the screen if it is not already clear.

Press the (TAB) key once and type the first paragraph.

Press (F4) for Indent, and type the second paragraph.

> Note how the paragraph wraps to the new indented margin 1 inch in from the original left margin.

Press (SHIFT)-(F4) twice for Left/Right Indent, and type the third paragraph.

> Note how the paragraph's left and right margins are indented an additional 2 inches from the original margins.

Put your work disk in drive B and save your document ((F10)) under the name B:LESSON5.

> It is a good idea to press (F10) every few minutes or every few pages. That way, if there is a power failure or a hardware problem, all your hard work will not be erased.

The Tab key moves the cursor to the next tab position. You can use it when you only want to indent the first line of the paragraph. It was used to indent this paragraph.

Like the tab key, the Indent key moves the cursor to the next tab position. In addition, it sets a temporary margin at the tab stop. It was used to set the new left margin for this paragraph.

The Left/Right indent key temporarily moves the left and right margins to the next tab stop. It was used to create this paragraph.

WP–15 Practice document for Lesson 5.

You can insert and delete text in these paragraphs and they will still retain the indent form you gave them.

Place the cursor after the words "right margins" in the last paragraph and delete the phrase "to the next tab stop".

Press Ⓓ to realign the text.

> Notice that the entire paragraph is still indented 2 inches from the left and right margins.

Move the cursor to the end of the second paragraph after the period.

> If you see the Typeover prompt in the lower left-hand corner of the status line on your screen, press the (INS) key once to turn off Typeover mode.

Press the space bar twice, then type **The new margin is effective until the Enter key is pressed.**

Press Ⓓ to realign the text.

Changing Tab Stops

WordPerfect automatically sets **tab** stops at every ½ inch. You can tailor the tab stops to your own needs by using the Format command ((SHIFT)-(F8)).

Move the cursor to the top of the document by pressing (PGUP)

Press (SHIFT)-(F8)

> The Format screen appears.

Type **1** to select the Line menu.

> (*Note:* In WordPerfect 4.2, select option 2 for Tabs.)

Type **8** to select Tab Set.

> As shown in Figure WP–16, the Tab Set menu appears on the bottom of the screen.

```
        The Tab key moves the cursor to the next tab position.  You
use it only when you want to indent the first line of the
paragraph.  It was used to indent this paragraph.

        Like the tab key, the Indent key moves the cursor to the next
tab position.  In addition, it sets a temporary margin at the
tab stop.  It was used to set the new left margin for this
paragraph.  The new margin is effective until the Enter key
is pressed.

                The Left/Right indent key temporarily moves
                the left and right margins.  It was used to
                create this paragraph.




L....L....L....L....L....L....L....L....L....L....L....L....L....L....L...
|    ^    |    ^    |    ^    |    ^    |    ^    |    ^    |    ^    |    ^
     20h      30h      40h      50h      60h      70h      80h
Delete EOL (clear tabs); Enter Number (set tab); Del (clear tab);
Left; Center; Right; Decimal; .= Dot Leader
```

WP–16 Document with the Tab Set menu.

In the Tab Set menu, the tab settings are marked with an L for left tab. You can create tabs by moving the cursor to the position where you want the tab and typing L, R, C, or D (L-Left tab; R-Right tab; C-Center tab; D-Decimal tab). To set a new tab at the 2.5-inch position, begin by erasing the current tabs.

Press CTRL-END for Delete EOL.

> All the tab settings to the end of the line ("EOL") have been erased.

Type **2.5** and press ENTER

Now you will practice erasing a tab. To erase the new tab:

Place the cursor on the tab stop (L) at the 2.5-inch position.

> You can use ← and → to move the cursor in the Tab Set menu.

Press DEL to erase the tab stop.

WordPerfect provides a quick method for setting a series of tabs at even intervals. Suppose you wanted to set tabs at every inch starting at position 0. You would type the position number of the first tab, type a comma, then type the interval number (in inches).

Type **0,1** and press ENTER

Press F7 twice

> Notice that the change in tab setting has altered your paragraphs.

Clear the screen (F7, **N, N**) without saving.

Creating Hanging Indents

WordPerfect gives you powerful methods for creating **hanging indents**. If you are not familiar with hanging indents, they are shown in Figure WP–17. Hanging indents are useful for creating lists or highlighting numbered items. To learn about hanging indents, you will type the text in Figure WP–17.

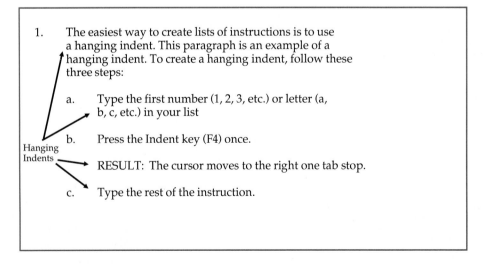

1.   The easiest way to create lists of instructions is to use a hanging indent. This paragraph is an example of a hanging indent. To create a hanging indent, follow these three steps:

    a.   Type the first number (1, 2, 3, etc.) or letter (a, b, c, etc.) in your list

    b.   Press the Indent key (F4) once.

        RESULT: The cursor moves to the right one tab stop.

    c.   Type the rest of the instruction.

Hanging Indents

WP–17   Practice document with hanging indents.

Type the first character (**1.** in this instance) and press F4 for Indent.

> This creates a hanging indent because the number "1." will be at the left margin, but the rest of the text will be indented to the first tab stop. When you press ENTER to end the paragraph, the cursor will return to the original left margin.

Type the first paragraph and press ENTER twice.

> Notice that the remaining text of the paragraph is indented.

Press TAB and type **a.**

Press F4 for Indent and then type the second paragraph.

> In the second paragraph, the letter "a." will be at the first tab stop, and the rest of the text will be indented.

Press ENTER

> Again, pressing ENTER ends the Indent option.

Type the rest of the text.

This completes Lesson 5. Clear the screen (F7 , **N, N**) and do the following practice exercise. After completing the exercise, if you wish to exit WordPerfect, type F7, **N, Y.**

Practice

By following the instructions below, type the letter in Figure WP–18 (shown on the following page).

1. Set tabs every 1 inch with an additional tab at the 2.5-inch position for the text of the numbered items.

2. Use a hanging indent on the three numbered items.

3. Use Left/Right Indent for the three paragraphs starting with "Your employment..." and ending with "August 1, 1989)."

4. Underline the heading "How Extended Coverage Works."

5. Bold the words "New Normal," "Regular," "Part Time," "Intermittent," and "Temporary."

6. Save the document as PRAC5 on your work disk.

Aromax Corporation
1721 North Pierce Street
Grand Junction, CO 81501

Dear Aromax Employees:

Effective January 1, 1991 in accordance with the Consolidated Omnibus Budget Reconciliation Act of 1985 the company will offer new extended coverage for the:

1)   Employee Health Care Plan for all exempt and non-exempt employees at Aromax.
2)   Dependent Health Care Plan for all married couples employed by Aromax.
3)   Vision Care Plan for employees and dependents.

<u>How Extended Coverage Works</u>

You and your dependents may have coverage expanded from <u>18 months</u> if any of the following "qualifying events" occur:

Your employment with Aromax is terminated for any reason other than gross misconduct, or you are laid off;

Your employment classification changes from **New Normal** or **Regular**, to **Part Time**, **Intermittent**, or **Temporary**; or

You retire with less than 10 years of service with the Company (If you were hired on or after August 1, 1989).

Should you have any questions regarding your extension, please call (303) 248-6171 between 8:00 a.m. and 5:30 p.m.

Sincerely,

Health Care Claims
Administration

WP–18   Practice letter for Lesson 5.

Lesson 6

Searching and Replacing Text

After completing this lesson, you will be able to:

✔ Search for text forwards and backwards through a document

✔ Search for text and automatically replace it with other text

✔ Search for hidden codes

Searching for Text

WordPerfect enables you to search forwards or backwards through a document to find text. You will find the name "Williams" in the letter you typed in Lesson 3.

Clear the screen and retrieve LESSON3 from your work disk.

Use the Retrieve command ((SHIFT)-(F10)) or List Files ((F5)) to retrieve your letter.

Press (F2) for Search Forward.

You should see the search prompt in the lower left corner of the screen.

`-> Srch:`

Type **Williams**

"Williams" is called the **search string**, and it can be any word or combination of words.

Press (F2)

Note: If you press (ENTER) by mistake, press (BACKSPACE) once to erase the hard return [HRt] code.

The cursor has stopped after the last character in the first occurrence of the name. Now continue the Search.

Press (F2)

The following is displayed:

`->Srch: Williams`

Notice that WordPerfect remembers the last search string, in this case "Williams." You can search for a second occurrence of the word or enter another search string.

To begin searching again, press (F2)

The search has located the second occurrence of Williams.

Press (F2), (F2) again.

If there are no more occurrences of Williams in the document, you will see a "* Not found *" prompt at the bottom of the screen. You can search backwards by pressing (SHIFT)-(F2), (F2) or (F2), (↑), (F2)

The Search command is handy for searching for unique words. But what do you do if the search string you are using is also a part of a word? For example, look what happens when you search for the word "in." First, move the cursor to the top of the document.

Press (PGUP)

WordPerfect searches from the cursor forward, so you must begin the search with the cursor at the beginning of the document if you want to search the entire document.

Press (F2)

Type **in**

Press (F2)

Repeat the search ((F2), (F2)) until you see the "* Not found *" prompt. You probably noticed that the cursor stopped on the letters "in" contained inside words such as "winner," "Lincoln," and "again." To avoid this problem, you must press the space bar before and after typing the word, and then press (F2) or (ESC) to begin searching.

Searching for Format Codes

The Search command can also find format codes in the document. You will search for the bold code in the first paragraph.

Press (PGUP)

Press (F2) for Search.

Press (F6) for Bold.

> You should see the following prompt:

`->Srch: [BOLD]`

Press (F2) to begin searching.

> When the cursor stops, press Reveal Codes ((ALT)-(F3)). The [Bold] code that turns on boldface should be just to the left of the cursor. You can delete it by pressing (BACKSPACE). Alternatively, you can press (F2), (F2) again to search for other occurrences of the bold code. Be sure to turn off Reveal Codes ((ALT)-(F3)) when you have completed searching for format codes. You can search for codes with Reveal Codes either on or off.

Replacing a Search String

You can also replace a string with new text. You will change the name Williams to Kendrick using the Replace command ((ALT)-(F2)).

Press (PGUP) to start at the top of the document.

Press (ALT)-(F2) for Replace.

> You should see this prompt in the lower left corner of your screen:

`w/Confirm? (Y/N) No`

> The program is asking you if you wish to pause before replacing the old text, so you can confirm the correctness of each replacement.

Type **Y**

> The Search prompt now appears in the lower left corner of the screen.

Type **Williams**

Press (F2) for Search (do not press (ENTER))

> You should see this prompt in the lower left corner of your screen:

`Replace with:`

Type **Kendrick**

Press (F2)

> Each time the cursor stops on the name Williams, type Y to change it to Kendrick.

Setting the confirm option to Y helps you make the final decision on each replacement. Use this as a safety feature to make sure that you do not accidentally change a word or phrase that you do not want to.

This completes Lesson 6. Clear the screen ((F7), **N, N**) and do the following practice exercise. After completing the exercise, if you wish to exit WordPerfect, type (F7), **N, Y**.

Practice

Retrieve PRAC5 from your work disk and do the following.

1. Search for all occurrences of the word "extended" and change to "expanded."

2. Use the Search and Replace command to change all occurrences of the word "Aromax" to "Aromax and Family."

3. Search for all the bold codes in the file and delete them.

4. Save the document as PRAC6 on your work disk.

Lesson 7

Page Formatting, Headers and Footers

After completing this lesson, you will be able to:

✔ Set top and bottom margins

✔ Align text flush right

✔ Center text

✔ Automatically number pages

✔ Create headers and footers

Changing the Top Margin

WordPerfect has many features to help you create polished and professional documents. Insert the Student Data Disk in drive B and retrieve the file LESSON7. Assuming this file will be printed on stationary with a printed letterhead, you will need to change the top margin to 2 inches to accommodate the paper.

Press (SHIFT)-(F8) for Format.

(*Note:* In WordPerfect 4.2, press (SHIFT)-(F8), and do not type the 2 in the following instruction.)

Type **2** to select the Page menu.

The Format: Page menu will appear on the screen (see Figure WP–19).

Type **5** to select the Margins option.

Type **2** to change the top margin to 2 inches.

```
Format: Page

    1 - Center Page (top to bottom)    No

    2 - Force Odd/Even Page

    3 - Headers

    4 - Footers

    5 - Margins - Top                   1"
               Bottom                   1"

    6 - New Page Number                 1
        (example: 3 or iii)

    7 - Page Numbering                  No page numbering

    8 - Paper Size                      8.5" x 11"
               Type                     Standard

    9 - Suppress (this page only)

Selection: 0
```

WP–19 The Page options of the Format menu.

Press (ENTER) four times.

Note that you will not see the wider top margin on the screen. If the letter included a second page printed on plain paper, you would have to reset the top margin to 1 inch at the top of the second page.

Using the Flush Right Command

The top address and date would probably look best if it were flush right on the page.

Move the cursor to the first character of the address.

Press (ALT)-(F6) for Flush Right.

Flush Right moves the line to the right margin.

Move the cursor to the first character of the second line of the address.

Press (ALT)-(F6)

Move the cursor to the first character of the date.

Press (ALT)-(F6)

You can also enter text automatically flush right by pressing (ALT)-(F6) before typing text. The text will then move to the left as you type.

Centering Text

Next you will center text on the screen. Suppose you want to center the words DELINQUENT PAYMENT.

Move the cursor to the D in DELINQUENT.

Press (SHIFT)-(F6) for the Center command.

The text is centered on the page.

Press (↓)

As with Flush Right, you can center a line of text while typing it. For example, suppose you want to add the words FINAL NOTICE and center them beneath DELINQUENT PAYMENT.

Move the cursor to the line between DELINQUENT PAYMENT and "Dear Ms. Yoshino".

Press (SHIFT)-(F6)

The cursor will jump to the center of the screen.

Type **FINAL NOTICE** and press (ENTER)

Automatic Page Numbering

W
P

WordPerfect can automatically number each page of your document. You will now put a page number in the top right corner of the page.

Move the cursor to the first character of the first line of the first page.

Press (SHIFT)-(F8) for Format.

(*Note:* In WordPerfect 4.2, (ALT)-(F8).)

Type **2** to select the Page menu.

Type **7** to select Page Numbering.

(*Note:* In WordPerfect 4.2, select option 1, Page Number Position.) The Page Numbering menu will appear on the screen (see Figure WP–20). Notice that nine page numbering options are shown in a representation of a page: every page on the top left (1), top center (2), top right (3), bottom left (5), bottom center (6), bottom right (7); and alternating top (4), alternating bottom (8). The No Page Number option (9) is spelled out.

Type **3** for page numbering in the top right margin.

Notice that the option you chose, Top Right, now appears next to the Page Numbering option on the Format: Page menu.

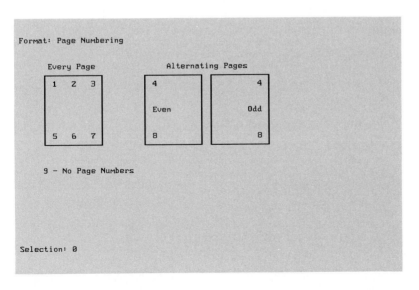

WP–20 The menu for Page Numbering.

Press (ENTER) twice to return to the document.

> The page number does not appear on the screen. To view how the final letter will turn out you must bring up the Print menu ((SHIFT)-(F7)) and select the View Document option.

Press (SHIFT)-(F7)

Type 6 to View Document.

> The View Document screen has four options for viewing the document, as shown below. (*Note:* This screen will appear somewhat different in WordPerfect 4.2.)

```
1   100%    2   200%    3   Full Page    4   Facing Pages
```

Type 1 to select the 100% option.

> You can use the cursor movement keys to scroll through the document if you like.

Press (F7) to exit the View Document option.

Creating Headers and Footers

A **header** is one or more lines of standard text that appears at the top of each page, and a **footer** is a line that appears at the bottom. They are used to insert titles, labels, and page numbers in books, reports and reference works. You can place them at the top or bottom of every page, every odd-numbered page, or every even-numbered page.

Like page numbers, headers and footers are invisible on the editing screen and only appear when printed, or in the View Document option of the Print menu ((SHIFT)-(F7), 6). You can also use the Reveal Codes command to verify that they have been correctly added.

When creating a header or footer, be sure that the cursor is on the first line of the first page you want the header to be printed on.

To create a header on every page:

Move the cursor to the first character of the first line of the first page.

Press (SHIFT)-(F8) for Format.

> (*Note:* In WordPerfect 4.2, press (ALT)-(F8), 2, 6 in place of the following.)

Type 2 to select Page.

Type 3 to select the Headers option.

> You should see this prompt in the lower left corner of your screen:

```
1   Header   A;   2   Header   B:   0
```

Type 1 to select Header A.

> Five options then appear at the bottom of the screen.

Type 2 to put a header on every page.

> The screen will go blank. It is now ready for you to type the text of your header. Two common headers are the title of a report or the page num-

ber. You can also use formatting such as bold, italics, or centering. For this example, you will create the header "Delinquent Payment."

Type **Delinquent Payment**

Press (F7) twice for Exit.

> Again, you won't see the header unless you use the View Document option on the Print menu ((SHIFT)-(F7), **6**).

You create a footer in the same way that you create a header, except you choose the footer option instead of the header option.

This completes Lesson 7. Clear the screen ((F7), **N, N**). If you wish to exit WordPerfect, type (F7), **N, Y**.

Practice

Retrieve PRAC6 from your work disk and do the following.

1. Change the top margin to 2.5 inches.

2. Enter the text CIRCULATE IMMEDIATELY flush right on the first line.

3. Using automatic page numbering, put a page number at the bottom center of the page.

4. Center the date.

5. Save the document as PRAC7 on your work disk.

Lesson 8

Merging Documents

After completing this lesson, you will be able to:

> ✔ Use a primary file and secondary file to create form letters that appear to be personalized for each recipient
>
> ✔ Create forms that can be filled in "on the fly"

Creating Merged Letters

In this exercise, you will create primary and secondary files that when **merged** will produce the three form letters shown in Figure WP–21. First you will create the **primary file** for the merge. The primary file consists of the actual letter. The date, recipient name and address, salutation ("Dear..."), and amount donated will differ from letter to letter, so these are called the **variable data** and will be represented by merge codes (^D, ^F1, ^F2, etc.) in the primary file.

Then you will create a **secondary file**, which consists of the actual data (names, addresses, etc.) to be substituted during the merge. When merged, these two files will print letters that appear to be customized.

WP–21 Three form letters after Merging files.

June 20, 1990

Mr. Bill Doolay
143 Beverly Blvd.
West Los Angeles, CA 91232

Dear Mr.Doolay:

Thank you for your generous wedding gift of a four piece set of Dansk table settings. Only last night Judy and I were talking about how your gift has added to our home!

Sincerely,

Mr. and Mrs. John Williams

June 20, 1990

Mrs. Mandy Reynault
23 Elsinor Drive
Seattle, WA 99492

Dear Mrs. Reynault:

Thank you for your generous wedding gift of an electric ice cream maker. Only last night Judy and I were talking about how your gift has added to our home!

Sincerely,

Mr. and Mrs. John Williams

June 20, 1990

Mr. and Mrs. Red Hebbard
1230 Market Street
San Francisco, CA 91234

Dear Mr. and Mrs. Hebbard:

Thank you for your generous wedding gift of red towels. Only last night Judy and I were talking about how your gift has added to our home!

Sincerely,

Mr. and Mrs. John Williams

Creating the Primary File

The primary file that you will create will have seven fields. A **field** is a distinct piece of information. The fields and their field code numbers are as follows:

```
^F1    name
^F2    street
^F3    city
```

```
^F4   state
^F5   zip code
^F6   salutation
^F7   gift
```

The collection of all these pieces of information (fields) in a single form (one individual's letter) is called a **record**.

When you have completed the following instructions, the primary file for the letter will appear as in Figure WP–22.

Clear the screen.

Press (SHIFT)-(F9) for Merge Codes.

(*Note:* In WordPerfect 4.2, press (ALT)-(F9).) You should see the following merge codes displayed in the status line.

```
^C;  ^D;  ^E;  ^F;  ^G;  ^N;  ^O;  ^P;  ^Q;  ^S;  ^T;  ^U;  ^V
```

Type **D**

This will insert the date code (^D) at the top of the letter. The ^D code will turn into the current date at the time you perform the merge that joins the primary and secondary files together.

Press (ENTER) twice.

This moves the cursor down two lines.

Press (SHIFT)-(F9) for Merge Codes.

(*Note:* In WordPerfect 4.2, press (ALT)-(F9))

Type **F** to insert the first field code.

You should see this prompt in the lower left corner of your screen:

```
Field:
```

Type **1** to complete the first field code.

This will be the recipient's full name when the files are merged.

Press (ENTER) twice.

Press (SHIFT)-(F9)

```
^D

^F1^
^F2^
^F3^,  ^F4^  ^F5^

Dear ^F6^:

Thank you for your generous wedding gift of ^F7^.  Only last
night Judy and I were talking about how your gift has added
to our home!

Sincerely,


Mr. and Mrs. John Williams
```

WP–22 The primary file.

Type **F** and **2** to insert the second field code.

> This will be the street address when the files are merged.

Press (ENTER) twice.

Press (SHIFT)-(F9).

Type **F** and **3** to insert the third field code.

> This will be the city when the files are merged.

Press (ENTER)

Type **,** (comma) and press the space bar.

Press (SHIFT)-(F9)

Type **F** and **4** to insert the fourth field code.

> This will be the state when the files are merged.

Press (ENTER)

Press the space bar once.

Press (SHIFT)-(F9)

Type **F** and **5** to insert the fifth field code.

> This will be the zip code when the files are merged.

Press (ENTER) three times.

> This enters the code and moves the cursor down two lines.

Type **Dear**

Press the space bar.

Press (SHIFT)-(F9)

Type **F** and **6** to insert the sixth field code.

> This will be the salutation.

Press (ENTER)

Type **:** (colon).

> Type the rest of the letter as it appears in Figure WP–22, entering the seventh field code after you type the word "of" ((SHIFT)-(F9), **F**, **7**, (ENTER)). After you finish typing the entire letter:

Press (F10)

> Save the file to your work disk under the name B:GIFTS.PF (PF stands for primary file). Although using PF is not required, it is a good idea to use a recognizable extension such as .PF to identify your primary files. Then use the same name with the SF extension to identify the corresponding secondary file.
>
> In this primary file that you have just created, each of the seven fields was unique. Thus the letter required seven field numbers. If, however, you wanted to use a field twice (for example, a person's full name in both the address and the salutation), you could use F1 in both places.

Note also that many addresses contain another line, besides the street address, for such things as box numbers, suite numbers, etc. In such cases, you would need to enter six field codes in the address instead of the five fields used in this primary file.

Clear the screen ((F7), N, N).

You must clear the screen before typing the secondary file containing the actual data.

Creating the Secondary File

The secondary file contains the information to be merged into the primary file. In the secondary file each field, such as name, street address, city, state, zip, and salutation, is separated by a Merge Return code (^R), and each record (all the fields for a single form letter) ends with a Merge End code (^E). you will type the secondary file as shown in Figure WP–23.

Type **Mr. Bill Doolay**

Press (F9) for Merge Return.

Instead of pressing (ENTER) at the end of the line, you press the Merge Return key ((F9)), which inserts the code and moves the cursor to the next line.

Type the remaining fields in the first record, pressing (F9) after each line.

The cursor will be on the line below the gift description.

Press (SHIFT)-(F9) for Merge Codes.

```
Mr. Bill Doolay^R
143 Beverly Blvd.^R
West Los Angeles^R
CA^R
91232^R
Mr. Doolay^R
a four piece set of Dansk table settings^R
^E
=========================================================
Mrs. Mandy Reynault^R
23 Elsinor Drive^R
Seattle^R
WA^R
99492^R
Mrs. Reynault^R
an electric ice cream maker^R
^E
=========================================================
Mr. and Mrs. Red Hebbard^R
1230 Market Street^R
San Francisco^R
CA^R
91234^R
Mr. and Mrs. Hebbard:^R
red towels^R
^E
```

WP–23 The secondary file.

Type **E** to insert the ^E code.

> (*Note:* In WordPerfect 4.2, it is not necessary to type E.) The code forces a hard page break when the form letters are generated and starts a new letter if more data exists in the secondary file.

Type the remaining two records in the secondary file.

> After you finish typing the secondary file:

Press (F10)

Save the file to your work disk under the name B:GIFTS.SF

> (Recall that PF stands for primary file and SF means secondary file.) As noted, it is a good idea to use the same first name for both the primary and secondary files. This helps tell at a glance that they belong together.

Clear the screen.

> Before merging the primary and secondary files to create the three letters, you must clear the screen.

Creating the Merged Letters

You are now ready to merge the primary and secondary files in order to create customized form letters. When WordPerfect finishes generating the form letters, they will appear on screen with a hard page break separating them.

Press (CTRL)-(F9) for Merge/Sort.

Type **1** to select Merge.

Type the name of the primary file, B:GIFTS.PF

Press (ENTER)

Type the name of the secondary file, B:GIFTS.SF

Press (ENTER)

> When the "* Merging *" message disappears, press (HOME), (HOME), (↑) to get to the top of the first letter. Use the (PGDN) key to scroll down through the letters to see if they are correct.

You can now print the letters ((SHIFT)-(F7)) or save them to a new file. You can also use the secondary file again with a different form letter (primary file), or use it to create envelopes or mailing labels from the names and addresses in the list. Table WP–4 summarizes the steps and commands used to merge documents.

Merging Without a Secondary File

Suppose Mr. Williams sporadically receives wedding gifts for several months after his wedding. Since the gifts arrive sporadically, it would not be possible to create a secondary file with all the names and addresses of those sending gifts. Instead, he can set up a form letter thanking each individual and use it whenever a gift is received.

Table WP–4 Summary of the Merge Process

1. *Create the Primary File*

    Type document

    Enter field codes

        (SHIFT)-(F9) (Merge Codes), **F**, the number of the field, (ENTER)

    Save the primary file ((F10)) with a .PF extension

    Clear the screen ((F7), **N, N**)

2. *Create the Secondary File*

    Enter records

        Press (F9) (Merge Return) at the end of each field

        Press (SHIFT)-(F9) (Merge Codes), **E** at the end of each record

    Save the secondary file ((F10)) with a .SF extension

    Clear the screen ((F7), **N, N**)

3. *Merge the Files*

    Press (CTRL)-(F9) (Merge Sort), **1**

    Type name of primary file, press (ENTER)

    Type name of secondary file, press (ENTER)

To use this method, you would create a form letter using codes that allow you to type the variable data (name, address, etc.) at the time of the merge. Because there is no secondary file, you would use this method only if you do not need to save the variable data in a file for later use.

In this exercise you will create a new version of the primary file acknowledging receipt of gifts, as shown in Figure WP–24. When you run the merge, the cursor stops at the code and waits for you to type something. For example, the first time it stops you will type the name and address of the person sending a gift. After you finish typing, you press (F9) (Merge Return) and the cursor moves to the next code, where you will type the salutation.

Clear the screen. Press (F7), N, N

Retrieve the GIFTS.PF file and erase all the field codes (^F1, ^F2, etc.).

```
^D

^C


Dear ^C:

Thank you for your generous wedding gift of ^C. Only last
night Judy and I were talking about how your gift has added
to our home!

Sincerely,


Mr. and Mrs. John Williams
```

WP–24 The primary file for Merging information from the keyboard.

In place of the five address field codes you will need to insert only one ^C code.

Press (SHIFT)-(F9) Merge/Sort.

Type **C**

Repeat the above two steps to insert a merge pause (^C) code for the salutation and the gift description.

Press (F7), **Y** to save the file under a new name, FORM.PF

Clear the screen.

Remember, before starting a merge, you must clear the screen.

You are now ready to generate a form letter by merging information from the keyboard with the primary file.

Press (CTRL)-(F9) for Merge/Sort.

Type **1** to select Merge.

Type the name of the new primary file, **FORM.PF**, and press (ENTER)

In this type of merge there is no secondary file, since the data will be entered "on the fly."

Press (ENTER) in response to the prompt asking for the name of the secondary file.

As soon as the merge begins, the first pause code (^C) disappears and the cursor stops at that position. This is your signal to type the information that belongs there.

Aromax and Family Corporation
1721 North Pierce Street
Grand Junction, CO 81501

^D

^F1^
^F2^
^F3^
^F4^

Dear ^F1^:

This will confirm your registration and attendance for the following class and dates:

^F5^   ^F6^

If you are unable to attend, please notify us at least one week in advance.

Thank you.

(your name)
Training Administrator

WP–25 Practice primary file for Lesson 8.

Type this name and address, pressing (ENTER) after each line:

Ms. Barbara Konn
445 Anton Avenue
San Bernardino, CA 90576

Press (F9) for Merge Return to move the cursor to the next field (salutation).

Type **Ms. Konn**

Press (F9) to move to the next field (gift).

Type **fine crystal** for the gift they sent.

Press (F9)

> Be sure to press (F9) after typing the data for the gift. Although no ^Cs are visible, the cursor must end up at the bottom of the document.

Print the letter ((SHIFT)-(F7)).

> If you wish to use the form again, just clear the screen and repeat these steps.

This completes Lesson 8. Clear the screen ((F7), **N**, **N**) to do the following practice exercise. If you wish to exit WordPerfect after the exercise, type (F7), **N**, **Y**.

Practice

Create the primary file shown in Figure WP–25. Then create the secondary file shown in Figure WP–26. Merge these files and save the final letters as PRAC8 on your work disk.

```
Tony Rogers^R
Systems Programmer^R
Room 412^R
General Office^R
Lotus 1-2-3^R
May 20, 1990^R
^E
Mary Godinez^R
^R
Room 316^R
General Office 1^R
WordPerfect^R
April 30, 1990^R
^E
Ted Homley^R
District Manager^R
Room 515^R
Boulder Office^R
Advanced Lotus^R
May 17, 1990^R
^E
```

WP–26 Practice secondary file for Lesson 8.

Lesson 9

File Management

After completing this lesson, you will be able to:

✔ Use the List Files menu to retrieve, copy, move, rename, and delete files

✔ Search all files for a word or phrase

✔ Make a new directory and change directories

✔ Create and use a document summary

✔ Use the Look option to view files on disk and see or use files in other directories

The difference between average and excellent word processing users often lies in the way they manage files. Good file management is essential for effective word processing—and yet is often ignored. **File management** is the ability to control and organize your files so that you can always find quickly the file you need.

Copying and Renaming Files

We will first look at a common file management mistake. You already know how to retrieve a document using List Files. But what happens when you try to retrieve a second document after you have already retrieved one?

Insert the Student Data Disk in drive B.

Press (F5) for List Files.

Type **B:** (or A: for a hard disk system) to indicate the default drive.

Press (ENTER)

Move the cursor onto the LESSON1 file.

Type **1** to retrieve it.

Now you will see what happens if you try to retrieve a second document without clearing the edit screen first.

Press (F5), type **B:** and press (ENTER)

Place the cursor on the file named LESSON3.

Type **1**

Do you see the prompt at the bottom of the screen:

```
Retrieve into current document?
```

WordPerfect is warning you that if you press Y, you will retrieve the LESSON3 file and add it to the document on the edit screen. Notice that No is the default response.

Press (ENTER), then press Exit ((F7)).

Pressing (ENTER) answers No to the prompt "Retrieve into current document?" and returns you to the edit screen. In this way you keep from adding LESSON3 to LESSON1.

Press Exit ((F7)) and type N, N to clear the screen.

Always remember to clear a screen before beginning work on another document.

Copying Documents Using List Files

List Files ((F5)) also enables you to copy a file to another disk or to a different file name. You will practice by copying a file to a new file name in the same directory.

Press (F5) for List Files.

Type B:

Press (ENTER)

Place the cursor on the file named LESSON1.

Type 8 to make a copy of the file.

You should see this prompt in the lower left corner of your screen:

```
Copy this file to:
```

Type TEST1 and press (ENTER)

You just created a second copy of LESSON1 called TEST1.

Press the space bar or (F7) to exit the List Files screen.

You can verify that TEST1 has been added to the directory by listing your files again.

Press List Files ((F5)).

Type B:

Press (ENTER)

Notice that a TEST1 file is now shown in the list. In the next step, you will use the Move/Rename option to rename it.

Renaming Files

WordPerfect has a name search feature to help you find files.

Type N to begin Name Search.

Type T

Did you notice how the cursor moved to the first file that started with the letter T? If it is not TEST1, type E, then S, then T, then 1, if necessary, until the cursor moves to TEST1.

To quit Name Search and use the List Files menu again.

Press the Exit key ((F7)).

> Note that TEST1 is still highlighted. You are now prepared to change its name.

Type 3 for the Move/Rename option.

> You should see this prompt in the lower left corner of your screen:
>
> `New name: B:TEST1`
>
> To rename this file, you just type the new name that you want. As soon as you type the first letter, the old name will disappear.

Type **NEWTEST1** and press (ENTER)

Press the Exit key ((F7)) or the space bar to return to the document.

In the next section you will create a new subdirectory named TEMP, then use the Move/Rename option to move the NEWTEST1 file there.

Creating a New Subdirectory

To create a new subdirectory:

Press List Files ((F5)).

Type **B:**

Press (ENTER)

Type **7** to select Other Directory.

> You should see this prompt in the lower left corner of your screen:
>
> `New directory = B:`

Type **B:\TEMP** and press (ENTER)

> Notice the prompt "Create TEMP (Y/N)?" The TEMP subdirectory you are about to create will be under the current (parent) directory.

Type **Y** to create the TEMP subdirectory.

> WordPerfect creates the TEMP subdirectory, and the name appears as follows in the list: TEMP <DIR>.

You will now move the File NEWTEST1 into the TEMP subdirectory.

Move the cursor to the file named NEWTEST1.

Type **3** to use the Move/Rename option.

> The "New Name:" prompt appears in the lower left corner of the screen.

Press (→) until the cursor is on the N in NEWTEST1 in the prompt.

Type **TEMP** and press (ENTER)

> This moves the NEWTEST1 file into the TEMP subdirectory. Now check the TEMP subdirectory to see if NEWTEST1 is really there.

Place the cursor on the TEMP <DIR>

Type **6** to select the Look option.

The "DIR" prompt should now appear in the lower left corner of the screen.

Press (ENTER) to use the Look option in the subdirectory.

You should see the contents of the TEMP subdirectory.

Place the cursor on the NEWTEST1 file and select the Look option by pressing (ENTER)

Notice that the contents of the file appears on the screen. You should be aware that you cannot edit the file in the Look mode. Look is useful when you want to know what is in a file without retrieving it.

Press the Exit key ((F7)) to exit from Look.

The List Files screen appears again.

Press (F7) to exit the List Files screen.

You should now be back in the edit screen.

Next, you will erase the TEMP subdirectory.

Removing a Subdirectory

To remove the subdirectory:

Press List Files ((F5)).

Type **B:**

Press (ENTER)

Move the cursor to the TEMP subdirectory.

Type **2** to delete it.

You should see this prompt in the lower left corner of your screen:

`Delete: B:\TEMP? (Y/N) No`

Type **Y**

The "ERROR: Directory not empty" message appears because WordPerfect will not let you delete a subdirectory if there are any files in it. You must delete the NEWTEST1 file before you can delete the TEMP subdirectory.

Press **6** (ENTER) to look at the TEMP subdirectory.

Place the cursor on the NEWTEST1 file.

Type **2** to select Delete.

The following prompt appears:

`Delete B:\TEMP\NEWTEST1? (Y/N) No`

Type **Y** to erase NEWTEST1.

The file name disappears, and you can see that the TEMP subdirectory is now empty.

Place the cursor on PARENT <DIR> and press (ENTER) twice.

You can now delete the TEMP directory.

Place the cursor on the TEMP <DIR>

Type **2** to select Delete.

Type **Y**

> The subdirectory name disappears from the screen.

Next, you will use the List Files key to narrow the list of displayed files to those that begin with the letter L.

Listing Specific Files

The List Files menu can fill up with files rather quickly. WordPerfect provides a method for you to display only those files that you want to work with at a time. Just as you can use wildcards in DOS, you can use wildcards in WordPerfect as well. Suppose you only want to display those files that begin with the letter L.

Press the space bar to return to the edit screen.

Press List Files ((F5)).

> You should see this prompt in the lower left corner of your screen:

> `DIR`

Type **B:L*** and (ENTER)

> This reduces the display to only those files that begin with the letter L. The asterisk (*) is called a wildcard, and it represents all characters. By using it after the L, the file names must begin with L but can include any other characters following the L. Similarly, you can tell List Files to display only those files with a particular extension. For example, using *.WP would list all the files ending with the extension WP.

Press the space bar to return to the edit screen.

Next, you will explore the Word Search option, which can be used to locate a file containing a certain word or words.

Searching the Files in a Directory

So far you have been using the List Files key ((F5)) to display the files in a directory or only certain files based on their file names. WordPerfect can also search the contents of a file to help you find what you are looking for. Suppose you need to retrieve a document that deals with your 1988 taxes, but after looking at List Files you cannot tell which document you want.

Press the List Files key ((F5)).

Type **B:** and (ENTER)

Type **9** to select Word Search.

> As shown in Figure WP–27, four options to search for words or text in your files are displayed at the bottom of the screen.

Type **4** to select Conditions.

```
10/06/89  11:02              Directory C:\WP50\*.*
Document size:    111042   Free:  1617920   Used:   2028581        Files:   92

. <CURRENT>   <DIR>    .          .. <PARENT>   <DIR>
ARTICLES.     <DIR>   10/29/88 21:24     ATWATER .   <DIR>   09/02/88 12:41
BLISS    .    <DIR>   09/02/88 12:30     BRIDGET .   <DIR>   10/25/88 08:15
DAD      .    <DIR>   05/10/89 17:30     DAVID   .   <DIR>   07/31/89 21:42
FONTS    .    <DIR>   08/31/88 09:09     GRAPHICS.   <DIR>   08/31/88 09:00
IDEAS    .    <DIR>   09/04/88 09:57     INVOICES.   <DIR>   07/19/89 17:47
LETTERS  .    <DIR>   11/15/88 17:57     MAGIC   .   <DIR>   09/02/88 12:14
SARAH    .    <DIR>   05/06/89 06:59     STERN   .   <DIR>   03/08/89 09:54
STORIES  .    <DIR>   08/31/88 09:00     TOWER   .   <DIR>   09/02/88 11:57
TRAINING.     <DIR>   09/25/88 05:00     TWISSEL .   <DIR>   08/31/88 09:00
WPBOOK   .    <DIR>   05/26/89 14:50     8514A   .WPD   3466  04/27/88 14:24
ALTA    .WPM      65  03/07/89 10:29     ALTB    .WPM    91  08/02/89 19:07
ALTC    .WPM      87  01/09/89 09:40     ALTD    .WPM   117  12/21/88 11:28
ALTE    .WPM      57  07/19/89 14:05     ALTF    .WPM    97  09/17/89 19:23
ALTG    .WPM      87  03/07/89 18:58     ALTI    .WPM    88  03/09/89 09:27
ALTJ    .WPM     171  03/07/89 10:18     ALTK    .WPM    85  04/30/89 20:51
ALTL    .WPM     118  09/04/89 11:10     ALTM    .WPM   151  03/07/89 10:32
ALTO    .WPM      57  03/09/89 09:26  ▼  ALTP    .WPM    79  09/01/88 10:02
ALTQ    .WPM      74  01/05/89 22:10     ALTR    .WPM   135  09/04/89 10:28

Search: 1 Doc Summary; 2 First Page; 3 Entire Doc; 4 Conditions: 0
```

WP–27 List files with the Word Search option.

The Word Search menu appears as shown in Figure WP–28. You will use it to restrict the word search to files created between 1/1/89 and 12/30/89 that contain the words "1988 taxes."

Type 4 to select File Date.

The "No" automatically changes to "Yes." Next, you will enter the dates.

Press (ENTER) and type 1/1/89

Press (ENTER) and type 12/30/89

Press (ENTER)

You also want to tell WordPerfect to look for the phrase "1988 taxes" anywhere in the document.

Type 6 to select Entire Doc.

Type 1988 taxes and press (ENTER)

Note that the cursor jumped to the bottom of the screen to option 1, Perform Search On All Files.

```
Word Search

  1 - Perform Search on        All 92 File(s)

  2 - Undo Last Search

  3 - Reset Search Conditions

  4 - File Date               No
        From (MM/DD/YY):       (All)
        To   (MM/DD/YY):       (All)

              Word Pattern(s)

  5 - First Page
  6 - Entire Doc
  7 - Document Summary
        Creation Date (e.g. Nov)
        Descriptive Name
        Subject/Account
        Author
        Typist
        Comments

Selection: 1
```

WP–28 The Word Search menu.

Press (ENTER) to perform the search.

> When WordPerfect has finished the search, the List Files screen will appear with asterisks marking each file that matches the search conditions. Use the (TAB) key to move the cursor to the marked files. You may wish to use the Look option to verify that these files contain the word "taxes."

Press Exit ((F7)), then (F7), N, N

> This takes you out of List Files and clears the edit screen.

Next, you will learn how to use the List Files key to change to a different subdirectory on your data disks in drive B.

Using the Document Summary

A common problem for people who use microcomputer word processing packages is how to keep track of all the document files. DOS file names like REPORT1.DOC are only marginally helpful when working with hundreds of files. WordPerfect provides a good method, called the Document Summary, for identifying and keeping track of files.

Clear the screen if there is text on it ((F7), N, N).

Press List Files ((F5)).

Type **B:**

Press (ENTER)

Place the cursor on WRDSRCH.EXM

Type **R** to retrieve it.

> As soon as the document is on screen you are ready to create a document summary for it.

Press Format ((SHIFT)-(F8)).

Type **3** to select the Document menu.

Type **5** to select the Summary menu.

> As shown in Figure WP–29, the Document Summary screen is displayed where you can type additional information about the document. The summary information will appear whenever you use the Look option, but will not appear when you print the file.

Type **1** to select Descriptive Filename.

Type **Letter to Mr. Naruko**

Press (ENTER)

Type **5** to select Comments.

Type **This letter was sent on July 13, 1990. Mr. Naruko's pending lawsuit is now closed.**

> Notice that the letter already appears in the Comments box. As you type, the text will move down.

```
Document Summary

        System Filename          A:\WRDSRCH.EXM

        Date of Creation         October 5, 1989

    1 - Descriptive Filename

    2 - Subject/Account

    3 - Author

    4 - Typist

    5 - Comments
   ┌──────────────────────────────────────────────────────┐
   │ July 12, 1989; Mr. Honest Naruko; 1527 Cypress; Hollywood Riviera, CA │
   │ 90273; Dear Mr. Naruko:  Regarding: 1988 taxes; After carefully reviewing │
   │ your 1988 file, we have determined that our department has made a │
   │ substantial error in your favor.  ; Please fine enclosed a check for │
   │ $15,432 and, also, please accept our humble apologies.   Sincerely,; │
   └──────────────────────────────────────────────────────┘

Selection: 0
```

WP–29 The Document Summary screen.

Press (ENTER) twice.

Press Exit ((F7)) twice.

The Edit screen is displayed again.

Press Exit ((F7)) and type Y in response to the Save document prompt.

WordPerfect supplies the old file name, WRDSRCH.EXM, for you to use as the name for the new version.

Press (ENTER) to accept the original file name, WRDSRCH.EXM

WordPerfect asks if you wish to replace the original file with the edited version that includes a document summary.

Type Y

This replaces the disk version of the file with the screen version, then clears the screen. WordPerfect then asks if you wish to exit.

Type N

Press List Files ((F5)).

Type B:

Press (ENTER)

Move the cursor to WRDSRCH.EXM

Type 6 to select the Look option.

The document summary that you just created is displayed in a box. To view the rest of the document:

Press (↓)

The document summary disappears and you see the letter. Remember, you cannot edit the file in Look mode.

Press Exit ((F7)).

The List Files menu is displayed again.

This completes Lesson 9. Clear the screen ((F7)) to do the following practice exercise. If you wish to exit WordPerfect, type (F7), **N**, **Y**

Practice

1.   Create a PRACTICE subdirectory on your work disk.

2.   Move all your practice files to this subdirectory (they should all begin with the letters PRAC).

3.   Using the Word Search function, find out which files contain the name "John Williams." How many files are there?

Lesson 10

Macros

After completing this lesson, you will be able to:

✔   Create a macro

✔   Use a macro

A **macro** is a sequence of keystrokes that is saved in a special file so that you can use it again whenever you wish, just by typing the name that you assigned to it. Anytime you find yourself repeatedly typing a sequence of commands or a word, phrase, or paragraph, you should consider creating a macro.

Creating a Macro

For the following exercise you will create a macro to print a company letterhead.

Press (CTRL)-(F10) for the Define Macro command.

You should see this prompt in the lower left corner of your screen:

`Define macro:`

Type **Opening**

Press (ENTER)

"Opening" will be the name of the macro. Like DOS file names, macro names can consist of one to eight characters. You will now see this prompt in the lower left corner of your screen:

`Description:`

Type **Opening for a letter**

Press (ENTER)

You should see this prompt in the lower left corner of your screen:

`Macro Def`

When you see this message, it means that any keys you press from now until you turn off Macro Definition will be recorded as part of the macro. If you make a mistake in typing, correct it using the editing methods you have learned.

Press (CAPS LOCK) and type:

FAROUT INDUSTRIES
224 WALNUT GROVE AVENUE
NIRVANA, CALIFORNIA 91778

Move the cursor to the F in the first line.

Press (ALT)-(F4) for Block.

Move the cursor to the 8 in the zip code.

> The three lines should be highlighted in reverse video.

Press (SHIFT)-(F6) to Center the block.

> You should see this prompt in the lower left corner of your screen:

`[Cntr?] (Y/N) No`

Type **Y**

Press (CAPS LOCK) and press (ENTER) four times.

Press (SHIFT)-(F5) for Date.

Type **1** to select the date.

Press (ENTER) twice to move the cursor down 2 lines.

Type **Dear Mr.** and press the space bar.

Press Macro ((CTRL)-(F10)) again to turn off the macro for the letterhead and salutation.

> The macro is automatically saved under the name Opening.

Press (F7), **N, N** to clear the screen.

Using Macros

Now you will learn how to use the macro. Once a macro is created, you can use, or **invoke**, it with the Invoke Macro command.

Press (ALT)-(F10) for Invoke Macro.

> This prompt should appear in the lower left corner of the screen:

`Macro:`

Type **Opening** and press (ENTER)

> The letterhead and salutation that you typed in the previous section will appear on the screen.

As you can see, creating macros for repeatedly used keystrokes can save you a lot of time and effort.

This completes Lesson 10. Clear the screen ((F7), **N, N**) to do the following practice exercise. If you wish to exit WordPerfect, type (F7), **N, Y**.

Practice

Create a macro called CLOSE that when invoked creates the following closing for a letter:

Sincerely yours,

your name

cc: A. Adams
B. Billings
C. Coleman

Lesson 11

Graphics

After completing this lesson, you will be able to:

✔ Create a graphics line

✔ Insert a graphics image in your document

WordPerfect can combine text and graphics into a single document. By combining graphics, charts, and other images with text, you can make your documents look more professional.

In this lesson, you will create the graphics document shown in Figure WP–30. To create this document, you will need the WordPerfect Graphics disk.

To begin, first retrieve LESSON1 from your work disk.

Creating a Graphics Line

First, you will insert a graphics line at the top of the document.

Press (ENTER) four times.

This moves the first line of the document down to line 5.

Press ⬆ twice.

This moves the cursor up to line 3.

Press (ALT)-(F9) for the Graphics command.

You should see this prompt at the bottom of your screen:

`1 Figure; 2 Table; 3 Text Box; 4 User-Defined Box; 5 Line: 0`

Type **5** to select Line.

You should see this prompt in the lower left corner of your screen:

`1 Horizontal Line; 2 Vertical Line: 0`

Type **1** to select Horizontal Line.

As shown in Figure WP–31, the Line menu appears on the screen.

Type **3** to select Width of Line.

WordPerfect 5 is one of the most powerful word processing programs available for IBM microcomputers and their compatibles. Over the years, WordPerfect has earned lavish and well-deserved praise, and is now widely acclaimed as one of the best word processing packages on the market.

This tutorial provides step by step instructions on how to use WordPerfect commands quickly and easily to create your reports, letters, and documents. These commands are all very basic to using WordPerfect, so you might consider doing the tutorial twice to make sure you can remember them without looking anything up.

W
P

WP-30 A document with graphics.

Type .1 and press (ENTER)

Press (ENTER) again to return to the Edit menu.

The graphics line you just created does not appear on the screen—you must either print or view the document from the Print menu to see it. You will now create a second line at the bottom of the document.

Move the cursor to the bottom of the document.

Press (ENTER) three times.

```
Graphics: Horizontal Line

    1 - Horizontal Position          Left & Right

    2 - Length of Line

    3 - Width of Line                0.01"

    4 - Gray Shading (% of black)    100%












Selection: 0
```

WP-31 The Graphics Line menu.

Press (ALT)-(F9) for Graphics.

Type **5** to select Line.

Type **1** to select Horizontal Line.

Type **3** to select Width of Line.

Type **.1** and press (ENTER)

Press (ENTER) again to return to the Edit screen.

Combining Text and Graphics

Now you will put a graphics image in the document.

Move the cursor to the W of the word "WordPerfect" at the beginning of the first paragraph.

Press (ALT)-(F9) for Graphics.

Type **1** to select Figure.

> You should see this prompt at the bottom of your screen:

```
Figure: 1 Create; 2 Edit; 3 New Number; 4 Options: 0
```

Type **1** to select Create.

> As shown in Figure WP–32, the figure menu appears on your screen.

Take your work disk out of drive B and insert the WordPerfect Graphics disk.

Type **1** to select Filename.

Type **B:BOOK.WPG** and press (ENTER)

> A prompt in the lower left corner should say that WordPerfect is loading the file. If the prompt says, "Error, file not found," you do not have the Graphics disk loaded correctly, or the file is missing from the disk. Use List Files to find another file that has the extension WPG and use this file instead.

```
Definition: Figure

    1 - Filename

    2 - Caption

    3 - Type                    Paragraph

    4 - Vertical Position       0"

    5 - Horizontal Position     Right

    6 - Size                    3.25" wide x 3.25" (high)

    7 - Wrap Text Around Box     Yes

    8 - Edit




Selection: 0
```

WP–32 The Figure menu.

Press (F7) to exit the menu and return to the edit screen.

Scroll down through the document.

Note that as you scroll, the document reformats around the graphic.

You have now combined a graphics image with text. To check your work, you can use the View option in the Print menu. If you are satisfied, print it.

This completes Lesson 11. You can do the following practice exercise without clearing the screen. If you wish to exit WordPerfect, type (F7), **N**, **Y**.

Practice

Scroll to the top of the LESSON1 document. Press (ALT)-(F9) and experiment with the fourth selection: Options. See how changing the border style affects the graphic. Be aware, however, that for the Figure options to affect a graphic image, you must invoke options *before* the actual Figure code.

KEY WORDS

Block	Format code	Merge	Tab
Cursor	Hanging indent	Primary file	Typeover mode
Field	Header	Record	Variable data
File management	Insert mode	Search string	Word wrap
Footer	Invoke	Secondary file	
Format	Macro	Status line	

REVIEW QUESTIONS

1. Why is it important to save your work to disk every few minutes?
2. What can you do if you delete text by mistake and want to restore it?
3. Why must you be careful when conducting a Word Search for a word like "the"?
4. When would you use the merge function?
5. Why is it important to clear the screen before retrieving a document?
6. Why is it sometimes desirable to view a document using the View option?

A COMPARISON OF SELECTED COMMANDS

Command	WordPerfect 5.0	WordPerfect 4.2
Format		
Margins	(SHIFT)-(F8), **1, 7**	(SHIFT)-(F8), **3**
Line spacing	(SHIFT)-(F8), **1, 6**	(SHIFT)-(F8), **4**
Page format	(SHIFT)-(F8), **2**	(ALT)-(F8)
Tabs		
Tab set	(SHIFT)-(F8), **1, 8**	(SHIFT)-(F8), **2**
Move		
Move block	(ALT)-(F4), (CTRL)-(F4), **1, 1**, (ENTER)	(ALT)-(F4), (CTRL)-(F4), **1**, (CTRL)-(F4), **5**
Merge		
Merge codes	(SHIFT)-(F9)	(ALT)-(F9)
E code	(SHIFT)-(F9), E	(SHIFT)-(F9)

Using Lotus 1–2–3

Hardware needed:

- ✔ IBM PC, IBM PS/2, or IBM-compatible microcomputer
- ✔ Two floppy disk drives, or one floppy disk drive and a hard drive

Software needed:

- ✔ DOS 2.01 or later version
- ✔ A blank, formatted disk
- ✔ Lotus 1-2-3 version 2.01 or later

When you have completed this tutorial, you will be able to:

- ✔ Move around a spreadsheet
- ✔ Identify the parts of a spreadsheet
- ✔ Enter text and data into a spreadsheet
- ✔ Use the Help facility
- ✔ Use formulas and functions for calculations
- ✔ Copy data from one part of a spreadsheet to another
- ✔ Change the appearance of a spreadsheet by changing column widths, inserting and deleting rows and columns, and underlining labels
- ✔ Use relative and absolute cell addressing
- ✔ Save and print a spreadsheet

Lotus 1–2–3 Tutorial

Tutorial Outline

What Is Lotus 1-2-3?

This tutorial is a series of six lessons that will introduce you to the use of Lotus 1-2-3, a very popular electronic spreadsheet package. An electronic spreadsheet is an automated version of the ledgers used by accountants. Packages like Lotus 1-2-3 are very powerful tools, allowing instantaneous calculation of numerical data.

This tutorial assumes you have completed the DOS tutorial. Before beginning, it may be helpful for you to review the section on spreadsheets found in the text. Note: In this tutorial the terms spreadsheet and worksheet are used synonymously.

To help lead you through the tutorial, all entries you are to type in are printed in bold type. To improve the appearance of alphabetic data, you can keep the (CAPS LOCK) key locked in uppercase, unless you specifically want lowercase text. If you press this key, the word "CAPS" will be highlighted in reverse video at the bottom of the screen.

Loading Lotus

If your computer has a hard-disk drive, then it is assumed that the Lotus program has been installed onto the drive. Your instructor or lab assistant will provide the information you need to load Lotus from a hard drive.

WARNING

If you are using a computer with a hard drive, you must keep in mind that when you are saving or retrieving the files you have created, the default on Lotus 1-2-3 will save them to the hard disk, that is, the C drive. You do not want to do this, because you want to save your files to your work disk so that you can keep them with you and reuse them regardless of which computer you may use in other tutorial lessons. Therefore, remember to save your files to the diskette in the floppy drive. You can do this by using the prefix "B:". When retrieving your files, you must look on the B drive. Even if your hard disk computer has only one floppy drive, you may still call it B.

If your computer does not have a hard-disk drive, follow these instructions for loading Lotus:

Place the DOS disk in drive A and turn on the computer.

If you are unsure how to turn on your system, you should review the "Using DOS" tutorial for instructions.

Enter the date and time as directed (unless you have a battery-operated calendar-clock).

Remove the DOS disk from drive A.

Insert the Lotus system disk into drive A, and your blank, formatted disk into drive B.

This blank disk will be used to store the spreadsheets that you create in this tutorial. We will refer to it as your work disk.

Type **lotus**

Press (ENTER)

This displays the Lotus Access System screen. This screen allows you to select different parts of the Lotus package. For example, the PrintGraph option would be used to print a graph. You need to select 1-2-3, the spreadsheet program. 1-2-3 is highlighted, so to choose it,

Press (ENTER)

The Lotus 1-2-3 program is loaded and the spreadsheet appears on your monitor.

A short-cut method of loading the spreadsheet program, without the need for using the Lotus Access system screen, is to type "123" instead of "Lotus."

Lesson 1

Introduction to the Lotus Spreadsheet

After completing this lesson, you will be able to:

✔ Identify the components of a spreadsheet

✔ Move the pointer around the spreadsheet

✔ Access the Help facility

The Components of a Spreadsheet

Your monitor displays a part of the spreadsheet (Figure SS–1). Note that the spreadsheet consists of a series of **columns** and **rows**. The columns are labelled A,B,C..., and the rows are labelled 1,2,3.... The actual spreadsheet is much larger than what can be displayed on your monitor at any one time, and consists of 256 columns and 8192 rows. After column Z come columns AA...AZ, BA...BZ, and so on through IA...IV. Later you will learn how to bring these other rows and columns into view on your screen.

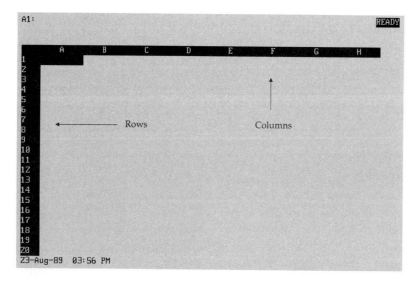

Figure SS–1

Key	Moves pointer or cursor
→ or ←	One cell to the right or left
↑ or ↓	One cell up or down
HOME	To cell A1
PGUP or PGDN	Up or down one screen
TAB	Right one screen
SHIFT-TAB	Left one screen
F5 and cell location	"Goto" specified cell

Table SS–1 Pointer Movement in a Lotus 1–2–3 Spreadsheet.

Each spreadsheet location where data is entered is called a **cell**. It is identified as the intersection of a column and a row. A1, for example, is where column A and row 1 intersect and is the first cell location.

When the spreadsheet is first displayed, the cursor, or **pointer**, highlights the cell that will receive the data that is typed in. Initially, cell location A1 is highlighted, but by using the cursor arrows, you can move the pointer right, left, up, and down throughout the spreadsheet.

The top line of the spreadsheet, called a **status line**, displays information about the spreadsheet. Currently it displays in the upper left-hand corner the cell where the pointer is located, A1. This is called the **active cell**. In the upper right-hand corner of the status line the word "READY" is displayed. This means that you are in the Ready mode and the spreadsheet is waiting for you to type in data or issue an instruction. The word "READY" is called the **mode indicator**.

The status line will show other information as data is entered in the spreadsheet. The other uses of the status line will be discussed as you work through this tutorial.

Pointer Movement

To enter data into the worksheet, you first move the pointer to the desired cell using the cursor arrow keys or any of the other keys shown in Table SS–1.

To see how the pointer moves around the spreadsheet, complete the following (begin with the pointer at A1):

Press →

This moves the pointer to B1 from A1.

Press →

This moves the pointer to C1 from B1.

Press ↓

This moves the pointer to C2 from C1.

Press PGDN

This moves the pointer to C22 from C2. PGDN moves the pointer 20 rows down.

Figure SS–2

Notice that the screen has scrolled down (Figure SS–2).

Press (F5)

This brings up the **Goto** prompt. The (F5) key allows movement anywhere in the worksheet. You enter the precise cell location you wish to "go to" after pressing (F5).

Type **E12**

This enters E12 as the cell to go to.

Press (ENTER)

This moves the pointer to E12.

Press (HOME)

This moves the pointer back to A1.

Note that, as you move around the worksheet, the status line indicates the cell location of the active cell.

The Help Facility

Lotus provides a **Help facility** in the form of a series of screens that help guide you through the use of the program. To access the Help facility, you press the (F1) key.

Press (F1)

A Help screen is displayed as shown in Figure SS–3. Note that the mode indicator changed to "HELP." This Help screen gives you information about the Ready mode. The Lotus Help facility is context sensitive. That is, the Help screen that appears after pressing (F1) is relevant to what you are doing. For example, if you were in the Print menu and you pressed (F1), the Help screen that appeared would provide information on printing a worksheet.

Near the bottom of the screen are options, such as Help Index and How to Use Help, that lead you through the Help facility. To select an option, use the (↓) key to move the pointer to it and then press the (ENTER) key.

```
A1:                                                                    HELP

─────────────────────────────────────────────────────────────────────────
READY Mode

The mode indicator, READY, in the upper right corner of the screen means you
can select a command or type a cell entry.  The first key you press
determines your action:

Formula or Number:    Type a digit (0..9) or one of the characters
                      +, -, ., (, @, #, or $.
Label:                Type any character except those that begin a
                      formula or number.  Start with a label-prefix character to
                      create a label of a particular type: ' for left-aligned,
                      " for  right-aligned, ^ for centered, or \ for repeating.
Command:              Type /.
Special Function:     Press a special key.

To learn more about this Help facility, press [END], then [RETURN].
─────────────────────────────────────────────────────────────────────────
Cell Entries          Mode Indicators
Help Index            How to Use Help

23-Aug-89  04:00 PM
```

Move the pointer to How to Use Help

Press (ENTER)

> A screen is displayed that gives you detailed information about how to
> use the Help facility. After reading the screen, you can leave the Help
> facility and return to the worksheet by pressing the (ESC) key.

Press (ESC)

Lesson 2

Creating, Saving, Retrieving, and Printing Worksheets

After completing this lesson, you will be able to:

✔ Distinguish between label and value entries

✔ Enter labels and values

✔ Correct errors in cell entries

✔ Enter formulas

✔ Use the menu system and commands

✔ Save, retrieve, and print worksheets

Entering Labels

Most worksheets are composed of headings or titles, called **labels**, and
numeric data, called **values**. See Figure SS–4 for an illustration. Labels must
begin with an alphabetic character. Values must begin with a number (0–9),
an arithmetic operator such as + or –, or a nontext character such as @ or $.
When you type a label entry, it will be left justified in a cell. When you type

a value (number) it is right justified in a cell. If you want to enter a number as a label item (for example, a date), type a single quotation mark (') as the first character of the entry so that the computer recognizes it as a label and left justifies it. A double quotation mark (") can also be used; this will right justify the label.

Complete the following to duplicate the worksheet in Figure SS–4. With the pointer at A1:

Type **ASSETS**

This enters the label ASSETS into A1.

Note: If you make a mistake in typing, simply move back to the error using the (BACKSPACE) key, and retype the label.

Press → three times.

This moves the pointer to D1.

Type your name.

This enters your name in D1.

Press ↓, ←, ←

This moves the pointer to B2.

Type **ASSET ANALYSIS REPORT**

Press (ENTER)

This enters the heading ASSET ANALYSIS REPORT in B2. Notice that this heading is longer than 9 characters, which is the standard cell width. Label entries longer than the cell width will automatically display in adjacent cells, as long as the adjacent cells are empty. But numeric data entries must fit the cell width. If 9 characters is insufficient for a cell width, it can be changed; we will show you how later.

Press ↓ twice.

This moves the pointer to B4.

Type **"1990**

Press ⟶

> This will enter 1990 as a label and move the pointer to C4. Note that we preface 1990 with a double quote mark so that the computer knows it is a label and not a numeric value. Also, 1990 will be right justified in the cell.

Type **"1991**

Press ⟶

> This will enter 1991 as a label and move the pointer to D4.

Type **"$INCR/**

Press ⟶

> This enters the label $INCR and moves the pointer to E4. Note, again, that the double quote mark causes the entry to be right justified within the cell.

Type **"%INCR/**

Press ⟓

> This enters the label and moves the pointer to E5.

Type **DECR**

Press ⟵

> This enters the label and moves the pointer to D5.

Type **DECR**

Press (ENTER)

> This enters the label.

Press ⟑

Press ⟵ three times.

> This moves the pointer to A4.

Type **ASSETS**

Press (ENTER)

> This enters ASSETS into A4.

You have completed entering all the labels across the top of the worksheet. Remember, labels that begin with a numeric character (1990, %INCR) must be prefixed by a quote mark so the computer will treat them as labels and not as numeric values. In this example we have used a double quote as a prefix. The result is to right justify the label in the cell.

Now complete the rest of the label entries, in column A, on your own. Remember, move the pointer, type the entry, and press (ENTER) or a pointer movement key.

Correcting Errors in Cell Entries

You can make corrections or changes to cell entries while entering data into a cell, or after entering it. We have already noted one way of correcting an error while making an entry in a cell; that is, before you press the (ENTER) key or move to another cell, use the (BACKSPACE) key to move back and erase one character at a time.

Alternatively, if you wanted to erase everything in a cell before moving to another cell, the (ESC) key clears all data that has been typed.

A third method of correction while in a cell uses the Delete ((DEL)) key. The (←) and (→) keys can be used to move to any character within the entry. Then the (DEL) key can be used to delete one or more characters at the cursor point.

Finally, characters can be inserted in a cell by pressing the Insert ((INS)) key and then typing the desired characters. Pressing (INS) again will turn the Insert mode off. Characters can then be entered that overwrite existing characters.

If an entry has been made in a cell and the (ENTER) or an arrow key has been pressed, changes can be made in two ways: First, simply returning to a cell and entering new data will erase any previous entry in the cell.

Alternatively, you can edit the entry with the (F2) key. Highlighting the cell and pressing (F2) makes the contents of the highlighted cell available for editing. This process is useful when the contents of the cell are relatively complex and only minor changes are needed; that is, you do not want to re-enter the entire cell contents.

Entering Values

Figure SS–5 shows the values entered into the worksheet. Duplicate these entries as follows:

Press (F5)

Type **B6**

Press (ENTER)

This brings up the Goto prompt, specifies B6 as the cell to go to, and moves the pointer to B6.

Type **15000**

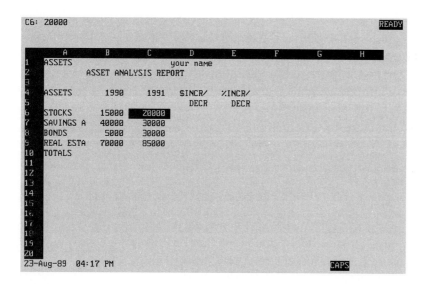

Figure SS–5

Press ⬇

> This will enter 15000 into B6 and move the pointer to B7.

Type **40000**

Press (ENTER)

> This will enter 40000 into B7.

Notice that the SAVINGS ACCOUNT entry is shortened, or **truncated**. This is because the cell width is 9 and will display only 9 characters if there is an entry in the adjacent (to the right) cell. Later you will learn how to increase the cell (column) width so that the entire heading is displayed. Also, notice that numeric entries are right justified in the cells.

> Now complete the other value entries on your own.

Entering Formulas

A spreadsheet would have limited value if all you could do was enter labels and numbers. **Formulas** allow you to reuse a spreadsheet, perform what-if analysis, and so on. In this section you will create the formulas required to compute the totals of investments. You are going to create a formula that will display the total of the contents of cells B6, B7, B8, and B9 in cell B10. Since this is a formula to sum the contents of several cells, it will be written +B6+B7+B8+B9.

Move the pointer to cell B10.

Type **+B6+B7+B8+B9**

Press (ENTER)

> This specifies the formula and enters it into cell location B10.

> Notice the immediate response. The worksheet displays 130000 and the status line shows the formula (Figure SS–6).

Now move the pointer to C10 and enter the formula that will sum the contents of cells C6, C7, C8, and C9.

Figure SS–6

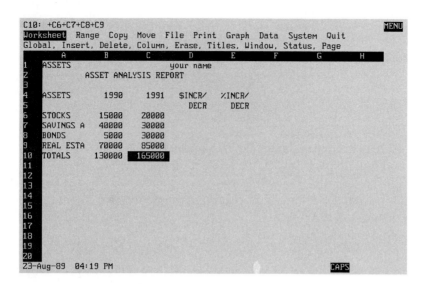

Figure SS–7

In formulas, any arithmetic operator can be used; that is, +, –, *, or /. But the formula must always begin with a +.

Using the Menu System and Commands

You have thus far learned how to enter labels, numbers, and formulas. Lotus also enables you to perform commands such as saving spreadsheets and later retrieving them. All commands are accessed by using the slash (/) key, which displays a main menu. When you first press the / key, two lines appear near the top of the spreadsheet. The first line (main menu) has a list of the basic commands, and the second line displays the subcommands or options available from the highlighted command. Figure SS–7 shows these lines.

Initially the Worksheet command is highlighted, and the options listed on the subcommand line refer to it. To select a different command, press the first letter of the command. Another way to select a command is to use the ⊖ and ⊙ arrow keys to highlight the desired command and then press (ENTER). The options listed change depending on which command is highlighted. For example, selecting the File command by pressing /F will provide the following options that then appear on line 1:

    Retrieve Save Combine Xtract Erase List Import Directory

That is, once a command is selected, the subcommand line moves to line 1 and the highlighted subcommand is explained on line 2.

Subcommands or options are selected in a similar way, by pressing the first letter of the option, or by using the arrow keys to highlight it and then pressing (ENTER).

To leave the command mode and return to the worksheet, press (ESC). Each time you press (ESC) you will return to a higher level command until you reach the main menu. Pressing (ESC) at that point will return you to the worksheet.

Using the Erase option from the Range command to erase an entry and leave the cell blank:

Action	Result
Move the pointer to the cell	
Press /	Displays the main menu
Press R	Selects the Range command
Press E	Selects the Erase option (Alternatively you could highlight the Erase option and press the (ENTER) key)
Press (ENTER)	Executes the command.

Using the Quit command to exit the Lotus program:

Action	Result
Press /	Displays the main menu
Press Q	Selects the Quit command
Press Y	Indicates Yes to confirm that you want to exit the Lotus program

The two examples in Table SS–2 show how this tutorial would direct you to use the menu system to execute commands. These are for reference only, so do not complete these steps at this time.

Table SS–2 Using the Menu System to Execute Commands

Saving and Retrieving Worksheets

The worksheet you have created exists only in your computer's temporary memory (RAM). Since RAM memory disappears as soon as the computer is turned off, it is essential that you save your worksheet to a disk. To save your worksheet onto your work disk, you will use the Save command. Make sure your data disk is in drive B.

Press /

This displays the main menu.

Press F (or highlight the File command by pressing (→) 4 times and then pressing (ENTER))

This selects the File command.

Press S

This selects the Save option.

Near the top of the screen is the prompt, "Enter save file name:" (Figure SS–8). Note: If A: or C: appears after the prompt, press the (ESC) key to clear it.

Type B:ASSETS2B

This specifies the file name and the drive (B) on which it should be saved.

Press (ENTER)

This saves the worksheet.

Figure SS–8

When you save a worksheet, Lotus automatically adds the file extension
.WK1 to the file name. This makes it easier to identify all spreadsheet or
worksheet files created by Lotus.

Now clear the worksheet from the screen with the Erase option.

Press /

This displays the main menu with all the commands.

Press **W**

This selects the Worksheet command.

Press **E**

This selects the Erase option. A prompt appears to verify that you want
to erase the entire worksheet. Your choices are Yes and No.

Press **Y**

This specifies Yes, and the worksheet is erased from the screen.

Now you will retrieve the worksheet from your disk. To load the ASSETS2B
data file back into storage, select the Retrieve command as follows:

Press /

Press **F**

This displays the main menu and selects the File command.

Press **R**

This selects the Retrieve option and a prompt (Figure SS–9) is displayed
asking for the name of the file to retrieve. Note: If A: or C: appears after
the prompt, press the (ESC) key to clear it.

Type **ASSETS2B**

Press (ENTER)

This specifies the file name and retrieves the worksheet. Note that even
though the ASSETS2B file has a .WK1 extension, you need not specify it
here.

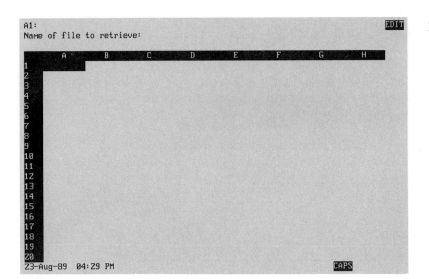

Printing a Worksheet

The Print command is used to print a worksheet. Before continuing, make sure that your computer is hooked up to a printer, that the printer is ready, and that the paper is aligned. Also, we assume that Lotus has been installed for use with your specific type of printer. Complete the following to print the ASSETS2B worksheet.

Press /

This displays the main menu.

Press P

This selects the Print command.

Press P

This selects the Printer option. This means that the output will be sent directly to the printer, rather than to a disk.

Press R

This selects the Range option. A prompt appears asking for the Print range, that is, that area of the spreadsheet you want to print. You specify a **range** (in this case a rectangle) by typing the upper left cell location, two periods, and the lower right cell location.

Type A1..E10

Press (ENTER)

This specifies the range to print.

Press A

This selects the Align option that tells the program that the paper is correctly positioned in the printer.

Press G

This selects the Go option, and the worksheet is printed.

Press P

This advances the paper to the top of the next page.

Press Q

This returns you to the worksheet.

This completes Lesson 2. If your practice time is up, you can exit the program and retrieve the worksheet later. To exit Lotus,

Press /

Press Q

This selects the Quit command from the main menu.

Press Y

Lesson 3

Changing Column Widths, Copying Data, and Using Functions

After completing this lesson, you will be able to:

✔ Adjust column widths

✔ Use the Copy command to copy formulas

✔ Understand the concept of relative addressing

✔ Understand the concept of functions

✔ Use the SUM and AVG functions

Adjusting Column Widths

In the last lesson you discovered that entering values in column B caused some of the labels in column A to be truncated. In this exercise you will increase the width of column A so that labels can be longer than 9 characters. It is fairly common to need to increase the width of column A since it most often contains labels. If the ASSETS2B worksheet is not already on your screen, retrieve it by pressing \FR and typing the file name. You will first move the pointer to column A, the column to be widened.

Press (HOME)

Press /

This moves the pointer to A1 and displays the main menu.

Press W

Press C

This selects the Worksheet command and then the Column option. The following options are displayed:

```
Set-Width Reset-Width Hide Display
```

Press S

```
A1: [W18] 'ASSETS                                              READY

          A            B       C       D       E     F     G
1   ASSETS                                your name
2                    ASSET ANALYSIS REPORT
3
4   ASSETS                 1990    1991   $INCR/  %INCR/
5                                         DECR    DECR
6   STOCKS                15000   20000
7   SAVINGS ACCOUNTS      40000   30000
8   BONDS                  5000   30000
9   REAL ESTATE           70000   85000
10  TOTALS               130000  165000
11
12
13
14
15
16
17
18
19
20
23-Aug-89  04:31 PM                                    CAPS
```

This selects the Set-Width command. A prompt appears asking you to enter the number of spaces you want the new column width to be.

Type **18**

Press ENTER

This changes the column width to 18. Column A is now wide enough to display the labels (Figure SS–10).

Using the Copy Command

In this section you will use the Copy command to copy a formula from one cell into a range of cells. As you copy a formula, the cell references change to reflect the new locations. That is, if the formula +B6+C6 is copied from A6 to A7, the formula at A7 is adjusted to read +B7+C7. This is called **relative cell addressing** and is performed automatically when formulas are copied.

In this exercise, you will enter into cell D6 the formula: +C6–B6 (this reflects the dollar amount of the increase or decrease from 1990 to 1991). Then you will copy this formula into cell locations D7, D8, D9, and D10. A single Copy command can be used which will make the proper row adjustments. That is, when this formula is copied down column D, the formula changes to +C7–B7, +C8–B8, and so on.

Complete the following to enter and copy the formulas for columns D and E. You will need to specify where to copy from and where to copy to.

Move the pointer to D6.

Type **+C6–B6**

Press ENTER

This specifies the formula and enters it into D6.

Press /

This displays the main menu.

Press **C**

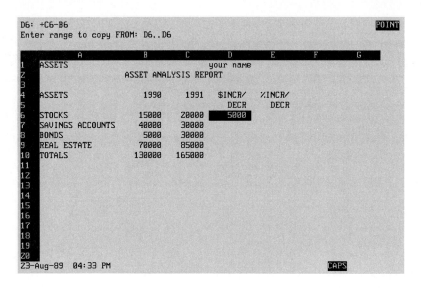

This selects the Copy command. A prompt appears at the top of the spreadsheet asking for the range to copy FROM (Figure SS–11). This should contain the cell location(s) that you want to copy. The default is cell location D6, because the pointer is located at D6. This will be displayed as the range D6..D6 at the top of the spreadsheet.

Press (ENTER)

This accepts D6 as the cell to copy from.

A prompt then appears at the top of the spreadsheet asking for the range to copy TO. Unless you moved the cursor, this, too, will display D6..D6. You can change this range to include D7 through D10 by typing D7..D10. Alternatively, you could use the pointer to specify the range to copy to. To specify a range of cells for any operation, move the pointer to the beginning cell location, press . (period), and then move the pointer to the ending cell location. The range selected will be highlighted.

Press ⬇

This moves the pointer to D7.

Type .

This marks, or anchors, the beginning of the cell range at D7.

Press ⬇ three times.

This moves the pointer to D10 and completes the range of cells to copy to. The range will be highlighted on the screen. D7..D10 will appear on the "copy TO" line at the top of the spreadsheet.

Press (ENTER)

This completes the copy.

To obtain the percent of increase (or decrease) in 1990, we divide the dollar increase (or decrease) by the corresponding 1991 values.

Move pointer to E6.

Type +D6/B6

Press (ENTER)

This enters the formula for percent of increase or decrease of stocks from 1990 to 1991.

Use the Copy command to copy the %INCR/DECR formula to the other column E entries.

Using Functions

In this section you will add the same cells you did previously, but this time you will use the built-in functions of Lotus. **Functions** allow you to perform a wide range of mathematical calculations such as summing a column of values or finding the average of a group of values.

Functions such as summation operate on ranges, where a range is a group of cells. When using a function, you will need to specify the range that will be used. For example, if you want to add the values in cells C6, C7, C8, and C9, the range would be (C6..C9). You can specify a range for a row, column, or block, where a block is a contiguous rectangle of columns and rows that make up a unit. The way to specify a range is to type a parenthesis, the first cell location, one or two periods, the last cell location, and another parenthesis. Alternatively, you can specify a range by using the pointer to highlight the range, as described in the previous section.

The format for a function is:

@function name (range)

For example, @SUM(C6..C9) would add the values in cells C6 through C9 and place the result in the cell where the pointer is located. This is the same as entering +C6+C7+C8+C9. @SUM is easier to enter where a long range of cells needs to be specified. Complete the following to enter the SUM function into C10.

Move the pointer to C10.

Type **@SUM(C6..C9)**

This specifies the SUM function (Figure SS–12).

```
C10: +C6+C7+C8+C9                                          VALUE
@SUM(C6..C9)

        A              B        C        D        E      F      G
1   ASSETS                            your name
2                  ASSET ANALYSIS REPORT
3
4   ASSETS                1990     1991    $INCR/  %INCR/
5                                          DECR    DECR
6   STOCKS            15000    20000     5000 0.333333
7   SAVINGS ACCOUNTS  40000    30000   -10000    -0.25
8   BONDS              5000    30000    25000       5
9   REAL ESTATE       70000    85000    15000 0.214285
10  TOTALS           130000   165000    35000 0.269230
11
12
13
14
15
16
17
18
19
20
23-Aug-89   04:37 PM                               CAPS
```

Figure SS–12

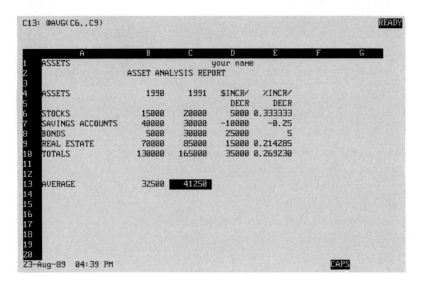

Press (ENTER)

> This enters the SUM function into C10 and displays the results.

Next, use the pointing process to enter a SUM function into cell B10.

Press (←)

> This moves the pointer to B11.

Type @SUM(

> This begins the @SUM function.

Press (↑) four times.

> This moves the pointer to B6, which is the beginning of the range.

Press . (period).

> This anchors the beginning of the range (B6).

Press (↓) three times.

> This moves pointer to B9. Notice how the range is highlighted as you press the (↓) key.

Type)

Press (ENTER)

> This closes the parentheses and completes the entry. Alternatively, you could have typed @SUM(B6..B9).

You will now use the AVG (average) function to place the average of cell locations B6 through B9 and C6 through C9 into cells B13 and C13 respectively (Figure SS–13).

Move the pointer to A13.

Type AVERAGE

Move pointer to B13.

Type @AVG(B6..B9)

Press (ENTER)

This enters the AVG function into cell B13 and displays the result.

Copy the function in cell B13 to cell C13.

Lotus provides other commonly used functions such as @MIN (lowest number in a range), @MAX (highest number in a range), and @COUNT (number of numbers in a range) as well as a wide variety of other functions.

This completes Lesson 3. If your practice time is up, save this worksheet (/FS) and then use the Quit command to exit the program.

Lesson 4

Enhancing Spreadsheet Appearance

After completing this lesson, you will be able to:

✔ Use the Global Column-Width command

✔ Display values as currency or percentages

✔ Use the Insert and Delete commands to add and delete rows

✔ Use the repeating character function to enter dashed lines

Formatting Cells

You have created an electronic spreadsheet that functions properly but does not look as neat as you might like. To make the spreadsheet more readable, you could display the dollar amounts with dollar signs, decimal points, and commas. You could also display the values in column E as actual percentages, as shown in Figure SS–14. You will use the Format command to duplicate Figure SS–14. First, however, you will widen all of the columns, using the Global Column-Width command, so that they can accommodate

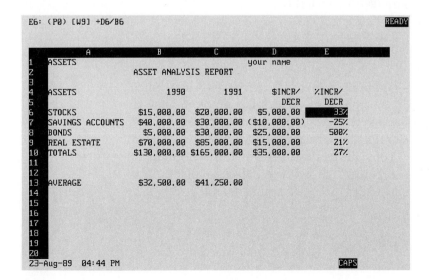

Figure SS–14

the extra characters (such as $) which will be added when the spreadsheet is reformatted. Retrieve the ASSETS2B worksheet if it is not already on your screen.

Press /

Press **W**

> This displays the main menu and selects the Worksheet command.

Press **G**

Press **C**

> This selects the Global submenu and then selects the Column-Width option. A prompt appears asking you to enter the number of spaces of the new column width.

Type **12**

Press (ENTER)

> This specifies 12 as the column width and widens all columns to 12 characters, except column A, which was previously widened to 18 characters.

Next you will format the values on the entire spreadsheet to display a dollar sign ($) and two decimal places using the Currency format option.

Press /

Press **W**

> This displays the main menu and selects the Worksheet command.

Press **G**

Press **F**

> This selects the Global submenu and selects the Format option.

Press **C**

> This specifies Currency (dollars and cents) as the format option, and a prompt appears asking for the number of decimal places. Two is the default value. You can press (ENTER) to select two.

Press (ENTER)

> This specifies two as the number of decimal places and completes the formatting process.

/ W G F C (ENTER) reformats all numeric values into currency format. Since most of the numeric values in the cells represent dollar amounts, it was logical to use the Global command to change all cells to currency format. But the values in column E need to be displayed as percentages, so you will need to reformat just this column. You will use the Percent format option to display the values in column E as percentages with zero decimal places. You will start by reducing column E's width to 9, the original default width.

Move the pointer to E6.

Press /

Press **W**

This displays the main menu and selects Worksheet command.

Press **C**

Press **S**

This selects the Column submenu and selects the Set-Width option.

Type **9**

Press (ENTER)

This specifies 9 as the column width and changes column E to this width.

Now use the Percent command to format the values in column E.

Press **/**

Press **R**

This displays the main menu and selects the Range command.

Press **F**

This selects the Format submenu.

Press **P**

This selects the Percent option. A prompt appears asking for the number of decimal places.

Type **0**

Press (ENTER)

This specifies zero decimal places. A prompt appears asking for the range to format. E6 is displayed because it is where the pointer is located.

Press ⊙ four times.

This moves the pointer to E10 to complete the range. Alternatively, you could type E6..E10.

Press (ENTER)

This displays the values in E6 through E10 as percents.

Inserting and Deleting Rows

Your spreadsheet is looking much better, but you might like to add some blank rows and dashed lines to improve the appearance. Notice the dashed lines in row 6 and row 11 in Figure SS–15. If you review Figure SS–14, you will see that a blank row must be added at row 6 to accommodate the dashed line. In this section of the exercise you will use the Insert and Delete commands to add and delete rows. Blank rows are inserted immediately above the cell where the pointer is located. Blank columns can also be inserted and would appear immediately to the left of the pointer location.

After insertions or deletions, the spreadsheet program automatically makes adjustments to the columns and rows used in formulas so that recalculations are not necessary. That is, if E6 contained the formula +D6/B6 and we add a row at line 6, then E7 would now contain the formula +D7/B7. Adjustments of this kind are made automatically by the Lotus package.

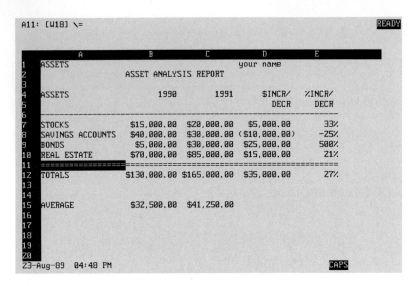

Start by using the Insert command to add a blank row at row 6. Make sure the pointer is at E6.

Press /

Press **W**

This displays the main menu and then selects the Worksheet command.

Press **I**

Press **R**

This selects the Insert submenu and then selects the Row option. A prompt appears asking for the row insert range. The default is E6 because the pointer is on row E6.

Press (ENTER)

This specifies row 6 and inserts a blank row.

Now use the same process to insert a blank row at row 11.

When using the Delete command, data in the columns or rows where the pointer is located will be deleted. To be safe, you may want to save the worksheet before using the Delete command. The way to delete a row or column (do not carry these steps out at this time) is to bring up the main menu and select the Worksheet command. Then select the Delete submenu and specify either row or column. Then indicate which row or column to delete.

Entering Dashed Lines

In this section you will create dashed lines by using the **repeating character** function. A single dashed line is created by filling a cell with the minus sign (–); it is then copied across the worksheet to appear as an underline. The minus sign is made to repeat across the cell by being prefaced with a backslash (\). (Note: This is not the same character as the slash (/) used to display the main menu.) If you type a backslash followed by another character, that character will repeat to fill the cell. Use this function to create the dashed lines as follows:

Move the pointer to cell A6.

Type \–

Press (ENTER)

> This specifies that – (minus sign) will be a repeating character and will fill cell A6 with dashes.

Now use the Copy command to copy the dashes in A6 to cells B6 through E6:

Press /

Press C

> This displays the main menu and selects the Copy command. A prompt appears asking for the range to copy from. If the pointer is still at A6,

Press (ENTER)

> This specifies the "copy from" range as A6. A prompt appears asking for the range to copy to.

Type B6..E6

Press (ENTER)

> This specifies the "copy to" range as B6 through E6 and copies the dashes to this range of cells. Alternatively, you could move the pointer to B6, anchor it by pressing the period, then use the pointer to move from B6 to E6. This would highlight the "copy to" range as B6..E6.

Now use the repeating character function to enter a double dashed line, or equal sign (=), in row 11.

When done save the worksheet to your work disk under the file name B:ASSETS2C. Then clear the worksheet.

This completes Lesson 4. If your practice time is up, you can exit the program by using the Quit command.

Lesson 5

Changing Print Default Settings and Creating Headers

After completing this lesson, you will be able to:

✔ Change printer margin settings

✔ Create headers that will print on all pages

✔ Print a worksheet so that formulas are displayed

Changing Margin Settings

The Print command prints a worksheet using the default, or built-in, setting in Lotus. Before printing you can change default settings, such as those for margins. In this lesson you will change the top, bottom, left, and right margins and you will create a header. Begin by retrieving the ASSETS2C worksheet. Then change the top margin from the standard 2 lines to 9 as follows:

Press /

Press **P**

> This displays the main menu and selects the Print command.

Press **P**

> This selects the Printer submenu.

Press **O**

> This specifies Options.

Press **M**

> This selects Margins, and the options Left, Right, Top, and Bottom appear on the screen.

Press **T**

> This selects Top margin, and the following prompt appears:

`Enter Top Margin (0..32): 2.`

Type **9**

Press (ENTER)

> This changes the top margin from 2 lines to 9 lines.

Use the same procedure to do the following:

Change the bottom margin from 2 lines to 9.

Change the left margin to 10.

Change the right margin to 75.

Press **Q**

> This quits the Margins option and returns you to the Printer submenu.

Next you will have to specify the range of cells to print as follows:

Press **R**

> This selects the Range option, and a prompt asks for the Print range.

Type **A1..E15**

Press (ENTER)

> This specifies the range of the spreadsheet to be printed as A1 through E15.

Creating Headings

Before printing the worksheet, however, you will create a header for the spreadsheet showing the date along the left margin and the title, ANNUAL ASSET REPORT, centered. A **header** is text that is printed at the top of all pages. In addition to entering text, there are three special characters that may be used in headers. If you type an @, the current date will be printed at its location. If you type a #, the page number will be printed. If you type |, what follows is centered, and if you type | |, what follows is right justified.

Complete the following to enter the date and center the heading, ANNUAL ASSET REPORT.

Press O

This selects the Options submenu.

Press H

This specifies the Header option.

Type @ | ANNUAL ASSET REPORT

Press (ENTER)

This enters the header that will be printed at the top of all pages. The date (represented by @) will be left justified on the page, and the heading will be centered (indicated by |).

Press Q

Press A

This selects the Quit option and sets the line counter to zero so that the printer executes page breaks correctly. Check to see that the printer is on and the paper is aligned at the print head.

Press A

Press G

This selects the Align and Go options, and the spreadsheet is printed.

Press P

This selects the Page option that moves the paper to top of next page.

Press Q

This returns you to the worksheet.

Printing Cell Contents

Another print option is to print out the contents of the cells. This is useful to check your work to insure that formulas were entered and copied correctly. This prints the formulas instead of the values created by the formulas. To print the contents of the cells, complete the following:

Press /

Press P

This displays the main menu and selects the Print command.

Press **P**

Press **O**

This selects Printer submenu and specifies Options.

Press **O**

This selects the Other option, and the following prompt appears on your screen:

```
As-Displayed Cell-Formulas Formatted Unformatted
```

Press **C**

This selects Cell-Formulas.

Press **Q**

Press **A**

This selects the Quit option and sets the line counter to zero so that the printer executes page breaks correctly. Check to see that the printer is on and the paper is aligned at the print head.

Press **G**

This selects Go, and the spreadsheet is printed.

Press **P**

This selects the Page option that moves the paper to the top of the next page.

Press **O** twice.

This Selects the Options submenu and specifies Other.

Press **A**

This specifies As-Displayed.

Press **Q** twice.

This returns you to the spreadsheet.

Now erase the worksheet.

This completes Lesson 5. If your practice time is up, use the Quit Command to exit the program.

Lesson 6

Working with Absolute Cell Addresses

After completing this lesson, you will be able to:

✔ Understand the difference between relative and absolute cell references

✔ Use absolute addresses in copying a formula

We have seen that when a formula is copied from one cell to another, cell references are adjusted. Relative addresses work very well when you copy

```
G18: 4000                                                      READY
            A      B      C       D       E     F      G      H
        1 PROFIT                        your name
        2                         WEEKLY PROFIT ANALYSIS
        3          NAME   INCOME  EXPENSES PROFIT  %INCOME  %PROFIT
        4 ================================================================
        5 WILLIAM  SMITH   1000    500     500
        6 SARA     ADAMS   3000    800    2200
        7 MARY     JONES   3500    800    2700
        8 JUNE     CARTER  2000   1700     300
        9 MARY     SMITHE  3000    300    2700
       10 SAM      JOHNSON 5000   3000    2000
       11 WILLIAM  FOSTER  7000    500    6500
       12 ANN      JONES   4000    200    3800
       13 SUSAN    YAH     6000   2000    4000
       14 ADAM     LEE     5000    400    4600
       15 -----------------------------------------------------------------
       16          TOTALS 39500  10200   29300
       17
       18 MONTHLY INCOME AND PROFIT QUOTAS            5000     4000
       19
       20
       23-Aug-89  04:53 PM                                       CAPS
```

Figure SS–16

and move data, because they adjust to the new locations. But there are times when one of the elements in a formula is located in a specific location which you want to remain fixed as the location of the formula is changed or the formula is copied. We call this fixed cell location an **absolute cell address**.

To identify a cell address as absolute instead of relative, insert dollar signs around the specific cell location in the formula. To practice this you will create the worksheet in Figure SS–16 and save it as PROFIT.

Duplicate the worksheet in Figure SS–16.

When done, move the pointer to cell F5.

Creating Absolute Cell References

Next you will specify an absolute cell reference when creating the formulas for columns F and G. To obtain %Income in the F column cells, you will divide the corresponding C column cells (Income) by F18, a fixed value. In F5 you want +C5/F18; in F6 you want, correspondingly, +C6/F18; and so on. That is, the C column cells will vary in the formula depending on the row, but the F18 cell is to remain fixed. The initial formula, then, in F5 will be +F5/$F$18. This formula will then be copied. F5 will be a relative cell location and F18 will be an absolute cell location. Then you will create a similar formula for %Profit in the G column.

Type **+C5/$F$18**

This specifies an absolute cell reference for F18 ($F$18).

Press ⟶

This enters the formula into F5 and moves the pointer to G5.

Type **+E5/$G$18**

Press ⟦ENTER⟧

This specifies an absolute cell reference and enters the formula into G5.

Now copy each of these formulas down the columns.

Press /

Press **C**

Press (ENTER)

> This brings up the main menu, selects the Copy command, and specifies the range to copy from as G5.

Type **G6..G14**

Press (ENTER)

> This specifies G6 through G14 as the range to copy to and copies the formula.

Press (←)

Press /

Press **C**

Press (ENTER)

> This brings up the main menu, selects the Copy command, and specifies the range to copy from as F5.

Type **F6..F14**

Press (ENTER)

> This specifies F6 through F14 as the range to copy to and copies the formula.

Now move the pointer down the F column. Notice that the C5 changes to C6, C7, and so on, but the $F$18 remains the same. Absolute addressing can be obtained by typing the $ before and after the column letter. Alternatively, absolute addressing can be accomplished by pressing the (F4) function key after typing the cell location that is to be absolute.

Finally, using the Percent format option,

Format the F and G columns for percents with no decimal places.

> The completed worksheet should look like Figure SS–17.

Save the worksheet to your work disk as B:PROFIT.

This completes Lesson 6. If your practice time is up, use the Quit command to exit the program.

Following are three exercises that help you practice the skills you have learned.

Practice

You will complete the first exercise in modules. Save your work periodically as you complete the modules. Note: Not all the keystrokes are specified. Also, in some cases the keystrokes that are listed show the command names. For example, the instruction:

/FS (File-Save) BUDGET1 (ENTER)

Figure SS–17

```
F5: (P0) +C5/$F$18                                              READY

      A         B         C         D         E         F         G        H
 1 PROFIT                                    your name
 2                               WEEKLY PROFIT ANALYSIS
 3            NAME      INCOME   EXPENSES PROFIT    %INCOME  %PROFIT
 4 ===================================================================
 5 WILLIAM  SMITH       1000       500      500       20%       13%
 6 SARA     ADAMS       3000       800     2200       60%       55%
 7 MARY     JONES       3500       800     2700       70%       68%
 8 JUNE     CARTER      2000      1700      300       40%        8%
 9 MARY     SMITHE      3000       300     2700       60%       68%
10 SAM      JOHNSON     5000      3000     2000      100%       50%
11 WILLIAM  FOSTER      7000       500     6500      140%      163%
12 ANN      JONES       4000       200     3800       80%       95%
13 SUSAN    YAH         6000      2000     4000      120%      100%
14 ADAM     LEE         5000       400     4600      100%      115%
15          -------------------------------------------------
16          TOTALS     39500     10200    29300
17
18 MONTHLY INCOME AND PROFIT QUOTAS                  5000      4000
19
20
01-Jan-80  12:07 AM                                            CAPS
```

means press /FS, type BUDGET1, and press the (ENTER) key. This would save the worksheet with the file name BUDGET1.

1. Figure SS–18 shows the completed worksheet called BUDGET. Complete the following to duplicate this worksheet.

Enter Labels

In cell A1 enter the name of this worksheet, **BUDGET**.

In cell B1 enter your name.

In cell B3 enter the column heading **JAN**.

Move the pointer to C3.

Continue entering the month headings until you have entered **DEC** into cell M3.

Press the (HOME) key to return to cell A1.

Move the pointer to A5.

```
A1: [W18] 'BUDGET                                              READY

      A              B            C            D            E
 1 BUDGET         your name
 2
 3                   JAN          FEB          MAR          APR
 4
 5 GROSS INCOME   $2,500.00    $2,500.00    $2,500.00    $2,500.00
 6 ---------------------------------------------------------------
 7 EXPENSES
 8 SAVINGS         $125.00      $125.00      $125.00      $125.00
 9 RENT            $450.00      $450.00      $450.00      $450.00
10 FOOD            $500.00      $500.00      $500.00      $500.00
11 UTILITIES       $150.00      $150.00      $150.00      $150.00
12 INSURANCE        $30.00       $30.00       $30.00       $30.00
13 PARKING         $100.00      $100.00      $100.00      $100.00
14 RECREATION      $375.00      $375.00      $375.00      $375.00
15 ---------------------------------------------------------------
16 TOTAL EXPENSES $1,730.00    $1,730.00    $1,730.00    $1,730.00
17 ===============================================================
18 NET INCOME        $0.00
19 SAVINGS TO DATE               $125.00
20
16-Jul-89  03:10 PM
```

Figure SS–18

Enter the row label **GROSS INCOME**.

Move the pointer to A7. Continue typing the row labels as shown below. Press the ⊙ key after each entry.

Cell	Label
A7	**EXPENSES**
A8	**SAVINGS**
A9	**RENT**
A10	**FOOD**
A11	**UTILITIES**
A12	**INSURANCE**
A13	**PARKING**
A14	**RECREATION**
A15	**TOTAL EXPENSES**
A16	**NET INCOME**
A17	**SAVINGS TO DATE**

Press (HOME) to return to cell A1.

Enter Values

Move the pointer to cell B5.

Enter your monthly income as **2500**, then move the pointer to B7. (Do not be concerned with losing part of the labels in column A.) Continue entering the values as shown below. Press ⊙ after each entry.

Cell	Value
B7	No entry
B8	No entry, to be computed later
B9	**450**
B10	**500**
B11	**150**
B12	**30**
B13	**100**
B14	No entry, to be computed later
B15	No entry, to be computed later
B16	No entry, to be computed later
B17	No entry for the first month, deposits are made at the end of each month

Press (HOME) to return to A1.

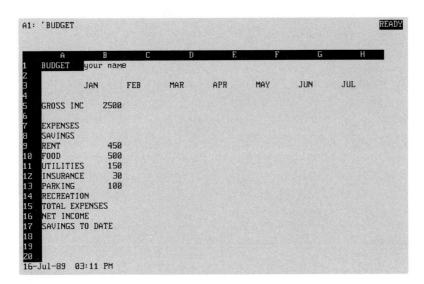

The first eight columns of your spreadsheet should look like the spreadsheet BUDGET1 shown in Figure SS–19. Use the following command to save your worksheet:

/FS (File/Save) **B:BUDGET1** (ENTER)

Enter Dashed Lines

To make the worksheet more readable, enter a single dashed line between the GROSS INCOME row and the EXPENSES row; between the RECREATION row and the TOTAL EXPENSES row; and a double dashed line between the TOTAL EXPENSES row and the NET INCOME row.

Move the pointer to cell A6.

Type \- and press (ENTER)

Move the pointer to cell A15.

Use the **/WIR** (Worksheet/Insert/Row) command to insert a blank row 15.

With the pointer at A15, type \– and press (ENTER)

Move the pointer to cell A17 and insert a blank row.

With the pointer at A17, type \= and press (ENTER)

Press (HOME) to return to cell A1.

Create Formulas

Savings   In cell B8 enter a formula to put 5% of your GROSS INCOME into your savings. The formula in cell B8 should be **+B5*.05**. After entering the formula, press ⊙ to move the pointer to B14.

Recreation   You enjoy life, so you plan to spend 15% of your gross pay for recreation. In cell B14 enter the formula **+B5*.15**.

Total Expenses   The TOTAL EXPENSES are the sum of the expenses displayed in cells B8 through B14. In cell B16 enter the formula @SUM(B8..B14).

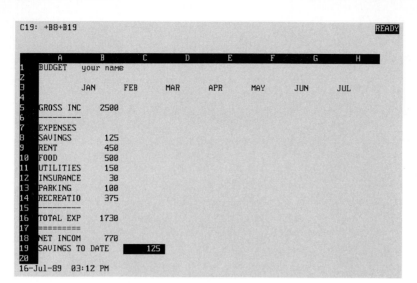

Figure SS–20

Net Income   The NET INCOME is the difference between GROSS IN-COME and TOTAL EXPENSES. In cell B18 enter the formula **+B5–B16**.

Savings Deposits   Savings deposits are made at the end of each month, so the SAVINGS TO DATE value in January is zero. For February add the amount saved in January to the beginning balance.

> Enter the following formula in C19: **+B8+B19**.

> > The first eight columns of your worksheet should resemble the worksheet in Figure SS–20.

Use the Copy Command

You have now entered most of the labels, formulas, and values you need in columns A and B of this worksheet. You need to copy some of these values and formulas to the rest of the worksheet.

Copy Values and Formulas   Until now you have copied one cell at a time. Lotus allows you to copy several cells at once. You will use the Copy command to copy the values and formulas in column B across the worksheet as follows:

> Move the pointer to B5.

> /C (Copy)

> The FROM range is **B5..B18**.

> The TO range is **C5..M5**.

Copy Other Data   Use the Copy command to copy the dashed lines across the spreadsheet one row at a time.

Format Labels and Values

Your worksheet contains the necessary labels and values, but the appearance of the worksheet can be improved.

Position the Labels in Row 3   Labels, by default, are left justified. To have the month labels properly positioned above the values, you need to have the labels right justified. Enter the following commands to right justify the month labels:

/RLR (Range-Label-Right) and define the range as **B3..M3**.

Widen Column A   You want to widen column A so that all of the labels will be displayed. With the pointer in A1, enter the following command:

/WCS (Worksheet-Column-Set-width)

Type **18**

Press (ENTER)

Format All Values to Currency   Since most values in this worksheet represent dollar and cents amounts, set the format for the entire worksheet for currency with two decimal places as follows:

/WGFC (Worksheet-Global-Format-Currency)

Type **2**

Press (ENTER)

Widen All Columns   With the extra characters inserted by the currency format, some of the cells are not wide enough to display the entire amount. Widen the remaining columns with the following command:

/WGC (Worksheet-Global-Column-width)

Type **12**

The worksheet is now complete. Save the worksheet.

/FS (File-Save) **B:BUDGET2** (ENTER)

Print the Worksheet

Modify Page Length   Begin by changing the page length to 33 so that two pages of the worksheet will print on the same sheet of paper.

/PPOP (Print-Printer-Options-Pg-length)

Type **33**

Add Headers   Create a header for the worksheet showing the date along the left border, the title ANNUAL BUDGET REPORT centered, and the page number at the right border. While still in the Options function:

Press **H** to select Header

Type **@ | ANNUAL BUDGET REPORT | PAGE-#**

Note: The date is displayed in a header wherever the @ is placed, and the page number is displayed wherever the # is placed.

Print Column Labels on All Pages   Complete the following to have the headings in column A printed on each page.

Press **Q Q** to return to the worksheet.

/PPOBC (Print-Printer-Options-Borders-Column)

Type **A1**

Now specify the range and print the worksheet. Because the heading in column A will be printed on all pages, do not specify column A in the range. Make sure the printer is on and the paper is aligned properly.

Press **Q R** to select range.

Type **B1..M19** (ENTER)

Press **A G** for Align-Go

Press **P** to advance the page.

This completes the first practice exercise.

2.   A friend who was impressed with your BUDGET worksheet asked you to prepare one for her for next year. In addition to the categories you have in your budget, she would like to add the following:

WITHHOLDING TAXES

TAKE-HOME PAY (GROSS INCOME – WITHHOLDING TAXES)

Following is the information she gave you.

*   Her salary is currently $5,000 per month, and she anticipates getting a 10% raise in June.

*   She estimates that 28% of her gross pay will be withheld for taxes.

*   She plans to put 10% of her take-home pay in a savings account.

*   Her apartment rent is $450 a month.

*   She spends about $500 a month on food.

*   Her utilities are $150 a month.

*   She contributes $30 a month to her church.

*   In June she contributes an additional $470 to her college alumni fund.

*   In November and December she will give $270 and $370 to charities for the Thanksgiving and Christmas holidays.

*   The parking garage rent is $100 a month.

*   She plans to set aside 15% of her take-home pay for recreation activities.

*   In April she has to pay a $1,500 insurance premium.

*   Her vacation expenses will be $3,000 in July and $2,000 in August.

Refer to the worksheet FINAL BUDGET, Figure SS–21, to see how the first four months of your spreadsheet should look after all of the values and formulas have been entered.

Now create the worksheet using formulas where appropriate. When done, save this file as **FINAL** on your work disk.

After you have completed and saved the above report, she asks you to enter the following changes:

A1: [W18]   READY   **Figure SS–21**

```
        A              B         C         D         E
1                          FINAL BUDGET         Cutler
2
3                         JAN       FEB       MAR       APR
4   GROSS INCOME      $5,000.00   5000.00   5000.00   5000.00
5   WITHHOLDING TAXES   1400.00   1400.00   1400.00   1400.00
6
7   TAKE-HOME PAY       3600.00   3600.00   3600.00   3600.00
8   EXPENSES
9
10  SAVINGS              360.00    360.00    360.00    360.00
11  RENT                 450.00    450.00    450.00    450.00
12  FOOD                 500.00    500.00    500.00    500.00
13  UTILITIES            150.00    150.00    150.00    150.00
14  CHARITIES             30.00     30.00     30.00     30.00
15  PARKING              100.00    100.00    100.00    100.00
16  RECREATION           540.00    540.00    540.00    540.00
17  MISCELLANEOUS                                     1500.00
18
19  TOTAL EXPENSES      2130.00   2130.00   2130.00   3630.00
20  ==================================================
16-Jul-89  03:13 PM
```

◆ Her salary will start at $6,000, not $5,000.

◆ She will put 15% of her take-home pay into savings.

◆ She will move into a new apartment with rent of $600 a month.

◆ After you have entered the above changes, save this new file as **FINALR** and print it.

This completes the second practice exercise.

3. The Able Sales Company wants you to create a worksheet showing net income projections for the coming year. The initial estimates are:

◆ January sales will be $10,000.

◆ Sales will increase at a rate of 5% a month.

◆ Variable expenses run at 70% of sales.

◆ Fixed expenses are $2,000 each month.

They want to be able to change any of the above factors and see the effect on the projected income values. This is called "what-if" analysis. One of the major advantages of a spreadsheet package is to be able to create a worksheet and determine the effects of projected changes with a few keystrokes. Be sure to use absolute cell references when you use these addresses in a formula.

Refer to the worksheet FORECST1, Figure SS–22, to see the format of the spreadsheet.

◆ FORMULA1 in cell B12 displays the January sales estimate.

◆ FORMULA2 in cells C12 through M12 multiplies the sales estimate by the sales increase factor in cell B5 and adds it to the value in C12.

◆ FORMULA3 in cells B14 through M14 multiplies the sales values in row 12 by the variable expense rate in cell B6.

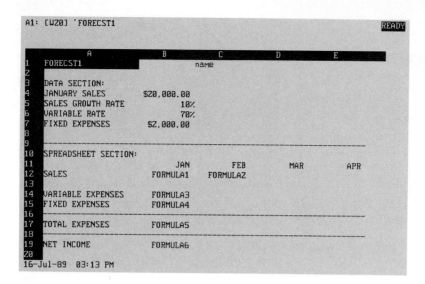

Figure SS–22

- FORMULA4 in cells B15 through M15 should contain the amount of fixed expenses in cell B7.

- FORMULA5 computes the total of fixed and variable expenses.

- FORMULA6 subtracts total expenses from the amount of sales.

- Copy the above formulas to cells through column M. Compare your results with Figure SS–23. Save the worksheet as FORECST2.

Now change the January sales value to $20,000 and the sales growth rate to 10%. Compare the results with Figure SS–24.
    This completes the third practice exercise.

KEY WORDS

Absolute cell addressing	Header	Repeating character
Active cell	Help facility	Row
Cell	Label	Status line
Column	Mode indicator	Truncate
Formula	Pointer	Value
Function	Range	
Goto	Relative cell addressing	

REVIEW QUESTIONS

1. Why is it necessary to preface a year entry such as 1991 with a quote mark?
2. When is it desirable to use the SUM function for adding cell values?
3. What happens if you try to enter data into a cell that already contains data?
4. What does the Currency function do?
5. Why is it important to use absolute cell addressing in some formulas?

```
B19: (,2) +B12-B17                                          READY

        A              B          C          D          E
1  FORECST1                   name
2
3  DATA SECTION:
4  JANUARY SALES      $10,000.00
5  SALES GROWTH RATE        5%
6  VARIABLE RATE           70%
7  FIXED EXPENSES      $2,000.00
8
9  _____
10 SPREADSHEET SECTION:
11                       JAN        FEB        MAR        APR
12 SALES            10,000.00  10,500.00  11,025.00  11,576.25
13
14 VARIABLE EXPENSES 7,000.00   7,350.00   7,717.50   8,103.38
15 FIXED EXPENSES    2,000.00   2,000.00   2,000.00   2,000.00
16                  _____
17 TOTAL EXPENSES    9,000.00   9,350.00   9,717.50  10,103.38
18                  _____
19 NET INCOME        1,000.00   1,150.00   1,307.50   1,472.88
20
16-Jul-89  03:14 PM
```

```
B5: (P0) 0.1                                                READY

        A              B          C          D          E
1  FORECST1                   name
2
3  DATA SECTION:
4  JANUARY SALES      $20,000.00
5  SALES GROWTH RATE       10%
6  VARIABLE RATE           70%
7  FIXED EXPENSES      $2,000.00
8
9  _____
10 SPREADSHEET SECTION:
11                       JAN        FEB        MAR        APR
12 SALES            20,000.00  22,000.00  24,200.00  26,620.00
13
14 VARIABLE EXPENSES 14,000.00  15,400.00  16,940.00  18,634.00
15 FIXED EXPENSES     2,000.00   2,000.00   2,000.00   2,000.00
16                  _____
17 TOTAL EXPENSES    16,000.00  17,400.00  18,940.00  20,634.00
18                  _____
19 NET INCOME         4,000.00   4,600.00   5,260.00   5,986.00
20
16-Jul-89  03:15 PM
```

S
S

Developing Graphs With 1-2-3

Hardware needed:

✔ IBM PC, IBM PS/2, or IBM-compatible microcomputer with graphics capabilities

✔ Two floppy disk drives, or one floppy disk drive and a hard drive

✔ Printer with graphics capabilities (for printing graphs)

Software needed:

✔ DOS 2.01 or later version

✔ Lotus 1-2-3 version 2.01, 2.2, or 3.0

✔ Work Disk with the files you created in the Using Lotus tutorial

When you have completed this tutorial, you will be able to:

✔ Create pie, bar, stacked-bar, and line graphs

✔ Store graph settings within a worksheet file

✔ Save graphs to print files

✔ Print graphs

Graphs Tutorial

Tutorial Outline

What Is a Graph?

A graph is a visual representation of numeric data. Lotus 1-2-3 allows you to develop, display, save, and print graphs using data in a worksheet. With Lotus you can create bar, pie, and line graphs. You can enhance a graph by adding titles, grid lines, legends, and so on. Then you save and print the graph.

This tutorial will show you how to use Lotus 1-2-3 to create, save, and print graphs. You must have completed the previous Lotus tutorial before starting this one, since you will use the worksheets that you created in that tutorial to develop graphs.

Loading Lotus

If your computer has a hard-disk drive, then it is assumed that the Lotus program has been installed onto the drive. Your instructor or lab assistant will provide the information you need to load Lotus from a hard drive.

REMINDER

If you are using a computer with a hard drive, you must keep in mind that when you are saving or retrieving the files you have created, the default on Lotus 1-2-3 will save them to the hard disk, that is, the C drive. You do not want to do this, because you want to save your files to your work disk so that you can keep them with you and reuse them regardless of which computer you may use in other tutorial lessons. Therefore, remember to save your files to the diskette in the floppy drive. You can do this by using the prefix "B:". When retrieving your files, you must look on the B drive. Even if your hard disk computer has only one floppy drive, you may still call it B.

If your computer does not have a hard-disk drive, follow these instructions for loading Lotus:

Turn on the computer with the DOS disk in drive A.

Enter the date and time if directed.

Remove the DOS disk from drive A, insert the Lotus system disk into drive A and your work disk into drive B.

> The work disk is where you will keep the files you create in the course of this tutorial.

Type **lotus**

Press (ENTER)

> This displays the 1-2-3 Access System screen. This screen allows you to select different parts of the Lotus package. For example, the PrintGraph option would be used to print a graph. At this point you need to select 1-2-3, the spreadsheet program. 1-2-3 is highlighted, so to choose it simply press (ENTER). (Alternatively, you could have typed "123" at the C> prompt instead of "lotus" to bypass the Access System screen and go directly to the spreadsheet.)

Press (ENTER)

GRAPH

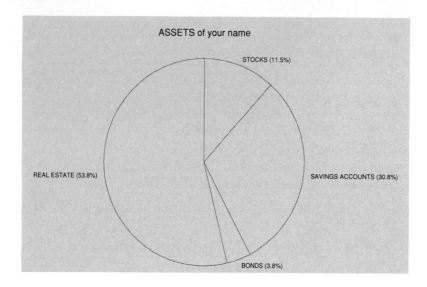

The Lotus 1-2-3 program is loaded and the spreadsheet appears on your monitor.

Developing a Pie Graph

In this section you will use the ASSETS2C worksheet to develop a **pie graph**, with titles, and save it. The completed graph that you will create is shown in Figure GR–1. A pie graph displays data in the form of slices that represent parts (percentages) of a whole. The pie graph you will develop shows what part stocks, savings accounts, bonds, and real estate are of the total 1990 assets.

Retrieve the worksheet ASSETS2C

Press /

This displays the main menu.

Press G

This selects the Graph command.

Figure GR–2 shows the Graph menu. The options are:

◆ **Type**   Allows you to select the graph type, such as line, bar, xy, stacked-bar, or pie.

◆ **X**   Specifies the range of cells in the worksheet to be used as labels for the graph. For example, notice in Figure GR–1, the labels STOCKS, SAVINGS ACCOUNTS, BONDS, and REAL ESTATE are listed next to their slices. These labels come from the spreadsheet cells A7 through A10. You use this X option to specify this range.

◆ **A–F**   Specifies the ranges of cells with the values that make up the graph. In a pie graph you only use one range of data, specified by the A option. For example, in Figure 1 the values for STOCKS, SAVINGS AC-COUNTS, BONDS, and REAL ESTATE make up the pie. These values come from the spreadsheet cells B7 through B10. You use the A option to specify this range. The other options (B–F) can be used with a bar or line graph in

```
A11: [W18] \=                                              MENU
Type  X A B  C  D  E  F  Reset  View  Save  Options  Name  Quit
Set graph type
            A          B          C          D         E
1  ASSETS                                 your name
2              ASSET ANALYSIS REPORT
3
4  ASSETS              1990       1991     $INCR/   %INCR
5                                          DECR     DECR
6  ─────────────────────────────────────────────────────
7  STOCKS        $15,000.00 $20,000.00   $5,000.00    33%
8  SAVINGS       $40,000.00 $30,000.00 ($10,000.00)  -25%
9  BONDS          $5,000.00 $30,000.00  $25,000.00   500%
10 LAND          $70,000.00 $85,000.00  $15,000.00    21%
11 ═══════════════════════════════════════════════════════
12 TOTALS       $130,000.00 $165,000.00 $35,000.00    27%
13
14
15 AVERAGE       $32,500.00 $41,250.00
16
17
18
19
20
24-Aug-89  02:12 PM
```

GR–2

which you want to plot more than one range of cells. For example, you could develop a bar graph which has both the 1990 and 1991 values. You would use the A option for the 1990 values and the B option for the 1991 values. Further ranges (up to six) would be specified with the other options (C–F).

◆ **Reset**   Cancels part or all of the graph settings.

◆ **View**   Displays the current graph on the monitor.

◆ **Save**   Saves the current graph in a special graph file that can be used later for printing. Note: This is not the same as saving a worksheet.

◆ **Options**   Allows you to enhance the graph by adding features such as titles, legends, and grid lines.

◆ **Name**   Stores one or more graphs as part of a worksheet file. That is, you can create several graphs using data in a single worksheet. If you name each graph and then save the worksheet, the graphs are stored with the worksheet. Later, when you retrieve the worksheet, the graphs can be used.

◆ **Quit**   Returns you to the worksheet.

Now you will create the graph in Figure GR–1.

Press T

This selects the **Type** option and lists the types of graphs at the top of the screen:

Line   Bar   XY   Stacked-Bar   Pie

Press P

This selects the Pie type and returns you to the Graph menu. (You could also use the cursor arrow keys to highlight Pie and then press (ENTER) to select it.) At this point you need to specify the range of cells that contain the values and the labels to be used in the graph.

Press X

G R A P H

```
A11: [W18] \=                                          EDIT
Enter first data range: B7..B10

          A           B          C          D          E
1  ASSETS                                  your name
2                   ASSET ANALYSIS REPORT
3
4  ASSETS              1990       1991      $INCR/    %INCR/
5                                            DECR      DECR
6  ─────────────────────────────────────────────────────────
7  STOCKS          $15,000.00 $20,000.00   $5,000.00    33%
8  SAVINGS ACCOUNTS $40,000.00 $30,000.00 ($10,000.00)  -25%
9  BONDS            $5,000.00 $30,000.00  $25,000.00   500%
10 REAL ESTATE     $70,000.00 $85,000.00  $15,000.00    21%
11 ═══════════════════════════════════════════════════════════
12 TOTALS         $130,000.00 $165,000.00 $35,000.00    27%
13
14
15 AVERAGE         $32,500.00 $41,250.00
16
17
18
19
20
24-Aug-89  02:22 PM                                    CAPS
```

This selects the X range option, and a prompt appears at the top of the screen asking for the range. This range will have the cells that contain the labels you want on your graph.

Type A7..A10

Press (ENTER)

This specifies the range of cells that contain the labels to be used in the graph, then returns you to the Graph menu. Next you will select the range of data to be graphed.

Press A

This selects the A range. A prompt appears at the top of the screen asking you to enter the first data range. To specify the range of cells containing the values to be graphed:

Type B7..B10

This specifies the data range, as shown in Figure GR–3.

Press (ENTER)

You are returned to the Graph menu. Note that the numeric values to be graphed can be in currency form as well as in standard numeric form.

Now you can use the View option to display the graph.

Press V

This displays the graph on your monitor. After viewing the graph, you can press (ENTER) to return to the Graph menu.

Press (ENTER)

The last thing you need to do is create a title for the graph. Complete the following to enter the title "ASSETS OF [your name]."

Press O

This selects the **Options** submenu as shown in Figure GR–4. Only the Title option has relevance for our pie chart; the other options are explained in Table GR–1.

```
A11: [W18] \=                                              MENU
Legend  Format  Titles  Grid  Scale  Color  B&W  Data-Labels  Quit
Specify data-range legends
         A              B         C         D          E
1  ASSETS                              your name
2               ASSET ANALYSIS REPORT
3
4  ASSETS                  1990      1991     $INCR/    %INCR/
5                                             DECR      DECR
6  ─────────────────────────────────────────────────────────
7  STOCKS            $15,000.00 $20,000.00  $5,000.00    33%
8  SAVINGS ACCOUNTS  $40,000.00 $30,000.00 ($10,000.00) -25%
9  BONDS              $5,000.00 $30,000.00 $25,000.00   500%
10 REAL ESTATE       $70,000.00 $85,000.00 $15,000.00    21%
11 ==================================================
12 TOTALS           $130,000.00 $165,000.00 $35,000.00   27%
13
14
15 AVERAGE           $32,500.00 $41,250.00
16
17
18
19
20
24-Aug-89  02:27 PM                                      CAPS
```

GR–4

The **Title** option allows you to create a title of up to two lines. To give your graph a title:

Press T

> This selects the **Titles** option and displays four choices:

```
First      Second      X-Axis      Y-Axis
```

The **First** and **Second** options specify title lines at the top two lines of the graph. The **X-Axis** and **Y-Axis** options specify titles for the horizontal and vertical axes in graphs that use X and Y axes such as Line and Bar types.

Press F

> This selects First, and a prompt appears near the top of the screen. Now enter the title, using your name, as shown in Figure GR–5.

Type ASSETS of (your name)

G
R
A
P
H

Option	Action
Legend	Creates legends for data ranges. Used in line and bar graphs.
Format	Allows you to change the appearance of the lines used in line graphs. You can specify different symbols, such as + or x, to indicate the data points in the graph.
Titles	Allows you to give your graph a title of up to two lines long, and it allows you to create titles for the horizontal (x) and vertical (y) axes.
Grid	Allows you to add and delete horizontal and vertical grid lines in the graph.
Scale	Allows you to set the scales for the x and y axes manually.
Color	Displays the graph in color, if you have a color monitor.
B&W	Displays the graph in black and white.
Data-Labels	Specifies a range of cells whose contents will be used to label the data points of a data range.

Table GR–1 The Options Submenu Choices.

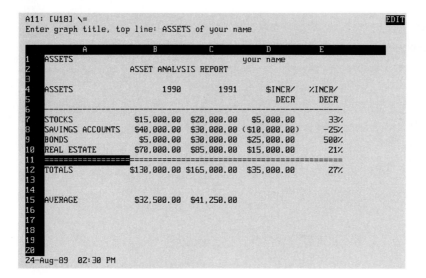

```
A11: [W18] \=                                              EDIT
Enter graph title, top line: ASSETS of your name

              A            B           C          D          E
1  ASSETS                                     your name
2                    ASSET ANALYSIS REPORT
3
4  ASSETS                  1990        1991      $INCR/    %INCR/
5                                                 DECR      DECR
6  ----------------------------------------------------------------
7  STOCKS            $15,000.00  $20,000.00   $5,000.00     33%
8  SAVINGS ACCOUNTS  $40,000.00  $30,000.00 ($10,000.00)   -25%
9  BONDS              $5,000.00  $30,000.00  $25,000.00    500%
10 REAL ESTATE       $70,000.00  $85,000.00  $15,000.00     21%
11 ===========================================================
12 TOTALS           $130,000.00 $165,000.00  $35,000.00     27%
13
14
15 AVERAGE           $32,500.00  $41,250.00
16
17
18
19
20
24-Aug-89  02:30 PM
```

Press (ENTER)

Press Q

> This enters the title line and returns you to the Graph menu. Now select the View option to display the graph with the titles.

Press V

> This displays the pie graph with the title you entered.

Press (ENTER)

> This returns you to the Graph menu.

Naming and Storing a Graph

To store a graph as part of a worksheet, you use the Name/Create command. First select the **Name** option from the Graph menu.

Press N

> The following options are displayed:
>
> `Use  Create  Delete  Reset`
>
> The **Use** option is selected when you have more than one graph stored with a worksheet and you want to recall one. **Delete** erases a named graph, and **Reset** erases all named graphs. The **Create** option stores a graph.

Press C

> This selects the **Create** option, and the following prompt appears near the top of the screen:
>
> `Enter graph name:`
>
> Enter PIEGRAPH as the name.

Type PIEGRAPH

Press (ENTER)

This names the current graph PIEGRAPH and returns you to the Graph menu. Later you will save the worksheet, so that the graph will be stored with the worksheet.

Developing a Bar Graph

Next you will use the ASSETS2C worksheet to develop a **bar graph** with one data range, as shown in Figure GR–6. The graph in Figure GR–6 has one data range for 1990 values. Later you will create a second bar graph with two data ranges for 1990 and 1991 values. Start by clearing the current graph settings with the Reset option.

Press **R**

A list of choices appears near the top of the screen:

`Graph X A B C D E F Quit`

Graph cancels all the current graph settings. **X** cancels the current settings in the label range. **A–F** cancel the current settings in the data range you choose. Since you want to cancel all settings:

Press **G**

This selects Graph, cancels all the current graph settings, and returns you to the Graph menu.

Press **T**

Press **B**

This selects the Type option and specifies Bar as the type of graph to develop.

Next you will specify the labels to be entered along the horizontal or **X axis** of the graph.

Press **X**

This selects the X data range, which will specify the labels for the X axis, and displays a prompt asking for the range.

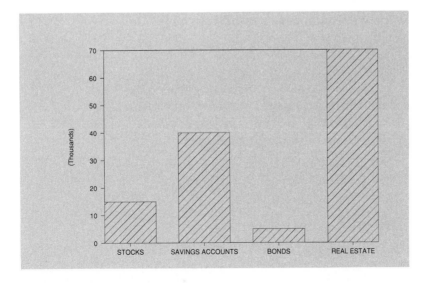

GR–6

Type **A7..A10**

Press (ENTER)

> This specifies the X axis range as A7 through A10 (the labels) and returns you to the Graph menu.

Next you will specify the range of data to be graphed.

Press **A**

> This selects the first data range and displays the prompt asking for the range. You want to specify the values for 1990.

Type **B7..B10**

Press (ENTER)

> This specifies B7 through B10 as the first data range of values to be used in the bar graph and returns you to the Graph menu.

Press **V**

> This selects the View option and displays the bar graph on the screen. Your bar graph should look like the one in Figure GR–6. Note that the vertical or **Y axis** values have been automatically set by Lotus 1-2-3, with the label "Thousands" indicating that the Y axis values represent numbers in the thousands.

Press (ENTER)

> This returns you to the Graph menu.

Now you will add a second data range (1991 values) to this bar graph, as shown in Figure GR–7.

Press **B**

Type **C7..C10**

> This selects the second data range (B) and specifies the range of cells (C7 through C10) that contain the 1991 values to be used in the graph.

Press (ENTER)

Press **V**

> This returns you to the Graph menu and selects the View option to display the graph.

Entering Legends

The two data ranges have been plotted in two sets of bars, distinguished by different patterns of cross-hatching. However, there is no way of determining the two years, 1990 and 1991. To identify each cross-hatching pattern, you need to create **legends**. This is done with the Legend option of the Graph menu.

Press (ENTER)

Press **O**

> This returns you to the Graph menu and selects Options.

Press **L**

This selects the Legend option, and a list of the data ranges (A–F) appears near the top of the screen.

Press **A**

This selects the A range and a prompt asking you to enter the legend. When you display the graph, the legend will appear at the bottom.

Type **1990**

Press (ENTER)

This specifies 1990 as the legend for the A data range.

Press **L**

Press **B**

Type **1991**

This specifies 1991 as the legend for the B data range.

Press (ENTER)

Press **Q**

This enters the legend for the B data range and selects Quit to return you to the Graph menu.

Press **V**

This selects View and displays the bar graph with the legends.

Now, to complete the graph, enter two title lines.

Press (ENTER)

Press **O**

Press **T**

This returns you to the Graph menu, selects Options, and specifies Titles.

Press **F**

Type **ASSET ANALYSIS**

Press (ENTER)

This selects the First line option and enters a title.

Press **T**

Press **S**

Type **by year**

This selects the Title option again, specifies Second, and enters a title.

Press (ENTER)

Press **Q**

Press **V**

This returns you to the Graph menu, selects the View option, and displays the bar graph with titles. Your bar graph should now look like the one in Figure GR–7.

Press (ENTER)

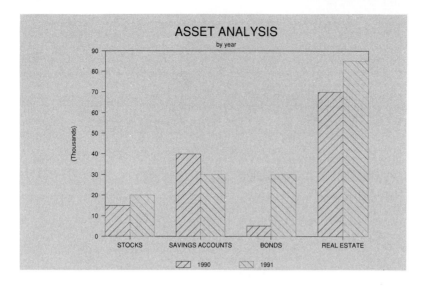

This returns you to the Graph menu.

To enhance the graph and make it easier to read, you can add horizontal **grid lines** as shown in Figure GR–8. This is done using the Grid option from the Options submenu.

Press **O**

Press **G**

This selects Options and specifies Grid. Grid is used to make a graph look like it was created on graph paper. With grid markings, it is easier to view graph values. The displayed options are:

```
Horizontal Vertical Both Clear
```

Press **H**

Press **Q**

Press **V**

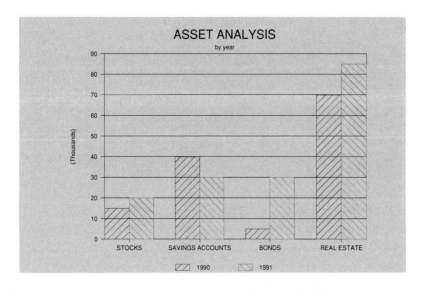

This specifies Horizontal grid lines, quits the Options submenu, and displays the graph.

Now name this graph BARGRAPH so that it is stored with the worksheet.

Press (ENTER)

Press N

Press C

Type **BARGRAPH**

Press (ENTER)

This returns you to the Graph menu, selects the Name option, and specifies Create. The name BARGRAPH is entered and you are returned to the Graph menu.

Developing a Stacked-Bar Graph

A variation of the bar graph is the **stacked-bar graph** as shown in Figure GR–9. In a stacked-bar graph, data ranges are stacked one above the other rather than side-by-side. This allows you to view the values from each year in proportion to the total for both years.

Now you will change your bar graph to a stacked-bar graph. Because the data ranges are already specified, all you need to do is select the Stacked-bar type. The same graph values can be used for creating other types of graphs.

Press T

Press S

Press V

This selects the Type option, specifies Stacked-bar, then displays the graph.

Press (ENTER)

This returns you to the Graph menu. Before continuing, clear the grid lines.

GR–9

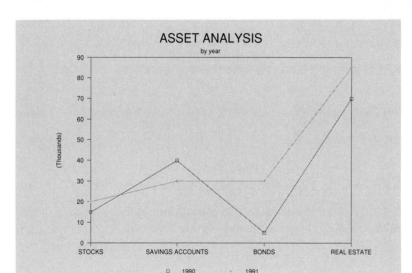

GR–10

Press **O**

Press **G**

Press **C**

Press **Q**

> This selects the Options submenu, specifies Grid, clears the grid lines, and returns to the Graph menu.

Developing a Line Graph

Figure GR–10 shows a **line graph**. In a line graph, data is displayed as a set of points along a line. The line graph you will create will use the same data ranges (1990 and 1991 values) as the bar graph. Because of the similarity of the bar and line graphs (they both use X and Y axes), it is easy to move from one to the other.

Press **T**

Press **L**

Press **V**

> This selects the Type option, specifies Line, and then displays the graph. Notice that Lotus 1-2-3 has created legends identifying each line. A box is used for the 1990 line and a plus sign is used for the 1991 line.

Press (ENTER)

> This returns you to the Graph menu.

Use the Name/Create command to name this graph LIN-GRAPH and store the graph settings in this worksheet file.

Figure GR–11 shows the same line graph with a third line created by specifying a C data range of cells D7 through D10 (the dollar change from 1990 to 1991). Complete the following to duplicate Figure GR–11. Assume that all other settings have remained the same.

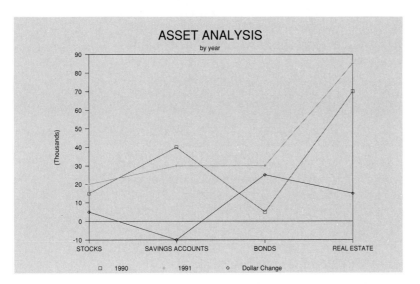

Press **C**

Type **D7..D10**

Press (ENTER)

> This selects the third data range (C) and enters D7 through D10 as the range of cells that contain the values to be used.

Press **V**

> This displays the graph with the three lines. Notice that the third line has a negative value. Now you need to specify a legend for this line.

Press (ENTER)

Press **O**

Press **L**

Press **C**

> This returns you to the Graph menu, selects Options, then Legend, and specifies the C data range. A prompt appears asking you for the legend.

Type **Dollar Change**

Press (ENTER)

> This enters Dollar Change as the legend for the C range.

Press **Q**

Press **V**

> This quits the submenu and displays the graph.

Use the Name/Create command to name this graph LIN-GRPH2 and store the graph settings in this worksheet file.

This completes the graphs you will develop using the ASSETS2C worksheet. To illustrate how these graphs have been stored with the worksheet, you will: save the worksheet; exit the program; retrieve the worksheet; and display the graphs. Remember, you must save the worksheet after naming

G
R
A
P
H

graphs so that they are stored with the worksheet. Make sure your work disk is in drive B. You will save the worksheet with the new name ASSETS2G.

> Press **Q**

> Press **/**

> Press **F**

> Press **S**

>> This returns you to the worksheet, displays the main menu, and selects the File command and the Save option.

> Type **B:ASSETS2G**

> Press (ENTER)

>> This saves the worksheet as ASSETS2G onto your work disk.

> Quit the Lotus program and return to the DOS prompt.

> Load the Lotus program.

> Retrieve the ASSETS2G worksheet.

>> From the Ready mode, you can view the current graph by pressing (F10). The last graph you created and named is LINGRPH2.

> Press (F10)

>> This displays the LINGRPH2 graph.

To display any of the other graphs that you created and named, you must select the Use option from the Name submenu. Select the bar graph as follows:

> Press (ENTER)

> Press **/**

> Press **G**

>> This returns you to the worksheet, displays the main menu, and selects the Graph command.

> Press **N**

> Press **U**

>> This selects the Name option and specifies Use. A prompt appears asking for the name of the graph to make current.

> Type **BARGRAPH**

> Press (ENTER)

>> This specifies BARGRAPH as the one to use and displays it.

> Press (ENTER)

>> This returns you to the Graph menu.

```
Copyright 1986 Lotus Development Corp.  All Rights Reserved. Release 2.01 MENU

Select graphs for printing
Image-Select  Settings  Go  Align  Page  Exit

  GRAPH      IMAGE OPTIONS                    HARDWARE SETUP
  IMAGES     Size                Range Colors   Graphs Directory:
  SELECTED   Top        .395     X Black          A:\
             Left       .750     A Black        Fonts Directory:
             Width     6.500     B Black          C:\LOTUS
             Height    4.691     C Black        Interface:
             Rotate     .000     D Black          Parallel 1
                                 E Black        Printer Type:
             Font                F Black          Eps FX,RX/lo
             1  BLOCK1                          Paper Size
             2  BLOCK1                            Width      8.500
                                                 Length    11.000

                                              ACTION OPTIONS
                                               Pause: No   Eject: Yes
```

GR–12

Printing Graphs

Lotus does not have a graph print command that would allow you to send a graph image directly from the screen to your printer. Instead you must save the graph using the Graph/Save command, which creates an image in a separate graph file. Then you can use another part of the Lotus package, PrintGraph, to print out this graph image. When you use the Graph/Save command, you will specify a file name. Lotus will automatically append the extension .PIC to indicate that this is a graph file. Note: To print a graph your computer must be connected to a printer that can print graphic images.

To illustrate graph printing, you will print the bar graph. Start by using the Save option from the Graph menu to create the graph file with the file name BAR.PIC. With your work disk in drive B:

Press S

This selects the Save option, and a prompt is displayed near the top of the screen asking for a file name.

Type B:\BAR

Press (ENTER)

This saves the graph as a graph image with the file name BAR.PIC.

Quit the Lotus program and return to the DOS prompt.

Next you must load the PrintGraph program.

Insert the PrintGraph disk of Lotus 1-2-3 into drive A.

Type PGRAPH

Press (ENTER)

Figure GR–12 shows the main menu for the PrintGraph program.

Press I

This selects the Image option and displays the .PIC files. Using the cursor arrow keys:

G
R
A
P
H

Highlight the BAR file.

Press space bar.

> This marks the file. The graph file is now ready for printing.

Press (ENTER)

> This returns you to the main menu.

Press A

> This selects the Align option, which sets the line counter on the printer.

Press G

> This selects Go and begins the print process. The printing may take several moments. When it is complete, exit the PrintGraph program as follows:

Press E

Press Y

> This selects the Exit option and Yes, and you exit Lotus 1-2-3.

You have learned how to create and display graphs using worksheets developed with the Lotus 1-2-3 package. You have also learned how to store graphs as part of the worksheet file and save them as graph images for later printing. Table GR–2, which follows on page GR–18, summarizes these steps. Complete the exercise below to practice the skills you have learned.

Practice

Using the PROFIT worksheet, develop the following graphs:

1. A pie graph showing the income of each person. (Hint: Use the C incomes as the A data range and the last names as the X label range). Include a title for the graph and store the graph as EXPPIE.

2. A bar graph showing the income for each person. Include a title and grid lines. Store the graph as EXPBAR.

3. A line graph showing the income and the expenses for each person. Include a title and legend. Store the graph as EXPLINE.

4. A stacked bar graph of the income and expenses. Include a legend and title. Store the graph as EXPSTACK and print the graph.

KEY WORDS

Bar graph	Legend	Stacked-bar graph
Graph	Line graph	X-axis
Grid lines	Pie Chart	Y-axis

REVIEW QUESTIONS

1. What are the steps to follow in creating a graph based on information contained in a already existing worksheet?
2. What additional steps are involved in preparing the graphs you create to be able to print them?
3. How many different kinds of graphs can be created with Lotus 1-2-3?

1. Create the spreadsheet.
2. Design the graph.
3. Display the graph to ensure its accuracy.
4. Use the Graph/Name command to store the graph settings in the spreadsheet file.
5. Use the Graph/Save command to save the graph in a file that can be printed later. The file extension .PIC will automatically be appended to the graph name.
6. Use the File/Save command to save the spreadsheet and its graph files.
7. Quit the spreadsheet program and return to the DOS prompt.
8. Insert the PrintGraph disk of Lotus 1-2-3 into drive A.
9. To load the program, type PGRAPH and press (ENTER)
10. To view a graph from the PrintGraph program:

Press **I**	Displays the .PIC files
Highlight the desired file.	
Press (ENTER)	
Press (F10)	Displays graph in desired file
Press (ENTER)	Returns to submenu
Press (ENTER)	Returns to main menu

11. To print a graph image file:

Press **I**	Displays the .PIC files
Highlight the desired file.	
Press the space bar.	Marks the file
Press (ENTER)	Returns to main menu
Press **A**	Selects Align
Press **G**	Selects Go

Table GR–2 Steps to Creating and Printing Graphs.

G R A P H

Creating and Using Macros in Lotus 1-2-3

Hardware needed:

✔ For release 2.01 or 2.2: IBM PC, IBM PS/2, or an IBM-compatible

✔ For release 3.0: IBM AT, IBM PS/2, or an IBM-compatible equipped with an Intel 80286 or 80386 microprocessor, a hard-disk drive, and a minimum of 1 megabyte of RAM.

Software needed:

✔ DOS 2.01 or later version

✔ Lotus 1-2-3 version 2.01, 2.2, or 3.0

✔ Work disk with the files you created in previous Lotus tutorials

When you have completed this tutorial, you will be able to:

✔ Plan and organize a macro

✔ Create a macro

✔ Document a macro

✔ Create and use a macro library file

✔ Use the pause command to allow user input

✔ Edit a macro

M
A
C
R
O

Macros Tutorial

Tutorial Outline

What Is a Lotus 1-2-3 Macro?

This tutorial helps you develop the skills to create and use macros in your Lotus 1-2-3 worksheets. A Lotus 1-2-3 macro is a series of instructions that can be executed repeatedly just by pressing one or two keys. Macros enable you to automate and customize the way you work in Lotus 1-2-3.

You should have completed both the Using Lotus tutorial and the Lotus Graphs tutorial before starting this one.

Loading Lotus

If your computer has a hard disk drive, then it is assumed that the Lotus 1-2-3 program has been installed onto this drive. Your instructor or lab assistant will provide the information you need to load the program from the hard drive. Make sure your work disk is in the floppy drive.

REMINDER

If you are using a computer with a hard drive, you must keep in mind that when you are saving or retrieving the files you have created, the default on Lotus 1-2-3 will save them to the hard disk, that is, the C drive. You do not want to do this, because you want to save your files to your work disk so that you can keep them with you and reuse them regardless of which computer you may use in other tutorial lessons. Therefore, remember to save your files to the diskette in the floppy drive. You can do this by using the prefix "B:". When retrieving your files, you must look on the B drive. Even if your hard disk computer has only one floppy drive, you may still call it B.

If your computer does not have a hard disk, follow these instructions for loading Lotus 1-2-3:

Turn on the computer with the DOS disk in drive A.

Enter the date and time if directed.

Remove the DOS disk from drive A, insert the Lotus 1-2-3 system disk into drive A, and your work disk into drive B.

Type **Lotus**

Press (ENTER)

This displays the Lotus Access System screen.

Press **1**

This selects the 1-2-3 option and starts Lotus 1-2-3. Alternatively, you may load Lotus by typing 123 after inserting the Lotus 1-2-3 disk into drive A.

Lesson 1

Creating Simple Macros

After completing this lesson you will be able to:

✔ Plan and organize a macro

✔ Create a simple keystroke macro

✔ Document a macro

✔ Use the range name command to name your macro

A **macro** is a series of keystrokes that is executed automatically whenever the macro name is typed in. These keystrokes can consist of any that you can make from the keyboard. Therefore, your macros can include any values or labels that you wanted entered in the worksheet as well as any Lotus 1-2-3 commands that you wish to be used.

A macro is actually a program you write for using the Lotus package in a specific way. You use a macro to execute a series of often-used Lotus commands that would otherwise require numerous keystrokes each time the sequence of instructions needed to be executed.

To create a macro in release 2.01, you first need to enter all the keystroke instructions that you wish the macro to use. You may enter all of your macro keystroke instructions in a single cell of the worksheet (as long as they do not exceed 240 characters), or you may enter them in separate cells as long as they are part of a single range.

The next step is to assign a one-letter name to the macro by using the /Range Name Create command. Finally, after naming the macro with this command, you can execute it by pressing the (ALT) key along with the letter you assigned in its range name.

Starting a Macro Library Worksheet

You will save all the macros you create in the following exercises in a separate **macro library** worksheet. At the end of this tutorial, you will learn how to use this macro library when creating a new worksheet and how to attach these macros to existing worksheets.

If necessary, begin by taking the following steps to clear the worksheet display. (If you have just loaded Lotus 1-2-3, you can skip these steps.)

Type / **W E Y**

> This clears the worksheet display so you can enter your macros in a new worksheet.

Next, you will move the pointer to a new area of the worksheet where you will locate your macros. With the pointer in cell A1:

Press (TAB) three times.

> This moves the pointer to cell Y1.

Press (PGDN) three times.

> Your pointer should be in cell Y61.

> You will call this worksheet MACROLIB, which stands for macro library. Create this file with the /File Save command:

Type / **F S**

> You will get the following message: **Enter save file name:** Press [Esc] to clear any default drive designation that may appear after this message.,

Type **b: macrolib**

Press (ENTER)

Planning and Organizing Your Macros

When creating macros, it is best to adopt a three-column layout in which the first column contains the macro name, the second column immediately to the right contains all the keystroke instructions, and the third column to its right documents the functions of the keystrokes.

To demonstrate how macros work, you will first create a very simple one. You will create a macro to save your work to the current worksheet. The usual way of saving to the current worksheet involves three commands:

/ to open the menu at the top of the screen

F to select the File option

S to select the Save option

You are going to automate this process by creating a macro to carry out these three steps with just two keystrokes:

(ALT)-**R**

Later you will learn how to automate a more complicated series of commands with a two-stroke macro.

To begin you have to assign the macro a name. Macro names consist of a \ (backslash) and a letter. In release 2.01, you can create up to 26 different macros in a single worksheet, with the names \A through \Z.

You will name this macro \R. In keeping with the layout scheme described above, you will enter the macro name \R in cell Y61.

Type ' (apostrophe).

> This enters the name as a label.

Type **\R** (→)

> This enters \R in cell Y61 and moves the pointer to cell Z61. Note that you needed to preface \R with the apostrophe to prevent the program from interpreting the backslash as the repeating label prefix, which would result in a string of Rs across the width of the cell.

Entering Keystroke Instructions

Now you are ready to enter the keystroke instructions for your save macro. First we will review the steps involved in saving a worksheet.

To save a worksheet file under the same file name, you would first type /FS to select the /File Save command. Lotus 1-2-3 then displays the existing file name after the prompt, requesting you to enter the name of file to be saved. (Do not perform these keystrokes at this time.)

To accept the file name and save your changes under it at this point, you would ordinarily press the (ENTER) key. However, when creating a macro in Lotus 1-2-3, the (ENTER) key must be represented by a special keystroke instruction, the tilde (~). Anytime you want the macro to execute the (ENTER) key, you type a ~ as the keystroke instruction.

After the (ENTER) key is pressed to accept the existing file name, the program displays the menu options Cancel and Replace. To complete the /File Save procedure, you would select the Replace option by pressing **R**.

The following sections explain how to enter the keystroke instructions for your macro using release 2.01, 2.2, and 3.0 of Lotus 1-2-3. For an overview of the differences between versions 2.01, 2.2, and 3.0, see Appendix C.

If you are using release 2.01 (or earlier) of Lotus 1-2-3, you must step through the commands to save your worksheet under the existing file name, writing down each key that you press. Then you enter these keystroke instructions as a label in cell Z61. If you are using release 2.01 or earlier, skip to the section "Entering Keystroke Instructions in Release 2.01" to enter the macro.

In release 2.2 or 3.0 of Lotus 1-2-3, you can have the program automatically record all these keystroke instructions as you perform the actual /File Save command procedure. If you are using release 2.2, you can use its LEARN mode to record the keystrokes for this macro. These steps are listed under "Entering Keystroke Instructions in LEARN Mode (Release 2.2)."

If you are using release 3.0, you should use its new Record key ((ALT)-(F2)) to record and enter the keystroke instructions for this macro. You will find these steps listed under "Entering Keystroke Instructions from the Record Buffer (Release 3.0)."

Entering Keystroke Instructions (Release 2.01)

Type ' (apostrophe).

You begin by entering the apostrophe label prefix to force the keystroke instructions for selecting the /File Save command to be entered as a label.

Type / F S

This enters the /File Save command.

Type ~ (tilde).

This executes the (ENTER) key.

Press R (→)

This enters the keystroke instructions /FS~R as a label in cell Z61 and moves the pointer to cell AA61. Your worksheet should resemble the one shown in Figure MAC–1.

You can now skip to the section, "Documenting Your Macro."

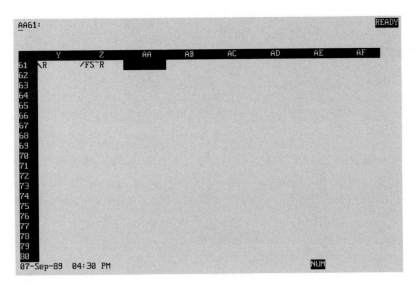

Entering Keystroke Instructions in LEARN Mode (Release 2.2)

In release 2.2, you can have Lotus 1-2-3 record all your keystrokes in LEARN mode. To turn LEARN mode on and off, you press the Learn key ((ALT)-(F5)). When LEARN mode is on, the program records all your keystrokes until you turn it off.

Before you can use LEARN mode, however, you must define a Learn range with the /Worksheet Learn Range command. When defining Learn range, always be sure to make it large enough to contain all the keystrokes you want included in the macro. This is because Lotus 1-2-3 stops recording your keystrokes as soon as the Learn range is full.

Create the Learn range for your \R macro with the pointer in cell Z61.

Type / **W L R**

> You should now see the prompt "Enter learn range: Z61."

Type **.** (period).

Press ⬇ seven times.

> This moves the pointer to cell Z68, making the Learn range Z61..Z68.

Press (ENTER)

> This sets the Learn range for your \R macro to the range Z61..Z68, which is more than adequate to contain all the keystroke instructions for this simple macro.

Now you are ready to turn on LEARN mode and step through the /File Save procedure:

Press (ALT)-(F5)

> Notice that the LEARN indicator appears at the bottom of the screen: This indicates that all keystrokes from this point forward will be recorded.

Type / **F S**

Press (ENTER)

M
A
C
R
O

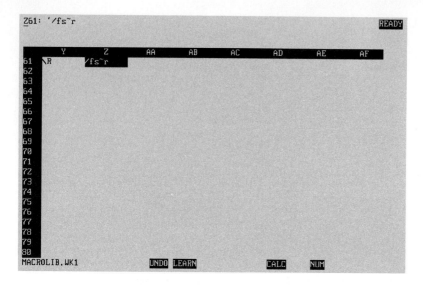

Type **R**

Now you are ready to turn off LEARN mode.

Press (ALT)-(F5)

The LEARN indicator disappears only to be replaced by the CALC indicator. To have the program enter the recorded keystrokes in the LEARN range, you need to press either the Calc key ((F9)) or the (ENTER) key.

Press (ENTER)

You now see the keystroke instructions /**fs~r** (Lotus 1-2-3 enters them in all lowercase letters) in cell Z61 as shown in Figure MAC–2. Next, you must turn off LEARN mode.

Press (ALT)-(F5)

The LEARN indicator disappears from the bottom of the screen, letting you know that the program is no longer recording your keystrokes.

You can now skip to the section, "Documenting Your Macro."

Entering Keystroke Instructions from the Record Buffer (Release 3.0)

In release 3.0, the program always keeps a running log of the keystrokes that you make (up to 512 characters worth). This temporary keystroke log is stored in a special place in your computer's memory referred to as the record buffer. You can use the Record key ((ALT)-(F2)) either to play back or copy any of the keystrokes stored in this log.

Before you can play back or copy the keystrokes for your \R macro, you need to add them to the record buffer by manually executing the /File Save command procedure. At cell location Z61:

Type / **F S**

Press (ENTER)

Type **R**

To copy these keystrokes now stored in the record buffer, you must press the Record key.

Press (ALT)-(F2)

This brings up the four menu options: Play back, Copy, Erase, and Stop. To copy keystrokes into cell Z61 that save your file under the existing name from the record buffer, you need to select the Copy option.

Press C

The program now displays all of the keystrokes you made since you began work on your macro library worksheet. Notice that the last five keystrokes in the record buffer are /FS~R, the ones you want to copy into your macro.

Press (CTRL)-(←)

This positions the cursor five spaces to the left, which in this case places it on the / (slash) of the keystrokes /FS~R, the first one of those that you wish to copy.

Press (TAB)

This anchors the cursor on the / (slash).

Press (END)

This highlights all five keystroke instruction—/FS~R—as shown in Figure MAC–3.

Press (ENTER)

The program now prompts you for the range you want to copy these keystrokes to. Notice that the current cell A:Z61 is the default.

Press (ENTER)

Cell Z61 now contains the keystroke instructions /FS~R.

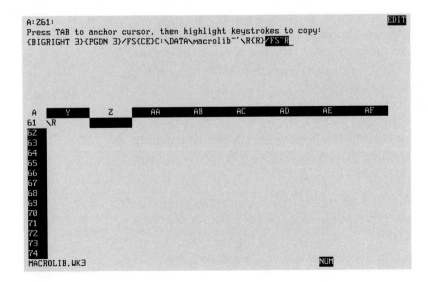

MAC–3

Documenting Your Macro

No matter which version of Lotus 1-2-3 you are using or which method you used to enter the keystroke instructions for your macros, you always need to describe, or **document**, their purpose and function. Therefore, you will now enter a comment in cell AA61 that documents what this macro does. With the pointer in cell AA61, enter this comment:

Type **Save worksheet under existing file name**

Press (ENTER)

> You have now documented your macro.

Assigning a Range Name to Your Macro

After naming the macro at Y61, defining it at Z61, and documenting it at AA61, you must assign the range name \R to the keystroke instructions in cell Z61. Though you have already entered the macro's range name in cell Y61, this name has not yet been recorded in the macro. You can use the /Range Name Labels Right command to assign the label in cell Y61 to cell Z61. To do this, you must first position the pointer back in cell Y61.

Press (←) twice.

Press /

Type **R N L R**

> The program now prompts you to enter the label range. Use the (ENTER) key to accept the default range of Y61..Y61.

Press (ENTER)

Notice that you did not have to enter the range name \R again. It was automatically assigned to the macro keystroke instructions in Z61 by the Range Name Labels Right command.

Executing Your Macro

Whenever you create a new macro, you should always save the worksheet that contains it *before* you use the macro for the first time. In this case, however, since the \R macro's function is to save all updates to the current worksheet, you can combine these two steps.

A macro is **executed** by pressing (ALT) and the macro letter name (in this case, **R**).

When you press (ALT)-**R** to execute this macro, be sure to watch the drive light on your computer. You should see it go on, however briefly, when you execute the macro.

Press (ALT)-**R**

> You should have seen the light on drive B go on for a few seconds as it saves this file to your work disk.

The \R macro has executed, and the worksheet is saved under its current file name, MACROLIB.

Creating a First-Time Save Macro

The \R macro can only *successfully* be used after you have already created and saved a worksheet under a file name. This is because Lotus assumes the existing file name that you originally loaded (MACROLIB in our example). If you have not saved a file yet, there is no default name.

For your second macro, you will create a variation of the \R macro that can be used when you have not yet saved a new worksheet or wish to save changes to an existing worksheet under a new name. You will call this macro \S. Note that, regardless of which release of Lotus 1-2-3 you are using, from now on you will type in the keystroke instructions for the rest of the macros that you create in this tutorial. This method works with all versions.

You will place the \S macro below the \R macro in your macro library worksheet. You must, however, be sure that you leave at least one blank cell between the macro instructions for the \R macro and those for the \S. This blank cell indicates where the \R macro instructions end and the \S instructions begin. This will prevent Lotus 1-2-3 from executing the macro keystrokes for the \S as part of the \R macro.

> Press ⬇ twice.
>
> This positions the pointer in cell Y63 where you will enter the macro's name.
>
> Type ' (apostrophe) \S
>
> Press ➔
>
> This enters the macro name \S in cell Y63 and positions the pointer in cell Z63.

Now you are ready to enter the macro instructions in cell Z63. For this macro, you only need to enter the commands /File Save when using it to save a new worksheet for the first time. However, you should add the keystroke instructions for pressing the (ESC) key for those times when you wish to use \S to save your worksheet with a new file name. Pressing (ESC) after pressing /File Save when the worksheet already has a file name causes the program to delete the file name from prompt line, whereupon you can then type in a new file name.

The (ESC) key, like the (ENTER) key, is another one of those keys which requires a special keystroke instruction in order to be entered in a macro. To include it in a macro, you must type its name enclosed in a pair of curly brackets, as in {ESC} (in either uppercase or lowercase letters).

As you continue working with macros, you will find that Lotus 1-2-3 uses a similar method for entering keystroke instructions for other special keys on the keyboard. For instance, to have your macro move the cell pointer directly to cell A1 using the (HOME) key, you would enter the keystroke instruction {HOME}. To have the macro move the pointer one cell to the right with the ➔ key, you would enter the keystroke instruction {RIGHT}.

Now enter the keystroke instructions for your \S macro in cell Z63.

> Type ' (apostrophe) / **F S**

M
A
C
R
O

Type {ESC}

Press →

> This enters in cell Z63 the keystroke instructions to select the /File Save command and press the (ESC) key. You have also moved the pointer to cell AA63.

Now you are ready to document the function of this macro.

Type **Save new worksheet or change file name**

Press (ENTER)

> This enters the comment on the purpose of the \S macro in cell AA63. Your macro library worksheet should be similar to the one shown in Figure MAC–4.

> Next, you need to assign the range name \S to the macro instructions in cell Z63. You should be at AA63.

Press ← twice.

> This moves the pointer back to cell Y63, which contains the label \S.

Type / **R N L R**

Press (ENTER)

> This assigns the range name \S to the macro instructions in cell Z63. Save your macro library worksheet before you execute the new save macro.

Press (ALT)-**R**

> This saves your new \S macro in the MACROLIB file. Now use your \S to save another copy of this worksheet under the file name MACROTST.

Press (ALT)-**S**

Type **b:macrotst**

Press (ENTER)

This completes Lesson 1. If you wish to exit Lotus 1-2-3 at this time, use the Quit command (\QY).

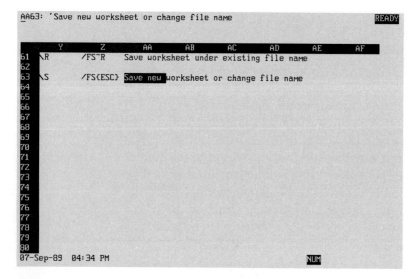

MAC–4

Lesson 2

Creating More Complex Macros

After completing this lesson you will be able to:

✔ Create a macro to automate a Lotus 1-2-3 command

✔ Use the macro pause command to allow user input

✔ Edit a macro

Creating a Macro for Changing Column Widths

Keystroke macros are most useful for automating those simple Lotus 1-2-3 command procedures that you find yourself using over and over again when creating a worksheet. One such commonly used command sequence is the one for modifying the width of various columns in your worksheet.

The next macro you are going to create will be called \W, and it will play back the keystrokes to perform the /Worksheet Column Set–width command. This macro will not, however, supply a new width for the column; you will do that manually whenever you use your \W macro. This enables you to use the same macro anytime you want to set a column width.

Retrieve your MACROLIB file. You will place the \W macro in row 65 (remember that you must separate the macro instructions by at least one blank cell). Begin by positioning the pointer in cell Y65. If the pointer is at W65:

Press ⬇ twice.

> This positions the pointer in cell Y65 where you will enter the macro's name.

Type ' (apostrophe) \W

Press →

> This enters the macro name \W in cell Y65 and positions the pointer in cell Z65.

The keystroke instructions for this macro are simply /WCS for /Worksheet Column Set–width; then the macro will terminate. With the pointer in cell Z65, do the following:

Type ' (apostrophe) / W C S

Press →

> This enters the appropriate keystroke instructions in cell Z65 and moves the pointer to AA65. Now, in cell AA65, you are ready to document the function of this macro.

Type **Change width of current column**

Press (ENTER)

This enters the comment on the purpose of the \W macro in cell AA65.

Next, you need to assign the range name \W to the macro instructions in cell Z65. At AA65:

Press (←) twice.

This moves the pointer back to cell Y65 that contains the label \W.

Type / **R N L R**

Press (ENTER)

This assigns the range name \W in cell Y65 to the macro instructions in cell Z65.

Save the new \W macro in the original macro library worksheet (named MACROLIB) before you execute it. To do this, you can use your \S macro.

Press (ALT)-**S**

Type **b:macrolib**

Be sure you are saving to your work disk.

Press (ENTER)

Type **R**

This saves the new \W macro in your MACROLIB worksheet.

Now you are ready to execute the macro. Do this by using it to widen column Z of the worksheet. First, move the pointer into column Z (cell Z65, specifically). Then:

Press (ALT)-**W**

You should see the prompt "Enter column width (1..240): 9" at the top of the screen.

Type **15**

Press (ENTER)

(Alternatively, you could press (→) 6 times.) The column-width indicator should now read 15 as shown in Figure MAC–5.

Press (ENTER)

Pausing Macros

Macros can contain more that just a series of keystroke instructions. They can also include any number of advanced commands from the macro command language included in Lotus 1-2-3. While an in-depth study of this Lotus Macro Language is beyond the scope of this introductory macro tutorial, there is one advanced macro command of which you should be aware: This is the command to pause a macro.

The **macro pause** is represented by a question mark enclosed in a pair of curly brackets, as in {?}. When a macro encounters this advanced command in the macro instructions, it suspends execution and waits for user input. It

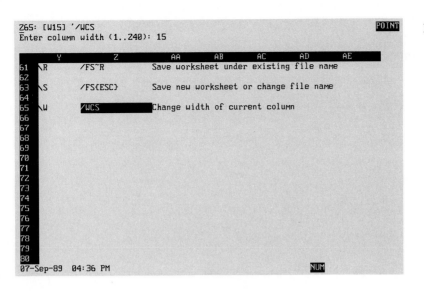

will not begin again until you press the (ENTER) key. As soon as (ENTER) is pressed, the macro execution resumes with the keystroke or command following the pause. Macro execution then continues until the macro encounters another pause or the end of the macro instructions.

To see how a macro pause works, you will modify your \W macro to include a pause. Strictly speaking, the macro does not require a macro pause to work. However, because it is so easy to forget to press (ENTER) when setting a new column with the ⬅ or ➡ keys, the macro will benefit from the addition of such a pause.

Modifying an Existing Macro

To modify an existing macro by adding a macro pause, you will edit the macro instructions using the Edit key ((F2)). With the pointer on cell Z65, make the following changes to the keystroke instructions of your \W macro:

Press (F2) (Edit key).

This returns the contents of cell Z65 to the edit line.

Type {?}

This adds the pause in the macro which will allow the user to modify the width of the current column.

Press ~ (tilde).

You added the keystroke ~ so that the macro will press (ENTER) to set the new column width as soon as *you* press (ENTER) to resume macro execution after the pause.

Press (ENTER)

This enters the keystroke instructions /WCS{?}~ in cell Z65.

To see how this pause can help you remember to press (ENTER) to set a new column width, you need to execute the \W macro again. First, however, save the changes to the worksheet with your macro.

Press (ALT)-R

M
A
C
R
O

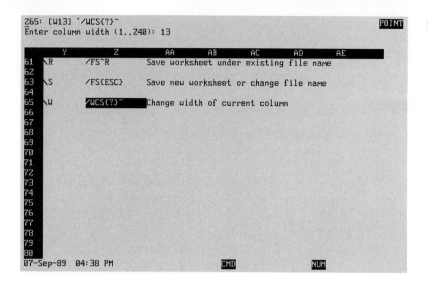

Now, with the pointer still in cell Z65, try your modified \W macro.

Press (ALT)-**W**

> This time the macro plays back the keystrokes /WCS and then suspends execution. This is indicated by the presence of the CMD indicator on the status line at the bottom of your screen.

Press (←) twice.

> This narrows the column width from 15 to 13 characters as shown in Figure MAC–6. Notice, however, that the CMD indicator remains on the screen, reminding you that you need to press (ENTER) to resume macro execution.

Press (ENTER)

> As soon as you press E, the macro resumes execution, the CMD indicator disappears, and the macro presses the (ENTER) key (represented by the final tilde), which sets the new column width.

Creating a Print Macro

The last macro that you will create will be a print macro that pauses to enable you to input the print range, and then prints that range using the program's printing default settings.

You have already had practice printing with Lotus 1-2-3 in two of the earlier tutorials. If need be, refer back to the section entitled "Printing a Worksheet" in the previous tutorial (Using Lotus 1–2–3) to review the keystrokes that will be required by this macro. This macro will differ from the ones you have created in your macro library worksheet up to this point because you will not enter all of its keystroke instructions in one cell.

You will start this macro in row 67 of your worksheet. If you are at Z65:

Press (←)

Press (↓) twice.

> This positions the pointer in cell Y67 where you will enter the macro's name as \P. Remember that row 66 must be blank.

Type ' (apostrophe) \ P

Press (→)

> This enters the macro name \P in cell Y67 and positions the pointer in cell Z67.
>
> The first part of the \P keystroke instructions in cell Z67 will play back the keystrokes /Print Printer Clear Range, which clear any currently defined print range.

Type ' (apostrophe) / P P C R

Press (↓)

> This enters the keystrokes /PPCR in cell Z67 and moves the pointer down to cell Z68. Here, you will enter the keystrokes to select the Range option before pausing the macro to enable you to specify the new print range:

Press R

> This selects the Range option and pauses the macro.

Type {?}

> When the macro is executed, you will key in a range to be printed.

Press ~ (tilde).

Press (↓)

> This enters the keystrokes R{?}~ in cell Z68, and moves the pointer to Z69. Note that only Z67 begins with an apostrophe; Z68 and Z69 are considered part of the same macro.

After specifying the range to be printed, you must add the keystrokes that send the report to the printer. You will enter these keystrokes in cell Z69. At Z69:

Type A G P Q

Press (ENTER)

> This enters the keystroke instructions AGPQ in cell Z69, which select the Align Go Page Quit options from the /Print Printer menu.
>
> Although you split the keystroke instructions up into three separate cells (notice, however, that they form a contiguous range), the program will execute them as though /PPCRR{?}~AGPQ were all entered in a single cell.

Next, you need to document the function of the keystrokes. Start by documenting the purpose of the instructions in cell Z67.

Press (→)

Press (↑) twice.

> This positions the pointer in cell AA67.

Type **Select Print menu & clear existing print range**

Press (↓)

Type **Select Range & pause to input new print range**

```
AA69: 'Print report, advance last page, & quit menu                    READY
```

MAC–7

```
          Y        Z          AA      AB      AC      AD      AE
61  \R     /FS~R        Save worksheet under existing file name
62
63  \S     /FS{ESC}     Save new worksheet or change file name
64
65  \W     /WCS{?}~     Change width of current column
66
67  \P     /PPCR        Select Print menu & clear existing print range
68         R{?}~        Print report & pause to input new print range
69         AGPQ         Print report, advance last page, & quit menu
70
71
72
73
74
75
76
77
78
79
80
07-Sep-89  04:41 PM                                            NUM
```

Press ⤓

Type **Print report, advance last page, & quit menu**

Press (ENTER)

> Your macro library worksheet should resemble the one shown in Figure MAC–7.

Next, you need to assign the range name \P to Z67, the first cell that contains macro instructions. At AA69:

Press ↑ twice.

Press ← twice.

> This positions the pointer in cell Y67.

Type / **R N L R**

Press (ENTER)

> This assigns the range name \P in cell Y67 to the macro instructions in cell Z67.

Before you can test this macro, you need to save your macro library worksheet.

Press (ALT)-R

> Make sure that your printer is turned on and that the printhead is positioned at the top of form (if you are using a laser printer, omit this last step).

Now you are ready to test your print macro.

Press (ALT)-P

> You should now see the prompt "Enter print range: Y67" at the top of the screen.

Press ↑ six times.

> This positions the pointer in cell Y61.

Type **.** (period).

> This anchors the print range on cell Y61.

Press (END)

Press (HOME)

> This extends the print range to Y61..AA69.

Press (→) five times.

> This extends the print range to column AF so that the print range is currently listed as Y61..AF69.

Press (ENTER)

> When you press the (ENTER) key, Lotus 1-2-3 resumes macro execution, thereupon sending the report to the printer.

This concludes Lesson 2. If you wish to exit Lotus 1-2-3 at this time, use the Quit command.

Lesson 3

Using Your Macro Library

After completing this lesson you will be able to:

✔ Use your macro library when you begin a new worksheet

✔ Attach your macro library to an existing worksheet

Your macro library worksheet now contains quite a few useful macros that you will want to be able to use when building worksheets in Lotus 1-2-3. You can start a new worksheet using as a basis the macro library worksheet, or you can copy the macros from your library to any existing worksheets.

To use the macros in this library when you begin a new worksheet, you would simply use the /File Retrieve command and specify MACROLIB as the file name to load. After the program retrieves this worksheet, you would then rename the worksheet with the /File Save command, using a new file name that is appropriate to the worksheet you are about to begin work on. This new spreadsheet will contain all of the macros in MACROLIB.

Attaching Macros to an Existing Worksheet File

You can also attach the macros in your library worksheet file to existing worksheet files. That way, you can use your macros to make it easier to complete or modify the spreadsheets. Following are the steps to attach your macros to an existing worksheet. Do not perform any of the keystrokes at this time.

To attach the macros in your MACROLIB worksheet to an existing file, you must first use the /File Retrieve command to load the worksheet you wish to work on. Then you must use the /File Combine Copy command to copy the macros from the MACROLIB worksheet into the current worksheet. The /File Combine Copy command copies only the macro instructions; it does not copy the macro range names. So, as a final step you must use the /Range Name Labels Right command to reassign the ranges names to your macros.

In this last example you will learn how to use this technique to attach the macros in your MACROLIB library worksheet to the ASSETS2C worksheet that you created earlier in Lesson 4 of the Using Lotus tutorial. Before you retrieve this worksheet, however, you must make one other addition to your library worksheet: You will assign a range name to the entire cell range that contains the macro names, keystroke instructions, and comments. You can then use this name instead of the cell addresses when you use the /File Combine Copy command to attach your macros to ASSETS2C.

If you have not already done so, retrieve your macro library worksheet. To assign a range name, you use the /Range Name Create command:

Press (F5) (Goto key).

Type Y61

Press (ENTER)

> This moves the pointer to cell Y61, the first cell of the range you are about to name.

Type / R N C

> This selects the /Range Name Create command. You are now prompted to enter a name for your range.

Type macros

Press (ENTER)

> You are now prompted to enter the range to be named.

Press (END)

Press (HOME)

> This moves the pointer to cell AA69, thereby making the range to name Y61..AA69.

Press (ENTER)

The cell range Y61..AA69 is now named MACROS. Before combining files, you must save this worksheet with the new range name. Use your \R macro to do this:

Press (ALT)-R

Now you are ready to retrieve your ASSETS2C worksheet.

Type / F R

Type b:assets2c

Press (ENTER)

The macros from your macro library should be placed in an out-of-the-way area of your ASSETS2C file, that is Y61..AA69. That way, you can use them to continue building this worksheet without having to worry that your changes to the worksheet data will adversely affect the macros you add. To do this, you should move the pointer to a new area that is well below and to the right of the area currently occupied by your worksheet data.

Press (F5) (Goto key).

Type **Y61**

Press (ENTER)

Now you are ready to use the /File Combine Copy command to copy the macros from your MACROLIB worksheet into your ASSETS2C worksheet. When you use this command, you can either choose to have the entire file copied or just a specific range. In your case, you will just copy the range named MACROS.

Type / **F C C**

> This selects the /File Combine Copy command. You must now choose between the Entire-File and Named/Specified-Range option. You will use the Named/Specified-Range option.

Type **N**

Type **macros**

Press (ENTER)

> You are now prompted to enter the name of the file that contains the range named MACROS:

Type **b:macrolib**

Press (ENTER)

> The program now copies the macro names, keystroke instructions, and documenting comments into your ASSETS2C worksheet starting at cell Y61.

There is still one more step to be completed before you can use the macros you have just copied from your MACROLIB worksheet; you must use the /Range Name Labels Right command to assign the range names in column Y to the macro instructions in column Z.

Type / **R N L R**

Press (↓) six times.

> This extends the label range so that it is now Y61..Y67.

Press (ENTER)

Your macros are now ready for use. Test this out by using the \W macro to widen column Z:

Press (→)

> This moves the pointer to cell Z61.

Press (ALT)-**W**

Press (→) five times.

> This increases the width of column Z to 14 characters.

Press (ENTER)

> This sets the new column width.

To complete this exercise, there is one more thing that you should do: assign a range name to the range that contains your macros. Remember that when you use the /File Combine Copy command, range names are not copied. Assigning your macros a range name makes it easier to locate or move them in your ASSETS2C worksheet.

Press (←)

> This positions the pointer back on cell Y61.

Type / **R N C**

Type **macros**

Press (ENTER)-(END)-(HOME)

> This highlights the range Y61..AA69.

Press (ENTER)

> Now save the worksheet with your \R macro.

Press (ALT)-**R**

This completes the tutorial on creating and using macros. To exit the program use the Quit command.

Practice

Using the MACROLIB worksheet, develop the following macros:
1. \O macro that prints the currently defined print range without pausing. (Hint: Use your \P macro as a guide, omitting the keystroke instructions that clear the currently defined print range as well as those that select the Range option and pause the macro.)
2. \E macro that erases the contents of the current cell (that is, the one that contains the pointer). (Hint: You use the /Range Erase command to erase the contents of any cell or cell range in the worksheet.)
3. \C macro that selects the Currency format with two decimal places and then pauses to allow you to indicate the cell range to be formatted before pressing the (ENTER) key for you. (Hint: Remember that you use the /Range Format Currency command to format monetary values in the worksheet.)

KEY WORDS

Document	Macro
Execute	Macro library

REVIEW QUESTIONS
1. Why are the macros in the macro library placed in an out-of-the-way part of the file?
2. What are macros most useful for?
3. What is a macro library?

Using dBASE IV

Hardware needed:

- ✔ IBM PC, XT, AT, or 100% PC-compatible; IBM PS/2 Models 30, 50, 60, 70 or 80; COMPAQ Portable II or III; or DESKPRO 286 or 386
- ✔ 640K RAM or more
- ✔ One 5-$\frac{1}{4}$" floppy and a hard-disk drive ; one 3-$\frac{1}{2}$" floppy and a hard-disk drive; or a floppy drive and network access

Software needed:

- ✔ Student Data Disk
- ✔ Work disk
- ✔ DOS 2.0 or later version
- ✔ dBASE IV installed on the hard-disk drive or the Local Area Network system

When you have completed this tutorial, you will be able to:

- ✔ Create a database structure
- ✔ Enter and edit data in a database file
- ✔ Make a backup copy of your database
- ✔ Create and use view queries to display selected data
- ✔ Link two database files
- ✔ Add and delete records
- ✔ Modify a database structure
- ✔ Sort records in a specified order
- ✔ Design and print records and labels

D
B
A
S
E

Tutorial Outline

What Is dBASE IV?

A DBMS, or database management system, such as dBASE IV is a set of programs that allows you to manage data using a computer. You may add, delete, change, sort, search for or calculate information from a database using a DBMS. Your college or university may use a DBMS to store information about you and your courses on a computer. The information in a database is stored in database files, much like it would be stored in file folders. The files are stored on disks, much like file folders are stored in filing cabinets. dBASE IV allows you to enter and use the information in your database file just like you would with data in file folders, except that the computer quickly performs searches, sorts, calculations, and reports. The examples presented in this tutorial are just illustrations. They could, however, be used by many small businesses in their day-to-day operations.

There are many uses or applications for dBASE IV, including:

- Mailing lists (membership and subscription lists)
- Accounting (bookkeeping and accounting information)
- Scientific research (experimental data, scientific journals)
- Business information (customers, vendors, inventories)
- Personal use (home record tape, book library)
- Library and government databases (scientific, academic, and agency publications)

As the DOS tutorial indicated, it is possible for you to use an application effectively without total proficiency in DOS commands. It is also possible for you to use dBASE IV without knowing all of its commands and capabilities. However, you need to know the basics of dBASE IV to create and use databases. This tutorial shows you how to use the menus and commands that are available in dBASE IV. It takes you through the steps to set up a database and to use it to enter, retrieve, sort, edit, and print reports using its data. These are the things that are commonly done in dBASE IV.

Now you will start dBASE IV, and in Lesson 1 you will do several things to familiarize yourself with the system. This tutorial assumes that dBASE IV has been installed on drive C, and that your work disk is in drive A. You should keep these drives, or the ones you are using, in mind as you progress through the tutorial. If you have difficulty running dBASE IV or finding your data files, you should check to see that dBASE IV is using the appropriate drive.

Before you begin to create databases and store data in them, you should be aware that the information in "open" database files is at least partially contained in memory. If you want to save the information on disk, you must either "close" the database files or exit from dBASE IV properly. If you do not, you will either lose some information or damage your database files, making them useless and forcing you to repeat some or all of the tutorial in order to complete and save the work.

WARNING

Remember, always close files when you have finished using them, always exit properly from dBASE IV, and never turn off the computer before you have exited to the DOS prompt.

In this tutorial, instructions for you to type in are given in **bold letters**. When you see (ENTER), you are to press the Enter key.

The cursor movement keys are indicated by arrows. For example, (→) indicates the right arrow key on the cursor movement keypad. Function keys are indicated by (F1) to (F10). A combination of keys, such as holding down the (SHIFT) key while pressing (F2), is denoted with a hyphen, as in (SHIFT)-(F2). The Escape key is indicated by (ESC).

For the sake of consistency and clarity, we recommend that you keep the (CAPS LOCK) key locked in uppercase, unless you specifically want to enter lowercase text. The (NUM LOCK) key should be off in order to use the cursor keys on older keyboards (keyboards without separate cursor keys and number pad keys).

Starting dBASE IV

Boot up the computer to the C> prompt, as described in the DOS tutorial.

Insert your work disk in drive A, label up, with the read/write slot in first. Close the drive door.

At the C> prompt (in the subdirectory with the dBASE IV program):

Type **DBASE**

Press (ENTER)

The system displays the dBASE IV logo and the copyright message, as shown in Figure DB–1. At the bottom of the copyright screen, a message appears:

Press Enter to assent to the License Agreement and begin dBASE IV.

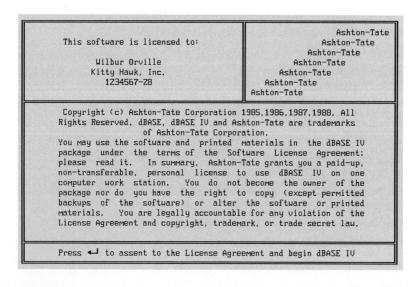

DB–1 The dBASE IV copyright screen.

DB–2   The Control Center.

```
  Catalog   Tools   Exit                                    7:42:52 am
                         dBASE IV CONTROL CENTER
                         CATALOG: C:\UNTITLED.CAT

     Data         Queries       Forms        Reports       Labels     Applications
 ┌───────────┐┌───────────┐┌───────────┐┌───────────┐┌───────────┐┌───────────┐
 │ <create>  ││ <create>  ││ <create>  ││ <create>  ││ <create>  ││ <create>  │
 │           ││           ││           ││           ││           ││           │
 │           ││           ││           ││           ││           ││           │
 │           ││           ││           ││           ││           ││           │
 │           ││           ││           ││           ││           ││           │
 │           ││           ││           ││           ││           ││           │
 └───────────┘└───────────┘└───────────┘└───────────┘└───────────┘└───────────┘

     File:          New file
     Description: Press ENTER on <create> to create a new file

     Help:F1  Use:↵   Data:F2  Design:Shift-F2  Quick Report:Shift-F9  Menus:F10
```

Press (ENTER)

The dBASE IV Control Center appears on the screen (Figure DB–2).

The dBASE IV program is now ready for you to use.

Lesson 1

Creating Database Files

After completing this lesson you will be able to:

✔ Create a database file from the Control Center or the dot prompt

✔ Use the Help facility

✔ Print a database file structure

✔ Open and close database files

✔ Enter records into a database file

✔ Make a backup copy of a database

✔ Exit dBASE IV

The Control Center

The **Control Center** is one of several full-screen utilities available in dBASE IV. On the top line of the screen are three menu options: Catalog, Tools, and Exit. The menu options in full-screen utilities can be accessed by pressing the (F10) key. When a menu option on the top line is selected, a **pull-down menu** appears, allowing you to select different options. You will use this feature shortly.

DB–3 The DOS Utilities screen.

The bottom line of the screen, called the **status line**, indicates special keystrokes you can use, like (F1) for Help. In the middle of the screen are six **panels**: Data, Queries, Forms, Reports, Labels, and Applications. Near the top of the screen, below the title "dBASE IV CONTROL CENTER," the name of the **catalog** in use is displayed. Your screen may show C:\UN-TITLED.CAT. The catalog is actually a special database file that contains the names of files that are used in a particular application. Files in the catalog in use are accessible from the Control Center panels.

Setting the Default Drive and Path

You are using a work disk in drive A, so you need to set the default drive and path. The default drive is the disk drive where dBASE IV expects to find your data files. You will need to set the default drive each time you enter dBASE IV. The default drive and path can be changed from the Control Center by using the appropriate menus.

Note that the bottom line of your screen shows "Menus:F10" at the right. To access the pull-down menus from the options at the top of the screen:

Press (F10)

A pull-down menu appears below Catalog on the top line. You can use the ⭠ and ⭢ keys to go to the pull-down menus for other options on the top line, or you can press (ESC) to close the pull-down menus and return to the cursor on the panels in the middle of the screen.

Press ⭢ to move to the Tools option.

To select the fourth option on the menu, DOS Utilities:

Press ⭣ to highlight that option.

Press (ENTER)

The DOS Utilities screen appears (Figure DB–3). This utility has many uses. One use is to change the default drive and directory. To change the default drive, you use the DOS menu option on the top line.

Press (F10)

This accesses the menu options displayed at the top of the screen. To select the third option in the DOS pull-down menu, Set Default Drive: Directory:

Press ⬇ to highlight that option.

Press (ENTER)

Type **A:**

Then, to blank out all trailing letters and characters:

Press (DEL) repeatedly.

Press (ENTER) when done.

This changes the default drive and directory. Now you should return to the Control Center.

Select the menu option, Exit (you should know how to do this by now).

A prompt appears: "Exit to Control Center."

Press (ENTER)

The Control Center screen reappears. Now, the catalog in use is A:\UN-TITLED.CAT. You will use this catalog for the dBASE IV tutorial.

To review: You have used the pull-down menus in full-screen utilities to reset the default drive and directory to your work disk in drive A.

The Dot Prompt

The Control Center is a powerful feature of dBASE IV. You use it by selecting options from menus, or by selecting files to use from the panels in the center of the screen. You can operate in the Control Center with just a few keys: the cursor movement keys, (ENTER), and the (F10) key to access the pull-down menus. This lets you use dBASE IV without having to type out the commands.

Another mode of dBASE IV operation also exists, called the **dot prompt**, because its prompt is a period (dot). This mode is command-line oriented, meaning that you type commands when you are at the dot prompt.

Moving Between the Control Center and the Dot Prompt

You can move from the Control Center to the dot prompt with the following steps.

Press (F10)

This takes you to the top level of commands.

Press (→) twice.

This selects the Exit option. The top option, Exit to Dot Prompt, will be highlighted; you can select it by simply pressing (ENTER).

Press (ENTER)

The screen changes to the one shown in Figure DB–4. It consists of a highlighted **status bar** near the bottom, with a dot on the line above the status bar.

The dot prompt puts you in **command mode** where you can enter your own commands. It allows you to do some things that are not available from the Control Center, and it allows you to do some things faster than selecting from menus, if you know the command to use. It is also important because the commands that are entered from the dot prompt can be placed together in a program, to allow the user to perform complicated and specific user-defined applications. These commands can then be saved in a file for future processing. We find that the easiest way to build user-specific applications programs in dBASE IV is to write programs using the commands that are used at the dot prompt.

We will be introducing both the Control Center options and the command mode. Sometimes, when you are working in the Control Center, you may inadvertently do something that causes you to exit to the dot prompt. It is easy to return to the Control Center. To return to the Control Center from the dot prompt:

Type **ASSIST**

ASSIST is a command that may be entered at the dot prompt.

Using the Help Facility

If you encounter difficulties or have a question during a session, the dBASE IV Help facility may provide some assistance. Help is available from within dBASE IV. When you are using the Control Center, pressing (F1) gets help relating to what you are currently doing. This is called context-sensitive help. The screen provides the information you need to obtain more detail on any selected item. When you have finished, you exit Help by pressing (ESC). The status line on the bottom of the screen reminds you that help can be obtained by pressing (F1).

At the dot prompt, you can access the Help facility by typing the command HELP and pressing (ENTER). Or, if you want to know about a particular command or function, type that command name after HELP, such as HELP DISPLAY (ENTER). The Help facility has several levels of detail. The information on the screen provides the information you need to find out how to use dBASE IV commands and functions.

Creating a Database File Structure

A database file holds the data that is used in an application. For example, an accounts receivable master file should contain the relevant information about each account. A database file can be pictured as a table, with rows and columns. Each row represents a **record**. In an accounts receivable master file, there is one record for each account. Each element in a record represents a **field**. The accounts receivable master file needs fields for such things as the account number, the customer name and address, the balance, and the credit limit.

In dBASE IV, each field is defined with a name and data type. The process of naming and specifying fields creates the structure of the database file. When the structure has been created, the database file exists and data may be entered. Field names begin with a letter and consist of 1 to 10 characters (letters, digits, or the underscore). Use meaningful names for fields. For example, DEPTNO is more meaningful than DNO or just D.

Several field types are used in dBASE IV, although we focus on only two in our first example. **Numeric field types** are used for fields which contain numbers that are to be used in arithmetic. **Character field types** are used for fields containing words or symbols, such as names, addresses, and telephone numbers. These fields also need to have their widths specified. For numeric fields we also must indicate the number of decimal positions. Since these two field types are the most common, we will focus on them for now.

You will create a file named MASTER (accounts receivable master file) with a structure as illustrated in Table DB–1. You will use the Control Center to establish the file structure specified.

If you are not currently at the Control Center, return to the Control Center by entering the command ASSIST (ENTER). At this point, the cursor

	Field Name	Field Type	Width	Dec
1	ACCT_NUM	Character	6	
2	CUST_NAME	Character	10	
3	STREET	Character	10	
4	CITY_STATE	Character	10	
5	ZIP	Character	5	
6	BEGIN_BAL	Numeric	8	2
7	UPDAT_BAL	Numeric	8	2
8	CR_LIMIT	Numeric	8	2

Table DB-1 Master file structure.

D
B
A
S
E

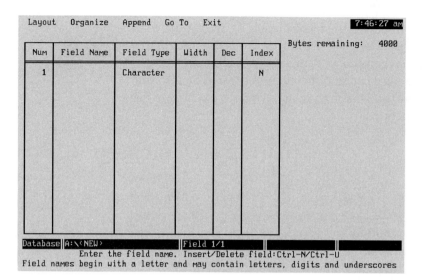

DB–5 Database Utility
screen.

highlights the word "<create>" in the Data panel:

Press (ENTER)

Figure DB–5 shows the full-screen Database utility.

In the Database utility screen, you enter one database field in each row, as shown in Table DB–1. Each character field requires a width, and each numeric field needs a width and the number of digits to the right of the decimal point (DEC). The last column on the screen, Index, will not be used now. Make sure N (for No) is entered in this column for each field.

Now you will enter the first field name, ACCT_NUM (use the underscore, not the hyphen):

Type **ACCT_NUM**

Press (ENTER)

The cursor will automatically move to Field Type.

As you type in the database structure, dBASE IV defaults each field type as a character field. If you want a character field, you may either type C or press (ENTER) to accept the default. If you want a numeric field, type N.

Type **C** (do not press (ENTER))

This selects a character Field Type. Even though ACCT_NUM will contain all numbers, we set it up as a character field because it will not be used for arithmetic.

Now you must enter the width for this field.

Type **6** (ENTER)

This selects a width of 6 characters.

Press **N**

This selects No for Index. Alternatively, you can simply press (ENTER), since N is the default.

You have now specified the first field. dBASE IV is ready for the next field specification.

Type in the remaining lines from Table DB–1, starting with CUST_NAME and ending with CR_LIMIT.

> When you have finished, check Table DB–1 to see if your results match. If there is an error, use the cursor keys to move to any row and column where a correction is needed, and retype the information.
>
> After creating the final field (CR_LIMIT) in the structure, you will be at the next field name.

Press (ENTER)

> This terminates the procedure.

Since you created the file structure from the Control Center, dBASE IV prompts with a box that states, "Save as:". You are to enter a file name. File names must follow the DOS file naming conventions as described in the DOS tutorial. dBASE IV automatically adds the extension .DBF to database files. You will name this file MASTER.

Type MASTER (ENTER)

> The computer will respond with the message, "please wait..." and then the following prompt:
>
> ```
> Input data records now? (Y/N)
> ```

Type N

> You are returned to the Control Center. The Data panel contains the file MASTER which you just created. The file name is above the horizontal line in the panel, indicating that it is OPEN, or being used.

Printing the Database Structure

You need to keep track of the structure of each database file. One way to do that is to get a printout of the structure. From the Control Center:

Press (SHIFT)-(F2)

> This returns you to the Database utility and accesses the Organize option.

Press (←)

> This moves the cursor to the Layout menu.

Press (ENTER)

> This selects the option, Print Database Structure, and your screen changes to that shown in Figure DB–6.
>
> Make sure your printer is ready to print.

Highlight Begin Printing

Press (ENTER)

> This prints the database structure.
>
> Your printout should say Page # 1 on the first line, followed by lines identifying the file name, number of records, and last update, then the eight field names and types and a line that shows the total width of the database record.

To return to the Control Center:

```
 Layout   Organize   Append   Go To   Exit          7:47:39 am
┌─────────────────────────────────────────┐
│ Print database structure        │ Dec │ Index │  Bytes remaining:   3935
│ ┌───────────────────────────────┐       │
│ │ Begin printing                │       │  N
│ │ Eject page now                │       │  N
│ │───────────────────────────────│       │  N
│ │ Use print form  {}            │       │  N
│ │ Save settings to print form   │       │  N
│ │───────────────────────────────│       │  N
│ │ ▶ Destination                 │   2   │  N
│ │ ▶ Control of printer          │   2   │  N
│ │ ▶ Output options              │   2   │  N
│ │ ▶ Page dimensions             │       │
│ └───────────────────────────────┘
│
│
│
│
│
│
│Database║A:\MASTER         ║Field 1/8
          Position selection bar: ↑↓   Select: ↵   Leave menu: Esc
                Start printing, using current print settings
```

DB–6 The Print Database Structure screen.

Press (F10)

Select the Exit option.

> You have the option of saving or abandoning changes. Since you have not made any changes to the database structure:

Select the option, Abandon Changes.

> You will be returned to the Control Center.

To review: You created a database file from the Control Center and specified the file structure. Then you printed the file structure. You will do this again, from the dot prompt, later in this lesson.

Opening and Closing Database Files

You may have several database files in the catalog, but only one can be opened at a time from the Control Center. It is easy to open and close files. Remember, whenever a file is open and you are making additions or changes, some of the data may reside only in memory. If power should fail while a file is open, you may lose some recently entered data or, worse, the file may be severely damaged. When a file is closed, all the data is safely saved to disk.

> To close an open data file from the Control Center:

Highlight the file name, MASTER

Press (ENTER)

> A box appears on the screen, as shown in Figure DB–7. The options in the box indicate what you can do to the file.

Highlight the Close File option.

Press (ENTER)

> The highlight cursor returns to <create>, and the file name is below the horizontal line, indicating that it is a closed file.

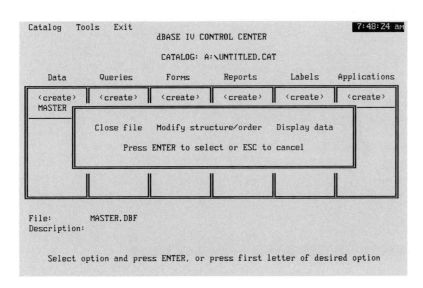

DB–7 Closing a file.

To open a data file from the Control Center, you highlight a file name that appears below the horizontal line.

Highlight MASTER

Press (ENTER)

Highlight the option, Use File

Press (ENTER)

The file name is above the horizontal line in the Data panel, indicating that the file is open.

Thus, file names that appear above the horizontal line in the Data panel are open files, and those that appear below the horizontal line are closed files.

Entering Data

Recall that you have only defined the structure for MASTER. Next, you will enter records into this database file. To enter data into an existing file.

Highlight the file name MASTER in the Data panel.

Press (ENTER)

The options box again appears. The third option, Display data, is used to enter data into the file.

Press (→) **twice.**

This selects Display Data.

Press (ENTER)

The full-screen Edit utility appears, as shown in Figure DB–8.

The status bar at the bottom of the screen indicates that you are looking at record 1 of 1 in file A:\MASTER. The screen shows that the record is empty. The highlighted areas by each field name are where you enter data.

DB–8 The full-screen Edit utility.

You can begin adding data into your database by entering the appropriate information for each field in the first record, and continuing to do so for subsequent records. You will add the five records shown in Table DB–2 and save them. The account number for the first record is 2145.

Type 2145

Press (ENTER)

The cursor moves to the next field. The customer name is JONES.

Type JONES

Press (ENTER)

The cursor moves to the third field.

Finish entering data for the first record.

When your data completely fills the field width, like the zip code, the computer beeps and the cursor automatically jumps to the next field. When you are entering data, you can use the cursor movement keys to correct data already entered. When you have entered data for the last field in the record, a new, blank, record appears for you to enter data in the next record.

	Rec 1	Rec 2	Rec 3	Rec 4	Rec 5
ACCT_NUM	2145	4115	4155	6598	6155
CUST_NAME	JONES	ADAMS	BROWN	FOSTER	WHITE
STREET	412 ELY	23 OAK	345 ELM	986 OAK	98 ELM
CITY_STATE	MAR, CA	LEE, IL	LEE, IL	LEE, IL	OAK, CA
ZIP	95485	78374	78374	78374	96254
BEGIN_BAL	100.00	200.00	300.00	300.00	400.00
UPDAT_BAL	150.00	200.00	300.00	500.00	400.00
CR_LIMIT	4000.00	1000.00	1000.00	1000.00	1000.00

Table DB–2 Data for master records.

Complete entering data for the remaining records.

When you have finished entering the data from Table DB–2:

Press (F10)

Select the Exit option.

This returns you to the Control Center.

Viewing Data from the Browse and Edit Screens

You can easily view the data in your file. There are two ways to do this: the Browse facility and the Edit facility. With the Browse facility each record is displayed on a single line, and each field is displayed in a column. With the Edit facility, one field is displayed per line. The (F2) key toggles between the Browse and Edit display modes. That is, pressing it once puts you in Browse mode, pressing it twice puts you in Edit mode.

From the Control Center, with the cursor on the file name in the Data panel:

Press (F2)

(You might have noticed "Data: F2" on the bottom of the screen, to remind you of the key to use to enter data.) The Edit screen appears, displaying the last record you entered.

Press (PGUP) several times.

Each time you press (PGUP), you move to the previous record. The (PGDN) key moves to the next record.

Move to the first record in the file.

Be careful, since any letters or numbers you type may be entered into the data file!

Press (F2)

The data is displayed in the full-screen Browse utility, as shown in Figure DB–9. To exit:

| Records | Fields | Go To | Exit | | | | 7:48:58 am |

ACCT_NUM	CUST_NAME	STREET	CITY_STATE	ZIP	BEGIN_BAL	UPDAT_BAL	CR_LIMIT
2145	JONES	412 ELY	MAR, CA	95485	100.00	150.00	4000.00
4115	ADAMS	23 OAK	LEE, IL	78374	200.00	200.00	1000.00
4155	BROWN	345 ELM	LEE, IL	78374	300.00	300.00	1000.00
6598	FOSTER	896 OAK	LEE, IL	78374	300.00	500.00	1000.00
6155	WHITE	98 ELM	OAK, CA	96254	400.00	400.00	1000.00

| Browse | A:\MASTER | | Rec 1/5 | | File | | |

View and edit fields

DB–9 Data displayed in the Browse screen.

	FIELD NAME	FIELD TYPE	WIDTH	DEC
1	ACCT_NUM	Character	6	0
2	REF_NO	Numeric	6	0
3	TRAN_CD	Numeric	1	0
4	PROD_CD	Numeric	2	0
5	AMOUNT	Numeric	8	2
6	AGE_CD	Numeric	1	0
7	DATE	Date	8	

Table DB–3   Transact file structure.

Press (F10)

Select the Exit option.

Select the option to return to Control Center.

To review: You entered data into a database file from the Control Center and then viewed the file in the Edit and Browse modes.

Now, close the file.

If you do not remember how to do this, review the previous section, "Opening and Closing Database Files."

Creating a Database File from the Dot Prompt

You can create database files from the dot prompt instead of from the Control Center. For this you need to learn specific commands. As a practice exercise, you will create a transaction file for accounts receivable. Again, you need to design the structure first. Table DB–3 shows the structure for TRANSACT, the accounts receivable transaction file. It contains seven fields. Note that the last field is a **date field**, which is a third field type that we will discuss. Note that date fields are eight characters by default with a format of month/day/year.

To exit to the dot prompt:

Press (F10)

Select the Exit option.

Select the Exit to Dot Prompt option.

Alternatively, you can press (ESC) and highlight Yes in response to the question asking if you want to abandon the operation.

Now, you are ready to create the database file. The dot prompt command to create a database file is CREATE, followed by the file name.

Type **CREATE TRANSACT** (ENTER)

The Database utility appears. You used the Database utility earlier to enter the structure for MASTER. This time, you will enter the structure for TRANSACT. Using the information from Table DB–3:

Enter the information for the seven fields.

Select N for the Index column for each field. To enter a Date field type for the last field, press D in the field type column. You need not enter a width for Date because it must be eight characters with an MM/DD/YY format.

After you have completed entering the seventh field:

Press (ENTER)

You will see a message on the screen, asking you to confirm the end of the operation.

Press (ENTER)

The screen displays the question, "Input data records now? (Y/N)."

Press N

You will be returned to the dot prompt.

In the Control Center, you printed the file structure by making menu selections. From the dot prompt, you will print by issuing a command. The DISPLAY STRUCTURE command displays the file structure on the screen, and the LIST STRUCTURE TO PRINT command prints out the file structure. At the dot prompt:

Type **DISPLAY STRUCTURE**

Press (ENTER)

The structure of the record will be displayed on your screen. Next, to print the data structure:

Type **LIST STRUCTURE TO PRINT** (ENTER)

The file now exists in memory.

Remember, you save a file to disk by closing it. The best method for closing files from the dot prompt is to use the command CLOSE ALL. This command closes all the files that are currently open.

Type **CLOSE ALL** (ENTER)

To review: You created a file, TRANSACT, from the dot prompt. You then displayed its structure on the screen and listed the structure to the printer. You used the command CLOSE ALL to save the file on disk.

Entering Data at the Dot Prompt

To enter data into a file, the file must be open, or in use. From the dot prompt, you open a file by entering the command USE, followed by the file name.

Type **USE TRANSACT** (ENTER)

The file name appears on the status line at the bottom of the screen. It contains no records.

To add data to a file from the dot prompt, use the APPEND command.

Type **APPEND** (ENTER)

Table DB–4 Data for MASTER records.

TRANSACT	Rec 1	Rec 2	Rec 3	Rec 4
ACC_NUM	6598	6155	2145	4155
REF_NO	11458	11459	77145	77146
TRAN_CD	4	4	1	1
PROD_CD	0	0	45	39
AMOUNT	–75.00	–13.50	50.00	10.00
AGE_CD	1	1	0	0
DATE	011788	011788	011788	011788

The system displays the Edit screen, which you use for entering the data. Using the data in Table DB–4:

Enter data for the four records.

After entering the data for these four records, return to the dot prompt.

Select the Exit option.

To view data on the screen using the dot prompt, you can use the LIST command.

Type LIST (ENTER)

The screen displays the data you entered into the currently open file, which is TRANSACT. If you see some errors, do not try to correct them now. You will learn how to edit data later.

The LIST command is also used to print data. The command to print data is LIST TO PRINTER. However, you will not print the data at this time.

Making a Backup Copy of Your Database

In business, the accounts receivable master file is very important: It indicates how much money customers owe the company. If it were to become lost or seriously damaged, the company could suffer devastating consequences. Therefore, many businesses maintain a rigorous backup policy with regard to crucial computer files. You can copy a disk file in dBASE IV from the dot prompt. The following steps copy the file MASTER to a backup file, MASTERBU. As you will see, to copy the database file, you must first open it. Then you copy it to a file of another name.

Type USE MASTER (ENTER)

The status bar indicates that A:\MASTER is open.

Type COPY TO MASTERBU (ENTER)

A message appears, indicating that 5 records were copied.

You can check that the copy procedure worked. To check the copy:

Type DIR (ENTER)

You should see that the "# Records and Size" of both MASTER.DBF and MASTERBU.DBF are identical.

If the two files are not identical, you will need to erase the backup file and perform the copy again. To erase the backup file from the dot prompt, you would type in the command ERASE MASTERBU.DBF.

You have created a backup copy of MASTER in case any damage occurs. This copy will also be useful when you modify your original database in later lessons. That is, you will still have a copy of your original database. From time to time in the tutorial, you will use the backup copy of the database.

It is a good idea to back up your database files regularly. If the information is important, like an accounts receivable file, you should make more than one copy and store at least one copy on a different disk in a different location from your computer and original data. (The command COPY TO B:MASTERBU copies the file to a disk in drive B.) This will ensure the safety of your database files and prevent the loss of valuable time and data.

Exiting dBASE IV

You have completed the first lesson. Now you will exit dBASE IV to the DOS prompt. There are two ways to exit dBASE IV: from the dot prompt and from the Control Center.

To exit dBASE IV from the dot prompt:

Type **QUIT** (ENTER)

You are now returned to the DOS prompt.

When you are in the Control Center, use the Exit menu option to exit dBASE IV properly.

Press (F10)

Select Exit.

Select the second option, Quit to DOS.

You are returned to the DOS prompt.

Use one of these methods now to exit to the DOS prompt.

To review: There are two ways to exit dBASE IV properly. It is important to use one of the two methods to safely close all files.

WARNING

Wait until the DOS prompt appears before turning off the computer.

Turn off the computer.

Remove your work disk from drive A.

Safely store your work disk. You will use it in later lessons.

1a1

REVIEW QUESTIONS

1. How do you start dBASE IV?
2. What should you do to quit or exit the program?
3. How do you move back and forth between the Control Center and the dot prompt?
4. How is a file created in the Control Center of dBASE IV?
5. How is data entered into a database file once it is created? Give two ways this can be done!
6. How do you make sure your database file is saved on your disk (as opposed to existing in RAM memory)?
7. What is an alternative to the Control Center?
8. How do you go between the dot prompt and the Control Center?
9. How do you list the structure of a file on the screen?
10. How do you print a file's structure?

Lesson 2

Displaying Data and Ordering the Database

After completing this lesson you will be able to:

✔ Create views for displaying data and linking databases

✔ Modify data in a view

✔ Display selected data from the dot prompt

✔ Arrange records in a database using sorting and indexes

Creating and Using Views

Views are a powerful feature of dBASE IV. A view is a way of displaying or printing the data in a database file. You will learn how to create and use views in this lesson, using selected fields from both MASTER and TRANSACT, which were created in the previous lesson. In this way, you can link, or relate, database files.

You will now start dBASE IV and set the default drive for your work disk. If necessary, review the instructions for starting a dBASE IV session, which were given at the beginning of Lesson 1.

Start dBASE IV.

Insert your data disk into drive A.

Set the default drive for your data disk, as you did in Lesson 1.

When you use a view, you can display selected fields or selected records. You might use a view because you need data from only a few fields for a particular application. You would use a view if the data in some fields is confidential, but a clerk needs access to other data in the file. A view can be used if you want to see the information in selected records only, like salespeople with less than $1,000 in commissions per month. Also, you can display the data in a specified sequence, if desired.

A view can also display the relevant data that exists across two files. In the previous lesson, you created an accounts receivable master file and a similar transaction file. Both files have fields for the account number. The master file has customer names and account information, and the transaction file has transaction codes and amounts. You can create a view to display names, account information, transaction codes and amounts as though the data were in a single file. However, when you use a view consisting of two or more files, the view is read-only; that is, you cannot edit the data from the view.

The ability to interrelate data from more than one file is a major component of DBMSs, which provides them with far more power than other file management packages.

A view is one of two kinds of **queries** in dBASE IV. The other kind of query is the update. An update can perform specified operations on one database file, depending on data in another file. Queries are useful because they can be saved as files on disk and they can be opened and closed, much like a database file. However, a query file does not contain data. Rather, it specifies the way that an existing database file is displayed.

In the following exercise you will create a view query for the MASTER database file. You should now be in the Control Center. If you are at the dot prompt:

Type **ASSIST**

Press (ENTER)

Now, open the MASTER database file for use.

Highlight MASTER at the Data panel.

Press (ENTER)

Select Use File.

That brings the file above the horizontal line.

Press (→) to highlight <Create> in the Queries panel.

Press (ENTER)

The full-screen Query Design utility appears, as shown in Figure DB–10.

The Query Design screen has five menu options on the top line: Layout, Fields, Condition, Update, and Exit.

The boxed area below the menu options is the file "skeleton" for MASTER.DBF. It is called a skeleton because it shows only one column for each field in the file. (TAB) and (SHIFT)-(TAB) control the highlight movement in the skeleton. That is, if you press the (TAB) key, the highlight bar will move to the next field; if you press the (SHIFT)-(TAB) keys, the highlight bar moves to the previous field. The skeleton may extend beyond the screen to the left or right. In the area beneath the field names, where the highlight is located, you can specify which records to use and which order to display the records.

DB–10 The Query Design screen.

Use the (TAB) key to move the highlight to all the fields in the file skeleton.

> After the last field, the highlight returns to MASTER.DBF. The boxed area near the bottom of the screen is the view skeleton. It shows which fields are selected for viewing when the query is in use. Initially, it shows all the fields of MASTER.

In the previous lesson, you accessed the menu options on the top line of any full-screen utility by pressing (F10). An alternate way to access a menu option is to hold down the (ALT) key while typing the first letter of the desired menu option. For example, to access the Fields menu option you could press (F10), use the (→) to highlight Fields, and then press (ENTER). Alternatively, you could type (ALT)-F, without having to press (ENTER).

> Suppose you would like to remove the STREET field from view.

Move the highlight to the STREET column.

Press (ALT)-F

> The pull-down menu under Fields appears.

Move the cursor to the second highlight, Remove Field From View.

Press (ENTER)

> The STREET field is removed from the view skeleton. Using the same procedure:

Remove the CITY_STATE and ZIP fields from the view skeleton.

Now you can look at the data display for the view query you are working on by using the Browse facility. As you learned in Lesson 1, the (F2) key accesses the Browse or Edit screens and toggles between the two.

Press (F2)

> It takes several seconds for dBASE IV to process the query. Then, the Edit or Browse screen appears. If the Edit screen appears first:

```
    Records      Fields      Go To      Exit                    8:14:11 am
   ┌────────┬─────────┬─────────┬─────────┬────────────────────────────────┐
   │ACCT_NUM│CUST_NAME│BEGIN_BAL│UPDAT_BAL│CR_LIMIT                        │
   ├────────┼─────────┼─────────┼─────────┼────────────────────────────────┤
   │2145    │JONES    │  100.00 │  150.00 │4000.00                         │
   │4115    │ADAMS    │  200.00 │  200.00 │1000.00                         │
   │4155    │BROWN    │  300.00 │  300.00 │1000.00                         │
   │6598    │FOSTER   │  300.00 │  500.00 │1000.00                         │
   │6155    │WHITE    │  400.00 │  400.00 │1000.00                         │
   │        │         │         │         │                                │
   ├────────┴─────────┴────┬────┴─────────┴─────┬──────────┬────────────────┤
   │Browse   A:\<NEW>       │      Rec 5/5       │  View    │                │
   └───────────────────────┴────────────────────┴──────────┴────────────────┘
                        View and edit fields
```

DB–11 Displaying data in a view.

Press (F2)

The Browse screen appears as shown in Figure DB–11.

Modifying Data in a View

You can modify the data that is displayed in the view, using the Browse utility as you would with the full database file. You will edit the data in the CUST_NAME field by adding "Mr.," "Ms.," or "Mrs." to the names.

Press (TAB) to move the cursor to the CUST_NAME field.

Edit the five names there as follows: **Mr.** JONES, **Ms.** ADAMS, **Mr.** BROWN, **Ms.** FOSTER, **Mrs.** WHITE

Cursor arrows can be used to move from one field to another, but (TAB) is quicker.

You have done two things. First, you created a view query for MASTER that displays all records of selected fields. Second, you edited the data in MASTER through the Browse utility within the view. Now you will save the view as a file.

Saving a View

Press (ALT)-E to exit.

Select the option Transfer to Query Design.

This displays the Query screen.

Press (ALT)-E to exit.

Select the option, Save Changes and Exit.

A box appears on the screen: "Save as:".

Type **VIEW1** (ENTER)

This view is now saved as VIEW1.QBE. The QBE extension that dBASE IV automatically adds to the query file name stands for "Query By Example."

The Control Center reappears. Notice "VIEW1" in the Queries panel. You have created and saved a view query named VIEW1. You can make it active (above the horizontal line) just like a database file, and you can browse or edit its data by highlighting the file and pressing (F2).

Linking Database Files

Next, you will make a view that links MASTER and TRANSACT. To do so, you must first add TRANSACT to the catalog.

Move the cursor to the Data panel.

Press (ALT)-C

> This accesses the Catalog menu.

Press (ALT)-A

> This selects the option Add File to Catalog. A **pick menu** opens, containing the names of database files on the default disk. From this menu, you "pick" the file to be added to the catalog. You will pick TRANSACT.

Highlight TRANSACT.

Press (ENTER)

> Another window opens with the message:
>
> ```
> Edit the description of this .dbf file.
> ```

You will now write a label describing what the file contains. This will be more informative than the abbreviated title and will help remind you of the contents of the TRANSACT file when you select it later on.

Type **ACCOUNTS RECEIVABLE TRANSACTION FILE**

Press (ENTER)

> The Data panel now contains MASTER and TRANSACT.

You can create a new view from scratch, or you can modify an existing view. You will modify VIEW1.

Move the cursor to the Queries panel.

Highlight VIEW1

Press (ENTER)

> A window opens with three options.

Select Modify Query.

> The Query Design screen appears, with the design for VIEW1. You will add TRANSACT to the view.

Press (ALT)-L

> This accesses the Layout menu. The top option is Add File to Query. To select that option:

Press (ENTER)

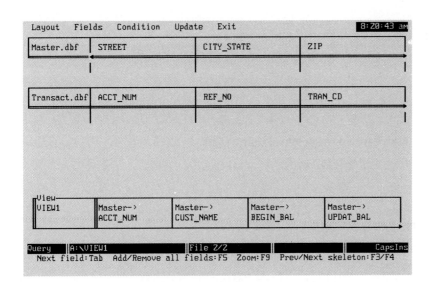

DB-12 Query Design screen with two files.

A pick menu of all database files on the logged disk appears for you to select the file to add. We added TRANSACT to the catalog because the pick menu shows only the files in the catalog.

Highlight TRANSACT.

Press (ENTER)

The Query Design screen now contains both MASTER and TRANSACT file skeletons (Figure DB–12).

In this view, you will include only the TRAN_CD (transaction code) and AMOUNT fields.

Move the highlight to the TRAN_CD column.

Press (ALT)-F

The Fields menu appears.

Select the top option, Add Field to View.

The arrow that precedes TRAN_CD indicates that this field was added to the view skeleton. Using the same procedure:

Add the AMOUNT field to the view skeleton.

You have created the view skeleton that you want to use. The (F3) and (F4) keys allow you to move the cursor between the various skeletons on the screen. To move to the view skeleton:

Press (F4)

Use (TAB) and (SHIFT)-(TAB) to see the fields that are contained in the view.

The next step is to relate, or link, the two files. The files have the ACCT_NUM field in common. This field will be used to link the files.

Press (F4)

This moves the cursor to the MASTER file skeleton.

Move the cursor to the ACCT_NUM column.

Access the Layout menu.

D
B
A
S
E

Select the option, Create Link by Pointing.

> The word LINK1 appears under ACCT_NUM in the MASTER.DBF file structure.

You now need to indicate the file and field that is associated with this field.

Press (F4)

> This moves you to the TRANSACT file skeleton. Using (TAB):

Move the cursor to the ACCT_NUM cell.

Press (ENTER)

> This completes the link, and the word LINK1 appears at the cursor. LINK1 serves as a label to link the two files.

To see the results of your labors, you can view the data.

Press (F2)

> If the Edit screen appears, press (F2) again to get the Browse screen.
>
> Your screen should look like Figure DB–13.
>
> The screen displays four records—the records that had links between the two files; that is, four records had ACCT_NUM that were the same in both the MASTER and TRANSACT files. More important, the display cannot be distinguished from a Browse screen of a single file except that the status bar contains the notice "ReadOnly." Now, if you try to edit information, you are prevented.

Next, you will return to the Query screen and save the changes as a second view query file.

Press (ALT)-E

Select the option, Transfer to Query Design.

From the Query screen, if you exit and save changes you overwrite VIEW1. You want to keep VIEW1, but you want to save this new view, too. You do this through the Layout menu.

Access the Layout menu.

Records	Fields	Go To	Exit			8:24:42 am
ACCT_NUM	CUST_NAME	BEGIN_BAL	UPDAT_BAL	CR_LIMIT	TRAN_CD	AMOUNT
2145	Mr. JONES	100.00	150.00	4000.00	1	50.00
4155	Mr. BROWN	300.00	300.00	1000.00	1	10.00
6598	Ms. FOSTER	300.00	500.00	1000.00	4	-75.00
6155	Mrs. WHITE	400.00	400.00	1000.00	4	-13.50

`Browse` `A:\VIEW1` `Rec 1/5` `View` `ReadOnly` `CapsIns`

View and edit fields

DB–13 Displaying data in a view of linked databases.

Select the option, Save This Query.

> A window opens with the message:
>
> `Save as: VIEW1.QBE.`

Change the file name to VIEW2.QBE

Press (ENTER)

You will now exit the query design screen without saving the changes.

Access the Exit menu.

Select the option, Abandon Changes.

> A box appears asking if you are sure you want to abandon the operation.

Press **Y** (do not press (ENTER)).

> The Control Center is displayed. You now have two query files: VIEW1.QBE and VIEW2.QBE.

To review: You have created a view for MASTER.DBF and saved it as VIEW1.QBE. You modified VIEW1.QBE and linked MASTER.DBF to TRANSACT.DBF. You designed the view skeleton to contain only selected fields from the database files. You browsed the data using (F2), as you would a database file. A view of a single database file can be edited, but a multiple-file view is read-only.

Displaying Data from the Dot Prompt

When you create a view, you can save it as a file and use it again. You can also enter commands from the dot prompt to display data. You will practice using some display commands from the dot prompt.

Exit from the Control Center to the dot prompt.

> You should begin by making sure that all databases and views are closed.

Type **CLOSE ALL** (ENTER)

> You may have entered changes to MASTER earlier in this lesson, while browsing the data in the first view. You will restore the original data from the backup file.

Type **USE MASTERBU** (ENTER)

Type **COPY TO MASTER** (ENTER)

> The message "File already exists" appears because MASTER.DBF already exists. You can either overwrite MASTER or cancel the command. You will overwrite it.

Type the letter **O** (do not press (ENTER))

> A message indicates that 5 records were copied to the new file. Now you can use MASTER.

Type **USE MASTER** (ENTER)

> When one database file is in use and you give the command to use another, the first database is automatically closed. The easiest way to see the data is to use the DISPLAY command.

```
. COPY TO MASTER
      5 records copied
. USE MASTER
. DISPLAY
Record#  ACCT_NUM CUST_NAME STREET      CITY_STATE ZIP    BEGIN_BAL UPDAT_BAL CR_
LIMIT
      1  2145     JONES     412 ELY     MAR, CA    95485    100.00    150.00  40
00.00
. DISPLAY ALL
Record#  ACCT_NUM CUST_NAME STREET      CITY_STATE ZIP    BEGIN_BAL UPDAT_BAL CR_
LIMIT
      1  2145     JONES     412 ELY     MAR, CA    95485    100.00    150.00  40
00.00
      2  4115     ADAMS     23 OAK      LEE, IL    78374    200.00    200.00  10
00.00
      3  4155     BROWN     345 ELM     LEE, IL    78374    300.00    300.00  10
00.00
      4  6598     FOSTER    896 OAK     LEE, IL    78374    300.00    500.00  10
00.00
      5  6155     WHITE     98 ELM      OAK, CA    96254    400.00    400.00  10
00.00
.
Command  A:\MASTER              Rec EOF/5       File            CapsIns
```

DB–14 Using DISPLAY to display all records in a file.

Type **DISPLAY** (ENTER)

The screen shows the data for all fields of the current record (the first record), including the record number.

Type **DISPLAY ALL** (ENTER)

As shown in Figure DB–14, the screen shows all records in the file. Each record is displayed on two lines. When the file contains more records than can be displayed on the screen, the display pauses when the screen is full and prompts you to press any key to continue.

You do not really need to see the record numbers. To turn off the display of record numbers:

Type **LIST OFF** (ENTER)

The DISPLAY and LIST commands are very similar. LIST does not pause when the screen is full (you can press (CTRL)-**S** at any time to pause the screen during LIST), so it is more suitable for printing data. The OFF parameter causes the display to omit record numbers.

Positioning the Record Pointer

LIST and DISPLAY, each without any parameters (such as ALL), perform differently. LIST displays all records, while DISPLAY shows only the current record.

Type **LIST** (ENTER)

All the records in the file are displayed.

Type **DISPLAY** (ENTER)

Nothing is displayed.

The current record, shown on the status bar, is EOF, or End Of File. You must reset the **record pointer**. Rec EOF/6 on the status line at the bottom of the screen alerts you to the fact that you are at the end of the file. Always check to be sure you are at the beginning of a file when displaying data. To get to the beginning of the file:

Type **GOTO RECORD 1** (ENTER)

> You have reset the record pointer to the first record. You could also have entered the command as GO TOP. The computer will respond: "MASTER: Record No 1." You may want to enter the command HELP GO to see the options that are used with the GOTO command.

Displaying Selected Fields

If you do not want to display all the fields in the file, you can specify only those fields to be displayed using the DISPLAY or LIST command. Suppose you just want to see the data for three specific fields in the file.

Type **DISPLAY CUST_NAME, UPDAT_BAL, ZIP** (ENTER) (the commas are optional).

> The screen displays the data for those fields in the first record of the file.
>
> Now, try this with the transaction file.

Type **USE TRANSACT** (ENTER)

Type **LIST ACCT_NUM, REF_NO, AMOUNT** (ENTER)

> The data for those three fields is displayed for all the records in the file.

Displaying Selected Records

You can select the records you want displayed, rather than displaying all the records in the file. You do this by specifying the condition that has to be met for a record to be displayed. The condition follows the command word FOR. For example, you might want to display only those records with the AMOUNT less than zero (negative).

Type **DISPLAY FOR AMOUNT <0 ACCT_NUM,AMOUNT** (ENTER)

To select records based on a numeric field, the arithmetic relation that must be met is specified in the LIST or DISPLAY command. You can try another example.

Type **USE MASTER** (ENTER)

Type **DISPLAY FOR UPDAT_BAL>300 CUST_NAME, UPDAT_BAL** (ENTER)

> The expression you gave for selecting records is for the UPDAT_BAL to be more than 300. Records that did not meet that criterion were not displayed.

To display selected records depending on the contents of character fields, the contents of the character field must be enclosed in single or double quotes.

Type **DISPLAY FOR CITY_STATE='LEE, IL'** **CUST_NAME, CITY_STATE** (ENTER)

> This displays records with a city and state of LEE, IL. The screen displays only those records where the contents of the field match *exactly* what you have between the quotes, including the comma and the case of the letters.

D
B
A
S
E

It is important that you type in the contents of the field in the same case as used in the file. That is, "LEE, IL" is not considered equal to "Lee, IL," because the latter contains lowercase letters.

Sometimes you want to match part of the contents of a field. The $ operator is used in place of the = operator in such a situation.

Type **LIST FOR 'CA' $ CITY_STATE** (ENTER)

You could read the command as "List for 'CA' contained in CITY_STATE." If you had an entry of ITHACA, NY in CITY_STATE, that record would also match the criterion specified in the above command because ITHACA contains a CA.

The SUM, COUNT, and AVERAGE Functions

There are several useful functions within dBASE IV that are available from the dot prompt. SUM, COUNT, and AVERAGE are three functions that are easy to use.

Type **SUM UPDAT_BAL** (ENTER)

Type **SUM UPDAT_BAL FOR CITY_STATE='LEE, IL'** (ENTER)

Type **AVERAGE UPDAT_BAL FOR CITY_STATE='LEE, IL'** (ENTER)

Type **COUNT FOR CITY_STATE='LEE, IL'** (ENTER)

Your screen should look like Figure DB–15. If there is a misspelling or a mismatch when selecting records based on character field criteria, then the message "No records" appears.

To review: You have used the DISPLAY and LIST commands from the dot prompt. You have learned how to display specific fields and specific records. You also used the SUM, AVERAGE, and COUNT commands from the dot prompt.

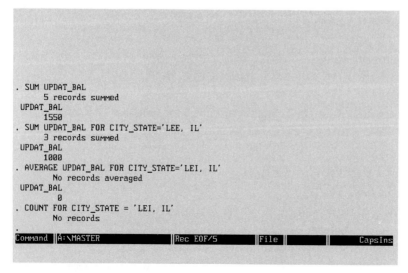

DB–15 Using the SUM, COUNT, and AVERAGE functions.

Ordering Records in the Database

Sorting Files

There are several ways to organize the records in your database. One way is to create a new, sorted file. You can rearrange the records in either ascending or descending order according to any field in the database. This produces a sorted database. The disadvantage is that the sorted file is static, even when you add new records. You must perform a new sort each time you add records or edit the data.

To illustrate the SORT command in dBASE IV, you will sort the MASTER file on customer name. First, you display records in the file before the sort.

Type **LIST CUST_NAME, UPDAT_BAL, ZIP** (ENTER)

Next, you sort the file by customer names.

Type **SORT ON CUST_NAME TO MASTER1** (ENTER)

A new file, MASTER1.DBF, is created with the records sorted by customer name. You can display the new file to verify the sort.

Type **USE MASTER1** (ENTER)

Type **LIST CUST_NAME, UPDAT_BAL, ZIP** (ENTER)

This verifies that the records are sorted by customer name.

You should try some other sorts, for practice.

Type **SORT ON UPDAT_BAL TO MASTER2** (ENTER)

Type **SORT ON ZIP TO MASTER3** (ENTER)

This creates two new files sorted by update balance and zip code. You should be able to check the new files and verify that the sorts were performed.

Creating Indexes

In contrast to the SORT command, the INDEX command creates a file that maintains the database in logical order even when new records are added. Thus, just as a view file makes the database file *appear* to contain only certain fields and records, or makes two database files *appear* as a single file, the index file makes the database file *appear* to be in a specified order when it is displayed. The manipulation in either case is done in RAM and does not affect the physical order of the database. That is, the record numbers are not affected by indexing.

You will again use MASTER. This time you will create index tags for keeping it ordered.

Type **USE MASTER** (ENTER)

Type **INDEX ON CITY_STATE TAG CITY_STATE** (ENTER)

A message indicates that 5 records were indexed.

You created an **index tag** named CITY_STATE that keeps the file in alphabetical order based on the contents of the field CITY_STATE. The index tag is part of a production multiple-index file, MASTER.MDX, and is always kept current. This means that if records are added the index is automatically updated.

To verify that the file has been organized as specified:

Type LIST ALL (ENTER)

You can see that the record numbers are no longer in order, but the CITY_STATE field contents determine the order of display.

Upon creation, the index tag is used to organize the records, and is called the **master index**. In subsequent use of the database, the master index is specified by typing the tag name after the word ORDER. For example, to use the MASTER file as ordered by the master index CITY_STATE, you would type: USE MASTER ORDER CITY_STATE.

To index the file on customer names, you create another index tag:

Type INDEX ON CUST_NAME TAG CUST_NAME (ENTER)

In the above example, you named the tag differently from the field it uses. That tag is now active. You can verify the results.

Type LIST CUST_NAME, CITY_STATE (ENTER)

The file is now organized by the CUST_NAME tag. To illustrate the dynamic quality of indexing, you will add another record to the file.

Type APPEND (ENTER)

Enter data for a new customer as follows:

Account number:	3456
Name:	ALLEN
Street:	116 MAIN
City, State:	ELY, NV
Zip:	89301
Begin Balance:	100.00
Update Balance:	100.00
Credit Limit:	2000.00

After the record has been entered, exit APPEND.

Press (ALT)-E (ENTER)

To see where the new record is listed:

Type LIST ALL (ENTER)

To review: You have created sorted databases and index tags for keeping database files ordered.

You may recall, during the file creation, that you repeatedly entered N in the Index column for each field. During file creation, you have the option of creating index tags. As you create files you will use this feature in a later lesson.

Type CLOSE ALL (ENTER)

Properly exit from dBASE IV.

Remove your work disk and save it.

Turn off the computer.

REVIEW QUESTIONS

1. What are the two types of query produced with the Query Design screen?
2. Why would you use views rather than database files?
3. What are the parts of the Query utility screen?
4. How do you add or delete fields from the view?
5. How do you link two database files in a view?
6. What happens if you misspell or change the case in a character field criterion in SUM, AVERAGE, or COUNT commands?
7. What is the result of the DISPLAY command?
8. What is the purpose of the $ in the LIST FOR command?
9. What is the smallest part of a record that can be displayed?
10. What is the difference between a sorted and an indexed file?
11. Which way of ordering is adaptable to new entries?
12. How do you specify the index tag to be the master index?

Lesson 3

Modifying the Database

After completing this lesson you will be able to:

✔ Edit data in a database file

✔ Add and delete records

✔ Add records to a database file from another database file

✔ Recall deleted records

✔ Pack a database file to remove delete records

✔ Modify a database structure

✔ Understand what is meant by a logical field

The first lesson demonstrated how to create database files and enter data. The second lesson demonstrated how to display and view the data. This lesson shows you how to edit data and how to modify the database structure.

Start dBASE IV.

You are initially in the Control Center. You need to set the default drive to A and then select A:\UNTITLED.CAT for the catalog (refer to Lesson 1 if necessary).

Insert your work disk into drive A.

Set the default drive for your work disk.

Set the catalog to A:\UNTITLED.CAT if necessary.

D
B
A
S
E

MASTER should appear on the Data panel. If not, you need to add MASTER to the catalog (refer to Lesson 2 if necessary).

Editing Data in Database Files

There are many reasons why the contents of a database file might change. The balance fields in an accounts receivable master file must be continually updated to reflect the current balances of customers. Occasionally, customers move or change names, and addresses and names may need to be updated. Also, data entry errors require correction. In addition to making changes to existing records, when the business acquires new customers, new records need to be added to the database file; and when customers close their accounts, their records need to be deleted from the database file.

Editing from the Control Center

Suppose that several data entry errors in MASTER.DBF have been brought to your attention. The name ADAMS should have been entered as AD-DAMS, and the address of WHITE should have been entered as 198 ELM. In the next several steps, you will make these changes or corrections from the Control Center.

Using the cursor arrows, highlight MASTER in the Data panel.

Press (ENTER)

A window opens in the middle of the screen with three options: Use File, Modify Structure/Order, and Display Data.

Select Display Data.

Either the Edit screen or the Browse screen appears. Remember that (F2) allows you to toggle between the Browse and Edit windows. The first field on the status bar near the bottom of the screen indicates which you are in. If it is the Browse screen:

Press (F2) to get to the Edit screen.

The data for the first record, JONES, appears.

In the Edit mode, you will use the (PGUP) and (PGDN) keys to move to the previous and next records in the file, respectively.

Press (PGDN) once.

The record for CUST_NAME ADAMS should appear.

Press (ENTER)

This moves the cursor from the first field, ACCT_NAME, to the second, or CUST_NAME, field.

You wish to add the letter D. To insert a letter, the Insert mode must be on. The (INS) key is a toggle key that turns Insert mode on and off. To ensure that when a key is pressed a character will be added, not replaced, look for the message "Ins" near the right end of the status bar. If it is not displayed, press the (INS) key to turn Insert mode on.

The (INS) key toggles between the Insert and Overwrite (replacement) modes. When you want to add a character in the middle of an entry, the Insert mode is more useful.

Press → to move the cursor to the D in ADAMS.

Type D

The name now reads ADDAMS.

You have corrected the name in the second record. Next, you will correct the street address in the fifth record.

Press (PGDN) until the record for CUST_NAME WHITE appears.

Press (ENTER) twice.

This moves the cursor to the STREET field. Making sure Ins is on:

Type 1

The address now reads 198 ELM.

You have made two manual changes to the data in the database file. Manual entry of changes is often used to correct data entry errors and to enter changes in names and addresses of people.

When you have finished editing the file, you can save the changes and exit the Edit screen. You previously saved and exited using the menu option. This time, you will use a different way to exit.

Press (CTRL)-(END)

This saves the changes and returns you to the Control Center.

To review: From the Control Center, you can edit data using either the Edit or Browse screens. To edit data, first select the required file. Then place the cursor at the appropriate record and field and make the change. In Edit mode, use (PGDN) to move from one record to another. In Browse mode, use the cursor arrow to move from one record to another.

Editing from the Dot Prompt

The dot prompt in Command mode provides greater flexibility for editing in several ways. We will explore some of these ways in the next few steps.

Exit from the Control Center to the dot prompt.

The status bar shows that MASTER is in use. The record pointer is located on the fifth record in the file.

From the dot prompt, the EDIT command is used to access the Edit screen. However, when you need to change data in a file, you often know which record you want to change. For example, if BROWN now lives at 100 ELM, you know that you want to change data in the record in which the content of the customer name field is BROWN. You can specify the record to edit from the dot prompt. Remember that the contents of character fields must be enclosed in quotes.

Type EDIT FOR CUST_NAME = "BROWN" (ENTER)

Be sure that BROWN is enclosed in quotation marks and that BROWN and the field's name itself are both in uppercase. The record for BROWN appears on the screen for editing.

By specifying the record you want to edit in the EDIT command with a FOR clause, the program finds the appropriate record for you.

Use ⬇ to move to the STREET field.

Change the data in the STREET field to 100 ELM.

Press (CTRL)-(END)

This saves the change and exits the Edit screen. To see the new contents of the record:

Type DISPLAY (ENTER)

Sometimes, you may know the record number of the record you want to change. If you need to check or edit the data in record 4, you can do so from the dot prompt.

Type EDIT RECORD 4 (ENTER)

The Edit screen appears showing the data for FOSTER. The status line confirms that this is record 4 in the file. You will now exit from the Edit screen to the dot prompt.

Press (F10)

Highlight Exit.

Select Exit to Dot Prompt.

Although the Edit screen is useful, sometimes you need to change the data in several records. For example, suppose the zip code for LEE, IL has been changed to 78327. Your database might have several records with LEE, IL physically scattered throughout it. You can use a single REPLACE command to do all the editing. Note that ZIP was designated as a character field, even though all its contents are digits. That is because it is not used for calculations. Therefore, since it is a character field, changes entered using the REPLACE command need to be enclosed in quotation marks.

Type REPLACE ZIP WITH "78327" FOR CITY_STATE = "LEE, IL" (ENTER)

Be sure to include the quotation marks around 78327 and LEE, IL as shown. Note that "LEE,IL" (without a space after the comma) is not equal to "LEE, IL " (with a space). Note too that uppercase and lowercase letters are not considered equal (that is, "A" does not equal "a"). A message appears on the screen:

    3 records replaced.

Type DISPLAY FOR CITY_STATE = "LEE, IL" CUST_NAME, STREET, ZIP (ENTER)

The three records with LEE, IL for CITY_STATE are displayed. All their zip codes are now 78327.

Sometimes, the contents of a field in all the records need to be updated. Again, a single command from the dot prompt can do it. Suppose that a 5 percent fee is assessed to all accounts, and thus all updated balances need to be increased by 5 percent. That is, the new updated balance should be 1.05 times the present value. A single dBASE IV command accomplishes this.

First, move to the top or beginning of the file.

Type **GOTO TOP** (ENTER)

Type **REPLACE ALL UPDAT_BAL WITH UPDAT_BAL * 1.05** (ENTER)

> A message appears indicating that all 6 records were updated. You can then see the results of the 5 percent increase by displaying the data.

Type **DISPLAY ALL CUST_NAME, CITY_STATE, ZIP, UPDAT_BAL** (ENTER)

> Note that all the UPDAT_BAL fields have the new values (Figure DB–16).

Thus, you have seen how to edit a record, using either the record number or the content of a field in the record to select the one desired. You have learned how to replace the contents of a specified field of several, or even all, records with a single command from the dot prompt.

After making these changes, you should copy the contents of this file to another database file for backup purposes.

Type **COPY TO MASTERBU** (ENTER)

> You see the following message:

```
File already exists,
Overwrite   Cancel
```

> The file MASTERBU already exists; you created it in a previous lesson.

Press **O** for Overwrite.

> The contents of MASTER.DBF are copied to MASTERBU.DBF.

To review: You have learned how to edit the contents of your database file. You learned how to get to the Edit screen from the Control Center and how

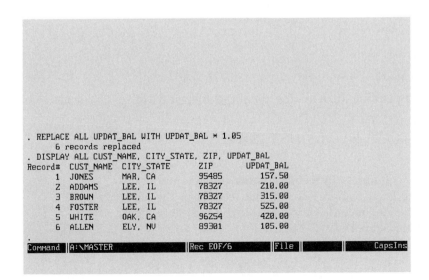

```
. REPLACE ALL UPDAT_BAL WITH UPDAT_BAL × 1.05
      6 records replaced
. DISPLAY ALL CUST_NAME, CITY_STATE, ZIP, UPDAT_BAL
Record#  CUST_NAME  CITY_STATE    ZIP     UPDAT_BAL
      1  JONES      MAR, CA      95485      157.50
      2  ADDAMS     LEE, IL      78327      210.00
      3  BROWN      LEE, IL      78327      315.00
      4  FOSTER     LEE, IL      78327      525.00
      5  WHITE      OAK, CA      96254      420.00
      6  ALLEN      ELY, NV      89301      105.00
.
Command  A:\MASTER                Rec EOF/6      File              CapsIns
```

DB–16 Using REPLACE to change all updated balances.

D
B
A
S
E

	Rec. 7	Rec. 8	Rec. 9
ACCT_NUM	1975	5280	2250
CUST_NAME	GREEN	BOYD	BLACK
STREET	301 MAIN	777 MILL	270 HILL
CITY_STATE	TEMPE, AZ	TAOS, NM	OMAHA, NB
ZIP	85281	87571	88101
BEGIN_BAL	400.00	200.00	250.00
UPDAT_BAL	0.00	100.00	0.00
CR_LIMIT	1000.00	2000.00	1000.00

Table DB–5 Data for records to append to MASTER.DBF.

to edit specific fields in specific records. You may exit the Edit screen and save your work at any point by pressing (CTRL)-(END). You also learned how to get to the Edit screen from the dot prompt. You learned several ways to specify which record to edit. You also learned how to use the REPLACE command to change data in several or all the records with a single command.

Adding Records to the Database File

The contents of many databases change with time. A growing business, for example, often experiences an increase in the number of customers it serves. The database needs to be updated by adding, or appending, new records to the existing database file. In the following example, you will append three records to the existing data in MASTER. At the dot prompt:

Type **APPEND** (ENTER)

> The Edit screen appears with a blank record for editing. The status bar indicates that this is the seventh and last record in the database file.
>
> The three new accounts that you are to enter are shown in Table DB–5.

Enter the data for three records in Table DB–5.

> When you are finished, a new record (Rec 10/10) appears.

Press (ENTER)

> This exits the APPEND mode.

To examine the effects of appending data to the database file, you can display some of the fields.

Type **DISPLAY ALL ACCT_NUM, CUST_NAME, UPDAT_BAL** (ENTER)

> The screen displays four columns—the record number, account number, customer name, and updated balance—for all the records in the file (Figure DB–17). The appended records were added to the end of the file. With DISPLAY ALL you need not GOTO TOP first.

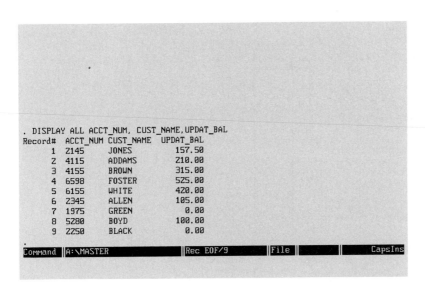

DB–17 Appending new records to an existing file.

Using Existing Index Tags

In the previous lesson, you created index tags on the CITY_STATE and CUST_NAME fields. You can view the data sorted in alphabetical order by either of these fields. The SET ORDER command is used to specify the index tag that is used for arranging the data.

Type **SET ORDER TO CUST_NAME** (ENTER)

Type **DISPLAY ALL ACCT_NUM, CUST_NAME, UPDAT_BAL** (ENTER)

The records are sorted alphabetically by customer name, as shown in Figure DB–18.

You can append records to the end of the database file without worrying about the order in which they are to be displayed. When you use the SET ORDER command to make an index tag the master index, the display is arranged according to that index tag specification even if records have been added.

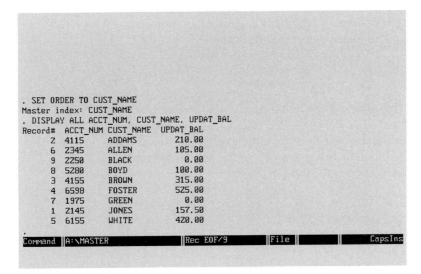

D
B
A
S
E

DB–18 Data sorted in alphabetical order.

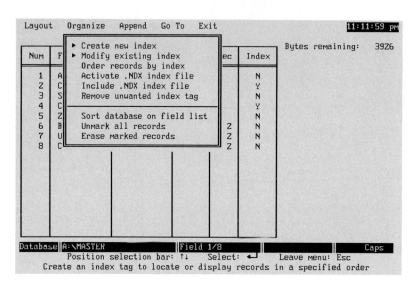

DB–19 The Design index menu.

You can also arrange the order of the data display from the Control Center.

Type **ASSIST** (ENTER)

You are returned to the Control Center. MASTER is still open in the Data panel.

Suppose you need to print out data from MASTER.DBF arranged by account numbers. You can do that by creating an index tag for ACCT_NUM and making it the master index.

On the bottom line of the screen, the message "Design: SHIFT-F2" appears. This option can be used to create, modify, or use index tags. With MASTER highlighted:

Press (SHIFT)-(F2)

The Database screen appears, overlaid by a window, as shown in Figure DB–19.

On the top line of the screen, the Organize menu option is open for organizing the data according to an index tag. In the window, the third option, Order Records by Index, can be used whenever an index tag already exists. You may not remember whether you created an index tag on ACCT_NUM. You can find out by selecting this option.

Highlight Order Records by Index.

Press (ENTER)

A list appears with the index tags you previously defined for MASTER.DBF. The list includes CITY_STATE and CUST_NAME. As you highlight each index tag, a window shows the expression that the index tag uses to arrange the data. Since there is no tag for the account number, you will create one.

Press (ESC)

This exits the Order Records by Index option.

Select the option, Create New Index.

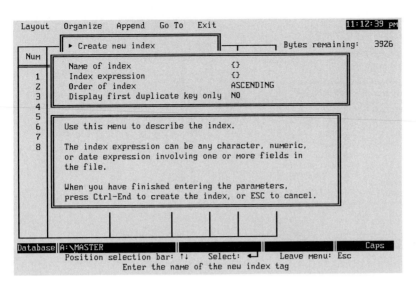

DB–20 Creating an index tag.

A window opens in the middle of the screen, as shown in Figure DB–20.

You need to name the index tag, specify the expression (the field name) that is to be indexed, indicate whether the index is ascending or descending, and finally indicate whether duplicate keys display only the first entry.

The option regarding duplicate keys may seem confusing. A **key** is the content of the index expression, or in this case, the content of the field indexed. For example, MASTER is indexed on CUST_NAME, so CUST_NAME is a key. If, however, there were several customers named BROWN, then you would want duplicate keys to be displayed to distinguish the different BROWNs. In this example, there should be no duplicate account numbers, so it makes no difference whether duplicate keys are displayed.

You will fill in the information in the upper window. With Name of Index highlighted:

Press (ENTER)

Index-tag-naming rules are the same as for field names: The name must begin with a letter, it must consist of letters, digits, or the underscore, and it must be one to ten characters long. When you index on a field name, you can name the tag the same as the field name, as you did from the dot prompt during the previous lesson, or you can give it another name. Here, you will name the tag ACCOUNT.

Type **ACCOUNT** (ENTER)

The index expression is the field name used for arranging the records. With Index Expression highlighted:

Press (ENTER)

You can type in ACCT_NUM or use a pick list to select ACCT_NUM. Using the pick list avoids problems of mistyping the entry.

Press (SHIFT)-(F1) to display the pick list.

A list of the field names appears, as shown in Figure DB–21.

Highlight ACCT_NUM

D
B
A
S
E

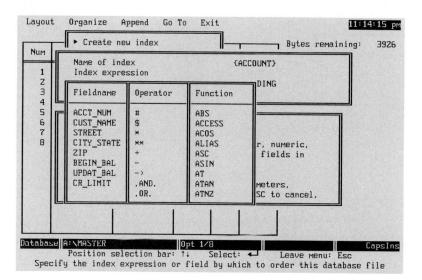

DB–21 The "pick" list.

Press (ENTER)

ACCT_NUM appears at the cursor.

Press (ENTER) to terminate the entry.

The next option allows you to specify whether the display should be in ascending or descending order. You do not need to change it from the default, ascending. The option to display only the first of duplicate keys, defaulted to No, is also acceptable. Thus, you have completed the specification for the index tag.

Press (CTRL)-(END) to save the entry for the index tag.

The new index tag is immediately used for the master index. You can display the data in ACCT_NUM sequence by pressing (F2).

Press (F2)

Either the Browse screen or Edit screen appears. If the Edit screen appears:

Press (F2) to toggle to the Browse screen.

If you are not at the top of the file:

Press (PGUP) until you are at the top of the file.

As shown in Figure DB–22, the records are arranged by account numbers. If you move the cursor up and down to the different records, you will notice that the record numbers shown on the status bar are not in order. Each record keeps its original record number, but the order of display is determined by the contents of the ACCT_NUM field.

Press (ESC) to exit Browse to the Control Center.

To review: You have used an existing index tag to arrange the data according to the contents of a field. The index tag keeps the data in order, even if new records are appended. You also learned how to create and use index tags from the Control Center.

```
  Records    Fields    Go To    Exit                      11:15:19 PM
 ┌────────┬─────────┬──────────┬────────────┬──────┬─────────┬──────────┬─┐
 │ACCT_NUM│CUST_NAME│ STREET   │ CITY_STATE │ ZIP  │BEGIN_BAL│UPDAT_BAL │C│
 ├────────┼─────────┼──────────┼────────────┼──────┼─────────┼──────────┼─┤
 │ 1975   │ GREEN   │ 301 MAIN │ TEMPE, AZ  │85281 │  400.00 │    0.00  │ │
 │ 2145   │ JONES   │ 412 ELY  │ MAR, CA    │95485 │  100.00 │  157.50  │ │
 │ 2250   │ BLACK   │ 270 HILL │ OMAHA, NB  │68101 │  250.00 │    0.00  │ │
 │ 2345   │ ALLEN   │ 116 MAIN │ ELY, NV    │89301 │  100.00 │  105.00  │ │
 │ 4115   │ ADDAMS  │ 23 OAK   │ LEE, IL    │78327 │  200.00 │  210.00  │ │
 │ 4155   │ BROWN   │ 100 ELK  │ LEE, IL    │78327 │  300.00 │  315.00  │ │
 │ 5280   │ BOYD    │ 777 MILL │ TAOS, NM   │87571 │  200.00 │  100.00  │ │
 │ 6155   │ WHITE   │ 198 ELM  │ OAK, CA    │96254 │  400.00 │  420.00  │ │
 │ 6598   │ FOSTER  │ 896 OAK  │ LEE, IL    │78327 │  300.00 │  525.00  │ │
 │        │         │          │            │      │         │          │ │
 ├────────┴─────────┴──────────┴────────────┴──────┴─────────┴──────────┴─┤
 │Browse   A:\MASTER              Rec 7/9          File          CapsIns  │
 └────────────────────────────────────────────────────────────────────────┘
                      View and edit fields
```

DB–22 Records sorted in ascending order by account number.

Deleting Records from a Database File

There are several ways to delete records from a database file. However, before you continue the lesson, it is important to understand some of the terminology that dBASE IV uses with regard to deleting records. When a record is deleted, it is considered to be "marked for deletion," but not physically deleted from the database. Deleted records can be recalled, which means that their "marks for deletion" can be erased.

A database file that accumulates many deleted records takes up excessive file space on disk because the records marked for deletion are still actually in the file. It can be cleaned up by **packing**, which means that records not marked for deletion are copied to another file, the original database file is erased, the new file is renamed to the original file name, and all the indexes are rebuilt. This process may take several minutes for large database files, but the command to do this is simple. First, however, you will back up your database file again.

Exit the Control Center to the dot prompt.

> MASTER.DBF should be in use. You will use the COPY command to copy the file to MASTERBU.DBF.

Type **COPY TO MASTERBU.DBF** (ENTER)

To delete a single record, you can position the record pointer to that record and give the DELETE command. Suppose you want to delete the record for customer GREEN. You can locate the record by setting the master index to the customer name field, then seeking the name.

Type **SET ORDER TO CUST_NAME** (ENTER)

Type **SEEK "GREEN"** (ENTER)

> (Be sure to enter quotation marks around GREEN.) The record pointer is located on the appropriate record. You know how to display the contents of that record.

D
B
A
S
E

```
. SET ORDER TO CUST_NAME
Master index: CUST_NAME
. SEEK "GREEN"
. DISPLAY
Record#  ACCT_NUM CUST_NAME  STREET      CITY_STATE      ZIP       BEGIN_BAL UPDA
T_BAL CR_LIMIT
      7  1975     GREEN      301 MAIN    TEMPE, AZ       85281        400.00
   0.00  1000.00
. DELETE
        1 record deleted
. DISPLAY
Record#  ACCT_NUM CUST_NAME  STREET      CITY_STATE      ZIP       BEGIN_BAL UPDA
T_BAL CR_LIMIT
      7 ×1975     GREEN      301 MAIN    TEMPE, AZ       85281        400.00
   0.00  1000.00
.
Command  A:\MASTER              Rec 7/9        File                   CapsIns
```

DB–23 The record "GREEN" marked for deletion.

Display the contents of the current record to be sure you are at the record for GREEN.

Now you can delete the record.

Type **DELETE** (ENTER)

The message "1 record deleted" appears.

Type **DISPLAY** (ENTER)

The record is displayed again, but an asterisk appears after the record number, indicating that the record is marked for deletion (Figure DB–23).

The DELETE command can be used with modifiers. You can delete a specific record by specifying its record number. As an exercise, you will delete the first record in the database file.

Type **DELETE RECORD 1** (ENTER)

Now two records are marked for deletion. You can see these with the following command.

Type **DISPLAY ALL ACCT_NUM, CUST_NAME** (ENTER)

Asterisks appear after the record numbers for GREEN and JONES, indicating the deleted records.

To unmark (that is, undelete) these records, you use the RECALL command.

Type **RECALL ALL** (ENTER)

The message "2 records recalled" appears.

The DELETE command can also be used to select several records that meet a specific condition. Suppose you want to delete the records for all customers with an updated balance of 0.

Type **DELETE FOR UPDAT_BAL = 0** (ENTER)

The message "2 records deleted" appears.

Type **LIST CUST_NAME, UPDAT_BAL** (ENTER)

This displays all the records and indicates with an asterisk that the records for customers BLACK and GREEN (those with UPDAT_BAL = 0) are marked for deletion.

As mentioned earlier, a database file may eventually contain many deleted records. You can physically remove them from the database file by packing the file.

Type **PACK** (ENTER)

The messages indicate that 7 records were copied and the indexes were rebuilt for the database file.

Type **LIST CUST_NAME, UPDAT_BAL** (ENTER)

The deleted records are no longer displayed. They no longer exist with the database file.

When you pack a file, it is no longer possible to recover deleted records with the RECALL command. Thus, to physically delete records you must first mark them for deletion with the DELETE command, and then re-create your file, eliminating records marked for deletion with the PACK command.

The final example of removing records from a database file involves deleting all the records and packing the file. This can be done with a single command. When *all* the data in a database file is to be deleted and erased, but the file structure is to remain intact, then a single command, ZAP, deletes and packs the database file. An example is given in the following steps.

Type **ZAP** (ENTER)

A message such as the following appears:

```
Zap A:\MASTER.DBF? (Y/N)
```

Type **Y** (do not press (ENTER))

Messages appear indicating that the indexes were rebuilt.

The status line indicates that there are no records in MASTER. If you should accidentally delete some or all records from MASTER, you can copy them from MASTERBU.

Type **APPEND FROM MASTERBU** (ENTER)

A message indicates that 9 records were appended to MASTER.

Note: If you use Browse to view the records, you will notice that they are in order by account numbers. That is because the last time you copied MASTER to MASTERBU, MASTER was in order by account number. Even though the physical records of the database file have changed, you can still use all the indexes you earlier built for MASTER.

To review: You learned how to add records to your database file using APPEND. You also learned how to mark for deletion selected records from your database file using the DELETE command. The RECALL command was used to undelete records, and the PACK command was used to remove all the deleted records from the database file. The ZAP command was used to delete all the records from the database file and pack the file. The

APPEND FROM command was used to add records to the database file from another database file.

Modifying the Structure of a Database

So far in this lesson, you have seen how dBASE IV can be used to modify the contents of one or more records and how you can append and delete records from the database file. These operations dealt with the data contained in the database file. In dBASE IV, you can also modify the database structure, even if the database contains data. The contents of the database are not lost when you modify the structure. In the next several steps, you will modify the structure of MASTER in several ways. First, you will increase the widths of two of the fields. Then, you will add a new field to the database structure.

It is also possible to delete fields from the structure (in which case the data in those fields is lost), to change field names, and even to change field types, although these modifications are not covered in this tutorial.

Changing the Width of Existing Fields

Suppose you need to increase the width of CITY_STATE to 15 characters and ZIP to 9 characters. You do not need to create a new database file and copy all your data from MASTER. Rather, you can modify the structure of MASTER, keeping all the data intact.

At the dot prompt, using MASTER.DBF, the MODIFY STRUCTURE command is used to change the database structure.

Type **MODIFY STRUCTURE** (ENTER)

> The Database screen appears. The work surface in the middle of the screen contains the field names, types, and widths. The fourth field, CITY_STATE, has a width of 10. If you need to enter data for a customer from LOS ANGELES, CA, then you need a field at least 15 characters wide. You will increase the width of the field to 15.

Move the cursor to field 4 (CITY_STATE).

Press (ENTER) twice to move to the width column.

Type **15**

Press (ENTER)

Increasing the width of a character or numeric field is easily performed. Next, you will increase the width of ZIP from 5 to 9.

Move the cursor to the width column of field 5 (ZIP).

Type **9**

Press (ENTER)

To exit the Database screen and save the changes you have made to the structure, you use (CTRL)-(END).

Press (CTRL)-(END)

> A message appears stating that you have changed the structure of the database file. It asks if you are sure that you want to save the changes.

Press Y (do not press (ENTER))

> To view your changes:

Type **DISPLAY STRUCTURE** (ENTER)

> To see the data in the new structure:

Type **BROWSE** (ENTER)

> The contents of the modified fields were not lost by increasing the widths.

Exit Browse to the dot prompt.

Adding a New Field to the Database Structure

Another way to modify the database structure is to add new fields. You will add a new field, GOODCREDIT, that will be a **logical field type**, containing either T (for true) or F (for false). After you have modified the structure, you will enter data into GOODCREDIT.

Type **MODIFY STRUCTURE** (ENTER)

> The Database screen appears. You will add the new field below the CR_LIMIT field.

Press ⬇ until you are on the line below CR_LIMIT.

Type **GOODCREDIT**

> The cursor moves to the Field Type column. To indicate a logical field:

Type **L** (do not press (ENTER))

> The field width of 1 is automatically inserted. The cursor jumps to the next row.

> Logical fields contain a single character that indicates one of two "logical states," either TRUE or FALSE. TRUE is represented by T, t, Y, or y (standing for true or yes) and FALSE is indicated by F, f, N, or n (standing for false or no).

To terminate changes to the database structure:

Press (CTRL)-(END)

> The message indicating that you have made changes to the structure again appears. To confirm that you want to save the changes:

Press Y (do not press (ENTER))

> You are returned to the dot prompt.

You can display the contents of a single record to see the effects of the changes you have made.

Type **DISPLAY** (ENTER)

> Your screen should look like Figure DB–24. The contents of the record were preserved, and GOODCREDIT was added to the database structure. The new field contains .F. initially, indicating logical FALSE. You will set all the credit ratings to TRUE, and later change the ratings as appropriate.

Type **REPLACE ALL GOODCREDIT WITH .T.** (ENTER)

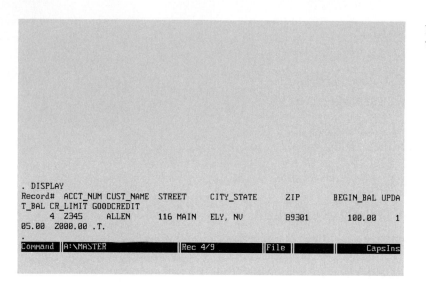

DB–24 Displaying a record with new field added.

Be sure to enclose the T in periods; it represents the logical value TRUE.

Edit the database and change GOODCREDIT to F for customers BROWN, WHITE, GREEN, and BLACK.

When done, return to the dot prompt.

Note: If you assign a value to a logical field with the REPLACE command, the value is enclosed in periods, like .T. or .F., to indicate the logical values.

Logical fields are often used to indicate whether or not to perform certain processing operations for the record. For example, you might want to display all customers with either good or bad credit ratings. The next two examples show this.

Type DISPLAY CUST_NAME, GOODCREDIT FOR GOODCREDIT (ENTER)

FOR GOODCREDIT means FOR values of T, t, Y, or y in the field. Only the records with a GOODCREDIT of TRUE are displayed (Figure DB–25).

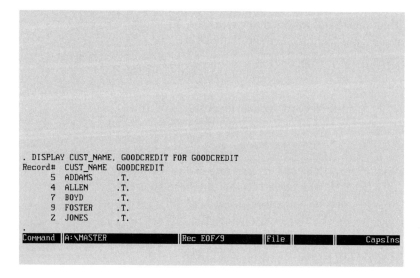

DB–25 Displaying records with good credit ratings.

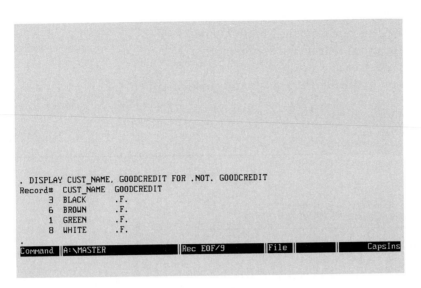

```
. DISPLAY CUST_NAME, GOODCREDIT FOR .NOT. GOODCREDIT
Record#  CUST_NAME  GOODCREDIT
      3  BLACK       .F.
      6  BROWN       .F.
      1  GREEN       .F.
      8  WHITE       .F.
.
Command  A:\MASTER              Rec EOF/9      File              CapsIns
```

Type **DISPLAY CUST_NAME, GOODCREDIT FOR .NOT. GOODCREDIT** (ENTER)

> This displays Customer Name and Good Credit for records where GOODCREDIT is F, f, N, or n (Figure DB–26).

> The two FOR clauses in the above examples indicate how to select logical records that are true or false. The word .NOT. is enclosed in periods to indicate that it is a logical operator.

To review: You have modified the database structure to increase the widths of two fields and to add a logical field. You have accessed certain records with the logical field that is considered either TRUE or FALSE.

Type **CLOSE ALL** (ENTER)

Exit dBASE IV to the DOS prompt.

Turn off the computer.

Remove your work disk from drive A and safely store it.

REVIEW QUESTIONS

1. What is the purpose of the (CTRL)-(END) key combination?
2. From the dot prompt, how can you specify which record to edit from the Edit screen?
3. What are two dot commands used to edit data? What determines which command is better to use?
4. How do you create an index tag from the Control Center?
5. How do you specify an index tag to be the master index from the dot prompt?
6. How do you specify an index tag to be the master index from the Control Center?
7. How could you delete records from MASTER.DBF with credit limits of less than 3000?
8. How do you undelete records?
9. How do you delete and pack all the records in a file?
10. How do you copy all the records from a backup file back into an empty database file?

11. How do you modify a database structure from the Control Center?
12. How do you modify a database structure from the dot prompt?
13. In what ways can you modify a database structure?
This is the end of the third lesson in dBASE IV. You should close MASTER and properly exit dBASE IV.

Lesson 4

Creating Reports and Labels

After completing this lesson you will be able to:

✔ Generate Quick Reports

✔ Design and print custom reports

✔ Use functions to perform calculations on reports

✔ Create and print mailing labels

✔ Print selected records

The first three lessons covered many of the operations that are frequently performed in a DBMS. This lesson shows you how to create and print reports and labels.

The instructions for starting dBASE IV were given at the beginning of Lesson 1.

Start dBASE IV.

> You are initially at the Control Center. You need to set the default drive to A and then select A:\UNTITLED.CAT for the catalog (refer to Lesson 1 if necessary).

Insert your work disk into drive A.

Set the default drive for your work disk.

If necessary, set the catalog to A:\UNTITLED.CAT.

> MASTER and TRANSACT should appear on the Data panel. If not, you need to add MASTER and TRANSACT to the catalog. (Refer to Lesson 2 if necessary.)

Creating and Printing Reports

A **report** is a printout containing information from a database. There are many ways that a report can be formatted, or laid out on the printed page. A simple report design consists of report columns for the various database fields that are selected for printing. The report has a title, and each report column contains a descriptive heading of its contents. The body of the report may consist of one line for each record to be printed. At the end of the report, there may be a footer that displays totals, if required.

It is not necessary to print all the fields, or even all the records, in a database. The selection of the fields to print is determined by the report design process. The selection of the records to print is determined at the time of printing. Therefore, we will cover the report design process first. Then, we will cover report printing.

You should be aware of one other thing about reports and labels in dBASE IV. When a report or label is generated, the design instructions you have given are processed by the computer to generate a fast-running set of instructions. Each process may take a minute or so, but the subsequent printing of reports is fast. Each time you modify a report or label format, the process needs to be performed again.

The first report you print will contain all the data in TRANSACT.DBF. You will create the report from the Control Center, using dBASE IV's Quick Report facility.

Generating Quick Reports

To generate a Quick Report, you need to select a database or a view for the report to use. You will use TRANSACT.DBF, which you created in the first lesson.

Select TRANSACT in the Data panel.

Then select Use File.

> Quick Report is a feature of dBASE IV that prints an untitled report with the field names as the report column titles. All the records are printed, and sums are printed for all the numeric fields. A Quick Report is useful for checking data. Quick Reports can be generated from the Control Center, the Browse or Edit screens, or the Query design screen by pressing (SHIFT)-(F9).

Press (SHIFT)-(F9) to generate a Quick Report.

> A menu appears (Figure DB–27). This time, you will view the report on the screen.

Highlight the option, View Report on Screen.

Press (ENTER)

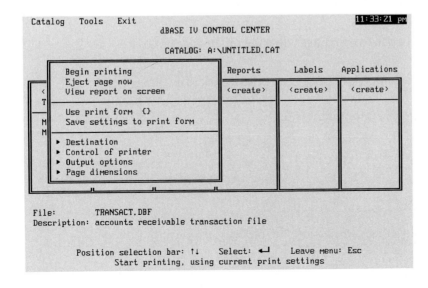

DB–27 The Quick Report menu.

```
Page No.   1
09/12/89

ACCT_NUM    REF_NO   TRAN_CD  PROD_CD      AMOUNT  AGE_CD  DATE

6598        11458        4        0       -75.00       1  01/17/88
6155        11459        4        0       -13.50       1  01/17/88
2145        77145        1       45        50.00       0  01/17/88
4155        77146        1       39        10.00       0  01/17/88
            177208      10       84       -28.50       2




                 Cancel viewing: ESC,  Continue viewing: SPACEBAR
```

DB–28   A Quick Report of TRANSACT.

It may take up to two minutes to produce and compile the Quick Report. When the process is completed, the report appears on the screen. As Figure DB–28 shows, the report includes all the data in TRANSACT. Each column header is the field name, and all the records in the database are printed.

You return to the Control Center by pressing (ESC), then pressing any key, as instructed at the bottom of the screen.

Press (ESC)

Press (ENTER)

You are returned to the Control Center.

There are two drawbacks to Quick Reports. First, each time you produce one, you must wait while the computer recompiles. For example, let us produce the same Quick Report, this time selecting the Begin Printing option (rather than View Report on Screen). First, make sure your printer is ready to print.

Press (SHIFT)-(F9) for a Quick Report.

Select Begin Printing.

Again, there is a delay of up to two minutes while the report is compiled. This time, the report is printed.

The delay each time you print a Quick Report is one drawback. The other drawback is its rigidity of design. To illustrate this, you will display a Quick Report of MASTER on the screen. At the Data panel:

Select MASTER.

Select Use File.

Press (SHIFT)-(F9)

Select View Report on Screen.

After the expected wait during compilation, the report is displayed on the screen, as shown in Figure DB–29.

DB–29 Quick Report of MASTER.

```
Page No.   1
09/12/89

ACCT_NUM  CUST_NAME   STREET      CITY_STATE      ZIP       BEGIN_BAL   UPDAT
_BAL      CR_LIMIT  GOODCREDIT

1975       GREEN      301 MAIN    TEMPE, AZ       85281       400.00
0.00      1000.00   N
2145       JONES      412 ELY     MAR, CA         95485       100.00       15
7.50      4000.00   Y
2250       BLACK      270 HILL    OMAHA, NB       68101       250.00
0.00      1000.00   N
2345       ALLEN      116 MAIN    ELY, NV         89301       100.00       10
5.00      2000.00   Y
4115       ADDAMS     23 OAK      LEE, IL         78327       200.00       21
0.00      1000.00   Y
4155       BROWN      100 ELK     LEE, IL         78327       300.00       31
5.00      1000.00   N
5280       BOYD       777 MILL    TAOS, NM        87571       200.00       10
0.00      2000.00   Y
6155       WHITE      198 ELM     OAK, CA         96254       400.00       42
0.00      1000.00   N
6598       FOSTER     896 OAK     LEE, IL         78327       300.00       52
          Cancel viewing: ESC,  Continue viewing: SPACEBAR
```

There are too many database fields to fit on one line, so the report is difficult to read. Since many databases will contain more fields than can fit on one line, you often need to design your own reports so that they are more readable. This is the same problem you encounter with the command DISPLAY ALL.

Return to the Control Center.

Designing Custom Reports

The report-generation facility in dBASE IV is easy to use. You will now design a credit report for use with MASTER. The report should contain account numbers, customer names, and the three numeric fields (beginning balance, updated balance, and credit limit).

To generate a report, you begin by selecting the <Create> option in the Reports panel after opening the Database or Query file you want to use. MASTER.DBF is already open. At the Reports panel:

Press (TAB) to highlight <create> option.

Press (ENTER)

The Report Generation screen appears, as shown in Figure DB–30. Initially, the Layout menu is open, with the Quick Layout option highlighted. This is how Quick Reports are designed. For now, you will close the menu option.

Press (ESC) to close the menu.

The Report Design screen (Figure DB–31) has seven menu options at the top: Layout, Fields, Bands, Words, Go To, Print, and Exit. Beneath these is the Ruler line. The ruler indicates left and right page margins with "[" and "]," and tab stops with little triangles. The numbers 1, 2, 3, and so on indicate where columns 10, 20, 30, and so on are located.

Before continuing, you will set the margins of the report to columns 8 and 72. To do this, you must access the Words menu.

Press (ALT)-W

DB–30 The Report Generation screen.

The Words menu is displayed. One of the options in the menu is Modify Ruler.

Select Modify Ruler.

Press (ENTER)

After you press (ENTER), the cursor is located on the Ruler line, but you are not sure what to do. Here is where dBASE IV's context-sensitive Help facility is useful.

Press (F1) **to get help.**

The help window (Figure DB–32) indicates what you can do to the ruler. Note that entering [or], for example, sets the margins. To exit the Help facility:

Press (ESC)

To select column 8 as the left margin:

Press (TAB) **to move the cursor to the first tab stop at column 8.**

DB–31 The Report Design screen.

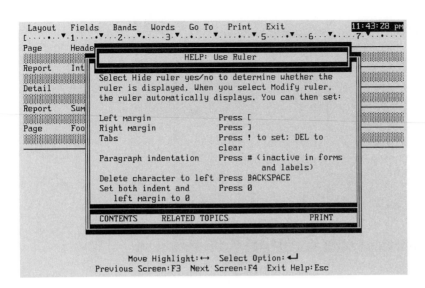

DB–32 The Help window for Use Ruler.

Press [to set the left margin.

Notice that the [on the ruler line has moved from position 0 to position 8. Now you will set the right margin.

Press (TAB) several times until the cursor is located in column 72.

Press] to set the right margin.

The triangle that denotes a tab stop has been changed to a], indicating the right margin.

Press (↓) to move the cursor off the Ruler line.

You have set the margins for the report. A left margin of 8 and a right margin of 72 are good settings for printing 10 characters per inch on 8 1/2-inch-wide paper.

Notice that the main body of the work surface consists of several bands. Each band has some purpose in designing the printed report. You will use several bands in preparing the report. Each band is described as you get to it.

After pressing the (↓) key, the cursor will be located in the Page Header band separator. The Page Header band describes what is to be printed out on the top of each page in the report. Typically, this includes a report title, and perhaps a date and page number. Suppose that you would like the page header to read "Credit Report on MM/DD/YY," where the date is automatically inserted in the title.

Press (↓) to move the cursor off the Page Header band separator.

The cursor is located in line 0, column 8 of the Page Header band, as the status bar shows.

Press (ENTER)

A second line appears. The cursor moves to line 1, column 8, as the status bar shows. What you type now is entered into the Page Header band and used for the first line of the page heading.

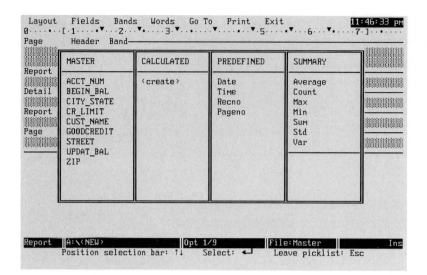

DB–33 The Add a Field window for report layout.

Type "Credit Report on "

Leave a space after "on," but do not press (ENTER). You want to include the date in the title. You do this by adding the DATE field. The contents of the field are displayed during printing.

Press (F5) to add a field.

A window with four sections appears, as shown in Figure DB–33. This window indicates the fields you can select. The left column shows fields in your database. Of interest now is the DATE field, at the top of the third column. To select the DATE field:

Highlight DATE.

Press (ENTER)

Another window appears, as shown in Figure DB–34. This window is used to determine how a selected field is to be displayed in the report. For the DATE field, you can select the defaults, MM/DD/YY. To accept the default settings:

Press (CTRL)-(END)

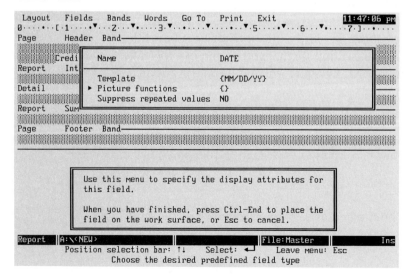

DB–34 Window for specifying how a field will be displayed in a report.

```
   Layout   Fields   Bands   Words   Go To   Print   Exit        11:47:48 pm
   0······[·1·····▼····2···▼·····3·▼··▼······▼·····▼·5·····▼···6···▼····7·]·····
   Page        Header   Band────────────────────────────────────────────────

                                   Credit Report on MM/DD/YY
   Report      Intro    Band────────────────────────────────────────────────

   Detail               Band────────────────────────────────────────────────

   Report      Summary  Band────────────────────────────────────────────────

   Page        Footer   Band────────────────────────────────────────────────




   Report   A:\<NEW>              Line:1 Col:33    File:Master           Ins
            Add field:F5  Select:F6  Move:F7  Copy:F8  Size:Shift-F7
```

DB–35 Report title centered on page.

The date is represented by MM/DD/YY in the title.

Next, you want to center the title on the page. To do this, you need to go to the Words menu.

Press (ALT)-W

Select the Position option.

Another window opens.

Select the Center option.

The work surface indicates that the title has been centered on the page, as shown in Figure DB–35. Now, you would like two blank lines beneath the title.

Press (END)

Press (ENTER) twice.

This generates two new lines in the Page Header band.

You have completed the page header. The next step is to generate the details of the report. The Detail band is used to specify where and how each data field is to be printed in the main body of the report. That means, you indicate in this band which fields are printed in which columns. Each record that is printed follows the specifications of the Detail band. For now we will skip over the Report Intro band, but we will return to it later.

Press ⤓ until you are in the work space beneath the Detail band separator.

You want the account number located at the left margin. To move the cursor to the left margin:

Press (HOME)

The status line should read "Line: 0, Col: 8."

Press (F5) to select a field.

The menu of fields to select appears.

D
B
A
S
E

Highlight ACCT_NUM in the leftmost column.

Press (ENTER)

> The window for field display appears. To accept the default settings:

Press (CTRL)-(END)

> The six Xs indicate where the ACCT_NUM field is placed. Next, you want to enter the customer names, starting in column 16.

Press (TAB) to move the cursor to column 16.

Press (F5) to add a field.

Select the CUST_NAME field in the left column.

Press (CTRL)-(END) to accept the default settings.

> The Detail band work surface indicates the two report columns that have been defined. The third report column, BEGIN_BAL, should begin in column 32.

Press (TAB) to locate the cursor at column 32.

Add field BEGIN_BAL with its default settings using the same steps as for the previous fields.

> The template for BEGIN_BAL shows 9s and a decimal point, indicating a numeric field. The Xs for the first two report columns indicate that those fields are character fields.

Add UPDAT_BAL with its default settings beginning at column 48.

Add CR_LIMIT with its default settings beginning at column 64.

You have completed designing the Detail band of the report. As previously mentioned, this band specifies how each record prints on the page.

Next, you can design the Report Intro band, which we skipped over. The Report Intro band is used to format the report column titles. In the Quick Report, the column titles were the field names by default. If you want column titles like Account Number rather than ACCT_NUM, you can set the Report Intro line accordingly.

Press (↑) until the cursor is located in the work surface within the Report Intro band.

Press (HOME) to move the cursor to the left margin.

> The Report Intro band will consist of three lines. The column titles will take two lines each, and the third line will be blank, to place a space between the column titles and the data. To enter text, you type it in, using the cursor arrow keys, rather than the space bar and (ENTER), to move around in the work surface. The space bar and (ENTER) keys make changes to the work surface; that is, to the lines to be printed within the Report Intro band.

Type "Account" (do not press (ENTER)).

Press (TAB) to move the cursor to column 16.

Type "**Customer**" (do not press (ENTER)).

Press (TAB) twice to move the cursor to column 32.

Type "**Beginning**" (do not press (ENTER)).

Press (TAB) to move the cursor to column 48.

Type "**Updated**" (do not press (ENTER)).

Press (TAB) to move the cursor to column 64.

Type "**Credit**"

You have completed entering the first line of the Report Intro band. To generate a second line:

Press (ENTER)

The second line will have the second words of the titles.

Enter the words **Number, Name, Balance, Balance,** and **Limit** under the existing first words of the column titles.

Refer to Figure DB–36 as necessary.

Press (ENTER) to generate a third line in the band.

You have completed specifying the Report Intro band. This band prints the column labels. The next band you need to specify is the Report Summary band. This band is printed at the end of the report. It can be used for printing sums of numeric fields. You will use it to print the sums of the three numeric fields in your report.

Use ⊥ to locate the cursor in the work surface for the Report Summary band.

Press (ENTER) to expand the band to two lines.

Next, you must locate the cursor where you want the field to be placed. The sum for BEGIN_BAL should be immediately beneath where BEGIN_BAL is located in the Detail band.

Press (TAB) to move the cursor to column 32.

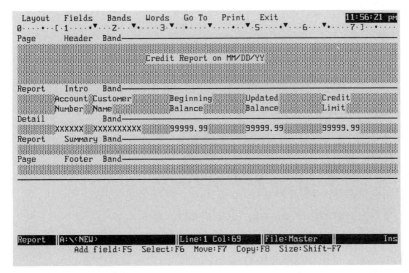

DB–36 The completed Report Intro band.

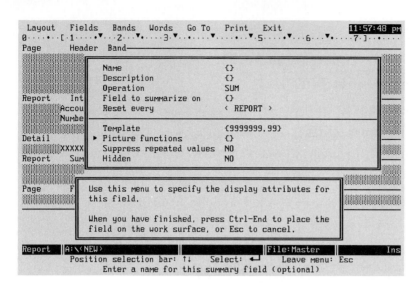

DB–37 Window to specify
which field to be summed.

Now, you add the field. The summed field is specified slightly differently than the actual database fields were specified.

Press (F5) to add a field.

> The right column of the window contains several functions that can be performed. Among them are **SUM, MAX, MIN,** and **AVERAGE.**

Select the SUM function.

> A specification window appears, as shown in Figure DB–37. The window is used to specify which field is to be summed.

Locate the cursor on the fourth option, Field to Summarize On.

Press (ENTER)

> A list of fields appears. Only numeric fields may be selected.

Select BEGIN_BAL.

> The template in the window indicates 9999999.99, or ten characters wide. The field only needs to be eight characters wide. Two of the leading 9s can be deleted.

Select the Template option.

> To move the cursor to the beginning of the template:

Press (HOME)

Press (ENTER)

> To shorten the field by two characters:

Press (DEL) twice.

> In this way you can make any changes necessary to the size of a field.

> You have finished the specifications for the field.

Press (CTRL)-(END) to place the template on the work surface.

> The template is placed beneath the Detail band field.

In column 48, repeat the above steps to get the sum of UPDAT_BAL.

In column 63, repeat the above steps, except shorten the field length by only one character, to get the sum of CR_LIMIT.

You have finished specifying the Report Summary band. This concludes designing the report. We will not use Page Footer, which prints a line at the bottom of each page. Before leaving the Report Design screen, you should view the report on the screen.

Press (ALT)-**P** to open the Print menu.

Select View Report on Screen.

Recall that report compilation may take up to two minutes. The screen indicates the files that are used in this operation. The report appears on the screen (Figure DB–38). If it is correct, you can exit and save it. If there is an error, you will need to go back and fix the error. When you have corrected any errors, you can save the report. To return to the Report Design screen:

Press (ESC)

Press (ENTER)

Then, exit the Report Design screen.

Press (ALT)-**E**

Select the option, Save Changes and Exit.

A message appears: "Save as:". You will save this report under the name CREDIT.

Type **CREDIT** (ENTER)

It takes up to two minutes to compile and save the report. When finished, the Control Center appears on the screen.

```
                    Credit Report on 09/12/89

         Account Customer      Beginning    Updated     Credit
         Number  Name          Balance      Balance     Limit

          1975   GREEN           400.00         0.00     1000.00
          2145   JONES           100.00       157.50     4000.00
          2250   BLACK           250.00         0.00     1000.00
          2345   ALLEN           100.00       105.00     2000.00
          4115   ADDAMS          200.00       210.00     1000.00
          4155   BROWN           300.00       315.00     1000.00
          5280   BOYD            200.00       100.00     2000.00
          6155   WHITE           400.00       420.00     1000.00
          6598   FOSTER          300.00       525.00     1000.00

                                2250.00      1832.50    14000.00


          Cancel viewing: ESC,  Continue viewing: SPACEBAR
```

DB–38 A View of the Credit Report for MASTER.

Printing Custom Reports

Now that you have generated the custom report, CREDIT, you can print it. The printing process is fast, because the report has already been compiled.

Highlight CREDIT in the Reports panel.

Press ENTER

A window appears.

Select the Print Report option.

Another window appears.

Select the Begin Printing option.

In about 10 to 20 seconds, the report begins printing.

To review: You used the Quick Report facility in dBASE IV and saw its limitations. You used the Report design screen to design a custom report, CREDIT, that formats the data in MASTER.DBF for printing. You then printed the report from the Control Center.

Creating Labels

Labels are another type of printout that uses information from a database. Whereas reports print one line for each record, labels print a grouping of fields for each record. An excellent example of labels is mailing labels. You will produce mailing labels for MASTER.DBF. Like reports, producing labels consists of two steps. The first involves formatting, or specifying which fields are printed and how they are to be laid out. The second step involves the actual printing.

In the Control Center, with MASTER in use in the Data panel:

Highlight <create> in the Labels panel.

Press ENTER

The Label Design screen appears, as shown in Figure DB–39. The central area on the screen is the label work surface, similar to the report work surface you just used. It has a Ruler line above it and is of a fixed size, 5 lines by 35 columns. The cursor is located in the upper left corner, at line 0, column 0, as noted on the status line.

A mailing label has the name on the first line, so you will enter the CUST_NAME field first.

Press F5 to add a field.

Select the CUST_NAME field.

Press CTRL-END to select the default settings of the template.

The template for CUST_NAME appears on the first line of the label, with Xs to indicate that it is a character field. You want to enter the street address on the second line. To move the cursor to column 0 of the next line:

Press ENTER

DB–39 The Label Design screen.

Press (F5) to add a field.

Select the STREET field.

Press (CTRL)-(END) to select the default settings of the template.

> The STREET field appears on the second line of the label.

Next, you want CITY_STATE on the third line of the label. Following the steps given above:

Enter the CITY_STATE field on the third line.

You want CITY_STATE to be followed by a space, then ZIP. With the cursor at the first position after the CITY_STATE template on the work surface:

Press the SPACE BAR once.

Enter the ZIP field.

You have completed specifying the layout of data in the labels. Next, you want to specify the layout of labels on the page. You want three labels across on a page. To do this in 80 columns, you need to change the width of each label from 35 to 25. To do this, you need to access the Dimensions menu.

Press (ALT)-D

> The Dimensions menu appears.

Select the second option, Width of Label.

Type 25 (ENTER)

> This resets the label width.

Select the option, Columns of Labels.

Type 3 (ENTER)

> This changes the setting to three labels across the page. Now, exit the Dimensions menu.

Press (ESC)

> The work surface for the label is resized.

Before exiting the Label Design screen, you should view the labels on the screen to verify that they have been correctly defined.

Press (ALT)-P to access the Print menu.

Select the option View Labels on Screen.

> The compilation may take as long as a minute before labels appear on the screen. When done viewing the output:

Press (ESC)

Press (ENTER)

> You are returned to the Label Design screen. Correct any errors you noticed when viewing the labels.

When you have finished you should exit, saving the specifications.

Press (ALT)-E for the Exit menu.

Select the option, Save Changes and Exit.

> A message "Save as:" appears.

Type MAIL (ENTER)

> It takes up to a minute to compile and save the label formatting you just specified. You are returned to the Control Center.

Printing Labels

From the Control Center, it is easy to print labels. MASTER is in use in the Data panel and MAIL is highlighted in the Labels panel.

Press (ENTER)

Select the Print Labels option.

Select the Begin Printing option.

> The labels are printed.

To review: You created a label form for use with MASTER to generate mailing labels. You then printed labels using the form.

Printing Selected Records from the Dot Prompt

The report and label forms generated from the Control Center can be used from the dot prompt with FOR clauses like you used in other instructions during the previous lessons. The command to print a report is REPORT FORM, and the command to print a label is LABEL FORM. The optional modifier TO PRINTER causes the report or labels to be printed. Otherwise, they are displayed on the screen.

Exit the Control Center to the dot prompt.

> The status bar indicates that MASTER.DBF is in use.

Type REPORT FORM CREDIT TO PRINTER FOR GOODCREDIT (ENTER)

The report prints only those records in the database that have GOODCREDIT equal to logical TRUE. The records are printed as specified in the CREDIT report created previously, with the same headings, field specifications, and summaries.

Type **LABEL FORM MAIL TO PRINTER FOR GOODCREDIT** (ENTER)

The labels print three across for records in the database that have GOODCREDIT equal to logical TRUE. That is, the command uses the label called MAIL that we created previously, which includes all print specifications.

To review: You have used the report and label forms you created earlier and printed selected records from the database.

This concludes the tutorial of the most commonly used features of dBASE IV. Table DB–6 reviews cursor movement keys used in dBASE IV. See Appendix B for a summary of the function key commands used in dBASE IV.

The exercises included in the practice section below will allow you to practice what you have learned. You may close MASTER.DBF now and properly exit dBASE IV.

Type **CLOSE ALL** (ENTER)

Exit dBASE IV to the DOS prompt.

Turn off the computer.

Remove your work disk from drive A and safely store it.

REVIEW QUESTIONS
1. How do you get a Quick Report of a database file?
2. What are the Quick Report limitations?
3. What are the Page Header, Report Intro, Detail, and Page Footer bands used for?
4. How do you get the sum of a numeric field to print in a report?
5. How do you create a label form?
6. How do you specify which fields are included in the form?
7. How do you change the dimensions of each label?

Practice

These exercises allow you to review, learn, and consolidate what you have already learned in this tutorial. You will need to use the files on your Student Data Disk supplied with this text. Make sure that you have your Student Data Disk in the floppy drive and that the default for the Student Data Disk is set to drive A (or whichever drive you are using for data). For all of these exercises it is assumed that you will be using dBASE IV and that it is already loaded. Press (F2) if not already in the Control Center.

1. From the Control Center, use the database BUSMAIL and make the following changes:
   a. Change the order. Sort the list by each of the following fields:

   1) Business
   2) City
   3) State
   4) Contact
   b. Name each of these files after the field on which you are sorting.
   c. Print out each of these files to show that you have sorted them.
2. It is inconvenient to sort each time a change or addition is made to BUSMAIL.
   a. Index each of the four fields.
   b. In the Control Center, make the appropriate changes to index BUSMAIL on each of the above fields.
   c. With each of the four indexes as the master file in turn, list the file to the printer to illustrate the effects of indexing.
3. Append records to BUSMAIL and see if they are reflected in the indexes.
   a. Add the following record: Ozone Industries, Los Angeles, CA, Mr. Airborne.
   b. Change the name of Divot Industries to Mac Divott Industries.
   c. Change the location of Hershey to Carmel, CA.
   d. Again, with each of the indexes as the master index, list the file to the printer to see the effects of the changes and additions.

KEY WORDS

Catalog	Key	Pull-down menu
Character field type	Label	Query
Command mode	Logical field type	Record
Control Center	Master index	Record pointer
Date field type	Numeric field type	Report
Dot prompt	Pack	Status bar
Field	Panel	Status line
Index tag	Pick menu	View

Key	Work Surface	Movement or Action
→		Right one position
←		Left one position
↓		Down one row
ENTER	Edit	Next field
↑		Up one row
↑	Edit	Previous field
PGDN	Browse, Edit, Layout	Display next screen
PGUP	Browse, Edit, Layout	Display previous screen
END	Edit	End of field
END	Browse	Last field in record
END	Layout	Last text/field on line
END	Query	Last column of skeleton
HOME	Edit	Beginning of field
HOME	Browse	Beginning of record
HOME	Layout	Left margin
BACKSPACE		Delete previous character
CTRL-BACKSPACE	Layout	Delete previous word
TAB	Edit, Browse	Next field
TAB	Layout	Next tab stop
TAB	Query, Control Center	Next column

Table DB–6 Cursor Navigation Keys. (Note: Layout Work Surface refers to both Report and Label design screens.)

D
B
A
S
E

APPENDICES

Glossary

Absolute addressing Copying a cell address in a spreadsheet formula so that it remains constant in every new location in which the formula appears; contrast with relative addressing.

Access time The time needed to locate a disk record, typically measured in thousandths of a second.

Acoustic coupler A type of modem that communicates with the computer by sending audio signals through the telephone handset rather than by direct connection to a telephone jack.

Ada A highly powerful, sophisticated general-purpose programming language developed for the Department of Defense, based on the structured concepts of Pascal; specifically designed for real-time and embedded computer systems.

Algorithm A set of rules for solving a problem.

Alphanumeric data field A unit of information in a record which may contain any kind of data—numbers, letters, or special symbols.

Analog signals Signals in the form of electronic waves which are often transmitted over telephone lines.

Application generator A type of fourth-generation programming language that allows the user to alter databases in connection with report generators and query languages.

Application programmer A computer professional who writes, debugs, and documents programs for specific business tasks.

Application software Software used to manipulate input data in order to provide users with meaningful information.

Arithmetic-logic unit (ALU) A component of the CPU that performs arithmetic functions such as addition or subtraction, and logic functions such as the comparison of two numbers.

Artificial intelligence Simulated human decision-making using a computer.

ASCII Acronym for American Standard Code for Information Interchange (pronounced ass-key). A binary code used for representing data in many computers and for transmitting data over communications lines.

Assembler A program that translates assembly language statements into machine language.

Assembly language A second-generation programming language in which each individual operation is translated into a machine instruction; it is a very efficient, but not very user-friendly, programming language.

Audio response Output in the form of verbal responses.

Audio response unit A device that provides users with a verbal response using a voice simulator or a series of prerecorded messages.

Auditor The accounting and computer specialist responsible for assessing the effectiveness and efficiency of the computer system and for maintaining the overall integrity of a system's programs and data.

Automated design tools Tools used to improve computer system development.

Automatic teller machine (ATM) A specialized form of interactive terminal that is part of an on-line banking system in which data entered at the point of transaction automatically and immediately updates banking records.

Auxiliary storage A series of devices that store data in electronic form so that the data can conveniently be used again. Also called secondary storage. Examples of auxiliary storage are a floppy or hard disk for micros or the packs of large, hard disks used on minicomputers and mainframes.

Band printer A type of line printer that uses a flexible stainless-steel print band that is photoengraved with print characters.

Bar code reader An input device that reads the black-and-white bars (the Universal Product Code, or UPC) that you see on most consumer goods.

Baseband A type of LAN (local area network) that operates on only one communication channel at medium speed.

BASIC An easy-to-learn high-level programming language that is most often used for interactive processing; an acronym for Beginner's All-Purpose Symbolic Instruction Code.

Batch processing   A data processing method in which input is entered off-line and the entire set of data is processed as a batch; batch processed files are only current periodically, after they are updated.

Baud rates   A measure of the speed with which information is transmitted over communication lines.

Benchmark test   A test that compares the performance of various computers using a company's sample data as input.

Binary numbering system   A numbering system in which there are only two possible digits: 0 and 1. Computers use a binary-coded system for representing data and instructions.

Bit   Short for binary digit—a single on- or off-state signal; characters are represented by 7- or 8-bit computer codes.

Bit-mapped graphics   Graphic images created in a painting program that consist of patterns of dots.

Bits per inch (bpi)   A measure of the density of data recorded on a magnetic tape. This term is a misnomer, since it really measures bytes per inch, i.e., the number of characters per inch of tape.

Bits per second (bps)   An expression of the speed with which information is transmitted over communication lines.

Block   In a word processing program, a group of text on the screen that you define in order to perform an operation such as moving, copying or deleting.

Bootlegging   Making an unauthorized copy of software.

Bridge   A type of network software that connects normally incompatible networks in a way that is transparent to the users.

Broadband   A type of LAN (local area network) that can handle data, voice, and video transmission at high speed along numerous channels.

Budgetary constraints   Limits on the time and money that an analyst can spend analyzing and designing a system.

Bus configuration   A type of network configuration where each node can access not only the host computer but also every other node as well.

Bus   The electronic tracks on which data moves between memory and the CPU.

Business functions   A set of procedures designed to perform a business operation.

Business system   A set of procedures used to achieve business goals.

Byte   A unit of data consisting of a group of eight bits or binary digits. A single storage position that typically contains a character of data.

C   A structured, middle-level programming language combining the advantages of assembly language and high-level languages; the UNIX operating system was written in C.

Cache memory   A type of memory that can double the speed of a computer by using a scheme of storing and retrieving data from lower-speed mass storage devices.

Callback system   Security method to ensure that a user on a phone line is calling from an authorized telephone number and not from some other location.

Case structure   One of the four logic structures in programming in which a series of single-alternative decision structures check for a series of conditions. When a condition is true, the specified action is taken.

Case-insensitive   An application in which you can type commands using either upper- or lowercase letters and get the same results.

Cathode ray tube (CRT)   A TV-like screen that displays your instructions and the computer's responses. Also called video display terminal (VDT) or monitor.

CD-ROM   (Compact Disk Read-Only Memory). A type of memory that uses the same technology as CD audio disks, and cannot be written to; it can only be read. The disks are suitable for storing large amounts of fixed data that need frequent reference.

Cell   The intersection of a row and column in a spreadsheet program.

Central processing unit (CPU)   The part of the computer system that controls all computer operations.

Centralized data processing   A single computer facility that serves the entire information needs of an organization.

Chain printer   A type of mainframe line printer that has one print hammer for each print position in a line.

Check byte   A byte added to the end of a record of data that is used to ensure the appropriate parity of each bit position in each byte of the record as a method of verifying the accurate transmittal of information.

Chief programmer   The computer professional responsible for the overall design and coordination of all programs to be used in the information system.

CISC   An abbreviation for complex instruction set computer; most micros are CISC computers.

Clock speed   The rate at which a computer can process data, as determined by the CPU's clock; in micros, it is measured in megahertz (MHz).

Clone   A machine comparable to the IBM PC, sometimes with additional features, such as faster processors; usually clones are sold at a lower price.

Coaxial cable   A central cylinder surrounded by a series of wires that carry data at very high speeds; used instead of twisted-pair cables for high-quality data transmission.

COBOL   An early, high-level programming language especially developed for use in business applications; an acronym for Common Business Oriented Language.

Coding   The process in which the programmer writes the instructions in a programming language after the logic has been designed.

Common carrier   A company that builds and maintains public data networks for those who cannot afford their own networks.

Communication channel   The medium that passes data between CPUs and terminals. The three basic types are: hardwired, telephone lines, and alternative channels such as leased lines, microwave, or satellite links.

Communications controller   Includes multiplexers and front-end processors; a device that integrates the use of terminals and reduces data communications costs.

Communications satellite   A method of data transmission that uses microwave relay stations for high-volume data transmission.

Communications software   Software that specifies the communications protocol for exchanging files with a host computer through acoustic couplers and direct-connect modems.

Compiler   A program used to translate a source program into an object program. Compiling is a separate step that must be completed before a program can be run on the computer.

Compound document   A document that integrates data from different applications—text, data, spreadsheet, graphic, image, and voice information—for use by a cohesive information system.

Computer output microfilm (COM) unit   A device that can be linked to a CPU to create output on microfilm or microfiche at very high speeds.

Computer system   A group of machines, commonly called hardware, that together with programs reads data, processes it, and produces information.

Computer-aided software engineering (CASE) tool   A tool used to improve computer system development.

Computer-aided design and drafting (CAD) software   Drawing programs that offer additional features specifically required by architects and engineers.

Configuration   The manner in which the host computer and nodes are organized in a network. Three common configurations are: star, ring, and bus.

Continuous recognition system   A voice recognition system that enables users to speak in a normal cadence with words running into one another.

Continuous-form paper   Printer paper with small holes on either side that allow it to be fed through the printer at the right speed without interruption.

Control keys   Keys on a terminal or microcomputer keyboard with arrows pointing in four directions; in general, the arrows are used for positioning the cursor on the screen.

Control unit   A component of the computer's CPU that monitors the operations performed by the entire system.

Controls   Systems and programming techniques that users implement to minimize errors, such as double-checking computations and cross-checking data between employees.

Coprocessor   A special chip that can be added to microcomputers to speed up certain kinds of operations; for example, a math coprocessor is used to speed up the processing of mathematical operations for applications such as statistical analysis.

Copy protection   Preparing software in such a way that it cannot be copied to other disks, or can only be copied a limited number of times; copy protection is designed to prevent bootlegging.

Cost-benefit analysis   A report by a systems analyst outlining the costs associated with an existing system that compares these costs to those associated with a proposed system.

Cursor   A small blinking underline or rectangle that indicates where your input will actually appear on the screen.

Customized program   A program designed to meet the specific needs of users and written by programmers within an organization, by outside consultants, or by self-employed programmers.

Daisywheel printer   A type of impact printer that prints fully formed characters from a flat disk that has petal-like projections containing individual characters.

Data   Anything to be processed by the computer.

Data communications   The group of technologies that enable computers to pass data electronically to one another from input/output devices to a host computer at a different location.

Data definition language (DDL)   A set of technical specifications for a database's fields and the relationships between data in the database.

Data dictionary   In a DBMS, a data dictionary contains descriptions of the fields, records, and files and the relationship between them.

Data encryption   Encoding data so that it cannot be understood unless it is first decoded; used to protect data from unauthorized access.

Data flow diagram   A diagram used by analysts to depict a system, with the emphasis on where the data originates and where it goes.

Data hierarchy   The organization of data at different levels so that it can be stored and retrieved efficiently.

Data integrity   The need to keep the database from being corrupted by input or programming errors or by deliberate attempts to tamper with the data.

Data manipulation languages (DML)   A computer language, typically a proprietary part of a database management package, that allows users to create custom-designed applications. Query languages are data manipulation languages.

Data verification   Checking the validity of data.

Database   A collection of related files that are stored electronically and can be cross-referenced.

Database administrator   The individual responsible for organizing, designing, and maintaining the database and all other data used by the organization.

Database application   A specific use for a DBMS package.

Database file   A collection of records used in a given application, such as payroll or accounts receivable.

Database management system (DBMS)   A software package that makes it possible to create, maintain, and access databases.

Database security   The measures needed to protect databases against unauthorized use.

Debugging   Finding and correcting errors ("bugs") in a program.

Decentralized system   Separate computer facilities for each department, as opposed to centralized or distributed data processing.

Decimal system   The numbering system we use every day, based on units of ten.

Decision structure   One of the four logic structures in programming whereby a condition is tested to determine what sequence of instructions is to be executed next in the program.

Decision support system (DSS)   A flexible information system that allows managers to access corporate and other databases and to create their own reports and applications, even their own specialized databases. Such systems are used by managers to help them make decisions.

Default setting   A standard setting on a software package established by the manufacturer at a commonly used value; default settings can be changed by users if the need arises.

Demodulaton   The process of converting an analog signal to a digital signal.

Desk-checking   Debugging by manually tracing through the program from beginning to end, visually checking for errors.

Desktop organizer   A program that allows microcomputer users to keep track of information such as names, addresses, telephone numbers, notes, to-do lists, and appointment schedules. Also called a personal information manager.

Desktop publishing   Tools offering advanced capabilities that allow users to do page design at a level used in publications such as newsletters, magazines, and books.

Digital signals   Signals in the form of on/off electronic pulses.

Direct conversion   A method of system conversion in which the company simply stops using the old system and begins using the new one with no overlap.

Direct-access file   A method of database organization in which the key field is used to calculate the record's address itself, eliminating the need to look for the record in the index.

Direct-access storage   A type of storage in which data can be accessed without the need for a sequential search.

Direct-connect modem   A modem directly attached to a computer by cable; it can be either inside the computer or outside.

Director of information systems   An executive, typically a vice-president, with overall responsibility for all computer operations and for the entire staff of programmers, analysts, and other computer professionals.

Discrete recognition system   A voice recognition system that requires the user to pause between words to help the system identify word breaks.

Disk pack   A removable set of hard disks mounted together on a spindle; used with mainframe and minicomputer systems.

Distributed processing   The procedure of transmitting computer power throughout an organization.

Distributed system   A system consisting of terminals, micros, or minis linked in a network to a centralized computer, usually a mainframe.

Documentation   That which is used to explain programs to people, such as a printed manual or on-line help.

Documentation package   A total record of the precise procedures and techniques a new system uses, as well as the technical specifications for all the hardware and software used.

Dot-matrix printer   An impact printer that creates characters using a grid of pins that press against a carbon ribbon to print on paper.

Double-alternative decision structure   A variation of one of the four logic structures in programming, the decision structure; using this structure, one action is taken if the condition is true, and another action is taken if it is false.

Download   To copy files located in a host computer's storage to a local level, typically at a microcomputer station.

Draft-quality output   The crudest, fastest quality available from a dot-matrix printer.

Drum printer   A type of line printer that uses a cylindrical steel drum embossed with print characters.

Dumb terminal   A computer terminal that can only send data via the keyboard and receive data from the CPU on the screen without the ability to do any local processing.

EBCDIC   Acronym for Extended Binary Coded Decimal Interchange Code (pronounced eb-c-dick). The standard 8-bit computer code for most IBM and IBM-compatible mainframe computers.

Editing   Altering, deleting, replacing, moving, or copying data already entered in a document, spreadsheet, or database.

EEPROM   An acronym for Electronically Erasable Programmable Read-Only Memory. A ROM chip that allows program information to be changed by software without removing the chips from the computer.

Electroluminescent (EL) display   A type of flat-screen technology that makes possible display screens without the use of cathode ray tubes; often used in laptop computers.

Electronic filing   Computer-defined storage and retrieval of data or information.

Electronic mail   Using electronic means to send, store, and deliver messages that you would otherwise deliver verbally by phone or send by mail.

Electronic spreadsheet   A software productivity tool that uses a row-and-column format for storing data and performing calculations; any data that can be displayed in this row-and-column format, like ledger sheets used by accountants, can be prepared using this tool.

Embedded systems   Computer systems built into other systems, such as those in a video cassette recorder or on an airplane.

Emulation   A technique that enables a microcomputer to act exactly like a mainframe terminal.

End-user productivity tool   A software package that increases productivity by enabling users to do a specific type of task more efficiently.

EPROM   An acronym for Erasable Programmable Read-Only Memory. A ROM chip that must be removed from the computer for re-programming and requires the use of a special process to erase old programs.

Equipment constraints   Limits on the design of a new system due to computer hardware and other devices that already exist in a company.

Ergonomics   The science of adapting machines and work environments to people.

Even parity   A method of verifying the accurate transmittal of data by checking to ensure that an even number of bits are always in the on-state at any given time. Some computers use even-parity and others use odd-parity.

Exception report   A report that calls attention to unusual situations in which certain predefined conditions occur.

Executive information system (EIS)   A specialized form of decision-support system that requires no expertise on the part of the user and is often designed around the information needs of a single executive.

Expert system   A system consisting of a database and software that simulates the knowledge and analytical ability of an expert in a particular field.

Explanation subsystem   The part of an expert system that explains to users why the system has chosen to ask a certain question or how it has reached specific conclusions.

External hard disk   A separately housed fixed disk for micros that operates just like an internal fixed disk, but has the advantage of being portable.

Feasibility study   A top-down and thorough technical evaluation of the overall computer equipment needs of an organization.

Feedback   The process of periodically evaluating an information system to determine how well it meets user needs.

Fiber optic cables   A communication channel that uses light impulses that travel through clear flexible tubing half the size of a human hair to transmit data at very high speeds with few or no errors.

Field   An individual data item within a record.

Fifth-generation programming language (5GL)   A nonprocedural language used to query databases; often closely linked to artificial intelligence and expert systems.

File   A collection of related records.

File conversion   The process of changing computer files as part of implementing a new system.

File management system   A limited system for storing simple data such as a personal address book in which one file cannot be linked in any way to data in another file. Also called a file manager.

File server   The central processor in a network; also called the host computer.

Financial planning language (FPL)   A fourth generation programming language that provides sophisticated mathematical, statistical, and forecasting methods for analyzing data.

Firmware   Another name for ROM chips that contain built-in programming functions.

First generation programming language   Another name for machine language, because it was the earliest type of programming language developed.

Fixed disk   Another term for a hard disk.

Fixed-length record   A record with fields that are always the same size.

Flat-file database system   A database system that can only access a single file at a time.

Flat-screen technology   A technology that makes possible a display screen without the use of a cathode ray tube; often used in laptop computers.

Floppy disk or diskette   A small flexible Mylar disk, coated with iron oxide, on which data is stored. Called floppy disk, diskette, or floppy; most often used with microcomputers.

Flowchart   A pictorial representation of the logic flow to be used in a program, illustrating the major elements and how they are logically integrated.

Formatting   The way output is arranged to make it pleasing to look at and easy to read and understand.

FORTRAN   An early high-level programming language best suited for scientific and engineering applications; an acronym for Formula Translator.

Fourth-generation programming language (4GL)   An easy-to-write nonprocedural programming language that simply states the needed output using English-like terms, without specifying each step required to obtain it.

Friction feed   A type of printer mechanism that enables the paper to be fed through the printer one sheet at a time.

Front-end processor   A controller, which is itself a computer, that performs simple processing of data from remote terminals so that the host computer is free to do the types of processing that maximize its efficient use.

Full-duplex line   A communications channel that permits data to move in both directions at the same time, such as a telephone line.

Function keys   Keys numbered F1 through F10 or F1 through F12 on a microcomputer; each key typically performs a specific operation depending on the software package being used.

Functions   Specialized mathematical calculations in a spreadsheet program, such as @SUM, @AVERAGE, and @COUNT.

Gantt chart   A chart that depicts timelines which graphically show how long projects are scheduled to take and at what points parts of the project development can overlap.

Gas plasma display   A form of flat screen technology for laptop computers that sandwiches a neon/argon gas mixture with grids of vertical and horizontal wires.

Gateway   Software that connects small local area networks to mainframe systems.

Gigabyte   Approximately 1 billion bytes.

Graphics   Pictorial displays of data or information.

Graphing and charting package   A program used for presenting business graphics; its artwork can be output as transparencies or as black-and-white or color graphs on paper.

Half-duplex line   A communications channel that permits data to move in two directions, but not at the same time, like a CB radio.

Hard card   A series of circuit boards that can be added to a microcomputer by plugging them into the computer's internal expansion slots; functions like a hard disk.

Hard copy   Output on paper from a computer.

Hard disk drive   A microcomputer storage device that can typically store between 10 and 100 or more million characters.

Hard-dollar value   The benefits in business processes that can be measured in actual costs and savings.

Hard-sectored   Diskettes that come with some already defined sectors when you buy them. These have evenly-spaced holes around the hub, one for each predetermined sector.

Hardware   The set of devices that together with sets of instructions perform information-processing functions.

Hardwired   Devices that are directly and permanently linked by cable, such as a terminal and a central processor.

Head crash   The loss of all data on a hard disk when a read/write head impacts with the disk itself.

Header label   A programmed label that appears before the first record and that identifies a database or file.

Help screen   A screen that displays information about the functions that are currently being used; help screens, available with many software packages, may be obtained by pressing a specified key, commonly the F1 function key.

Hierarchical database   A database organized like an upside-down tree with the root or main segment at the top in a one-to-many, or parent-child, relationship. Each data item or group of data items shown in the tree diagram is called a segment, or sometimes a record.

Hierarchy chart   A program-planning tool that graphically demonstrates how a program can be divided into subprograms and how the subprograms relate to one another.

High-level language   A symbolic programming language that is similar to English, such as COBOL or BASIC.

Horizontal package   A software package that is useful in a broad range of business and personal situations.

Host computer   The central processor in a network.

Hypertext   An application that allows users to link files together associatively; a way of creating documents that can be read in relation to other documents.

Icon   A small symbol displayed on a screen that represents files and other objects that commonly appear on a desktop.

Illustration package   A graphics program that performs paint and draw operations.

Impact printer   A printer that uses some form of strike-on method to press a carbon or fabric ribbon against paper, much as typewriters do.

Implementation   The stage of a system life-cycle in which management approves the final design of a new system, then the hardware and software packages are purchased, and conversion from the old procedures to the new design is completed.

Index   A file that contains two lists: the disk address of each record in the main file and a matching key field.

Indexed file   A method of database organization that uses an index based on the key field of the records. The most common method of organization for storing records on disks.

Inference engine   In an expert system, the software that examines facts and rules to draw conclusions.

Information   Output, or processed data.

Information resource management (IRM)   A group in certain companies that specializes in asset management techniques and supervises the flow of information within the organization.

Information resource manager   A computer professional responsible for coordinating the corporate computing systems and monitoring the acquisition of hardware and software by the company's functional areas.

Information system   A combination of the computer hardware—the computer system—and the software, output, and procedures needed to perform the function of a business system.

Ink-jet printer   A type of nonimpact printer based on shooting tiny dots of ink onto paper.

Input   Raw data fed into the computer.

Input devices   The part of the system that accepts data from the user, such as a keyboard or a mouse.

Insert mode   A text-editing feature in which text is moved to the right as new characters are typed.

Instruction register   A temporary storage location within the CPU.

Integrated circuit   A circuit consisting of hundreds of electronic components, thousands of which are imprinted onto a silicon microchip.

Integrated package   Software that integrates all three of the productivity tools—word processing, spreadsheets, and database management —in one package so that users can easily move data from one application to another.

Intelligent terminal   A computer terminal that can send and receive data, and can also independently run application software without using the main CPU's capabilities; microcomputers frequently function as intelligent terminals.

Interactive processing   The immediate processing of entered data so that updated information can be quickly provided to all system users. Also known as real-time processing.

Internal analyst   A systems analyst employed by an organization on a long-term basis.

Interpreter   A translator program that converts programs in a high-level language into machine language one statement at a time as the program is being run on the computer.

Iteration   One of the four logic structures in programming, in which a program executes a series of steps repeatedly. Also called a looping structure.

Jukebox   A device that manipulates optical disks to process images.

Justification   The ability of a word processing package to make both left and right margins align.

Kernel   The part of the operating system that manages the computer's resources including the CPU, primary storage, and peripheral devices; also called the supervisor.

Key field   A major field on which records can be indexed in some logical order for fast access.

Key users   Users in a business organization who have a strong interest and technical expertise in computers who may be asked to develop systems for their work areas.

Key-to-disk   A method for preparing large quantities of input data in which operators enter data from source documents by typing on a keyboard and the keystrokes are captured on magnetic disks as tiny magnetized spots.

Key-to-tape   A method for preparing large quantities of input data in which operators enter data from source documents by typing on a keyboard and the keystrokes are captured on magnetic tape as tiny magnetized spots.

Keyboard   A device that resembles a typewriter keyboard; this is the most common unit for entering data and for coding or using program instructions.

Keyboarding   Entering data into a computer by typing.

Keypunch card   One of the first input media used by mainframes; data is keyed in by using a keypunch machine that punches small holes in card columns, where the combination of holes punched represents a letter, number, or special character.

Kilobyte (K)   Approximately 1,000 bytes (actually 1,024 bytes).

Knowledge acquisition subsystem   A part of an expert system that enables the knowledge engineer to define and encode the expert's problem-solving ability, and also allows the engineer to easily insert and delete knowledge in the system.

Knowledge base   The part of an expert system that translates the knowledge from human experts into rules and strategies.

Knowledge engineer   A computer professional who creates a knowledge base in an expert system.

Laser memory   A nonmagnetic type of storage the uses light energy rather than magnetic fields to store characters.

Laser printer   A type of non-impact printer that uses laser technology to produce very high-quality characters by beaming whole pages at a time onto a drum; then the paper is passed over the drum and the image is picked up with toner, like that used in xerographic copiers.

Legal constraints   Limits on the design of an information system due to legal requirements, such as compliance with Social Security payroll deductions.

Letter-quality printer   A printer capable of the best quality output. Each letter is composed of solid lines, just like typewriter output.

Light pen   A pen-shaped device that uses a laser beam to transmit signals to the CPU by "writing" on the screen.

Line printer   A type of impact printer that prints an entire line at a time. These include band printers, chain printers, and drum printers.

Liquid crystal display (LCD)   A type of flat-screen based on running a current through liquid crystals sandwiched between two sheets of polarized material.

Local area network (LAN)   A network that connects computers and terminals that are all located in nearby offices or buildings, with a range of about 50 miles.

Logic data field   Fields in a record that allow only Yes/No or True/ False responses.

Logic error   A program error caused by mistakes in the sequencing of instructions or by instructions that do not include all the needed steps.

Longitudinal parity   A method of verifying the accurate transmittal of data in which a check byte is added to the end of each record that is transmitted, and each bit of the check byte is used to preserve the appropriate parity of each bit position in each byte of the record.

Looping   One of the four logic structures in programming, in which a program executes a series of steps repeatedly. Also called an iteration structure.

Low-level language   A symbolic programming language that resembles machine language.

Machine language   A complex language that uses actual machine addresses and operation codes in order to execute a program; all programs must be in machine language in order to be executed.

Magnetic bubble memory   A nonvolatile type of computer storage consisting of magnetized spots on a thin film of semiconductor memory.

Magnetic ink character reader (MICR)   A device that reads magnetic ink numbers and special symbols printed at the bottom of bank checks.

Mail merge   A word processor feature that allows letters to be personalized to every recipient on a mailing list.

Main memory   The computer's primary storage, commonly called random access memory (RAM).

Mainframe computer   A faster, more powerful, and more expensive machine than a minicomputer.

Maintenance programmer   A computer professional who modifies existing programs to make them more current or efficient.

Management information system (MIS)   A business information system designed to integrate the information needs of the entire organization, beginning at the top, with the company-wide goals set by high-level managers.

Manager's use of output   Use of computer-produced information at a managerial level to support decision-making, without necessarily having a working knowledge of the software used.

Master file   The main collection of records relating to a specific application area.

Megabyte (MB)   Approximately 1 million bytes.

Menu   A list of choices displayed on the screen from which required operations can be selected.

Microcomputer   The smallest and least expensive of all computers.

Microform   Miniaturized photographic copies of documents that take up very little storage space, such as microfilm and microfiche.

Microprocessor   A tiny silicon chip, about the size of a child's fingernail, on which electronic circuitry has been etched. The microprocessor manages computer processes, including the transfer of data to and from RAM.

Microsecond   One millionth of a second.

Millions of instructions per second (MIPS)   A measurement of a computer processor's speed.

Minicomputer   A computer larger than a micro with more computing power, that does not incur the prohibitive expense associated with some mainframe systems.

MIS control software   Software that acts as an operating system for the MIS or as an interface with the hardware's operating system.

Modem   A device that enables digital data to be transmitted over telephone lines by converting digital signals to analog signals and vice-versa.

Modula-2   A structured, high-level programming language developed as an improvement over Pascal.

Modulation   The process of converting a digital signal to an analog signal.

Module   A subprogram contained within a main program that performs a fixed set of operations.

Monitor   A TV-like screen that displays your instructions and the computer's responses. Also called video display terminal (VDT) or cathode ray tube (CRT).

Monochrome monitor   A CRT with only one color, typically green or amber against a black background.

Mouse   A hand-held device with a ball-type roller on the bottom and one or more buttons on the top, that you slide around the desktop to electronically move an arrow on the computer screen, eliminating the need to type commands.

Multiple virtual storage (MVS)   The high-end operating system for IBM's batch-oriented mainframe systems.

Multiplexer   A type of device that collects messages from numerous terminals at one location and transmits them collectively at high speeds over one communication channel.

Multiprocessing   Linking two or more CPUs to optimize the handling of data.

Multiprogramming   On large computer systems, the ability to store more than one program in the CPU at the same time, thereby permitting several different jobs to be run at the same time.

Multitasking   A variation of multiprogramming implemented on many high-end microcomputers that allows the user to access several programs at the same time.

Nanosecond   One billionth of a second.

Natural-language interface   An interface for an expert system that allows users to conduct dialogues with the computer that seem as natural as talking to another human being.

Near-letter-quality printer   A type of dot-matrix printer that improves print quality by moving the print head over letters more than once so that the spaces between dots get filled in with other dots.

Network   A data communication system that links terminals, microcomputers, minis, and/or mainframes so that they can operate independently but also share data and other resources.

Network database   Similar to a hierarchical database, except that more than one parent per child is permitted, as is a child with no parent.

Network operating system   An operating system that works in conjunction with the normal computer operating system to facilitate basic network management functions such as transmitting files, communicating with other systems, and performing diagnostics.

Nodes   The terminals, micros, or minis linked to the host computer in a network.

Nonprocedural languages   Another name for fourth-generation programming languages; they are called nonprocedural because they only specify output, not the procedure by which the output is to be obtained.

Nonimpact printer   A printer that produces images by methods other than striking, such as thermal, ink-jet, and laser printers.

Nonvolatile memory   A type of memory composed of magnetic bubbles so that data stored in it can be retained for some time even after the power is shut off.

Numeric data field   A field in a record that has only numbers in it.

Numeric keypad   A section of a keyboard containing numbers; used to facilitate numeric data entry.

Object program   A program that has been translated into machine language.

Object-oriented   An interface that uses graphic images called icons to represent various objects, such as files.

Odd parity   A method of verifying the accurate transmittal of data in which an odd number of bits must always be in the on-state at any given time. A computer is said to be even-parity or odd-parity.

Off-line operation   Data entry in which data is entered on computers or terminals that are not connected to the main CPU. Used for collecting data for future batch processing.

On-line operation   Data entry in which data is entered on computers or terminals that are directly connected to the main CPU.

Operating system   Software used to monitor, or supervise, the overall operations of the computer system.

Operations manager   A computer professional with responsibility for the day-to-day functioning of the computer and data entry operations.

Optical character recognition (OCR) device   An input device that reads typed or even handwritten data from a source document.

Optical disk   Platters about the size of long-playing records that can contain about 40,000 pages of images and text.

Optical mark reader   A device that detects the presence of pencil marks on predetermined grids. Used to read test answer sheets and market research forms. Also called a mark-sense reader.

Optical memory   A nonmagnetic type of storage that uses light energy rather than magnetic fields to store characters.

Organization chart   A schematic drawing showing the hierarchy of formal relationships between groups of employees.

Output   Information, or processed data.

Output device   The part of the system that produces the processed data, called information. These include monitors and printers.

Outside consultant   A systems analyst or programmer hired temporarily by companies when they need expertise that is not available within the organization.

Packaged program   A program designed for general use in many companies and sold or leased by computer vendors, self-employed programmers, or software houses.

Paper tape   One of the first input media used by mainframes, with data keyed in by using a keypunch machine that punches small holes in the paper tape's columns, where the combination of holes punched represents a letter, number, or special character.

Parallel conversion   A method of system conversion in which the old system and the new system are used simultaneously for a short time, and output from both are compared to make sure the new system is functioning correctly.

Parallel processing The use of many microprocessor chips to do different processing tasks simultaneously.

Parallel run A method of converting to new software by temporarily continuing to use the old system along with the new one, comparing results for completeness and accuracy.

Parity bit A single bit attached to each byte used to verify the accurate transmittal of data.

Pascal An easy-to-learn, highly structured high-level programming language.

PC-compatible A machine built on the same standard as the IBM PC, sometimes with additional features, such as faster processors, and usually at a lower price.

Periodic report A report generated at regular intervals, such as a quarterly financial report.

Peripheral device Any input/output device that has access to the CPU.

Personal information manager (PIM) A software package that allows microcomputer users to keep track of information such as names, addresses, telephone numbers, notes, to-do lists, and appointment schedules. Also called a desktop organizer.

PERT chart A chart that provides a method for keeping track of the progress of a project. PERT is an acronym for Program Evaluation and Review Technique.

Phased conversion A gradual method of system conversion.

Picosecond One trillionth of a second.

Pilot conversion A method of system conversion in which the new system is first implemented in a single department or division.

Pixel A tiny point of light or picture element on a monitor or screen.

PL/1 A high-level programming language designed to meet the needs of both business and science, combining the advantages of both FORTRAN and COBOL.

Plotter A printer that produces high-quality line drawings in colors by moving either pens or electrostatic charges with different colors of ink over the paper.

Point-of-sale (POS) terminal A terminal used in retail establishments to enter data at the actual location where a sale is transacted.

Polling A checking method in a LAN ring configuration that prevents two computers from sending a message at the same time.

Portable Adjective for the ability of some high-level languages such as COBOL and Pascal to be executed on many types of computers with minimal changes.

Positional numbering system A numbering system in which the position of the number helps to determine its value, such as the decimal system.

Presentation graphics Programs designed to produce graphic representations of data for business presentations.

Prewired function A function contained in ROM (Read-Only Memory). See firmware.

Primary storage The computer's main memory, commonly called random access memory (RAM).

Printer A peripheral device that converts output into hard copy.

Privacy A concern by computer professionals that personal information, such as employment and credit history, will be used properly.

Problem definition A report prepared by a systems analyst that analyzes the basic problem areas in existing procedures and highlights those areas needing improvement.

Procedural language Another name for a third-generation programming language; the term "procedural" means that the programmer must develop the logic necessary to carry out each procedure.

Processing speed The time required to access data in memory; typically measured in microseconds, or millionths of a second.

Processor The part of the system that transforms input data into useful information.

Productivity tools Computer applications that can be used by almost any kind of worker to do his/her job more effectively.

Program A set of instructions for processing data.

Program testing Executing the program with different sets of data to determine whether it always produces correct results.

Programmer A computer professional who writes programs, or sets of instructions, for each application, debugs and then documents them.

Programmer analyst A computer professional who serves as both a programmer and systems analyst in a smaller company.

Programming manager A computer professional who supervises the work of other programmers.

Project management software Software used by managers to keep track of complex projects.

PROM An acronym for Programmable Read-Only Memory. A ROM chip that must be removed from the computer for programming and requires the use of a special process to erase old programs.

Protocol A standard set of rules that regulates the way data is transmitted between two computers.

Prototype system A small-scale model of an expert system or an information system.

Prototyping A system-design approach whereby systems analysts provide all essential system elements as soon as possible to users, but before all of the systems interfaces and software modules have been designed.

Pseudocode A program planning tool that uses words to depict the logical structures to be used in the program.

Qualitative evaluation An evaluation method that assigns a soft-dollar value to the benefits of both current and proposed systems.

Quantitative evaluation An evaluation method that assigns a hard-dollar value to the contribution of both current and proposed systems.

Query Extracting selected information from a database.

Query language A type of fourth-generation programming language that allows the user to retrieve information and create custom-designed applications in databases by following simple syntax rules.

Random-access memory (RAM) The computer's main memory, also called primary storage.

Read into memory To copy a program or data file into primary storage or RAM.

Read-only memory (ROM) Prewired instructions that cannot be altered by programmed instructions. Examples of ROM instructions are built-in procedures for starting the system or for calculating a square root.

Read/write head A mechanism for reading and writing data from disk or tape.

Real-time processing Processing data and producing updated information online, interactively, so that it is available almost immediately.

Record A collection of related fields.

Register A specialized storage area where the CPU holds data while performing operations on it.

Relational database A type of DBMS package that presents files in table format to the users, with the records as rows and the fields as columns; relational databases enable numerous files to be linked together.

Relational database management system A database system organized so that separate data files are linked.

Relative addressing In a spreadsheet, the automatic changing of cell locations in a copy or move operation to reflect their new location; contrast with absolute addressing.

Remote data entry An application in which data is entered using terminals that are not physically at the same site as the central computer, such as in point-of-sale systems.

Remote job entry An application in which users write or run programs from terminals.

Report generator The component of a DBMS that produces customized reports using data stored in a database.

Request for proposal (RFP) A document prepared by an analyst to specify technical information about the type of computer needed in order to invite cost bids from vendors and to ask for information about the vendor itself.

Resolution The crispness of images and characters on a monitor or screen as affected by the number of pixels.

RGB monitor A color monitor in which the pixels each have a dot of red, green, and blue that can create many hues and colors.

Ring network A network configuration that connects computers in a circle of point-to-point connections, with no central host computer.

RISC technology RISC is an acronym for Reduced Instruction Set Computer. RISC technology that makes it possible for CPUs to have fewer and simpler instructions programmed into ROM but still be capable of complex tasks by combining simple instructions; this greatly reduces processing time.

ROM See read-only memory

Rules An approach for encoding knowledge in an expert system expressed in an IF-THEN format.

Save To write output to disk before exiting an application so that it will not be lost.

Scanner A device that converts pictures and text into machine-readable data.

Scientific programmer A computer professional who writes, debugs, and documents programs for specific scientific applications.

Scrolling Text that flows rapidly past on the screen.

Search and replace A word processing feature that searches for every instance of a specified word or phrase and replaces it with another, either automatically or after pausing for the user to verify the change.

Search feature   A word processing feature that allows the computer to look for a particular word or place in a text.

Second-generation programming language   Another name for assembly language, which is one step removed from machine languages.

Secondary storage   A set of devices that store data and programs in electronic form so that they can be accessed by computer. Also called auxiliary storage. Examples of auxiliary storage are floppy disks or the packs of large, hard disks used on minicomputers and mainframes.

Sector   A wedge-shaped segment of a track on a disk.

Security   Protecting computer systems and data from fire, sabotage, and espionage, as well as from various kinds of theft.

Sequence structure   One of the four logic structures in programs whereby a series of statements are executed in the order in which they appear in the program.

Sequential file   A file that is stored in some sequence or order, and that can only be accessed sequentially.

Serial printer   An impact printer that prints one character at a time.

Shell   The user interface to the operating system.

Simplex lines   Communications channels that permit data to flow in one direction only, such as from CPU to printer.

Single-alternative decision structure   A variation of one of the four logic structures in programs. With this structure, an action is taken if the condition is true; otherwise no action is taken.

Smart terminal   A computer terminal that has some independent abilities such as the capability to edit input before it is sent to the CPU; smart terminals, however, cannot run independent application programs.

Soft copy   On-screen output.

Soft-dollar value   Those benefits in business processes that result in a better financial position but are difficult to quantify.

Soft-sectored diskette   A diskette with a small hole near the center hub that tells the disk drive where the tracks begin. These do not have sectors already defined when you buy them.

Software   The total set of programs that enables a computer system to process data. Consists of both operating system and application programs.

Software development cycle   The steps involved in creating a program. These include: developing the program specifications and designing a solution; coding the program and translating it into machine language; debugging, testing, installing, maintaining, and documenting the program.

Source document   A document such as a purchase order, vendor invoice, or payroll change report that contains data that could be input into a computer.

Source program   The program as it exists in symbolic language, before it is translated into machine language.

Speaker-dependent system   A voice recognition system that requires users to train the system to recognize their specific speech profiles.

Speaker-independent system   A voice recognition system that can be used without training the system to recognize a particular voice.

Special report   A report prepared on an as-needed or on-demand basis.

Spelling checker   A word processing feature that enables users to compare each word in a document with an electronic dictionary to catch errors.

Spreadsheet package   A type of application that computerizes the record keeping function of spreadsheet ledgers or any worksheet that can be divided into rows and columns.

SQL   Structured Query Language. A non-proprietary data manipulation language that has become a standard for many database applications.

Star network   A network configuration in which one or more small computers is connected to a host computer that coordinates the messages between the nodes.

Statistical package   A program used to perform statistical operations on large quantities of data, including the ability to calculate standard deviations and variances.

Status line   An on-screen line, usually at the top or bottom of the screen that an application package uses for providing key information about the current status of that application.

Storage capacity   The amount of data each disk or computer can hold; measured in megabytes or gigabytes.

Storage devices   The parts of the system that permanently store the program, input, or output so that they can be used again later.

Stored-program device   A computer that requires a set of instructions to be entered and stored before data can be processed.

Structured analysis   A top-down method used by systems analysts to describe a system.

Structured programming   A standardized approach to creating a program using logical control constructs that makes the program easier to write, read, debug, maintain, and modify.

Structured walkthrough   A method of making programs more standardized and reducing debugging time by having a group of programmers work together to review the design.

Style sheet   A set of design choices for each document in a desktop publishing program as to what typeface to use, spacing required, and so on.

Subprogram   An element of a program that fits together with other subprograms, or program modules, to accomplish an overall procedure.

Subscriber service   A service that permits users with a modem to send and receive electronic mail, have access to databases, games, shopping services, and electronic bulletin boards.

Supervisor   The part of the operating system that manages the computer's resources including the CPU, primary storage, and peripheral devices; also called the kernel.

Swapping   A process that, using virtual memory, permits a very large program to be executed by a computer with limited storage capacity; parts of the program are loaded into memory at different times, overlaying parts that have already been executed.

Switched line   A standard telephone line used by common carriers that connects telephone lines to each other using central office switching equipment.

Switched service   A service offered by common carriers that connects telephone lines to each other using central office switching equipment.

Symbolic language   A programming language that uses instructions such as ADD or + instead of complex operation codes, and allows the programmer to assign symbolic names to storage locations.

Syntax error   An error that occurs when the programmer violates the grammatical rules of the programming language.

System flowchart   A chart used by analysts to depict the relationships between inputs, processing, and outputs, in the system as a whole.

System life cycle   The five stages in the creation of a business system: planning and analysis, design, implementation, operation and maintenance, and replacement.

Systems analyst   A specially trained computer professional who studies the information needs of various groups in an organization and works with user groups to design a system plan. If customized programs are required, the analyst supervises the work of programmers who actually write the software needed to meet the specifications in the system design.

Systems manager   A computer professional who oversees the activities of all systems analysts in an organization.

Systems programmer   A computer professional who develops operating systems, compilers and other programs designed to maximize the processing efficiency of the computer system.

Table   A method used for representing data in a database; rows correspond to records and columns correspond to fields.

Telecommunications   A special form of data communications that can transmit data via communications facilities such as telephone systems.

Telecommuting   Using data communications facilities so that employees with on-line terminals or microcomputers in their homes can do word processing, access corporate data, and communicate with colleagues, all without having to be physically present in the office.

Template   A form that contains the shell of an application including all the necessary design elements so that the user need only enter data.

Terminal   Any input/output device that is not at the same site as the CPU; is usually a remote keyboard and monitor connected to a separate CPU by cable or telephone.

Text and retrieval program   A program which stores the entire contents of a document in a database and retrieves text either by searching from the beginning of a document to the end or by using special search algorithms.

Text-oriented   A software feature that uses words rather than graphic images to represent various objects, such as files.

Thermal printer   A type of nonimpact printer that creates whole characters on specially treated paper that responds to patterns of heat produced by the printer.

Thermal transfer printer   A type of nonimpact printer that uses a heat-and-wax method that produces high-quality output, in color, and on regular paper.

Third-generation programming language (3GL)   A high-level, symbolic language that uses English-like commands to instruct the computer. Also called a procedural language.

Time-sharing   The ability of some large computers to be shared by numerous users who access the computer using terminals at remote locations.

Time-slicing   A time-sharing method that allocates a small amount of time to each user so that one user cannot monopolize the system at the expense of others.

Token ring network   A type of LAN (local area network) ring configuration in which a single set of messages passes from computer to computer.

Top-down design   A type of system design that is organized around the goals and informational needs of top managers.

Touch-sensitive screen   A user-friendly input device that displays choices and instructions and needs only to be touched to perform operations.

Track   Invisible concentric circles on a disk that are segmented into wedge-shaped units called sectors.

Tractor feed   A type of printer mechanism that feeds continuous-form paper through without interruption.

Traditional systems approach   An approach to designing information systems that assumes that if each business system within an organization functions efficiently, then the organization as a whole will run smoothly.

Transaction file   A file of changes to be made to the master file.

Transaction processing   A form of interactive processing that allows a user to input data and complete a transaction on the spot.

Transfer rate   The speed at which data is transferred from disk to main memory, measured in megabytes per second.

Transmission protocol   A set of procedures established by communications software that permits electronic impulses to move across either simplex, half-duplex, or full-duplex lines.

Twisted-pair cable   The typical telephone wires used in your house, consisting of two individual copper wires that are twisted for physical strength.

Typeover mode   A text editing feature in which text that is currently on the screen will be overwritten by the new text you enter.

Universal Product Code (UPC)   The bar code on most consumer goods, which includes a code for the manufacturer as well as the product's code.

Upload   To send data and programs to a central computer for a mini or micro.

Upward compatibility   The ability of a computer system to adapt to being upgraded to successively larger systems.

User   Anyone who uses a computer.

User friendly   Hardware or software that is easy to use and learn.

User interface   The part of the operating system that permits you to communicate with the hardware.

Utilities   The components of a DBMS that allow you to maintain the database by editing data, deleting records, creating new files, and so on. Can also be a set of programs that perform standard procedures such as sorting files, merging files, etc.

Value-added network (VAN)   A communications network offered by value-added carriers that offers extra services over and above those offered by the common carriers.

Variable-length record   A record that uses only as much storage per field as is needed.

Vector graphics   A graphic image created in a drawing program using combinations of lines, arcs, circles, squares, and other shapes.

Vertical package   A software package designed to meet the highly specialized needs of a specific industry or business.

Video display terminal (VDT)   A TV-like screen that displays your instructions and the computer's responses. Also called cathode ray tube (CRT) or monitor.

Virtual machine   A concept whereby the real machine simulates a number of virtual machines, each capable of interfacing with its own operating system, so that it performs as though there were a number of separate systems.

Virtual memory   Memory that allows the computer system to operate as if it had more primary storage than it actually does by segmenting the application program and storing parts of it on auxiliary storage. Also called virtual storage.

Voice recognition   A process that turns analog, or sound, signals into digital information that machines can understand.

Voice recognition device   The most user-friendly input device, one that can "hear" the human voice and correctly interpret a small vocabulary of words.

Voice response system   A system that turns words into digital information, compresses the digitized words, stores them in libraries of words and phrases, and later uses these words to build responses.

Voice store-and-forward system   A system that turns analog voice signals into digital format so that voices can be stored, retrieved, and distributed like any other form of electronic information.

Voice synthesis system   A system that turns digital information into sound waves—an audible voice with a potentially unlimited vocabulary.

Volatile memory   A type of memory composed of microprocessor chips in which programs and data disappear when the computer is turned off or loses power.

Wide area network (WAN)   A network that uses microwave relays and satellites to reach users over long distances around the world.

Window   A displayed portion of a worksheet or other document; several windows can be opened at once, allowing you to switch between applications.

Word   Technical term meaning a unit of data consisting of clusters of consecutive bytes. A word is the number of bits that can be transferred to a register in the CPU's control unit in a single operation.

Word wrap   A feature of word processing packages that automatically moves the cursor from the right margin to the left margin of the next line when the line is full, so there is no need to press the [Enter] key.

Word processing   Typing that uses software to record words electronically, making it possible to rearrange paragraphs and sentences and make deletions and insertions by using simple keystrokes.

Worksheet   A document that is divided into a row-and-column format. Also called a spreadsheet.

Write to disk   To store output of some kind after processing by copying data from RAM to disk, where it will not be lost when the power is turned off.

Write-protect notch   A feature of diskettes that allows you to protect the data by covering the notch, which prevents the disk from being written to, accidentally or otherwise.

WYSIWYG   "What you see is what you get" (pronounced wizzy-wig). A term describing a word processing or desktop publishing package that displays the text on the screen in exactly the same format as how the printed output will look.

Command Summaries

DOS

Command	Action
CHDIR or CD	Changes the current directory.
CHKDSK	Checks for disk's available space and specifies whether there are faulty files.
COPY	Copies files.
DATE	Allows current date to be set or changed.
DEL	Deletes files.
DIR	Displays any disk's directory.
DISKCOPY	Formats a disk and copies all files from one disk to another.
ERASE	Erases files.
FORMAT	Initializes diskettes.
MKDIR or MD	Creates new directories on the disk.
RENAME or REN	Renames files.
RMDIR or RD	Removes the current directory.
TIME	Allows current time to be set or changed.
TYPE	Displays the contents of a file.
VER	Displays the DOS version number.

WordPerfect 4.2

Key(s)	Action	Key(s)	Action
CTRL-F1	Shell (Access to DOS)	CTRL-F2	Spell Checker
SHIFT-F1	Superscript/Subscript	SHIFT-F2	Reverse Search
ALT-F1	Thesaurus	ALT-F2	Search and Replace
F1	Cancel	F2	Forward Search
CTRL-F3	Screen Options	CTRL-F4	Move
SHIFT-F3	Switch Doc 1/Doc 2	SHIFT-F4	Left/Right Indent
ALT-F3	Reveal Codes	ALT-F4	Block
F3	Help	F4	Left Indent
CTRL-F5	Text In/Out from DOS files	CTRL-F6	Tab Align
SHIFT-F5	Date	SHIFT-F6	Center
ALT-F5	Mark Text	ALT-F6	Flush Right
F5	List Files	F6	Bold
CTRL-F7	Footnote	CTRL-F8	Format Print
SHIFT-F7	Print Menu	SHIFT-F8	Format Line
ALT-F7	Math/Columns Options	ALT-F8	Format Page
F7	Exit	F8	Underline
CTRL-F9	Merge/Sort	CTRL-F10	Define Macro
SHIFT-F9	Merge E	SHIFT-F10	Retrieve Document
ALT-F9	Merge Codes	ALT-F10	Macro
F9	Merge Return (^R)	F10	Save

WordPerfect 5.0

Key(s)	Action	Key(s)	Action
CTRL-F1	Shell (Access to DOS)	CTRL-F2	Spell Checker
SHIFT-F1	Setup Menu	SHIFT-F2	Reverse Search
ALT-F1	Thesaurus	ALT-F2	Search and Replace
F1	Cancel	F2	Forward Search
CTRL-F3	Screen Options	CTRL-F4	Move
SHIFT-F3	Switch Doc 1/Doc 2	SHIFT-F4	Left/Right Indent
ALT-F3	Reveal Codes	ALT-F4	Block
F3	Help	F4	Left Indent
CTRL-F5	Text In/Out from DOS files	CTRL-F6	Tab Align
SHIFT-F5	Date/Outline	SHIFT-F6	Center
ALT-F5	Mark Text	ALT-F6	Flush Right
F5	List Files	F6	Bold
CTRL-F7	Footnote	CTRL-F8	Fonts
SHIFT-F7	Print Menu	SHIFT-F8	Format Menu
ALT-F7	Math/Columns Options	ALT-F8	Style
F7	Exit	F8	Underline
CTRL-F9	Merge/Sort	CTRL-F10	Define Macro
SHIFT-F9	Merge Codes	SHIFT-F10	Retrieve Document
ALT-F9	Graphics	ALT-F10	Macro
F9	Merge Return (^R)	F10	Save

Lotus 1–2–3

Key or Command	Action
(HOME)	Moves pointer to cell A1
(PGUP)	Up one screen - 20 rows
(PGDN)	Down one screen - 20 rows
(TAB)	Right one screen
(SHIFT)-(TAB)	Left one screen
(F1)	Help
(F2)	Makes the contents of a highlighted cell available for editing
(F5), cell location	"Go To" specified cell
(F10)	Graph
(ESC)	Return to previous menu or screen
' (apostrophe)	Designates the cell as a label, flush left
" (quote mark)	Designates the cell as a label, flush right
/	Displays the main menu
/ File Save, filename	Saves the worksheet
/ Worksheet Erase	Clears the worksheet from the screen
/ File Retrieve	Retrieves a file
/ Print Printer Range Align Go Page Quit	Send specified part of worksheet to printer
/ Quit	Exit the program
/ Worksheet Column Set-Width	Changes column width
/ Copy	Copies contents of specified cells
@SUM(range)	Adds the values in specified cells
@AVG(range)	Takes the average of the values in specified cells
/ Worksheet Global Column-Width	Sets column width for the entire worksheet
/ Worksheet Global Format	Formats the values on the entire worksheet
/ Range Format	Formats the values for specified cells
/ Worksheet Insert Row	Inserts blank rows in specified location
/ Worksheet Insert Column	Inserts blank columns in specified location
/ Worksheet Delete Row	Deletes specified rows
/ Worksheet Delete Column	Deletes specified columns
/ Print Printer Options Margins Quit	Sets left, right, top, and bottom margins for printing
/ Print Printer Options Header Quit	Allows you to create a header for printed document
/ Print Printer Options Cell-Formulas Quit Align Go Page Options Other As-Displayed Quit Quit	Prints out the contents of the cells, such as formulas, instead of values
/ Graph	Displays the Graph submenu
/ Graph Type	Selects a type of graph
/ Graph X	Specifies the label range for the graph
/ Graph (A-F)	Selects the data ranges for the graph

Key or Command	Action
/ Graph Reset	Cancels all or part of the graph settings
/ Graph View	Displays the current graph on the monitor
/ Graph Options	Enhances the graph with titles, legends, and grid lines
/ Graph Save	Saves current graph in a file
/ Graph Name	Stores one or more graphs as part of a worksheet file
/ Range Name Labels	Assigns range name to macro instructions
/ File Combine Copy	Copies all or part of one worksheet onto another
/ Range Name Create	Allows you to create a range name

dBASE IV

Commands invoked with the Function Keys

Key(s)	Command	Action
F1	Help	Displays help on-screen
F2	Data	Switch to Edit or Browse
F3	Previous	Moves to the previous field in Browse, Edit, Query or Help.
F4	Next	Moves to next field in Browse, Edit, Query, or Help
F5	Field	Adds field to layout surface or view skeleton
F6	Select	Selects contiguous text and fields
F7	Move	Moves selected text and fields
F8	Copy	Copies selected text and fields
F9	Zoom	Enlarges or shrinks memo fields, condition boxes and some data fill-ins, and file skeletons
F10	Menus	Gives access to menus for current screen
SHIFT-F1	Pick	Displays a list of items available for current fill-in
SHIFT-F2	Design	Displays the design screen
SHIFT-F3	Find Previous	Locates previous occurrence of each search string
SHIFT-F4	Find Next	Locates next occurrence of each search string
SHIFT-F5	Find	Finds specified search string
SHIFT-F6	Replace	Replaces search string with another string
SHIFT-F7	Size	Changes size of design elements and column widths
SHIFT-F8	Ditto	Copies data from corresponding field of previous record into current field
SHIFT-F9	Quick Report	Prints a Quick Report of data
SHIFT-F10	Macros	Accesses macros prompt box

Commands invoked from the Dot Prompt

Command	Action
ASSIST	Returns to the Control Center
CREATE	Creates a database file, followed by the file name
DISPLAY STRUCTURE	Displays the file structure on screen
TO PRINT	Following a command such as LIST, prints the onscreen information
LIST STRUCTURE	Lists the file structure
CLOSE ALL	Closes and saves all files currently open
USE	Followed by file name, opens a file
APPEND	Displays the Edit screen for adding data to a file
COPY TO	Followed by the name of the destination file, copies the file in use
DIR	Displays directory of files, including the number of records and size
LIST	Shows the data for all fields of the current record; since it cannot be stopped from scrolling, it is best used for printing
DISPLAY	Shows the data for all fields of the current record; scrolling can be controlled
DISPLAY ALL	Shows all records in the file
OFF	Following a command such as LIST, causes the display to omit record numbers
GOTO	Resets the record pointer to a specified record in a file
GO TOP	Resets record pointer to the first record of a file
HELP	Followed by another command, displays a Help message screen about the command
SUM	Adds up amounts in a field corresponding to a specified criterion
AVERAGE	Gives the average amount of each cell in a field corresponding to a specified criterion
COUNT	Counts the number of entries in a field corresponding to specified criteria
FOR	Following a command, specifies entries in a field to which to apply the command
SORT	Rearranges records in a file
SORT ON	Rearranges records in a file according to specified criteria
INDEX	Creates an index fle that keeps the database in logical order
EDIT	Accesses the edit screen
EDIT FOR	Accesses a particular record to edit
REPLACE	Replaces data in fields of specified records
SET ORDER TO	Used to specify an index tag that is used for arranging data
DELETE	Marks specified records for deletion
SEEK	Locates the record pointer on a specified record
RECALL	Unmarks records that were marked for deletion
PACK	Re-creates a file eliminating records marked for deletion
ZAP	Deletes and erases all the data in a database file while leaving the file structure intact
MODIFY STRUCTURE	Modifies a files structure while leaving the data intact
BROWSE	Accesses the Browse screen
REPORT FORM...TO PRINTER	Prints a specified report
LABEL FORM...TO PRINTER	Prints a specified set of labels

Lotus 1-2-3 Release 2.2 and 3.0 New Features Summary

Release 2.2

System Requirements:

IBM PC, IBM PS/2, or IBM-compatible with DOS 2.0 or higher and a minimum of 320K of system RAM. A hard disk and a minimum of 512K of system RAM is required to run the Allways add-in program included as part of Release 2.2.

Significant New Features:

Undo key (ALT-F4)   Cancels any changes to the worksheet since the program was last in READY mode. This feature allows you to recover from errors as well as toggle between the state of the worksheet before and after you used the Undo key to undo the changes made to it.

Minimal recalculation   Recalculates only those cells whose formulas depend upon the most recently changed value.

Settings sheets   Display all of the current settings for a particular operation in one screen. There are settings sheets for the global, default, print, graph, data query, data parse, and data regression settings.

/File Save Backup   Renames the previous version of the current worksheet file with the extension .BAK and saves your updates under the original file name.

/Worksheet Column Column-Range   Allows you to set a new width for a range of adjacent columns in one operation.

/Range Search   Allows you to find or replace a string in labels or formulas, or in both labels and formulas, in a particular cell range.

Enhanced overall graph appearance   Includes hatch patterns that progress from dark to light patterns, long legends wrapped onto two lines, X-axis labels staggered to avoid overlap, and tic marks placed within the graph frame. Also, in bar and stacked-bar graphs, grid lines do not run through the bars, and the first and last bars no longer touch the graph frame.

/Graph Group   Allows you to define all the graph ranges in a single operation.

File linking   Allows you to create formulas that use values from other worksheet files on disk. (Note that these linking formulas are limited to bringing forward single values from worksheets on disk.)

Learn mode   Records your keystrokes as you make them and then copies them into the worksheet where they can be used as macro instructions.

Run key ((ALT)-(F3))   Allows you activate a macro that has any range name, thus superseding the previous limit of 26 macros named \A through \Z in a single worksheet found in Release 1A, 2.0, and 2.01 of Lotus 1-2-3.

Macro Library Manager   Stores macros saved in special library files (given the extension .MLB) in RAM so that they can be used with any worksheet you are working on without having first to be copied into that worksheet.

Enhanced STEP mode   Displays the macro instruction and its current cell address as you execute it, thus making it easier to determine the exact place at which the macro fails to execute properly.

Allways spreadsheet publishing add-in program   Gives you what-you-see-is-what-you-get (WYSIWYG) control over the output of worksheet reports. This program allows you to enhance your reports with its own fonts, shading, line, and box drawing, as well as special printing effects including italics, boldface, and single and double underlining. This add-in program also makes it possible to print your Lotus 1-2-3 graphs along with your worksheet data in your printed reports.

Built-in network compatibility   Includes file locking that prevents another user from saving changes to the same worksheet file. To facilitate this record locking on a network, Release 2.2 includes new /File Admin Reservation commands that allow a user to release or get control of a worksheet file on the network.

Release 3.0

System Requirements:

IBM AT, IBM PS/2, or IBM-compatible equipped with an Intel 80286 or 80386 microprocessor and hard disk. DOS 3.0 or higher or OS/2 1.1 or 1.2. Under DOS, a minimum of 1 MB of system RAM is required (2 MB recommended). Under OS/2, a minimum of 3 MB of system RAM is required (4 MB recommended).

Significant New Features:

Undo key ((ALT)-(F4))   Cancels any changes to the worksheet since the program was last in READY mode.

Minimal recalculation   Recalculates only those cells whose formulas depend upon the most recently changed value.

Background recalculation   Enables you to continue to add or edit worksheet data while the program is recalculating dependent formulas.

Expanded edit line   Wraps characters to a new line that extend beyond the 80-character line length. In Release 3.0, the maximum number of characters allowed in a single cell has been increased from 240 to 512 characters.

Automatic cell formatting   Allows you to format a cell entry at the same time you enter it simply by typing the entry in the appropriate format. For example, you can apply the Currency format to a value when Automatic format is on by including the dollar sign, commas, and decimal places, as in $1,250.75. Note that in previous versions of Lotus 1-2-3 to achieve the same result you would have to enter 1250.75 and then select the /Range Format Currency command with two decimal places to have it displayed as $1,250.75

Automatic file naming   Assigns the next available numeric file name between FILE0001.WK3 through FILE9999.WK3 if you fail to specify a name after selecting the /File Save command.

/File Save Backup   Renames the previous version of the current worksheet file with the extension .BAK and saves your updates under the original file name.

/Worksheet Column Column-Range   Allows you to set a new width for a range of adjacent columns in one operation.

/Range Search   Allows you to find or replace a string in labels or formulas or both labels and formulas in a particular cell range.

Formulas or values   Can be annotated with comments that document their purpose in the worksheet by terminating the formula or number with a semicolon and then typing the text of the comment (up to 512 characters total).

/Worksheet Window Map   Displays a symbolic overview of the current worksheet that indicates the type of entry of each occupied cell. In this view all columns are displayed two characters wide with " in cells that contain labels, # in cells that contain numbers, and + in cells that contain formulas or annotated numbers.

/Range Name Note   Allows you to annotate a range name with comments describing the contents of the named range. When you create a range name table with the /Range Name Table command in Release 3, the program includes any attached notes in the resulting table.

Many new and enhanced graph types   Includes Hi-Lo-Open-Close graphs, combined line and bar graphs, area graphs, horizontal bar graphs, graphs using two different Y axes, and logarithmic graphs.

Automatic graph feature   Enables the program to draw a graph when you press the Graph key ([F10]) based on the location of the pointer in a range of data even when no graph ranges have been assigned.

/Graph Group   Allows you to define all the graph ranges in a single operation.

/Worksheet Window Graph   Allows you to split the worksheet display into two windows with one displaying the current graph and the other displaying worksheet data alongside it. This enables you to see immediately the effect that adding a new enhancement from the /Graph menu or changing a graphed value in the worksheet has on the current graph.

Advanced graph options   Allow you to select the colors and/or hatch patterns and fonts to be used in your graphs.

Note options   Allow you to annotate your graphs with up to two lines of footnotes.

Three-dimensional worksheets   Allow you to insert up to 256 different worksheets (A through Z) in a single worksheet file.

Group mode   Enables you to simultaneously format all the worksheets in a single file as you apply formats and column widths to the current worksheet.

Multiple worksheet files in memory   Permits you to open as many worksheet files as the memory of your computer can hold. Once open, you can copy or transfer data between files with the /Copy or /Move command or create formulas that dynamically link the data from different files.

/Worksheet Window Perspective   Displays three windows in one screen view that show part of three consecutive worksheets or files in memory. You can use the Zoom key (ALT-F6) to switch back and forth between a full-screen view of the current worksheet and the three-window perspective view showing parts of three worksheets.

File linking   Allows you to create formulas that use values from other worksheet files either open in memory or still on disk.

Graphs can be printed from the /Print menu   without having to use a separate PrintGraph program as you did in earlier versions of Lotus 1-2-3.

Background printing   Allows you to continue work on your worksheet after sending a report to the printer. This feature makes it possible to establish a print queue, load it with different reports and graphs, and have them printed one after the other. New print options allow you to suspend, resume, or cancel the printing.

Multiple ranges can be printed in a single report   by including them as part of the print range.

The worksheet frame can be included in the printout   without having to add the corresponding column letters and row numbers to the worksheet and include them as part of the print range as in previous versions of Lotus 1-2-3.

Advanced print options   Enable you to select different fonts for the print range, headers and footers, borders, or worksheet frame without having to use setup strings as in previous versions of Lotus 1-2-3.

Print settings can be named and saved   as part of the worksheet. You can then reuse the particular settings and apply them to a range that you are about to print simply by selecting the appropriate name.

/Data Sort Extra Key   Allows you to sort data ranges or database tables in a worksheet on up to 253 additional sorting keys on top of the primary and secondary sort keys supported by previous versions of Lotus 1-2-3.

/Data Query Modify   Enables you to extract records from a database table that meet your criteria, make your changes to the records, and then return them to the database table.

Databases can consist of multiple data tables   (although each database table must reside in its own worksheet). You can also perform a join operation with different database tables, allowing you to extract data from each table using a common key field.

/Data External   Enables you to query data in external database files created with other PC database management programs, such as dBASE III database files created with mainframe or minicomputer database management programs.

/Data Fill   Allows you to generate date and time sequences by entering starting and ending dates or times and then specifying the type of interval such as D for days, W for weeks, M for months, Q for quarters, Y for years, S for seconds, MIN for minutes, and H for hours.

Data Table Labeled   Enables you to generate a data table with as many input cells and input variables as you wish (previous versions of Lotus 1-2-3 could generate only one-input or two-input data tables).

Record key (ALT-F2)   Records your keystrokes as you make them and then copies them into the worksheet where they can be used as macro instructions.

Run key (ALT-F3)   Allows you to activate a macro that has any range name, thus superseding the previous limit of 26 macros named \A through \Z in a single worksheet found in previous versions of Lotus 1-2-3.

Built-in network compatibility   Includes file locking, which prevents another user from saving changes to the same worksheet file. To facilitate this record locking on a network, Release 3.0 includes new /File Admin Reservation commands that allow a user to release or get control of a worksheet file on the network.

/File Admin Seal File   Prevents access to a file's worksheet and reservation settings, thus making it impossible to do more than browse data and change data in unprotected cells when the worksheet's global protection is enabled and the user does not know the password.

Structured BASIC Programming for the PC

- ✔ Write structured BASIC programs in their entirety
- ✔ Use the logical control constructs of sequence, selection, iteration, and case in your programs
- ✔ Use coding techniques that make your programs easier to read, maintain, and modify
- ✔ Test and debug simple and intermediate-level BASIC programs

Appendix D

BASIC Outline

The Nature of BASIC

BASIC is designed to be an easy-to-learn programming language that you can use for writing programs in many applications areas.

BASIC as a Universal Language

BASIC is an acronym for Beginner's All-Purpose Symbolic Instruction Code. It was developed in the early 1960s by John G. Kemeny and Thomas E. Kurtz at Dartmouth College and was, at the time, one of very few existing symbolic programming languages. It gained immediate and widespread popularity because it is easy to learn and easy to use, and at the same time is both powerful and flexible.

Today, there are dozens if not hundreds of versions of BASIC available for microcomputers as well as for mainframes. In fact, when micros were introduced in the 1970s, BASIC was the first, and in most instances, the only, symbolic programming language available for them. It remains the most widely used symbolic language for microcomputers and is still widely used on mainframes as well.

The Most Commonly Used Versions for Micros

Although there are numerous versions of BASIC for micros, the main versions currently available are: IBM's Advanced BASIC, commonly referred to as BASICA (or GW-BASIC on most IBM compatibles), and Microsoft's QuickBASIC™. We will focus on BASICA because QuickBASIC is totally compatible with BASICA; in addition, we will provide a section at the end of this appendix that indicates advanced features of QuickBASIC not available with BASICA. Note that BASICA and GW-BASIC are essentially the same.

One main difference between BASICA and many other versions of BASIC, including QuickBASIC, is that it is interpreted, not compiled. Compiled versions can save the translated, machine language code in a program file that can then be executed over and over again without the need for repeated translations. Thus compiled versions of BASIC are more useful for regular production runs than is BASICA, which must be retranslated before each run. Also, compiled versions of BASIC tend to translate and run faster. Most of these compiled versions of BASIC for microcomputers are fully compatible with BASICA, which means that programs written in BASICA can be translated and then executed with little or no modification using these compilers.

BASICA is typically supplied as part of the DOS disk(s) so that its actual cost is negligible. As a result, it is the most widely used version for IBM micros and their compatibles. Compiled versions of BASIC, including QuickBASIC, must be purchased separately, but they typically sell for under $100. There is an educational version of QuickBASIC as well that is even cheaper.

In this text, we will provide a common core of BASICA instructions that are likely to run, with perhaps very minor adjustments, with all versions of BASIC.

Steps Involved in Writing Programs

Before discussing BASICA in depth, let us review the steps involved in writing programs and the techniques that should be used for creating well-designed programs.

1. **Obtain the program requirements and specifications** from a systems analyst or from the user, depending upon who the programmer interacts with at the company.

2. **Plan the program** using standard planning tools such as pseudocode and hierarchy charts.

3. **Write the program** and desk-check it before keying it in.

4. **Key in the program** and desk-check again, this time for typos.

5. **Translate the program** using either a BASIC compiler or interpreter. If there are any rule violations or syntax errors, they will be displayed on the screen. Fix them and retranslate the program until there are no more syntax errors.

6. **Run the program** using test data that includes a sample of what the actual data is likely to look like. Using pencil and paper, manually determine the results you should get and compare them with the computer-produced results. If there are discrepancies, find the error(s), fix them, retranslate, and rerun the program until all the results are correct.

7. **Perform a conversion** to ensure that the program runs smoothly in a normal operating environment.

8. **Document the program** so that users can run it as necessary without your intervention.

Techniques for Good Program Design

Before you begin to write actual programs in BASIC, it is a good idea to review some fundamental techniques of good program design.

Structured Programming

The most important technique for coding well-designed programs is called **structured programming**. Structured programming is an effort to standardize program design so that all programs, regardless of the language in which they are written, will have a similar form. In general, structured programs are easier to read than nonstructured programs. They are also easier to debug and modify, if changes are required at a later date. Moreover, they are easier to evaluate so that programming managers and systems analysts are better able to assess programmers' skills and the quality of their programs.

For those of you who have had some previous programming experience, you may have encountered nonstructured techniques that include frequent use of GOTOs, which is another term for a branch instruction. One major purpose of structured programming is to simplify debugging by reducing the number of entry and exit points or "GOTOs" in a program. For that reason, structured programming is sometimes referred to as GOTO-less programming. Using the techniques of structured programming, the GOTO statement is avoided entirely. In BASIC, this means writing programs where sequences are controlled by WHILE loops or some other logical control statement.

Modular Programming

Long and complex structured programs are sometimes subdivided into **modules**, also called subroutines, subprograms, or procedures. These are separate sets of instructions that accomplish distinct functions. Programs that are subdivided into modules are called modular programs. That is, subroutines, subprograms, or procedures are written as separate sections and are called into the main body of a modular program when they are needed.

Modules of a program are not only written separately but also can often be tested separately as well. This makes it possible to segment a large or complex program into individual sections so that, if necessary, different programmers can code and debug these different sections. In summary, modular programs consist of individual sections that are executed under the control of a main module.

Top-Down Programming

Another important design technique that makes programs easier to read and more efficient is called **top-down programming**. Top-down programming implies that proper program design is best achieved by designing and coding major modules before minor ones. Thus, in a top-down program, the main modules are coded first, after which intermediate modules and then minor ones are coded. By coding modules in this top-down manner, the organization or flow of the program is given primary attention.

This standardized top-down technique provides an excellent complement to structured programming for achieving efficient and effective program design.

In this appendix we will use structured techniques in all our programs and avoid the use of GOTOs entirely. In addition, we will use a top-down approach in our more advanced programs so that you will learn to program in a style that is widely accepted as a standardized and effective one.

A Sample BASIC Program

To understand the nature of BASIC, we will first look at a sample program that solves a typical business problem.

Definition of the Problem

A computer center of a company is assigned the task of calculating weekly wages or gross pay for all nonsalaried personnel. The employee name, hourly rate, and number of hours worked are supplied as input for each employee, and the weekly wages figure is to be computed as follows:

Weekly Wages = Hours Worked x Hourly Rate

efore processing can begin, the incoming data or input must be in a m that is "readable" by the computer. The input may be keyed in or read in from a disk or other storage medium.

Input Layout

Let us assume that the employee data will be keyed in using a keyboard. As we will see later, the device used for entering the input does not really affect the program's logic.

Each employee's data consists of three fields called **variables.** A variable is a storage area that will contain data. We will name the three variables that will contain input data EMPNAME$, HOURS, and RATE. Later on, when we discuss rules for forming variable names, you will see that the $ in EMPNAME$ is required because you are defining a variable that can contain alphabetic data.

Output Layout and Definition

For each EMPNAME$, HOURS, and RATE entered on the keyboard, we will print on a printer the employee's name and his or her weekly WAGES, which will be calculated as HOURS multiplied by RATE.

The Program Illustrated

To examine the program in detail, we will first look at its specifications, then the coding guidelines, and finally the instructions themselves.

Reviewing the Specifications   Recall that the program development process begins when the programmer obtains the program specifications. The program specifications for this problem include the formats of both the input and output and a description of the processing to be performed. This has already been provided in the previous sections.

Once these specifications have been supplied, the programmer should plan the program's design. This means mapping out the logic to be used in the program. The following illustrates the pseudocode that describes the logic to be used in the sample program. We include pseudocode as a planning tool here because we believe you should become familiar with reading pseudocode even before you prepare your own. The basic rules for writing your own pseudocode are provided in the next section.

```
START
    Print a message to user describing the input to be entered
    Input EMPNAME$, HOURS, and RATE
    WHILE there is still input
        Calculate WAGES as HOURS x RATE
        Print the results
        Input EMPNAME$, HOURS, and RATE
    WEND
    Print a message indicating End of Report
STOP
```

After the program has been planned using pseudocode or another planning tool, the programmer is ready to code it. Recall that a program is a set of instructions that operate on input to produce output. The following is a simplified BASICA program that inputs employee data keyed in using a keyboard and creates a printed payroll report containing the computed wages for each employee along with the employee's name.

```
10    'This Program Calculates Weekly Wages
20    PRINT "Enter Name, Hours and Rate"
30    INPUT EMPNAME$, HOURS, RATE
40    WHILE HOURS < 999
50       LET WAGES = HOURS * RATE
60       LPRINT "Weekly Wages For "; EMPNAME$; " is "; WAGES
70       INPUT EMPNAME$, HOURS, RATE
80    WEND
90    LPRINT "End of Report"
100   END
```

(handwritten annotations: STOP, 999,999; control; "control")

The numbers 10–100 on the left are line numbers. As you will see, BASICA programs are executed in line number sequence.

This BASICA program is likely to be executable as it is with most versions of BASIC. At worst, minor modifications might be necessary.

Note that business programs typically operate on numerous data items; the number of such items is often unknown when the program is written. Moreover, if the program is run periodically, the number of input data items can change. That is, the number of employees can be 100 in one week, 98 the next week, 103 the third, and so on. For this reason, most business programs use a WHILE **loop** to specify repeated execution of a series of steps. In this instance, WHILE there is still valid data to process, the program continues to do so. WHILE ... WEND in the program above delimits the loop. Some versions of BASIC use WHILE ... LOOP (VAX), WHILE ... NEXT, and so on in place of WHILE ... WEND. Even though the actual words or syntax may vary slightly, the important thing to remember is that the instructions within the WHILE loop will be executed repeatedly until there is no more data to process.

Coding Guidelines   Each line in a BASICA program must have a line number, but these are optional for QuickBASIC and some other versions. We use multiples of 10 in our line numbering (10, 20, etc.) so that we can easily make insertions if the need arises. If a line needs to be added between lines 20 and 30, for example, we can number it as line 25. Note, however, that with BASICA, instructions are executed in line number sequence, regardless of how they are entered. If you accidentally code:

```
10
30
20
```

the instructions will be executed as follows:

BASICA	*Some other versions, including QuickBASIC*
in line number sequence: (10,20,30)	in the sequence entered: (10,30,20)

This is an important difference between BASICA and QuickBASIC.

As a matter of style, capitalize all BASIC key words such as PRINT, INPUT, and WHILE, as well as variables such as EMPNAME$, HOURS, and RATE. This is a convention we use in our programs but it is not a requirement. BASIC is a case-insensitive language, which means that the translator ignores the distinction between upper- and lowercase letters. PRINT, print, Print, or even PRInt, for example, are all interpreted as the same word. Some versions of BASIC such as BASICA and QuickBASIC automatically convert key words to uppercase; BASICA also converts the names of variables to uppercase.

The Instructions   Each instruction in a BASIC program is executed in sequence unless a logical control construct such as WHILE is performed.

Let us consider each instruction in sequence. The first line in the program is:

```
10    'This Program Calculates Weekly Wages
```

This numbered line 10 is a comment line, which means it is coded just for information purposes and has no effect on either the translation or execution of the program. Comment lines begin with an ' (apostrophe or single quote) or with the abbreviation REM for REMARK. Once an ' or REM is sensed on any line, the rest of the line is treated as a comment and is not translated or executed in the program. Any instruction line can have a comment as its only entry, as above, or an instruction can have a comment added to it. For example, the following END instruction includes a comment that is not compiled or executed:

```
100    END REM This is the last line of a program
```

or

```
100    END 'This is the last line of a program
```

We recommend that you use comments freely in your programs because they help others understand your coding and logic, and they can even help remind you of some details later when you are testing the program.

The second line in the program is:

```
20    PRINT "Enter Name, Hours and Rate"
```

This line, when executed, will display a message on the screen to the user. It is intended to help the user determine the input to be entered and the form that the input should take. In a PRINT statement, the words between the double quotation marks are displayed on the screen as is. When the program is executed, these words appear on the screen where input and output is displayed.

When keying in double quotes to delimit both the beginning of the message and the end of the message, use the keyboard's double quote symbol. This symbol is the same for "open quote" and "close quote."

The message in the PRINT instruction is called a **literal** or **string constant**. Do not confuse this PRINT instruction with a comment line. A comment appears within the program itself only as a remark to the programmer. A PRINT instruction, when executed, prints a message to the user at the time the program is run.

Consider the next instruction in our sample program:

```
30    INPUT EMPNAME$, HOURS, RATE
```

string

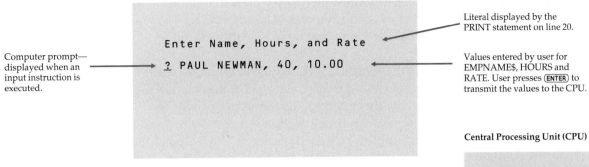

Computer prompt— displayed when an input instruction is executed.

Literal displayed by the PRINT statement on line 20.

Values entered by user for EMPNAME$, HOURS and RATE. User presses (ENTER) to transmit the values to the CPU.

Central Processing Unit (CPU)

When the user presses (ENTER), the computer transmits the data to the variables or storage areas called EMPNAME$, HOURS, and RATE.

This INPUT instruction accepts three values to be entered by the user on the keyboard. When the INPUT instruction is executed the computer prints a ? on the screen. The ? is called a **prompt** because it signals the user that the computer is waiting for input to be entered. In this case, three values are expected—one each for EMPNAME$, HOURS, and RATE. The three values must be keyed in by the user, each separated by a comma. After the three values have been entered, the user must press (ENTER) on the keyboard to transmit the values to the computer, and the next instruction in sequence will be executed. Recall that the Enter key is sometimes marked ↵ or may be called Return, as on a typewriter.

In summary, line 20 displays a message to the user on the screen and line 30 accepts input. Figure D–1 is an example of what might be entered and how it would be stored in the computer when the PRINT and INPUT instructions are executed.

D–1 How data is transmitted to the CPU.

The next five instructions in the sample program are treated as a unit:

```
40    WHILE HOURS < 999
.     .
.     .
.     .
80    WEND
```

The WHILE ... WEND structure in BASICA is called a **logical control construct**. It instructs the computer to execute the series of steps between the WHILE instruction on line 40 and the WEND instruction on line 80 and to continue executing these instructions for as long as the specified condition on the WHILE line is met. The WHILE in the example tests to see if the HOURS entered is less than 999 (< is the symbol for less than). This means that the instructions within the WHILE ... WEND structure will be executed repeatedly until HOURS is entered as 999 or more. In other words, each time that a value less than 999 is entered for HOURS, the instructions between the WHILE and the WEND will be executed.

In summary, the program begins with a comment that describes the processing to be performed. It then displays a message to the user, who should then input a set of values for the first employee. The WHILE ... WEND structure processes this first set of data, prints the result, and then transmits the next employee's data that the user enters. This WHILE ...

WEND structure is executed repeatedly until the three values that are entered include a quantity of 999 or more for the number of hours worked. The value of 999 is intended to signal the computer that there is no more input to process.

We indent instructions within the WHILE ... WEND just to highlight the fact that they are under the control of a logical structure. The translation process in BASICA is not, however, affected by indentation or spacing of any kind.

The value 999 in the HOURS variable is called a **trailer** or **sentinel value**, which means the user should only enter it after all valid data values have been input and processed. A value of 999 for HOURS serves to indicate that there is no more data. The number 999 was selected as a trailer or sentinel value because it could never be an actual value. That is, we chose 999 to signal an end-of-job condition because it is impossible for any employee actually to work 999 or more hours in any given week.

Thus the instructions within the WHILE ... WEND will be executed repeatedly until the user enters a trailer or end-of-job value of 999 for the HOURS variable. Suppose we use this program to process 15 employee entries. To end the run we might enter STOP, 999, 999 as the last line to be input; that is, the 15 employee lines would be followed by a 16th trailer line with STOP, 999, 999. This would cause the WHILE ... WEND to terminate because HOURS would be equal to 999. Note that all three entries— EMPNAME\$, HOURS, RATE—must be entered when the INPUT instruction is executed, even though only HOURS is tested by the WHILE. It is, however, the value of 999 in the variable called HOURS that terminates the loop.

The main body of all our programs will follow this same structured format:

```
        INPUT first set of values

        ⎧ WHILE one variable is not equal to a trailer value
        ⎪     process data
loop  ⎨      INPUT next set of values
        ⎩ WEND
                    .
                    .
                    .
```

The pseudocode planning tool for most of our programs will also have the same form, with WHILE ... WEND the terminology used to denote a loop in a pseudocode structure. All other words used in pseudocode (such as input, enter, and read) need not follow any specific rules:

```
Enter input
WHILE there is still input
            .
            .
            .
        Enter input
WEND
```

The first instruction within the WHILE ... WEND of our BASICA program processes the first set of data variables:

```
50    LET WAGES = HOURS * RATE
```

Line 50 calculates WAGES as the HOURS worked times the hourly RATE. The * is the symbol for multiplication. The LET or assignment statement will be discussed in detail later.

Let us walk through the logic in the program to see how the data is processed. When the INPUT instruction is executed, the computer prompts the user for input, and the user keys in the values for the three variables, as illustrated previously.

Program instruction:	Example of user-supplied input:
30 INPUT EMPNAME$, HOURS, RATE	? LINDA EVANS, 40, 8.00

The LET instruction on line 50 calculates WAGES as 40 x 8.00, which is 320. The computer stores the result in the variable called WAGES.

Line 60 is an output operation that prints on the printer a combination of literals or string constants and the contents of the variables called EMPNAME$ and WAGES:

```
60    "Weekly Wages For ";    EMPNAME$;    " is "    WAGES
```

String constant is printed
Contents of EMPNAME$ is printed
String constant is printed
Contents of WAGES is printed

Each LPRINT prints one line on a printer. While the PRINT on line 20 displays data on a screen, the LPRINT prints data on a printer. The LPRINT instruction can print string constants or literals as messages, along with the contents of variables. Constants or messages are enclosed in quotation marks. Hence LPRINT "Weekly Wages For " will print the words enclosed in quotes. LPRINT EMPNAME$ will print the contents of the variable called EMPNAME$. Elements to print are most often separated by semicolons.

The above instruction will print the following on the printer:

```
Weekly Wages For LINDA EVANS is 320
```

Contents of EMPNAME$
Contents of WAGES

Line 70 inputs the next set of values for Employee Name, Hours Worked, and Hourly Rate:

```
70    INPUT EMPNAME$, HOURS, RATE
```

Recall that the user enters the values for EMPNAME$, HOURS, and RATE all on one line, separated by commas. The three values will be transmitted to the computer when (ENTER) is pressed.

Line 80 indicates the end of the WHILE structure or loop:

```
80    WEND
```

When the program encounters the WEND statement or loop terminator, it repeats the series of instructions beginning with WHILE if the specified condition (HOURS < 999) is still met. That is, the next set of input is entered when the instruction on line 70 is executed, and the instructions within the

WHILE loop will be repeated if the HOURS entered on line 70 is less than 999.

In summary, when the computer executes the WEND, control returns to the WHILE statement, which processes the next set of input if the HOURS just entered is less than (<) 999. Suppose HOURS is entered for the second employee as a number less than 999. Then the second set of input will be processed and a second line printed. A third set of input values will then be read. The process of calculating and printing WAGES and reading new input is repeated until the user enters 999 or more for HOURS. At that point, the WHILE ... WEND is terminated and the statement following the WEND is executed. The statement following the WEND is another LPRINT instruction:

```
90    LPRINT "End of Report"
```

This will print the literal or constant "End of Report" as the last printed line after all weekly wages are printed.

This LPRINT instruction is executed only after the WHILE ... WEND is terminated. That is, when the user enters a value for HOURS that is 999 or more, along with an EMPNAME$ and RATE, the final LPRINT is executed.

The last instruction in a BASIC program is an END instruction:

```
100   END
```

We include this instruction in all our programs to indicate explicitly when a program is complete.

A Review of the Elements of a BASIC Program

All BASIC programs include the following elements:

- **Line numbers.** These are required for BASICA but are optional for some other versions.

- **Comments**. These provide information about the program. Comments begin with an apostrophe or single quote mark, or with REM for RE-MARK. Comments can be on a line by themselves or at the end of any instruction line. To highlight comments, we sometimes use the * or = characters as borders:

```
10 '*******************************
20 ' This is a payroll program
30 '*******************************
```

or

```
10 '===============================
20 ' This is a payroll program
30 '===============================
```

- **Reserved words**. These have special meaning to the translator (compiler or interpreter) and are used to perform operations (such as PRINT, INPUT, WHILE, LET, LPRINT, WEND, END). As a convention, we use uppercase letters for reserved words.

♦ **Variables**. These are areas in storage to hold data (for example, EMP-NAME$, HOURS, RATE, WAGES). We use uppercase letters for variables also. In addition, we use a $ at the end of a variable that holds either alphabetic data or data that may contain letters, digits, and special characters; such data is called *alphanumeric data.*

♦ **Operators**. These may be used in arithmetic: + (addition), – (subtraction), * (multiplication), / (division), and ^ (exponentiation).

♦ **Constants**. Data that is fixed in the program (for example, the trailer value of 999 on line 40 and the literal "End of Report" on line 90).

♦ **Relational tests** can also be performed in a WHILE ... WEND and in conditional tests (such as WHILE HOURS < 999). These include: < (less than), <= (less than or equal to), > (greater than), >= (greater than or equal to), = (equal to), and <> (not equal to).

BASIC is a free-form language, which means that no spacing rules are required. We recommend, however, that you include spaces between elements of an instruction for ease of reading. 10LET A=B+7 is not as easy to read as 10 LET A = B + 7. Similarly, we recommend that you indent instructions within logical control constructs such as WHILE ... WEND.

Interacting with Your Computer's Operating System and BASIC Translator

To run your BASIC programs you will be using an IBM microcomputer or compatible, another type of micro, or a larger mini or mainframe. Let us begin by focusing on how to use BASIC on IBM micros.

DOS Versions of BASIC for IBM Micros and Their Compatibles

Two DOS versions of BASIC can be used with IBM and IBM-compatible micros—they are BASIC and BASICA (the same as GW-BASIC).

BASIC and BASICA   One version of BASIC is built into ROM on IBM PC's and IBM PS/2's, but not always on their compatibles. This is called BASIC (not BASICA). You can access this version by booting up a dual-diskette system with no disks in any drive. The following message appears:

```
The IBM Personal Computer BASIC
Version A3.30 Copyright IBM Corp. 1981, 1982, 1983, 1984, 1985, 1986, 1987
60225 Bytes free
OK
```

Note, however, that this version is very limited and we do not recommend you use it. For one thing, it does not enable you to save programs easily, making it useful only as an experimental tool. You can get this same limited version of BASIC (when using an IBM micro) from the DOS operating system by typing **BASIC** at the A>, B> or C> prompt, depending upon which disk you have booted up with.

BASICA (or GW-BASIC), the focus of this Appendix, is also a BASIC translator supplied along with the DOS operating system. To access it, first

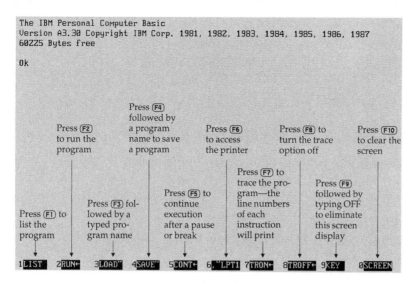

D–2 BASICA screen display.

load the operating system, and then type **BASICA** (or **GW-BASIC**) in response to the A>, B> or C> prompt, depending on where your operating system is located. The BASICA (or GW-BASIC) interpreter will then be loaded in as a program, and the screen display in Figure D–2 will appear.

Making Corrections to a Program   You can begin to enter your program by line numbers at this point. Each line is transmitted to the CPU when you press (ENTER). If you make a mistake before pressing (ENTER), you may use the backspace key to erase characters up to the error, or you may use the cursor arrow keys to return to an error point (without erasing characters) and fix the error. That is, using the cursor arrow keys does not erase as the cursor moves. To replace one character with another, use the cursor arrow key to move to the character to be replaced and then key in the replacement. To add or delete characters, use the cursor arrow keys to go to the point of insertion or deletion and then press (INS) and the character to be inserted, or press (DEL) to delete a character.

If you realize an error has been made after you press (ENTER), you may:

♦ Rekey the entire line with the same line number at any point in the program. If more than one line 30 appears in a program, for example, the last one replaces all previous references to that line.

♦ Use the cursor arrow keys to return to the error point and fix the error. Be sure you press (ENTER) at the end of the line after the change has been made; if you do not, the change or changes will not be transmitted.

If you need to insert a line between two previously entered lines, just give it an appropriate line number. That is, if you need two additional instructions between line numbers 20 and 30, enter them at any point as lines 24 and 28, for example. Remember that in BASICA, instructions are executed in line number sequence regardless of the order in which they are entered.

If you want to delete a line, just re-enter it with the same line number and no instructions.

BASICA System Commands BASIC instructions such as INPUT, PRINT, and so on are used to process data. There are also BASIC **commands** that are used for communicating with the translator itself. For example, to run a program you must type a RUN command that would not have a line number because it is not an instruction. Commands do not have line numbers.

Several BASICA commands appear on the bottom of the screen; you can execute them by typing either a key word or a function key. See Figure A–2.

Important BASICA system commands that you will need for running programs include:

- RUN—To execute a program (you may press (F2) in place of typing **RUN**)

- LIST—To display on the screen the program in line number sequence (you may press (F1) in place of typing **LIST**)

- LLIST—To print on a printer the program in line number sequence

- NEW—To enter an entirely new program

- SAVE "program name"—To save a BASICA program: a program name should be 1–8 characters long; preface the name with a drive letter, if necessary (such as SAVE "B:PROG1"); the system automatically gives it an extension of .BAS (you may press (F4) in place of typing **SAVE**)

- LOAD "program name"—To load back into memory a previously saved program (you may press (F3) in place of typing **LOAD"**)

- SYSTEM—To leave BASICA and return to DOS

Entering and Running a BASIC Program Using Another Translator or Computer

If you are using a version of BASIC other than BASICA or a different type of computer, you will probably find that many commands to the BASIC translator are either identical (such as RUN, SAVE, LOAD) or very similar. We provide the QuickBASIC command structure at the end of this appendix.

The following is a brief list of questions to ask before beginning a BASIC session with some computer or translator other than those discussed here:

1. How to log on (for mainframes) or boot up (for micros).

2. How to access or load in the BASIC translator.

3. How to transmit a line (usually by pressing (ENTER)).

4. How to make insertions and deletions to a program file.

5. How to perform full-screen text editing (typically you use cursor arrow keys to move to the error point and then either replace, insert, or delete characters as described previously).

6. How to save a program and load it back in memory.

7. How to run a program using test data.

A Brief Overview of Pseudocode as a Program Planning Tool

A program such as that for payroll, illustrated in this appendix, would first be planned using pseudocode to map out the logic. This planning tool is particularly useful in helping programmers determine the best type of structure for their programs. Moreover, for complex programs, this tool is essential for ensuring that the program is properly designed.

Fundamental Rules for Interpreting Pseudocode

♦   Pseudocode begins with a START and ends with a STOP.

♦   All instructions within the pseudocode are read in sequence.

♦   There is no set rule for specifying instructions in pseudocode. That is, "Enter input," "Read data," and "Input a name" are all acceptable ways for specifying that an input instruction should be coded.

♦   In pseudocode, to indicate a loop or the repeated occurrence of a series of instructions for all valid input we will write:

WHILE there is still input
    .
    .
    .
WEND

We have selected WHILE and WEND as pseudocode expressions for a loop. "WHILE there is still input" could be written as "DO WHILE more data," or "DO WHILE not end-of-job," or any other phrase that conveys the same meaning.

♦   The instructions between the WHILE ... WEND in the pseudocode are executed repeatedly until there is no more input to process. We indent these instructions in pseudocode, as in a program, so that the overall structure is highlighted.

♦   A conditional or test may be specified in pseudocode as:

IF condition THEN
    .   ⎰Statements to be executed if the
    .   ⎱ condition is met
    .

ELSE
    .   ⎰Statements to be executed if the
    .   ⎱ condition is not met
    .

ENDIF

(There will be more on this later.)

Example 1   Pseudocode for a program to calculate an average grade:

```
START
Enter three Exams
WHILE there is still more data
        Compute Average
        Print Average
        Enter three Exams
WEND
STOP
```

Example 2   Pseudocode for a program that will calculate sales commission:

```
START
Enter a SalesAmount
WHILE there is still more data
        IF    SalesAmount > 100.00 THEN
              Commission = .10 x SalesAmount
        ELSE
              Commission = .05 x SalesAmount
        ENDIF
        PRINT Commission
        Enter a SalesAmount
WEND
PRINT "End of Job"
STOP
```

SELF-TEST

1. (T *or* F) Structured programs are sometimes called GOTO-less programs.
2. Some versions of BASIC are translated by using a(n) _____, which scans the code and executes it all in one process, while more efficient versions are translated using a _____, which translates first, then executes the program, and can also save the program in executable form.
3. (T *or* F) BASICA instructions are compatible with most popular interpreted versions of BASIC for IBM microcomputers.
4. The two most common tools for planning a program are _____ and _____.
5. BASIC is an acronym for _____.
6. (T *or* F) Structured programs are easier to read, debug, modify, and maintain than nonstructured programs.
7. (T *or* F) Line numbers are required in BASICA but optional with some other versions.
8. The _____ instruction is used to display information on the screen, while the _____ instruction writes the information on the printer.
9. A comment in BASIC begins with _____ or _____.
10. In the instruction WHILE AMT < 9999, 9999 is called a _____. The WHILE ... WEND loop will be executed repeatedly until _____.

SOLUTIONS

1. True
2. interpreter; compiler
3. True
4. pseudocode; hierarchy charts
5. Beginner's All-Purpose Symbolic Instruction Code
6. True
7. True
8. PRINT; LPRINT
9. REM or ' (apostrophe)
10. trailer or sentinel value; the user enters an AMT as 9999 or more

"5-ON" ASSIGNMENT

ı on your computer the Sample Payroll Program discussed previously, run ... with sample data, save it, and then load it back into memory.

Writing Elementary BASIC Programs

In the following sections you will gain experience in BASIC by writing simple programs. First we will look at a few general programming principles.

Input-Process-Output

Most programs read in data or **input**, process it in some way, and produce information called **output**. Input can be entered as a series of entries using a keyboard, as shown in Figure D–3. Input can also be read in from a disk file or other storage medium, as shown in Figure D–4.

Input is processed by either performing arithmetic operations or selecting operations to be performed, depending on the contents of the input. In the sample payroll program that was illustrated, the variable (input) was multiplied by a rate variable (also input) to produce the weekly wages (output). Output can be information that is displayed on a screen, printed on a printer, or stored on disk or other storage medium for future processing.

In this section we will consider some elementary input, processing, and output operations. After you have read the section, you will be able to write simple BASICA programs in their entirety.

All our programs will use the structured programming technique discussed in the previous sections:

```
INPUT ...
            'This is the initial read
WHILE there is still input
            process input
            produce output
       INPUT ...
WEND
```

Defining Variable Names

The concept of a variable is very important in BASIC. The following sections discuss how you define variable names as well as what types of variables are allowed.

An Overview of Variables   A **variable** is a data element that may be different each time the program is run. For example, customer numbers, prices of items, quantities, and so on may be read in as variable input each

```
Enter Unit Price

? 5.00

Enter Qty                   ──── Input entered using a keyboard

? 4.0

The Total is $20.00
```

D–3 Entering input in BASIC.

File of Accounts Receivable Records on Disk							
Record 1				Record 2			
ACCTNO	NAME	UNIT PRICE	QTY	ACCTNO	NAME	UNIT PRICE	QTY
001	NEWMAN, PAUL	3.00	2	002	EVANS, LINDA	5.50	2

time the program is run or executed. Similarly, the output information will also be variable because it depends on the input.

D-4 A sample of records that can be input using a BASIC program.

Variable data elements are given variable names in a program. If you say INPUT PRICE, for example, PRICE is called a variable name. Each variable name refers to a location or address in the computer's memory where the data is actually stored. Data elements or variables can be read in as input, given a value as a result of some processing, or produced as output.

The rules for defining variable names depend on whether the data to be stored is either numeric or alphanumeric. A **numeric variable** contains numbers, an optional decimal point, and an optional plus or minus sign; such variables may be used in arithmetic operations. An **alphanumeric** or **string variable** can contain letters or symbols as well as numbers and is never used in arithmetic operations. A variable that contains an address or a name, for example, is considered alphanumeric.

Numeric Variables We begin by considering the rules for forming numeric variable names, which are areas in storage that will store numeric values:

- The name must begin with a letter.

- In BASICA the name can contain up to 39 characters; other versions of BASIC may have different length limitations.

- The name can use periods as word separators (such as SALES.AMT).

- Blanks are not permitted within a variable name (for example, the variable NEWSALARY is okay, as is NEW.SALARY, but NEW SALARY is not).

- Reserved words such as INPUT or PRINT are not permitted as variable names. At the end of this appendix, we list all BASICA reserved words.

We recommend that you use meaningful names to define a variable. This makes programs easier to read and debug.

Recall that BASIC, in general, is a case-insensitive language. That means that you can use upper- and lowercase letters interchangeably. Thus, upper- and lowercase letters will be recognized by the BASIC translator as the same characters. To the translator, then, the variable Amt is the same as AMT or even AMt. However, the BASICA interpreter will convert all variables and reserved words to uppercase.

The following are examples of invalid numeric variable names:

Invalid Name	Reason
UNIT.PRICE.IN.$	The $ is not permitted in a numeric variable name. (UNIT.PRICE.IN.DOLLARS is okay.)
2NDAMT	A numeric variable must begin with a letter. (AMT2 is okay.)
EMPLOYEE WAGES	Blanks are not permitted within a numeric variable name. (EMPLOYEE.WAGES or EMPLOYEEWAGES is okay.)
OUTPUT	This is a BASIC reserved word. (OUTPUTAMT or OUTPUT.AMT is okay. See the list of BASICA reserved words at the end of this appendix.)

String Variables   The preceding variables are used to store numeric data. These numeric variables can be used in arithmetic operations. Other variables, however, are needed to store alphanumeric data (letters, blanks, and/or special symbols, as well as numbers). These are called *string variables*.

String variable names are formed according to the same rules as for numeric variables except that a string variable name ends with a $. Thus, EMPLOYEENAME$, ADDRESS$, and MARITAL.STATUS$ are all valid names for string variables.

Defining Literals or String Constants

As you have seen, a literal or string constant is a value that is always the same regardless of the input. It is coded directly in the program as a fixed value. The value 999 that was used in the instruction WHILE HOURS < 999 is an example of a numeric constant. Similarly, the value "End of Report" in the PRINT "End of Report" instruction is an example of a string constant.

Just as there are two types of variables (numeric and string) in a BASICA program, there are two types of constants as well:

Type of Constant	Valid Characters	Examples
Numeric Constant	Digits.	46
	An optional decimal point.	12.47
	An optional + or – sign to the left of the number.	–12.3
String Constant	Any set of characters enclosed in double quotes (" ") is permitted in a string constant. This includes letters, digits, blanks, and special symbols, such as %, #, and @.	"This is a Constant" "Input Error #412"

The INPUT Statement

You have already seen that an INPUT statement is used first to prompt the user for input and then to enter the data to be processed. Both numeric variables and string variables can be entered as input, as in the following examples:

```
10    INPUT AMOUNT       'AMOUNT is a numeric variable
20    INPUT NAMEIN$      'NAMEIN$ is a string variable
```

When an INPUT statement is executed, the computer prompts the user for an entry. The prompt for input is displayed as a question mark (?) when the program is run. After the input is entered, the user must press (ENTER) to transmit or send it to the computer so that the next instruction in the program can be executed.

Entering Numeric Variables   The characters permitted in a numeric variable are the same as for numeric constants:

♦ Digits

♦ An optional decimal point

♦ An optional + or – sign to the left of the number

Hence, the following are all valid as numeric input that the user may key in, as a response to a ? prompt:

115	.25	+1278	12.5	–16.5

For example, each of the above could be correctly input into a numeric variable such as AMOUNT.

Other characters, such as a comma or dollar sign, are not permitted in a numeric variable. Note again that characters that are valid as numeric input are also valid in a numeric literal or constant. This means that the program itself could include numeric constants of 115, .25, and so on.

Let us consider the statement 10 INPUT AMOUNT. Suppose you are prompted to enter a value for the AMOUNT variable during program execution, and you respond with any one of the following. The values will be incorrect for the reasons specified:

Incorrect Data Entry	*Explanation*
? 1,000	Commas are not permitted in numeric variables or numeric constants. The computer interprets the comma to mean the end of the value.
? a	a is not valid in a numeric field. Any non-numeric input entered for a numeric variable is stored as 0.
? $12	The $ is not valid in a numeric field.
? 12 –	The – is simply ignored because it is not to the left of the digits.

In each of the above instances, the translator will respond *Redo from start* (or with some similar message), if an incorrectly input value is entered.

Note that when entering input, you can erase incorrect keystrokes with the backspace key if you have not yet pressed (ENTER). It is best, then, to carefully check the input on the screen before pressing (ENTER).

Entering String Variables

A string or alphanumeric variable may also be entered as input. Recall that string variable names end with a $. When you input data to a string variable, any character is acceptable, but note that the string variable that is stored may not be used in arithmetic operations even if the value entered contains all numbers. The following, then, is invalid:

```
10    INPUT AMOUNT$
20    LET AMOUNTOUT = AMOUNT$ + 3    'AMOUNT$ may not be used in arithmetic
```

You will get a syntax error when the second instruction is translated by the computer because AMOUNT$, as a string variable, may not be used in an arithmetic operation.

You can also use quotation marks to delimit input strings. For example, consider the following:

```
10    INPUT CUST.NAME$
20    PRINT CUST.NAME$
```

Suppose you enter the following at the ? prompt:

```
? Newman, Paul
```

A *Redo from start* error message (or a similar error message) will be displayed because a comma was entered between the last and first names. Once the computer senses the comma, it assumes that the data to be entered in the variable CUST.NAME$ is complete. To enter string data that is itself to contain a comma, as above, use quotation marks to delimit the value:

◆ **Program**

```
10    INPUT CUST.NAME$
20    PRINT CUST.NAME$
```

◆ **Run**

```
? Newman, Paul
Newman, Paul
```

The Assignment Statement

In BASIC, you set a variable to be equal to a computed expression by using an assignment statement. This allows you to move data, copy it, and perform arithmetic operations such as addition and subtraction on it.

Performing BASIC Arithmetic Operations Using an Assignment Statement

◆ **The Format**   Arithmetic operations are performed in BASIC by using a LET statement, which is also called an *assignment statement*. This type of instruction sets a variable equal to a computed value. The format of the instruction is as follows:

```
[LET] variable = expression
```

The above statement is called a **format**, as indicated. A format specifies the precise rules for using an instruction. The word LET, for example, is bracketed, which means that it is optional. The expression in the format consists of operators and operands (variables and constants) that compute a result.

The expression can operate on numeric variables and numeric constants with the following basic operators:

```
+    Addition
–    Subtraction
*    Multiplication
/    Division
^    Exponentiation
```

All variables and constants, including the resultant variable to the left of the = sign, *must be numeric*. The ^ used for exponentiation is a special character above the number 6 on the main keyboard. Look at the following examples:

Valid Assignment Statements	*Explanation*
`LET TOTAL = AMT1 + AMT2`	The variable to the left of the equal sign, TOTAL, will be set equal to the sum of AMT1 and AMT2.
`LET WAGES = HOURS * RATE +` `    OVERTIME`	An expression to the right of the equal sign can include more than one arithmetic operator. In this case, WAGES will be set equal to the computed result of HOURS x RATE + OVERTIME.
`LET TAX = .05 * PRICE`	An assignment statement can be used to set a variable equal to an expression that contains variables as well as constants. In this case, the variable PRICE is multiplied by the numeric constant .05, and the result is placed in TAX.
`LET AREA = 3.14 * RADIUS ^ 2`	This instruction computes the area of a circle as Pi x R^2 (Pi = 3.14 and R = the radius) and places the result in a numeric variable called AREA.
`COMMISSION = SALES * .10`	The word LET is optional in an assignment statement.

The following are invalid for the reasons noted:

Invalid Assignment Statements	*Reason for Error*
`LET .0751 * SALARY = SOCSECTAX`	A variable, not an arithmetic expression, must appear after the word LET; that is, to the left of the = sign. The correct statement is LET SOCSECTAX = .0751 * SALARY.
`LET NEWSALARY = $1,000+SALARY`	$1,000 is not a valid numeric constant because it includes a $ and a comma. The correct statement is: LET NEWSALARY = 1000 + SALARY.
`LET OVERTIME = 2HOURS`	If 2HOURS means "2 times HOURS," the multiplication symbol, *, is necessary (such as in LET OVERTIME = 2 * HOURS). Note also that 2HOURS cannot be a numeric variable because all variables must begin with a letter.
`LET BONUS$ = AMT / 10`	BONUS$ may not be the result of an arithmetic operation because it is a string or alphanumeric variable.

◆   **A Sample Program that Performs Arithmetic Operations**   Let us consider a program that reads in a series of Celsius temperatures and displays their Fahrenheit equivalents. End the program when a Celsius temperature of 999 is entered as a trailer or sentinel value. Recall that a trailer value indicates that there is no more data to process; it is entered after all "real" data has been input and processed. This value should not itself be processed as "real" data. The formula for calculating Fahrenheit temperature is:

Fahrenheit = (9/5 * Celsius) + 32

As noted, all our programs are structured. This means that we use an initial INPUT statement to read in the first Celsius value; we then use a WHILE ... WEND loop to process this first value and to read additional values until there is no more input. We will use a basic PRINT statement in our examples to output the results on the screen. Other options for printing are discussed later. The pseudocode for this problem is as follows:

```
START
        Input a Celsius < value
        WHILE there is more input
                Calculate Fahrenheit
                Print the result
                Input a Celsius value
        WEND
        Print a closing message
STOP
```

Standard pseudocode should begin with a START and end with a STOP. The instructions within the WHILE ... WEND are part of a logical control sequence called a **loop**. The words used in each instruction need not follow any programming language's syntax because pseudocode, as a planning tool, is language-independent.

The BASICA program is as follows:

```
10      INPUT CELSIUS
20      WHILE CELSIUS < 999
30          LET FAHRENHEIT = 9/5 * CELSIUS + 32
40          PRINT FAHRENHEIT
50          INPUT CELSIUS
60      WEND
70      PRINT "That's all folks!"
80      END
```

$$9/5 = 1.8$$

In the above program, 999, 9, 5, and 32 are numeric constants, and CELSIUS and FAHRENHEIT are numeric variables. "That's all folks!" is a string constant. Because the fraction 9/5 could be written as 1.8, line 30 could also be coded as LET FAHRENHEIT = 1.8 * CELSIUS + 32.

After the program has been translated and there are no syntax errors, it is ready to be run. When the computer executes the INPUT instruction, a ? prompt appears on the screen. This means that the computer is waiting for input from the user. Suppose you enter 25 at the cursor point or prompt.

After you press (ENTER), 25 is transmitted to and stored in the variable named CELSIUS. Then the FAHRENHEIT equivalent of the CELSIUS temperature of 25 is computed. The input expected on each line must be in numeric form with no symbols such as commas or dollar signs.

The PRINT instruction will print the value 77 (9/5 x 25 + 32). The next INPUT instruction on line 50 will cause the prompt to appear again, which is a request for another CELSIUS temperature. This series of instructions or loop continues repeatedly until you enter a CELSIUS temperature of 999 (or more); the trailer value of 999 terminates the loop and causes the closing string constant or message ("That's all folks!") to print.

Using indented instructions makes it easier to understand the program's structure. Indentation is most easily accomplished by pressing Tab, which is the key marked (TAB) on the left-hand side of the keyboard.

SELF-TEST

Solutions to Questions 1-2 require full BASIC programs. In each case, the program should be able to process numerous input variables. All programs should be structured. Begin by planning the program with pseudocode.

1. Write a program to input the number of gallons of gas used in a trip and the number of miles traveled. Print miles per gallon. Use a WHILE ... WEND loop to enable the program to continue processing for other values to be input.
2. Write a program to input Sales Amounts and to print a commission as 15 percent of each Sales Amount.

SOLUTIONS

1. Pseudocode:

```
START
        Enter No of Gallons and Miles Traveled
        WHILE there is still input
            Calculate Miles Per Gallon
            Print the result
            Enter No of Gallons and Miles Traveled
        WEND
        Print an end-of-run message
STOP
```

BASICA Program:

```
10    REM This program computes miles per gallon
20    INPUT NOOFGALLONS, MILESTRAVELED
30    WHILE NOOFGALLONS < 99
40        MILESPERGALLON = MILESTRAVELED / NOOFGALLONS
50        PRINT MILESPERGALLON
60        INPUT NOOFGALLONS, MILESTRAVELED
70    WEND
80    PRINT "End of Job"
90    END
```

2. Pseudocode:

```
START
        Enter Sales Amount
        WHILE there is still input
                Calculate Commission
                Print the result
                Enter Sales Amount
        WEND
                Print an end-of-run message
STOP
```

BASICA Program:

```
10    ' This program calculates Sales commissions
20    INPUT SALESAMOUNT
30    WHILE SALESAMOUNT < 99999
40        COMMISSION = .15 * SALESAMOUNT
50        PRINT COMMISSION
60        INPUT SALESAMOUNT
70    WEND
80    PRINT "DONE!"
90    END
```

◆ **Hierarchy of Arithmetic Operations**   The sequence in which arithmetic operations are performed may affect the results of a computation. Consider the following:

```
10     INPUT AMT1, AMT2, AMT3
20     WHILE AMT2 <> 99
30        LET TOTAL = AMT1 - AMT2 * AMT3
40        PRINT TOTAL
50        INPUT AMT1, AMT2, AMT3
60     WEND
70     END
```

Suppose you initially enter AMT1 as 10, AMT2 as 5, and AMT3 as 2. You need to determine whether the computer will perform AMT1 – AMT2 * AMT3, which is equal to $10 - 5 \times 2$, as:

(a) $(10 - 5) \times 2 = 10$

or

(b) $10 - (5 \times 2) = 0$

If the computer performs the subtraction operation first as in (a) and then the multiplication, the result will be different from that obtained by performing the multiplication first as in (b).

The following are the hierarchy rules used by computers in most programming languages:

◆ Arithmetic operations are performed in the following order:

    1. Exponentiation first.
    2. Multiplication and division next.
    3. Addition and subtraction last.

◆ If an instruction has two or more operations on the same level, they are executed in sequence from left to right.

◆ The use of parentheses overrides all other hierarchy rules.

Let us look again at our previous assignment statement:

```
30     LET TOTAL = AMT1 - AMT2 * AMT3
```

According to the above rules, the multiplication is performed first and then the subtraction. That is, TOTAL will contain the following when the arithmetic operations are executed:

$10 - 5 * 2 = 10 - 10 = 0$

As noted, the basic hierarchy rules can be overridden with the use of parentheses. Thus, to obtain AMT1 – AMT2 multiplied by AMT3, we would write LET TOTAL = (AMT1 – AMT2) * AMT3.

Example   Input three exam grades for every student in a class and calculate the average grade for each student. The pseudocode and BASICA program follow:

◆ **Pseudocode**

    START
        Enter three Exam Grades

```
            WHILE there is still data
                    Calculate Average
                    PRINT Average
                    Enter three Exam Grades
            WEND
        STOP
```

♦ **BASICA Program**

```
10      INPUT EXAM1, EXAM2, EXAM3     'Get initial data
20      WHILE EXAM1 <> 999              'Check for trailer value
30          LET AVERAGE = (EXAM1 + EXAM2 + EXAM3) / 3
40          PRINT AVERAGE
50          INPUT EXAM1, EXAM2, EXAM3
60      WEND
70      END
```

In this instance, the parentheses in the LET or assignment statement are required for obtaining the proper order of evaluation. The following will not produce a correct average:

```
30      LET AVERAGE = EXAM1 + EXAM2 + EXAM3 / 3
```

Based on the hierachy rules, the computer performs the additions before the division; hence only EXAM3 would be divided by 3 if parentheses were omitted. Thus AVERAGE would be set equal to EXAM1 + EXAM2 + EXAM3/3.

In summary, when an operation or a series of operations is to be performed in an order different from those specified in the hierarchy rules, you enclose the operation(s) in parentheses. In the above, you want the three exams to be added before the division is performed, so you must use parentheses.

Note, too, that any attempt to divide by zero will result in an error.

SELF-TEST

Indicate the result in Questions 1–2:
1. 10 LET TOTAL1 = 4 + 2 / (5 – 3)
2. 10 LET TOTAL3 = 4 * 5 + 2

Indicate the error in Questions 3–4:
3. 10 LET C = 2A + D
4. 10 PRINT "THE ANSWER IS ; F

Write a BASIC instruction to perform the following:

5. $A = \dfrac{3 + C}{D + 7}$

SOLUTIONS
1. 4 + 2 / 2 = 4 + 1 = 5
2. 4 * 5 + 2 = 20 + 2 = 22
3. 2A must be coded as 2 * A: 10 LET C = 2 * A + D
4. A quotation mark is missing: 10 PRINT "THE ANSWER IS "; F
5. 10 LET A = (3 + C) / (D + 7)   'The parentheses are required

---

♦ **Obtaining Running Totals**   As you have seen, an assignment statement can be used to perform an arithmetic operation and place the result in the variable indicated. For example, the statement LET NET = PRICE –

DISCOUNT causes DISCOUNT to be subtracted from PRICE and the result placed in NET.

You could also use an assignment or LET statement to replace the value in a variable. That is, 10 LET AMT = 30 places the value of 30 in AMT. Similarly, 20 LET TOTAL1 = TOTAL2 copies the value stored in TOTAL2 into the variable called TOTAL1.

You could also use an assignment statement to place a string value into a string variable. That is, 10 LET CODE$ = "ABC" or 20 LET CODE1$ = CODE2$ are also valid statements.

Incrementing Counters Assignment statements are also used for incrementing the contents of a variable. Consider the following: 10 LET COUNTER = COUNTER + 1. This statement is not a valid mathematical expression, but it is a valid BASIC statement that performs the following:

1. One is added to the value in the variable called COUNTER.

2. The sum of one plus the value in the variable COUNTER then replaces the original contents of COUNTER.

Thus if COUNTER had an initial value of 10, 1 would be added to it, and 11 would be placed back into COUNTER. That is, the effect of the instruction LET COUNTER = COUNTER + 1 is to add one to COUNTER. This type of assignment statement is frequently used to increment counters or to add to totals. 10 LET TOTAL = TOTAL + AMT1 adds AMT1 to TOTAL.

In general, an assignment statement of this kind is used to obtain a running total that increments a variable, or adds to the contents of that variable. To accumulate the sum of all transaction amounts read in, for example, you write:

```
10      LET SUM = 0              'Initialize SUM at 0
20      INPUT AMOUNT             'Get an initial AMOUNT
30      WHILE AMOUNT <> 999      'Trailer value for AMOUNT is 999
40         LET SUM = SUM + AMOUNT    'Add AMOUNT to running total
50         INPUT AMOUNT          'Get another input AMOUNT
60      WEND
70      PRINT SUM                'Only one final total is printed
80      END
```

Each time the computer executes the WHILE ... WEND loop, SUM is increased by the value of each AMOUNT that is entered as input. Thus, the LET instruction on line 40 accumulates a running total of all values of AMOUNT the user enters.

Note that the first program line is used to initialize the variable called SUM at 0. Although BASIC automatically initializes numeric variables at 0, it is always good practice to explicitly set to 0 all variables that will be used as running totals. Other programming languages may not initialize variables automatically, so we advise programmers to develop the habit of setting numeric variables to 0 before adding to them. Note, however, that a variable such as AMOUNT, in the preceding illustration, need not be initialized, because it will always contain values the user enters.

Example   For all salaries that are entered, provide for a $100 raise and print the new salaries. The pseudocode and BASICA program are shown below.

◆ **Pseudocode**

```
START
        Enter Salary
        WHILE there is still input
                Increase Salary by $100
                Print New Salary
                Enter Salary
        WEND
STOP
```

◆ **BASICA Program**

```
10    REM This program increases each salary by $100
20    INPUT SALARY              REM Get initial Salary data
30    WHILE SALARY < 999999     REM Test for trailer value
40        NEWSALARY = SALARY + 100
50        PRINT NEWSALARY
60        INPUT SALARY          REM Get more data
70    WEND
80    END
```

Coding Guidelines for Assignment Statements

◆ As noted, the word LET is optional in an assignment statement. It is best to either use it consistently or omit it in all your programs.

◆ Spaces are not required on either side of the arithmetic operators (=, *, +, and so on) but they will make your program easier to read if you use them (for example, 10 AMT = 5 * PRICE rather than 10 AMT=5*PRICE).

SELF-TEST

For both questions, full programs are required. In each case, the program should be able to process numerous input variables. All programs should be structured. Begin by planning the program with pseudocode.

1. Write a program to input numerous lines of data where each line contains an employee's name, gross pay, and taxes. Print, on the printer, each employee's name and net pay, where net pay = gross pay – taxes.

2. Input Daily Sales totals for Monday, Tuesday, Wednesday, Thursday, and Friday all on a single line. Display the Average Daily Sales on the screen.

SOLUTIONS

1. Pseudocode:

```
START
        Enter Name, GrossPay and Taxes
        WHILE there is still input
                Calculate Net Pay
                Print the result
                Enter Name, Gross Pay and Taxes
        WEND
STOP
```

BASICA Program:

```
10    'This program calculates NetPay
20    INPUT EMPNAME$, GROSSPAY, TAXES
30    WHILE TAXES < 99999
40        NETPAY = GROSSPAY - TAXES
50        LPRINT EMPNAME$; NETPAY
60        INPUT EMPNAME$, GROSSPAY, TAXES
```

```
70    WEND
80    END
```

2. Pseudocode:

```
START
        Enter 5 daily sales figures
        WHILE there is still input
            Calculate an average
            Print the result
            Enter 5 daily sales figures
        WEND
STOP
```

BASICA Program:

```
10    'This program calculates average weekly sales
20    INPUT MSALES, TSALES, WSALES, THSALES, FSALES
30    WHILE MSALES < 99999
40        AVERAGE = (MSALES + TSALES + WSALES + THSALES + FSALES) / 5
50        PRINT AVERAGE
60        INPUT MSALES, TSALES, WSALES, THSALES, FSALES
70    WEND
80    END
```

The PRINT and LPRINT Statements

The two fundamental ways you can obtain output with BASIC are:

- PRINT—Displays output on a screen

- LPRINT—Prints output on a printer

PRINT   All output generated by the PRINT instruction will appear on the screen. This output will be displayed interactively with any input that the user enters.

LPRINT   If the output is to be retained in hard-copy or printed form, use an LPRINT instruction in place of a PRINT.

You will see later that it is often more meaningful to print the input as well as the output on the printer so that the user has a hard-copy record of what each result means.

Rules for using the PRINT and LPRINT are identical, so we will consider them together.

The format of the PRINT and LPRINT is as follows:

$$\begin{Bmatrix} \text{PRINT} \\ \text{LPRINT} \end{Bmatrix} \text{[expression list] [;]}$$

Both the PRINT and LPRINT instructions have the same format. That is, either PRINT or LPRINT could be used in the above.

The expression list may be:

- A series of variables and/or literals (for example, 10 PRINT AMT1 displays the contents of AMT1 and 20 LPRINT "DONE!!" prints the literal or constant DONE!!)

- An arithmetic expression (for example, 10 PRINT AMT1 * 2 will print the product of AMT1 x 2).

Items within a PRINT or LPRINT expression list may be separated by a semicolon or comma. For now, we will use semicolons as separators in our illustrations because a semicolon ensures that each entry appears directly to the right of the previous entry on a single line. Commas as separators place each expression in a separate zone that is 14 characters long.

The bracket in the format above means that an expression list is optional. The instruction PRINT or LPRINT by itself is valid and will display or print a blank line.

Note that when using semicolons as separators, string variables and constants will print adjacent to each other unless blanks or spaces are included. For example:

Syntax	Meaning
`10 PRINT "Name is "; LASTNAME$`	Displays the string constant "Name is " along with the contents of the string variable LASTNAME$, both on the same line. The space after "Name is "in the constant is required because without it the Last Name would collide or print adjacent to the s in "is" (for example, Name isJohnson).

As noted, string variables and literals require this space as a separator in the expression list. Positive or unsigned numeric variables and constants, however, always print with a space before the value, so that a " " or blank as a separator is not necessary. That is, +12 or 12 entered as input will print as 12 with a leading blank.

Negative numbers, however, do not automatically print with a space before the number, so that provision must be made for appropriate spaces. If a variable called AMT, for example, will contain a negative number, code 10 PRINT "The negative number is "; AMT, rather than 10 PRINT "The negative number is"; AMT, which has no space after the s in "is".

In summary, all numbers, both positive and negative, are always followed by a space, but only positive numbers are always preceded by a space.

Coding Guidelines

♦ The rules about spaces before and after positive and negative numbers may be confusing and are often forgotten. To avoid any potential collisions, always include a space between all variables and values to be printed.

♦ Although an arithmetic operation may be included in a PRINT or LPRINT statement, we recommend that you separate such instructions into two statements:

```
10    LET TOTAL = AMT1 + AMT2
20    PRINT "The Total is "; TOTAL
```

rather than

```
10    PRINT "The Total is "; AMT1 + AMT2
```

The former is easier to read and debug.

Output More Readable

You can use several techniques to make your output more readable, as shown in the following sections.

Printing Literals with Variables for More Meaningful Output   We typically PRINT (or LPRINT) a string expression along with a computed result to make the output more meaningful. For example, code 50 PRINT "The Sum Is "; SUM, rather than 50 PRINT SUM.

Printing Explanatory Messages to User Before Data Is Input   We   also use a PRINT instruction to provide the user with some information about how data is to be entered. Explanatory messages should precede the first INPUT statement when they are intended as instructions to the user.

◆   **Program**

```
10     PRINT "Enter Two Amount Fields Separated By a Comma"
20     PRINT "Enter 999, 999 When Done"
30     INPUT AMT1, AMT2          'Get initial amounts
40     WHILE AMT1 < 999          'Check trailer value
50        TOTAL = AMT1 + AMT2
60        PRINT "The Total Is "; TOTAL
70        INPUT AMT1, AMT2       'Get additional Amounts
80     WEND
90     PRINT "End Of Job"
100    END
```

◆   **Run**

```
Enter Two Amount Fields Separated By a Comma
Enter 999, 999 When Done
? 10, 15
The Total Is 25
? 999,999
End Of Job
```

The two explanatory PRINT statements are executed only once, at the beginning of the run, but you may repeat them within the loop before the second INPUT statement if you wish. This will result in the message printing before each input prompt.

Editing Printed Data

A record on a disk file may, for example, have two amount fields with the following data: 450 and 38726.58. Although these fields are acceptable as is in disk files, the printed report should contain this information in edited form to make it more meaningful to the user. For example, $450.00 and $38,726.58 are clearer methods of presenting the data.

Editing will be defined as the process of making fields of data clearer, neater, and more useful. In this section, we will focus on the types of editing that can be performed on both numeric and string variables.

The following editing functions will be discussed in this section:

◆   Suppressing leading zeros.

◆   Printing a specified number of digits to the right of the decimal point regardless of the number of decimal digits in the variable.

◆   Printing commas and dollar signs.

The editing functions described in this section may only be performed on numeric variables or fields.

Consider the following:

◆   **Program**

```
10      INPUT AMT
20      WHILE AMT <> 9
30          LPRINT AMT
40          INPUT AMT
50      WEND
60      END
```

◆   **Run**

```
? 12.75
? 0
? 125000
```

The output would be printed on the printed page as:

```
12.75
0
125000
```

The results would be more readable if they were printed, instead, as follows:

```
$      12.75
$       0.00
$ 125,000.00
```

In the latter case, notice that:

◆   The numbers are aligned on the decimal point.

◆   A dollar sign precedes each value.

◆   A comma has been inserted in the last number to make it easier to read.

To do this type of editing, you use an LPRINT USING or PRINT USING statement.

The LPRINT USING and PRINT USING Statements

The LPRINT USING and PRINT USING statements allow you to format and edit your output.

Format   Two of the major purposes of the LPRINT USING and PRINT USING statements are as follows:

◆   To provide proper alignment of results.

◆   To edit the results.

In this context, editing means making the results more readable and useful by adding edit characters such as dollar signs and commas.

The format for the LPRINT USING and PRINT USING statements is:

$$\left\{ \begin{array}{l} \text{LPRINT} \\ \text{PRINT} \end{array} \right\} \text{USING format string; expressionlist [;]}$$

The format string is a string constant or variable that describes the way the expression list is to be formatted.

The expression list includes the numeric variables to be printed. If more than one variable or field is to be printed on the line, they may be separated by commas, spaces, or semicolons. We typically use semicolons.

The format string that describes the editing to be performed is enclosed in double quotation marks (") and is followed by a semicolon, which is then followed by the variable(s) to be formatted.

As noted, the PRINT USING statement may use exactly the same format string as the LPRINT USING. The only difference is that with PRINT USING, the output is displayed rather than printed.

```
                                                    ┌────────── Formats the variable that follows it
                                          ┌───────────────── Indicates the variable to be formatted
10     PRINT USING "######"; AMT
```

Editing Numeric Fields   You will often need to edit numeric fields—for example, you might want to align numbers with each other or on the decimal place or to insert commas in large numbers and dollar signs before dollar values.

◆   **Aligning the Contents of Numeric Variables**   The symbol # is used in the format string of the LPRINT USING or PRINT USING statement to indicate that a numeric variable is to be printed in right-justified or right-aligned form. Right-justified output is aligned so that the three numbers, 87, 387, and 2826, for example, would print as:

```
   87
  387
 2826
```

Note that the numbers print with the rightmost or units positions aligned.

The symbol # in the format string not only right-justifies data but also fills leading or leftmost zeros with blanks. Thus, 0026, 087, 382, respectively, would print as:

```
  26
  87
 382
```

This type of editing ensures that all data is printed with units positions aligned properly and with leading zeros suppressed. The expression in the LPRINT USING or PRINT USING is separated from the variable by a semicolon. Consider the following:

```
10    LPRINT USING "######"; AMT
```

The values for AMT will print as follows:

Value of AMT	LPRINT or PRINT USING format string	Printed Results
1234	"######"	1234
26	"######"	26
374	"######"	374
26873	"######"	26873
987261	"######"	987261
7522117	"######"	%7522117

Without the PRINT USING, the output would print left-justified. The column marked "Value of AMT" in the above has data listed in left-justified form; that is, with numbers aligned on the left. It is far more appropriate to print numbers right-justified so that the units position of each number prints in the same relative position, and the tens position of each number prints in the same relative position, etc. To get right-justification, you use the LPRINT USING or PRINT USING.

Note again that the rules for LPRINT USING and PRINT USING are the same. The format string "######" indicates that the value of the variable can be any number from 1 to 6 integers. If AMT has a value greater than six integers or whole numbers, such as 7522117 in the last example above, it would print as %7522117. The % indicates that the variable is too large for the format string specified.

You can edit several variables with the same format string. For example, coding 10 PRINT USING "######"; AMT1, AMT2, AMT3 will right-justify all three Amount fields.

◆ **Aligning Fields with Decimal Places**   If the number to be printed contains a decimal point, include the decimal point in the format string along with the number of decimal positions to be printed, as in the following:

```
10    LPRINT USING "######.##"; AMT
```

Consider the following examples:

Value of AMT	LPRINT or PRINT USING format string	Printed Results
12.75	"######.##"	12.75
8.60	"######.##"	8.60
125000.50	"######.##"	125000.50
4	"######.##"	4.00
4.1	"######.##"	4.10
14.7685	"######.##"	14.77
87.67	"######.##"	87.67
−6.48	"######.##"	−6.48
−.25	"######.##"	−0.25

First, the format string right-justifies the number. Second, the printed results print exactly two decimal digits for each variable.

The variables in the expression list can each have up to six integers and any number of decimal places. That is, the number of integers in the variable should not exceed the number of #s before the decimal point in the format string. In the above, if the number of integers actually stored in the variable is more than six, then a % precedes the output indicating that a size error has occurred. This means that the variable has too many integers for the formatted output string.

But the number of decimal positions (that is, positions to the right of the decimal point) in the variable itself is not limited. If there are more decimal digits in the variable than are specified in the format string, this is not considered an error. Suppose AMT has three or more decimal positions. A PRINT USING or LPRINT USING with ".##" will mean that the results will be rounded to two decimal places rather than truncated to two decimal places. Thus if AMT has a value of 12.755 and you code it as 10 LPRINT USING "##.##"; AMT then AMT will print as 12.76. If AMT has fewer than two decimal places, zeros will be added to print to two decimal places. That is, an AMT equal to 4 will print as 4.00 and 4.1 will print as 4.10 using the above format string.

Using the LPRINT or PRINT USING "##.##"; AMT, if AMT has only decimal positions with no integers as in the last example above (.25), it will print with a leading zero (0.25).

♦ **Double-Precision Numbers**   Single-precision numeric variables or fields are accurate only up to seven integers. Hence if you wish to store a numeric variable that has more than seven integers, you should establish the variable as a double-precision number. If you do not define a long numeric variable as double precision and the user enters a number with more than seven digits, it will print as a floating-point number, with an E to denote where the decimal point should be positioned. For example:

```
10    INPUT AMT1
20    PRINT AMT1
```

If AMT1 is entered as 111111111, which is a number larger than seven digits, it will print as 1.111111E+08. This means that the decimal point should be moved eight positions to the right. To avoid long numbers printing with the E or exponential format, define them as double precision by using a # at the end of the numeric variable name. AMT#, for example, is a double-precision numeric variable.

As a guideline, when there is a possibility that a variable may exceed seven whole numbers or integers, establish it as a double-precision variable.

Because of the way the computer represents numbers, you may find that large values, when edited, are rounded by the computer. Making the variables double precision will avoid this rounding.

♦ **Inserting Commas in Numeric Fields**   If you want one or more commas to separate integers in a number that is output, you can simply include the commas in the format string of the PRINT USING or LPRINT USING statement. All data will remain decimally aligned and right-justified. Consider the following:

```
10    LPRINT USING "#,###.##"; AMT
```

If AMT has a value of 1500.50, for example, it will print as 1,500.50. Commas will print only if the value of AMT has enough significant or nonzero integers; otherwise commas will be suppressed or replaced with blanks. Thus, if AMT has a value of 532.50, for example, it will print without the commas as ƀ ƀ 532.50, where ƀ denotes a blank space. All data will be aligned on the decimal point.

The following are examples of the LPRINT USING or PRINT USING where commas are to be printed:

Value of AMT	LPRINT or PRINT USING format string	Printed Results
4872.8	"###,###.##"	4,872.80
873586.487	"###,###.##"	873,586.49
287.05	"###,###.##"	287.05
31.621	"###,###.##"	31.62
2876543.92	"###,###.##"	%2876,543.92

Note: % in the last example indicates that the variable is too long for the format string. The format string allows for a maximum of six integers or whole numbers (that is, six places to the left of the decimal point).

◆ **Inserting Dollar Signs in Numeric Fields**   If you want a dollar sign to print with the contents of a field, include the dollar sign in the LPRINT or PRINT USING statement. For example:

```
10    LPRINT USING "$#,###.##"; AMT
```

If AMT contained a value of 3546.23, it would print as $3,546.23.

Consider the following examples:

Value of AMT	LPRINT or PRINT USING format string	Printed Results
28.73	"$#,###.##"	$ 28.73
4872.26	"$#,###.##"	$4,872.26

◆ **Using a Floating Dollar Sign**   Sometimes printing a dollar sign as above is not sufficient. If there is the possibility that blanks in the output can be tampered with, as on checks, for example, you would not want spaces between the $ and the first significant digit.

If AMT contained 1.93, the output would print as follows: $ 1.93. In this case, a series of blanks separate the dollar sign from the first significant character. Someone could easily type in values so that $ 1.93 would appear as $99991.93. This is particularly dangerous if the output is a check.

By including two dollar signs at the beginning of the format string of the LPRINT or PRINT USING statement, you can ensure that the dollar sign prints adjacent to the first significant character. That is, the use of two dollar signs will cause the $ to float, suppressing both leading commas and leading zeros so that the $ prints next to the first significant digit of the number. In this instance, the $ is called a floating dollar sign.

Consider the following examples:

Value of AMT	LPRINT or PRINT USING format string	Printed Results
28.73	$$#,###.##	$28.73
4872.26	$$#,###.##	$4,872.26
927.163	$$#,###.##	$927.16
.06	$$#,###.##	$0.06

Value of AMT	LPRINT or PRINT USING format string	Printed Results
87262.00	`$$#,###.##`	`$87,262.00`

To display or print two values on a single line, only one of which is to be edited, use two PRINT or LPRINT instructions where the first ends with a semicolon (;) which means that there is more to print on that line. For example:

```
10    PRINT NAME.IN$;
20    PRINT USING "##.##"; AMT
```

Both NAME.IN$ and AMT will be displayed on the *same line* because the first PRINT ends with a semicolon.

Selection Using the IF Statement

Using special control structures allows you to write BASIC instructions that are executed conditionally. For example, if a certain condition is met, your program will do one thing; if it is not met, your program will do another. This gives you a great deal of flexibility in writing programs that will operate under various conditions. The following sections will look in detail at such control structures.

An Overview of the Four Logical Control Structures

Thus far you have learned syntax rules for a number of BASIC instructions. You have seen that instructions are executed in sequence unless a WHILE ... WEND loop changes the order of execution. The order in which instructions can be executed is controlled by logical control structures.

The four types of logical control structures that may be used in any programming language are as follows:

♦ Sequence

♦ Selection (IF-THEN-ELSE)

♦ Iteration (WHILE ... WEND or other loop)

♦ Case (ON GOSUB)

Sequence   The pseudocode specification for a sequence is as follows:

START

.
. } Sequence of steps goes here
.

STOP

This is an example in BASICA:

```
10    'This program calculates a total
20    INPUT AMT1, AMT2
30    LET TOTAL = AMT1 + AMT2
40    PRINT "THE TOTAL IS "; TOTAL
50    END
```

All instructions are executed in **sequence** unless one of the other logical control structures such as the WHILE ... WEND alters the order.

Selection   **Selection** is a logical control structure that executes instructions depending on whether a condition or conditions are met. Selection is sometimes referred to as an **IF-THEN-ELSE** structure because it has the following pseudocode format:

IF (condition is met or is "true") THEN

. ⎰ Indicates the sequence of instructions
. ⎬ to be executed only if the condition
. ⎱ is met or is true

ELSE

. ⎰ Indicates the sequence of instructions to
. ⎬ be executed if the condition is not met or
. ⎱ is "false"

ENDIF   Terminates the scope of the IF structure in a pseudocode

Most programming languages have an IF-THEN-ELSE logical control structure similar to this pseudocode. We discuss the selection structure in BASIC in this section. First we will briefly outline the other two logical control structures so that you are aware of all four ways instructions can be executed.

Iteration   **Iteration** is the logical control structure that enables a sequence of instructions to be executed repeatedly. We have thus far used a WHILE ... WEND loop for iteration. The next section will focus on the full range of BASIC instructions that can be used for iteration.

The pseudocode specification for a WHILE ... WEND loop is:

WHILE condition is met

. ⎫
. ⎬ Sequence of steps to be performed
. ⎭

WEND

An example in BASICA is:

```
10    INPUT AMTIN
20    WHILE AMTIN < 99999
30        PRINT AMTIN
40        INPUT AMTIN
50    WEND
60    END
```

Case   A **case** structure is a logical control structure that enables the user to choose which task the computer should perform from a list of possible tasks. For example, suppose you are updating payroll data. The program may display a menu that indicates the type of update to be performed. The menu may indicate that the user should press 1 to change an employee's salary, press 2 to change an employee's name, and so on. The case structure is used to designate which path to follow, depending on a value entered by the user.

The IF Statement

In this section we focus on the IF-THEN-ELSE (selection) structure, which permits you to execute an instruction or series of instructions depending on the contents of variables. The IF-THEN-ELSE structure is coded in BASIC with the **IF statement**.

The Instruction Format for an IF Statement   A **conditional statement** is one that performs operations depending on whether or not some condition is met or is "true." Such statements begin with the word IF and are called IF-THEN-ELSE or selection structures.

The basic instruction format for IF statements is as follows:

IF condition THEN

```
.
.  }  statement(s)
.
```

[ELSE

```
.
.  }  statement(s) ]
.
```

Relational operators used in an IF expression are as follows:

Operand 1	Relational Operator	Operand 2	Meaning
literal-1 or variable-1	=	literal-2 or variable-2	IF Operand 1 equals Operand 2
	<		IF Operand 1 is less than Operand 2
	>		IF Operand 1 is greater than Operand 2
	<=		IF Operand 1 is less than or equal to Operand 2
	>=		IF Operand 1 is greater than or equal to Operand 2
	<>		IF Operand 1 is not equal to (that is, if it is less than or greater than) Operand 2

The operands specified in a conditional are either literals (constants) or variables. The operands used in the condition must be of the same type, meaning that string variables or literals can only be compared to other string variables or literals, and numeric variables can only be compared to numeric variables or literals. The following are examples of valid conditions using relational operators:

```
10    IF TAX = .25 THEN ...
10    IF SALARY1 <> SALARY2 THEN ...
10    IF SALES >= 500.00 THEN ...
10    IF EMP.NAME$ = "Paul Newman" THEN ...
```

Examples of Invalid Comparisons	Reason Comparison Is Invalid
10 IF TAX = ".25" THEN ...	TAX, a numeric variable, cannot be compared with ".25," a string constant.
10 IF CODE1 <> CODE2$ THEN ...	CODE1, a numeric variable, cannot be compared with CODE2$, a string variable.
10 IF SALES$ >= 500.00 THEN ...	SALES$, a string variable, cannot be compared with 500.00, a numeric constant.

The outcome of an IF statement will depend on whether the condition is true or false. Consider the following IF statement:

```
10     IF HOURS > 40 THEN PRINT "Overtime Pay Required"
       ELSE PRINT "Regular Pay Only"
```

If the variable called HOURS has a value greater than 40, then the constant "Overtime Pay Required" is displayed. If HOURS is not greater than 40 (if it is <= 40) then the constant "Regular Pay Only" is displayed.

Thus, by using the IF statement, you test the initial condition; if it is met or is "true," you perform the instruction(s) specified. By using ELSE, you can perform an operation or operations if the initial condition is not met or is "false." The ELSE clause is itself optional.

With pseudocode, an IF statement must end with a scope terminator of ENDIF to signal the end of the structure. This is not necessary in BASICA, which uses line numbers; that is, the IF instruction is coded with a line number and the computer understands that this IF, which may be coded on several lines, ends when a new line number is coded. Therefore an IF statement may be coded on several lines, but only its first line is given a line number. Because the computer assumes the full IF structure is terminated when it reaches the next line number, no ENDIF or scope terminator is necessary.

Note that using separate lines for an IF-THEN-ELSE requires special handling in BASICA. (This special handling of separate lines in an IF statement does not apply to other versions of BASIC.) Although you will be coding each IF-THEN-ELSE structure on several lines, it is actually just a single instruction. Hence, pressing (ENTER) at the end of each physical line, which means the instruction is complete, will convey the wrong message to the computer. To tell the computer that you wish to end a line but *not* end the instruction, press (CTRL), and while it is still depressed, press (ENTER). We designate this as (CTRL)-(ENTER). It tells the computer to continue the instruction on the next line. To end or terminate the entire instruction after the last ELSE statement, press (ENTER) in the usual way.

Note that only the last line of the IF structure, the line prior to the next line number, is transmitted by pressing (ENTER). The other lines are considered part of the structure and are terminated by pressing (CTRL)-(ENTER).

Each BASICA instruction, regardless of the number of clauses it uses, is restricted to 255 characters, including blanks. Thus, if you are using an 80-column screen format, you are essentially limited to 3 lines (80 x 3) and a small portion of a fourth line.

This means that you will need to condense your IF statements some-what. That is, if more than one instruction is to be executed if a given condition is met, you put them all on one line, or at most two lines, separated by a colon (:). Similarly, use one line, or at most two, for the ELSE clause.

```
IF ... THEN statement-1 : statement-2      'The entire instruction
ELSE statement-3 : statement-4             'can use a maximum
                                           'of 3 lines
```

All lines except the last end by pressing (CTRL)-(ENTER). If numerous state-ments are required when a condition is met, you have some flexibility but are still limited to three lines. For example:

```
10    IF AMT > 0 THEN PRINT "AMT IS POSITIVE" : TOTAL = TOTAL + 1:
         CTR = CTR + 1                                              Press (CTRL)-(ENTER) to end these lines
      ELSE PRINT "AMT <= 0"                                         Press (ENTER) to end this line
```

Indent CTR = CTR + 1 to indicate that it is part of the IF condition. The first two lines end by pressing (CTRL)-(ENTER); the last ends by pressing just (ENTER). Use colons to separate a series of instructions to be executed IF the condition is met or after the ELSE clause.

Later you will see that if numerous instructions are to be executed after the IF-THEN or after the ELSE, you can execute them as a separate module or subroutine. For now, code the IF-THEN on one or two lines and the ELSE on one or two lines, using colons (:) to separate instructions, but be sure that the full IF-THEN-ELSE does not exceed three lines.

The preferred format of coding each IF-THEN and ELSE on a separate line (terminated by pressing (CTRL)-(ENTER)), and indenting clauses within the IF and ELSE clauses makes it easy to follow the structure of an IF statement. It also makes the program easier to read and debug. Note, however, that this format does not affect the translation process. That is, this coding technique is not a requirement, even though we strongly recommend you use it. You can press (TAB) to indent eight spaces.

Note that more than one statement can be executed if the condition is true or is met, and, similarly within the ELSE clause, more than one state-ment can be executed if the condition is false or is not met. The following will perform two operations if WEIGHT is > 200, and two different operations if WEIGHT is not > 200:

♦ **Pseudocode**

```
IF WEIGHT exceeds 200 THEN
        PRINT a message
        Add 1 to OVERWEIGHTCTR
ELSE
        PRINT a message
        Add 1 to OKWEIGHTCTR
ENDIF
```

♦ **BASICA Program**

```
10    IF WEIGHT > 200 THEN PRINT "Diet":OVERWEIGHTCTR - OVERWEIGHTCTR + 1
      ELSE PRINT "OK Weight" : OKWEIGHTCTR = OKWEIGHTCTR + 1
20    ...
```

Example 1   The following pseudocode plans a program that inputs sales amounts and, for each, calculates and prints a commission. If a sales amount is less than $500.00, the commission is 5 percent. Otherwise the commission is 10 percent.

♦ **Pseudocode**

```
START
        Input Sales Amount
        WHILE there is still input
             IF Sales Amount is less than $500.00 THEN
                  Commission is 5% of Sales Amount
             ELSE
                  Commission is 10% of Sales Amount
             ENDIF
             Print Commission
             Input Sales Amount
        WEND
STOP
```

The full BASICA program to calculate and print the commission is:

♦ **BASICA Program**

```
10      'This program calculates and prints commission
20      PRINT "Enter Sales Amount - Type 99999 When Done"
30      INPUT SALES.AMOUNT
40      WHILE SALES.AMOUNT < 99999
50         IF SALES.AMOUNT < 500 THEN              'Press Ctrl-Enter to end line
                COMMISSION = .05 * SALES.AMOUNT    'Press Ctrl-Enter to end line
           ELSE COMMISSION = .10 * SALES.AMOUNT    'Press Enter
60         PRINT "Commission is "; COMMISSION
70         INPUT SALES.AMOUNT
80      WEND
90      END
```

Example 2   The following pseudocode plans a program that will print the average salaries of males and females. The sex and salary for each employee in the company will be entered as input on a single line.

♦ **Pseudocode**

```
START
        Initialize Counters and Totals
        Input Sex and Salary
        WHILE there is still input
             IF Sex is Female THEN
                  Add 1 to Female Counter
                  Add Salary to Total Female Salaries
             ELSE
                  Add 1 to Male Counter
                  Add Salary to Total Male Salaries
             ENDIF
             INPUT Sex and Salary
        WEND
        Calculate and Print Average Female Salary
        Calculate and Print Average Male Salary
STOP
```

The full BASICA program to print the average salary for males and females is as follows:

◆ BASICA Program

```
10    'This program calculates average salaries for males and females
20    FEMALECTR = 0
30    MALECTR = 0
40    TOTFEMALESALARIES = 0
50    TOTMALESALS = 0
60    PRINT "Enter Sex (M, F) and Salary"
70    PRINT "Enter 9, 999999 when done"
80    INPUT SEX$, SALARY
90    WHILE SEX$ <> "9"
100      IF SEX$ = "F" THEN FEMALECTR = FEMALECTR + 1 :
            TOTFEMALESALARIES = TOTFEMALESALARIES + SALARY
          ELSE MALECTR = MALECTR + 1 : TOTMALESALS = TOTMALESALS + SALARY
110      INPUT SEX$, SALARY
120    WEND
130    AVERAGEFEMALESALARY = TOTFEMALESALARIES / FEMALECTR
140    AVERAGEMALESALARY = TOTMALESALS / MALECTR
150    PRINT "The Average Salary for Females is "; AVERAGEFEMALESALARY
160    PRINT "The Average Salary for Males is "; AVERAGEMALESALARY
170    END
```

◆ Run

```
Enter Sex (M, F) and Salary
Enter 9, 999999 when done
? M, 1000
? F, 500
? F, 500
? M, 1000
? 9, 999999
The Average Salary for Females is 500
The Average Salary for Males is 1000
```

SELF-TEST

Plan each program with pseudocode first.

1. Write a program to input a series of Employee Names and then Gross Pay, each on a single line. For each employee, calculate Federal Income Tax as 20 percent of Gross Pay if the employee earns less than $50,000. Otherwise the Federal Income Tax rate is 25 percent. Print each employee's name and federal income tax owed.

2. Write a program to input employee names and salaries, each on a single line. Give employees who earn 25000 or less a 10 percent bonus, and give employees who earn more than 25000 an 8 percent bonus. Print each employee's name and bonus. At the end of the run, print the sum of all bonuses that the company will pay.

SOLUTIONS

1. Pseudocode:
```
START
      Input Name and Gross Pay
      WHILE there is still input
          IF Gross Pay < 50000 THEN
              Federal Tax is 20% of Gross Pay
          ELSE
              Federal Tax is 25% of Gross Pay
          ENDIF
          Print Name and Federal Tax
          Input Name and Gross Pay
      WEND
STOP
```

BASICA Program:

```
10  'This program calculates federal income tax
20  PRINT "Enter Name and Gross Pay "
30  PRINT "Type Stop, 999999 when done"
40  INPUT EMPNAME$, GROSSPAY
50  WHILE GROSSPAY < 999999
60     IF GROSSPAY < 50000 THEN FEDLTAX = .20 * GROSSPAY
          ELSE
              FEDLTAX = .25 * GROSSPAY
70        LPRINT EMPNAME$; " owes "; FEDLTAX
80        INPUT EMPNAME$, GROSSPAY
90  WEND
100 END
```

2. Pseudocode:

```
START
        Enter Name and Salary
        Initialize Total Bonus
        WHILE Salary > 0
            IF Salary <= 25000 THEN
                Bonus is 10% of Salary
            ELSE
                Bonus is 8% of Salary
            ENDIF
            Print Name and Bonus
            Add Bonus to Total Bonus
            Enter Name and Salary
        WEND
        Print Total Bonus
STOP
```

BASICA Program:

```
10  'This program prints bonuses and calculates total bonuses paid
20  TOTAL.BONUS = 0
30  PRINT "Enter Name and Salary"
40  PRINT "Type END, 0 When Done"
50  INPUT EMPNAME$, SALARY
60  WHILE SALARY > 0
70     IF SALARY <= 25000 THEN BONUS = .10 * SALARY
          ELSE
              BONUS = .08 * SALARY
80        LPRINT "Bonus for "; EMPNAME$," is "; BONUS
90        TOTAL.BONUS = TOTAL.BONUS + BONUS
100       INPUT EMPNAME$, SALARY
110 WEND
120 LPRINT "Total Bonus is "; TOTAL.BONUS
130 END
```

How Comparisons Are Performed   In BASIC, numeric comparisons are performed algebraically, but string comparisons follow a different set of rules, as you will see in the following sections.

- **Comparing Numeric Variables**   When comparing numeric variables, the following are all considered equal:

    012   12.00   12   +12

That is, numeric comparisons are performed in BASIC algebraically. Thus, the number of digits being compared in numeric operands will not affect the comparison. The number $001 = 01 = 1$ even though each value has a different number of digits. Moreover, positive numbers are recognized as equal to unsigned numbers.

- **Comparing String Operands**   The number of characters in string variables always affects the comparison. Also, string variables are compared alphabetically, so that "ABC" < "BBC" < "ZBC". But how would "ABC" be compared with "ABCD"?

If two string variables being compared are of unequal length but have equal values up to the length of the shorter one, then the shorter string operand will be considered less than the longer one regardless of the right-most characters in the longer string. Consider the following examples of comparing string data:

"ABC" < "ABCD"	If a shorter string has the same
"DOG" < "DOGS"	leftmost characters as a longer
"DOG" < "DOG "	string, the shorter is considered "<"
"DOG " < "DOG "	the longer.
"tes" < "test"	

Note that a string variable can be assigned a value such as "DOG" by coding 10 LET X$ = "DOG" or it can be assigned the same value by coding 10 INPUT X$. During the run, the user could input DOG or "DOG" in response to the ? prompt. To input rightmost or leftmost blanks such as "DOG" or "DOG " in place of simply "DOG", the user must key in quotation marks around the value as indicated—for example, "DOG " instead of "DOG".

As a rule, when comparing string operands of different lengths, the number of characters compared is determined by the size of the shorter string.

String operands are not compared algebraically as are numeric operands. That is, "123" is greater than "0123" because the high-order, or leading, "1" is greater than the high-order "0." This is true even though a numeric variable with the contents 123 would be considered equal to a numeric variable with the contents 0123. Similarly " abc" is considered less than "abc" because the first operand has a high-order, or leftmost, blank.

The ASCII Collating Sequence   When performing an alphanumeric comparison, the hierarchy of the comparison, called the **collating sequence**, is determined by the computer.

The internal code that is most commonly used for representing data in microcomputers is ASCII, an abbreviation for American Standard Code for Information Interchange. Characters are compared with one another in ASCII as shown in Figure D–5.

On ASCII computers, a numeric comparison will be performed properly, as noted. That is, the number 012 is less than 022, which is less than 042, and so on. Uppercase and lowercase alphabetic comparisons are performed properly. Thus, the computer will also be able to determine if data is arranged alphabetically because "A" is considered less than "B", which is less than "C", and so on. Thus, "ABCD" < "BBCD" < "XBCD", and so on. Similarly, "a" < "b" < "c" ... < "z".

Note, however, that on ASCII computers uppercase letters are considered less than lowercase letters, so that "A" < "a", "Z" < "z", "TEST" < "test", and so on.

Thus, if upper- and lowercase letters are mixed when entering data or when assigning a string value to a string variable, a comparison could

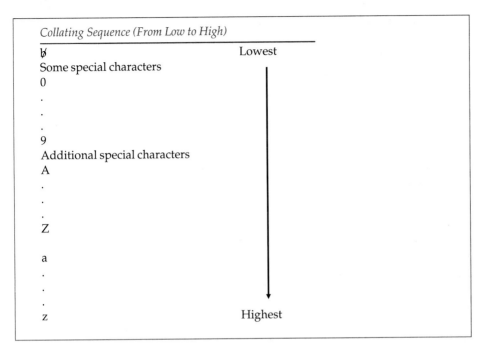

Collating Sequence (From Low to High)

b̸	Lowest
Some special characters	
0	
.	
.	
.	
9	
Additional special characters	
A	
.	
.	
.	
Z	
a	
.	
.	
.	
z	Highest

D–5 ASCII collating sequence.

produce unexpected results. Consider the following examples of comparing mixed upper- and lowercase letters:

"ABC" < "abc"
"Abc" < "abc"
"ZIP" < "apple"
"ZIP" < "ZIp"

When you enter a value for a string variable or use an assignment statement to assign a value to a string variable, use either all uppercase letters, all lowercase letters, or an initial uppercase letter followed by all lowercase letters. In this way, you will minimize the risk of erroneous processing when comparing string operands. Note that there is a UCASE$ and a LCASE$ function to change strings into either all uppercase or all lowercase. These functions will keep case differences from affecting a comparison. You can make the contents of a variable called CODE$ all uppercase by coding LET CODE$ = UCASE$(CODE$). This ensures that CODE$ contains all uppercase letters.

Note, too, that, on ASCII computers, numbers are less than letters, so that "ROUTE 109," for example, in an address variable, is greater than "100 MAIN ST" because the first character, R, compares as "greater than" the number 1.

If you are using an IBM mainframe version of BASIC, the collating sequence for your computer may be EBCDIC rather than ASCII. EBCDIC, an abbreviation for Extended Binary Coded Decimal Interchange Code, is the other main computer code for representing data, but it is used mostly on IBM mainframes. In EBCDIC's collating sequence, letters are less than numbers and uppercase letters are less than lowercase letters.

SELF-TEST

1. What is wrong with the following statement?

   10 IF AMT = 0
         PRINT "Amt Is Zero"

2. Write a routine to move the smallest of three numbers AMT1, AMT2, and AMT3 to a variable called PRINTSMALL and print it.

For questions 3–5, indicate the results if the following groups of two literals are compared:

3. "IBM" "ibm"

4. "BASIC" "BASICA"

5. "123" 123

6. Write a BASIC program to input per line a Name, Hours worked, and Code. If the Code = 1, the rate of pay is 5.00; if the Code = 2, the rate of pay is 7.00, and if the Code = 3, the rate of pay is 10.00. Print Name and Wages for each input line. First plan the program with pseudocode.

SOLUTIONS

1. The word THEN is missing from the first line of the IF statement.

2. Routine:

```
10    PRINTSMALL = AMT1
20    IF AMT2 < PRINTSMALL THEN     'Press Ctrl-Enter keys
            PRINTSMALL = AMT2        'Press Enter key
30    IF AMT3 < PRINTSMALL THEN     'Press Ctrl-Enter keys
            PRINTSMALL = AMT3        'Press Enter key
40    PRINT PRINTSMALL
```

3. "IBM" < "ibm" (uppercase is < lowercase)

4. "BASIC" < "BASICA" (shorter string < longer string if strings are equal up to length of the smaller string)

5. This comparison is not valid because string variables and numeric variables cannot be compared. To do so will cause a syntax error.

6. Pseudocode:

START
        Enter Name, Hours and Code
        WHILE there is still input
            Initialize Rate
            IF Code = 1 THEN
                Rate = 5.00
            ENDIF
            IF Code = 2 THEN
                Rate = 7.00
            ENDIF
            IF Code = 3 THEN
                Rate = 10.00
            ENDIF
            Calculate Wages
            Print Wages
            Enter Name, Hours and Code
        WEND
STOP

BASICA Program:

```
10  'This program computes wages for employees
20  PRINT "Enter Name, Hours and Code"
30  PRINT "Type End, 99, 9 when done"
40  INPUT EMPNAME$, HOURS, CODE
50  WHILE CODE <> 9
60    RATE = 0
70    IF CODE = 1 THEN
        RATE = 5.00
80    IF CODE = 2 THEN
        RATE = 7.00
90    IF CODE = 3 THEN
        RATE = 10.00
```

```
100    WAGES = HOURS * RATE
110    PRINT EMPNAME$; " earned "; WAGES
120    INPUT EMPNAME$, HOURS, CODE
130  WEND
140  END
```

Nested Conditional

A **nested conditional** is a conditional in which an IF statement can itself contain additional IF clauses. Consider the following example.

IF ... THEN IF ... as a Nested Conditional   A format for nested conditionals is as follows:

```
IF condition-1 THEN IF condition-2 statement-1
     ELSE statement-2
ELSE statement-3
```

◆ **Example:**

```
10    IF DEPT = 1 THEN IF HOURS > 40 THEN BONUS = 3 * HOURS
         ELSE BONUS = 2 * HOURS
      ELSE BONUS = 0
20    PRINT BONUS
```

This example conforms to the original format specified for an IF instruction, but if the first condition specified is true, then another test is performed. This is one type of nested conditional. The tests performed are:

1. If DEPT is not equal to 1, the last ELSE is executed, and BONUS is then set equal to 0.

2. If DEPT = 1, the second condition is tested as follows:

◆ (If DEPT = 1) and HOURS is greater than 40, BONUS is set equal to 3 * HOURS.

◆ (If DEPT = 1) and HOURS is not greater than 40, the first ELSE clause is executed and BONUS is set equal to 2 * HOURS.

The use of an indented clause in the above example will help to interpret the structure of the nested conditional. Be sure that the full instruction, however, does not exceed 255 characters.

A nested conditional is really a shortcut method of writing a series of simple conditionals. Thus, any nested conditional may be written with simple conditionals. Note that each line except the last in the example is terminated by pressing Q-E. Only the last line is terminated by pressing E.

IF ... THEN ... ELSE IF ... as a Nested Conditional   Another format for nested conditionals is as follows:

```
IF condition-1 THEN statement-1
     ELSE IF condition-2 THEN statement-2
ELSE statement-3
```

◆ **Example:**

```
10    IF SALARY > 99999 THEN PRINT "Six Figure Salary"
         ELSE IF SALARY > 60000 THEN PRINT "Salary Between 60000 and 99999"
      ELSE PRINT "Salary Less Than or Equal to 60000"
```

hen coding a nested conditional, as with any conditional, use at least
ine for each IF or ELSE clause in the statement as long as you do not
exceed three lines; indent where possible; use (CTRL)-(ENTER) when ending a
clause within the statement and (ENTER) to terminate the entire statement;
and be sure the instruction does not exceed 255 characters. (Recall that these
special coding rules for IF statements apply to BASICA only.)

SELF-TEST

1. A store that sells VCRs is having a sale, where the color of the price tag
   indicates the discount on that item:

Color	Code	Discount
Red	R	30%
Green	G	25%
Blue	B	20%

   Write a program that reads in the color code and the list price and then
   outputs the selling price. Use nested conditionals.

2. Use an IF statement to code the following: Enter, on each line, Student Name
   and NoOfCredits. If NoOfCredits is 12 or less, then the Tuition is $200 x
   NoOfCredits. If NoOfCredits is 13–15, the tuition is a flat $2600; if NoOfCred-
   its is 16–18 the tuition is a flat $3200. Print an error message if NoOfCredits is
   in excess of 18. Use nested conditionals.

SOLUTIONS

1. Program:

```
 10  PRINT "Enter Code (R, G, or B) and Price"
 20  PRINT "Enter X, 0 to Exit"
 30  INPUT CODE$,PRICE
 40  WHILE CODE$ <> "X"
 50     IF CODE$ = "R" THEN DISCOUNT = .30 ELSE IF CODE$ = "G" THEN DISCOUNT = .25
            ELSE IF CODE$ = "B" THEN DISCOUNT = .20
            ELSE PRINT "No discount": DISCOUNT = 0
 60     SELLINGPRICE = PRICE - PRICE * DISCOUNT
 70     PRINT "Selling Price is "; SELLINGPRICE
 80     INPUT CODE$, PRICE
 90  WEND
100  PRINT "End of Program"
110  END
```

2. Program:

```
 10   PRINT "Enter Student Name and Number of Credits"
 20   PRINT "Enter STOP, 99 when done"
 30   INPUT STUDNAME$, CREDITS
 40   WHILE CREDITS < 99
 50     IF CREDITS <= 12 THEN TUITION = CREDITS * 200
           ELSE IF CREDITS < 16 THEN TUITION = 2600
           ELSE IF CREDITS < 19 THEN TUITION = 3200 ELSE PRINT "ERROR"
 60   PRINT "Tuition for "; STUDNAME$; " is "; TUITION
 70   INPUT STUDNAME$, CREDITS
 80   WEND
 90   END
```

Compound Conditionals

You have seen that the selection structure provides programs with a great
deal of logical control capability. The **compound conditional** provides even
greater flexibility for selection and enables the IF statement to be used for
more complex problems. With the compound conditional, the programmer
can test for several conditions in a single IF-THEN-ELSE structure.

OR in a Compound Conditional   To perform an operation or a series of operations if any one of several conditions is met, a compound conditional with conditions separated by OR is used. This means that if any one of several conditions is met, the statement(s) specified will be executed:

```
IF  condition-1  OR  condition-2  THEN  ...
```

Note that, as in all conditionals, the ELSE IF and the ELSE clauses may be used, but they are optional. For example:

```
10      IF AMT1 < AMT3 OR AMT1 = AMT4 THEN
            LET TOTAL = TOTAL + AMT1
        ELSE LET TOTAL = 0

10      IF SEX$ = "M" OR SEX$ = "F" THEN
            PRINT "Sex Code Is Correct"
```

By using OR in a compound conditional, any of the conditions specified will cause execution of the statement(s) specified. If none of the conditions is met, the computer will execute either the ELSE or ELSE IF clause, if used, or the statement on the next line number. Any number of conditions separated by ORs may be specified in a single statement.

In the first example above, TOTAL is set equal to 0 only if AMT1 is greater than or equal to AMT3 *and* AMT1 is not equal to AMT4. If *either* AMT1 is less than AMT3, or AMT1 is equal to AMT4, AMT1 will be added to TOTAL and then the statement on the next line number will be executed.

In the second example above, recall that string constants that are being compared with string variables must be enclosed in quotes.

Keep in mind that each condition must include operands of the same type. Separate conditions may, however, include either a string or numeric comparison:

```
        IF DEPT = 1 OR LOCATION$ = "New York" THEN
            PRINT "Attend the meeting"
```

As with any conditional, only the first line has a line number. Use (CTRL)-(ENTER) to terminate all lines until the last, which is terminated by pressing (ENTER). Be sure the instruction does not exceed 255 characters.

AND in a Compound Conditional   If a statement or statements are to be executed only when all of several conditions are met, use the word AND in the compound conditional as in IF condition-1 AND condition-2 ... THEN ...

All conditions must be met when AND is used in a compound conditional. The ELSE or ELSE IF option (if specified) will be performed if any one of the stated conditions is not met.

For example, suppose you want to print "This is a male under 6 ft and < 200 lbs" if all of the following conditions are met:

Sex$ = "M"; Height less than 72 inches; Weight less than 200 pounds

Otherwise, you want to print "This person does not meet all three conditions". That is, if one or more of these conditions is not met, you want to print the latter phrase. You can use a compound conditional for this:

```
10      IF SEX$ = "M" AND HEIGHT < 72 AND WEIGHT < 200 THEN
            PRINT "This is a male under 6 ft and < 200 lbs"
        ELSE PRINT "This person does not meet all three conditions"
```

The ELSE clause is executed in the preceding if *any one* of the specified conditions is not met.

Using Both AND and OR in the Same Statement   You can use both AND and OR in a single compound conditional. For example:

```
10     IF SEX$ = "F" OR SEX$ = "M" AND AGE > 25 THEN
          PRINT "Regular Insuree"
       ELSE PRINT "Assigned Risk"
```

When using both AND and OR in the same compound conditional, as in the above, the order of evaluation of each condition tested is critical. Consider the following:

```
       (1) SEX$ = "F" OR SEX$ = "M"
AND    (2) AGE > 25
```

In this case, "Regular Insuree" will print if SEX$ is "F" or "M" *and* AGE > 25. That is, any male or female who is over 25 years old will be considered a Regular Insuree. Alternatively, for anyone who is 25 or under, "Assigned Risk" prints.

Suppose, however, that the above IF statement is evaluated in the following order:

```
       (1) SEX$ = "F"
OR     (2) SEX$ = "M" AND AGE > 25
```

If this is the order of evaluation, then "Regular Insuree" will print for females *or* males over 25 years old.

The following hierarchy rules indicate which of the above orders of evaluation is actually used:

◆   Conditions surrounding the word AND are evaluated first.

◆   Conditions surrounding the word OR are evaluated last.

◆   When there are several AND or OR connectors, the AND conditions are evaluated first, as they appear in the statement, from left to right. Then the OR conditions are evaluated, also from left to right.

◆   To override Rules 1–3, use parentheses around conditions to be evaluated first.

Using these hierarchy rules to evaluate the above example, "Regular Insuree" prints if:

```
       (1) SEX$ = "F"
OR     (2) SEX$ = "M" AND AGE > 25
```

This is the same as the second order of evaluation specified above.

To change the order so that the hierarchy rules are overridden, use parentheses.

As a general rule, to simplify coding, to minimize errors, and to clarify a program, it is best to use parentheses in a compound conditional with ANDs and ORs even if they are not required.

You can also test for values of a variable between two endpoints. For example, let us print the literal "It fits!" for values of AMT1 between 10 and

13 inclusive of the endpoints. "Inclusive of the endpoints" means including the values 10 and 13:

```
10    IF AMT1 >= 10 AND AMT1 <= 13 THEN
         PRINT "It fits!"
```

This is the most efficient method for coding the program excerpt correctly.

Negating Conditionals

All relational operators can be negated:

```
IF NOT condition THEN
   .
   .
   .
```

Example:

Negating a Simple Conditional	Alternative Coding
1. IF NOT AMT < 7	(same as IF AMT >= 7)
2. IF NOT AMT > 7	(same as IF AMT <= 7)

The following two statements, then, are equivalent:

◆ **Statement (a)**

```
IF AMT >= 0 THEN
    PRINT "AMT is zero or positive"
ELSE PRINT "AMT is negative"
```

◆ **Statement (b)**

```
IF NOT AMT < 0 THEN
    PRINT "AMT is zero or positive"
ELSE PRINT "AMT is negative"
```

In all instances, the word *NOT* follows the word *IF* and precedes the condition to be tested. That is, we code IF NOT AMT = 7 THEN ... . To code IF AMT NOT = 7 will cause a syntax error.

As a rule, it is easier to read and walk through a program that tests if a condition is true rather than using a NOT to test if a condition is false.

SELF-TEST

1. What, if anything, is wrong with the following statement? Correct the errors.

```
IF A < 21 OR A = 21 AND A = 5 OR A > 5 THEN PRINT "A OK"
```

2. Write a single statement to print "A OK" if A is between 10 and 20, inclusive of the endpoints.
3. Find the absolute value of A. (The absolute value of a number is its distance from 0 regardless of sign. The absolute value of 3 is 3; the absolute value of –3 is 3.)
4. Determine if a string variable called Code$ contains numeric data.
5. Calculate weekly wages based on input values of hourly rate and hours worked. For employees who have worked more than 40 hours, pay them time-and-a-half for overtime. An hours worked figure of 99 denotes the end of the job. Plan your program first using pseudocode.
6. A certain club will only admit members who are 21 years old or over. In addition, all members must either have an income over $40,000 or an availa-

ble credit line of at least $5000. Write an IF-THEN-ELSE statement to reflect the club membership's selection criteria.

7. Write an IF-THEN-ELSE statement for the following problem. If your year-end bonus is more than $2500 and your outstanding bills are less than $2000, then display "Go On Vacation" on the screen; otherwise display "Stay Home This Year."

SOLUTIONS

1. There should be parentheses around conditions to make the statement logical:

```
10    IF (A < 21 OR A = 21) AND (A = 5 OR A > 5) THEN
        PRINT "A OK"
```

2.
```
10    IF A <= 20 AND A >= 10 THEN
        PRINT "A OK"
```

3.
```
10    IF A >= 0 THEN PRINT "Absolute Value of "; A; " is " A
      ELSE PRINT "Absolute Value of "; A; " is "; -1 * A
```

4.
```
10    IF Code$ > "9" OR Code$ < "0" THEN PRINT Code$;" IS NOT NUMERIC"
      ELSE PRINT Code$; " IS NUMERIC"
```

5. Pseudocode:

```
START
        INPUT Hourly Rate and Hours Worked
        WHILE Hours Worked <> 99
            IF Hours Worked <= 40 THEN
                Wages = Hours Worked * Hourly Rate
            ELSE
                Wages = 40 * Hourly Rate + (Hours Worked - 40) * (Hourly Rate * 1.5)
            END IF
            PRINT Wages
            INPUT Hourly Rate and Hours Worked
        WEND
STOP
```

BASICA Program:

```
10    PRINT "Enter Rate and Hours - Type 99,99 when Done"
20    INPUT HOURLYRATE, HOURSWORKED
30    WHILE HOURSWORKED <> 99
40        IF HOURSWORKED <= 40 THEN WAGES = HOURSWORKED * HOURLYRATE
          ELSE REGULARWAGES = 40 * HOURLYRATE:OVERTIMEWAGES = (HOURSWORKED - 40) * (HOURLYRATE * 1.5):
              WAGES = REGULARWAGES + OVERTIMEWAGES
50        PRINT WAGES
60        INPUT HOURLYRATE, HOURSWORKED
70    WEND
80    END
```

6. With compound conditionals:

```
IF AGE >= 21 AND (INCOME > 40000 OR CREDIT >= 5000) THEN
    PRINT "Meets Criteria"
ELSE PRINT "Does Not Meet Criteria"
```

With nested conditionals:

```
IF AGE < 21 THEN PRINT "Does Not Meet Criteria"
ELSE IF INCOME > 40000 OR CREDIT >= 5000 THEN PRINT "Meets Criteria"
ELSE PRINT "Does Not Meet Criteria"
```

7. Statement:

```
IF YEAR.END.BONUS > 2500 AND OUTSTANDING.BILLS < 2000 THEN
    PRINT "Go On Vacation"
ELSE PRINT "Stay Home This Year"
```

Iteration, Looping, and Subroutines for Logical Control and Top-Down Programming

As noted in the previous section, the logical control structures used in all programs regardless of the programming language are:

Logical Control Structure	Meaning
Sequence	Program steps are executed in the order they appear.
Selection	An IF-THEN-ELSE selects the instruction or instructions to be executed, depending on whether or not a condition is met.
Iteration	A series of steps are executed repeatedly; continued execution is based on whether or not a given condition or conditions are met.
Case	One of a number of steps will be executed, depending on the contents of a variable or variables.

In this section we will focus specifically on iteration or **looping**. We will provide additional information on the WHILE ... WEND and then discuss other iterative techniques.

Iterative Techniques

The WHILE ... WEND loop, nested iterations, and FOR ... NEXT statements are all types of iterative techniques. We will look at them in detail in the following sections.

More on the WHILE ... WEND Loop for Iteration   A WHILE (condition) ... WEND is executed repeatedly until the condition specified is no longer true or met. When the loop is terminated, execution continues with the statement following the word WEND. Note: WHILE ... WEND is used for iteration in BASICA; other versions may use different delimiters such as DO WHILE ... LOOP (VAX), WHILE ... NEXT, etc. All, however, are used in the same way for looping.

If the condition tested in the WHILE ... WEND is not met initially, the loop is not executed at all. Note that the test for the specified condition is made even before the series of steps is executed even once. That is, consider the following:

```
10     WHILE AMT1 <> 9999
         .
         .
         .
90     WEND
```

Suppose AMT1 is entered initially as 9999, meaning that there are no valid AMT1 variables at all. Before the statements within the WHILE ... WEND loop are executed, AMT1 is compared with 9999. Since AMT1 equals 9999 at the beginning, the condition in the WHILE loop is not met, even initially. In this case, the statements within the WHILE ... WEND will not be executed at all. Thus, execution would continue with the statement following WEND. This would be the correct procedure because if a trailer value is entered initially, then there is no valid data to process and you would want to bypass the loop entirely.

Repeating or iterating a series of steps any number of times as in the above is called *looping*. You use WHILE AMT1 <> 9999, in the preceding, because you have an unknown number of input variables that are to be processed; in such cases, a trailer value is entered to force the WHILE ... WEND to terminate. This trailer value is entered after all "real" input, regardless of what the number of input variables to be processed actually is.

Sometimes, however, you know in advance the exact number of times you want to execute a loop. In such cases you can use a counter along with a WHILE ... WEND to control the number of times a procedure is repeated or iterated. Instead of testing for a trailer value to terminate the loop, we test the counter to see if the loop has been executed the required number of times.

For example, you can use a counter to process a fixed number of variables. Suppose you input customer data as follows:

Customer Name
Street Address
City State Zip (Assume no commas between city, state, and zip).

The following will print one mailing label for each of 25 customers:

```
10     PRINT "Enter Name on Line 1, Street Address on Line 2"
20     PRINT "Enter City State Zip on Line 3"
30     LET LABEL.CTR = 0
40     WHILE LABEL.CTR < 25
50         INPUT CUST.NAME$
60         INPUT ST.ADDR$
70         INPUT CITY.STATE.ZIP$
80         LPRINT CUST.NAME$
90         LPRINT ST.ADDR$
100        LPRINT CITY.STATE.ZIP$
110        LPRINT    'Prints a blank line between labels
120        LET LABEL.CTR = LABEL.CTR + 1
130    WEND
140    PRINT "End of Job"
150    END
```

The following list of steps may be used for iteration in which a loop is to be executed a fixed number of times:

1. Initialize a counter before looping.

2. Increment the counter each time you execute the loop.

3. Use the WHILE statement to test the counter. This ensures that the loop is executed the required number of times.

Note that a common error when using a counter is to forget either to initialize it at the beginning or to increment it within the loop.

For another example, let us see how you can add 5 input amounts to a total. Suppose you code the following, which contains a logic error:

```
10     LET TOTAL = 0
20     LET COUNTER = 0
30     WHILE COUNTER < 5
40         INPUT AMT1
```

```
50        LET TOTAL = TOTAL + AMT1
60        WEND
70        PRINT TOTAL
80        END
```

The WHILE ... WEND loop is incorrect because within its sequence of steps there is no instruction to increase or increment the COUNTER. Thus, COUNTER is initialized at 0 and remains at 0 throughout. Because COUNTER will always be less than 5, values for AMT1 are entered and added to TOTAL indefinitely. This error condition is called an infinite loop. That is, the computer will execute the above procedure continually prompting for input until the programmer or user realizes there is an error and terminates the program.

The correct coding for the preceding program is:

```
10        LET TOTAL = 0
20        LET COUNTER = 0
30        WHILE COUNTER < 5
40           INPUT AMT1
50           LET TOTAL = TOTAL + AMT1
60           LET COUNTER = COUNTER + 1        'Counter must be incremented
70        WEND
80        PRINT TOTAL
90        END
```

Once the COUNTER is equal to 5, the WHILE ... WEND loop will no longer be executed. TOTAL will then print and the run will terminate.

If a program with an infinite loop is run on a mainframe, the computer's internal clock will sense that the statements are being executed longer than would normally be required by any program and will automatically terminate the job. On microcomputers using BASIC, you can press (CTRL) and, while holding it down, press (BREAK) to exit an infinite loop.

SELF-TEST

How many times will the WHILE ... WEND be executed in each of the following cases (1–4)?

```
1. 10    LET CTR = 5
   20    LET TOTAL = 0
   30    WHILE CTR <= 10
   40       INPUT AMT
   50       LET TOTAL = TOTAL + AMT
   60       LET CTR = CTR + 1
   70    WEND
   80    PRINT TOTAL

2. 10    LET CTR = 10
   20    LET TOTAL = 0
   30    WHILE CTR >= 5
   40       INPUT AMT
   50       LET TOTAL = TOTAL + AMT
   60       LET CTR = CTR - 1
   70    WEND
   80    PRINT TOTAL

3. 10    LET CTR = 10
   20    LET TOTAL = 0
   30    WHILE CTR >= 10
   40       INPUT AMT
   50       LET TOTAL = TOTAL + AMT
   60    WEND
   70    PRINT TOTAL
```

```
4. 10   LET CTR = 0
   20   LET TOTAL = 0
   30   WHILE CTR <= 5
   40      LET CTR = CTR + 1
   50      INPUT AMT
   60      LET TOTAL = TOTAL + AMT
   70   WEND
   80   PRINT TOTAL
```

5. Write a program to calculate and print the sum of even integers from 2 to 2000.

SOLUTIONS

1. 6 times
2. 6 times
3. Infinite loop—CTR is not changed within the loop
4. 6 times
5. Program:

```
10   'This program prints the sum of even numbers from 2 - 2000
20   LET SUM = 0
30   LET EVENNO = 2
40   WHILE EVENNO <= 2000
50      LET SUM = SUM + EVENNO
60      LET EVENNO = EVENNO + 2
70   WEND
80   PRINT "The sum is "; SUM
90   END
```

Nested Iterations   All forms of iteration can be **nested**, which means that any one iteration may appear within another.

For example, suppose you want to again prepare mailing labels. This time you want 25 labels for each customer, and the number of customers is variable. In this case, you read one line of input containing (1) name, (2) street address, and (3) city state and zip. (Assume there are no commas between city, state, and zip.) You print 25 labels for each input line entered. You end processing when a customer name is entered as "LAST"; that is, "LAST" is a trailer value indicating that there is no more data. You use an initial input statement and a trailer value here because you do not know how many customers you have.

One method for accomplishing this procedure is to use a WHILE (more data) ... WEND loop and within that, a WHILE ... WEND that is executed exactly 25 times. Within the major WHILE ... WEND loop you establish a counter that begins as zero. Within the minor loop this counter is increased by one each time a label is written. In this way, when the counter is 25, you know you have written 25 labels for each set of input variables. The BASICA program for this problem appears in Figure D–6.

This program illustrates the use of nested iteration. The major loop is defined by:

```
WHILE CUSTNAME$ <> "LAST"
  .
  .
  .
WEND                   'Outer loop refers to 1st WHILE
```

The loop structure WHILE CUSTNAME$ <> "LAST" to the WEND on line 150 is the major iteration. All instructions from WHILE up until the last

```
10    'This program prints 25 mailing labels for each customer
20    INPUT CUSTNAME$, STADDR$, CITYSTATEZIP$
30    WHILE CUSTNAME$ <> "LAST"
40       LET COUNTER = 0
50       WHILE COUNTER < 25
60          LPRINT CUSTNAME$
70          LPRINT STADDR$
80          LPRINT CITYSTATEZIP$
90          LPRINT
100         LET COUNTER = COUNTER + 1
110      WEND
120      LPRINT 'Space after each set of labels
130      LPRINT 'Space after each set of labels
140      INPUT CUSTNAME$, STADDR$, CITYSTATEZIP$
150   WEND
160   PRINT "End of Job"
170   END
```

D-6 BASICA program showing nested iterations.

WEND are part of it. As long as CUSTNAME$ is not equal to "LAST", the entire structure is executed repeatedly. When CUSTNAME$ is finally entered as "LAST", the computer proceeds to the statement following the last WEND, which in this case prints an end-of-job message. Then it executes an END, where the program is terminated.

The minor or inner loop is delimited by WHILE COUNTER < 25 on line 50 to the WEND on line 110. Before the minor iteration or module is executed 25 times, the COUNTER must be set to zero. You then execute the minor loop or module 25 times, or until COUNTER = 25. COUNTER is set to 1 after one label is written, to 2 after the second label is written, and so on. This means that when 25 labels have been written, COUNTER will be 25. The minor or inner WHILE ... WEND will then no longer be executed, and control will pass to the next step after the inner loop on line 120. The LPRINTs that follow provide two lines of space between labels, and then the next set of variables is read. This entire process is repeated until a trailer value with a CUSTNAME$ equal to "LAST" is entered, at which point the program ends.

Although setting COUNTER to 0 initially is not required because all numeric variables are automatically set to 0, the outer loop requires this instruction. This is because you need to have COUNTER set to 0, not only at the beginning but also each time through the major loop.

You could, alternatively, initialize COUNTER at 1 instead of 0 and then code WHILE COUNTER <= 25.

The use of a WHILE within a WHILE as above is called **nested WHILEs**. The main or outer WHILE usually means that an entire routine or module is to be executed for as long as you have input. This routine or module may itself have some iteration or sequence of steps to be repeated that calls for another WHILE. Keep in mind that the *last* or outer WEND statement refers to the *first* WHILE, and inner WEND statements refer to inner WHILEs. We recommend that you indent instructions within loops for clarity, as shown in Figure D–7. When coding, remember that each WHILE is matched to the closest WEND.

FOR ... NEXT Statements

A loop is a form of iteration in which a sequence of instructions is executed repeatedly. We have used several types of loops for iteration. FOR ... NEXT statements can perform many loop control functions automatically. In this section we consider the FOR ... NEXT for looping.

♦   **FOR ... NEXT as Another Iterative Technique**   Suppose you want to compute the amount of money you will accumulate at the end of one, two, and three years if you deposit a specified amount at a given interest rate. Assume that the interest is compounded annually, which means that in year 2, the new principal will be the original principal plus the interest from year 1 and that the rate of return is based on this increased value for the principal.

The new principal for each of the three years is:

New principal after year 1 = Original Principal (1 + Rate)

The principal after year 2 = Original Principal $(1 + Rate)^2$

The principal after year 3 = Original Principal $(1 + Rate)^3$

The general formula for computing compound interest is:

$P_n = P_0 (1 + r)^n$ where:

P_0 = original principal

P_n = principal after n years

r = Interest rate

n = Number of years

When n is 1, P_n is equal to the total amount of money after one year of investment of an initial amount (P_0) at a given rate of interest (r). When n is 2, P_n is equal to the total amount after two years of investment. When n is 3, P_n is equal to the total amount after three years of investment.

Let us begin with an illustration that focuses on compound interest for this three-year period.

The input to be entered consists of a principal amount (P_0) and interest rate (r). The number of years to be invested (n) will be predefined as 3.

The output will consist of a chart indicating the value of the principal plus interest for each of three years of investment. The following provides an example of the displayed input and output:

```
ENTER PRINCIPAL AMOUNT:

? 2000

ENTER INTEREST RATE: (e.g., 8% AS 8.0):

? 10.0

INVESTMENT CHART FOR 2000 AT 10% INTEREST
YEAR AMOUNT
1    2200
2    2420
3    2662
```

We will now write a program that computes the total, where values of P (principal) and r (rate of interest) are to be entered as input. We are interested in the results when n equals 1, 2, and 3. The following method does not use any loops:

```
 10 PRINT "Enter Principal Amount:"
 20 INPUT PRINCIPAL
 30 PRINT "Enter Interest Rate (e.g., 8% as 8.0):"
 40 INPUT RATE
 50 PRINT
 60 PRINT "INVESTMENT CHART FOR "; Principal; " AT "; RATE; "% INTEREST"
 70 PRINT "   YEAR   AMOUNT"
 80 LET RATE = RATE / 100
 90 LET AMOUNT1 = PRINCIPAL * (1 + RATE) ^ 1
100 PRINT "     1       "; AMOUNT1
110 LET AMOUNT2 = PRINCIPAL * (1 + RATE) ^ 2
120 PRINT "     2       "; AMOUNT2
130 LET AMOUNT3 = PRINCIPAL * (1 + RATE) ^ 3
140 PRINT "     3       "; AMOUNT3
150 END
```

The screen display would be:

```
Enter Principal Amount:
? 100
Enter Interest Rate (e.g., 8% as 8.0):
? 5.0
```

This is followed by:

```
INVESTMENT CHART FOR 100 AT 5.0% INTEREST
   YEAR    AMOUNT
    1        105
    2        110.25
    3        115.7624969482422
```

To represent all values as dollars and cents figures, use a PRINT USING as follows:

```
100 PRINT "     1      ";              '; means line is not terminated
105 PRINT USING "###.##"; AMOUNT1
```

Lines 100 and 105 would replace line 100 in the program.

Notice that the boxed entries within the program have several lines that are similar. That is, the arithmetic operations use the same basic formula. For year 1, (1 + RATE) is multiplied by the principal. For year 2, $(1 + RATE)^2$ or $(1 + RATE) \times (1 + RATE)$, is multiplied by the PRINCIPAL. For year 3, $(1 + RATE)^3$, or $(1 + RATE) \times (1 + RATE) \times (1 + RATE)$, is multiplied by the PRINCIPAL. Any sequence of steps that is repeated with an incremented set of values is best coded with a loop that executes a single sequence repeatedly.

In the above, one routine could be coded to compute the three values. This one routine could use a variable exponent called NO.OF.YEARS, for example, which begins as 1 and is incremented by one each time the routine is executed until the variable exceeds 3. That is, a loop can be established to be executed three times, varying NO.OF.YEARS from 1 to 3.

The next method uses a WHILE ... WEND structure.

```
10     PRINT "Enter Principal Amount:"
20     INPUT PRINCIPAL
30     PRINT "Enter Interest Rate (e.g., 8% as 8.0):"
40     INPUT RATE
50     PRINT
60     PRINT "INVESTMENT CHART FOR "; PRINCIPAL; " AT "; RATE; "% INTEREST"
70     PRINT "   YEAR    AMOUNT"
80     LET RATE = RATE / 100
90     LET NO.OF.YEARS = 1
100    WHILE NO.OF.YEARS <= 3
110       LET AMOUNT = PRINCIPAL * (1 + RATE) ^ NO.OF.YEARS
120       PRINT "      "; NO.OF.YEARS; "      "; AMOUNT
130       LET NO.OF.YEARS = NO.OF.YEARS + 1
140    WEND
150    END
```

Notice that this program uses a WHILE ... WEND loop. The sequence of instructions to be repeated is within the WHILE routine. Because NO.OF.YEARS is not greater than 3, the statements within the WHILE ... WEND loop are executed for the first time with NO.OF.YEARS = 1. Then 1 is added to NO.OF.YEARS, and the computer tests again to see if NO.OF.YEARS is greater than 3. Since it is now 2, which is not greater than 3, the statements within the WHILE ... WEND loop are executed again with NO.OF.YEARS = 2. Then with NO.OF.YEARS = 3, the WHILE ... WEND loop is executed again. After the third time through this loop, 1 is added to NO.OF.YEARS, which makes it 4. Because 4 is greater than 3, the loop is not performed again and the program ends.

You have seen from the previous solution that you want to perform a series of operations using a variable NO.OF.YEARS that begins as 1 and is incremented until it reaches 3. The FOR ... NEXT statement is typically used when you want to perform a loop a predefined number of times in which a variable needs to be incremented, as in this case.

The FOR ... NEXT structure performs several functions. It establishes a variable, increments the variable, and specifies the range in which the variable is to vary. Thus for this problem you would have:

```
100     FOR NO.OF.YEARS = 1 TO 3
110        LET AMOUNT = PRINCIPAL * (1 + RATE) ^ NO.OF.YEARS
120        PRINT AMOUNT
130     NEXT NO.OF.YEARS
```

The statements within the FOR ... NEXT structure will be executed for the first time with the variable NO.OF.YEARS equal to 1. The instruction FOR NO.OF.YEARS = 1 TO 3 means that the computer will repeat the steps within the FOR ... NEXT structure first with NO.OF.YEARS = 2 and then NO.OF.YEARS = 3.

Thus the procedure is executed three times, first with NO.OF.YEARS = 1, then NO.OF.YEARS = 2, and finally NO.OF.YEARS = 3. The program will continue then with the statement after the NEXT, which in this case is the end of the program. With the FOR ... NEXT loop there is no need to initialize the counter (NO.OF.YEARS here) to 1 or to increment it by 1 each time through the loop. This is handled by the FOR ... NEXT structure itself.

The full program using the FOR ... NEXT loop follows:

```
10      PRINT "Enter Principal Amount:"
20      INPUT PRINCIPAL
30      PRINT "Enter Interest Rate (e.g., 8% as 8.0):"
40      INPUT RATE
50      PRINT
60      PRINT "INVESTMENT CHART FOR "; PRINCIPAL; " AT "; RATE; "% INTEREST"
70      PRINT "   YEAR   AMOUNT"
80      LET RATE = RATE / 100
90      FOR NO.OF.YEARS = 1 TO 3
100        LET AMOUNT = PRINCIPAL * (1 + RATE) ^ NO.OF.YEARS
110        PRINT "    "; NO.OF.YEARS; "      "; AMOUNT
120     NEXT NO.OF.YEARS
130     END
```

The output will be the same regardless of which method you use for coding the program.

The initial screen display will be:

```
Enter Principal Amount:
? 100
Enter Interest Rate (e.g., 8% as 8.0):
? 5.0
```

This is followed by:

```
INVESTMENT CHART FOR 100 AT 5.0% INTEREST
   YEAR   AMOUNT
    1       105
    2       110.25
    3       115.7624969482422
```

Use the FOR ... NEXT structure whenever a sequence is to be repeated a fixed number of times and a variable needs to be incremented each time through the sequence.

Remember to use a PRINT USING to display the amounts as dollars-and-cents values.

◆ **Refinements of the FOR ... NEXT Structure**   You have thus far used numeric literals in FOR ... NEXT loops for the starting and ending points of the variable NO.OF.YEARS (such as FOR NO.OF.YEARS = 1 TO 3). The starting and ending points or delimiters of the FOR ... NEXT could also be numeric variables. Moreover, the starting delimiter need not be 1. Consider the following two examples:

Example 1

```
10    LET S = 1
20    FOR N = S TO 10              'N will vary from 1 to 10
      .
      .
      .
100   NEXT N
```

Example 2

```
10    LET T = 5
20    FOR N = 1 TO T               'N will vary from 1 to 5
      .
      .
      .
100   NEXT N
```

However, keep in mind that if the beginning delimiter is greater than the ending delimiter in a FOR ... NEXT, the loop is not executed at all. In the following, the FOR ... NEXT loop does not get executed at all:

```
10    LET I = 10
20    LET J = 5
30    FOR N = I TO J
      .
      .
      .
90    NEXT N
```

Also, you can increment the variable in a FOR ... NEXT loop by a value other than one. Consider the following:

```
10    FOR I = 1 TO 5
      .
      .
      .
100   NEXT I
```

The computer executes the loop 5 times. The first time I has a value of 1, then 2, until it reaches 5. When I is 5, the loop is executed a fifth time, and then the statement following the NEXT is executed.

Thus I is incremented by 1 each time the loop is executed. Using a STEP clause, however, you can increment I by any value you wish.

Suppose you want to sum the odd numbers from 1 to 101, inclusive of the end points, using a FOR ... NEXT loop. You could code the following:

```
10    LET T = 0
20      FOR I = 1 TO 101 STEP 2
30          LET T = T + I
40      NEXT I
50      PRINT "The Sum of Odd Numbers from 1-101 is "; T
```

In this FOR ... NEXT loop, I is set equal to 1 initially. T is incremented by the value of I, and then I is incremented by 2. I continues to be incremented by 2 until it equals 101 and the FOR ... NEXT loop is terminated.

The STEP clause could specify a variable instead of a value. Thus the preceding example could be coded as:

```
10    LET S = 2
20    FOR I = 1 TO 101 STEP S
30       LET T = T + I
40    NEXT I
```

Moreover, you can use the STEP clause to decrease the values in the variable. The following is also correct:

```
10    FOR I = 101 TO 1 STEP - 2
20       LET T = T + I
30    NEXT I
```

If the STEP clause is omitted, the default STEP value is 1. This means that the computer assumes you want to increment the variable by 1 each time. Thus the following two instructions produce identical results.

```
10    FOR I = 1 TO 5        and       10    FOR I = 1 TO 5 STEP 1
```

Do not change the variable used with a FOR ... NEXT loop within the loop itself. The following type of coding could produce errors.

```
10    FOR I = 1 TO 5
         .
         .
         .
90       LET I = ...
100   NEXT I
```

That is, I is the variable in this FOR ... NEXT loop. It should not be used as a receiving variable or changed by the programmer as above.

Do not use the variable defined by a FOR ... NEXT outside the loop. Consider the following invalid coding:

```
10    FOR I = 1 TO 5
         .
         .
         .
100   NEXT I
110   PRINT I   'I should not be accessed outside the loop
```

As I varies from 1 to 5 in the FOR ... NEXT, you might assume that 5 or 6 will print when the above is executed. In fact, I has predictable values only within the FOR ... NEXT loop and should not be accessed outside the loop.

FOR ... NEXT loops, like all other iterative structures, can be nested, which means that you may include FOR ... NEXTs within FOR ... NEXTs. When nesting FOR ... NEXT loops, be sure to keep in mind the rule that each NEXT is matched to the closest FOR. Consider the following invalid coding:

```
10    FOR N = 1 TO 5
         .
         .
         .
100   FOR M = 1 TO 10
         .
         .
         .
200   NEXT N
         .
```

.
.
.

```
300    NEXT M
```

The NEXT N and NEXT M instructions must be reversed to make this structure work properly. That is, the initial FOR N = 1 TO 5 is the major loop and must be linked to the outermost NEXT N. The minor or second FOR M = 1 TO 10 should be linked to the first or inner NEXT M. If the minor FOR ... NEXT loop were indented in the preceding, it would have been easier to detect the error.

Note that as a coding guideline we indent a FOR ... NEXT within a FOR ... NEXT loop, and all statements within the minor loop are indented as well. This makes the program easier to read and debug. Press (TAB) once to indent eight spaces on a line; press it again to indent another eight spaces.

Which Iterative Technique to Use

An iterative structure can be coded using either a WHILE ... WEND or a FOR ... NEXT structure. Most programmers prefer to use a WHILE ... WEND loop when the number of iterations is unknown or variable each time the program is to be run. That is, if the number of iterations is dependent on the input, it is best to use a WHILE ... WEND structure. If, however, the number of times an iteration is to be executed is fixed, it is best to use a FOR ... NEXT loop.

SELF-TEST

1. What is wrong with the following?
```
10    FOR N = 1 TO 4
20        INPUT AMT
30        PRINT AMT
40    NEXT I
```

2. Print a multiplication table as follows using FOR ... NEXT looping:

1	2	3	4	5
2	4	6	8	10
3	6	9	12	15
4	8	12	16	20
5	10	15	20	25

3. Code the above using a WHILE ... WEND loop.

4. Using a FOR ... NEXT loop, write a program to calculate and print the sum of even numbers from 2 to 2000 inclusive of the end points.

5. Calculate N Factorial (N!) where N is an input variable. N Factorial = N x (N − 1) x ... 1. (for example, 5! = 5 x 4 x 3 x 2 x 1 = 120).

SOLUTIONS

1. The NEXT statement should be NEXT N.

2. Program:
```
10    FOR N = 1 TO 5
20        LPRINT N, N * 2, N * 3, N * 4, N * 5
30        LPRINT
40    NEXT N
50    END
```

The displayed output will be as follows:

```
        1     2     3     4     5
        2     4     6     8    10
        3     6     9    12    15
        4     8    12    16    20
        5    10    15    20    25
```

3. WHILE ... WEND loop:

```
10    N = 1
20    WHILE N <= 5
30        LPRINT N, N * 2, N * 3, N * 4, N * 5
40        LPRINT
50        N = N + 1
60    WEND
70    END
```

4. FOR ... NEXT loop:

```
10    TOTAL = 0
20    FOR NUMBER = 2 TO 2000 STEP 2
30        TOTAL = TOTAL + NUMBER
40    NEXT NUMBER
50    PRINT TOTAL
60    END
```

5. N Factorial (N!):

```
10    TOTAL = 1
20    INPUT N
30    FOR CTR = N TO 1 STEP -1
40        TOTAL = TOTAL * CTR
50    NEXT CTR
60    PRINT N; "FACTORIAL = "; TOTAL
70    END
```

An Introduction to Subroutines for Top-Down Modular Programming

Thus far in this text, you have focused on BASICA syntax and three of the four logical control constructs necessary for writing well-designed programs. You have also learned how to use pseudocode to map out the logic in your programs before you begin coding. Moreover, you have been introduced to the concept of top-down programming in several discussions.

In this section we will consider top-down modular programming in detail. Top-down modular programs are easy to code, debug, maintain, and modify. We define a module as a routine or a group of instructions that function as a unit and that performs a specific set of operations.

Subroutines Defined   One method for including modules in a top-down BASICA program is with the use of **subroutines**. Subroutines have the following features:

◆ **Subroutines Can Minimize Duplication of Effort**   Consider the following program excerpt:

Each of the boxed entries represents a module or sequence of steps that accomplishes a given function; in this case, the module prompts for input and enters the input as well.

Note that both boxed entries are the same. They appear in two places—as part of an initial read routine and then, again, at the end of the WHILE ... WEND loop.

```
 10     PRINT "Enter Customer No:"
 20     INPUT CUSTNO
 30     PRINT "Enter Part Description:"
 40     INPUT PARTDESCRIPTION$
 50     PRINT "Enter Unit Price:"
 60     INPUT UNITPRICE
 70     PRINT "Enter Qty Ordered:"
 80     INPUT QTYORDERED
 90     WHILE CUSTNO < 999
100         LET BALDUE = UNITPRICE * QTYORDERED
110         LPRINT "Customer "; CUSTNO; "Owes: "
120         LPRINT BALDUE; "For Part "; PARTDESCRIPTION$
130         PRINT "Enter Customer No:"
140         INPUT CUSTNO
150         PRINT "Enter Part Description:"
160         INPUT PARTDESCRIPTION$
170         PRINT "Enter Unit Price:"
180         INPUT UNITPRICE
190         PRINT "Enter Qty Ordered:"
200         INPUT QTYORDERED
210     WEND
220     LPRINT "End of Report"
230     END
```

To repeat the boxed set of instructions twice is not only cumbersome but it increases the risk of errors. A subroutine can be written as a separate series of statements, or **module**, and can then be executed in the program whenever it is needed.

A GOSUB is a statement that causes execution of a separate subroutine. After the computer executes the subroutine, it then returns control to the statement following the GOSUB.

GOSUB *line #* is the instruction that causes execution of the statements at the subroutine specified by the label. You could write, therefore:

```
10      GOSUB 1000
20      WHILE CUSTNO < 999
30          LET BALDUE = UNITPRICE * QTYORDERED
40          LPRINT "Customer "; CUSTNO; "Owes: "
50          LPRINT BALDUE ; "For Part "; PARTDESCRIPTION$
60          GOSUB 1000
70      WEND
80      LPRINT "End of Report"
```

GOSUB 1000 instructs the computer to execute a module located at line 1000. The module itself will follow the END statement. The GOSUB causes execution of all the instructions within that module; it must end with a RETURN statement. After all the instructions within the subroutine are executed, control returns to the statement in the main program following the GOSUB. The return point will be line 20 after the first execution of the GOSUB and will be line 70 after every other execution of the GOSUB.

The subroutine that begins at line 1000 is itself coded after the END and must have a RETURN as a scope terminator.

```
10   GOSUB
 .
 .
 .
100   END
1000  '*****************************************
1010  ' This subroutine prompts for & gets input
1020  '*****************************************
```

```
1030   PRINT "Enter Customer No:"
1040   INPUT CUSTNO
1050   PRINT "Enter Part Description:"
1060   INPUT PARTDESCRIPTION$
1070   PRINT "Enter Unit Price:"
1080   INPUT UNITPRICE
1090   PRINT "Enter Qty Ordered:"
1100   INPUT QTYORDERED
```

Note that the subroutine at line 1000 is executed twice from the main program. The actual sequence of steps in the subroutine is, however, coded only once at the end of the program. Any number of subroutines may be included after the END statement.

A sequence of instructions that appears more than once in a program can be coded as a separate subroutine and executed from the main program with a GOSUB instruction, as in the above. Even sequences that appear only once are often best coded as a subroutine, if they represent a cohesive entity. This is especially true in IF statements where you are restricted to three lines of coding. For example:

```
10   IF AMT1 = AMT2 THEN
 .    ⎧ Sequence of steps to be executed
 .    ⎨ if AMT1 and AMT2 are equal
 .    ⎩

ELSE
 .    ⎧ Sequence of steps to be executed
 .    ⎨ if AMT1 and AMT2 are unequal
 .    ⎩
```

Each sequence is a cohesive set of instructions that is collectively executed under certain conditions. The preferred form for the above is:

```
10   IF AMT1 = AMT2 THEN
        GOSUB 1000    'This will have the processing for AMT1 = AMT2
        ELSE GOSUB 2000    'This will have the processing for AMT1 <> AMT2
```

In this way, each GOSUB can have separate instructions on separate lines without the need for using colons to separate instructions in an IF statement and without having to worry about exceeding 255 characters in the entire IF statement.

Using Subroutines in Top-Down Modular Programming   When planning a program such as the above, it would be unwise to begin by focusing on the syntax in the subroutines. Rather, it is best to develop the logic by focusing on the structure of the program first, leaving the details in a subroutine for later.

Thus, when coding a program, you may include a GOSUB in the main program to designate any subroutine or sequence of instructions that we wish to code in detail later. This technique is called **top-down programming**, and each subroutine is called a **module**. Long and complex programs could contain many GOSUBs, which keeps the main module clear and free from details; as noted, the details are left for subroutines.

We encourage you to code top-down programs in this way. That is, any sequence of steps that represents a related set of operations such as printing headings or entering a series of variables should be coded as a module or subroutine. The purpose of this top-down approach is to allow the programmer to focus on the structure rather than the syntax in the main body of the program. Similarly, any series of steps that are executed from more than one place in a program should be coded in a subroutine and executed from the main program with a GOSUB. Consider the following example:

```
10    'This program prints 25 amounts per page
20    GOSUB 1000
30    INPUT AMT1
40    WHILE AMT1 < 999
50        LPRINT "Amount = "; AMT1
60        LINECTR = LINECTR + 1
70        'LineCtr keeps track of the number of lines printed
80        IF LINECTR = 25 THEN
                  GOSUB 1000        'We want 25 lines per page
90        INPUT AMT1
100   WEND
110   END
1000  '**********************************
1010  ' This subroutine prints headings
1020  '**********************************
1030      LPRINT "            DETAIL REPORT     "
1040      LINECTR = 0            'Reinitializes Line Counter
1050  RETURN
```

The subroutine at 1000 that prints headings is performed at the beginning of the program and then again whenever LINECTR = 25. After the RETURN is executed, control returns to the statement following the GOSUB instruction. Initially, after the PrintHeadings module beginning at line 1000 is executed, control returns to the first INPUT statement on line 30. If GOSUB 1000 is executed from within the loop, then control returns to the INPUT AMT1 statement on line 90.

Line number 1000 was used for the subroutine just because it is a nice round number; any line number after 110 (the END statement) could have been used.

All logical control constructs, including GOSUBs, can be nested. This means any such construct can include the same construct within it. A GOSUB, for example, can be written in a module that is itself executed by a GOSUB.

Subroutines can appear in any order as long as they follow the END statement. We recommend, however, that you code major subroutines before minor ones to make your programs top-down.

Common GOSUB Errors   There are two common causes of GOSUB errors:

- Failure to include a RETURN with a GOSUB will result in a logic error.

- Failure to include an END statement in its proper place will cause an error. Be sure that the END statement precedes the first subroutine in the program. Failure to include this will result in a logic error.

ON ... GOSUB for the CASE Structure   We have seen that there are four logical control constructs: sequence, IF-THEN-ELSE, iteration, and CASE. The CASE structure, which consists of selecting a module from a series of items or menu, is coded using ON ... GOSUB.

Consider the following menu that may appear on a screen:

```
        Payroll  Procedure  Menu

   Salary  Change            [ 1 ]

   Name  Change              [ 2 ]

   Address  Change           [ 3 ]

   Department  Change        [ 4 ]

   Type  a  Number  1-4      [   ]
```

The user enters a number from 1 to 4; different procedures will be executed, depending on which number is entered. Although you could use simple IF statements to test the value entered, a CASE construct is clearer and more efficient. The pseudocode for this structure is:

```
CASE MenuItem
        WHEN 1 Process Salary Change
        WHEN 2 Process Name Change
        WHEN 3 Process Address Change
        WHEN 4 Process Department Change
END CASE
```

This structure can be coded in BASICA with an ON GOSUB (some versions of BASIC have not only ON GOSUB but additional CASE structures):

```
10   '*******************************************
20   'An Example of a Case Structure
30   ' The program begins with a main module first
40   '*******************************************
50   INPUT MENU.ITEM
60   ON MENU.ITEM GOSUB 1000, 2000, 3000, 4000
      .        .
      .        .
      .        .
999  END
1000 '*******************************************
1010 ' This subprogram defines the Salary
1020 ' Change Procedure
1030 '*******************************************
      .        .
      .        .
      .        .
```

```
1999  RETURN    ' This instruction returns you to main module
2000  '***********************************************
2010  ' This subprogram defines the Name
2030  ' Change Procedure
2040  '***********************************************
      .         .
      .         .
      .         .
2999  RETURN    ' This instruction returns you to main module
3000  '***********************************************
3010  ' This subprogram defines the Address
3020  ' Change Procedure
3030  '***********************************************
      .         .
      .         .
      .         .
3999  RETURN    ' This instruction returns you to main module
4000  '***********************************************
4010  ' This subprogram defines the Department
4020  ' Change Procedure
4030  '***********************************************
      .         .
      .         .
      .         .
4999  RETURN    ' This instruction returns you to main module
```

Each of the separate subroutines is a module that is executed if the specified condition is met. That is, if MENU.ITEM = 1, the first line number specified in the ON ... GOSUB is executed; thus, module 1000, which handles a Salary Change Procedure, would be executed. If MENU.ITEM = 2, the second line number in the ON ... GOSUB would be executed; that is, module 2000, which handles a Name Change Procedure, would be executed, etc.

Advantages of Using GOSUBS in Top-Down Modular Programs

◆ Programs are easier to read and maintain.

◆ Duplicate coding is avoided.

◆ The logic in the program is easier to follow.

◆ The structure of the program is easier to design.

Guidelines for Coding Subroutines

◆ Each subroutine should be a self-contained unit representing a single type of operation or function.

◆ Keep subroutines single-purpose (for example, use two separate subroutines to perform two separate tasks).

◆ Keep subroutines short.

◆ Code subroutines in a top-down or hierarchical manner.

SELF-TEST

Consider the following subroutine:

```
1000  'SUBROUTINE 1
1010    SUM = SUM + EVENNUM
1020    EVENNUM = EVENNUM + 2
1030  RETURN
```

1. Write a program that calls the above subroutine to calculate the sum of even numbers from 2 to 2000, including the end points.
2. Write a program that calls the above subroutine to calculate the sum of even numbers from 50 to 3002, including the endpoints.
3. Write a program that calls a subroutine to calculate the sum of integers from 1 to 2500, excluding the endpoints. Then code the subroutine.
4. Write a program that calls a subroutine to calculate N! (referred to as "N factorial") where N! = (N) x (N − 1) x (N − 2) x ... x 1 (for example, 5! = 5 x 4 x 3 x 2 x 1 = 120). Then code the subroutine.
5. Indicate what is wrong with the following program excerpt:

```
50 GOSUB 1000
   .
   .
   .
1000
   .
   .
   .
2000 RETURN
```

SOLUTIONS

1. Program:
```
10    SUM = 0
20    EVENNUM = 2
30    WHILE EVENNUM <= 2000
40       GOSUB 1000
50    WEND
60    PRINT SUM
70    END
```

2. Program:
```
10    SUM = 0
20    EVENNUM = 50
30    WHILE EVENNUM <= 3002
40       GOSUB 1000
50    WEND
60    PRINT SUM
70    END
```

3. Program:
```
10 SUM = 0
20 NUMBER = 1
30 WHILE NUMBER < 2499
40    GOSUB 1000
50 WEND
60 PRINT SUM
70 END
1000 'Add numbers
1010    NUMBER = NUMBER + 1
1020    SUM = SUM + NUMBER
1030 RETURN
```

4. Program:

```
  10 RESULT = 1
  20 INPUT NUMBER
  30 FOR FACTOR = NUMBER TO 1 STEP -1
  40    GOSUB 1000 'Calculates Factorial
  50 NEXT FACTOR
  60 PRINT NUMBER; "Factorial = "; RESULT
  70 END
1000 'Calculates Factorial
1010    RESULT = RESULT * FACTOR
1020 RETURN
```

5. There must be an END statement prior to line 1000.

Array Processing

Arrays are used in programming to input and process a series of variables. These variables may be either all numeric or all string. The major uses of arrays include:

♦   Storing a series of data elements each of the same type (for example, all numeric or all string variables)

♦   Storing a series of totals to which input amounts are added; after all data is accumulated, the totals can be printed

♦   Storing a table to be used for "looking up" values

Using an Array to Store a Series of Data Elements All of Which Are Either Numeric or String Variables

Suppose you want to read in and process 20 exam grades, one for each student in a class. Using traditional methods, you would need to input 20 separate variables, one for each exam:

```
 10    INPUT EXAM1
 20    INPUT EXAM2
         .
         .
         .
200    INPUT EXAM20
```

Moreover, obtaining an average of the 20 exams would also require a great deal of tedious coding:

```
 10    AVERAGE = (EXAM1 + EXAM2 + ... EXAM20) / 20
```

The dots or ellipses (...) above mean that the programmer would need to specifically list all 20 variables to be used in calculating the average.

All 20 exams are numeric variables that can be defined with a single name called an **array**.

Using the DIM Statement to Define the Size of the Array

The name and size of an array may be defined with a DIMension statement. To store 20 exam values in an array where you access the first as EXAM(1), the second as EXAM(2), and so on, you could code the following:

```
 10    DIM EXAM (20)
```

The following is an example of how the EXAM array would appear in storage:

DIM EXAM (20)

0th EXAM	1st EXAM	2nd EXAM	....	20th EXAM
(Unused)	Exam (1)	Exam (2)	....	Exam (20)

Exam is called an array, and each variable is an element in that array. There are actually 21 elements in an array set up as DIM EXAM(20). They are EXAM (0) (not used), EXAM (1), EXAM (2), ... EXAM (20). The 0th is not used, and the first through the twentieth are referred to as EXAM(1) through EXAM(20), respectively.

All elements in an array must be of the same type. In this case, each element is a numeric variable. As noted, if you establish an array as DIM EXAM (20), EXAM(1) refers to the first exam that you will reference, and EXAM(20) refers to the last EXAM you will reference. To avoid confusion, you do not use the 0th element at all.

The DIM statement that defines an array should precede all instructions that process the array. Thus the following sequence is incorrect:

```
10    LET EXAM (20) = 0
        .
        .
        .
100   DIM EXAM (20)              'DIM must precede the assignment above
```

A DIM statement is not required for all arrays. If you do not include a DIM statement but use an array in your processing, BASIC assumes that the array has a maximum of 11 elements. In this example it also assumes that the elements are numbered Exam (0) through Exam (10).

```
10    INPUT EXAM (0)            'This is the first element of the array
20    INPUT EXAM (1)            'This is the second element of the array
        .                       '11 is the maximum array
        .                       'size unless you use a DIM
100   INPUT EXAM (10)
```

In summary, if a DIM statement does not precede the above INPUT instructions, the default is DIM EXAM (10), which has elements numbered EXAM (0) ... EXAM (10). No error message occurs when referencing an EXAM as long as you do not reference any element outside that range (0–10). That is, to code INPUT EXAM (11) without a preceding DIM statement would cause a syntax error.

Coding Guidelines

To ensure proper handling and to make your programs clearer, always use DIM statements when processing an array. Using the statement DIM array (m), 0 is the lowest element number in the array, and m is the highest element number in the array.

Accessing an Array Element Using a Subscript   Let us consider the EXAM array established with DIM EXAM (20), and let us assume that you have already entered input into EXAM (1) through EXAM (20)—remember that EXAM (0) is not used. To access any one of the 20 exams, you use the array name, EXAM, along with the entry within parentheses, which is called a **subscript**. The subscript indicates which of the 20 entries (1–20, respectively) you want to access. (Although a subscript of 0 refers to a valid array element, we do not use this element here.) For example, you would access the first student's grade as EXAM (1), the second student's grade as EXAM (2), and so on. If the 20 exams were already entered and stored in the computer, you could print the fifth student's grade by coding:

```
50    PRINT "GRADE FOR STUDENT 5 IS "; EXAM (5)
```

The subscript, then, specifies the particular element in the array that you want to access. Using a DIM EXAM (20) as above, the subscript will be the number of the actual element you want. This is because the subscripts will vary from 1 to m, where m is the number of array elements.

You use a subscript along with the array name to refer to any element within the array. In this example, if DIM EXAM (20) is coded, you use the subscript for EXAM that can have a value from 1 to 20. Any other value (except 0) would result in an error:

```
10    PRINT EXAM (.5)
20    PRINT EXAM (21)
```

Subscripts: Integers, Variables, or Arithmetic Expressions   Thus far we have focused on subscripts that are integers. A subscript, however, may also be a variable that contains an integer. Suppose you define a numeric variable along with the EXAM array as follows:

```
10    DIM EXAM (20)
20    LET I = 1
```

You could then print the first exam grade with either of the following:

```
30    PRINT EXAM (I)     or    30    PRINT EXAM (1)
```

Subscripts, then, identify specific items in an array, and they can be either integers or variables that contain integers. Using a variable rather than a fixed integer as a subscript enables you to vary the contents of the subscript so that you can process a series of items within a single procedure. Suppose you want to find the average of the 20 exams that have been stored in an array. You can use integers as subscripts, but to do so does not reduce the coding at all:

```
10    AVERAGE = (EXAM (1) + EXAM (2) + ... EXAM (20)) / 20
```

It is far more efficient to write a loop that adds one exam at a time to a total where the exam is referenced by a variable subscript. You can vary the contents of the subscript from 1 to 20 so that all 20 exams are added to the total.

Using FOR ... NEXT for Processing an Array

Assume that all 20 exams are already stored in the EXAM array. The procedure for calculating an average can be coded with a FOR ... NEXT loop as follows:

```
10    'Calculate an Average assuming Exam1-Exam20
20    'Have already been entered
30    DIM EXAM (20)
40    TOTAL = 0
50    FOR I = 1 TO 20
60        TOTAL = TOTAL + EXAM (I)
70    NEXT I
80    AVERAGE = TOTAL / 20
90    PRINT "Average = "; AVERAGE
100   END
```

We used a FOR ... NEXT for initializing and incrementing subscripts until the entire array was processed. You could have used a WHILE ... WEND loop as well, but you would then need to initialize and increment the subscript with additional instructions. The FOR ... NEXT loop does this automatically.

Coding Guidelines

Any iterative structure (FOR ... NEXT or WHILE ... WEND) can be used to process elements in an array. We recommend using the FOR ... NEXT statement when processing all array elements because the subscript or index variable is automatically initialized and incremented properly. This results in shorter, clearer code.

Let us consider additional examples of procedures that process an array. For example, to find the highest exam grade in the class, we can code the following procedure:

```
10    'Find highest grade
20    'Assume array already entered
30    DIM EXAM (20)
40    HIGHEST = 0 'Initialize Highest
50    FOR I = 1 TO 20
60        IF EXAM (I) > HIGHEST THEN
              HIGHEST = EXAM (I)
70    NEXT I
80    PRINT "Highest Grade is "; HIGHEST
```

To print the number of the student who has the highest score, you need to save the subscript number of the grade in HIGHEST as well as the grade itself:

```
10    'Find Student with the highest grade
20    'Assume array already entered
30    DIM EXAM (20)
40    HIGHEST = 0
50    FOR I = 1 TO 20
60        IF EXAM (I) > HIGHEST THEN
              HIGHEST = EXAM (I) : STUDENT = I
70    NEXT I
80    PRINT "Student "; STUDENT; "Has Highest Grade "
```

To find the number of students who received a grade of 80 or more, you would code the following:

```
10       'Find the number of students
20       'With a grade of 80 or more
30       'Assume array already entered
40       DIM EXAM (20)
50       COUNT = 0
60       FOR I = 1 TO 20
70          IF EXAM (I) >= 80 THEN
                COUNT = COUNT + 1
80       NEXT I
90       PRINT "No. of Students with a Grade of 80 or More is "; COUNT
```

Reading Data into an Array

Thus far we have assumed that data has already been read and stored in our EXAM array. Let us now consider the routine to input the 20 exams:

```
10       'Input data to an array
20       DIM EXAM (20)
30       FOR I = 1 TO 20
40          PRINT "Enter Exam Score "; I
50          INPUT EXAM (I)
60       NEXT I
```

Note that the array need not be initialized to 0 because data will be input to it.

For example, the following code will load into an array 7 daily sales totals:

```
10       DIM SALES (7)
20       FOR I = 1 TO 7
30          PRINT "Enter Sales Total for "; I
40          INPUT SALES (I)
50       NEXT I
```

Then, assuming that the array is loaded, you can calculate the weekly total with:

```
10       TOTAL = 0
20       FOR I = 1 TO 7
30          TOTAL = TOTAL + SALES (I)
40       NEXT I
50       PRINT "The Total Sales is "; TOTAL
```

Assuming that the array is loaded, you can print the total number of days that sales exceeded $1000.00 with the following code:

```
10       CTR = 0
20       FOR I = 1 TO 7
30          IF SALES (I) > 1000 THEN
                CTR = CTR + 1
40       NEXT I
50       PRINT "Total No. of Days with Sales > 1000 is "; CTR
```

SELF-TEST   Consider the following:

```
10   INPUT VAR1
20   INPUT VAR2
30   INPUT VAR3
40   INPUT VAR4
50   INPUT VAR5
```

1. An array could be used in place of defining each Var separately because _____.

2. Suppose VAR3 and VAR5 were defined as VAR3$ and VAR5$, that is, they were string variables. Could one array be used to define the five variables? Explain your answer.

3. Recode the above instructions, using an array to define the variables and inputting five numeric variables into VAR1–VAR5.

4. Suppose you establish an array that contains 24 hourly temperatures for a given day. You could code the DIM statement for the array as DIM TEMP(24), which would allow you to access elements _____ through _____, although you would use only elements _____ through _____.

5. The numbers in parentheses in the above are called _____.

Assume the following array is in storage:

```
DIM Temp(24)
TEMP(1) has the temperature for 1 A.M., TEMP(2) has the temperature for 2 A.M.,
and so on.
```

6. Write a routine to find the average temperature for the day.

7. Write a routine to find the lowest temperature for the day.

8. Write a routine to print the time when the temperature was the lowest.

9. Write a routine to find the number of hours in the day when the temperature fell below 20°.

SOLUTIONS

1. An array, defined properly, will reserve the same amount of storage space as if you defined each variable individually. Also, you may access each array element just as if it were a separate variable.

2. No. When an array is defined, it must be defined either as all strings or all numeric data.

3. Code:

```
10   DIM VAR(5)
20   FOR I = 1 TO 5
30      INPUT VAR(I)
40   NEXT I
50   END
```

4. TEMP(0); TEMP(24); TEMP(1); TEMP(24)

5. subscripts.

6. Routine:

```
10   TOTAL = 0
20   FOR I = 1 TO 24
30      TOTAL = TOTAL + TEMP(I)
40   NEXT I
50   AVERAGE = TOTAL / 24
60   PRINT "The average temperature was "; AVERAGE
```

7. Routine:

```
10   LOW.TEMP = 999
20   FOR I = 1 TO 24
30      IF TEMP(I) < LOW.TEMP THEN
            LOW.TEMP = TEMP(I)
40   NEXT I
50   PRINT "The low for the day was " ; LOW.TEMP
```

8. Routine:
```
10    LOW.TIME = 0
20    LOW.TEMP = 999
30    FOR I = 1 TO 24
40       IF TEMP(I) < LOW.TEMP THEN
              LOW.TEMP = TEMP(I)
              LOW.TIME = I
50    NEXT I
60    PRINT "At "; LOW.TIME; ":00 the temperature was "; LOW.TEMP
```
9. Routine:
```
10    COUNT = 0
20    FOR I = 1 TO 24
30       IF TEMP(I) < 20 THEN
              COUNT = COUNT + 1
40    NEXT I
50    PRINT "The temperature fell below 20 "; COUNT;" hours"
```

Reserved Words in BASICA

Note: These words cannot be used as variable names.

ABS	CVI	EXP	LET	OFF	RETURN	THEN
AND	CVS	FIELD	LINE	ON	RIGHT$	TIME$
ASC	DATA	FILES	LIST	OPEN	RMDIR	TIMER
ATN	DATE$	FIX	LLIST	OPTION	RND	TO
AUTO	DEF	FNxxxxxxxx	LOAD	OR	RSET	TROFF
BEEP	DEFDBL	FOR	LOC	OUT	RUN	TRON
BLOAD	DEFINT	FRE	LOCATE	PAINT	SAVE	USING
BSAVE	DEFSNG	GET	LOF	PEEK	SCREEN	USR
CALL	DEFSTR	GOSUB	LOG	PEN	SGN	VARPTR
CDBL	DELETE	GOTO	LPOS	PLAY	SHELL	VARPTR$
CHAIN	DIM	HEX$	LPRINT	POINT	SIN	VIEW
CHR$	DRAW	IF	LSET	POKE	SOUND	WAIT
CINT	EDIT	IMP	MERGE	POS	SPACE$	WEND
CIRCLE	ELSE	INKEY$	MID$	PRESET	SPCI	WHILE
CLEAR	END	INP	MKD$	PRINT	SQR	WIDTH
CLOSE	ENVIRON	INPUT	MKDIR	PRINT#	STEP	WINDOW
CLS	ENVIRON$	INPUT#	MKI$	PSET	STICK	WRITE
COLOR	EOF	INPUT$	MKS$	PUT	STOP	WRITE#
COM	EQV	INSTR	MOD	RANDOMIZE	STR$	XOR
COMMON	ERASE	INT	MOTOR	READ	STRIG	
CONT	ERDEV	KEY	NAME	REM	STRING$	
COS	ERDEV$	KEY$	NEW	RENUM	SWAP	
CSNG	ERL	KILL	NEXT	RESET	SYSTEM	
CSRLIN	ERR	LEFT$	NOT	RESTORE	TAB	
CVD	ERROR	LEN	OCT$	RESUME	TAN	

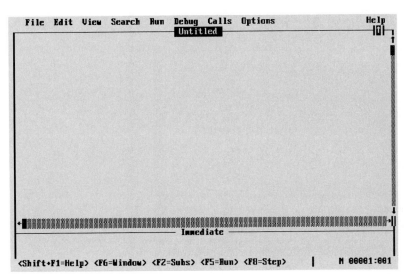

D–8 QuickBASIC screen display.

A Brief Introduction to QuickBASIC

The following sections provide an overview of QuickBASIC that you can use for quick reference. QuickBASIC features not covered previously in this appendix are presented to provide a more complete introduction to this version of the language.

QuickBASIC Features

To load the QuickBASIC compiler, place the disk with QB.EXE in the A or C drive, depending on your system, and type **QB**. Depending on which version you have, your main screen display will appear similar to Figure D–8.

The QuickBASIC commands appear at the top of the screen. To use one of them, hold down (ALT) and press the first letter of the desired command. Pressing (SHIFT)-(F1) at any point provides context-sensitive help.

When you select a command, you will see a pull-down menu from which you can make additional selections. Figure D–9 illustrates the pull-down menu for the File command. You may use the 'or' cursor and then

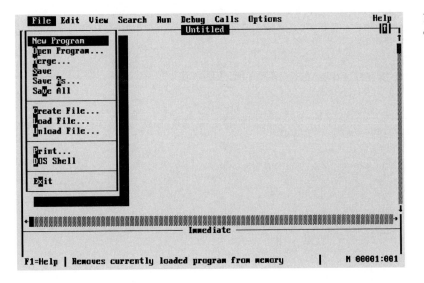

D–9 QuickBASIC's File command pull-down menu.

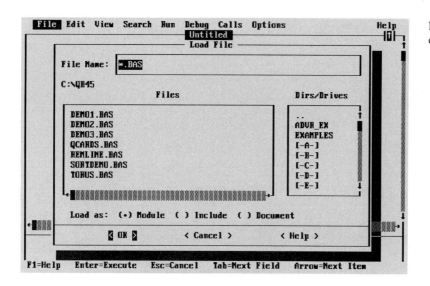

D–10 A QuickBASIC dialog box.

press (ENTER) to select an item from a pull-down menu, or you can key in the highlighted letter from the pull-down menu's item.

Pull-down menu items that end with ... will, when selected, display a dialog box requesting user information. For example, (ALT)-F(ile) , L(oad) File ... requires you to key in some data, in this case a file name. A dialog box would then be displayed requesting you to enter the name of the file to be loaded in. See Figure D–10 for an illustration of a dialog box.

The following is a brief summary of QuickBASIC commands.

Command	Use
File	To load, save, or define a program file
Edit	To alter a program file by moving, deleting, or copying portions of the text
View	To display various segments of a program or to display and/or change options selected
Search	To find specified elements in a program and/or change them
Run	To compile and execute a program
Debug	To select various debugging aids when testing a program
Calls	To reference other modules in a program

The following is a summary of special keys used in QuickBASIC.

Key(s)	Use
F1 function key	To display context-sensitive help
(CTRL)-Y	To delete a line at the cursor
(HOME)	To go to the beginning of a program line
(END)	To go to the end of a program line

The following is a list of global cursor moves.

Key(s)	Use
(PGDN) or Page Down	Scrolls a full page down
(PGUP) or Page Up	Scrolls a full page up
(CTRL)-(HOME)	Cursor moves to the beginning of the file
(CTRL)-(END)	Cursor moves to the end of the file
(CTRL)-(→)	Cursor moves to the beginning of the next word
(CTRL)-(←)	Cursor moves to the beginning of the previous word

The following is a list of special commands.

Key(s)	Use
(ALT)-F(ile), P(rint ...)	To print part or all of a currently loaded program
(CTRL)-(F10)	To eliminate the Immediate window from the QuickBASIC Screen ((CTRL)-(F10) is a toggle switch)
(ALT)-R(un) (then (ENTER)) or (SHIFT)-(F5))	To run an existing program.

Logical Control Constructs in QuickBASIC

Like all programming languages, QuickBASIC has four logical control constructs: sequence, selection, iteration, and case structure.

Sequence   Statements are executed in the sequence entered, not in line number sequence as in BASICA. Line numbers are not required.

Selection   IF-THEN-ELSE statements are not limited in length to 255 characters as with BASICA. IF-THEN-ELSE statements are coded as follows, ending with END IF:

```
IF  condition THEN
        statement–1          Each statement can be on a
        statement–2          separate line, ended by
          .                  pressing (ENTER)
          .
          .
ELSE
        statement–3          Each statement can be on a
        statement–4          separate line, ended by
          .                  pressing (ENTER)
          .
          .
    END IF            The IF block ends with an END IF as in pseudocode
```

Iteration   WHILE ... WEND and FOR ... NEXT are permitted as with BASICA. You may also use a DO WHILE ... LOOP in place of WHILE ... WEND, or you may use a DO UNTIL ... LOOP. The following are equivalent:

```
DO WHILE CTR <= 20          DO UNTIL CTR > 20
  .                           .
  .                           .
  .                           .
LOOP                        LOOP
```

Case Structure   In place of ON GOSUB, you use SELECT CASE ... END
SELECT with GOSUBs. A GOSUB label can be used in place of GOSUB line
number.

Example:

```
INPUT MENU.ITEM
SELECT CASE MENU.ITEM
     CASE 1
        GOSUB SALARY.CHANGE    'Labels may be used with GOSUBs
     CASE 2
        GOSUB NAME.CHANGE
     CASE 3
        GOSUB ADDRESS.CHANGE
     CASE 4
        GOSUB DEPT.CHANGE
     CASE ELSE
        GOSUB PRINT "ERROR"
END SELECT
```

Procedures

QuickBASIC permits separate modules to be coded in which the programmer can control the data passed from the main program to the procedure
and back again.

Arrays

DIM EXAM(1:20) will establish a 20-element array, which is referenced as
EXAM(1) to EXAM(20).

Debugging

The following debugging options are available with QuickBASIC:

1. The Trace feature allows you to step through the program as it is
executed, one line at a time.

◆   To manually step through a program, press F8.

◆   To automatically step through a program as each line is executed, select
the Trace On option of the Debug command.

◆   Use the TRON instruction within the program itself to trace a program
or segment when the instruction is encountered (TROFF is an instruction
that terminates tracing).

2. To display the contents of variables as a program is traced or executed,
select the Add Watch option of the Debug command and then enter variables to be watched. These variables will be displayed above the program,
and their values will change as the program is traced or executed.

3. When a portion of a program functions properly or need not be tested at
some point during debugging, you may want to bypass it. Preface such
instructions with a single quote or apostrophe so that the compiler treats
them as comments.

4. To select a breakpoint (a line(s) or instruction(s) at which you wish to
suspend program execution so that you can analyze results or variables

selected by the Add Watch option), move the cursor to the instruction to serve as a breakpoint. Then press (F9) or select the Toggle Breakpoint option of the Debug command (ALT)-D(ebug), B(reakpoint). The instruction selected will be highlighted. When the instruction is to be executed, the program is suspended. To clear the breakpoint, select the Clear All Breakpoints option of the Debug command.

The QuickBASIC Environment

The following outline summarizes how you interact with your computer while working in QuickBASIC.

I.   Customizing the QuickBASIC Screen

    A. Use (ALT)-V(iew), O(ptions)

    B. By using the cursor arrow keys, you can set foreground and background colors for the following elements:
        1. Normal Text
        2. Current Statement (the statement being traced)
        3. Breakpoint Lines

    C. You can set a highlight for each of the above; Current Statement and Breakpoint Lines can also be set for Blink or Underline.

    D. Scroll Bars
        1. Use the scroll bars to size a screen with a mouse.
        2. The default is to set scroll bars on, but they can be set off if you are not using a mouse.

    E. Tab Stops
        1. The default for indentation is 8 characters when (TAB) is pressed.
        2. You can change it to any number.

    F. Setting Options in the Dialog Box
        1. To move from option to option, use (TAB).
        2. To change a color, use the cursor arrows when at the required option.
        3. To change highlighting, use the space bar when you are at the required option.
        4. To omit scroll bars, use the space bar.
        5. To return to previous lines or to skip lines, enter the highlighted letter.
        6. Press (ENTER) to store changes; press (ESC) to cancel changes.

II. Working with the Immediate Window

    A. Use this window for executing from 1 to 10 instructions immediately.

    B. To adjust the size of the Immediate Window:
        1. Press (ALT)-+ (plus key) to increase the size one line at a time.
        2. Press (CTRL)-(F10) to increase the size of the window to the full screen. (CTRL)-(F10) is a toggle.

III. Creating Executable Files

    A. An executable file is a debugged program file in machine language that does not require the QuickBASIC editor and compiler for loading and translating. That is, it can be run directly from DOS.

    B. Press (ALT)-R(un), X for Make **EXE** file to create such a file.

    C. To run the program, type *program name* from DOS.

    D. The following QuickBASIC files are required to create an executable file: BC.EXE   LINK.EXE   BRUN45.LIB   BCOM45.LIB

IV. Saving Files

    A. You can save QuickBASIC files in QuickBASIC form, only readable by the QuickBASIC system, or in a format readable by other BASIC compilers. When you type (ALT)-F(ile), S(ave), the computer will enable you to specify which format you want the file saved in. Use (TAB) to select a format. The default is to save the file in QuickBASIC form.

    B. After working on a program and saving it, select (ALT)-F(ile), N(ew) Program before loading in a new program.

V. Using the Edit Menu

    A. If you make a change to a previously entered program line, you can undo the change by pressing (ALT)-E(dit), U(ndo) or (ALT)-(BACKSPACE) while the cursor is on the designated line.

    B. Moving and Copying Blocks of Instructions. Use (SHIFT)-(→) to designate characters as part of a block of text or (SHIFT)-(↓) to designate a line as part of a block of text.

    C. To move a block of text, designate the block, select (ALT)-E(dit), (Cu)t to delete the text; then move the cursor to the desired point and press (ALT)-E(dit), P(aste) to move it.

    D. To copy a block of text, designate the block, select (ALT)-E(dit), C(opy); move the cursor to the desired position; then press (ALT)-E(dit), P(aste) to copy it.

    E. To delete a block of text, designate the block, press (ALT)-E(dit), (Cu)t to delete it temporarily and (ALT)-E(dit), (Cl)e(ar) to delete it permanently.

VI. Using the Search Command

    A. To find and/or change elements in a program, use the Search command.

    B. You can make changes globally, or you can verify each change before it is made.

VII. Using a Mouse

    You can use a mouse in place of a keyboard for pointing to elements in a dialog box and selecting required entries.

VIII.You can size screens by using a mouse or pressing the (ALT) + (plus key) or (ALT) – (minus key).

SUMMARY

I.   An Overview

A. Data Organization

1. Data that changes value during the execution of a program is known as variable data. This includes entered data, totals, and counters.

2. Data that maintains the same value throughout the entire program is known as constant or literal data.

3. Data may be numeric or string. Numeric variable names consist of letters and digits and begin with a letter. String variable names are similar to numeric variable names, except that they must end with a $. A numeric variable may contain digits, a decimal point, and a leading sign. A string variable can contain any character.

B. BASIC Input and Output Statements

1. The INPUT statement is used to enter data from the keyboard.

2. The LPRINT statement causes output to be sent to the printer, and the PRINT statement causes output to be displayed on the screen.

3. A comment line may be designated by using the REM statement or by beginning any line with a single quote ('). Comments may also be added to any statement with the use of the single quote:

    T = 15.3   '15.3 is the value in T

C. Performing Arithmetic Operations

1. A numeric variable is specified to the left of the equal sign in an assignment statement (for example, LET TOTAL = ... or TOTAL = ...).

2. All arithmetic operations are specified to the right of the equal sign.

3. The order of evaluation of arithmetic operations is as follows:

    ^   Exponentiation
    * or /   Multiply or divide
    + or −   Add or subtract

All operations on the same level are performed in sequence from left to right. *Note:* Parentheses ( ) override normal hierarchy rules.

II. Using Simple Relationals

A. Relations

IF a variable or literal is <, >, =, <=, >=, or <> a second variable or literal THEN a series of instructions is performed.

B. Comparisons

1. Numeric operands are compared algebraically.

    12.0 = 12.00 = 12 = +12

2. String operands should contain the same number of characters for a logical comparison.

    a. "ABC" is equal to "ABC" only if both variables are the same length. Note that " ABC" < " ABC" < "ABC". (To store " ABC" or " ABC" in a string variable, you must use an assignment statement or input it with quotation marks as " ABC".)

    b. Shorter string operands are considered 'less than' longer ones if all characters up to the length of the shorter field are equal. That is, "ABC" < "ABC " and "ABC " < "ABCD".

3. The collating sequence used with most micros is called ASCII. With ASCII, numbers are less than letters. Also, uppercase letters are less than lowercase letters. That is, numbers are always compared correctly (0 < 1 < 2 ...), uppercase letters are compared correctly ("A" < "B" < "C" ...), and lowercase letters are also compared correctly ("a" < "b" < "c" ...). But keep in mind that 0 < 1 < ... 9 < "A" ... < "Z" < "a" ... < "z"

   C. Compound Conditionals
       1. Format
         IF (condition-1) OR (condition-2) THEN ...
         IF (condition-1) AND (condition-2) THEN ...
       2. Hierarchy
           a. If ORs and ANDs are used in the same statement, ANDs are evaluated first from left to right, followed by ORs.
           b. Parentheses can be used to override this hierarchy rule.

III. The Four Logical Constructs

   A. Sequence
       Program steps are executed in the order they appear.

   B. Selection
       An IF-THEN-ELSE selects the instruction or instructions to be executed, depending on whether a condition is met.

   C. Iteration
       A series of steps are executed repeatedly, based on whether a given condition or conditions are met.

   D. Case
       One of a number of steps will be executed, depending on the contents of a variable or variables.

IV. Iterative Techniques

   A. A WHILE ... WEND may be used to accomplish iteration.
       1. The loop is repeated until the condition is no longer met.
       2. If the condition is not met initially, the loop will never be executed, because the test is performed before the first execution of the loop.

   B. All forms of iteration can be nested.

V.   FOR ... NEXT Statements

   A. The FOR ... NEXT statement is used when you want to perform a loop a predefined number of times in which a variable needs to be incremented (or decremented) by the same amount each time the loop is repeated.

   B. The FOR ... NEXT accomplishes the following:
       1. Establishes and initializes a variable.
       2. Increments (or decrements) the variable.
       3. Specifies the range in which the variable is to vary.

VI. Subroutines for Top-Down Modular Programming

   A. A module, or subroutine, is a set of instructions that functions as a unit and performs a specific set of operations.

   B. Subroutines minimize duplication of effort.

   C. A GOSUB statement causes execution of a separate routine and then returns control to the statement following the GOSUB.

   D. Subroutines are coded after the END statement.

   E. Each subroutine is terminated by a RETURN that is coded on a line by itself.

   F. Subroutines implement top-down modular design.

   G. A subroutine is identified by a line number. In GOSUB 1000, for example, 1000 is a line number.

   H. GOSUB statements may be nested.

VII. Arrays are used to store a series of variables, all with the same format.

KEY WORDS

Alphanumeric variable
Array
Case
Collating sequence
Command
Compound conditional
Conditional statement
Constant
Editing
Format
IF-THEN-ELSE
Input

Iteration
Literal
Logical control construct
Loop
Module
Nested conditional
Nested iteration
Nested while
Numeric variable
Output
Prompt
Selection

Sentinel value
Sequence
String constant
String variable
Structured
    programming
Subroutine
Subscript
Top-down
    programming
Trailer value
Variable

SELF-TEST

What, if anything, is wrong with the statements in 1–2? Correct the errors.

1. 10 IF A = B OR IF A = C THEN
         PRINT "A OK"

2. 10 IF A < 21 OR A = 21 AND A = 5 OR A > 5 THEN
         PRINT "A OK"

3. The hierarchy rule for evaluating compound conditionals states that conditions surrounding the word _____ are evaluated first, followed by the conditions surrounding the word _____.

4. Write a single statement to print "A OK" if A is between 3 and 13, inclusive of the endpoints.

5. Write a single statement to print "A OK" if A is between 3 and 13, exclusive of the endpoints.

6. (T *or* F) A loop should be used whenever one set of instructions is to be executed when a condition is true, and another set is to be executed when the condition is false.

7. (T *or* F) All subroutines should be coded after the END statement.

8. (T *or* F) A subroutine may be referenced from only one place in a program.

Identify the errors in each of the following FOR statement (9–10):

9. FOR CTR = 1 TO 4 STEP – 1

10. FOR NAME$ = 1 TO 10

11. What will happen if the counter or variable in a loop is not modified?

12. Why is it best to use a top-down modular approach to designing and coding programs?

SOLUTIONS

1. The word IF should appear only once.

2. There should be parentheses around the condition to make the statement logical.
   10 IF (A < 21 OR A = 21) AND (A = 5 OR A > 5)

3. AND; OR

4. IF A <= 13 AND A >= 3 THEN
   PRINT "A OK"

5. IF A > 3 AND A < 13 THEN
   PRINT "A OK"

6. False. A loop is coded when a section of code is to be executed repeatedly.

7. True.

8. False. A subroutine may be referenced from more than one location in the program.

9. The STEP must specify a positive increment.

10. The counter variable must be numeric.

11. If the counter loop is not modified, the loop will repeat indefinitely (an infinite loop) because the loop condition will never be met.

12. A top-down modular approach makes it easier to debug and modify your code. In addition, it leads to better designed programs.

TRUE-FALSE QUESTIONS

1. (T *or* F) A BASIC program that compiles without any errors will always run properly.
2. (T *or* F) BASIC programs must be converted into machine language before execution can occur.
3. (T *or* F) A comment in BASIC programs begins with REM or with an apostrophe (single-quote mark).
4. (T *or* F) Instructions are typically executed in sequence unless a WHILE ... WEND or other logical control structure alters the flow.
5. (T *or* F) A trailer value is used to indicate that there is no more data to be processed.
6. (T *or* F) The LPRINT instruction is used to display data on a screen.
7. (T *or* F) The IF statement is used to implement the iteration control structure.
8. (T *or* F) An ELSE clause is a required part of the IF statement.
9. (T *or* F) A string variable cannot be compared with a numeric variable in a conditional.
10. (T *or* F) When an IF statement includes both an AND or an OR, the conditions surrounding the AND are evaluated first.

PRACTICE PROGRAMS

1. Write a program (1) without subroutines and (2) using subroutines to print the class average of a final exam for each of 10 classes. Each class has exactly 20 students, and each student has taken every exam. Thus 200 lines will be entered. Assume that the first 20 lines are for students in Class 1, the next 20 are for students in Class 2, and so on.

Without Subroutines:
```
10   '*****************************************
20   'This program calculates the class average
25   'for 10 classes each with 20 students in it
30   'Subroutines are not used
40   '*****************************************
50   LET CLASSCTR = 1
60   WHILE CLASSCTR <= 10
70      LET STUDNO = 1
80      LET TOTAL = 0
90      WHILE STUDNO <= 20
100        INPUT EXAM
110        LET TOTAL = TOTAL + EXAM
120        LET STUDNO = STUDNO + 1
130      WEND
140      LET AVERAGE = TOTAL / 20
150      PRINT "Class Average for Class "; CLASSCTR; " is "; AVERAGE
160      CLASSCTR = CLASSCTR + 1
170   WEND
180   END
```

With Subroutines:
```
'****************************************************
' This program prints a class average for 10
' classes with 20 students per class
'
' We do not need an initial read because we
' know precisely how many variables we will
' be processing
'****************************************************
  10 LET CLASSCTR = 0
  20 WHILE CLASSCTR < 10
  30      GOSUB 1000
  40      WHILE STUDNO < 20
  50         GOSUB 2000
  60      WEND
  70      GOSUB 3000
  80 WEND
```

```
  90 PRINT "End of Job"
 100 END
 110 'Subroutines go here
1000 'Initialize
1010    LET STUDNO = 0
1020    LET TOTAL = 0
1030 RETURN
2000 'Input and Total 120 Exams
2010       INPUT EXAM
2020       LET TOTAL = TOTAL + EXAM
2030       LET STUDNO = STUDNO + 1
2040 RETURN
3000 'Class Average Module
3010       LET CLASSCTR = CLASSCTR + 1
3020       LET AVERAGE = TOTAL / 5
3030       PRINT "Class Average for Class "; CLASSCTR; " is "; AVERAGE
3040 RETURN
```

PROGRAMMING ASSIGNMENTS

1. A company pays its 15 salespeople (numbered 01–15) a monthly salary of $2500 plus a 2 percent commission. Write a program to input Salesperson Number and Amount Sold and calculate and print the amount sold and the Salary plus Commission for each salesperson.

2. Print a table that will show the square and square root of all integer numbers between 1 and 100. Note that no input is required.

3. Write a program to calculate FICA (Social Security tax), where a variable called SALARY is entered as data. FICA is equal to 7.51 percent of SALARY up to $48,000. Salary in excess of $48,000 is not taxed.

4. Doughnuts cost $ .25 each if a customer purchases less than a dozen. The doughnuts are $ .18 each if 12 or more are purchased. Write a program to read in the number of doughnuts purchased and calculate the total price. The program should be able to operate on a variable number of input lines entered. Plan the program first with pseudocode.

5. A school cafeteria charges $ .60 for a cup of coffee that costs $ .29 if less than 100 cups are sold in a day, and $ .24 if 100 or more cups are sold in a day. Write a program to input the number of cups sold per day and to print the profit made each day. Plan the program first with pseudocode.

Microsoft BASIC Command Summary

Legend: Uppercase letters are required keywords. You must supply items within <>'s. You must select one of the entries within { }'s. Items within [ ]'s are optional. Three ellipsis points (...) indicate that an item may be repeated as many times as you wish. The symbol Ƀ represents a blank character.

Summary of BASIC Statements

BEEP
Causes the speaker on the PC to beep for a quarter of a second.

CHAIN <"filespec"> [,line number] [,ALL]
Instructs the PC to stop executing the current program, then load another program from auxiliary storage and start executing it.

CIRCLE <(x, y), radius> [,color [,start,end [,shape]]]
Causes the PC to draw an ellipse, circle, arc, or wedge with center at (x,y).

CLOSE [#] [filenumber] [,[#] [filenumber]]
Closes specified files.

CLS
Erases the information on the first 24 lines of the screen and places the cursor in the upper-left corner of the screen.

COLOR [background] [,palette]
In medium-resolution graphics mode, sets the color for the background and palette of colors.

COLOR [foreground] [,background] [,border]
In the text mode, defines the color of the foreground characters, background, and border around the screen.

COM(n) {ON or OFF or STOP}
Enables or disables trapping of communications activity on adaptor n.

COMMON <variable> [,variable]...
Passes specified variables to a chained program.

DATA <data item> [,data item]...
Provides for the creation of a sequence of data items for use by the READ statement.

DATE$ = mm{/ or –}dd{/ or –}yy[yy]
Sets the system date, where mm = month, dd = day, yy = year, yyyy = 4-digit year.

DEF FN <name> [(variable [,variable]...)] = <expression>
Defines and names a function that can be referenced in a program as often as needed.

DIM <array name(size)> [,array name(size)]...
Reserves storage locations for arrays.

DRAW <string expression>
Causes the PC to draw the object that is defined by the value of the string expression.

END
Terminates program execution and closes all opened files.

ERASE <array name> [,array name]...
Eliminates previously defined arrays.

FIELD <#filenumber, width AS string variable> [,width AS string variable]...
Allocates space for variables in a random file buffer.

FOR numeric variable = initial TO limit [STEP increment]
Causes the statements between the FOR and NEXT statements to be executed repeatedly until the value of the numeric variable exceeds the value of the limit.

GET <(x_1, y_1) – (x_2, y_2), array name>
Reads the colors of the points in the specified area on the screen into an array.

GET <[#]filenumber> [,record number]
Reads the specified record from a random file and transfers it to the buffer that is defined by the corresponding FIELD statement.

GOSUB <line number>
Causes control to transfer to the subroutine represented by the specified line number. Also retains the location of the next statement following the GOSUB statement.

GOTO <line number>
Causes an unconditional branch to the line number.

IF <condition> THEN [clause]
Causes execution of the THEN clause if the condition is true

IF <condition> THEN [clause] ELSE [clause]
Causes execution of the THEN clause if the condition is true. Causes execution of the ELSE clause if the condition is false.

INPUT [;]["prompt message" {; or ,}] <variable> [,variable]...
Provides for the assignment of values to variables from a source external to the program, like the keyboard.

INPUT <#filenumber, variable> [,variable]...
Provides for the assignment of values to variables from a sequential file in auxiliary storage.

Key {ON or OFF}
Turns the display of the ten function keys on line 25 of the screen to on or off.

KEY(n) {ON or OFF or STOP}
Activates or deactivates trapping of the specified key n.

[LET] <variable> = <expression>
Causes the evaluation of the expression, followed by the assignment of the resulting value to the variable to the left of the equal sign.

LINE [(x₁, y₁)] <–(x₂, y₂)> [,color] [,B[F]][,Style]
Draws a line or a box on the screen.

LINE INPUT [;]["prompt message";] <string variable> or LINE INPUT <#filenumber,> <string variable>
Provides for the assignment of a line of up to 255 characters from a source external to the program, like the keyboard or a sequential file.

LOCATE [row] [,column] [,cursor] [,start] [,stop]
Positions the cursor on the screen. Can also be used to make the cursor visible or invisible and to control the size of the cursor.

LPRINT [item] [{, or ; or ƀ}item]...
Provides for the generation of output to the printer.

LPRINT USING <string expression;> <item> [{, or ; or ƀ} item]...
Provides for the generation of formatted output to the printer.

LSET <string variable> = <string expression>
Moves string data left-justified into an area of a random file buffer that is defined by the string variable.

MID$ <(string var, start position [,number]> = <substring>
Replaces a substring within a string.

NEXT [numeric variable] [,numeric variable]...
Identifies the end of the For loop(s).

ON COM(n) GOSUB <line number>
Causes control to transfer to the line number when data is filling the communications buffer (n).

ON ERROR GOTO <line number>
Enables error trapping and specifies the first line number of an error-handling routine that the PC is to branch to in the event of an error. If the line number is zero, error trapping is disabled.

ON <numeric expression> GOSUB <line number> [,line number]...
Causes control to transfer to the subroutine represented by the selected line number. Also retains the location of the next statement following the ON-GOSUB statement.

ON <numeric expression> GOTO <line number> [,line number]...
Causes control to transfer to one of several line numbers according to the value of the numeric expression.

ON KEY(n) GOSUB <line number>
Causes control to transfer to the line number when the function key or cursor control key (n) is pressed.

ON PEN GOSUB <line number>
Causes control to transfer to the line number when the light pen is activated.

ON PLAY(n) GOSUB <line number>
Plays continuous background music. Transfers control to the line number when a note (n) is sensed.

ON STRIG(n) GOSUB <line number>
Causes control to transfer to the line number when one of the joystick buttons (n) is pressed.

ON TIMER(n) GOSUB <line number>
Causes control to transfer to the line number when the specified period of time (n) in seconds has elapsed.

OPEN <filespec> FOR <mode> AS <[#]filenumber> [LEN = record length] or
OPEN <mode, [#]filenumber, filespec> [,record length]
Allows a program to read or write records to a file. If record length is specified, then the file is opened as a random file. If the record length is not specified, then the file is opened as a sequential file.

OPTION BASE {0 or 1}
Assigns a lower bound of 0 or 1 to all arrays.

PAINT <(x, y)> [[,paint] [,boundary]]
Paints an area on the screen with the selected color.

PEN(n) {ON or OFF or STOP}
Enables or disables the PEN read function used to analyze light pen activity.

PLAY <string expression>
Causes the PC to play music according to the value of the string expression.

PRESET <(x, y)> [,color]
Draws a point in the color specified at (x, y). If no color is specified, it erases the point.

{PRINT *or* **?} [item] [{,** *or* **;** *or* **b}item]...**
Provides for the generation of output to the screen.

{PRINT *or* **?} <#filenumber,> [item] [{,** *or* **;** *or* **b}item]..**
Provides for the generation of output to a sequential file.

PRINT USING <string expression;> <item> [{, *or* **;** *or* **b} item]...**
Provides for the generation of formatted output to the screen.

PRINT <#filenumber,> USING <string expression;> <item> [{, *or* **;** *or* **b}item]...**
Provides for the generation of formatted output to a sequential file.

PSET <(x, y)> [,color]
Draws a point in the color specified at [x, y].

PUT <(x$_1$, y$_1$), array name> [,action]
Writes the colors of the points in the array onto an area of the screen.

PUT <[#]filenumber> [,record number]
Writes a record to a random file from a buffer defined by the corresponding FIELD statement.

RANDOMIZE [numeric expression]
Reseeds the random number generator.

READ <variable> [,variable]...
Provides for the assignment of values to variables from a sequence of data items created from DATA statements.

{REM *or* **'} [comment]**
Provides for the insertion of comments in a program.

RESTORE [line number]
Allows the data items in DATA statements to be reread.

RESUME {line number *or* **NEXT** *or* **0** *or* **b}**
Continues program execution at the line number, or the line following that which caused the error, after an error-recovery procedure.

RETURN [line number]
Causes control to transfer from a subroutine back to the statement that follows the corresponding GOSUB or ON-GOSUB statement.

RSET <string variable> = <string expression>
Moves string data right-justified into an area of a random file buffer that is defined by string variable.

SCREEN [mode] [,color switch] [,active page] [,visual page]
Sets the screen attributes for text mode, medium-resolution graphics, or high-resolution graphics.

SOUND <frequency, duration>
Causes the generation of sound through the PC speaker.

STOP
Stops execution of a program. Unlike the END statement, files are left open.

STRIG(n) {ON *or* **OFF** *or* **STOP}**
Enables or disables trapping of the joystick buttons.

SWAP <variable$_1$, variable$_2$>
Exchanges the values of two variables or two elements of an array.

TIME$ = hh[:mm[:ss]]
Sets the system time where hh = hours, mm = minutes, and ss = seconds.

TIMER {ON *or* **OFF** *or* **STOP}**
Enables or disables trapping of timed events.

VIEW [[SCREEN] (x$_1$, y$_1$) – (x$_2$, y$_2$)] [,color] [,boundary]
Defines a viewport.

WEND
Identifies the end of a While loop.

WHILE <condition>
Identifies the beginning of a While loop. Causes the statements between WHILE and WEND to be executed repeatedly while the condition is true.

WIDTH {40 *or* **80}**
Erases the information on the first 24 lines of the screen, sets the width of the line on the screen to 40 or 80 characters, and places the cursor in the upper-left corner of the screen.

WINDOW <[SCREEN] (x$_1$, y$_1$) – (x$_2$, y$_2$)>
Redefines the coordinates of the viewport. Allows you to draw objects in space and not be bounded by the limits of the screen.

WRITE [expression list]
Writes data to the screen. Identical to the PRINT statement except that it causes commas to be inserted between items displayed; causes strings to be delimited with quotation marks; and positive numbers are not preceded by blanks.

WRITE <#filenumber,> [item] [{, *or* **;** *or* **b}item]...**
Writes data to a sequential file. Causes the PC to insert commas between the items written to the sequential file.

Summary of BASIC Commands

AUTO [line number] [,increment]
Automatically starts a BASIC line with a line number. Each new line is assigned a systematically incremented line number.

CLEAR
Assigns all numeric variables the value zero and all string variables the null value.

CONT

Resumes a system activity, like the execution of a program, following interruption due to pressing the Control and Break keys simultaneously or execution of the STOP or END statement.

DELETE [lineno₁] [–lineno₂]

Deletes line numbers lineno₁ through lineno₂ in the current program.

EDIT <line number>

Displays a line for editing purposes.

FILES ["device name:]

Lists the names of all programs and data files in auxiliary storage as specified by the device name.

KILL <"filespec>

Deletes a previously stored program or data file from auxiliary storage.

LIST [line number₁] [–line number₂] [,"filespec]

Causes all or part of the BASIC program currently in main storage to be displayed on the screen. The LIST command can also be used to copy lines to a file in auxiliary storage.

LLIST [line number₁] [–line number₂]

Causes all or part of the BASIC program currently in main storage to be displayed on the printer.

LOAD <"filespec>

Loads a previously stored program from auxiliary storage into main storage.

MERGE <"filespec>

Merges the lines from a program in auxiliary storage with the program in main storage. The program in auxiliary storage must have been saved using the A (ASCII) parameter.

NAME <"old filespec"> AS <"new filespec">

Changes the name of a program or data file in auxiliary storage to a new name.

NEW

Causes the BASIC program currently in main storage to be erased and indicates the beginning of a new program to be created in main storage.

RENUM [new line number] [,[old line number] [,increment]]

Renumbers the program uniformly with a new line number and increment.

RUN {line number *or* "filespec [",R] *or* ƀ}

Causes the BASIC program currently in main storage to be executed. This command can also be used to begin execution at a specified line number of the program in main storage or to load and execute a program from auxiliary storage.

SAVE <"filespec> [,A]

Saves the current program into auxiliary storage for later use. The parameter A instructs the PC to save the file in character format (ASCII) rather than binary format.

SHELL

Places the current BASICA session in a temporary wait state and returns control to the operating system (DOS). When the operating system prompt appears, you can enter DOS commands. To return to the BASICA session, type EXIT.

SYSTEM

Causes the PC to permanently exit BASICA and return control to the operating system (DOS).

TROFF

Turns off the program trace feature.

TRON

Turns on the program trace feature.

Summary of BASIC Functions

ABS(N)

Returns the absolute value of the argument N.

ASC(X$)

Returns a two-digit numeric value that is equivalent in ASCII code to the first character of the string argument X$.

ATN(N)

Returns the angle in radians whose tangent is the value of the argument N.

CHR$(N)

Returns a single string character that is equivalent in ASCII code to the numeric argument N.

COS(N)

Returns the cosine of the argument N where N is in radians.

CVI(X$), CVS(X$), CVD(X$),

Returns the integer, single-precision, or double-precision numeric value equivalent to the string X$. Used with random files.

EOF(filenumber)

Returns -1 (true) if the end of file has been sensed on the sequential file associated with filenumber. Returns 0 (false) if the end of file has not been sensed.

EXP(N)

Returns e(2.718281...) raised to the argument N.

FIX(N)

Returns the value of N truncated to an integer.

FRE(N)

Returns the number of unused bytes within BASIC's data space. N is a dummy argument.

INPUT$(N)

Suspends execution of the program until a string of N characters is received from the keyboard.

INSTR(P, X$, S$)

Returns the beginning position of the substring S$ in string X$. P indicates the position at which the search begins in the string X$.

INT(N)

Returns the largest integer that is less than or equal to the argument N.

LEFT$(X$, N)

Returns the leftmost N characters of the string argument X$.

LEN(X$)

Returns the length of the string argument XS.

LOC(#filenumber)

With a random file, it returns the number of the last record read or written. With a sequential file, it returns the number of records read from or written to the file.

LOF(#filenumber)

Returns the number of bytes allocated to a file.

LOG(N)

Returns the natural log of the argument N where N is greater than 0.

MID$(X$, P, N)

Returns N characters of the string argument X$ beginning at position P.

MKI$(N), MKS$(N), MKD$(N)

Returns the string equivalent of an integer, single-precision or double-precision value. Used with random files.

PEN(n)

Reads the light pen.

PLAY(n)

Returns the number of notes currently in the music background buffer.

PMAP (c, n)

Returns the world coordinate of the physical coordinate c or vice versa. The parameter n varies between 0 and 3 and determines whether c is an x or y coordinate and whether the coordinate is to be mapped from the physical to the world coordinate or vice versa.

POINT {(x, y) *or* (n)}

With the argument (x,y), the PC returns the foreground color attribute of the point (x,y). With the argument n, the PC returns the physical or world x or y coordinate of the last point referenced. The parameter n varies in the range 0 to 3.

POS(N)

Returns the current position of the cursor on the screen. N is a dummy argument.

RIGHT$(X$, N)

Returns the rightmost N characters of the string argument X$.

RND(N)

Returns a random number between 0 (inclusive) and 1 (exclusive). If N is positive or not included, the next random number is returned. If N is 0 (zero), the previous random number is returned. If N is negative, the random number generator is reseeded before a random number is returned.

SCREEN(row, column)

Returns the ASCII code for the character at the specified row (line) and column on the screen.

SGN(N)

Returns the sign of the argument N: -1 if the argument N is less than 0; 0 if the argument N is equal to 0; or +1 if the argument N is greater than 0.

SIN(N)

Returns the sine of the argument N where N is in radians.

SPACE$(N)

Returns a string of N spaces.

SPC(N)

Displays N spaces. Can be used only in an output statement, like PRINT or LPRINT.

SQR(N)

Returns the square root of the positive argument N.

STR$(N)

Returns the string equivalent of the numeric argument N.

STRIG(n)

Returns the status of the joystick buttons.

STRING$(N, X$)

Returns N times the first character of X$.

TAB(N)

Causes the PC to tab over to position N on the output device. Can be used only in an output statement, like PRINT or LPRINT.

TAN(N)

Returns the tangent of the argument N where N is in radians.

TIMER

Returns a value that is equal to the number of seconds elapsed since midnight.

VAL(X$)

Returns the numeric equivalent of the string argument X$.

Summary of Special Variables

CSRLIN
Equal to the vertical (row) coordinate of the cursor.

DATE$
Equal to the current date (mm-dd-yyyy).

ERL
Equal to the line number of the last error. Used for error trapping.

ERR
Equal to the error code of the last error. Used for error trapping.

INKEY$
Equal to the last character entered from the keyboard.

TIME$
Equal to the current time (hh:mm:ss).

Summary of All Operators

Order of Precedence	Operator	Symbol
Highest	Arithmetic	$\wedge$ – (Unary minus sign) * or / \ MOD + or –
	Concatenation	+
	Relational	=, >, >=, <, <=, or <>
	Logical	NOT AND OR or XOR EQV IMP
Lowest		

Summary of Function Keys in BASIC

(F1) LIST
(F2) RUN (ENTER)
(F3) LOAD"
(F4) SAVE"
(F5) CONT (ENTER)
(F6) ,"LPT1:" (ENTER)
(F7) TRON (ENTER)
(F8) TROFF (ENTER)
(F9) KEY
(F10) SCREEN 0, 0, 0 (ENTER)

Summary of Keyword Entries Using (ALT)

(ALT)-A	AUTO	(ALT)-M	MOTOR
(ALT)-B	BSAVE	(ALT)-N	NEXT
(ALT)-C	COLOR	(ALT)-O	OPEN
(ALT)-D	DELETE	(ALT)-P	PRINT
(ALT)-E	ELSE	(ALT)-R	RUN
(ALT)-F	FOR	(ALT)-S	SCREEN
(ALT)-G	GOTO	(ALT)-T	THEN
(ALT)-H	HEX$	(ALT)-U	USING
(ALT)-I	INPUT	(ALT)-V	VAL
(ALT)-K	KEY	(ALT)-W	WIDTH
(ALT)-L	LOCATE	(ALT)-X	XOR

Summary of Keyword Entries Using Special Characters

?	PRINT
'	REM

Summary of Special Keys

(CAPS LOCK)   Acts as a toggle switch for changing the keyboard to the uppercase or lowercase mode. Non-letter keys are not affected.

(CTRL)-(ALT)-(DEL)   Resets the PC. Used to "warm start" (i.e., reboot) the PC.

(CTRL)-(BREAK)   Terminates a PC activity, like the execution of a program, automatic line numbering or the listing of a program.

(CTRL)-(END)   Erases from the cursor position to the end of the current line.

(CTRL)-(ENTER)   Inserts blanks through the end of the current line.

(CTRL)-(HOME)   Clears the screen and places the cursor in the upper-left corner of the screen.

(CTRL)-(NUM LOCK)   Stops the PC. Press any key (except Shift, Break, or Ins) to resume.

(CTRL)-[PrtSc]   Acts as a toggle on/off switch. Directs output to the printer as well as the screen.

(DEL)   Deletes the character at the cursor position on the screen.

(END)   Moves the cursor to the end of the line.

(ESC)   Cancels any changes to the current line.

(HOME)   Moves the cursor to the upper-left corner of the screen.

(INS)   Enters or exits the insert mode.

(NUM LOCK)   Acts as a toggle switch to turn the numeric keypad on or off.

(SHIFT)-[PrtSc]   Prints the contents of the screen onto a printer.

[Space bar]   Transmits a blank character and advances the cursor one position to the right

(SHIFT)   Causes characters pressed while this key is held down to be displayed in uppercase form (lowercase if the keyboard is in the uppercase mode).

(BACKSPACE)   Backspaces the cursor one position and erases the character that was to the left of the cursor.

(ENTER)   Used to enter a line and place the cursor in position 1 of the next line.

(→) (←) (↑) (↓)   These four keys are used to move the cursor in the indicated directions.

(TAB)   Moves the cursor to the next tab position. Inserts 8 blanks in the Insert mode.

Index